T0332730

Security, Privacy, and Forensics Issues in Big Data

Ramesh C. Joshi
Graphic Era University, Dehradun, India

Brij B. Gupta
National Institute of Technology Kurukshetra, India

A volume in the Advances in Information Security, Privacy, and Ethics (AISPE) Book Series

Published in the United States of America by
    IGI Global
    Information Science Reference (an imprint of IGI Global)
    701 E. Chocolate Avenue
    Hershey PA, USA 17033
    Tel: 717-533-8845
    Fax: 717-533-8661
    E-mail: cust@igi-global.com
    Web site: http://www.igi-global.com

Library of Congress Cataloging-in-Publication Data

Names: Joshi, R. C., editor. | Gupta, Brij, 1982- editor.
Title: Security, privacy, and forensics issues in big data / Ramesh C. Joshi
  and Brij B. Gupta, editors.
Description: Hershey, PA : Information Science Reference, an imprint of IGI
  Global, [2020] | Includes bibliographical references and index.
Identifiers: LCCN 2019007879| ISBN 9781522597421 (hardcover) | ISBN
  9781522597438 (softcover) | ISBN 9781522597445 (ebook)
Subjects: LCSH: Big data. | Cyber intelligence (Computer security) | Privacy,
  Right of. | Digital forensic science.
Classification: LCC QA76.9.B45 S43 2020 | DDC 005.8--dc23 LC record available at https://lccn.loc.gov/2019007879

This book is published in the IGI Global book series Advances in Information Security, Privacy, and Ethics (AISPE) (ISSN: 1948-9730; eISSN: 1948-9749)

British Cataloguing in Publication Data
A Cataloguing in Publication record for this book is available from the British Library.

All work contributed to this book is new, previously-unpublished material. The views expressed in this book are those of the authors, but not necessarily of the publisher.

For electronic access to this publication, please contact: eresources@igi-global.com.

Advances in Information Security, Privacy, and Ethics (AISPE) Book Series

Manish Gupta
State University of New York, USA

ISSN:1948-9730
EISSN:1948-9749

MISSION

As digital technologies become more pervasive in everyday life and the Internet is utilized in ever increasing ways by both private and public entities, concern over digital threats becomes more prevalent.

The **Advances in Information Security, Privacy, & Ethics (AISPE) Book Series** provides cutting-edge research on the protection and misuse of information and technology across various industries and settings. Comprised of scholarly research on topics such as identity management, cryptography, system security, authentication, and data protection, this book series is ideal for reference by IT professionals, academicians, and upper-level students.

COVERAGE

- Internet Governance
- Security Classifications
- Security Information Management
- Computer ethics
- Cyberethics
- Data Storage of Minors
- Electronic Mail Security
- Information Security Standards
- IT Risk
- Privacy Issues of Social Networking

IGI Global is currently accepting manuscripts for publication within this series. To submit a proposal for a volume in this series, please contact our Acquisition Editors at Acquisitions@igi-global.com or visit: http://www.igi-global.com/publish/.

Titles in this Series

For a list of additional titles in this series, please visit: www.igi-global.com/book-series

701 East Chocolate Avenue, Hershey, PA 17033, USA
Tel: 717-533-8845 x100 • Fax: 717-533-8661
E-Mail: cust@igi-global.com • www.igi-global.com

Editorial Advisory Board

Table of Contents

Detailed Table of Contents

Chapter 1
    Michael Robinson, Airbus, UK
    Kevin Jones, Airbus, UK

This chapter explores how organizations can seek to secure a public cloud environment for use in big data operations. It begins by describing the challenges that cloud customers face when moving to the cloud, and proposes that these challenges can be summarized as a loss of control and visibility into the systems and controls around data. The chapter identifies thirteen areas where visibility and control can be lost, before progressing to highlight ten solutions to help regain these losses. It is proposed that planning is the most significant step a customer can take in ensuring a secure cloud for big data. Good planning will enable customers to know their data and pursue a risk-based approach to cloud security. The chapter provides insight into future research directions, highlighting research areas which hold the potential to further empower cloud customers in the medium to long term.

Chapter 2
    P. Lalitha Surya Kumari, Geethanjali College of Engineering and Technology, India

This chapter gives information about the most important aspects in how computing infrastructures should be configured and intelligently managed to fulfill the most notably security aspects required by big data applications. Big data is one area where we can store, extract, and process a large amount of data. All these data are very often unstructured. Using big data, security functions are required to work over the heterogeneous composition of diverse hardware, operating systems, and network domains. A clearly defined security boundary like firewalls and demilitarized zones (DMZs), conventional security solutions, are not effective for big data as it expands with the help of public clouds. This chapter discusses the different concepts like characteristics, risks, life cycle, and data collection of big data, map reduce components, issues and challenges in big data, cloud secure alliance, approaches to solve security issues, introduction of cybercrime, YARN, and Hadoop components.

Chapter 3

Over recent years, the extensive development of information technology has dramatically advanced the way that people use the internet. The fast growth of the internet of things and mobile crowdsensing applications raise challenging security and privacy issues for the society. More often than before, malicious attackers exploit human vulnerability as the weakest link to launch cyberattacks and conduct fraudulent online activities. How to profile users' daily behavior becomes an essential component for identifying users' vulnerable/malicious level and predicting the potential cyber threats. In this chapter, the authors discuss human factors and their related issues in cyber security and privacy. Three categories of human behaviors—desktop behavior, mobile behavior, and online behavior—and their corresponding security and privacy issues are demonstrated in detail to estimate the vulnerabilities of internet users. Some future directions related to human-factor based security and privacy issues are proposed at the end of this chapter.

Chapter 4

Big data refers to enormous amount of information which may be in planned and unplanned form. The huge capacity of data creates impracticable situation to handle with conventional database and traditional software skills. Thousands of servers are needed for its processing purpose. Big data gathers and examines huge capacity of data from various resources to determine exceptional novel awareness and recognizing the technical and commercial circumstances. However, big data discloses the endeavor to several data safety threats. Various challenges are there to maintain the privacy and security in big data. Protection of confidential and susceptible data from attackers is a vital issue. Therefore, the goal of this chapter is to discuss how to maintain security in big data to keep your organization robust, operational, flexible, and high performance, preserving its digital transformation and obtaining the complete benefit of big data, which is safe and secure.

Chapter 5

A cloud-based public key infrastructure (PKI) utilizing blockchain technology is proposed. Big data ecosystems have scalable and resilient needs that current PKI cannot satisfy. Enhancements include using blockchains to establish persistent access to certificate data and certificate revocation lists, decoupling of data from certificate authority, and hosting it on a cloud provider to tap into its traffic security measures. Instead of holding data within the transaction data fields, certificate data and status were embedded into smart contracts. The tests revealed a significant performance increase over that of both traditional and the version that stored data within blocks. The proposed method reduced the mining data size, and lowered the mining time to 6.6% of the time used for the block data storage method. Also, the mining gas cost per certificate was consequently cut by 87%. In summary, completely decoupling the certificate authority portion of a PKI and storing certificate data inside smart contracts yields a sizable performance boost while decreasing the attack surface.

Chapter 6

Prabha Selvaraj, VIT-AP University, India
Sumathi Doraikannan, VIT-AP University, India
Vijay Kumar Burugari, KL University, India

Big data and IoT has its impact on various areas like science, health, engineering, medicine, finance, business, and mainly, the society. Due to the growth in security intelligence, there is a requirement for new techniques which need big data and big data analytics. IoT security does not alone deal with the security of the device, but it also has to care about the web interfaces, cloud services, and other devices that interact with it. There are many techniques used for addressing challenges like privacy of individuals, inference, and aggregation, which makes it possible to re-identify individuals' even though they are removed from a dataset. It is understood that a few security vulnerabilities could lead to insecure web interface. This chapter discusses the challenges in security and how big data can be used for it. It also analyzes the various attacks and threat modeling in detail. Two case studies in two different areas are also discussed.

Chapter 7

Mohammad Rasool Fatemi, University of New Brunswick, Canada
Ali A. Ghorbani, University of New Brunswick, Canada

System logs are one of the most important sources of information for anomaly and intrusion detection systems. In a general log-based anomaly detection system, network, devices, and host logs are all collected and used together for analysis and the detection of anomalies. However, the ever-increasing volume of logs remains as one of the main challenges that anomaly detection tools face. Based on Sysmon, this chapter proposes a host-based log analysis system that detects anomalies without using network logs to reduce the volume and to show the importance of host-based logs. The authors implement a Sysmon parser to parse and extract features from the logs and use them to perform detection methods on the data. The valuable information is successfully retained after two extensive volume reduction steps. An anomaly detection system is proposed and performed on five different datasets with up to 55,000 events which detects the attacks using the preserved logs. The analysis results demonstrate the significance of host-based logs in auditing, security monitoring, and intrusion detection systems.

Inspired computing is based on biomimcry of natural occurrences. It is a discipline in which problems are solved using computer models which derive their abstractions from real-world living organisms and their social behavior. It is a branch of machine learning that is very closely related to artificial intelligence. This form of computing can be effectively used for data security, feature extraction, etc. It can easily be integrated with different areas such as big data, IoT, cloud computing, edge computing, and fog computing for data security. The chapter discusses some of the most popular biologically-inspired computation algorithms which can be used to create secured framework for data security in big data like ant colony optimization, artificial bee colony, bacterial foraging optimization to name a few. Explanation of these algorithms and scope of its application are given. Furthermore, case studies are presented to help the reader understand the application of these techniques for security in big data.

Rapid growth of embedded devices and population density in IoT-based smart cities provides great potential for business and opportunities in urban planning. For addressing the current and future needs of living, smart cities have to revitalize the potential of big data analytics. However, a colossal amount of sensitive information invites various computational challenges. Moreover, big data generated by the IoT paradigm acquires different characteristics as compared to traditional big data because it contains heterogeneous unstructured data. Despite various challenges in big data, enterprises are trying to utilize its true potential for providing proactive applications to the citizens. In this chapter, the author finds the possibilities of the role of big data in the efficient management of smart cities. Representative applications of big data, along with advantages and disadvantages, are also discussed. By delving into the ongoing research approaches in securing and providing privacy to big data, this chapter is concluded by highlighting the open research issues in the domain.

Many sectors and fields are being computerized to make the work paperless, more transparent, and efficient. Banking is one such sector that has undergone enormous changes. Any amount from any part to any corner of the world is now possible around the clock. The dependency on technology for providing the services necessitates security, and the additional risks involved in cross-border nature of transactions of banks poses new challenges for banking regulators and supervisors. Many types of research are going in this area of banks big data processing, data analytics, and providing security for cross-border payments to mitigate the risks. Block chain is one such advancement for addressing the challenges in financial services. This chapter provides a brief overview of block chain usage, addressing the traditional issues and challenges for cross-border transactions.

Chapter 11

Hicham Amellal, University Mohamed V, Morocco
Abdelmajid Meslouhi, University Mohamed V, Morocco
Abderahim El Allati, Abdelmalek Essaadi University, Morocco
Annas El Haddadi, ENSA El-Hoceima, Morocco

With the advancement of communication and information technology, the internet has become used as a platform for computing and not only a way of communications networks. Accordingly, the large spread of cloud computing led to the emergence of different privacy implications and data security complexities. In order to enhance data security in the cloud, the authors propose in this chapter the use of an encryption box, which includes different cryptosystems. In fact, this step gives the user the opportunities to encrypt data with an unknown algorithm and makes a private key before the storage of data in the host company servers. Moreover, to manage the encryption database, the authors propose a quantum approach in search based on Grover's algorithm.

Chapter 12

Awanthika Senarath, University of New South Wales, Australia
Nalin Asanka Gamagedara Arachchilage, The University of New South Wales, Australia

There could be numerous reasons that drive organizations to provide privacy protections to end users in the applications they develop and maintain. Organizational motivations towards privacy affects the quality of privacy received by end users. Understanding these motivations and the approaches taken by organizations towards privacy protection would assist the policymakers and regulators to define effective frameworks encouraging organizational privacy practices. This study focuses on understanding the motivations behind organizational decisions and the approaches they take to embed privacy into the software applications. The authors analyzed 40 organizations different in size, scope, scale of operation, nature of data used, and revenue. they identified four groups of organizations characterized by the approach taken to provide privacy protection to their users. The taxonomy contributes to the organizational perspective of privacy. The knowledge presented here would help addressing the challenges in the domain of user privacy in software applications and services.

In today's internet world the internet of things (IoT) is becoming the most significant and developing technology. The primary goal behind the IoT is enabling more secure existence along with the improvement of risks at various life levels. With the arrival of IoT botnets, the perspective towards IoT products has transformed from enhanced living enabler into the internet of vulnerabilities for cybercriminals. Of all the several types of malware, botnet is considered as really a serious risk that often happens in cybercrimes and cyber-attacks. Botnet performs some predefined jobs and that too in some automated fashion. These attacks mostly occur in situations like phishing against any critical targets. Files sharing channel Information are moved to DDoS attacks. IoT botnets have subjected two distinct problems, firstly, on the public internet. Most of the IoT devices are easily accessible. Secondly, in the architecture of most of the IoT units, security is usually a reconsideration. This particular chapter discusses IoT, botnet in IoT, and various botnet detection techniques available in IoT.

Information system (IS) security threats are still a major concern for many organizations. However, most organizations fall short in achieving a successful adoption and implementation of IS security measures. In this chapter, the authors developed a theoretical model for the adoption process of IS security innovations in organizations. The model was derived by combining four theoretical models of innovation adoption, namely diffusion of innovation theory (DOI), the technology acceptance model (TAM), the theory of planned behavior (TPB), and the technology-organisation-environment (TOE) framework. The model depicts IS security innovation adoption in organizations, as two decision proceedings. The adoption process from the initiation stage until the acquisition of innovation is considered as a decision made by organisation while the process of innovation assimilation is assumed as a result of the user acceptance of innovation within the organization.

Digital processes for banks, insurances, or public services generate big data. Hidden networks and weak signals from frauds activities are sometimes statistically undetectable in the endogenous data respective to processes. The organic intelligence of human experts is able to reverse-engineer new fraud scenarios without statistically significant characteristics, but machine learning usually needs to be taught about them or fails to this task. Deep resonance interference network is a multidisciplinary attempt in probabilistic machine learning inspired from waves temporal reversal in finite space, introduced for big data analysis and hidden data mining. It proposes a theoretical alternative to artificial neural networks for deep learning. It is presented along with experimental outcomes related to fraudulent processes generating data statistically similar to legal endogenous data. Results show particular findings probably due to the systemic nature of the model, which appears closer to reasoning and intuition processes than to the perception processes mainly simulated in deep learning.

Chapter 16

Shingo Yamaguchi, Yamaguchi University, Japan
Brij Gupta, National Institute of Technology Kurukshetra, India

This chapter introduces malware's threat in the internet of things (IoT) and then analyzes the mitigation methods against the threat. In September 2016, Brian Krebs' web site "Krebs on Security" came under a massive distributed denial of service (DDoS) attack. It reached twice the size of the largest attack in history. This attack was caused by a new type of malware called Mirai. Mirai primarily targets IoT devices such as security cameras and wireless routers. IoT devices have some properties which make them malware attack's targets such as large volume, pervasiveness, and high vulnerability. As a result, a DDoS attack launched by infected IoT devices tends to become massive and disruptive. Thus, the threat of Mirai is an extremely important issue. Mirai has been attracting a great deal of attention since its birth. This resulted in a lot of information related to IoT malware. Most of them came from not academia but industry represented by antivirus software makers. This chapter summarizes such information.

Chapter 17

Chitra P., Thiagarajar College of Engineering, India
Abirami S., Thiagarajar College of Engineering, India

Globalization has led to critical influence of air pollution on individual health status. Insights to the menace of air pollution on individual's health can be achieved through a decision support system, built based on air pollution status and individual's health status. The wearable internet of things (wIoT) devices along with the air pollution monitoring sensors can gather a wide range of data to understand the effect of air pollution on individual's health. The high-level feature extraction capability of deep learning can extract productive patterns from these data to predict the future air quality index (AQI) values along with their amount of risks in every individual. The chapter aims to develop a secure decision support system that analyzes the events adversity by calculating the temporal health index (THI) of the individual and the effective air quality index (AQI) of the location. The proposed architecture utilizes fog paradigm to offload security functions by adopting deep learning algorithms to detect the malicious network traffic patterns from the benign ones.

Preface

Big Data refers to the study and applications of large-size datasets that are complex enough to be processed by traditional data-processing algorithms and software. Challenges associated with Big Data typically include capturing, storing, analyzing, searching, sharing, transferring, visualizing, querying, and updating data. Moreover, ensuring privacy of data and its source is also among these challenges. Public Clouds are resulting in the expansion of Big Data due to which security solutions defined for private computing infrastructures including firewalls, De-militarized Zones (DMZs) are not effective. In addition, security mechanisms in a Big Data environment are required to work over heterogeneous composition of diverse hardware, operating systems, and network domains.

With the fast pace increase in the use of Internet-connected devices, the volume of data collected, stored, and processed is also increasing day-by-day bringing newer challenges in terms of information security. Moreover, current security mechanisms are required to be extended in order to satisfy the mobility requirements of the users. These challenges can be categorized into infrastructure security, data privacy, data management and integrity, and reactive security. To develop effective security mechanisms, it is required to understand these aspects in detail.

This book contains chapters dealing with different aspects of security, privacy, and forensics of Big Data. These include Access control models and anonymization algorithms in big data, Data protection and integrity in big data, Security and privacy in big data mining and analytics, Threat detection using big data analytics, Privacy in Big Data end-point input validation and filtering, Privacy in parallel and distributed computation, Data mining security for Big Data, Cryptography in Big Data, Infrastructure Security, Secure Distributed Processing of Data, Security Best Actions for Non-Relational Data-Bases, Data Privacy, Data Analysis through Data Mining Preserving Data Privacy, Cryptographic Solutions for Data Security, Granular Access Control, Data Management and Integrity, Secure Data Storage and Transaction Logs, Data Provenance, Reactive Security, End-to-End Filtering & Validation, Supervising the Security Level in Real-Time and so on.

Acknowledgment

Many people have contributed greatly to this book on Security, Privacy, and Forensics Issues in Big Data. We, the editors, would like to acknowledge all of them for their valuable help and generous ideas in improving the quality of this book. With our feelings of gratitude, we would like to introduce them in turn. The first mention is the authors and reviewers of each chapter of this book. Without their outstanding expertise, constructive reviews and devoted effort, this comprehensive book would become something without contents. The second mention is the IGI Global staff, especially Courtney Tychinski, development editor and her team for their constant encouragement, continuous assistance and untiring support. Without their technical support, this book would not be completed. The third mention is the editor's family for being the source of continuous love, unconditional support and prayers not only for this work, but throughout our life. Last but far from least, we express our heartfelt thanks to the Almighty for bestowing over us the courage to face the complexities of life and complete this work.

Ramesh C. Joshi
Graphic Era University, India

Brij B. Gupta
National Institute of Technology Kurukshetra, India
June 3, 2019

Chapter 1
Securing the Cloud for Big Data

Michael Robinson
ⓘ https://orcid.org/0000-0002-4276-2359
Airbus, UK

Kevin Jones
Airbus, UK

ABSTRACT

This chapter explores how organizations can seek to secure a public cloud environment for use in big data operations. It begins by describing the challenges that cloud customers face when moving to the cloud, and proposes that these challenges can be summarized as a loss of control and visibility into the systems and controls around data. The chapter identifies thirteen areas where visibility and control can be lost, before progressing to highlight ten solutions to help regain these losses. It is proposed that planning is the most significant step a customer can take in ensuring a secure cloud for big data. Good planning will enable customers to know their data and pursue a risk-based approach to cloud security. The chapter provides insight into future research directions, highlighting research areas which hold the potential to further empower cloud customers in the medium to long term.

INTRODUCTION

Cloud has become the ideal platform for big data (Hashem, Yaqoob, Anuar, Mokhtar, Gani, & Khan, 2015): a seemingly limitless pool of computing resources which can be rapidly provisioned and scaled up or down as needed on a pay per use basis. Whilst being ideal for big data activities, the use of cloud presents new security challenges that do not exist when using an on-premise solution or private data centre (Singh, Jeong, & Park, 2016).

Many of these new challenges emerge from the fact that the customer relinquishes control over the infrastructure, processes and handling of data when moving to cloud (Behl, 2011). They instead place trust into the cloud provider that their data will be secure and that the service will be available for use when required. We propose that this trust is often given based upon the assurances from the cloud provider, contractual agreements and upon their reputation.

DOI: 10.4018/978-1-5225-9742-1.ch001

The aim of the chapter is to provide practical managerial guidance in deploying big data operations securely. The chapter begins by providing a review of areas where big data customers face security risks when moving to a public cloud environment. Following this, a survey of solutions which can address these risks is provided. Where appropriate, we provide links to ongoing research efforts which seek to improve and enhance big data security in the cloud and finish with a discussion on future research directions.

Background

The National Institute of Standards and Technology (NIST) defines cloud computing as "a model for enabling ubiquitous, convenient, on-demand network access to a shared pool of configurable computing resources" (Mell & Grance, 2011). It is a technology which fits many big data use cases well, removing upfront investment in hardware whilst providing agility, scalability and reliability in a pay-as-you-go context. As individuals and organisations continue to see the benefits of cloud for big data and other computing activities, it is an industry which continues to grow year on year. Evidencing the popularity of cloud, Gartner has predicted that the worldwide public cloud services market will grow 17.3 percent to total $206.2 billion in 2019 (Gartner Research, 2018).

Despite the benefits of cloud, organisations can be hesitant in their adoption for a number of reasons. Firstly, cyberspace is becoming an increasingly hostile environment. In 2015 Symantec reported that data breaches led to over half a billion personal records being lost or stolen globally (Symantec, 2016). A year later, this figure had doubled to just over one billion (Symantec, 2017). These cyber threats are not just coming from cyber criminals, but also from states and intelligence services which seek to conduct espionage (Hoboken & Rubinstein, 2014). In this hostile cyber environment, organisations are understandably cautious about sending data out of their perimeter, across the public internet to be received, stored and processed at a remote location by a third party.

These concerns are amplified due to the fact that national governments and regulators are strengthening legislation in regard to the protection of personal data. The European General Data Protection Regulation (GDPR) came into force in May 2018, with heavy fines for data controllers found to have failed in their duty to protect personal data. These penalties alone can be significant enough to threaten the financial health of an organisation, before reputational damage is even considered.

Cloud can also fundamentally change the architecture of systems and requires an understanding of new risks and controls to mitigate them (Gou, Yamaguchi, & Gupta, 2016; Singh, Jeong, & park, 2016). Without cloud expertise, the security of a deployment can be hard to assess and many customers accept that a level of control and transparency over their data will be lost in exchange for the benefits it brings (Flittner, Balaban, & Bless, 2016). This loss of control and increase in risk has been visualised by Saxena and Choudrey (2014) in Figure 1:

APPROACH

The focus of this chapter is to provide practical security guidance to those operating cloud based big data operation so that risks are lowered whilst control is raised. To achieve this goal, the flow of the chapter is as follows. We first describe thirteen areas where big data cloud customers face increased risks and

Figure 1. Relationship between risk and control when moving to cloud
(Adapted from Saxena and Chourey (2014))

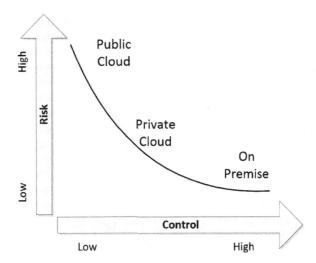

reduced control, discussing the main issues and providing links to further reading. We then move on to survey practical solutions and technologies which can be leveraged to reduce these risks and return control back into the customer's hands.

Risks and Control Losses

Regulatory Compliance

In a traditional data centre, the organisation controls where data is stored, how it is handled and how it is processed. It can implement controls as needed to comply with local laws and regulatory requirements. When moving to the public cloud, ensuring that operations comply with regulatory requirements becomes more challenging (Gozman & Willcocks, 2019). A prime example associated with cloud is personal data protection (Kemp, 2018). While data protection laws can vary by country, they commonly place conditions upon the movement of personal data across geographical borders. In a public cloud environment, customers lose direct control and visibility over the geographic location of where their data is stored and processed. In a big data environment, where there is potential for the use of personal data, the customer is at risk if they do not make specific efforts to regain control over data location. A practical example of this risk being realised can be found in the invalidation of the EU-US Safe Harbour Agreement, which had previously allowed US companies to transfer and store EU citizen data in the US. Upon its invalidation by a court, any organisation which processed and stored EU citizen data in US based cloud services was at risk of being in violation of data protection laws (Tracol, 2016). As a further challenge, there is uncertainty around the question of whether organisations using public cloud providers will be able to fully comply with EU GDPR regulations. The regulations set requirements and parameters for detecting and reporting security breaches, which some have suggested could be difficult to meet due to the challenges of cloud forensics (Duncan, 2018).

With big data having applications in multiple regulatory areas, including health and payment domains, customers must ensure that they remain compliant to laws and regulations in their respective areas. A comprehensive survey of these regulatory challenges has been conducted by Yimam and Fernandez (2016) and is recommended for further reading.

Legal Requests and eDiscovery

Electronic discovery is now central to legal proceedings and is defined as "any process in which electronic data is sought, located, and secured, with the intent of using it as evidence in a civil or criminal legal case." (Biggs & Vidalis, 2009). The challenges that cloud presents to the discovery phase of legal proceedings are well documented (Araiza, 2011) but from the perspective of a cloud customer running big data processes, the primary concern is maintaining visibility over legal requests for data and retaining the ability to respond and challenge it if necessary. Failure to do so may result in further legal action which can not only damage the financial health of the organisation, but also its reputation.

The legal requirements placed upon organisations and cloud providers are tightening. A contemporary example can be found in the U.S. CLOUD act (Daskal, 2018). This act enables U.S. law enforcement to make legal requests for data directly to U.S. based cloud providers, regardless of the physical storage location. It also allows for nations to enter into executive agreements with the U.S. administration, enabling them to make use of this streamlined approach to quickly access data stored with U.S. based cloud providers. The act has raised a number of privacy concerns (Rodriguez, 2018) and emphasises the need for customers to retain visibility and control over the legal aspects of their data. Further reading on the legal risks facing cloud users is available (Choo, 2014) (Brown, Glisson, Andel, & Choo, 2018).

Governance

Corporate governance has many definitions (Madini, Hussain, Ghashgari, Walters, & Wills, 2015) but can be most easily thought of as the policy, process, and internal controls that comprise how an organisation is run (Cloud Security Alliance, 2017). When big data operations are moved to public cloud, customers no longer have complete control over how their operations are governed. The customer's reputation and ability to conduct business becomes linked with the cloud provider's actions and choices. Customers must trust that the cloud provider will take prudent business decisions and operate in a stable, sustainable and ethical manner. Business risks taken by the cloud provider are shared with customers, since a bad decision at the cloud may have implications to customer operations. These implications may be operational, reputational or in the worst cases, the cloud provider may become financially troubled and cease operations. This has been referred to as the risk of vendor demise (Pearson & Benameur, 2010). It is therefore essential that any organisation looking to move big data operations into the cloud must be aware of and mitigate governance risks.

Portability

When using an on premise big data solution, it is possible to have full control over the format of data and the software used. If another product could produce a better result, work can begin to port data across. In a public cloud environment, this control can be lost: the data (including metadata) may be stored in a proprietary format. Cloud providers may not offer an easy method to export the data in bulk.

The portability of instances, configurations, code, data and metadata between providers can also be at risk (Silva, Rose, & Calinescu, 2013) if the cloud provider does not offer good portability features. Differing technologies, service level agreements, protocols, APIs, security features, and data formats have been identified as significant causes of poor portability (Opara-Martins, 2018) and in particular to those deploying big data operations (Lovas, Nagy, & Kovács, 2018).

Poor portability can lead to lock-in: Organisations are unable to change to a competitor or bring operations back on premise. They may find themselves unable to harness the latest technologies, take advantage of better service levels or lower costs by moving to another provider. This could hamper the effectiveness of a big data deployment both in the short and long term.

Disaster Recovery

Events such as hardware failure, human error, malicious attack or natural disasters can lead to business critical systems and data becoming lost, disclosed or unavailable. In a traditional IT environment, an organisation has full control over the handling of disaster scenarios. The most critical systems can be made more robust, whilst disaster recovery plans can be designed to meet an organisation's specific needs and priorities (Snedaker & Rima, 2014).

In a cloud environment, an organisation can architect for resiliency at the higher layers but must trust that the provider has suitable plans and controls in place at the infrastructure and metastructure layer. Major providers reassure customers that they have disaster recovery plans in place but specific details can be lacking. The customer also accepts a level of opaqueness in relation to fault resolution times. With no direct line of communication to front line fault resolution teams, customers must wait for official updates as they filter through the provider's chain of command for public release. This lack of visibility into the specifics of a failure may hamper an organisation's ability to manage the downtime. It may be difficult to estimate how long an outage will be, and therefore difficult to judge whether contingency plans should be put into action.

Incident Response and Forensics

Customers using a public cloud service can architect some security incident detection and forensic capability into their environments (Ruan, Carthy, Kechadi, & Crosbie, 2011). Since clouds are largely software defined, many activities can be logged such as user access, API calls, network activity and file activity. While this is useful for forensics, customers have little say over the types of logs that can be generated, or what format they are provided in: they use what the cloud vendor provides. Such logging is also limited to the customer environment: hypervisor logs or any other relating to the cloud metastructure will not be available for customer inspection. For breaches at the cloud infrastructure level the organisation must rely upon the cloud provider to detect incidents, conduct investigations and communicate the findings. Each organisation is likely to have different expectations on the timeliness of detection and the frequency and detail of reporting. This may not align with the level of incident response the vendor is able or willing to provide and again leads to a lack of visibility and control and ultimately a risk to be managed.

Applications and Tools

Cloud providers often make big data tools available for use by customers. Tools are available for interactive analytics, big data processing, data warehousing, dashboarding and more. Whilst these tools enable an organisation to quickly start-up big data operations, the customer has little control or visibility over how they are configured, coded or maintained. The customer trusts that the applications are coded securely, regularly tested and updated as necessary. The security challenges that insecure coding presents has been well documented (Mathew, 2012), (Acar, et al., 2017) and customers must therefore factor this concern into their risk assessment and seek out potential mitigations if it likely to generate a high risk.

Data Security

When opting to use a public cloud environment, an organisation must trust that their data will be handled securely. Data security is commonly considered at three stages:

1. **At Rest:** When the data is in storage.
2. **In Transit:** While the data is moving between components, across a network.
3. **In Processing:** While the data is being processed.

At each stage, the customer trusts that the confidentiality, integrity and availability of data will be protected. Encryption is the common control to ensure data security, but encryption alone cannot remove all need for trust. For example, the encryption keys themselves are often stored in the cloud provider's key management system (KMS). Customers can set access control policies to these keys, but it is ultimately the cloud provider that administrates these systems. Furthermore, data must be decrypted to be processed and is exposed at this point. When thinking about data security, the areas of physical and human security must also be considered: how is the data physically protected? How are staff vetted, trained and monitored? It is therefore unavoidable that some level of trust in the provider is needed, although solutions discussed later in this chapter can minimise that need.

Supply Chain and Outsourcing

Organisations using on premise solutions can choose suppliers, equipment and contractors according to their own policies, vetting processes and risk appetite. An organisation using a cloud service must trust that the provider has chosen subcontractors carefully, and that it monitors them for compliance with security procedures. Similarly, customers cannot express requirements for specific hardware or software suppliers and must trust the provider's judgement and processes. Some of the larger providers produce their own hardware (Richman, 2017). Publicly available details on this hardware will be minimal and external scrutiny of such devices (e.g. security testing) could be limited. This may be a case of security by obscurity, which tends to be a high-risk approach (Diehl, 2016). Customers therefore must trust that such hardware is securely designed, robustly tested and regularly maintained.

Capacity Planning

When moving big data operations to a public cloud, the customer must trust that the provider has enough spare capacity to absorb spikes in demand, not just from itself but from all of its customers. If the cloud provider under provisions, a spike in demand from multiple customers may lead to resource exhaustion and degradation of performance. Providers themselves have to strike the balance between having enough resources, but not too many (Jiang, Perng, Li, & Chang, 2012). Whilst it is rare for a major cloud provider to encounter significant capacity issues, it has been noted that common patterns in fail-over architecture could lead to potential issues. For example, *us-east-1* is a popular AWS region for many businesses in the United States, and many architect fail-over systems to switch to *us-east-2* if an outage occurs. This could lead to a tsunami of automatic migrations flooding into *us-east-2* and has the potential to cause a domino effect: as one region fails, others get a spike in demand and suffer performance issues. Customers must trust that the provider has mitigations in place, and that spikes in demand can be handled gracefully.

Billing

An on-premise solution generally provides predictable ongoing costs which can be budgeted for. The hardware has been purchased, and support contracts for maintenance are in place. Moving to the cloud involves a switch from predictable upfront investment to a potentially more unpredictable pay as you go service. By moving to a pay per use structure, organisations are accepting that an unexpected spike in resource consumption will lead to increased bills that may not be planned for. A surge in use can be legitimate, but could also be a bug in software consuming excessive resources (e.g. memory leaks), human error in configuration or an attack in the form of economic denial of service. An example of this was seen in 2015, when an organisation faced a $30,000USD daily bill from their cloud provider due to an economic denial of service attack (Somani, Gaur, Sanghi, Conti, & Buyya, 2017). It has also been noted that cloud billing is largely unobservable to the customer, asynchronous and often an aggregate of many individual events (Jellinek, Zhai, Ristenpart, & Swift, 2014). This may make it difficult for a customer to gain insight into how much their use is costing and deny them the ability to break the costs down into specific events and resource use.

Perimeter

Organisations with traditional on-premise IT systems have full control over the perimeter. They are able to lower risks by controlling which systems are internet facing, and limiting public access to sensitive systems with firewall rules or physical isolation. This is the fortress approach to security: a trusted inside protected from attack by a impenetrable wall. As cloud has risen in popularity, this traditional fortress approach to security has steadily become less relevant, along with all of its associated controls such as firewalls and intrusion detection systems (Amoroso, 2013).

In the cloud, assets are highly dispersed and shared between multiple customers. Credentials and access management become the critical control in protecting an environment from intruders. Customers must configure the access controls as needed, but again have no visibility or control over them at the infrastructure level. The customer therefore trusts that the software controlling these systems are robust, secure and well maintained.

Connectivity

Traditional IT deployments use local area networks to provide access to systems and enable staff to perform their duties. These networks can be private, carrying only the organisation's traffic. Performance can be monitored and failures can be addressed as a priority by local support teams. By moving to a cloud-based system, an organisation loses this control and visibility over connectivity. They instead place trust in public networks and all of the entities which use and control it. Internet providers, backbone carriers and other users all have the potential to impact a connection between an organisation and a cloud provider. Any failure by these external actors has the potential to disrupt connectivity and business functions. Malicious acts such as denial of service (Negi, Mishra, & Gupta, 2013) or even physical cable attacks must be considered here. These have the potential to degrade performance or cause unavailability, even if not specifically directed at the cloud provider or customer.

SOLUTIONS

It is clear that moving big data operations to public cloud comes not only with benefits, but also with risks. Customers relinquish control in a number of areas and instead place trust in the provider whilst accepting increased risks. In this section, we propose that a secure big data cloud deployment rests upon two fundamental overarching pillars: Planning and architecting for security. These pillars are visualised in Figure 2.

The rest of this chapter is dedicated to looking deeper into these two pillars, to explore the contents of each and how the specific solutions available to customers help secure their cloud environments.

Figure 2. The two pillars of secure cloud usage

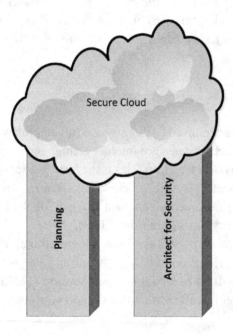

Planning

Before starting big data operations in the cloud, it is essential that customers plan for security. Planning is arguably the most important activity a customer can undertake and will help to inform later decisions regarding which security controls to implement. Planning enables an organisation to have clear goals in mind and a reference point to return to when faced with unexpected architectural or policy decisions.

The Cloud Security Alliance (CSA) propose a cloud security process model, which can be used as a high level roadmap towards planning and deploying big data applications into the cloud (Cloud Security Alliance, 2017). The model emphasises the importance of planning, so that risks can be identified and controls put into place. A visual representation of the model is shown in Figure 3.

The CSA model does not cover every aspect of planning, but can act as a high level framework for those seeking to move big data operations to a cloud environment. The first step is to identify the requirements: what is the system trying to achieve and what are the requirements to make that happen? The specifics of this step will vary, depending upon the size of the organisation and the data being used, but at a minimum the customer should think about the following:

- **Data Classification:** Know what data will be ingested into the platform and its security classification. Will confidential data be allowed? What about personal information such as names, telephone numbers etc.? Without having a solid understanding of the data, visibility and control over it can quickly be lost as it is ingested into the platform, placed into a data lake and mingled with other data for new results.
- **Roles:** Whilst the attraction of big data is that new insights can be generated by finding new meaning from a pool of data, the principle of least privilege should still be applied. With knowledge of the data classification, consider how users of the system should be assigned to roles. For example, data scientists with security clearance can access all types of data, whilst external staff are limited to less sensitive data. Similarly, someone designing a dashboard could be limited to a dummy set of data for the purposes of design and testing only.
- **Data Lineage:** For each dataset to be uploaded, keep a record of where it originally came from and who the owner was. Consider if technical measures will be needed to keep track of data as it transforms. In large organisations with many departments and responsible entities, it may be challenging to retroactively trace data back to its original source.
- **Risk Assessment:** Conduct risk assessments to identify your position in certain scenarios. For example, if certain datasets were leaked, tampered with or made unavailable. What would be the

Figure 3. Cloud security alliance security process model
(adapted from (Cloud Security Alliance, 2017))

impact? How much downtime would be acceptable? Once you have a clear understanding of how much risk you are willing to accept, this will influence the kinds of controls to be implemented.

With an understanding of what is required from the platform, the customer can begin to survey the cloud market for a suitable provider. A key tool in this process will be the study of a provider's contractual and service agreements.

Contracts and Cloud Service Agreements

The contract between the customer and the provider is one of the most significant ways in which a customer can gain visibility into how the provider operates. The Cloud Standards Consumer Council (CSCC) defines a Cloud Service Agreement (CSA) as "a set of documents or agreements that contain the terms governing the relationship between the cloud customer and the cloud service provider'' (Cloud Standards Customer Council, 2015). The CSA is valuable because it sets out each party's responsibilities. For example, the AWS customer agreement states that they will implement reasonable and appropriate measures designed to help you secure your content against accidental or unlawful loss, access or disclosure. It also sets out that the customer must take some responsibility, by taking appropriate actions to secure, backup and protect their data. This reduces uncertainty over who is responsible for certain aspects and provides the customer with legally binding assurances over how the provider will act.

A Service Level Agreement (SLA) also commonly exists. The SLA sets out the level of service the cloud provider promises to provide, and includes metrics such as guaranteed uptime and levels of performance. In practice, responsibility for detecting violations of the SLA falls upon the cloud customer who must identify a violation and submit a claim for compensation along with supporting evidence. Compensation is usually in the form of service credits, which serves the purpose of maintaining the customer's loyalty despite the violation.

CSAs provide visibility to customers but rarely control: public cloud providers are able to keep costs low by offering a fixed service which is suitable for the majority of customers. The terms are therefore non-negotiable in most cases. However, customers should read them carefully and ensure that they suit the requirements identified in the planning stage. This will provide the customer with visibility over what the cloud provider promises to do and where gaps remain that must be filled by the customer or by selecting another provider.

Unfortunately it has been noted that the majority of cloud SLAs today focus purely upon availability and performance – not security (Hoehl, 2015). Existing metrics included in cloud SLAs are commonly centred around the SMART principle (i.e. any metric should be Specific, Measurable, Achievable, Relevant and Timely (W Krag & Hinson, 2016). This suits parameters such as uptime, network latency and available storage, but finding metrics that are SMART in relation to confidentiality and integrity is an ongoing research challenge which poses multi-faceted problems for researchers (Jansen, 2009). Researchers have been active in addressing this gap. Some have proposed a set of security metrics on a per service basis (Hoehl, 2015). Others have proposed methods to quantitatively reason about cloud security using quantitative policy trees and hierarchical process techniques (Luna, Taha, Trapero, & Suri, 2015).

Implementing security metrics into cloud agreements would require buy-in by cloud providers, but if it does become offered it will be a useful resource for customers to measure and compare not just availability promises but also security promises. But until then, customers must turn to other methods to get security assurances, such as evaluative standards.

Evaluative Standards

Evaluative standards such as ISO27001 have established themselves as a means for service providers to demonstrate a commitment to information security, provide assurances to customers and prove that the organisation has passed a standardised set of information security criteria (Calder & Watkins, 2008). The following are standards that concern cloud computing in some form:

- **ISO/IEC 17789:2014:** Specifies the ISO/IEC cloud computing reference architecture.
- **ISO/IEC 27017:2015:** Also known as ITU-T X.1631, this standard provides guidelines to support the implementation of information security controls for cloud service customers and cloud service providers.
- **ISO/IEC 27018:2014:** Code of practice for protection of personally identifiable information (PII) in public clouds.
- **ISO/IEC 27001:** Widely regarded standard for information security assurance.
- **ITU-T X.1601:** Describes the security framework for cloud computing.
- **ISO/IEC 19086:2016:** Multi part series which describes standards for cloud SLAs.
- **ISO/IEC 27036-4:2016:** Defines guidelines supporting the implementation of information security management for the use of cloud services.
- **HIPAA Compliance:** US Health Insurance Portability and Accountability Act, for the protection of health data.
- **SOC:** System and Organization Control audit.
- **PCI DSS**: Payment Card Industry Data Security Standard - applies to entities that store, process, or transmit cardholder data or sensitive authentication data.
- **National Specific Schemes:** e.g. FedRAMP, DoD SRG for US. IRAP for Australian Government, ENS for Spain and so on.

Cloud providers know the value that customers place into evaluative standards, and the major three providers display the standards they are certified to on their respective websites. However, to complicate matters it must be noted that certifications held by cloud providers do not necessarily apply to all of its services. Customers therefore need to ensure that the specific services they are using are in the scope of the certification being presented.

Standardisation bodies such as ISO/IEC are continually updating and releasing new standards. For example, ISO/IEC NP TR 23613 is currently at the proposal stage and concerns cloud service metering and billing elements. However, it has been argued that the process of updating and releasing new standards is not quick enough to cover new threats which may arise as the pace of cloud service evolution increases (Di Giulio, et al., 2017). To address this, some have called for a shift to continuous auditing (Quinting, Lins, Szefer, & Sunyaev, 2017), whereby a provider must continually prove that it is compliant.

Once a customer has chosen a suitable cloud provider, they can then begin to think about the second pillar: architecting for security.

Architect for Security

Cloud providers take responsibility for securing the underlying infrastructure and metastructure of the service, but it is always the customer's responsibility to design and secure their own environment. This is our second pillar of cloud security: architecting for security.

Public clouds are highly software defined: the provider secures the underlying hardware and virtualisation systems, whilst the customer builds and connects virtual assets together using a web-based software interface (sometimes called the management plane) (Cloud Security Alliance, 2017). Although the customer has no control over the underlying hardware, they have full visibility and control over the virtual infrastructure they build on top of it. This enables a customer to architect their big data deployment for security. Architecting for security means that the customer creates their virtual infrastructure in a way that promotes security. At the core of virtual infrastructure design is the concept of a virtual private cloud (VPC). A VPC is the customer's virtual environment and can initially be thought of as an empty datacentre. Leveraging software defined networks the VPC can be populated with virtual machines, firewalls, routers, load balancers and so on. The VPC offers opportunities for secure design:

- **High Availability:** VPCs make automatic fail over and load balancing relatively simple, but the customer must architect their environment to take advantage of these capabilities.
- **Isolation:** Because everything is software defined, services can be highly isolated. A VPC could contain just one instance which performs a very specific task. This VPC may be configured to have no internet connectivity and only allow one other service to access it on a specific port. This reduces the attack surface as well as the blast radius, should that environment be compromised.
- **Firewalls:** Software defined firewalls tend to be more granular than physical firewalls. This can be leveraged to have tight control over not only which IP addresses may pass, but also to specific users and resources. Apply deny by default principles and be explicit in what is allowed, down to specific roles and assets.
- **Templating:** Because the virtual infrastructure is a software construct, known good configurations can be saved as a template. In the event of a security breach or undesirable change, the environment can simply be rolled back to a known good configuration with a few clicks of a mouse. Templating is also valuable in other ways. It can help to control billing since customers are less likely to end up with orphaned assets (i.e. instances or storage where the purpose or ownership is unclear) if everything is built via a validated template. It is also easier to estimate costs when everything in the environment is template based.
- **Logging and Alerting:** Because everything in a customer's virtual infrastructure is software and API based, there are opportunities for extensive logging and alerting. File and network activity, user actions, infrastructure changes and resource consumption can all be monitored and alerts automatically generated. Even features such as budget alerting can be leveraged to increased visibility: an unexpected rise in costs could indicate a security breach or misconfiguration. This capability needs to be architected in by the customer, but the amount of visibility good logging returns into operations is significant.
- **Private Connectivity:** Relying on the public internet to access the cloud results in a significant amount of trust being placed into multiple third parties. Denial of Service attacks (Negi, Mishra, & Gupta, 2013), failures and high latency all have the potential to degrade performance and lead

to a loss of availability. To reduce the need to trust the public internet, some providers offer private, dedicated end to end connectivity which does not utilise the public internet at all (Amazon, 2018). This should be considered in cases where the risk assessment has determined that degraded or interrupted communications would not be acceptable.

Depending upon the level of risk (as defined by the risk assessment), customers may wish to utilise some of the additional features that major cloud providers are now starting to offer:

- **Data Loss Prevention (DLP):** Many cloud providers offer native DLP tools to monitor the movement and access of files. DLP can return a significant amount of visibility and control into how data is being moved and accessed but as with all tools, the customer must architect their system to utilise it.
- **User/entity Behavioural Analytics (UEBA):** UEBA uses machine learning and statistical models to look for unusual user or entity activity (Yang, Liu, & Zou, 2011). This takes auditing of cloud activity beyond being reactive to being pro-active, allowing malicious activity to be spotted and potentially blocked as it is occurring. It is becoming increasingly offered as a native tool at major cloud providers and can return valuable visibility into unusual behaviour.
- **Legal Compliance Tools:** Cloud providers often offer tools which can help to increase control and visibility over legal compliance. For example, legal holds can be placed upon storage services at which point they become immutable, allowing it to be preserved and used as evidence.

Encryption

When thinking about data security in the cloud, and specifically big data, encryption is one of the key controls to architect into the environment. Major cloud providers such as AWS, Google and Microsoft offer encryption in transit and at rest by default. This encryption is largely invisible to customers: encryption, decryption and key management are handled automatically. The service agreement will commonly provide visibility into the type of encryption used and how keys will be managed. In cases where the data is non-sensitive, provider managed encryption will likely be suitable: it is simple to manage, low cost and offers adequate protection from data theft.

In cases where the data is more sensitive the customer may wish for increased control by implementing other solutions. There are a number of options here:

- **Customer Held Key:** Major providers now offer to let the customer hold and manage their own key. Data is still encrypted and decrypted at the cloud, but the key is sent with each API request and is only held in volatile memory until the requested operation is completed.
- **Cloud Based Hardware Security Module (HSM):** The provider offers to store the key in a cloud based HSM. The customer then has exclusive control over the key lifecycle. The provider can still use the key when necessary.
- **Client-Side Encryption:** The customer encrypts the data either before it is uploaded to the cloud or at the application layer at the cloud. Decryption takes place on premise or at the application layer using a process and keys defined and controlled by the customer. The cloud provider has no involvement in this process.

- **Proxy Encryption:** The customer employs a trusted third party to intercept and encrypt data before it reaches the cloud.

Whilst these solutions are applicable to protecting data at rest, they do not help to protect data in processing. Data that is being processed must be in its plaintext form, and is therefore exposed to the provider during this stage. If a customer regards this as an unacceptable risk, the field of homomorphic encryption (HE) holds potential to mitigate it. HE is a field of research aimed at allowing computation to take place upon encrypted data, without having to decrypt it first (Armknecht et al., 2015). This places a significant amount of control back into the hands of customers, since the data is never exposed in clear text form to the cloud provider. Whilst the research community continues to make advances, HE is not yet a technology suitable for common cloud computing tasks such as big data processing. However, it is always advancing and will likely become a viable control in the future.

Other technologies in this domain include searchable encryption. Searchable encryption schemes enable untrusted systems such as the cloud to conduct searches upon encrypted data without decrypting it and without learning anything about the clear text. Research into searchable encryption is not new: authors such as Song et al. (Song, Wagner, & Perrig, 2000) have been discussing the concept for a number of years, demonstrating schemes which allow searching of encrypted data. Over the years it has advanced to a point where it is starting to see some practical uses (Gupta, Agrawal, & Yamaguchi, 2016). A third solution to the problem of protecting data in processing is to use a trusted execution environment.

Trusted Execution Environments

An alternative solution to protecting data in processing is the use of trusted execution environments (TEEs). These are environments where code and data can be held and processed, whilst being protected from reads and writes from untrusted external sources. The concept behind TEEs is that whilst the customer may not trust the cloud vendor, they do trust the manufacturer of a TEE which is made available for use. A TEE can be software or hardware based.

A practical example of a hardware-based TEE can be found in Intel's Secure Guard Extension (SGX) technology. A processor using SGX protects the integrity and confidentiality of computation by providing a secure container, also known as an enclave. The secure enclave ensures confidentiality by isolating code and data from the outside environment, including firmware, the operating system and hypervisor (Costan, Lebedev, & Devadas, 2017). Data within the enclave can only be accessed by code which has also been loaded into the enclave by the customer. The integrity of the enclave is ensured through the use of software attestation. This is a process whereby the enclave can prove that the contents have not been tampered with, by presenting a cryptographic certificate and a hash of the loaded data.

Microsoft Hyper-V offers an example of a software based TEE: Virtual Secure Mode (VSM). This feature enables the hypervisor to segregate certain parts of physical memory away from an OS, providing an isolated enclave for sensitive data and code to run (Zylva, 2016). In both of these examples, the need for trust is reduced but never eliminated. In the software example (VSM), the customer must trust the hypervisor which has been coded and maintained by Microsoft. In the hardware example of SGX, the customer must trust Intel.

TEEs are not a new technology, but recent improvements in capability and availability brought by examples such as Intel SGX, VSM and Google's Asylo (Porter, Garms, & Simakov, 2018) have led to it becoming a viable solution for customers looking to reduce the need to trust cloud vendors. In 2017

Microsoft Azure announced availability of SGX in their early access program, and this has now been made available to the public. Others such as Google have also announced their intention to offer SGX and other hardware based solutions. As this technology continues to become more widely available it has the potential to work with encryption to ensure that data is protected at all stages: at rest, in transit and in processing. This will give a significant boost to security of data in the cloud.

Identity and Access Management (IAM)

One of the most important aspects of a secure cloud architecture is identity and access management. Strong access control is often the only barrier preventing an unauthorised party from accessing critical tools such as the management plane (Cloud Security Alliance, 2017). Cloud providers offer native IAM solutions and whilst these solutions are often powerful and secure, a customer seeking to regain some control and visibility may prefer to keep identity data on premise or at a trusted third party. There are generally three approaches to identity management in the cloud:

- **Cloud Identity:** Identity data is stored and managed fully in the cloud environment, commonly referred to as Identity as a service (IDaaS). IDaaS requires trust in the identity provider but can be low cost.
- **Synchronized Identity**: Identity data is managed on premise or at a trusted identity provider, but all identity data (including passwords) is synced to the cloud environment. Authentication then happens at the cloud. This reduces the amount of trust required, since the customer retains control over the data itself and maintains it locally.
- **Federated Identity**: Cloud service does not store or have access to any identity data: authentication and authorisation takes place on premise or at a trusted identity provider, who then informs the cloud of the result (e.g. via SAML assertion). This approach requires the least amount of trust in the cloud provider.

As with all aspects of cyber security, the choice taken by a customer should depend upon their risk assessment. Where there is low risk cloud identity may be the best choice. In cases where the risks are higher, federated identity would be suitable.

With regards to access control, providers offer high levels of granularity here and customers should take advantage of this to implement the roles identified in the planning stage. Attribute Based Access Control (ABAC) can provide high granularity over who is able to access data and in what context (e.g. time of day, device used etc.). This can be valuable when working with sensitive data and/or a large number of users from varying organisations. However, Role Based Access Control (RBAC) can also be suitable in cases where the use cases are relatively simple and the sensitivity of the data is low. As with most areas in security, customers must find their own balance between usability and security. The core cyber security principles of least privilege and deny by default remain true in all cases. This is why the planning phase is important: if a customer already knows how data will be grouped and the types of roles that will exist, access control can be implemented correctly and securely from the outset.

Penetration Testing

Once a customer has architected their deployment, it will be desirable to conduct some security testing in the form of a penetration test. Penetration tests are a valuable activity for ensuring the cyber security of IT systems (Xynos, Sutherland, Read, Everitt, & Blyth, 2010). They can include technical aspects (e.g. testing the robustness of login portals), social elements (e.g. calling and asking for passwords) and attempts to breach physical security at a site. Moving to a cloud environment, customers generally surrender control over the ability to conduct such tests upon the systems that store and process their sensitive data. Customers of cloud services must instead trust that the provider is performing the necessary testing (Jones, 2013).

Some cloud providers do allow limited forms of penetration testing against their services. For example, Google states that it is open to customers performing penetration tests upon its systems, and actively encourages such tests through the Google Vulnerability Reward Programme. This program is limited to technical penetration tests, and is further limited to specific types of attack. Denial of service tests tend not to be permitted by any provider, since the multitenant nature of public cloud means there is potential for multiple customers to be impacted.

A development in this area is the concept of virtual penetration testing. This involves the customer uploading a tool to their cloud based virtual environment, which then automatically performs a specific set of security tests at the customer's virtual network layer. Other pentesting products and services which specifically address cloud environments have also started to emerge (Nettitude, 2017). Despite these services, customers can rarely gain permission to test anything outside of their own virtual environment. This means that customers must still largely trust that the cloud provider is testing these aspects themselves and that any failings are addressed.

RECOMMENDATIONS

Looking at the risk areas, along with the various solutions that are available to mitigate them, it can be challenging for an organisation to determine which solutions will be necessary in a specific scenario. Planning and architecting for security will always be necessary, but the challenge comes in striking the balance between security, usability and cost. While it may be tempting to aim for maximum security, it must be remembered that cyber security is always a balance between risk and reward. Organisations should not seek to implement every solution in this chapter if the identified risks are low. Not only would it be costly in terms of implementation, but also in terms of stifling the high efficiency and performance that big data thrives upon. Instead organisations should identify critical areas in their specific context and apply mitigations to bring the risk down to an acceptable level. For example, if the data being worked on will be sensitive health data, extensive controls such as seeking a provider which is HIPAA compliant and investigating the use of trusted execution environments would be reasonable. However, if the data will be sensor information from geographically distributed IOT devices such as temperature sensors, the security requirement may be much lower. It is therefore recommended that while planning is essential in all cases, the use of other controls will largely depend upon the use case in question and the risk assessment produced. This is why the planning phase is so important: it informs the architecting phase and ensures that customers get this balance right.

FUTURE RESEARCH DIRECTIONS

Whilst many solutions are available for use today, the research community continues to propose and develop new methods to secure the cloud and place more control back into the hands of customers. One of the most promising areas is homomorphic encryption (HE). Today, HE schemes are too inefficient for use in practical scenarios but work to improve efficiency continues. Researchers at Microsoft have explored the benefits that neural networks can bring to solving the efficiency problem (Dowlin, et al., 2016). They developed a cryptonet: a neural network that uses homomorphic encryption to produce encrypted predictions on encrypted data in an acceptable amount of time. They were able to demonstrate that their system can make 51,000 predictions per hour with 99% accuracy while studying a stream of encrypted input images. This level of speed would make it suitable in some practical use cases, such as analysing medical scans in the cloud without endangering patient privacy. The speed of the predictions was bolstered due to an element of pre-preparation. The complexity of the mathematics involved in making the prediction was required to be fixed and known before hand, and the neural network custom designed to handle this and only this level of complexity. Other works have achieved efficiency improvements in the HElib software library (a library which implements homomorphic encryption). With their changes, they were able to achieve 30-75 times speed increases and a 33-55% reduction in key size (Halevi & Shoup, 2018). Further research should be encouraged in this area to bring HE to a commercially viable state.

Further developments are also needed in the field of certification. Researchers have noted that because cloud services evolve so rapidly, certifications achieved at a fixed point in time may not represent the current state of the service (Quinting, Lins, Szefer, & Sunyaev, 2017). This has led to calls for a shift to continuous auditing (Lins, Grochol, Schneider, & Sunyaev, 2016) and new methods to make certifications more relevant to a cloud context and the challenges faced by customers.

Cloud providers themselves have also been active in offering new ways for customers to gain greater visibility and control. For example, Amazon Web Services recently made Security Hub available, a single pane of glass into a high level overview of all accounts and their associated security alerts. As providers compete for customers, it is expected that such features will continue to evolve.

Whilst this chapter has surveyed both current and future solutions for how they can reduce risks, there is scope in future work to also consider costs. Many of the solutions described are already available from cloud providers either as part of existing subscription costs or at minor additional cost. Others are available from third parties for a range of prices. However, other costs such as the time and expertise required to implement and maintain them should be considered. Quantifying such costs would be an interesting area for future work, allowing organisations to better weigh up the risk vs reward for each solution.

CONCLUSION

This chapter has explored the security challenges faced by organisations when moving big data operations into the public cloud. It was proposed that risks increase, whilst control decreases. The chapter proposed that there are two fundamental pillars towards reducing these risks: planning and architecting for security. It was emphasised that not all big data operations should be aiming for the highest levels of security: an organisation's approach should be risk based and solutions applied only if they are mitigating a specific unacceptable risk. This highlights the importance of planning, knowing the data to be processed and the associated risks for a specific scenario.

REFERENCES

Acar, Y., Stransky, C., Wermke, D., Weir, C., Mazurek, M. L., & Fahl, S. (2017). *Developers Need Support, Too: A Survey of Security Advice for Software Developers. Cybersecurity Development (SecDev)* (pp. 22–26). Cambridge, MA: IEEE.

Amazon. (2018). AWS Direct Connect. Retrieved from https://aws.amazon.com/directconnect/

Amoroso, E. G. (2013). From the Enterprise Perimeter to a Mobility-Enabled Secure Cloud. *IEEE Security and Privacy, 11*(1), 23–31. doi:10.1109/MSP.2013.8

Araiza, A. (2011). Electronic discovery in the cloud. *Duke Law & Technology Review*, 1-19.

Armknecht, F., Boyd, C., Carr, C., Gjosteen, K., Jaschke, A., Reuter, C., & Strand, M. (2015). A Guide to Fully Homomorphic Encryption.

Bayramusta, M., & Nasir, V. A. (2016). A fad or future of IT?: A comprehensive literature review on the cloud computing research. *International Journal of Information Management, 36*(4), 635–644. doi:10.1016/j.ijinfomgt.2016.04.006

Behl, A. (2011). Emerging security challenges in cloud computing: An insight to cloud security challenges and their mitigation. In *Proceedings of the World Congress on Information and Communication Technologies* (pp. 217–222). Mumbai: Academic Press; . doi:10.1109/WICT.2011.6141247

Biggs, S., & Vidalis, S. (2009). Cloud Computing: The impact on digital forensic investigations. In *Proceedings of the International Conference for Internet Technology and Secured Transactions, (ICITST)*, London. doi:10.1109/ICITST.2009.5402561

Brandis, K., Dzombeta, S., Colomo-Palacios, R., & Stantchev, V. (n.d.). Governance, Risk, and Compliance in Cloud Scenarios. *Applied Sciences, 320*.

Brown, A. J., Glisson, W. B., Andel, T. R., & Choo, K.-K. R. (2018). Cloud forecasting: Legal visibility issues in saturated environments. *Computer Law & Security Review, 34*(6), 1278–1290. doi:10.1016/j.clsr.2018.05.031

Calder, A., & Watkins, S. (2008). *IT Governance: A Manager's Guide to Data Security and ISO 27001 / ISO 27002*. Kogan Page Ltd.

Choo, K.-K. R. (2014). Legal Issues in the Cloud. *IEEE Cloud Computing*, 94-96.

Chopra, R. (2017). *Cloud Computing: An Introduction*. Mercury Learning and Information.

Cloud Security Alliance. (2017). *Security Guidance for Critical Areas of Focus in Cloud Computing V4.0.*

Cloud Standards Customer Council. (2015, 4). *Practical Guide to Cloud Service Agreements Version 2.0.* Retrieved from https://www.omg.org/cloud/deliverables/practical-guide-to-cloud-service-agreements.htm

Costan, V., Lebedev, I., & Devadas, S. (2017). *Secure Processors Part I: Background, Taxonomy for Secure Enclaves and Intel SGX Architecture*. now. Retrieved from https://ieeexplore.ieee.org/xpl/articleDetails.jsp?arnumber=8186867

Daskal, J. (2018). Microsoft Ireland, the CLOUD Act, and International Lawmaking 2.0. *Stanford Law Review*.

Di Giulio, C., Sprabery, R., Kamhoua, C., Kwiat, K., Campbell, R. H., & Bashir, M. N. (2017). Cloud Security Certifications: A Comparison to Improve Cloud Service Provider Security. In *Proceedings of the Second International Conference on Internet of Things, Data and Cloud Computing* (pp. 1–12). Cambridge: ACM; . doi:10.1145/3018896.3025169

Diehl, E. (2016). Law 3: No Security Through Obscurity. In E. Diehl (Ed.), *Ten Laws for Security* (pp. 67–79). Springer.

Dowlin, N., Gilad-Bachrach, R., Laine, K., Lauter, K., Naehrig, M., & Wernsing, J. (2016). *CryptoNets: Applying Neural Networks to Encrypted Data with High Throughput and Accuracy*. Microsoft Research. Retrieved from https://www.microsoft.com/en-us/research/publication/cryptonets-applying-neural-networks-to-encrypted-data-with-high-throughput-and-accuracy/

Duncan, B. (2018). *Can EU General Data Protection Regulation Compliance be Achieved When Using Cloud Computing?* Barcelona: Cloud Computing.

Flittner, M., Balaban, S., & Bless, R. (2016). CloudInspector: A Transparency-as-a-Service Solution for Legal Issues in Cloud Computing. In *Proceedings of the IEEE International Conference on Cloud Engineering Workshop (IC2EW)*. Academic Press; . doi:10.1109/IC2EW.2016.36

Gartner Research. (2018). Gartner Forecasts Worldwide Public Cloud Revenue to Grow 17.3 Percent in 2019. Stamford.

Gou, Z., Yamaguchi, S., & Gupta, B. B. (2016). Analysis of Various Security Issues and Challenges in Cloud Computing Environment: A Survey. In B. Gupta, D. P. Agrawal, & S. Yamaguchi (Eds.), *Handbook of Research on Modern Cryptographic Solutions for Computer and Cyber Security* (pp. 393–419). Hershey, PA: IGI Global; . doi:10.4018/978-1-5225-0105-3.ch017

Gozman, D., & Willcocks, L. (2019). The emerging Cloud Dilemma: Balancing innovation with cross-border privacy and outsourcing regulations. *Journal of Business Research*, 97, 235–256. doi:10.1016/j.jbusres.2018.06.006

Gupta, B., Agrawal, D. P., & Yamaguchi, S. (2016). *Handbook of Research on Modern Cryptographic Solutions for Computer and Cyber Security*. Hershey, PA: IGI Global; . doi:10.4018/978-1-5225-0105-3

Halevi, S., & Shoup, V. (2018). Faster Homomorphic Linear Transformations in HElib.

Hashem, I. A., Yaqoob, I., Anuar, N. B., Mokhtar, S., Gani, A., & Khan, S. U. (2015). The rise of "big data" on cloud computing: Review and open research issues. *Information Systems*, 47, 98–115. doi:10.1016/j.is.2014.07.006

Hoboken, J. V., & Rubinstein, I. S. (2014). Privacy and Security in the Cloud: Some Realism About Technical Solutions to Transnational Surveillance in the Post-Snowden Era. *Me. L. Rev., 487*.

Hoehl, M. (2015). Proposal for standard Cloud Computing Security SLAs - Key Metrics for Safeguarding Confidential Data in the Cloud. Retrieved from https://www.sans.org/reading-room/whitepapers/cloud/proposal-standard-cloud-computing-security-slas-key-metrics-safeguarding-confidential-dat-35872

Indu, I., Anand, P. R., & Bhaskar, V. (2018). Identity and access management in cloud environment: Mechanisms and challenges. *Engineering Science and Technology, an International Journal*, 574-588.

Inukollu, V. N., Sailaja, A., & Srinivasa, R. R. (2014). Security issues associated with big data in cloud computing. *International Journal of Network Security & Its Applications, 45.*

Jansen, W. (2009). Directions in Security Metrics Research. Retrieved from http://csrc.nist.gov/publications/nistir/ir7564/nistir-7564_metrics-research.pdf

Jellinek, R., Zhai, Y., Ristenpart, T., & Swift, M. (2014). A day late and a dollar short: the case for research on cloud billing systems. In *Proceedings of the 6th USENIX conference on Hot Topics in Cloud Computing*, (pp. 21-21). Academic Press.

Jiang, Y., Perng, C.-s., Li, T., & Chang, R. (2012). Self-Adaptive Cloud Capacity Planning. In *Proceedings of the Ninth International Conference on Services Computing*, Honolulu, HI (pp. 73-80). IEEE.

Jones, G. (2013). Penetrating the cloud. *Network Security*, 5-7. doi:10.1016/S1353-4858(13)70028-X

Kemp, R. (2018). Legal aspects of cloud security. *Computer Law & Security Review*, *34*(4), 928–932. doi:10.1016/j.clsr.2018.06.001

Krag, W. B., & Hinson, G. (2016). *Pragmatic security metrics: applying metametrics to information security*. Auerbach Publications.

Lee, C. Y., Kavi, K. M., Paul, R. A., & Gomathisankaran, M. (2015). Ontology of Secure Service Level Agreement. In *Proceedings of the 2015 IEEE 16th International Symposium on High Assurance Systems Engineering*, (pp. 166-172). doi:10.1109/HASE.2015.33

Lins, S., Grochol, P., Schneider, S., & Sunyaev, A. (2016). Dynamic Certification of Cloud Services: Trust, but Verify! *IEEE Security and Privacy*, *14*(2), 66–71. doi:10.1109/MSP.2016.26

Lovas, R., Nagy, E., & Kovács, J. (2018). Cloud agnostic Big Data platform focusing on scalability and cost-efficiency. *Advances in Engineering Software*, *125*, 167–177. doi:10.1016/j.advengsoft.2018.05.002

Luna, J., Taha, A., Trapero, R., & Suri, N. (2015). Quantitative Reasoning About Cloud Security Using Service Level Agreements. *IEEE Transactions on Cloud Computing, PP*, 1-1. doi:10.1109/TCC.2015.2469659

Madini, A., Hussain, R. K., Ghashgari, G., Walters, R. J., & Wills, G. B. (2015). Security in organisations: governance, risks and vulnerabilities in moving to the cloud. *International Workshop on Enterprise Security*, 241-258.

Mathew, G. (2012). *Elements of application security in the cloud computing environment. Conference on Open Systems* (pp. 1–6). Kuala Lumpur: IEEE; . doi:10.1109/ICOS.2012.6417637

Mell, P., & Grance, T. (2011). *800-145. The NIST Definition of Cloud Computing*. SP: National Institute of Standards & Technology.

Negi, P., Mishra, A., & Gupta, B. B. (2013). Enhanced CBF Packet Filtering Method to Detect DDoS Attack in Cloud Computing Environment. *International Journal of Computer Science Issues*.

Nettitude. (2017). Cloud Penetration Testing. Retrieved from https://www.nettitude.com/uk/cloud-penetration-testing/

Oliveira, R. R., Martins, R. M., & Simao, A. d. (2017). Impact of the Vendor Lock-in Problem on Testing as a Service (TaaS). *International Conference on Cloud Engineering (IC2E)*. Vancouver. doi:10.1109/IC2E.2017.30

Opara-Martins, J. (2018). Taxonomy of Cloud Lock-in Challenges. In M. Khatib, & N. Salman, *Mobile Computing - Technology and Applications*. IntechOpen. doi:10.5772/intechopen.74459

Pearson, S., & Benameur, A. (2010). *Privacy, security and trust issues arising from cloud computing. Cloud Computing Technology and Science*. Indianapolis, IN: CloudCom.

Porter, N., Garms, J., & Simakov, S. (2018, 5 3). Introducing Asylo: an open-source framework for confidential computing.

Qiu, M. M., Zhou, Y., & Wang, C. (2013, 6). Systematic Analysis of Public Cloud Service Level Agreements and Related Business Values. In *Proceedings of the 2013 IEEE International Conference on Services Computing* (pp. 729-736). Academic Press. doi:10.1109/SCC.2013.24

Quinting, A., Lins, S., Szefer, J., & Sunyaev, A. (2017). Advancing the Adoption of a New Generation of Certifications--A Theoretical Model to Explain the Adoption of Continuous Cloud Service Certification by Certification Authorities. In *Proceedings of Wirtschaftsinformatik* (pp. 1–12). WI: Academic Press.

Ramachandra, G., Iftikhar, M., & Khan, F. A. (2017). A Comprehensive Survey on Security in Cloud Computing. *Procedia Computer Science, 110*, 465–472. doi:10.1016/j.procs.2017.06.124

Richman, D. (2017). *Amazon Web Services' secret weapon: Its custom-made hardware and network*. Geekwire.

Rodriguez, K. (2018, April 9). *The U.S. CLOUD Act and the EU: A Privacy Protection Race to the Bottom*. Electronic Frontier Foundation: Retrieved from https://www.eff.org/deeplinks/2018/04/us-cloud-act-and-eu-privacy-protection-race-bottom

Ruan, K., Carthy, J., Kechadi, T., & Crosbie, M. (2011). Cloud forensics: An overview. In *Proceedings of the 7th IFIP International Conference on Digital Forensics*, 16-25.

Saxena, T., & Chourey, V. (2014). A survey paper on cloud security issues and challenges. In *Proceedings of the Conference on IT in Business, Industry and Government (CSIBIG)* (pp. 1–5). Indore: IEEE; . doi:10.1109/CSIBIG.2014.7056957

Silva, G. C., Rose, L., & Calinescu, R. (2013). *A systematic review of cloud lock-in solutions. Cloud Computing Technology and Science*. Bristol: CloudCom.

Singh, S., Jeong, Y.-S., & Park, J. H. (2016). A survey on cloud computing security: Issues, threats, and solutions. *Journal of Network and Computer Applications*, *75*, 200–222. doi:10.1016/j.jnca.2016.09.002

Snedaker, S., & Rima, C. (2014). *Business Continuity and Disaster Recovery Planning for IT Professionals*. Syngress.

Somani, G., Gaur, M. S., Sanghi, D., Conti, M., & Buyya, R. (2017). DDoS attacks in cloud computing: Issues, taxonomy, and future directions. *Computer Communications*, *107*, 30–48. doi:10.1016/j.comcom.2017.03.010

Song, D. X., Wagner, D., & Perrig, A. (2000). Practical techniques for searches on encrypted data. In *Proceeding 2000 IEEE Symposium on Security and Privacy* (pp. 44-55). Academic Press. doi:10.1109/SECPRI.2000.848445

Symantec. (2016). *Internet Security Threat Report*.

Symantec. (2017). *Internet Security Threat Report*.

Tracol, X. (2016). "Invalidator" strikes back: The harbour has never been safe. *Computer Law & Security Review*, *32*(2), 345–362. doi:10.1016/j.clsr.2016.01.011

Xynos, K., Sutherland, I., Read, H., Everitt, E., & Blyth, A. J. (2010). Penetration testing and vulnerability assessments: A professional approach.

Yang, X., Liu, L., & Zou, R. (2011). A statistical user-behavior trust evaluation algorithm based on cloud model. In *Proceedings of the 2011 6th International Conference on Computer Sciences and Convergence Information Technology (ICCIT)* (pp. 598-603). Academic Press.

Yimam, D., & Fernandez, E. B. (2016). A survey of compliance issues in cloud computing. *Journal of Internet Services and Applications*, *7*(1), 5. doi:10.118613174-016-0046-8

Zylva, A. (2016, 3 2). Windows 10 Device Guard and Credential Guard Demystified.

ADDITIONAL READING

Cloud Security Alliance. (n.d.). CSA Security Guidance for Critical Areas of Focus in Cloud Computing v4.0. Retrieved from https://cloudsecurityalliance.org/guidance/

Fatima-Zahra Benjelloun and Ayoub Ait Lahcen, "Big Data Security: Challenges, Recommendations and Solutions" *Web Services: Concepts, Methodologies, Tools, and Applications*. IGI Global, 2019. 25-38. Web. 25 Jan. 2019.

Ibrahim, A. T. H., Yaqoob, I., Anuar, N. B., Mokhtar, S., Gani, A., & Khan, S. U. (2015). The rise of "big data" on cloud computing: Review and open research issues. *Information Systems*, *47*, 98–115. doi:10.1016/j.is.2014.07.006

Liu, F., Tong, J., Mao, J., & Robert, B. Bohn, John V. Messina, Mark L. Badger, Dawn M. Leaf, "NIST Cloud Computing Reference Architecture", 2011. https://www.nist.gov/publications/nist-cloud-computing-reference-architecture

Mather, T., Kumaraswamy, S., & Latif, S. (2009). *Cloud Security and Privacy: An Enterprise Perspective on Risks and Compliance*. O'Reilly Media.

Reddy, Y. (2018). *"Big Data Security in Cloud Environment," 2018 IEEE 4th International Conference on Big Data Security on Cloud (BigDataSecurity), IEEE International Conference on High Performance and Smart Computing, (HPSC) and IEEE International Conference on Intelligent Data and Security* (pp. 100–106). Omaha, NE: IDS; . doi:10.1109/BDS/HPSC/IDS18.2018.00033

Ronald, L. (2010). *Krutz and Russell Dean Vines, "Cloud Security: A Comprehensive Guide to Secure Cloud Computing*. John Wiley & Sons.

Singh, A., & Chatterjee, K. (2017). Cloud security issues and challenges: A survey. *Journal of Network and Computer Applications*, *79*, 88–115. doi:10.1016/j.jnca.2016.11.027

KEY TERMS AND DEFINITIONS

Data Loss Prevention: Technologies to monitor the movement of data and take action in response to rules defined by the customer.

Electronic Discovery: The process by which an entity obtains private electronically stored documents for use in legal proceedings.

GDPR: General Data Protection Regulation.

Governance: The manner in which an organisation is run.

Metastructure: The protocols and mechanisms that provide the interface between the infrastructure layer and the other layers of the cloud.

Portability: A desirable property of data in a cloud service. High portability means that the data (including metadata) can be moved between providers at low cost and without loss of information.

Service Level Agreement: The level of service the cloud provider promises to provide.

Chapter 2
Big Data:
Challenges and Solutions

P. Lalitha Surya Kumari
Geethanjali College of Engineering and Technology, India

ABSTRACT

This chapter gives information about the most important aspects in how computing infrastructures should be configured and intelligently managed to fulfill the most notably security aspects required by big data applications. Big data is one area where we can store, extract, and process a large amount of data. All these data are very often unstructured. Using big data, security functions are required to work over the heterogeneous composition of diverse hardware, operating systems, and network domains. A clearly defined security boundary like firewalls and demilitarized zones (DMZs), conventional security solutions, are not effective for big data as it expands with the help of public clouds. This chapter discusses the different concepts like characteristics, risks, life cycle, and data collection of big data, map reduce components, issues and challenges in big data, cloud secure alliance, approaches to solve security issues, introduction of cybercrime, YARN, and Hadoop components.

INTRODUCTION

This chapter updates the most important characteristic about how computing framework must be configured and intelligently administers to fulfill the main aspects related to security required by the applications of the Big Data. The place where the huge quantity of data is stored, extracted and processed is called Big Data. Big Data is the area with vast potential to handle datasets of the size which is beyond the capability of generally used software tools to capture, manage, and timely analyze that amount of data. The amount of data to be analyzed is estimated to be twice for every two years. The various sources of this unstructured data are medical records, scientific applications, sensors, social media, video and image archives, surveillance, business transactions, Internet search indexing, and system logs. As the number of connecting devices of Big Data like Internet of things increases attention towards Big Data also increased at unexpected levels. In addition, it is very common to acquire on-demand supplementary computing control and storage to carry out exhaustive data-parallel processing from public cloud providers. Thus,

DOI: 10.4018/978-1-5225-9742-1.ch002

privacy and security issues can be potentially increased by the variety, volume and wide area deployment of the system infrastructure to support Big Data applications. As Big Data expands with the help of public clouds, traditional security solutions tailored to private computing infrastructures, confined to a well-defined security perimeter, such as firewalls and demilitarized zones (DMZs) are no more effective. Using Big Data, security functions are required to work over the heterogeneous composition of diverse hardware, operating systems, and network domains. A clearly defined security boundary like firewalls and demilitarized zones (DMZs), conventional security solutions adapted to private computing infrastructures are no more effective for Big Data as it expands with the help of public clouds.

Using Big Data, security functions are required to work over the heterogeneous composition of diverse hardware, operating systems, and network domain. In this complicated computing environment, Big Data secure services upon the heterogeneous infrastructure are deployed efficiently by taking the abstraction capability of Software-Defined Networking (SDN). An abstraction concept of SDN separates the control (higher) plane from the underlying system infrastructure being controlled and supervised. Segregating network's control logic from the underneath physical routers and switches that forward traffic makes the system administrators to write high-level control programs that specify the behavior of an entire network, in contrast to conventional networks, whereby administrators (if allowed to do it by the device manufacturers) must codify functionality in terms of low-level device configuration. The intelligent management of secure functions simplifies the concepts of implementation of security rules; system (re)configuration; and system evolution using SDN. The main problem of a centralized SDN solution can be reduced by using a chain of controllers and/or through the usage of more number of controllers to control at least the most important functions of a system.

The National Institute of Standards and Technology (NIST) launched a framework with a set of voluntary guidelines to help organizations make their communications and computing operations safer (NIST, 2014). This could be accomplished by verifying the system infrastructure in view of security against threats, risk assessment, and ability to respond and recover from attacks.

Following the last verification principles, Defense Advanced Research Projects Agency (DARPA) is creating a program called Mining and Understanding Software Enclaves (MUSE) to enhance the quality of the US military's software. The design of this program is to develop more robust software to work with big datasets with no errors or break down under the huge volume of information (DARPA, 2014). Additionally, main concepts like privacy and security are becoming the most important aspects of Big Data aspects that need to be addressed. As the social networks made the people to share and distribute important copyrighted digital information in a very easy way, the copyright infringement behaviors like malicious distribution, illicit copying and usage, unauthorized access, and free sharing of copyright-protected digital contents, will become a much more common phenomenon. To alleviate these problems Big Data must provide solid solutions to protect security for author's privacy and author's copyrights. In addition, it has become a common trend to share personal data through their mobile devices and computers to social networks and cloud services and misplace data and content leads to a severe (serious) impact on their own confidentiality. Hence, a secure framework to social networks is one of the most important topics in research.

This chapter discusses the following in further sections.

1. Characteristics of Big Data like volume, variety, velocity, variability, value, and veracity that affect information security.
2. Risks include lifecycle (provenance, ownership and classification of data), the data creation and collection process, and the lack of security procedures.
3. Security and privacy issues and Challenges in big data.
4. MapReduce 2.0 Main Components
5. Challenges in Security of Big Data
6. Cloud Secure Alliance (CSA)
7. Approaches To Solve Security Issues
8. Introduction of Cybercrime
9. YARN and Hadoop components

Characteristic of Big Data

Big Data has specific characteristics that affect information security: volume, variety, velocity, variability, value, and veracity

1. **Volume**: Volume indicates 'size of the data'. The name 'Big Data' itself indicates that the size which is enormous. In most of the applications, size of data plays very crucial role to determine the output out of that data. To consider data as Big Data, volume of the data will be taken as measurement. Hence, 'Volume' is one characteristic which is required to be considered while dealing with 'Big Data'.
2. **Variety**: 'Variety' refers to the nature of data indicates both structured and unstructured data. Previously, databases and spreadsheets were the only sources of data used in most of the applications. Currently, data in the form of videos, photos, emails, audio, monitoring devices, PDFs, etc. is also being considered in the analysis applications. This type of unstructured data causes certain issues for storing, mining and analyzing data.
3. **Velocity**: Big Data Velocity deals with the speed at which data flows in from sources like Mobile devices, business processes, sensors, networks and social media sites, application logs, etc. The term 'velocity' refers to the speed at which data is generated. It also determines the potentiality of the data as velocity defines how fast the data is produced and processed to meet the demands. The data flow is massive and continuous.
4. **Variability**: Inconsistency of data in Big Data is referred by the character Variability' and can be shown by the data at times. Hence, obstructing the efficient handling of data.
5. **Value**: 'Value' refers to the significance of the data being extracted. Having continuous amounts of data is one thing, but unless it can be turned into value it is useless. While there is a clear link between data and insights, this does not always mean there is value in Big Data. The most important part of utilizing the big data is to understand the costs and benefits of collecting and analyzing the data to make sure that the data that is collected can be monetized finally.
6. **Veracity**: 'Veracity' is the quality or trustworthiness of the data. Just how accurate is all this data? For example, think about all the Twitter posts with hash tags, abbreviations, typos, etc., and the reliability and accuracy of all that content. Gleaning loads and loads of data is of no use if the qual-

Figure 1. Characteristic of big data

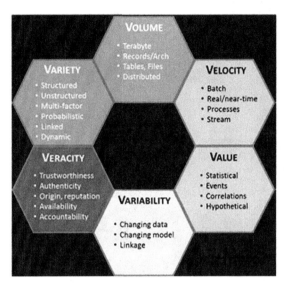

ity or trustworthiness is not accurate. Another good example of this relates to the use of GPS data. Satellite signals are lost as they bounce off tall buildings or other structures. When this happens, location data has to be fused with another data source like road data, or data from an accelerometer to provide accurate data.

Risks in Big Data

Risks include lifecycle (provenance, ownership and classification of data), the data creation and collection process, and the lack of security procedures.

Life Cycle of Big Data

To design a framework by any organization to perform any sort of work and to deliver clear insights from Big Data, it is better to follow as different stages of life cycle. Life cycle of Big Data provides the similar structure of traditional data mining life cycle as portrayed in CRISP methodology

CRISP-DM Methodology

CRoss Industry Standard Process (CRISP)

Data Mining Methodology is a cycle that explains different approaches used by experts to tackle difficulties faced in data mining. Observe the Figure 2. It depicts the correlation of different stages of CRISP-DM methodology. In 1996 CRISP-DM was designed and it was taken up as a European Union project under the funding agent ESPRIT. The project was led by five companies: SPSS, NCR Corporation, Teradata, Daimler AG and OHRA (an insurance company). Finally, the project was incorporated into SPSS.

Figure 2. Different stages of CRISP-DM methodology

Now, Let us understand all the stages involved in the CRISP-DM life cycle

- **Business Understanding**: This initial phase mainly focuses to identify the project objectives and requirements from a business point of view and then defines a data mining definition from this knowledge. A preliminary plan is aimed at achieving the objectives. A decision model, notably one built using the Decision Model and Notation standard can be used.

- **Data Understanding**: This phase starts initially with data collection and continues with other activities like identification of data quality problems, discovering first insights into the data or to detect interesting subsets to form hypotheses for secret information.
- **Data Preparation**: In this phase initial raw dataset is fed into tools to construct the final dataset. Data preparation tasks are needed to be performed many times without considering any order. These data preparation tasks consist of creation of a table, record, and attribute selection and also the transformation and clearing of data for modeling tools.
- **Modeling**: In the modeling phase, different modeling techniques are selected and applied so as to obtain optimal values to their parameters. Usually, there are a number of techniques for the similar data mining problem type. Some of the techniques have specific requirements depending on the type of data. Therefore, it is repeatedly required to go back to the data preparation phase.
- **Evaluation:** From the perspective of data analysis, a high-quality model (or models) was built at this stage of the project. It is important to evaluate and review the steps used to construct the model thoroughly, to be certain it properly achieves the business objectives before considering this model as a final deployment model.

The main objective of this phase is to determine any of the business issues has been over-looked/ considered insufficiently. By the end of this phase the decision as to the use of data mining results will be reached.

- **Deployment**: Construction of the model is usually not the end of the project. Even if the very purpose of the model is to boost the knowledge of the data, the information gained will need to be structured and demonstrated in such a way that it is useful to the customer. Based on the requirements, the deployment phase can be a simple task like producing a report or a complex task like applying a repeatable data scoring (e.g. segment allocation) or data mining process. In most of the cases, customer will carry out the deployment steps even if the analyst deploys the model. Main reason is that customer must also know the actions to be carried out to know how the created model can be used.

SEMMA Methodology

SEMMA is another methodology developed by SAS for data mining modeling. It stands for Sample, Explore, Modify, Model, and Asses. Here is a brief description of its stages –

- **Sample**: SEEMA methodology starts with data sampling. i.e. selection of dataset for modeling. The dataset must be big enough to contain adequate information to retrieve yet small enough to be used efficiently. It also deals with data partitioning.
- **Explore**: With the help of data visualization, this phase find out relationships like anticipated and unanticipated relationships among the variables and also abnormalities.
- **Modify**: The Modify phase consists (contains) routines to select, create and transform variables in the development of (preparation) for data modeling.
- **Model**: In this phase, the main objective (focus) is to apply different modeling techniques on the prepared variables to develop models to get expected outcome.
- **Assess**: The evaluation of the modeling results shows the reliability and usefulness of the created models.

The main difference between CRISM–DM and SEMMA is that SEMMA gives importance to the concepts of modeling aspect whereas CRISP-DM gives more importance to phases of the cycle like recognition of the business problem which is to be resolved and preprocessing the data to be used as input prior to model. Example: machine learning algorithms.

Big Data Life Cycle

Now days, these approaches are either insufficient or suboptimal for the applications of Big Data. For example, the SEMMA methodology ignores data collection completely and preprocessing of various data resources. These stages normally make up most of the work in a successful big data project.

A big data analytics cycle can be described by the following stage –

1. Business Problem Definition
2. Research

3. Human Resources Assessment
4. Data Acquisition
5. Data Munging
6. Data Storage
7. Exploratory Data Analysis
8. Data Preparation for Modeling and Assessment
9. Modeling
10. Implementation

In this section, we will discuss briefly about every stage of life cycle of Big Data.

1. **Business Problem Definition**: This is the common point in both big data analytics life cycle and traditional BI. Generally, it is the most important stage of a big data project to identify the problem and estimate accurately the potential gain it may fetch for a business. It is apparent that, it has to be calculated what are the estimated gains and costs of the project

2. **Research**: Analysis should be made of what other companies did in a similar situation. It also involves finding solutions that suit the company as per the requirements and resources it has. At this stage the methodology for future stages is defined.

3. **Human Resources Assessment:** After defining the problem, the next logical step would be to analyze the capability of the existing team as to whether it could complete the project successfully. The options of outsourcing and hiring more people for the project should be considered before the start of the project as the traditional BI teams may not possess the capability to deliver optimal solutions for all the problems at every stage.

4. **Data Acquisition:** This section is the essential phase of big data life cycle; it defines what outlines would be required to deliver the resultant data product. Data gathering is the most important step of the process; it normally involves collection unstructured data from different sources. For an example, it could involve writing a crawler to retrieve reviews from a website. This involves dealing with text, perhaps in different languages normally requiring a significant amount of time to be completed.

5. **Data Munging:** After retrieving data from web, it is required to store in an easy to-use format. Consider with the reviews examples; let us imagine the data is retrieved from various sites where each has a different display of the data.

Suppose one data source provides review's rating in terms of stars, hence, it is likely to represent this as a mapping for the response variable $y \in \{1, 2, 3, 4, 5\}$. A different data source provides review's rating using two arrows system, one for up voting and the other for down voting. This would imply a response variable of the form $y \in \{positive, negative\}$. In order to join both the data sources, one has to take a decision whether these two response representations equivalent. This can involve changing the representation of first data source response to the second one, considering one star as negative and five stars as positive. This process frequently requires a large time allocation for good quality to be delivered.

6. **Data Storage:** After the data is processed, it may needs to be stored in a database. Big data technologies offer a large number of alternatives regarding this point. The most widespread alternative is using the Hadoop File System for storage space that offers users a classified version of SQL and

Figure 3. Big data processes

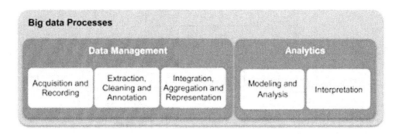

it is recognized as HIVE Query Language. From the perspective of a user, the task carried out by the analytics is similar to that of a traditional BI data warehouse. Apart from Hadoop other storage options that could be considered are MongoDB, Redis, and SPARK.

This stage of the cycle is associated with the human resources knowledge in terms of their capabilities to implement various architectures. Most of the large scale applications are still using modified versions of traditional data warehouses. Consider teradata and IBM offer SQL databases such as postgreSQL and MySQL that can handle terabytes of data and provide open source solutions for large scale applications are still being used. Solutions from the client side provide mostly SQL API even if there are variations in how the various storages work in the background. Therefore having a good knowledge of SQL is still a essential ability to have for big data analytics. Consequently this stage seems to be the most important topic, practically this is not true. It is not even a crucial stage. Generally, there is no need to formally store the data at all because most of possible solutions to implement Big Data applications are working with real-time data. Hence, we need only to gather data to develop the model and then implement it in real time.

1. **Exploratory Data Analysis:** The data exploration phase is mandatory after the data has been cleaned and stored in a way that insights can be retrieved from it. The objective of this stage is to quire the knowledge of the data, this is usually done with statistical techniques and also plotting the data. This is a correct (good) stage to evaluate whether the problem definition makes sense or is feasible.
2. **Data Preparation for Modeling and Assessment:** This stage involves remolding the cleaned data retrieved previously and using statistical preprocessing for feature selection and feature extraction, missing values imputation, normalization, outlier detection.
3. **Modelling:** The previous stage might have produced several datasets for testing and training, for example, a predictive model. This stage mainly performs different tasks like trying different models and to find solution to solve the business problem at hand. Generally, it is desired to have a model would give some insight into the business practically. Finally, the best model or combination of models is taken as a choice to evaluate its performance on a left-out dataset.
4. **Implementation:** In this stage, the developed model of data product is implemented in the data pipeline of the business organization. This also enhances the validation scheme to track its performance while the data product is working. Consider an example of implementing a predictive

Figure 4. Big data classification

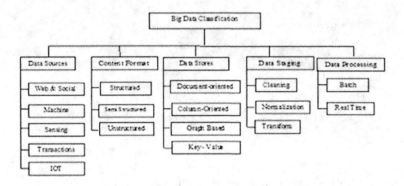

model, this stage make the model to apply on new data and once the response is available, evaluate the model.

Data Collection

Data collection plays a key role in the Big Data cycle. For a variety of topics, the Internet supplies almost unlimited sources of data. The significance of this area is based on the type of business, but traditional industries can attain a various source of external data and combine those with their transactional data. Consider an example to build a system that recommends restaurants. Data is gathered in the first step. In this step, reviews of restaurants from different websites are gathered and store them in a database. As we are interested in raw text, and would use that for analytics, it is not that relevant where the data for developing the model would be stored. This may leads to contradictory with the main technologies of big data, but to make big data application to implement us simply need to make it work in real time.

Above figure shown data sources include internet data, sensing and all stores of transnational information, ranges from unstructured to highly structured are stored in various formats. Most popular is the relational database that comes in a large number of varieties. As there are broad variety of data sources, the size of the data captured vary on the factors noise, redundancy and consistency etc.

Example: Twitter Mini Project

Once problem is defined, the next stage is to collect the data. This example is to work on collecting data from the web and structuring it to be used in a machine learning model. We will collect some tweets from the twitter rest API using the R programming language. First of all create a twitter account, and then follow the instructions in the twitteR package vignette to create a twitter developer account. This is a summary of those instructions –

- Go to https://twitter.com/apps/new and log in.
- After filling in the basic information, go to the "Settings" tab and select "Read, Write and Access direct messages".
- Make sure to click on the save button after doing this
- In the "Details" tab, take note of consumer key and consumer secret

- In the R session, the API key and API secret values are using.
- Finally run the following script. This will install the twitteR package from its repository on github.

REASONS FOR SECURITY AND PRIVACY ISSUES AND CHALLENGES IN BIG DATA

Security and privacy are major concerns of big data. The security concerns also grow proportionally along with the volume of big data that grows every day. As big data is widely accessible privacy and security have become major concerns of big data. Government agencies, doctors, business officials, normal people and scientists share data on large scale. However the tools and technologies that have been developed till date to handle these huge volumes of data are not efficient enough to provide adequate security and privacy to data. The technologies lack enough security and privacy maintenance features and the reason for this is because there is a lack of basic understanding about how to provide security to these huge volumes of data and sufficient training is not provided regarding how to provide security and privacy to these large scale data. The policies that maintain privacy and security of big data are inadequate and hence recent techniques or approaches are taken into consideration. Although current technologies are considered the maintenance of these concerns is not up to the expected level as there is continuous breach of security either intentionally or accidentally because of weak potentiality of current technologies. Continuously reassessment and also updation of current technologies must be done. Companies are not spending the required amount to protect security of big data. About 10% of a company's IT budget should be spent on security but below 9% is spent on an average thus making it tougher for themselves to protect their data.

MapReduce 2.0 Main Components

Client – Resource Manager

Generally, the process is initiated by a client by communicating with the RM (specifically the Applications Manager component of the RM). The foremost step is the client has to inform through "New Application Request" to the Applications Manager for the required application. In general the response of Resource Manager contains a newly created unique application ID along with the information of cluster resource capabilities need by the client for running the AM of application. After receiving information the client constructs and submits an "Application Submission Context" which generally includes scheduler queue, priority and user information and also the information required by the RM to start the AM. The "Container Launch Context" encloses the information of job files, application's jar, security tokens and any other required resources.

Resource Manager: Application Master

When the RM receives the application submission context from the client, it finds an available container meeting the resource requirements for running the AM, and it contacts the NM for the container to begin the AM process on client's node. The first step is for the AM to register itself with the RM. During the registration step handshaking procedure is performed and also communicates information like the RPC

Figure 5. MapReduce Architecture describing flow of tokens

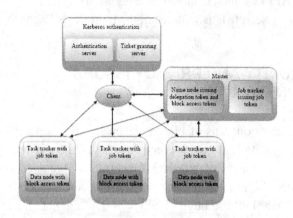

port that the AM will be listening on, the tracking URL to monitor the status and progress of application. The RM registration response will convey essential information for the AM master like minimum and maximum resource capabilities for this cluster. The AM will apply such information for calculation and requests for any resources required for the individual task of an application. The AM sends resource allocation request to the RM which mainly includes a list of containers requested and also containers released by this AM. Heartbeat and progress information are also relayed through resource allocation requests When the Scheduler component of the RM receives a resource allocation request, it computes, based on the scheduling policy, a list of containers that satisfy the request and sends back an allocation response which contains a list of allocated resources. Using the resource list, the AM starts contacting the associated node managers (as will be soon seen), and finally, when the job finishes, the AM sends a Finish Application message to the Resource Manager and exits.

Application Master: Container Manager

To start every container a requisition is send by AM to hosting NM.

While containers are running, the AM can request and receive a container status report respectively.

Challenges in Security of Big Data

With the increase of devices connected through Internet, the quantity of data gathered, stored, and processed is rising everyday and hence new challenges of information security have been raised. In reality, the existing security mechanisms like firewalls and DMZs are not efficient for Big Data infrastructure for the reason that the security mechanisms must be draw out of the perimeter of the network of the organization to accomplish the data/user motility requirements and the approaches of BYOD (Bring Your Own Device).

By taking into Consideration of these new developments, the valid question is that what security and privacy policies and technologies would meet the demands of the present top Big Data privacy and security (Cloud Security Alliance, 2013). The four different challenges in the concept of security of Big Data are Infrastructure Security i. e. security in MapReduce model, data privacy to protect confidential data, data management for secure storage and integrity and reactive security to control inconsistency and also attacks. Security and privacy issues are magnified by the three V's of big data: Velocity, Volume, and Variety. These factors consist of variables like variety of data sources and designs, large-scale cloud infrastructures, continuous nature of data acquirement and the progressively more high volume of inter-cloud migrations. As a result, conventional security systems, which are adapted to secure small-scale static data, often fail. The three step process followed by the CSA's Big Data Working Group is to reach a top level security and privacy challenges presented by Big Data.

Big Data Issues and Challenges Related to Characteristics of Big Data

- **Data Volume:** When we consider term data volume the very first concern that arises is storage. The amount of memory needed for efficient storage of data increases as volume of data increases. Also, there is a need for the huge volumes of data to be retrieved at a faster rate to get the results from them. In addition to above things, we need to look after the areas like Networking, bandwidth, cost of storing like in-house versus cloud storing. As the volume of data increases the value of data records have a tendency to decrease in proportion to time, style, richness and value. Nowadays, the data produced each day is in the order of terabytes due to increase in the development of social networking sites.
- **Data Velocity:** There is a simultaneous growth in the data consumption by the users in proportion to the high speed growth in the operational and analytical data. Whenever people wants all the data immediately that leads to what is called high-velocity data. High velocity data can mean millions of rows of data per second. To perform analytics on huge volumes of data which is in continuous motion then conventional database systems are not efficient.

Data generated through websites like data in E-commerce, twitter feeds and also log files generated by both devices and actions of human beings unable to collect as the modern technology can't handle that data

- **Data Variety:** The different forms of big data are like messages, updates and images from websites of social media, GPS signals from cell phones and sensors and many more. Many sources of big data are practically new or having age of the networking websites as per the statistics from social media, Facebook launched in 2004 and Twitter in 2006. Smart phones and other mobiles devices can be bracketed in the same category. While these devices are omnipresent the conventional databases that store most corporate information until recently are found to be poorly matched to these data. Most of the data requires rigorous decision-making techniques as data are cumbersome, unstructured and noisy in nature. Nowadays, the algorithms required to analyze these data are also a major concern.
- **Data Value:** Data are stored by different organizations to obtain awareness from them and utilize them for analytics for business intelligence. This storing creates a gap between the business organizers and professionals of IT industry. The main concern of business organizers is to add value to their business and gaining profits out of it. More the data more are the insights. Nevertheless, this doesn't turn out well with the IT experts as they have to handle the technicalities associated to store and process the large amounts of data

Big Data Management, Human Resource and Manpower Issues and Challenges

Management of Big data deals with administration, governance and organization of huge amounts of unstructured and structured data. The main objective is to ensure a high standard quality of data and ease of access for business intelligence and applications of big data analytics. Efficient data management helps organizations, agencies and companies in finding important information from huge sets of the order of terabytes and petabytes of data of semi structured or unstructured. Main sources are social media sites, call details and messages, system logs. Nevertheless, there are a few challenges with big data and its management: The biggest challenge of the users of big data is that they are new to big data and its management.

As organizations are new to big data it typically has inadequate data analysts and IT professionals having the skills to help interpret digital marketing data. The sources of big data are varied with respect to size, format and method of collection. Digital data taken from many sources like video recordings, sounds, drawings, documents, pictures, models and user interface designs, with or without metadata which outline about the data, its origin and how it was processed. Main problem of big data arises due to non familiarization of these latest data types and sources and also not suitable infrastructure of data management. This problem can be overcome by training and hiring new consultants and making progress by desirable quality of learning.

The talent of a data analyst must not be restricted to the technical field. He must also be expertise in the areas like creative, interpretive, analytical and research skills. Not only must the organizations that train for data scientist but also the universities or educational institutions too include knowledge about big data and data analysis to bring out skillful and expertise employees. Another problem is that investment on purchasing modern analytical tools by IT industries to handle bigger data and analyze with more complex data for better efficiency is not up to the expectation. It is difficult to start new projects owing to lack of governance, business sponsors and compelling ordnance due to lack of authority or guidance, business case.

Big Data Technical Issues and Challenges

- **Fault Tolerance:** With the emerging technologies like cloud computing, IOT the focus must be on that whenever failure occurs the damage occurred must be within suitable threshold so that the entire work need not done again. Fault-tolerant computing is very difficult and there is a need of tremendously complex algorithms. A cent percent perfect, reliable fault tolerant software or machine is simply a very good idea. To minimize the probability of failure to a satisfactory level we need to do. Divide the entire computation task into sub tasks and allocate these tasks to individual nodes for calculation. Make one node as a supervising node and examine all the remaining assigned nodes to check whether they are working correctly or not. In case of a problem that specific task will start again. However there are certain situations where the complete task can't be divided into separate tasks because a task can be recursive in nature and needs the output of the earlier computation to find the current result. This type of tasks can't be restated if error occurs. In this type of situations we need to use checkpoints to keep the status of the system at different intervals of time so that computation can be started again from the last checkpoint so recorded.
- **Data Heterogeneity:** 80% of data in today's world are unstructured data. It includes nearly every type of data and we create on a daily basis like document sharing, emails, social media interaction,

fax transfers, messages and many more. Working on unstructured data is a difficult task and also expensive. Converting unstructured data to structured data is not feasible as well. Data Quality: As has been stated before, storage space of big data is very costly and there is constantly a tiff between IT professionals and business leaders who look upon the quantity of data the organization or the company is storing. The primary thing need to be considered here is the quality of data. it is futile to store large sets of unrelated data as it is not used to draw conclusions and also better result cannot yield from them. Make sure that the quantity of data is adequate for a certain conclusion to be drawn or the data is the related data are further queries.

- **Scalability:** The concern (challenge) in scalability of big data has provided a route to cloud computing. It is accomplished by accumulating several different workloads with dissimilar performance goals into extremely large clusters. This requires complex level of distribution of resources that is quite expensive and also brings various challenges along with it like implementing various jobs. This makes the objective of every task to achieve successfully. System failures can be dealt efficiently because it is very common when large clusters of data have processed. Data being stored using solid state drives instead of hard disk drives as the hard disks are not enough to store big and phase change technology of big data is not having same performance between random and sequential data transfer. The difficulty that is looming in storage of big data is the kind of storage devices used.

Big Data Storage and Transport Issues and Challenges

As new storage medium is invented the amount of data also becoming more and more. The current disk has capacity of 4 terabytes so 1Exabyte can contain 25000 disks. Even if a particular computer system is able to process 1 Exabyte, working with that many of disks directly is well beyond its capability.

Accessing this flow of data beats present communication networks.

Big Data Processing Issues and Challenges

Efficient processing of big data involves massive parallel processing and also new analytical algorithms so as to supply rapid information. Often it may not be known how to handle very large and different quantities of data and whether all of it requires to be analyzed. Challenges also contain finding out data points that are really of importance and how to make use of the data to extract utmost benefit from it.

Big Data Privacy and Security Issues and Challenges

At the time of big data analysis, there is a merging of people's personal information with large external data sets either from social networking websites like facebook or from a database. Hence, confidential information of any person can be revealed to the outside world. It makes the people to go into the insights of people's lives of which they are unaware of. Often it take place that a more educated personality having better knowledge and concepts of big data analysis captures the advantage of predictive analysis over a person who is less educated than him.

Following this exercise, the Working Group researchers collect their list of the Top 8 challenges, which are as follows:

1. Secure computations in distributed programming frameworks
2. Security best practices for non-relational data stores
3. Secure data storage and transactions logs
4. End-point input validation/filtering
5. Real-Time Security Monitoring
6. Scalable and composable privacy-preserving data mining and analytics
7. Cryptographically enforced data centric security
8. Granular audits

The Expanded version of top 10 Big Data challenges addresses three new distinct issues. They are:

- **Modeling:** Standardize a risk model that envelops majority of the cyber-attacks or data-leakage situations
- **Analysis:** Getting good solutions based on the concept of threat model
- **Implementation:** Establishing the result in the present infrastructures.

The complete report investigates every challenge in depth, including an outline of different use cases for all challenges.

The aim of highlighting these challenges is to restore focus to make infrastructures of big data stronger.

Secure Computations in Distributed Programming Frameworks

Distributed programming frameworks make use of parallel computing and data storage for huge quantities of data. Consider an example of MapReduce framework. In this framework, input file is divided into several chunks. After division mapper of every chunk takes data, performs calculations or processing and produces outputs in the form of key/value pairs. All the unique key and outputs each chunk are combined by a reducer and gives results. Security of mapppers and protecting data from malicious mapper are the main concerns as erroneous results produced by mapper are not easy to detect and that leads to wrong comprehensive results. With very large data sets malicious mappers are too hard to be detected as well and they eventually damage essential data. Leakage of private data unintentionally or intentionally by mappers is also an issue of concern. MapReduce components are often affected to denial-of-service attack man-in-the-middle attack and replay attack. Received data can be replicated or altered MapReduce code can be delivered if malicious data nodes are added to the cluster. Alter copies of data can be introduced again by producing snapshots of legal nodes so that it is easy to attack in virtual and cloud environments and also not easy to detect.

Security Best Practices for Non-Relational Data Stores

Big data is stored using non relational databases mainly NoSQL databases. These databases handle many issues of big data analytics without any much concern over security problems. NoSQL databases contain security which is embedded in the middleware and no explicit security mechanism is required. Maintenance of Transactional integrity is neglected in NoSQL databases.

NoSQL databases can't have complex integrity constrains as it slows down its functionality of providing improved performance and scalability.

Authentication methodologies and password storage methods used in NoSQL databases are feeble. As they use Digest- based authentication or HTTP Basic NoSQL databases prone to man-in-the-middle attack. REST (Representational State Transfer) based on HTTP is vulnerable to cross-site request forgery, cross-site scripting and injection attacks like: schema injection, REST injection, array injection, JSON injection, GQL (Generalized Query Language) injection, view injection and others. The third party interference is also possible in NoSQL as it does not support blocking of third party. There are also some flaws in Authorization techniques in NoSQL. As NoSQL provides authorization at higher layers rather than at the layer at which data being are collected leads to inside attacks because of moderate security mechanisms. They may go unnoticed due to poor logging and log analysis methods along with other fundamental security mechanisms. They may not be observed due to substandard logging procedures and log analysis methodologies together with additional primary security mechanisms.

Secure Data Storage and Transaction Logs

Data and transactions logs are placed in multi-tiered memory space. Auto-tiering for big data storage came into existence because of issues of scalability and accessibility occurs due to continuous increase in size. Auto-tiering for big data storage do not keep track of where the data are stored in contrast to previous multi-tiered storage media where IT managers were able to know type of data and also when and where data is resided.

This leads to many new challenges for storage of data security. Always dishonest storage service providers often search for an opportunity to get some information that help them to connect user activities and data sets, able to know certain properties that are proved to be very important to them. Encipherment protects the data so that they cannot breech into the security of data. Data owner distributes the private key and cipher text to each and every user though he is not having right to access the data. However he may plan among users by exchanging the key and data thus he can gain data to which he is not authorized. In multi-user environment the service provider can produce roll back attack on users. He may provide outdated versions of data while the updated data are by now uploaded in the database. There is a conflict among the data storage provider and users due to tampering of data and data loss done by the malicious users.

End Point Input Validation/ Filtering

Whenever data is collected from different sources like software applications, hardware devices and endpoint devices, validation of the data and also the source is a challenge. Generally, harmful user tampers data collected device or data collecting application of a device during the installation so that malevolent data can enter into the central data collecting system.

After tampering, malicious users may create fake IDs and produces malignant data and put into the central data collecting system. ID cloning attacks such as Sybil attacks are primary in a Bring Your Own Device (BYOD) situation where a malignant user carries his own device, acts as a trusted device and produces malevolent data and sends into the central data collecting system.

Input data from sensors can also be operated like artificially altering the temperature from the temperature sensors and send as input to the process which collects temperature. GPS signals can also be operated in the same manner. These data signals can be changed during the transmission from generous source to the central data collection system by malignant user

The malicious user may change data while it is in transmission from a generous source to the central data collection system. It acts like man-in-the middle attack.

Real-Time Security Monitoring

Monitoring the security of Real-time systems has been a continuing challenge in the big data analysis development primarily due to the number of alerts produced by security devices. Main threats of infrastructure of big data include access of applications or nodes by dishonest admin, threats related to application and intruding through lines. This infrastructure is mostly collection different types of components. Hence, security of every component and the security amalgamation of these components need to be considered.

Consider an example of a Hadoop cluster run in a public cloud. Where public cloud is an ecosystem consists of components of storage, computing and network components and these components need to considered by providing security to the public cloud.

That means we need to consider security of the Hadoop cluster, the each node's security, the network connection among the nodes and the security of the data stored in a node. In addition to above security issues, monitoring the security of application which includes correlation rules of an application that must go after secure coding principles must also be considered. Not only that the security of the input data that comes from the source must also be taken into consideration.

Scalable and Composable Privacy-Preserving Data Mining and Analytics

Big data are prone to misuse of privacy, decrease of civil liberty, invasive marketing and enhance in corporate and state control. There is a possibility of an employee of a big data company misusing his power by violating privacy policies. He may resort to stalking people by monitoring their chats, if the big data company is into social networking and facilitates chatting. An unreliable business partner can penetrate into personal information and send it into the cloud as owner of data handles the cloud infrastructure.

Cryptographically Enforced Data-Centric Security

There are two primary approaches to manage visibility of data to systems, organizations and individuals. The first approach is to restrict access to operating systems or hypervisor. The second approach encapsulates data to protect itself using cryptography. As the first approach restricted to larger area there are more chances to attack the data. Many attacks like buffer overflow, privilege escalation etc., access the data by bypassing access control implementations. Protection of data through encryption from end-to-end grants a very small distinct attacking surface. As it is vulnerable to side-channel attack secret keys can be extracted though it is an impossible task. Different threats correlated with cryptographically forced access control routine done through encryption are: It must not be recognized by the challenger, the equivalent plaintext data considering for the cipher text even if incorrect or correct plan text has chosen. To facilitate filtering and searching encrypted data of cryptographic protocol an attacker must able to learn nothing regarding encrypted data outside the equivalent predicate, whether satisfied or not. This protocol assures that opponent cannot be able to counterfeit data that is sent from the authorized source for this may well be forged hence affecting data integrity.

Granular Audits

Notification given by the monitoring security system of Real time applications at the time of an attack is an actual challenge to be fulfilled. There may be frequently new attacks or ignored true positives. Audit information is needed to find out a missed attack. Audit information of any machine has to be comprehensive or at least the information must be given about what happened exactly and what mistake was made. To serve the main purpose the audit information must be accessed timely.

Cloud Secure Alliance (CSA)

Local chapters are necessary to our task to encourage the secured cloud computing. CSA chapter members are composed primarily of individual members. The minimum number of members of CSA is 20 members and they must be the established members. These members also represent a credible group which comprises of security experts of cloud for a particular region. These chapters provide a way to produce knowledge of security issues of cloud computing and challenges faced by local peers of networks in a secure cloud.

Cloud Secure Alliance (CSA) is a non-profit organization with a mission to promote the use of most excellent performances to provide security assurance in Cloud Computing. CSA has formed a Big Data Working Group to focus on the main challenges to implement Big Data services in a secure manner(Cloud Security Alliance, 2013) if there is an interest in establishishing a local chapter. The privacy and security challenges of Big Data are categorized by CSA into four different aspects. These aspects are Data Privacy, Reactive Security, Integrity and Data Management and Infrastructure Security. Every aspect has the following security constraints according to CSA.

1. Infrastructure Security
   a. Data is processed in a secured Distributed environment.
   b. Security Best Actions for Non-Relational Data-Bases
2. Data Privacy
   a. Data Analysis through Data Mining Preserving Data Privacy
   b. Cryptographic Solutions for Data Security
   c. Granular Access Control
3. Data Management and Integrity
   a. Secure Data Storage and Transaction Logs
   b. Granular Audits
   c. Data Provenance
4. Reactive Security
   ◦ End-to-End Filtering & Validation
   ◦ Supervising the Security Level in Real-Time

Table 1. Comparison of security algorithms

ALGORITM	CONTRIBUTOR	BLOCK SIZE	KEY LENGTH	SECURITY RATE	EXECUTION RATE
ECC	Neil, Victor	Varies	135 bits	Less	Fastest
RSA	Rivest, Shamir, Adleman	Varies	Based on no. of bits	Good	Slowest
DES	IBM75	64 bits	56 bits	Not enough	Slow
3-DES	Derived fom DES	64 bits	168, 112, 56 bits	Weak	Slow
AES	Rijman, Joan	128 bits	128,192,256 bits	Excellent	More fast
BLOW FISH	Bruce Schneier	64 bits	32 bits to 448 bits	Good	Fast

Approaches to Solve Security Issues

Security problems in Big Data can be resolved by means of some techniques like network encryption, data encryption and logging.

1. **Data Encryption:** Data encryption is the conversion of simple message into an encrypted form i.e. conversion of plain text into cipher text and is for data level issues. Approach solves the issues of data is Data encryption. Conversion of data into a secret message using encryption algorithms is called Data encryption. There different encryption algorithms are like DES, AES, ECC. RSA etc., Big data concerns with storing, processing and retrieval of data. The technologies used for these concerns are transaction management, memory management, networking and virtualization.

    For this reason, security problems of above technologies are also concerned to big data. The most significant security concerns of big data are data level, authentication level, network level and common issues. The most important thing must be considered about Big Data is security of data as it contains different types of data like public or private, irrelevant or relevant. In most of the applications of Big Data security issues arises if there is an involvement of private data or sensitive information. Hence, data requires to be protected from illegal access and release. The advancement of Big Data introduced a challenge in protecting the data. There is a necessity of research and methodologies to handle this huge amount of data efficiently and securely. Even if several new technologies and methodologies have been developed, but slightly they get declined when it is associated with huge amount of data.

2. **Approaches to Tackle Issues of Data Encryption:** Encryption is done at sender's side and decryption is done at receiver's side. If the data is encrypted then hacker finds it difficult to steal or modify data. For encryption/decryption process, two types of algorithms are, basically, used: Symmetric key cryptography and Asymmetric key cryptography. Symmetric key cryptography: This algorithms use the same key for both encryption and decryption. Examples are Data Encryption Standard (DES) and Advanced Encryption Standard (AES). Asymmetric key cryptography: This technique uses different keys for encryption and decryption. Examples are Rivest Shamir-Adleman

(RSA) and Elliptic curve cryptography (ECC). Network encryption: This approach is for network level issues. Since network is used for communication then network must be encrypted. If network is encrypted with appropriate algorithm then hacker is unable to crack the network and steal the data. Then data over the network will be secure enough from unauthorised access. RPC (Remote Procedure Call) mechanisms can also be used for communication but is insecure as it is not encrypted. RPC is secure only if it is used with some other techniques like SSL (Secure Socket Layer). SSL is a standard security technology for establishing an encrypted link between a server and a client. When data is sent between browsers and web servers is in the form of plain text which is vulnerable to eavesdropping. If an attacker is somewhat able to intercept all data being sent the information can be seen and used by them. In order to create an SSL connection, a web server requires an SSL Certificate. In order to activate SSL on web server, number of questions about the identity of website and company will be asked. Web server then creates two cryptographic keys a Private Key and a Public Key. The Public Key does not need to be secret and is placed into a Certificate Signing Request (CSR) - a data file also containing details. Then CSR will be submitted. During the SSL Certificate application process, the Certification Authority will validate details and issue an SSL Certificate containing details and allows using SSL. Then web server will match issued SSL Certificate to the Private Key. Web server will then be able to establish an encrypted link between the website and customer's web browser.

3. **Logging:** In order to prevent unauthorized access from malicious node, logging is used. Logging plays an important role in Big Data and used is for authentication level issues. It is used to keep an eye on all the activities and record them. If there is absence of logging then no activities will be recorded and data may be modified or deleted. If separate log is maintained by each and every node then each activity is recorded and malicious node can be detected easily.

4. **Authentication Level Issues:** In a cluster, different nodes with different priorities and rights are present. Accessing any type of data is allowed only to the nodes with administrative rights. If in any case, malicious node gets administrative property then it may alter or steal the secured data. In order to prevent unauthorized access from malicious node, logging is used. Logging plays an important role in Big Data. It is used to keep an eye on all the activities and record them. If there is absence of logging then no activities will be recorded and data may be modified or deleted. Data level issues: Data plays a very crucial role in Big Data. Data is no more than the information with variable priorities. Information obtained from the social networking sites, data from various government sites is increasing rapidly. Data level issues basically deals with data integrity and availability such as data protection and distributed data. In order to improve efficiency, big data environments like Hadoop, HDFs store the data as it is without encryption. If unauthorised access is possible then it may alter or modify the data. Information is stored in many nodes with replicas for quick access in distributed data storage. Network level issues: Various nodes are present in a cluster which performs processing of data computations. This processing of data can be done by any of the node in a cluster. It will then become difficult to find which node is active in processing. This arises to a problem that to which node security should be provided. Nodes can communicate to each other via network. RPC (Remote Procedure Call) mechanisms can also be used for communication but is insecure as it is not encrypted.

5. **General Level Issues:** In Big data, many technologies are used for processing. For security purposes, traditional tools are also used. But these tools may not perform well with new distributed environment of big data. Big data uses many new technologies for data storage, processing and retrieval. There may be complexities in using these traditional technologies.

INTRODUCTION OF CYBERCRIME

Types of Cyber Crimes

The Internet: Catalyst to crime, Viruses versus Worms, Computers' roles in crimes, Introduction to digital forensics, Introduction to Incident - Incident Response Methodology – Steps - Activities in Initial Response, Phase after detection of an incident.

The more sophisticated the technology, the higher the level of criminal activity. With the increasing number of organizations connected to the Internet, criminals of the World Wide Web are using personal information for their own gain. Large developing markets are not spared from the cybercriminals and even classified government information is compromised.

Many individuals, companies or banks suffer huge losses. The internet has become a breeding ground for illegal activities. Cyber attack is one of the crimes that can be experienced by anyone and is growing at an alarming rate with no end in sight in spite of taking adequate defense measures and enforcing stringent laws because of the inscrutability of the Internet.

Define Cybercrime?

Cybercrime is also called computer crime. It is a crime where a computer and Internet is used as an instrument to commit an offense like stealing personal information from other users(phishing and pharming). It also includes non-monetary offenses, such as creating and distributing viruses on other computers or posting confidential business information on the Internet.

Cybercrimes can generally be divided into two categories

Categories of Cybercrime

Cybercrimes are categorized based on types of methods used and difficulty levels. The three major categories that cybercrime falls into are: individual, property and government.

Table 2.

Crimes that target networks or devices	Crimes using devices to participate in criminal activities
Viruses	Phishing Emails
Malware	Cyberstalking
DoS Attacks	Identity Theft

- **Property**: In this category, Hacker gains access to person's bank details by stealing to utilize funds to make purchases online or to do phishing scams. Even the confidential information can be accessed through malicious software.
- **Individual**: In this category of cybercrime, hacker distributes illegal or malicious information through internet. This may leads to distributing pornography and trafficking, Cyberstalking.
- **Government**: This is the least common cybercrime, but is the most serious offense. Cyber terrorism is a crime against the Government cybercrime includes hacking military websites, government websites, or distributing propaganda. Generally, criminals involved in this category are enemy governments of other nations or terrorists.

Types of Cybercrime

DDoS Attacks

These are used to render an online service unavailable and bring the network down by overwhelming the site with traffic from various sources. Large networks of infected devices known as Botnets are created by depositing malware on users' computers. The hacker then hacks into the system once the network is down.

Botnets

Botnets are networks from compromised computers which are externally controlled by remote hackers. These remote hackers then send spam, or attack other computers using these Botnets. Botnets can also act as malware and perform malicious tasks.

Identity Theft

This cybercrime occurs when a cybercriminal gains access to a user's personal information with intent to steal funds, access confidential information, or commit tax/health insurance fraud. They may also open a phone/internet account under user name, use that name to plan a criminal activity or claim government benefits in user name. They may do this by obtaining passwords through hacking, gaining personal information from social media, or sending phishing emails.

Cyber-Stalking

This kind of cybercrime involves online harassment where the user is subjected to multiple online messages and emails. Typically cyber-stalkers use social-networking sites and search engines to intimidate a user. Usually, the cyber-stalker knows their victim, and instills fear with malicious intent.

Social Engineering

In this case, cybercriminals make direct contact with their victim, usually by phone or email. They wish to gain user's faith and usually pose as a customer service agent so that they obtain the information they need from user. The said information is typically a password, the company where the user works, or their bank account details. Cybercriminals will find out whatever they can about user through the internet and then attempt to add user as a friend on social media.

PUPs

PUPS or Potentially Unwanted Programs are a type of malware and are considerably less threatening than other the cybercrimes. They uninstall necessary software in the system including search engines and pre-downloaded apps. They can include spyware or adware, so it's a good idea to install an antivirus software to avoid malicious download.

Phishing

Such an attack is done by hackers who send malicious email attachments or URLs to users to gain access to their accounts or computer. Cybercriminals are becoming more sophisticated and many of these aforementioned email attachments are not flagged as spam. Users are tricked by emails claiming they need to change their password or update their billing information into giving cybercriminals illegal access.

Prohibited/Illegal Content

This cybercrime involves criminals sharing and distributing inappropriate content that can be considered highly distressing and offensive. Offensive content can include, but is not limited to, sexual activity between adults, videos with intense violence and videos of criminal activity, materials advocating terrorism-related acts and child exploitation content. Such content exists both on the everyday internet and on the dark web, which is an anonymous network.

Online Scams

These are usually ads or spam emails that include enticing offers that are "too good to be true", like promises of rewards or offers of unrealistic amounts of money, and when clicked on, can cause malware to interfere with and compromise/corrupt information.

Exploit Kits

Exploit kits require a vulnerability (a bug in the code of a software) in order to gain control of a user's computer. They are ready-made tools that criminals can buy online and use against anyone with a computer. Exploit kits are upgraded regularly, similar to normal software and are available on dark web hacking forums.

History of Cybercrime

The malicious tie to hacking was first documented in the 1970s when the early computerized phones began being targeted. Some tech-savvy people, known as "Phreakers", began finding ways around paying for long distance calls through a series of codes. They were the first hackers, who learnt to exploit the system by modifying its hardware and software to steal long-distance phone time. This made people realize the vulnerability of computer systems to criminal activity, and that the more complex the systems were, the higher was their susceptibility to cybercrime. FBI agents confiscated about 42 computers and over 20,000 floppy disks which were used by criminals for illegal usage of credit cards and telephone services. This operation involved over a hundred FBI agents and it took about two years to track down even a few of all the suspects. However, it was seen as a great Public-Relations effort, since it conveyed that hackers would be under surveillance and be prosecuted if necessary. The Electronic Frontier Foundation was formed as a response to the threats on public liberties which occur when the law enforcement makes a mistake or participates in unnecessary tasks to investigate any cybercrime. Their mission was to protect and defend all consumers from unlawful/unfair prosecution. While helpful, it also opened the door for loopholes and anonymous browsing where many criminal hackers practiced their illegal services. Cybercrime has become an increasing menace to modern society, even with the criminal justice system in place. Cybercriminals are highly skilled and are not easy to find, both in the public web space and the dark web.

Impact of Cybercrime on Society

Cybercrime poses a major threat to those who use the internet. Millions of users' information has been stolen within the past few years. It has caused a huge dent to the economies of several nations. IBM president and CEO GinniRometty described cybercrime as "the greatest threat to every profession, every industry and every company in the world."

Types of Cyber Crime

There are many ways in which cybercrime may be perpetrated against the user. In order to protect ourself from these, we need to know about the different ways in which our computer could be compromised, and our privacy infringed. In this section, we shall discuss about a few common tools and techniques employed by cyber criminals. This is not an exhaustive list by any means, but will give a comprehensive idea of the loopholes present in networks and security systems, which may be exploited by attackers, and also their possible motives for doing so.

Hacking

In simple words, hacking is committed by an intruder who accesses computer system without our permission and knowledge. Hackers (people who 'hack') are essentially computer programmers who have an advanced understanding of computers and commonly misuse this knowledge for devious reasons. They are usually technology buffs who have an expertise in a particular software program or language. As for their motives, there could be several, but the most common ones are pretty simple and can be explained by the lesser human tendencies such as greed for fame, power, money etc. Some people do it just to show-off their skills. Hacking ranges from relatively harmless activities such as modifying software or hardware to carry out tasks that are outside the creator's intent, others just to cause destruction.

Greed and sometimes even voyeuristic tendencies may cause a hacker to break into systems to try and steal personal banking information, a corporation's financial data, etc. They will also try and modify systems so they can execute tasks at their whim. Hackers displaying such destructive conduct are also called "Crackers", or "Black Hat" hackers. On the other hand, there are those who develop interest in computer hacking out of intellectual curiosity only, and some companies hire these computer enthusiasts to find flaws in their security systems and help to fix them. Referred to as "White Hat" hackers, they are against the abuse of computer systems. They attempt to break into network systems purely to alert the owners of flaws. It's not always altruistic though, because many do this for fame as well, in order to land jobs with top companies, or just to be termed security experts. "Grey Hat" is another term used to refer to hacking activities that are a cross between black and white hacking.

Some of the most famous computer geniuses were once hackers who later went on to utilize their skills for constructive technological development. Dennis Ritchie and Ken Thompson, the creators of the UNIX operating system (Linux's predecessor), were two of them. Shawn Fanning, the developer of Napster, Mark Zuckerberg of Facebook, and many more are examples. The first step towards preventing hackers from gaining access to our systems is to learn how hacking is done.

SQL Injections

An SQL injection is a technique which allows hackers to attack the security vulnerabilities of the software that runs a web site. It can be used to attack any type of SQL database which is not protected properly, or entirely unprotected. This process involves entering portions of an SQL code into a web form entry field – most commonly usernames or passwords – to give the hacker further access to the back-end of the site, or to a particular user's account. When the user enters login information into sign-in fields, this information is typically converted to an SQL command. This command checks the data that what user has entered against the relevant table in the database. If the input data matches the data in the table, the access can be granted, and if not, error is occurred that like error shown when we enter an incorrect password. An SQL injection is generally an additional command, that when inserted into the web form, tries to change the content of the database so as to reflect a successful login. It can also be used to retrieve information such as credit card details or passwords from unprotected websites.

Theft of FTP Passwords

This is another very common way to tamper with web sites. FTP password hacking exploits the fact that many webmasters store their website login information on their poorly protected PCs. The thief searches through the victim's system for the FTP login details, and then relays them to his own remote computer. He then logs into the web site via the remote computer and modifies the web pages as he pleases

Cross Site Scripting

Also known as XSS (formerly CSS, but renamed due to confusion with cascading style sheets), it is a very easy way of circumventing a security system. Cross-site scripting is a hard-to-find loophole in a web site, making it vulnerable to an attack. In a typical XSS attack, the hacker infects a web page with a malicious client-side script or program. When we visit this web page, the script is automatically down-loaded to our browser and executed. Typically, attackers inject HTML, JavaScript, VBScript, ActiveX or Flash into a vulnerable application as masquerader and steal confidential information. To protect PC from malicious hackers, investing in a good firewall is imperative. Hacking is done through a network, so it is very important to stay safe while using the internet.

Figure 6. Virus or malicious software

Logic Bomb

A logic bomb, also known as "slag code", is a malicious piece of code which is intentionally inserted into software to execute a malicious task when triggered by a specific event. It's not a virus, although it usually behaves in a similar manner. It is stealthily inserted into the program where it lies dormant until specified conditions are met. Malicious software such as viruses and worms often contain logic bombs which are triggered at a specific payload or at a predefined time. The payload of a logic bomb is unknown to the user of the software, and the task that it executes unwanted. Program codes that are scheduled to execute at a particular time are known as "time-bombs". For example, the infamous "Friday the 13th" virus which attacked the host systems only on specific dates; it "exploded" (duplicated itself) every Friday that happened to be the thirteenth of a month, thus causing system

Virus Dissemination

Viruses are computer software that attach themselves to or infect files or a system and have a tendency of circulating to all the computers on a network. They interrupt the operation of computer and affect the stored data either by modifying or deleting it in general. "Worms" carry out without any host to stick on unlike viruses. They simply reproduce data up till all the memory available in the system is completely affected. The word "worm" means self replicating "malware",. MALicious softWARE is the abbreviation of malware.

"Trojan horses" are different from viruses in their approach of transmission. They pretend to be as a valid file, like attachment through an email from a imaginary friend with a very authentic name, and do not circulate themselves. The user may install unknowingly an infected Trojan horse program through a drive at the time of downloads while visiting a website, through online games or applications run through internet. A Trojan horse can cause damage like other viruses, such as information theft or obstruct or interrupt the performance of computer

Figure 7. How malware can transmit; how does this happen?

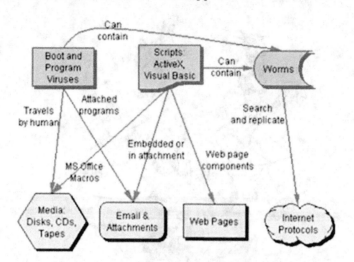

A simple diagram to show how malware can transmit How does this happen? The malicious code or virus is placed into the sequence of command so that when the program which got infected is run, the malicious code is also implemented or in some cases, malicious code runs as an alternative to the valid program. Viruses are generally seen as unrelated code attached to a host program, but this isn't always the case.

Sometimes, the whole environment is infected when uninfected legitimate program calls the virus infected program. This may almost infect all the executable files on the computer, even if code of those files was not really tampered with. Viruses include "cluster" or "FAT" (File Allocation Table) viruses, which transmit system pointers to infected files, associate viruses and viruses that change the Windows Registry directory entries so that their own code is implemented before any other authorized program.

Computer viruses generally spread through removable medium or the internet. A CD-ROM, flash disk, magnetic tape or other storage device infects all future computers when it is infected. Computer may also contract viruses by infected attachments send through e-mail, infected software and rogue web sites. They may spread to each and every system on the network.

Each and every computer virus software cause economic damages indirectly or directly. Based on this damage, viruses are categorized into two different ways:

1.   Those that distribute only but do not cause intentional damage.
2.   Programmers cause damage.

Even if they do distribution ample amount of memory, resources and time are utilized on the clean up job. Economic damages are caused directly when viruses modify the information through digital communication.

Significant expenditures are incurred by authorities, individual entities and firms to develop and execute the anti-virus tools for protecting the computer systems.

Logic Bombs

A logic bomb, also known as "slag code", is a malevolent piece of code which is intended to insert into software to make malicious task to execute when triggered by a definite event. Although it is not a virus it behaves like a virus. It is stealthily introduced into the program where it remains inactive until specific conditions are met. Logic bombs contained by the worms and viruses can be triggered at a predetermined time or definite payload

Logic bomb's payload is not known to the user of the software, and the task that it carries out is unwanted. Program codes that are planned to implement at a specific time are known as "time-bombs". For example, the infamous virus named "Friday the 13th" attacked the host systems only on particular dates; i.e. every Friday came on thirteenth of a month and causes the system slowdowns. Logic bombs are used by disgruntled people who work in the IT sector. There are situations we find "disgruntled employee syndrome" wherein angry employees who've been fired make use of logic bombs to remove the employer's databases, stultify the network for a short time or even accomplish insider trading. Triggers related to the execution of logic bombs can be a specific date and time, a misplaced entry from a database or not placing in a command at the normal time, indicates that the person doesn't work there any longer. Most logic bombs reside only in the network they were in employment. So in most of the cases, they are an insider job. It becomes easy for them to design and implement them than a virus. To protect network from logic bombs we must have continuous monitoring of data and use of efficient anti-virus software on every system of network. The piece of code embedded crash the software after a certain period of time or makes it useless until the user gives payment to use in further.

Although this piece of code uses the same technique as a logic bomb, it has a non-destructive, non-malicious and user-transparent use, and is not normally mentioned as one.

Denial-of-Service Attack

A Denial-of-Service (DoS) attack refuses service to intended users explicitly by attackers. It involves flooding of more requests into a computer resource than it can hold overwhelming its accessible bandwidth which results in overloading of server. This affects the resource to slow or crash down considerably so that nobody can access it.

By means of this technique, the attacker can make the web site unusable due to the huge amounts of traffic send to the intended site. A site may stop working completely or malfunction temporarily so that the system is unable to communicate effectively. All the policies of acceptance of the user of each and every Internet Service Providers are violated by DOS attacks. An alternative form of denial-of-service attack is "Distributed Denial of Service" (DDoS) attack where flooding of the network traffic is done by a number of topographically worldwide perpetrators. DOS attacks in general target servers of high profile web sites such as credit card payment gateways and banks. Even the websites of organizations like CNN, Amazon, Twitter, eBay! and Yahoo are not spared.

Phishing

A technique of extracting confidential information like username-password combination and credit card numbers by a masquerader who acts as a legitimate organizer. Phishing is usually accomplished by email spoofing.

Figure 8. How phishing can net some really interesting catches

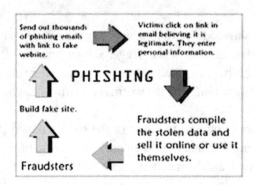

Email Bombing and Spamming

Email bombing means an abuser sends large volumes of email to an intended address which results in victim's email account or crashing of mail servers. There is an impact of DOS service attack if many mail servers are targeted. Spam filters can detect such mails easily if that mail arrives frequently into inbox. Usually, botnets carries email bombing as a DDoS attack. Botnets are private computers connected through internet whose security has been compromised by malware and it is under the control of attacker. These attacks are harder to control due to numerous source addresses and also the bots are programmed to defeat spam filters by sending different messages. "Spamming" is a variant of email bombing. Here unsolicited bulk messages are sent to a large number of users, indiscriminately. Continuous opening of links given in spam mails may leads to phishing web sites hosting malware. Spam mail may also contain attachments of infected files. Email spamming get worse if the receiver answers to the email so that all the original addressees to receive that answer. Spammers gather email addresses from newsgroups, customer lists, web sites, chat-rooms and viruses which gather address books of users and may also sell them to other spammers. A huge quantity spam is dispatched to email addresses which are not valid. Email filters cleaning out spam mail

The acceptable use policy (AUP) of all the ISPs is violated by continuous sending of spam. If the system suddenly becomes sluggish (email loads slowly or doesn't appear to be sent or received), the reason may be that processing a large number of messages through mail. Unfortunately, at this time,

Figure 9. Email bombing and spamming

Figure 10. Web jacking

there's no way to completely prevent email bombing and spam mails as it is not possible to predict the origin of the next attack. However, what we can do is identify the source of the spam mails and have our router configured to block any incoming packets from that address.

Web Jacking

Web jacking derives its name from "hijacking". Here, the hacker takes control of a web site fraudulently. In this contents of the original site can be changed and also redirect to another similar looking fake site controlled by web jacking. The owner of the web site has no more control and the attacker may use the web site for his own selfish interests. Cases have been reported where the attacker has asked for ransom, and even posted obscene material on the site. Clone of the web site can be created by the web jacking method attack and present with the other link to the victim informing that the site has moved.

Unlike usual phishing methods, when we observe closely, the URL presented will be the original one, and not the attacker's site. Website is opened and replaced quickly with the malevolent web server if new link is clicked. The name on the address bar will be some extent different from the original website that can trap the user to think whether it is a legitimate site. For example, "gmail" may direct to "gmail". Notice the one in place of 'L'. It can be easily overlooked.

Counterfeit message can be send by web jacker to the registrar managing the domain name registration. Registrar may ask to connect to IP address of webjacker by using false identity so that innocent customers of a particular domain name of a website are controlled by the webjacker.

Cyber Stalking

Cyber stalking is a new form of internet crime in our society when a person is pursued or followed online. A cyber stalker doesn't physically follow his victim; he does it virtually by following his online activity to harvest information about the stalkee and harass him or her and make threats using verbal intimidation. It's an invasion of one's online privacy. Cyber stalking uses the internet or any other electronic means and is different from offline stalking, but is usually accompanied by it. Most of the sufferers of this attack are women who are followed by children and men who are stalked by adult pedophiles and predators.

Cyber stalkers thrive on inexperienced web users who are not well aware of netiquette and the rules of internet safety. A cyber stalker can be a stranger, but could be the someone who knows about user.

Cyber stalkers harass their victims via email, chat rooms, web sites, discussion forums and open publishing web sites (e.g. blogs). The availability of free email / web site space and the anonymity provided by chat rooms and forums has contributed to the increase of cyber stalking incidents. Everyone has an online presence nowadays, and it's really easy to do a Google search and get one's name, alias, contact number and address, contributing to the menace that is cyber stalking. As the internet is increasingly becoming an integral part of our personal and professional lives, stalkers can take advantage of the ease of communications and the availability of personal information only a few mouse clicks away. In addition, the anonymous and non-confrontational nature of internet communications further tosses away any disincentives in the way of cyber stalking. Cyber stalking is done in two primary ways:

Internet Stalking: Here the stalker harasses the victim via the internet. Unsolicited email is the most common way of threatening someone, and the stalker may even send obscene content and viruses by email. However, viruses and unsolicited telemarketing email alone do not constitute cyber stalking. But if email is sent repeatedly in an attempt to intimidate the recipient, they may be considered as stalking. Internet stalking is not restricted to email; stalkers can use the internet more rigorously to harass the victims.

Computer Stalking

The more technically advanced stalkers use their computer skills to support them with the crime. They achieve unauthorized access of the victim's computer by making use of the internet and the Windows operating system. Although this is generally done by the skillful stalkers who have computer knowledge, instructions on how to carry out this without difficulty are also available on the internet. Now cyber stalking has spread over to social networking sites also. As the use of social media like Twitter, Face book, YouTube and Flickr is increased user's profile, status updates and photos are open for the world to see. When the user is online it gives immense information to make the user to become a possible victim of stalking without even being aware of the risk. The "check-ins", the "life-events", apps access confidential information and the need to assemble about everything that what and where the user is doing it, one doesn't actually leave anything for the followers to understand for themselves. Social networking technology provides a social and collaborative platform for internet users to interact, express their thoughts and share almost everything about their lives. Though it promotes socialization amongst people, along the way it contributes to the rise of internet violations.

Data Diddling

Data Diddling is unauthorized altering of data before or during entry into a computer system, and then changing it back after processing is done. It is not easy to track as the invader may alter the estimated output using this technique. In other words, the actual information entered may be changed through typing the data, a virus, the programmer of the database, an application, or anyone else engaged in the process of creating, recording, examining, encoding, converting checking or transmitting data.

The simplest of all methods of committing a computer-related crime is Data diddling because even a non computer professional can do it. Even though this is an effortless task, it can also have harmful effects. For example, a person responsible for accounting may change data about themselves or a friend or relative showing that they're paid in full. By altering or failing to enter the information, they're able

Figure 11. Credit card fraud

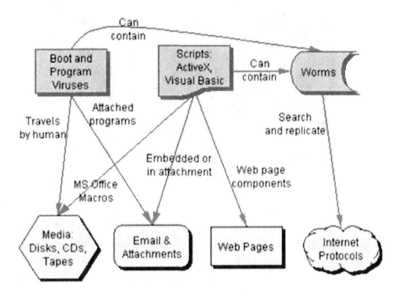

to steal from the enterprise. Other examples include forging or counterfeiting documents and exchanging valid computer tapes or cards with prepared replacements. Electricity boards in India have been victims of data diddling by computer criminals when private parties were computerizing their systems.

Identity Theft and Credit Card Fraud

Identity theft takes place when somebody steals one's identity and pretends to be that person to access credentials like bank accounts, credit cards and other benefits under his name. The pretender can also use his identity to commit other crimes. Crimes involved under identity theft are "Credit card fraud" where the masquerader uses credit card to fund his transactions. Credit card fraud is an identity theft in its simplest form. The most common case of credit card fraud is our pre-approved card falling into someone else's hands.

Credit card fraud is the most common way for hackers to steal money. He can use it to buy anything until the victim report to the authorities and get the card blocked. Several credit card companies can calculate the probability of fraud by software what they have. Generally, the issuer can even call to verify if user made a large transaction.

Habitually customers do not remember to collect their copy of the credit card receipt after paying through credit card at restaurants or elsewhere. These receipts contain credit card number and signature of customer for any person to see and use. With this information anyone can acquire anything through online or by phone. It will not be noticed until the monthly statement is received. We must ensure that website is secure and trustworthy when shopping online. Some hackers may get a hold of our credit card number by employing phishing techniques. Sometimes a tiny padlock icon appears on the left screen corner of the address bar on the browser which provides a higher level of security for data transmission. If we click on it, it will also tell the encryption software it uses. Most important thing is that use fake or stolen documents to open accounts to get the personal information so that they can do anything as a masquerader like taking loan on victim's name. These unscrupulous people may gather personal informa-

Figure 12. Software piracy

tion from the mailbox or trash (remember to shred all sensitive documents). Think of all the important details printed on those receipts, pay stubs and other documents. The user don't know a thing until the credit card people track the user down and tail until the user clear all their dues. With rising cases of credit card fraud, many financial institutions have stepped in with software solutions to monitor credit and guard user's identity. ID theft insurance can be taken to recover lost wages and restore the credit.

However before work on these services one must apply the common sense measures and no-cost to avoid such a crime.

Salami Slicing Attack

A "salami slicing attack" or "salami fraud" is a practice by which cyber-criminals take resources or money a bit at a time so that no one can notice size of the data. The perpetrator gets away with these little pieces from a large number of resources and thus accumulates a considerable amount over a period of time. The essence of this method is the failure to detect the misappropriation. The most classic approach is "collect-the-roundoff" technique. Most of the times, currency are rounded off to nearest number while doing calculations. If a programmer makes decision to gather these surplus parts of rupees to an account obviously there is no net loss to the system. This is made by transferring the amount carefully into the account of perpetrator.

Attackers carry out this task automatically by inserting a program into the system. Unsatisfied greedy people use logic bombs to exploit their knowledge about how to access the system and the network. In this technique, the criminal develops a program and makes the arithmetic calculator to modify the data while doing calculations like interest calculations etc., automatically. Stealing money electronically is the most common use of the salami slicing technique, but it's not restricted to money laundering. The salami technique can also be applied to gather little bits of information over a period of time to deduce an overall picture of an organization. This act of distributed information gathering may be against an individual or an organisation. Data can be collected from web sites, advertisements, documents collected from trash cans, and the like, gradually building up a whole database of factual intelligence about the target. As the amount of appropriation is just beneath the threshold of acuity, we need to be further cautious. Checking transactions, assets, and any other dealing including distribution of secret information to others carefully may help to decrease the probability of an attack by this method.

Software Piracy

Knowingly or unknowingly the internet piracy has become an essential part of our lives and we all contribute to. This leads to reduce the earnings of resource developers.

Piracy is rampant in India, but we knew that Software piracy is the unauthorized use and distribution of computer software. Software developers work hard to develop these programs and piracy curbs their ability to generate enough revenue to sustain application development. This affects the whole global economy as funds are relayed from other sectors which results in less investment in marketing and

The following constitute software piracy:

- Loading unlicensed software on the PC
- Using single-licensed software on multiple computers
- Using a key generator to circumvent copy protection
- Distributing a licensed or unlicensed ("cracked") version of software over the internet and offline

Cloning

"Cloning" is another threat. It happens if somebody copies the thought behind the software and develops his own software code. Always ideas are not copy protected across margins and it is not strictly against the law. A software "crack" is an illicitly acquired version of the software which works to prevent copy to be encoded.

Users of pirated software may use a key generator to generate a "serial" number which unlocks an evaluation version of the software, thus defeating the copy protection. Software cracking and using unauthorized keys are illegal acts of copyright infringement. Using pirated material comes with its own risks. The pirated software may contain Trojans, viruses, worms and other malware, since pirates will often infect software with malicious code. Users who use pirated software can may penalized by the law for illicit use of copyrighted material. Not only that the user do not get the software support that is provided by the developers. To protect oftware from piracy we must apply strong safeguards. Several websites put up for sale the software with a "digital fingerprint" that assists in track back the piratcd copies to the source. Another familiar technique is hardware locking. This locks license of the software for particular computer hardware such that it executes only on that computer. Woefully (Unfortunately), hackers carry on to discover their way around these measures.

Others

In a nutshell, any offence committed using electronic means such as net extortion, cyber bullying, child pornography and internet fraud is termed as cyber crime. The internet is a huge breeding ground for pornography, which has often been subject to censorship on grounds of obscenity. But what India considered as obscene which may not be considered by other countries. Since every country has a different legal stand on this subject matter, pornography is rampant online. However, as per the Indian Constitution, pornography is punishable by law and consider under the category of obscenity. Child pornography is a serious offence, and can attract the harshest punishments provided for by law. Pedophiles lurk in chat rooms to lure children. Internet crimes faced by the children are a matter of serious concern, and are being deal with by the authorities, but this problem is difficult to solve.

Figure 13. Aerial photo of the Federal Law Enforcement Training Center

CYBER FORENSICS

What is Forensics?

Forensics is a discipline that dates back at least to the Roman era (and possibly even to ancient China), when people accused of crimes (and the accuser) presented evidence in front of a public audience (the Latin word forensis, means "of or before the forum"). In modern times it has come to mean the application of scientific processes to recover evidence related to crime or other legal action.

Digital Forensics System

A new branch of Digital forensics came into existence as result of rapid growth in the field of personal computer during the late 1970s and early 1980s. The first crime in computers was identified in the 1978 Florida Computer Crimes Act that incorporated with legislation against the unauthorized deletion or modification of data on a computer system. As the number of computer crimes being committed increased laws were also passed to deal issues like child pornography, copyright, privacy and harassment. In 1980s, Federal laws were started to incorporate computer offences. The first country to pass legislation in 1983 is Canada. Next acts followed after this legislation was Abuse Act and US Federal Computer Fraud in 1986, Australian amendments for crimes in 1989 and the British Computer Abuse Act in 1990.

At this time traditional (and non-specialist) system administration tools were used to perform forensic analysis on "live" systems. Practitioners had only a few numbers of standards or guidelines so that the evidence produced by them was often rejected by courts.

Above photograph is an aerial photo of the Federal Law Enforcement Training Center where US digital forensics standards were developed in the 80s and 90s. In response to the growth in computer crime during the 1980s and 1990s law enforcement agencies began to establish specialized investigative groups, usually at the national level. Computer Analysis and Response Team was launched by FBI in 1984 and computer crime department was set up by UK within the Metropolitan Police fraud squad. Most of the members of these groups were computer specialists with law enforcement. During the 1990s there was high demand for the resources, eventually leading to the creation of regional and even local level units. For instance, the British National Hi-Tech Crime Unit was launched in 2001 to present a national structure; along with employees centrally in London and the different regional police forces (the unit was folded into the Serious Organized Crime Agency (SOCA) in 2006).

The great explosion of mobile devices at the early part of the 21st Century led to increase in crimes as well. These crimes are not restricted to simple text messages and phone calls. As the technology is developing mobile devices are also often contain photographs, chat, email and other types of communication or activity

Computer Security Incident

Computer security incident can be defined as any unlawful, unauthorized, or unacceptable action that involves a computer system or a computer network. Such an action can include any of the following events:

- Theft of trade secrets
- Harassment or Email spam
- Unlawful or Unauthorized intrusions into computing systems
- Embezzlement
- Possession or dissemination of child pornography
- Denial-of-service (DoS) attacks
- Tortuous interference of business relations
- Extortion

Some of the events violate public laws are actionable in civil or criminal proceedings and seriously affect the reputation of organization and its business also.

Incident Response and Computer Forensics

Breaking down of the procedure into logical steps makes incident response to manage easily.

What are the Goals of Incident Response?

Generally, in this methodology, we consider the goals of professionals of corporate security with concerns of legitimate business and also the concerns of officials of law enforcement. Finally, a methodology was developed by taking all into consideration that enhances a coordinated, interrelated response and accomplish the following:

- Avoids a disjointed, no cohesive response (which could be disastrous)
- Validates or dispels whether an incident occurred
- Encourages accumulation of accurate information
- Create controls for proper retrieval and handling of evidence
- Privacy rights protection established by law and policy
- Reduces disturbances to business and network operations
- Permission for criminal or civil action against perpetrators
- Produces accurate reports and useful recommendations

- Contribute rapid detection and containment
- Reduces exposure and compromise of proprietary data
- Provides security for organization's reputation and assets
- Train senior management
- Supports rapid detection and/or prevention of such incidents in the future

Members of the Incident Response Process

Incident response is a multifaceted discipline. Human resources such as personnel, technical experts, legal counsel, corporate security officers, security professionals, business managers, help desk workers, end users and other employees are involved in response to an incident of computer security. Computer Security Incident Response Team (CSIRT) is a team of individuals of a particular organization who responds for any incident of computer security. The CSIRT is a multidiscipline team with the appropriate legal, technical, and other expertise necessary to resolve an incident. While the CSIRT has members of special expertise incident response is not required at all times.

Incident Response Methodology

As the incident response process may demand so many characteristics and factors that affect its flow, it is rather a challenge to construct a simple process though maintaining high level of accuracy. This incident response process is both simple and accurate. The incidents of Computer security are always multifaceted and complex problems.

Pre-Incident Preparation

We need to take measures to prepare the CSIRT and the organization before an incident has happened. There is always a difference between the members of computer security incidents and those who investigate traditional crimes. Many organizations outline or define separate functionalities for personnel of corporate security as well as computer security. The CSIRT responds only to network attacks such as computer intrusions or DoS attacks. In this phase an incident response team is prepared successfully. Main objective of this phase is to provide proactive measures to assure the protection of assets and information of an organization by CSIRT. Preferably, this phase not only obtaining the developing techniques and tools react to incidents but also considering actions of networks and systems of any incident that required for investigation. There is enough chance to save and effort if we have control over the networks and hosts that are asked to investigate. Everyone will need to obtain and understand technical evidence. ole of the Corporate Computer Security Incident Response Team

- Recognition of incidents
- Recognize a possible computer security incident.
- Do an initial investigation by recording the essential details related to the incident, gathering the incident response team, and informing the individuals who have to to know regarding the incident.
- Prepare response strategy depends on the results of all the identified facts
- Decide the best response and acquire approval of management.

- Determine what criminal, civil, administrative, or additional actions are suitable to take, based on the conclusions drawn from the investigation.
- Investigate the incident Perform a thorough collection of data.
- Review the data collected to determine what happened, when it happened, who did it, and how it can be prevented in the future.
- Details which are useful for investigation must be sending to decision makers.

Preparing the Organization

This phase includes development strategies of all the corporate sectors that need to utilize for better position of an organization for incident response.

This includes the following:

- Execute the host-based measures for security
- Execute network-based security measures
- Train end users
- Make use of an intrusion detection system (IDS)
- Develop a strong access control
- Asses vulnerability periodically
- Ensure to take backups regularly

YARN and Hadoop Components

Get started quickly with some simple installation steps. They are as follows.

1. Download Apache Hadoop
2. Set JAVA_HOME
3. Create Users and Groups
4. Make Data and Log Directories
5. Configure core-site.xml
6. Configure hdfs-site.xml
7. Configure mapred-site.xml
8. Configure yarn-site.xml
9. Modify Java Heap Sizes
10. Format HDFS
11. Start the HDFS Services
12. Start YARN Services
13. Verify the Running Services Using the Web Interface

Connecting to port 50070 will bring up the web interface similar to what is shown in Figure
The following are the links related to YARN

- http://blog.cloudera.com/blog/2012/02/mapreduce-2-0-in-hadoop-0-23/
- http://hortonworks.com/blog/introducing-apache-hadoop-yarn/

Figure 14. As with HDFS services, the YARN services

- http://hortonworks.com/blog/apache-hadoop-yarn-background-and-an-overview/
- http://hadoop.apache.org/docs/stable/api/org/apache/hadoop/util/GenericOptionsParser.html

CONCLUSION

Along with the network requirements such as network resiliency, congestion, performance consistency, scalability, and partitioning, providing security and privacy must be considered while implementing an infrastructure for Big Data analytics. As current network infrastructures lacks the characteristics to implement Big Data network it is important to implement various tools, methods and techniques into networks in order to help support Map Reduce and Hadoop components. These tools and approaches help to manage and process the data more efficiently by breaking up the work to distribute simultaneously across the network. In conclusion, this chapter presents an overview of the operation principle of Big Data in the context of security and privacy issues especially explore network security concerns and mitigation strategies and also CSA, YARN and Hadoop components.

REFERENCES

Al-Kahtani, M. S. (2017, February). Security and Privacy in Big data. *International Journal of Computer Engineering and Information Technology*, *9*(2), 24–29.

Bhandari, R., Hans, V., & Ahuja, N. J. (2016). Big Data Security – Challenges and Recommendations. *International Journal on Computer Science and Engineering*, *4*(1).

Feng, X., & Zhao, Y.A. (2017). *Digital Forensics Challenges to Big Data in the Cloud.* IoTBDH-2017.

Kalaivani, R. (2017). Security Perspectives on Deployment of Big Data using Cloud: A Survey. *International Journal of Advanced Networking & Applications*, *8*(5), 5–9.

Lahmer, I., & Zhang, N. (2014). MapReduce: MR model abstraction for future security study. SIN '14 Proceedings of the 7th International Conference on Security of Information and Networks.

Maheswari, K. P., Ramya, P., & Devi, S. M. (2017). *Study and Analyses of Security Levels in Big Data and Cloud Computing*. RTESHM.

Moreno, J., Serrano, M. A., & Fernández-Medina, E. (2016). *Main Issues in Big Data Security*. Future Internet; doi:10.3390/fi8030044

Moura, J., & Serrão, C. (2016). *Security and Privacy Issues of Big Data*. Retrieved from: https://arxiv.org/abs/1601.06206

Murthy, A. (2014). Moving beyond MapReduce and Batch Processing with Apache Hadoop2. Hortonworks Inc. Arora, M., & Bahuguna, H. (2016). Big Data Security – The Big Challenge. *International Journal of Scientific & Engineering Research*, 7(12).

Tabassum, R., & Tyagi, N. (2016). Issues and Approaches for Big Data Security. International Journal of Latest Technology in Engineering, Management & Applied Science, 5(7).

Tarekegn, G. B., & Munaye, Y. Y. (2016, July–August). Big Data: Security Issues, Challenges and Future Scope. *International Journal of Computer Engineering & Technology*, 7(4), 12–24.

TechTarget. (n.d.). *Chapter 2: Introduction to the Incident Response Process*. Academic Press.

Toshniwal, R., Dastidar, K. G., & Nath, A. (2015). Big Data Security Issues and Challenges. *International Journal of Innovative Research in Advanced Engineering*, 2(2).

Vijayarani, S., & Sharmila, S. (2016). Research in Big Data – An Overview. *Informatics Engineering, an International Journal, 4*(3).

Zeng, G. (2015). Big Data and Information Security. *International Journal of Computational Engineering Research, 5*(6).

APPENDIX: REVIEW OF LITERATURE (RELATED WORK)

Mohammed S. Al-kahtani (2017) proposed possible solutions in network security of Big Data. This paper presents, classifies and compares different network security approaches and also show that their protective mechanisms reduce network vulnerabilities of software defined networks and Big Data.

Ibrahim Lahmer and Ning Zhang (2014) proposed a MapReduce, processes a huge amount of data using parallel programming in a distributed environment. Efforts are made to improve the efficiency of MapReduce's architecture from the beginning. One of its most accepted open source implementation is Hadoop. Some other recent practical MapReduce implementations like those by Facebook and IBM have propositions for the design of secure MapReduce. This paper put efforts to build a common MapReduce computation model expresses the main properties and features of the majority of recent implementations of MapReduce.

Renu Bhandari, Vaibhav Hans, and Neelu Jyothi Ahuja (2016) focuses mainly on key insights of architecture of big data which somehow lead to big data security risks and the use of best practices that must be considered for designing solution for big data so that thereby overcome these risks. In particular, this paper discusses the concerns and primary characteristics that should be taken into consideration to implement security of big data applications and technologies to handle the privacy concerns and risks related with big data analysis to increase the performance impact effectively, somehow these risks can be considered as a result of characteristics of big data architecture.

K.P. Maheswari, P. Ramya, and S. Nirmala Devi (2017) The service provider stores data in the cloud and has technique to ensure the security to protect data. But, the increased volume, variety and various data types made the scenario completely changed by the concept of Big Data. This paper made a comparative study on the security levels, which are considered as concerns common to Big Data and Cloud computing and the accomplished depending on the impact of those security levels.

Risha Tabassum and Dr. Nidhi Tyagi (2016) security of the confidential data is required as the size and continuous usage of Internet is increasing. The importance of Big Data does not depend on quantity of data rather depends on what to do with data. The review of security concerns and different approaches to surmount them was given in this paper

José Moura and Carlos Serrão (2016) revise the most significant aspects about how configuration of computing infrastructures should be done and also managed intelligently to accomplish the most remarkable security aspects involved in Big Data applications. Privacy is the most important of aspect of big data. SDN is an emerging solution and a convenient mechanism to employ security in applications of Big Data. This paper also discusses present relevant work in security and recognizes open issues.

Arun Murthy (2014) provides the best source of information for getting started with, and then mastering, the latest advancements in Apache Hadoop. Besides multiple examples and valuable case studies, a key topic in the book is running existing Hadoop 1 Applications on YARN and the MapReduce 2 Infrastructure.

Minit Arora and Dr Himanshu Bahuguna (2016) discuss the issues related to Big Data. Big Data is the vouluminous amount of data with variety in its nature along with the complexity of handling such data. In addition to the problem of mining information from Big Data, privacy is a big challenge for big data. In this paper we discuss the issues concerning privacy of this data and some of the existing techniques to ensure privacy of the data.

With the development of application of Internet/Mobile Internet, social networks, Internet of Things, big data has become the hot topic of research across the world, at the same time, big data faces security risks and privacy protection during collecting, storing, analyzing and utilizing. The functions of big data and the security threat faced by big data are introduced in this paper, and then propose the technology to solve the security threat, finally, big data applications in information security were discussed (Zeng, 2015).

Big data is a prominent term which characterizes the improvement and availability of data in all three formats like structure, unstructured and semi formats. There is a detailed study on history, basic concepts, technique, research issues, applications and tools of big data were made in this paper (Vijayarani & Sharmila, 2016).

Give details about the results achieved after the applying a efficient mapping study of security in the Big Data ecosystem. It is almost very difficult to perform thorough research in the security concepts, and the result of this research is, therefore, a major concern of security in a Big Data system, along with the most important solutions proposed by the research community (Moreno, Serrano & Fernancez-Medina, 2016).

Getaneh Berie Tarekegn and Yirga Yayeh Munaye (2016) discussed different concepts of big data. This comprises of the V's of big data which are volume, variety and velocity. This paper also discusses the processes involved in Big Data applications and reviews the Big Data's security aspects. It proposes a novel methodology for Security of Big Data and in conclusion the future scope of Big Data was presented.

Design an incident response process that will work with each type of incident you may encounter. This incident response process meets the needs of any organization or individual who must respond to computer security incidents and law enforcement or hired investigators should understand all of the stages of this method, even if they perform actions during only a portion of the entire process. It gives answers to the questions like What do we mean by a computer security incident? What are the goals of incident response? Who is involved in the incident response process? (TechTarget, n.d.)

The present paper highlights important concepts of Big Data. Definition and different parameters of Big Data were defined. The V's of Big Data like velocity, volume and variety are mainly focused. This paper also consider processes involved in big data applications and review the security concerns of Big Data and propose a novel methodology to improve the Security concepts of big data and concludes with the future scope of Big Data (Toshniwal, Dastdar & Nath, 2015).

As everything was digitized today, tons of petabyte and exabyte of data were generated by every organization, industry, business function and individual throughout the world. All our expensive data were present at various vendor clouds; there might be huge chances for our data to be exploited knowingly or unknowingly by others. This paper mainly concentrates on providing security to big data which was stored on cloud (Kalaivani, 2017).

As a new research area, Digital Forensics is a subject in a rapid development society. Cyber security for Big Data in the Cloud is getting attention more than ever. Computing breach requires digital forensics to seize the digital evidence to locate who done it and what has been done maliciously and possible risk/damage assessing what loss could leads to. In particular, for Big Data attack cases, Digital Forensics has been facing even more challenge than original digital breach investigations (Feng & Zhao, 2017).

Chapter 3
Human Factors in Cybersecurity:
Issues and Challenges in Big Data

Xichen Zhang
University of New Brunswick, Canada

Ali A. Ghorbani
University of New Brunswick, Canada

ABSTRACT

Over recent years, the extensive development of information technology has dramatically advanced the way that people use the internet. The fast growth of the internet of things and mobile crowdsensing applications raise challenging security and privacy issues for the society. More often than before, malicious attackers exploit human vulnerability as the weakest link to launch cyberattacks and conduct fraudulent online activities. How to profile users' daily behavior becomes an essential component for identifying users' vulnerable/malicious level and predicting the potential cyber threats. In this chapter, the authors discuss human factors and their related issues in cyber security and privacy. Three categories of human behaviors—desktop behavior, mobile behavior, and online behavior—and their corresponding security and privacy issues are demonstrated in detail to estimate the vulnerabilities of internet users. Some future directions related to human-factor based security and privacy issues are proposed at the end of this chapter.

INTRODUCTION

In recent years, the growth of online Cloud services and the increasing number of remote users rise more complex security and privacy issues. Hence, human factors play crucial roles in the pervasiveness of cyber threats and attacks. As the fast and extensive development of cybersecurity technologies, novel and sophisticated approaches are used for fighting against digital cybercrimes. As a result, hackers need to seek new hacking methods to launch cyberattacks. With non-professional personnel being the weakest link, most of the advanced attacks rely heavily on human factors. Human's interaction with the electric

DOI: 10.4018/978-1-5225-9742-1.ch003

devices and their performance in normal security procedure can bring potential cyber threats and vulnerabilities in daily actions. Under this circumstance, how to profile human's daily behavior and evaluate users' malicious and vulnerable level should be paid more attention in both academia and industry.

With the help of daily user behavior analysis, cyber defenders and experts can flag and report abnormal online actions that are potentially suspicious and anomalous. However, accurate user profiling analysis is still challenging, due to the complex, diverse, and dynamic nature of human's online behaviors. Most of the previous studies only focus on technological perspective of defending cyberattacks. The limited availability of related research poses great difficulties for both researchers and industrial participators. So, the motivation of this Chapter can be summarized as follows. (1) The current research of cyberattack analysis is not adequate to capture human-based factors in cyber space. There is an immediate need for understanding human's daily online behaviors and labeling the malicious level or vulnerable level of an Internet user. (2) The recent studies of human-based factors in cyber security and privacy are diverse in terms of objectives, methodologies and domains. It is necessary to summarize different types of online behaviors in a consistent format. This can provide practical conveniences and guidance for researchers. (3) With the development of computing technologies, new methodologies and application scenarios (e.g., *mobile crowdsensing*, *adversarial machine learning*) can bring new trends of challenges and difficulties. It is a necessity to present new information threats under these domains and propose promising approaches for addressing such issues. All in all, by consolidating malicious and vulnerable human daily behaviors, and extracting intelligent insights from human daily factors, cyber defenders and experts can effectively detect cyber attackers, and reduce the impact of those information threats.

In this chapter we first introduce the role of human factors in cyberspace, and the importance of profiling user behaviors in cybersecurity. Then, from the following three aspects of human factors: *desktop behaviors, mobile behaviors, and online behaviors*, we propose the potential security and privacy issues in daily human practices, and then present important concepts, technologies and solutions of modeling users' normal behavior patterns and detecting abnormal, vulnerable and malicious actions. The contributions of this Chapter are: (1) We group the Internet users' behaviors into three categories: *desktop behavior, mobile behavior, and online behavior*, which is useful for researchers and participates to understand the nature of user's daily online actions; (2) For each type of user behavior, we present a comprehensive and up-to-date survey on the typical and important cyber issues and vulnerabilities. And readers can have a clear understanding of why human become the important factor in cyberspace, what are the common human-based vulnerabilities, how hackers target victims, and how to profile users' daily behaviors based on the available information. (3) At the end of this Chapter, we also propose some interesting and important research directions that can be worked in the future.

The rest of this Chapter is organized as follows. Section "Background" discusses the definition of insider attack and outsider attack, and then demonstrates the importance of user profiling techniques in the existing cyber defending approaches. Section "Security and Privacy Issues in Human's Desktop Behaviors" summarizes the common security and privacy issues for desktop users, and then propose some typical risk desktop behaviors and the corresponding mitigation methods. Section "Security and Privacy Issues in Human's Mobile Behaviors" presents common security vulnerabilities and threats of individual mobile users, and then discusses the essential security and privacy issues in a new emerging data sharing environment – mobile crowdsensing. In Section "Security and Privacy Issues In Human's Online Behaviors", three common and risk online behaviors (financial behavior, online social media, online Cloud) are discussed in detail. In Section "future research directions", some promising research areas like security and privacy issues in smart home and smart city, location-based privacy preserving, and advanced data mining tasks are proposed and discussed. And Section "Conclusion" recaps the conclusions and contributions of this Chapter.

BACKGROUND

Nowadays, security and privacy issues have become the high-ranking priorities for every single online user. As the extensive development of big data technologies, a large amount of data is collected and used by multiple domains. And all the users' valuable information, such their personal data and the data extracted from their daily online behaviors, are profiled by IT companies, politics, and other organizations for different purposes. In this case, human factors become the most significant vulnerabilities in cyberspace. For example, typical human-factors based actions, such as the usage of desktop and mobile devices, can reflect the underlying natures of the users and their vulnerable level against cyberattacks. Attackers can exploit human-factors based information for targeting certain victims and launching cyberattacks. However, most of the previous research focuses solely on the operational or technological aspect of cyberattacks (Vieane, 2016), which aim to understand the attacking techniques to improve the security level of the cyber defense. Hence, the study of human-factors based security and privacy issues should be supported more for understanding human factors in cybersecurity and stopping cyberattacks and their prevalence.

Human-factors based online actions represent users' daily behavioral patterns, which can be used to infer users' behavioral tendencies and preferences (Chen M. a., 2019). So, on the one hand, human-factors based profiling can be used for distinguishing between malicious online users and legitimate online users. One the other hand, it can also be used to determine the malicious level or vulnerable level of a legitimate user who has no intention for malicious actions but may perform risky actions. As a result, profiling human daily behavior is essential for understanding the trending of cyberattacks and proposing practical solutions (Mittu, 2015). In this section, we introduce the necessary background of human factors in cybersecurity, and the importance of profiling human's daily behaviors in cyberspace.

Insiders and Outsiders in Cyberspace

Depending on the accessibility of the resources or information of a process in a company or an organization, a user can be categorized as *insider* or *outsider* in cyberspace (Legg, 2017). Insiders are those users who originally from within an organization, whereas outsiders are from external domains, who are not affiliated with the organization.

Insiders are either ordinary insiders or privileged insiders. Ordinary insiders, such as employees, operators, or guests have partial access to the database, infrastructure, resources, and computer systems. Privileged insiders, such as employers, managers, team leaders or administrators, have full access to everything related to the whole services or operations. Usually, privileged insiders have professional knowledge and extensive experiences in cyber operations. Compared with an outsider, a malicious insider can cause greater harm and damage, since they are legitimate and authorized to get access to essential resources and data, thus bring more privacy and security issues to the organization. It has been reported that more than half of fraud is perpetrated by malicious insiders (Legg, 2017), and almost half of all security breaches are caused by lack of user compliance (Chen M. a., 2019). The complexity of insider detection and the continuous development of human-centric cyber risks rise growing challenges for cyber defenders. It is essential to understand risky user behaviors clearly and fully characterize insider attacks and threats. And the problem of human-factors based privacy and security issues should receive more attention for both industrial and academic communities.

After understanding the insider and outsider definitions of human in cyberspace, it is necessary to describe human-based threats and attacks. According to (Nurse, 2014), there are two types of insider threats which pose potential risks to businesses, institutions, and governments: they are *malicious insider threat* and *non-malicious insider threat*. From this perspective, insiders can be categorized as *malicious insiders* who willfully cause cyber threats and attacks, and *non-malicious insiders* with the unintentional purpose for causing harms or damages. For malicious insider threat, the insider may intentionally take advantage of the privileged access for illegal gain. For example, by exploiting his privilege or accessed resources, the malicious insiders can steal personal or financial information from one company. However, a non-malicious insider threat can be considered as an accidental event. The users have no malicious intent, but their actions still cause harm to the confidentiality, integrity or availability of the organization's assets or resources. Most of such accidents are wholly or partially resulting from users' mistakes or errors. For example, if an employee fails to identify a phishing email and click a malicious website, then it is likely that his workstation may be attacked and some sensitive information may be leaked. Based on information from (Lord, 2017; Partners, 2018; Glaspie, 2017), we summarize the differences between insiders and outsiders in term of intentionality, motivation, major targets, common threats and approaches. The detailed information is listed in Table 1.

The Significance of Profiling Human Behavior in Cybersecurity

As mentioned above, profiling human's daily behaviors become useful and necessary for understanding the vulnerability of benign users and detecting potential malicious users. Also, by profiling users who may cause potential threats, cyber defenders can have precise knowledge of the possible cause, damage and underlying solutions for such threats. Attacker profiling is a technique used for security defenders to understand and identify attackers. It is significant for labeling the risky level of the attackers and understanding the nature of cyberattacks (Dantu, 2009). With attacker profiling, security administrators and experts can predict the potential severity and consequences of cyber threats by identifying the attackers' motivations, professional skills, level of system privileges, resource availability and so on.

Profiling human behavior also plays an essential role in the existing in intrusion detection and risk management systems. In this section, we mainly discuss how human behavior profiling techniques are used in those security and privacy protection systems.

Security Information and Event Management

Security Information and Event Management (SIEM) is a tool that responsible for centralizing and analyzing logging information by combining security information management and security event management (Elmrabit, 2015). The sources of the logs can be varied from client workstations to servers, firewalls and so on. At the same time, log analysis is an important aspect for malicious user profiling. By monitoring the logging data, cyber defenders can provide the overall suspiciousness of the users and predict their potential threats to the system. A lot of works have been done on identifying malicious insider activities

Table 1. Comparisons between insiders and outsiders

	Insiders and Insider Threats	**Outsiders and Outsider Threats**
Privilege	Partial or wholly access to the information and resources within an organization.	Have no access to the internal resources.
Examples	• Employees • Contractors • Administrators • Managers • Guests • Operators • Service providers	• Hackers • Cybercriminals • Random users • Spies • Terrorists
Intentionality	• Malicious (for malicious insiders) • Not malicious (for non-malicious insiders)	• Malicious
Target	• Intellectual property • Business plans and secrets • Employee information • Personal information • Financial information • Privileged account information • Source code	• Financial information • Personal information • Privileged account information • Database and infrastructure • Services and applications • Insiders
Most vulnerable IT assets	• Database • File servers • Cloud applications	• Network • Mobile devices • Remote servers
Resource availability	• Authentication information • Employee information • Both hardware and software • Database • System operation privilege	• Only external resources
Motivations or reasons	For malicious insiders: • Financial gain • Personal gain • Professional revenge For non-malicious insiders: • Weak or erroneous actions (e.g., weak/reused password, unlocked devices, unsecured network connection)	• Financial gain • Military gain • Political gain • Espionage
Common threats	For malicious insiders: • Physical theft • Privilege abuse • Copying or offloading sensitive data to personal drives For non-malicious insiders: • Unintentional data breach	• Social engineering • Hacking • Phishing • Malware • Denial of service attack • Web-based attack • Botnet • Viruses, worms and trojans

by integrating SIEM and user profiling techniques (Flynn, 2014) (Tep, 2015) (Soomro, 2016). With data mining and machine learning approaches, cyber defenders can detect abnormal cyber operations or identify evidence for forensic investigations after the cyber incident occurs (Elmrabit, 2015) (Homoliak, 2018).

Data Loss Prevention

Data Loss Prevention (DLP) is a strategy for preventing end users from sending sensitive information to malicious users or outsider networks. Accurate user profiling is vital for DLP, since it can help system classify authorized end users and protect confidential and critical information. It can also help benign users avoid disclose or share sensitive data accidentally. Since the possibility of data leakage is highly correlated to users' insecure actions, so user profiling is a fundamental aspect in DLP, and can enhance the functionality of DLP by detecting sensitive data in the users' network traffic, monitoring the users' PC based systems and their anomalous actions (Veracode, 2019).

Access Control

In the information security domain, Access Control is a technique that regulates who or what can view or get access to the resources in a computing environment (Searchsecurity, 2019). Again, user profiling plays an important role in Access Control, since it can help the Access Control system perform authorization of users and entities by evaluating user-based attributes. There are different types of Access Control, and user profiling is essential in Role-based access control. Role-based access control is widely used for restricting access to computer resources based on individuals and groups (Searchsecurity, 2019). The role-based security model relies on role-based user classification system using user profiling techniques. Since automatic user profiling can help Access Control system to perform well in the tasks like role authorization, role permission, and improve the overall performance effectively.

Human Error Modeling

Human error modeling, or human error assessment, is a technique used for evaluating the probability of a human error occurring throughout the completion of a specific task (Evans, 2016). Such analysis can reduce the potential risk and therefore improve the overall security level for a system or an organization. With advanced user profiling techniques, human error models can perform a comprehensive analysis of human actions and then output effective results on predicting hidden mistakes and accidents.

Personality Analysis

With the influx of cyber-attacks in recent years, there is an increased demand for understanding the relationship between users' personality and their vulnerabilities in the information security domain (Freed, 2014). It is reported that people who intend to enter cybersecurity careers are the people who tend to have personalities like high openness, rational decision-making style and investigative interests (Wee, 2016). The analysis of personality of a user in cybersecurity can be an interdisciplinary work, in which the knowledge from both sociology and psychology are necessities. In (Greitzer, 2010), a user-profiling based framework for malicious behaviors detection is proposed. In their system, the users' daily working actions (web traffic information, internet activities, working hours, etc.) are integrated as psychological indicators, which are finally used to assess potential malicious exploits and risk levels. Also, in their study, they summarize some important psychosocial indicators, such as disgruntlement, accepting feedback, anger issues, stress, confrontational behaviors, which are useful connections between personality characteristic and potential cyber risks.

Attacker Characteristic

Nowadays, as the development of social engineering, malicious attackers attempt to gain access to the resources by manipulating people's trust (Krombholz, 2015). As a result, it is important to think about the goals, motivations, and capabilities of likely adversaries against which we wish to protect our system (Carayon, 2005). So, attacker characteristics are significant since it can provide the nature and potential severity of the future cyberattacks. User profiling can be a reliable technique for characterizing attackers' background, knowledge, intention and capacity. Previously, there are lots of work on the categorization of attackers and the corresponding attacks (Heartfield, 2016). By integrating attacker's information such as inside/outside status, sophistication, level of privileges, resources availability, professionalism, creativity, cleverness and so on, a final attacker profiling can be achieved with the maliciousness level of the attacker (Carayon, 2005). Attacker characteristic with user profiling techniques can enhance the performance of the security system and create alerts before dangerous threats happen.

SECURITY AND PRIVACY ISSUES IN HUMAN'S DESKTOP BEHAVIORS

As the increasing popularity of information technology and the World Wide Web, the desktop has become one of the essential daily supplies in everybody's life. As a result, most of the cybercrimes are related to desktop security. According to (Hanus, 2016), desktop security can be defined as the protection of equipment and data stored on home users' desktop or laptop computers, as well as the recovery from potential attacks. Many desktop users have fallen victim to some computer virus or malware attacks. Also, the growth of cybersecurity techniques leads to more sophisticated attacking approaches, and many desktop users, due to the lack of professional knowledge and experience, do not usually understand their insecure behaviors that can be associated with potential cyber risks. In this section, we first discuss some common security and privacy issues for desktop users; then we present some typical risk desktop behaviors and their corresponding consequences. Finally, we briefly introduce some resources for desktop behavior analysis.

Security and Privacy Issues in Desktop Users

In this section, we mainly talk about some major and common security and privacy issues in desktop users.

Malware

In 2018, malware is one of the most common attacks with an average of US $2.4 million in defense (Sobers, 2019). Especially in recent years, malware experiences an unprecedented evolution, and both self-propagating malware and ransomware have drawn considerable attention from cyber defenders. Designed by cyber attackers, malware typically contains malicious code, and can cause extensive damage to data or operating system. Malware is usually delivered through website or attachments in an email, it can be installed and executed automatically, even without users' awareness. Virus, worm, Trojan horse, and toolkit are the most common malware. As the development of threat protection technology, the trending of malware is evolved, which may bring new information threats. According to Symantec Internet Security Threat Report 2018 (Symantec s. c., 2018), the number of new malware variants (e.g.,

Ransomware, WannaCry, Emotet, FBI Virus, Loyphish, Sirefef (Armendariz, 2018)) has increased more than 54% after 2017. Compared with traditional malware like trojans or spyware, new malware attack like Ransomware can hack the system in an automated and seamless manner, which can be more harmful to the organizations.

There are mainly two types of malware detection approaches: *signature-based approach* and *anomaly-based approach* (Chowdhury, 2017). In signature-based method, a specific pattern of a series of bytes or a cryptographic hash in a file is checked with a database of known malware samples. This method is efficient but not effective sometime, especially when new types of malware occur. Also, a large human involvement is required to update the database and maintain new types of malware. In anomaly-based detection, rather than focusing on patterns or signatures, the detection is based on heuristics or rules. Recently, machine learning and deep learning techniques are widely used for anomaly-based malware detection, and have been proven to be capable of monitoring new malware threats effectively (Kolosnjaji, 2016; Aijaz, 2018; Narudin, 2016; Rajeswaran, 2018; Xu, 2017). However, the shortcoming of machine learning based approach is the time-consuming in feature engineering during the training stage. There are some warning signs that non-professional personnel can use as clues to predict if the desktop or laptop is injected with malware. For example, if pop-up ads start showing everywhere, then it is likely that an ad fraud malware hacks a computer. Browser redirecting is another good indicator for redirection attacks. Also, users should be careful about some notable and abnormal web post. Such hackers usually use some fake news to draw users' attention and then lure them to click the link and fall into the malware attacks.

Data Breach

Data breach is the unintentional release of personal or sensitive data to untrusted entities. Both insiders and outsiders can cause a data breach. It is one of the most damaging privacy threats which can result in the loss of millions of private records. Data from healthcare, financial, government and military organizations are always the targets of cybercriminals. In 2016, personal information of more than 3 billion Yahoo accounts were leaked in a big data breach accident (Oath, 2016). Also, in 2016, over 57 million passengers and drivers found that their information was hacked through Uber database (Khosrowshahi, 2016). From 2017 to 2018, over 130 large-scale data breaches were happened in the U.S. annually, and the number was still increasing after that (Abbosh, 2019). In breach-focused attacks, adversaries can exploit the vulnerability of regular desktop users and trick them into exposing important information. For instance, a credential phishing website or a piece of surprising news can be used in these tactics. In this case, human factors become the weakest link in the attacks. Just like zero-day attacks (Zhang M. a., 2016), attackers can take advantage of users' vulnerability, and data breach can occur even without users' awareness. To avoid data breach, desktop users should cultivate secure behaviors, such as patching and updating software regularly, encrypting sensitive data and managing passwords in an organized way.

Phishing

Phishing is the fraudulent attempt to obtain confidential information such as usernames, passwords, and credit card details by disguising as a trustworthy entity in electronic communications (Ramzan, 2010). As aforementioned, hackers can use phishing attacks to distribute malware or cause a data breach. A "legitimate" email is the most commonly used way for launching phishing attacks, followed by other fraudulent activities. According to 2018 Symantec Internet Security Threat Report (Symantec s. c.,

2018), Internet users averagely received 16 phishing email per month. Proofpoint report (Proofpoint, 2018) mentioned that over 75% phishing emails contain malicious links or attachment.

The nature of phishing is exploiting the weakness and vulnerability of desktop users. And some social engineering techniques are often used to increase the chance of a successful phishing attack. There are three common phishing detection approaches: *content-based filtering*, *blacklisting*, and *whitelisting*. By extending spam filtering techniques, content-based filtering methods examine suspicious URLs and their context. The detection results are often based on statistical rules or heuristics. The mechanisms in blacklisting and whitelisting are similar. The difference is, in blacklisting, a list or collection of websites are collected as suspicious or malicious URLs. In whitelisting, the benign and trustworthy URLs are confirmed by human participators (Shahriar, 2016). Some studies (Sheng, 2010; Kumaraguru, 2010; Albladi, 2017) work on the vulnerabilities of different desktop users facing phishing attacks based on their demographic information. They find that men can always distinguish phishing websites with legitimate websites better than women. And people who are more neurotic is more likely to be the victims of phishing scams.

Others

There are still other types of security and privacy issues for desktop users, such as network traffic attacks, web-based attacks, SQL injection attack and so on. But since they are not related to human-based factors, so they are not the scope of this chapter.

Risk Desktop Behaviors

According to IBM 2018 X-Force report (IBM, 2018), a majority amounts of incidents involve human errors. With social engineering approaches, hackers can exploit the mistakes and weakness of human behaviors to launch a successful cyberattack. Outsider attackers always lure insiders to provide sensitive information, like account name, password, and intellectual property. To safeguard the cyber domain from the perspective of desktop users, it is essential to understand the typical and common daily human desktop errors. Since these behaviors can be considered poor cybersecurity practices and can lead to serious cyber threats and attacks. And in this section, some high-risk desktop behaviors and the corresponding consequences are discussed.

Among all risk desktop behaviors, *downloading behaviors*, *updating behaviors* and *patching behaviors* are the essential ones that highly related to users' vulnerable level. Attackers can inject malicious codes or files in a legitimate download process, and then compromise victims' computers. Updating systems and installing patches are useful ways to prevent desktop users from being exploited by malicious software (Temizkan, 2012). Usually, software vendors are responsible for updating patches available for download, and users are responsible for patching the software early and frequently.

Bilge (2017) proposes a semi-supervised model for predicting cyber risk attacks mainly based on downloading and patching behaviors. In their study, a useful and comprehensive feature set for malicious download behavior analysis is proposed. And they find that if users have abundant and varied downloading behaviors, then they likely to suffer higher cyber risks. And more extended working hours is also correlated with higher vulnerability. Beside downloading behaviors and patching behaviors, there are still some other actions for potential desktop victims. Table 2 lists some typical risky desktop behaviors and their corresponding consequences.

Table 2. Some typical risky desktop behaviors and their potential consequences

Risky daily behaviors	Potential consequence
● Share password with others	● Data leakage
● Use same or simple passwords in multiple websites	● Data leakage
● Do online banking/shopping with untrusted devices or public Internet	● Data leakage
● Download free anti-virus software/multimedia/applications/files from an unknown source	● Malware
● Do not updating systems or applications regularly	● Malware
● Do not patching applications regularly	● Malware
● Disable anti-virus software on desktop	● Malware
● Click untrusted URLs in browsers or in unsolicited emails	● Malware ● Phishing
● Sharing current location or too much personal information on the Internet	● Data leakage ● Phishing

Resources for Desktop User Analysis

There are three principal sources for desktop behavior analysis, and they are *logs*, *network traffics* and *history records*. (1) Logs are the standard documentation of events relevant to desktop devices. They record all the security-related events, like computer status, virus and malware detection, usage of software, and the communication information between different users. (2) Network traffic describes all the communications among computer networks. By recording and analyzing network traffics, researchers can understand and evaluate the network utilization. (3) Browsing history is the primary way to review users' online activity. They are all important sources for tracking user's desktop activities.

In the era of big data, a large amount of data is created every day, which makes profiling users' desktop behavior possible. Researchers can build both supervised and unsupervised models for extracting useful insights and patterns from logs or network traffics and predicting the vulnerable level or malicious level for the desktop users. For example, Yen (2013), Corney (2011), Jia (2017), Du (2017), and Gasser (2018) focus on suspicious activity detection based on analyzing different types of logs with data mining and deep learning techniques. Also, lots of studies are working on anomaly detection based on network traffics, include machine learning based anomaly detection (Silva, 2016; Stevanovic, 2016), statistical and information theoretic analysis (Lee, 2001; Tan, 2014) and unsupervised clustering approaches (Su, 2011; Syarif, 2012; Ahmed, 2015). With the help of these models, researchers and cyber defenders can either classify malicious cyber events or identify anomaly behaviors.

SECURITY AND PRIVACY ISSUES IN HUMAN'S MOBILE BEHAVIORS

Computing techniques are evolved from the large desktop computer systems to the mobile devices like smartphones, smart watches, and so on (Gupta B. a., 2016). Until January 2018, global smartphone population amounted to 3.7 billion unique users (Statista R., 2018). More and more malicious attacks shift their focus from desktop devices to mobile applications, and mobile security becomes a crucial aspect in cybersecurity. Rather than only smartphones, a considerable number of mobile sensing and computing devices are emerging, which fuel the development of mobile crowdsensing applications and the Internet of Things (IoT). Those mobile devices include music players, the global positioning system (GPS), Bluetooth devices, in-vehicle sensing devices, and so on. Due to the dynamic and unsecured nature of mobile communications, cybercriminals explore the limitations and the vulnerabilities of mobile devices to steal personal information and launch cyberattacks. There is an immediate need to establish a safeguarding architecture to protect personal credentials from being attacked and avoid unauthorized insiders/outsiders getting access to the utilization of such mobile devices (Gupta B. a., 2016). And it is essential to understand the potential risky mobile behaviors and address possible security and privacy issues among mobile devices.

In this section, we mainly discuss the security and privacy issues in human's mobile behaviors. And it contains two subsections. In the first subsection, we introduce common and typical security vulnerabilities of individual mobile users, which include mobile terminal issues, mobile network issues and mobile cloud issues. In the second subsection, we propose the essential security and privacy issues in a new emerging data sharing environment – mobile crowdsensing. Under this scenario, users are not considered individually but collaboratively. Typical problems contain insider attacks, outsider attacks and data privacy preserving in mobile crowdsensing.

Security and Privacy Issues in Mobile Users

According to Suo (2013), different types of security and privacy issues for mobile users can be categorized into the following three categories, *mobile terminal issues*, *mobile network issues*, and *mobile Cloud issues*.

Mobile Terminal Issues

Lots of third-party applications support the diverse functionalities of different mobile devices, however, they can lead to severe cyber threats for mobile users. Also, the operating systems and wireless Internet connections are also vulnerabilities of mobile devices. And in this section, we mainly talk about the security and privacy issues in the mobile terminal.

Mobile Malware

Mobile malware is malicious software specifically targets on smartphone or other wireless devices. As the widespread use of mobile devices, more and more attackers focus on distributing malware among mobile devices. After the mobile is compromised, attackers can steal user information and collapse the operating system. Lots of mobile malware targets only on Android systems, due to (1) Google Play is open source, and (2) the updates and patches of Android applications are always not inconsistent.

There are a large number of different types of attacks target on Android system, such as ransomware (Yang, 2015), spyware (Jiang, 2012), adware (rturk, 2012), financial malware (Kadir, 2018), and so on. Mobile malware is always the first enemy for smartphone users. In 2018, a mobile malware called *CopyCat* infected over 14 million Android devices worldwide and earned the attackers more than $ 1.5 million in fake ad revenues in just two months (Point, 2018). Accordingly, on the one hand, lots of studies are working on Android malware detection and classification (Yujuan, 2015; Hou, 2017; Ghaffari, 2016; Yun'an, 2017). One common and popular way is extracting both static features (e.g., Java code,

Permissions, Intent filters, Network address) and dynamic features (e.g., System calls, Network traffic, User interactions) for building supervised machine learning models (Feizollah, 2015). On the other hand, mobile users should behave better to protect their devices from being compromised by cybercriminals. Some useful and straightforward hints include: always download applications from Apple, Google stores; do not trust third-party application stores; do not jailbreak the devices and keep both the software and application of the devices updated regularly.

Software Vulnerability

Mobile devices are the subject of many security issues, one of them is software vulnerability. The software is the fundamental service of a mobile device, but it can also be exploited by attackers to intrude malicious activities. For example, if a user wants to share files or multimedia between phone and computer via File Transfer Protocol (FTP), then sensitive information like user name and password can be leaked through the transmission over the network. Hackers can get access to smart phone illegally, insert malicious codes, steal personal information and conduct malicious modification (Suo, 2013). Nowadays, as the speed of smartphone is faster, and the memory of the device is larger, more and more applications are installed on mobile devices, which can lead to a higher chance of suffering software vulnerability. Under this circumstance, patching and updating the applications play an essential role for safeguarding the mobile devices. (Bilge, 2017) conduct research on studying the relationship between users' patching behavior and their usage vulnerabilities. By profiling user behavior, they find that users who do not patch the software vulnerability shows low-security awareness and are likely to be infected in the future.

Others

There are also some other types of mobile terminal issues which related to the usage of the devices, such as password and authentication control, multiple user logging, and online banking and shopping, which also need mobile users to pay attention to. Notably, online banking and shopping, which are discussed in the next Section "Security and Privacy Issues in Online Behaviors".

Mobile Terminal Issues

A working mobile device can get access to many different types of networks, such like the phone signal network, the Short Message Service (SMS) network, the Internet through 3G, 4G, 5G networks, Wi-Fi, Bluetooth, and so on (Suo, 2013). A large number of ways for approaching different networks can bring more security issues and threats for mobile users.

Others Public Wi-Fi Connection

It is one of the typical mobile networks issue, and free public Wi-Fi is hackers' favorite platform for stealing personal data. One serious reason that public Wi-Fi is risky is that data transmission over the network is often unencrypted and unsecured, and adversaries can exploit this security flaw to launch a man-in-the-middle attack. In this cyberattack, hackers can get access to any information between the user and the destination website. As a result, all the personal information like passwords, account name can be exposed.

Rouge Hotspot

A rogue hotspot is another security vulnerability of public Wi-Fi connection. By mimicking legitimate hotspot, hackers can make the rogue hotspot not distinguishable with legitimate ones, and mobile users are easily be fooled. Once the link is established, hackers can intercept the data transmission and inject malware into the connected devices (Symantec, 2019).

Bluetooth Attack

As one of the important technologies in wireless communication, Bluetooth can provide fast and low-cost data transmission. Many mobile devices serve Bluetooth function, such as smartphones, printers, keyboards, earphones, mouse, and so on. Although Bluetooth offers convenience and ease of use, it lacks a centralized security infrastructure and has many serious security vulnerabilities. Especially the fast development of IoT rise the significant security issues in Bluetooth technology. Researchers comprehensively discuss the common Bluetooth attacks, such as Obfuscation, Surveillance, Sniffing, Man-in-the-middle, Unauthorized direct data access, Denial of service, and so on (Lonzetta, 2018).

Mobile Cloud Issues

The last category is mobile security issue related to Cloud storage and Cloud computing. In recent years, with the widely popularity of mobile devices, mobile Cloud storage and computing become the one of the most predominant services for online users, businesses, financial organizations, governments, and so on. Mobile Cloud computing is the terminology which refers to an infrastructure where both data storage and data processing operate outside of the mobile device (Stergiou, 2018). A vast number of mobile Cloud services and application rise great challenges for both industry and academia. Data security and privacy protections are the major problems that related to both mobile hardware and software in the Cloud architecture, which make the challenge even more difficult. And data integrity, data confidentiality, data availability and data privacy should be all considered as significant security and privacy threats for mobile users (Sun, 2014). All the traditional Cloud threats can be applied for mobile Cloud platforms. Some typical mobile Cloud security issues include data breaches, network security, data locality, data access, system vulnerabilities, account hijacking, malicious insiders, compromised credentials, broken authentication, and so on. More discussions can be seen in the next section "Security and Privacy Issues in Online Behaviors".

Security and Privacy Issues in Mobile Crowdsensing

The fast and extensive development of mobile computation technologies enables the emergence of mobile crowdsensing (MCS). As defined in (Ganti, 2011), in mobile crowdsensing, individuals with sensing and computing devices collectively share data and extract information to measure and map phenomena of common interest. Figure 1 shows the typical architecture of MCS applications. Raw data is collected from different sensors and smart devices, and then the data is transferred to a backend server and processed by

Figure 1. Typical architecture of MCS applications

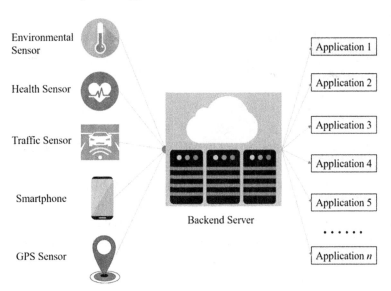

it for aggregation and mining. The data might be modified to preserve privacy and then can be used for extracting useful insights and knowledge based on different application scenarios, like natural environment monitoring, traffic information collection and management, urban dynamic sensing, healthcare monitoring, and social network-based analysis (Ganti, 2011; Liu, 2018).

In the big data era, mobile users will not use their devices individually. Instead, lots of online servers, data collectors and cloud offer platforms for mobile users to share, exchange and take advantage of data in more collaboratively, so MCS highly depend on the power of the crowds of mobile users. Based on the different purposes and functionalities of services, MCS application can be classified as 1) environmental application, 2) infrastructure application, and 3) social application. Mobile users can collect and upload various types of data through the Internet, ranging from general information (e.g., temperature, moisture, pollution information) to more specialized and personal information (e.g., personal location, mobility, driving pattern, health condition, voting intentions) (Ni, 2018).

However, due to the crowd, dynamic and uncertainty nature of MCS, large numbers of security and privacy issues should be addressed before MCS can provide better services.

Insider Attacks

The reliability of the shared data and the trustworthy of the participant are the major concerns of insider attacks in MCS. A good MCS service highly relies on the trustworthy of all the participants and the services providers. In an insider attack, a malicious mobile user can share some confusing or false data to mislead the computational results. On the other hand, if the misleading crowdsensing results may also affect users' motivation for further sharing personal data. Also, a suspicious data collector can easily exploit all the data to profile certain victims and launch malicious activities.

Outside Attacks

Just like cloud applications and IoT applications, MCS may also face dangerous outsider attacks. In Ni (2018), the author reports a good summary of outsider attacks for MCS, including man-in-the-middle attack, eavesdropping attack, forgery attack, impersonation attack, spam attack, and so on.

Data Privacy

Personal data sharing is the fundamental aspect of MCS applications. With all the data input, the MCS service provider can extract useful insights from the statistical analysis or pattern discovery computation. For example, a traffic monitoring system may need to keep track of mobile users' real-time location and mobility to report road condition and predict traffic accident. If the location-based data is exposed to malicious attackers, then users' daily routine, habit, and even social relationship can be profiled and extracted. Privacy-preserving technologies are essential tools to protect users' data from being leaked. Some popular approaches include anonymization, multiparty computation, and data perturbation.

SECURITY AND PRIVACY ISSUES IN HUMAN'S ONLINE BEHAVIORS

The increase in the use of and access to technology has recently witnessed a tremendous growth of online users, especially young users. However, due to the increasing popularity of the Internet, a massive amount of cyber vulnerabilities, threats, and attacks are distributed in Web surfing or online actions. Being extensively used for malicious purposes, the Internet has become a platform for delivering malicious and fraudulent activities. Also, we should pay attention to users' online vulnerabilities and their online behaviors. Some everyday risky online actions include sharing too much information on online social media, using the same passwords for every online logging in, always connecting to the public Wi-Fi, sharing current location in online services, agreeing with the private and security policies without even reading them, and so on. As mentioned before, if the malicious attackers exploit the risky online behaviors, then users' online experience will be further degraded, and more malicious activities need to be addressed. For safe online practices, it is essential for users to identify potential security and privacy issues and understand risky online actions.

In this section, the essential vulnerabilities of online actions are discussed regarding online financial behaviors, online social media, and online Cloud behaviors.

Security and Privacy Issues in Online Financial Behaviors

The development of the Internet and big data technology have significantly triggered the growth of e-commerce and online financial services. And with the technological advancements, a large number of customers are increasingly turning to digital channels for selling/buying products, doing online shopping and banking through many different online financial organizations. Directly related to money, the security issues in online financial behaviors can cause much more damaging results for Internet users. And in this section, we mainly talk about three different online financial options; they are online banking, online shopping and online trading.

Online Banking

Online banking is one of the most popular and commonly-used services offered by financial institutions. Users can access their banking accounts anytime and anywhere, and it is fast, mostly free and easy-to-use. As a result, more and more people are relying on online banking to pay their rental fee, pay their credit cards, transfer money to other people, pay the mortgage, and so on. Until 2018, nearly 70% Internet users use digital banking for daily routine purpose (Statista S., 2019). It is becoming an essential part of our daily behavior, and the security and privacy issues should be paid more attention. And all the customers need to be familiar with all the potential risks of online banking. Important online banking security issues include identity theft, phishing, account compromised, online fraud, unauthorized access, reused credentials, and so on.

Compromised Banking Apps

Nowadays, lots of online banking services can be accessed by mobile devices and banking apps. In 2018, 22 million mobile users managed their banking account via smartphones. By the end of 2019, mobile banking will overtake Internet banking in terms of the number of customers (Peachey, 2019). The vulnerability of banking apps can be a significant risk issue for online banking users. If the smartphones are compromised by dangerous hackers, then it is very risky to conduct any online banking behaviors using those mobile devices. With the help of techniques like reverse engineering and mobile malware infection, hackers can easily compromise the mobile devices and steal users' personal information. Also, the privacy of confidential financial data is another important aspect of online banking. Under this condition, evaluate and manage the risk level of banking applications is in high demand. In Bojjagani (2016), the authors propose a comprehensive system for testing the security threats in Android banking application at both code level, network level and device level.

Reused Credentials

Almost every online banking website need users' credential information, such as usernames and passwords before the users can get access to all the online services. All the sensitive information can be phished or stolen by hackers while users are using their online banking services. And this situation becomes worse when many online users use a single username and password for all their web accounts. For example, in 2014 Kickstarter's database is compromised and the customers' data was beached. And the hackers may use those stolen credentials into the victims' bank website (Kumparak, 2019).

Online Shopping

Over recent years, as the development of e-commerce, online shopping advances the way that people buy or sell goods and services. Users can easily search for a product of interest by visiting online shopping websites and paying the money online. In 2017, e-commerce was responsible for $2.3 trillion in sales around the world, the number is expected to be nearly $4.5 trillion by 2021. And it is estimated that 95% of purchases will be made via online shopping by 2040 (Osman, 2019). Different computers and devices are used for online shopping, includes desktop, laptops, tablet, smartphone, and so on. Similar with online banking, there are many major issues and risks in online shopping. For example, fake online reviews are intrusive in nearly every online website, which can direct costumers' opinion and the decision by exaggerating the fact or defaming the reputation of the products. A fake online shopping webpage can steal users' personal information and financial history by sending malicious URLs and email scams.

Fake Online Reviews

One good service provided by online shopping website is all the quality of the products and services are transparent, people can write their reviews and view other people's reviews. However, when users browse online shopping webpages, fake reviews are intrusive and everywhere. It can direct people's opinions and decisions by exaggerating the fact or defaming the reputation of some products. It may destroy the trust ecosystem of online shopping since consequently users are not believing in the online shopping websites and will not share their comments (USPS, 2019).

Lack of Disclosure

Another issue is that online users can not get access to the full cost disclosure of their online shopping, which might lead to additional fees like shipping. Also, sometimes users do not read the conditions and terms of a website carefully before becoming a member.

Reused Credentials Others

Some other security and privacy issues include fraudulent websites and emails, intercepting transactions, and vulnerable devices (USPS, 2019). Finally, all the risks related to online banking can also be the issues of online shopping, due to online shopping always ends up with paying the bills online. So, users should be more focusing on identity theft, online fraud, phishing, and financial malware.

Online Trading

Online trading, also known as online investing, is a process by which individual investors and traders buy and sell securities over the Internet, typically with a brokerage firm (Wikipedia, 2019). Usually, investors need to place an order through a stockbroker either in person or via telephone. As the development of information and technology, the Internet becomes a popular platform for trading and investing. Same as other online services and behaviors, there are still different risks in online trading. For instance, investment fraud is a deceptive practice that induces investors to make purchase or sale decisions based on false information. Personal information, like username and password can be hacked and leaked by malicious traders.

Security and Privacy Issues in Online Social Media

Over recent years, the growth of online social media has dramatically facilitated the way people communicate with each other. With the considerable data day in and out created by online social media like Twitter and Facebook, researchers and industrial participates can profile online users to understand their interest, opinions and decisions.

However, due to the popularity and exposure of social networks, online social media has become a platform for an illegal purpose. For example, malicious online users can distribute false or misleading information, which has the potential to cause serious problems. Many points to the 2016 U.S. presidential election campaign as having been influenced by fake news. The massive amount of incredible and misleading information can arise as a dangerous threat to online social communities, and online users.

In this section, we discuss the security and privacy issues in online social media behaviors. And it has two major components. In the first subsection, we present the potential security and privacy issues for users in online social networking. Such problems are: *online fake information* (includes online fake news, fake reviews, fake advertisements, fake political statements, etc.), *identity theft and data leakage* (includes identity theft, financial information leakage, personal data leakage), *third party threats* (include fake and malicious apps, financial malware, malicious links), *profile hacking* (such as phishing, keylogging, session hijacking, DNS spoofing, botnet, etc.), *spamming* (like fraud request from spamming account), and so on.

Fake Information in Online Social Media

Due to the increasing popularity of online social network, it has become a major platform for distributing fake news, misleading data, rumors, fake political statements, and so on. And online fake information via social media rises big threat and vulnerabilities to online social communities and may cause serious impact in social networking. Statista conducts a survey on random American Internet users, more than 50% of the respondents stated that they believed online news sources regularly published fake news stories (Report, 2019). As more and more users use online social media to share information, express feeling and opinion, exchange ideas, communicate with other people and make decision, it is essential to understand how fake information is transmitted and to identify how to detect fake information.

Malicious users or attackers always create fake online information for different purposes. For example, a fake review may be generated for misleading online customers' shopping preference and damaging the reputation of a product. Fake political news may be created by a politician to change citizen's voting decision. A fake advertisement may be created by an attacker to distribute malware or launch a phishing attack. Most of the time, the fake news is intentionally written to mislead online readers, so it is difficult to distinguish the authenticity of the news content. Moreover, identifying credible and trustable information from millions of real-time data is challenging, due to the heterogeneous and dynamic nature of online social communication. Under this circumstance, the credible of the news creator or news source become a strong indicator for the truthfulness of the online news (Kumar, 2018). And how to profile online news creators and detect malicious online users become an essential and fundamental aspect of online fake information detection.

Every user can be profiled and modeled with his/her *demographic information*, *content* and *context on social media* (Shu, 2017). (1) Demographic information includes gender, age, education, interest, occupation, income, marital status, and so on. (2) Social content is all the posted, shared, forwarded information on the online social media from the online user, includes both raw text messages and multimedia information. (3) Social context represents the communication of the targeted user with other users, which contains: 1) *network-based information* (like friends, followers, similar groups, etc.); 2) *distribution based information* indicates the propagation of the user's data, how the data is retweeted and reposted, and what is the in/out-degree of the user's ego net; 3) *temporal based information* describes the posting behavior of the user in a time manner and indicates suspicious posting actions, and 4) *spatial based information* such as locations and mobility of the user. With data mining algorithms and big data technologies, it is possible for researchers and cyber defenders to detect malicious users in online social media and help legitimate users avoid being the spreaders of false or misleading information.

Privacy-Related Threats

Privacy is of paramount importance in online social media, the unauthorized disclosure and improper use of users' private information can cause undesirable or damaging cyber consequences (Zhang C. a., 2010). And there are different types of privacy-related threats, like identity privacy, demographic privacy, location privacy, and communication privacy. As more and more websites can use Facebook or Twitter account for logging in, users should be careful about identity theft via the unknown or untrusted third-party websites. Also, hackers can take advantage of user profile information in online social media and conduct fraudulent activities (e.g., distribute fake news to specific users) and launch cybercriminals (e.g., lure users to visit malicious advertisement web pages based on their shopping preference). By tracking users' location and mobility, it is possible to figure out online users' important information, like their working place, daily habit and even their social relationship (Backes, 2017). Also, hackers can even extract useful personal information from users' communication data, like a temporal based pattern of the user, and how the communication information is distributed via social media.

As the fast development of deep learning algorithm, image recognition has become one of the hottest topics in both academia and industry. (Al Hasib, 2009) describes two image-based privacy issues in online social media, they are *face recognition* and *content-based image retrieval*. And they can help an adversary to collect substantially more personal information about an online user than intended.

Others

In addition, there are many other types of security and privacy issues in online social media. (Al Hasib, 2009) discusses some SNS based traditional network security threats like Spamming, Cross-site scripting, SNS aggregators, Phishing, and social based threats like Stalking, Corporate espionage. (Joe, 2014) proposes some image-based threats like Image tagging, Image hacking, and Dragging the image. Due to the dynamic nature of the Internet, online users' risky behavior is also the vulnerability of online social media. Some risky actions include forgetting to log out, being redirected to an untrusted third-party webpage, exposing too much information, adding strangers as friends, and so on.

Security and Privacy Issues in Online Cloud

Cloud computing is a well-known terminology that involves resources via remote servers to provide dynamic and scalable system virtualization (Gou, 2017). Cloud computing brings a list of advantages for the Internet users, business, government, and other organizations. It can reduce the cost and complexities of infrastructural configurations for computational platforms (Abbas, 2017; Sen, 2015). Also, online resources like servers, storages, applications, files, and services can be shared and provisioned rapidly and efficiently (Sen, 2015). Service-oriented architecture is the technical foundation of cloud computing, which enables the integration and collaboration of different online providers (Zhang Y. L., 2017).

However, the uncertainty of participators, and the flexible and scalable nature of Cloud pose significant challenges and cyber threats in both Cloud computing and Cloud storage. A misconfigured Cloud platform can cost serious damage and financial loss. In 2018, more than 70 million records were stolen or leaked from poorly configured S3 buckets, an Amazon online Cloud storage services (Symantec s. c., 2018). Like other emerging technology, Cloud can be abused, and Cloud security and privacy have become one of the most critical and severe issues for all Internet users. Until 2018, over 90% organizations are concerned about Cloud security, and about 18% of the organizations experienced a Cloud security incident in 2018. From 2019, around 49% of them will increase their budget in addressing Cloud security and privacy issues (Raphael, 2019). Nowadays, more and more IT cyber defenders and professionals start paying their focuses to the damages caused by Cloud security issues. The summarizations of security and privacy issues in Cloud computing are listed as follows.

Data Confidentiality, Integrity, and Availability

Data privacy is one of the most essential and critical problems to be considered in Cloud computing and storage (Rao, 2015). As multiple entities are involved in storage, transit, or computation, data authentication and authorization are practical methods for keeping Cloud data secure. In data privacy preserving, three security factors should be considered, they are: *data confidentiality*, *data integrity*, and *data availability* (Gou, 2017; Abbas, 2017; Zhang Y. L., 2017). (1) As data is stored in remote servers, confidentiality prevention mechanism should be designed to protect sensitive information from being accessed by malicious users or Cloud providers. (2) Integrity safeguards the consistency, trustworthiness and accuracy of the data in Cloud. To maintain integrity, data cannot be changed, modified, or altered by unauthorized users. (3) Data availability can ensure and maintain the daily operation of Cloud services. The hardware, operating systems, and servers should be kept in a correct and functioning environment and should be kept upgraded regularly.

Cloud Attacks

There are different types of cyberattacks related to Cloud computing and storage. According to Khan (2016), based on Cloud components, the categorizations of cyberattacks are *network-based attacks*, *Virtual Machine (VM)-based attacks*, *storage-based attacks*, and *application-based attacks*. (1) In network-based attacks, the malicious intruder may attack the Cloud architecture through the network that connect the client with the remote servers. Typical network-based attacks include *port scanning* (Riquet, 2012), *botnets* (Lin, 2012), and *spoofing attacks* (Riquet, 2012). (2) Multiple VMs are being hosted in the Cloud architectures for functionality or efficiency purposes. But they also bring cyber vulnerabilities which can be exploited by malicious attackers to launch different cyberattacks. Typical examples include cross *VM side channel attacks, VM creation attacks* (Fernandez, 2013), and *migration and rollback attacks* (Szefer, 2012). (3) Storage-based attacks related to Cloud data privacy and integrity. If private data is stolen by attackers, then the sensitive or personal information can be exploited by malicious entities for personal, financial, or political gains. *Data scavenging* (Chen D. a., 2012) and *data deduplication* (Kaaniche, 2014) are two typical examples of storage-based attacks. (4) The applications running on Cloud platforms can be utilized by attackers for performing malicious activities. In addition, a compromised application can exploit the vulnerabilities of other architectural components for malicious purposes. In Khan (2016), three types of application-based attacks are proposed as Cloud threats, they are *malware injection and steganography attacks* (Kourai, 2012), *shared architecture attacks* (Zhang Y. J., 2014), and *web services and protocol attacks* (Gruschka, 2009).

Others

Other unique cloud threats and risks include: limited human visibility and control, easily-compromised application programming interfaces (APIs) in cloud, and incomplete data deletion. With a high concentration of information access, the Cloud host may also be susceptible to cyberattacks. Both the data transmission in Cloud and the Cloud server are at high risk level, so as users' important personal information. So, the reliability of Cloud platform and data privacy protection become the major concerns for Cloud-specific vulnerabilities (Suo, 2013).

FUTURE RESEARCH DIRECTIONS

In this chapter, we presented the common and typical security and privacy issues in human-factor based cyber domain. Especially, potential threats and vulnerabilities in human desktop behaviors, mobile behaviors, and online behaviours are discussed. However, due to the limited scope of this chapter, some other important aspects of vulnerable human daily actions are not presented, such as security issues in privacy leakage issues in location-based problems, new challenges in the smart city and Internet of Things (IoT), and security threats in advanced data mining tasks.

In the future, the following work can be performed to extend the scope of this chapter.

Security and Privacy Issues in Smart Home and Smart City

Recently, the Internet of Things (IoT) is becoming increasingly widespread among in-home environments (Zeng, 2017). The wireless interaction and cooperation between mobile devices and remote objects can set things together as a combined entity and advance the way the people communicate with the living environment (Stergiou, 2018). In modern society, more and more customers install internet-connected sensors, remote controllers, artificial assistant, lights, and other appliances to enjoy the comfort, convenience and efficiency of the smart home. By the end of 2016, there are more than 21.8 million smart homes in North America. And according to a recent forecast study, there will be 73 million customers using smart appliances in their home in North America, which equals 55% of all households (DeviceHive, 2019). Similarly, some other smart concept such as smart transportation, smart community, smart grid, smart manufacturing, smart healthcare pushes the fast and extensive development of smart city. Nowadays, citizens are living in a smart environment that is entirely different with ten years ago. Even through the smart ecosystem can significantly improve efficiency and convenience for citizens, a various number of security and privacy issues need to be addressed and solved. From Nokia's Threat Intelligence Report 2019 (Nokia, 2019), IoT botnet distributed 78% malware events in the communication service among IoT devices in 2018, which is more than double the rate in 2016. Therefore, security and privacy issues of smart home and smart city as an essential aspect of human based cybersecurity can be studies and researched in detail in the future.

Location-Based Privacy Issues

The pervasive use of geo-location technologies poses many new and difficult challenges to personal data and privacy protection (Cheung, 2014). The extensive use of mobile devices enables a vast number of personal geo-location data available on the Internet, and how to preserve online users' geo-location privacy become an immediate necessity. Now, there are many location-based services and applications, which aim to provide user useful important based on short-distance tracking or location identification. But these applications offer excellent opportunities for malicious hackers to steal valuable location data and conduct some illegal and fraudulent activities. And the geo-location technologies become more passive, users sometimes are not even aware of when and where they have been tracked. Although some location-based privacy issues have been discussed in this chapter (e.g., the location privacy issues in mobile behaviours and online behaviours), they need to be further explained and addressed under the domain of human-factor based security and privacy issues.

Security and Privacy Issues in Data Mining Tasks

The era of big data promotes the advancement and development of data mining and knowledge discovery in both industry and academia. As business and organizations continue to face enormous challenges and opportunities in extracting useful insights and decisions from big data, there is a huge demand for data scientists and data analysts for technology firms and companies. Until recent years, the use of data mining and machine learning techniques become ubiquitous. There are even many online platforms that can run machine learning algorithms in Cloud, such as Google Cloud Platform, Machine Learning on AWS, and so on. However, these online computing platforms bring new cyber challenges and threats for researchers and scientists. *Adversarial machine learning* and *privacy preserving machine learning* are the typical examples of such threats. (1) Adversarial machine learning is a new emerging technique which attempts to fool the machine learning models through adversarial examples, in order to violate the statistical assumption and malfunction the results. Attackers can intentionally design adversarial examples to cause a model to make a mistake, for example, identify a stop sign as a yield sign. (2) Privacy preserving machine learning is a terminology which indicates the potential privacy issues when utilizing machine learning models. As the widely utilization of machine learning models, sometimes private or sensitive information is required which may expose significant personal privacy. And some sensitive insights can be extracted even when the data is anonymized. As the crowded, dynamic, and uncertain nature of Cloud computation, it is essential for researchers and scientists to understand the characteristics of the underlying mechanisms for different data mining tasks. This could help them to avoid and mitigate the potential privacy and security threats in such operations.

CONCLUSION

Nowadays, the rapid developments in the electronics business witness the large amounts of digital inventions including laptops, tablets, smartphone, palmtops, and so forth (Gupta B. B., 2018). In the age of big data, vast amounts of data are drawn from numbers of resources ranging from online social media, web browsing history, online Cloud, to the gathered databases of academic and government organizations. And these online data and information are stored and processed over desktop or mobile devices, most of which are highly sensitive and private. In the digital world, every single person can be represented as a string of flowing data. The information stored in the data is critical since it indicates all the significant aspects of human's daily life. However, hackers and malicious users can utilize the data as a powerful tool for implementing cyber attacks. And it is essential to establish adequate security measurements to safeguard sensitive information and quantify cyber threats and risks (Gupta B. B., 2018). As human being becomes the weak link in a cyber space, knowledge and awareness about the information and techniques for profiling malicious or risky human behaviors is unavoidable.

This chapter discussed the human-factors based security and privacy issues in the big data era. It presented risky human behaviors in terms of desktop behavior, mobile behavior, and online behavior. Structure and content of this Chapter is illustrated in Figure 2. (1) In Desktop Behavior section, we first discuss the common desktop security threats like malware, data breach, and phishing. Then we conclude some typical risk desktop behaviors and their corresponding consequences. Finally, the resources and approaches for detecting risk desktop behaviors are introduced. (2) In Mobile Behavior section, the cyber security and privacy issues are presented in two categories: individual mobile aspect and crowdsensing aspect. In individual aspect, mobile terminal threats, mobile network threats, and mobile Cloud threats are discussed accordingly. In crowdsensing aspect, insider attacks, outsider attacks, and crowdsensing related privacy issues are characterized. (3) In Online Behavior Section, three types of common online behaviors and their related cyber security threats are demonstrated, they are online financial behaviors (includes online banking, online shopping, and online trading), online social media (includes fake news distribution, privacy preserving issues, and so on), and online Cloud (includes data integrity, Cloud attacks, and so on). In this Chapter, the basic and essential concepts, technologies, and solutions for addressing human factor-based cyber security and privacy issues are introduced and discussed. Future works include more detailed human behavior analysis, such as privacy leakage issues in location-based problems, and new challenges in the smart city and Internet of Things (IoT), and the computation security issues in advanced machine learning and data mining operations.

Figure 2. The visual conclusions of the main content in the chapter

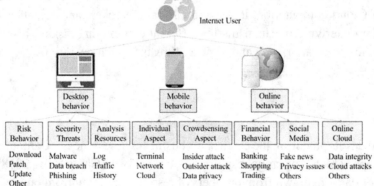

REFERENCES

Abbas, H., Maennel, O., & Assar, S. (2017). Security and privacy issues in cloud computing. *Annales des Télécommunications*, 72(5-6), 233–235. doi:10.100712243-017-0578-3

Abbosh, O. (2019). *Cybertech Europe*. Retrieved from Accenture: https://www.accenture.com/us-en/event-cybertech-europe-2017?src=SOMS#block-insights-and-innovation

Ahmed, M. A. (2015). Novel approach for network traffic pattern analysis using clustering-based collective anomaly detection. *Annals of Data Science*, 111-130.

Aijaz, U. N. (2018). Malware Detection on Server using Distributed Machine Learning. *Perspectives in Communication, Embedded-systems and Signal-processing-PiCES*, 172-175.

Al Hasib, A. (2009). Threats of online social networks. *International Journal of Computer Science and Network Security*, 88-93.

Albladi, S. M. (2017). *Personality traits and cyber-attack victimisation: Multiple mediation analysis. In Internet of Things Business Models, Users, and Networks*. IEEE.

Armendariz, T. (2018). *Top Malware Threats and How to Protect Yourself*. Retrieved from lifewire: https://www.lifewire.com/top-malware-threats-153641

Backes, M. A. (2017). walk2friends: Inferring Social Links from Mobility Profiles. In *Proceedings of the 2017 ACM SIGSAC Conference on Computer and Communications Security* (pp. 1943-1957). ACM. 10.1145/3133956.3133972

Bilge, L. A. (2017). RiskTeller: Predicting the Risk of Cyber Incidents. In *Proceedings of the 2017 ACM SIGSAC Conference on Computer and Communications Security* (pp. 1299 - 1311). ACM. 10.1145/3133956.3134022

Bojjagani, S. A. (2016). *Stamba: Security testing for Android mobile banking apps. In Advances in Signal Processing and Intelligent Recognition Systems* (pp. 671–683). Springer.

Carayon, P. K. (2005). Human factors issues in computer and e-business security. In Handbook of integrated risk management for e-business: measuring, modeling and managing risk (pp. 63-85). J. Ross Publishing.

Chen, D. A. (2012). Data security and privacy protection issues in cloud computing. In *International Conference on Computer Science and Electronics Engineering* (pp. 647-651). IEEE. 10.1109/ICCSEE.2012.193

Chen, M. A. (2019). A Survey on User Profiling Model for Anomaly Detection in Cyberspace. *Journal of Cyber Security and Mobility*, 8, 75–112.

Cheung, A. S. (2014). Location privacy: The challenges of mobile service devices. *Computer Law & Security Review*, 30(1), 41–54. doi:10.1016/j.clsr.2013.11.005

Chowdhury, M. A. (2017). *Protecting data from malware threats using machine learning technique*. IEEE. doi:10.1109/ICIEA.2017.8283111

Corney, M. A. (2011). Detection of anomalies from user profiles generated from system logs. In *Proceedings of the Ninth Australasian Information Security Conference* (pp. 23--32). Australian Computer Society.

Dantu, R., Kolan, P., & Cangussu, J. (2009). Network risk management using attacker profiling. *Security and Communication Networks*, *2*(1), 83–96. doi:10.1002ec.58

DeviceHive. (2019). *IoT Privacy and Security Challenges for Smart Home Environments*. Retrieved from hackernoon: https://hackernoon.com/iot-privacy-and-security-challenges-for-smart-home-environments-c91eb581af13

Du, M. a. (2017). *Deeplog: Anomaly detection and diagnosis from system logs through deep learning.* ACM. doi:10.1145/3133956.3134015

Elmrabit, N. H. (2015). Insider threats in information security categories and approaches. In *2015 21st International Conference on Automation and Computing (ICAC)* (pp. 1 - 6). IEEE.

Evans, M., Maglaras, L. A., He, Y., & Janicke, H. (2016). Human behaviour as an aspect of cybersecurity assurance. *Security and Communication Networks*, *9*(17), 4667–4679. doi:10.1002ec.1657

Feizollah, A., Anuar, N. B., Salleh, R., & Wahab, A. W. A. (2015). A review on feature selection in mobile malware detection. *Digital Investigation*, *13*, 22–37. doi:10.1016/j.diin.2015.02.001

Fernandez, E. B. (2013). Two patterns for cloud computing: Secure virtual machine image repository and cloud policy management point. *Proceedings of the 20th conference on pattern languages of programs*, 15.

Flynn, L. A. (2014). *Cloud Service Provider Methods for Managing Insider Threats: Analysis Phase 2, Expanded Analysis and Recommendations*. Carnegie-Mellon Univ.

Freed, S. E. (2014). *Examination of personality characteristics among cybersecurity and information technology professionals*. University of Tennessee at Chattanooga.

Ganti, R. K., Ye, F., & Lei, H. (2011). Mobile crowdsensing: Current state and future challenges. *IEEE Communications Magazine*, *49*(11), 32–39. doi:10.1109/MCOM.2011.6069707

Gasser, O. A. (2018). In Log We Trust: Revealing Poor Security Practices with Certificate Transparency Logs and Internet Measurements. In *International Conference on Passive and Active Network Measurement* (pp. 173--185). Springer.

Ghaffari, F. A. (2016). DroidNMD: Network-based Malware Detection in Android Using an Ensemble of One-Class Classifiers. *The Modares Journal of Electrical Engineering*, 40-47.

Glaspie, H. W. (2017). *Human Factors in Information Security Culture: A Literature Review*. Springer.

Gou, Z. a. (2017). Analysis of various security issues and challenges in cloud computing environment: a survey. In Identity Theft: Breakthroughs in Research and Practice (pp. 221-247). IGI Global. doi:10.4018/978-1-5225-0808-3.ch011

Greitzer, F. L. (2010). Combining traditional cyber security audit data with psychosocial data: towards predictive modeling for insider threat mitigation. In *Insider threats in cyber security* (pp. 85–113). Springer. doi:10.1007/978-1-4419-7133-3_5

Grobauer, B., Walloschek, T., & Stocker, E. (2011). Understanding cloud computing vulnerabilities. *IEEE Security and Privacy, 9*(2), 50–57. doi:10.1109/MSP.2010.115

Gruschka, N. a. (2009). Vulnerable cloud: soap message security validation revisited. In *IEEE International Conference on Web Services* (pp. 625-631). IEEE. 10.1109/ICWS.2009.70

Gupta, B. A. (2016). *Handbook of research on modern cryptographic solutions for computer and cyber security.* IGI Global. doi:10.4018/978-1-5225-0105-3

Gupta, B. B. (2018). *Computer and Cyber Security: Principles, Algorithm, Applications, and Perspectives.* CRC Press.

Hanus, B., & Wu, Y. A. (2016). Impact of users' security awareness on desktop security behavior: A protection motivation theory perspective. *Information Systems Management, 13*(1), 2–16. doi:10.1080/10580530.2015.1117842

Heartfield, R. A. (2016). *A taxonomy of attacks and a survey of defence mechanisms for semantic social engineering attacks. ACM Computing Surveys.*

Homoliak, I. A. (2018). *Insight into Insiders: A Survey of Insider Threat Taxonomies, Analysis, Modeling, and Countermeasures.* arXiv preprint arXiv:1805.01612

Hou, S. A. (2017). *Hindroid: An intelligent android malware detection system based on structured heterogeneous information network* ACM. doi:10.1145/3097983.3098026

IBM. (2018). *IBM X-Force Threat Intelligence Index 2018.* IBM.

Jia, T. A. (2017). *LogSeD: Anomaly diagnosis through mining time-weighted control flow graph in logs.* IEEE.

Jiang, X. A. (2012). *Dissecting android malware: Characterization and evolution.* IEEE.

Joe, M. M. (2014). A survey of various security issues in online social networks. *International Journal of Computer Networks and Applications,* 11-14.

Kaaniche, N. a. (2014). A secure client side deduplication scheme in cloud storage environments. In *6th International Conference on New Technologies, Mobility and Security (NTMS)* (pp. 1-7). IEEE. 10.1109/NTMS.2014.6814002

Kadir, A. F. (2018). Understanding Android Financial Malware Attacks: Taxonomy, Characterization, and Challenges. *Journal of Cyber Security and Mobility,* 1-52.

Khan, M. A. (2016). A survey of security issues for cloud computing. *Journal of Network and Computer Applications, 71,* 11–29. doi:10.1016/j.jnca.2016.05.010

Khosrowshahi, D. (2016). *2016 Data Security Incident.* Retrieved from Uber Newsroom: https://www.uber.com/newsroom/2016-data-incident/

Kolosnjaji, B. A. (2016). *Deep learning for classification of malware system call sequences.* Springer. doi:10.1007/978-3-319-50127-7_11

Kourai, K. A. (2012). A self-protection mechanism against steppingstone attacks for iaas clouds. In *International Conference on Autonomic Trusted Computing (UIC/ATC)*, (pp. 539–546). IEEE.

Krombholz, K. A. (2015). Advanced social engineering attacks. *Journal of Information Security and Applications*, 113-122.

Kumar, S. A. (2018). *False information on web and social media: A survey*. arXiv preprint arXiv:1804.08559

Kumaraguru, P. A. (2010). Teaching Johnny not to fall for phish. *ACM Transactions on Internet Technology*, 7.

Kumparak, G. (2019). *Kickstarter hacked, customer addresses and other infor accessed*. Retrieved from Techcrunch: https://techcrunch.com/2014/02/15/kickstarter-hacked-customer-addresses-and-other-info-accessed/

Lee, W. A. (2001). *Information-theoretic measures for anomaly detection*. IEEE.

Legg, P. A., Buckley, O., Goldsmith, M., & Creese, S. (2017). Automated insider threat detection system using user and role-based profile assessment. *IEEE Systems Journal*, *11*(2), 503–512. doi:10.1109/JSYST.2015.2438442

Lin, W. A. (2012). Traceback Attacks in Cloud--Pebbletrace Botnet. In *32nd International Conference on Distributed Computing Systems Workshops* (pp. 417-426). IEEE.

Liu, J. A. (2018). A survey of mobile crowdsensing techniques: A critical component for the internet of things. *ACM Transactions on Cyber-Physical Systems*, 18 - 43.

Lonzetta, A. A. (2018). Security Vulnerabilities in Bluetooth Technology as Used in IoT. *Journal of Sensor and Actuator Networks*, 28.

Lord, N. (2017). *Insiders vs. outsiders: What's the greater cybersecurity threat?* Retrieved from DATAINSIDER: https://digitalguardian.com/blog/insiders-vs-outsiders-whats-greater-cybersecurity-threat-infographic

Mittu, R. A. (2015). Foundations of Autonomy and Its (Cyber) Threats: From Individual to Interdependence. *AAAI Spring Symposium Series*.

Narudin, F. A., Feizollah, A., Anuar, N. B., & Gani, A. (2016). Evaluation of machine learning classifiers for mobile malware detection. *Soft Computing*, *20*(1), 343–357. doi:10.100700500-014-1511-6

Ni, J. (2018). *Security and privacy preservation in mobile crowdsensing*. University of Waterloo.

Nokia, N. (2019). *Threat Intelligence Report 2019*. Nokia.

Nurse, J. R. (2014). Understanding insider threat: A framework for characterising attacks. *Security and Privacy Workshops (SPW), 2014 IEEE*, 214 - 228.

Oath. (2016). *Yahoo provides notice to additional users affected by previously discussed 2013 data theft*. Retrieved from Oath: https://www.oath.com/press/yahoo-provides-notice-to-additional-users-affected-by-previously/

Osman, M. (2019). Ecommerce – *Chatbots, Voice, Omni-Channel Marketing*. Retrieved from KINSTA: https://kinsta.com/blog/ecommerce-statistics/

Partners, C. R. (2018). *Insider Threat 2018 Report.*

Peachey, K. (2019). *Banking by mobile app 'to overtake online by 2019'*. Retrieved from BBC: https://www.bbc.com/news/business-44166991

Point, C. (2018). *2018 Security Report: Welcome to the Future of Cyber Security*. Check Point Research.

Proofpoint. (2018). *Quarterly Threat Report.* Proofpoint.com.

Rajeswaran, D. a. (2018). *Function call graphs versus machine learning for malware detection*. Springer. doi:10.1007/978-3-319-92624-7_11

Ramzan, Z. (2010). Phishing attacks and countermeasures. In *Handbook of information and communication security* (pp. 433–448). Springer. doi:10.1007/978-3-642-04117-4_23

Rao, R. V., & Selvamani, K. (2015). Data security challenges and its solutions in cloud computing. *Procedia Computer Science, 48*, 204–209. doi:10.1016/j.procs.2015.04.171

Raphael, J. (2019). *7 mobile security threats you should take seriously in 2019*. Retrieved from CSO: https://www.csoonline.com/article/3241727/mobile-security/7-mobile-security-threats-you-should-take-seriously-in-2019.html

Report, S. (2019). *Frequency of online news sources reporting fake news U.S. 2018*. Retrieved from Statista: https://www.statista.com/statistics/649234/fake-news-exposure-usa/

Research, C. P. (n.d.). *2019 Security Report: Security the Cloud, Mobile and IoT*. Academic Press.

Riquet, D. A. (2012). Large-scale coordinated attacks: Impact on the cloud security. In *Sixth International Conference on Innovative Mobile and Internet Services in Ubiquitous Computing* (pp. 558-563). IEEE.

Rturk, E. (2012). A case study in open source software security and privacy: Android adware. In *World Congress on Internet Security (WorldCIS)*. IEEE; doi:10.1109/IMIS.2012.76.

Searchsecurity. (2019). *Access control*. Retrieved from https://searchsecurity.techtarget.com/definition/access-control

Sen, J. (2015). *Security and privacy issues in cloud computing*. IGI Global.

Shahriar, H. A. (2016). Mobile phishing attacks and mitigation techniques. *Journal of Information Security*, 206.

Sheng, S. A. (2010). Who falls for phish?: a demographic analysis of phishing susceptibility and effectiveness of interventions. In *Proceedings of the SIGCHI Conference on Human Factors in Computing Systems* (pp. 373 - 382). ACM. 10.1145/1753326.1753383

Shu, K. A. (2017). Fake news detection on social media: A data mining perspective. *ACM SIGKDD Explorations Newsletter*, 22-36.

Silva, A. S.-F. (2016). *ATLANTIC: A framework for anomaly traffic detection, classification, and mitigation in SDN*. IEEE.

Sobers, R. (2019). 60 Must-Know Cybersecurity. Retrieved from VARONIS: https://www.varonis.com/blog/cybersecurity-statistics/

Soomro, Z. A., Shah, M. H., & Ahmed, J. (2016). Information security management needs more holistic approach: A literature review. *International Journal of Information Management, 36*(2), 215–225. doi:10.1016/j.ijinfomgt.2015.11.009

Statista, R. (2018). *Mobile Internet - Statistics & Facts*. Retrieved 12 30, 2018, from Statista: https://www.statista.com/topics/779/mobile-internet/

Statista, S. (2019). *Share of population using digital banking in the United States from 2018 to 2022*. Retrieved from Statista: https://www.statista.com/statistics/946109/digital-banking-users-usa/

Statista. (2019). *Share of population using digital banking in the United States from 2018 to 2022*. Retrieved from https://www.statista.com/statistics/946109/digital-banking-users-usa/

Stergiou, C. G., Psannis, K. E., Kim, B.-G., & Gupta, B. (2018). Secure integration of IoT and cloud computing. *Future Generation Computer Systems, 78*, 964–975. doi:10.1016/j.future.2016.11.031

Stevanovic, M. A. (2016). On the use of machine learning for identifying botnet network traffic. *Journal of Cyber Security and Mobility*, 11 - 32.

Su, M.-Y. (2011). Using clustering to improve the KNN-based classifiers for online anomaly network traffic identification. *Journal of Network and Computer Applications, 34*(2), 722–730. doi:10.1016/j.jnca.2010.10.009

Sun, Y. A. (2014). Data security and privacy in cloud computing. *International Journal of Distributed Sensor Networks*, 9.

Suo, H. A. (2013). *Security and privacy in mobile cloud computing*. IEEE. doi:10.1109/IWCMC.2013.6583635

Syarif, I. B. (2012). Unsupervised clustering approach for network anomaly detection. In *International Conference on Networked Digital Technologies* (pp. 135-145). Springer. 10.1007/978-3-642-30507-8_13

Symantec, S. C. (2018). *2018 Internet Security Threat Report*. Author.

Symantec. (2019). *Why hackers love public Wi-Fi*. Retrieved from Norton by Symantec: https://us.norton.com/internetsecurity-wifi-why-hackers-love-public-wifi.html

Szefer, J. A. (2012). Architectural support for hypervisor-secure virtualization. *ACM SIGARCH Computer Architecture News*, 437-450.

Tan, Z. A. (2014). Enhancing big data security with collaborative intrusion detection. *IEEE Cloud Computing*, 27-33.

Temizkan, O., Kumar, R. L., Park, S. J., & Subramaniam, C. (2012). Patch release behaviors of software vendors in response to vulnerabilities: An empirical analysis. *Journal of Management Information Systems*, *28*(4), 305–338. doi:10.2753/MIS0742-1222280411

Tep, K. S.-K. (2015). *A taxonomy of cloud attack consequences and mitigation strategies: The Role of Access Control and Privileged Access Management. In Trustcom/BigDataSE/ISPA* (pp. 1073–1080). IEEE.

USPS. (2019). *Risks and Recommendations for Online Shopping*. Retrieved from CyberSafe at USPS: https://www.uspscybersafe.com/articles/individuals/risks-and-recommendations-for-online-shopping/

Veracode. (2019). *Data loss prevention guide: learn data loss tips*. Retrieved from https://www.veracode.com/security/guide-data-loss-prevention

Vieane, A., Funke, G., Gutzwiller, R., Mancuso, V., Sawyer, B., & Wickens, C. (2016). Addressing human factors gaps in cyber defense. *Proceedings of the Human Factors and Ergonomics Society Annual Meeting*, *60*(1), 770–773. doi:10.1177/1541931213601176

Wee, C. a. (2016). Understanding the Personality Characteristics of Cybersecurity Competition Participants to Improve the Effectiveness of Competitions as Recruitment Tools. In *Advances in Human Factors in Cybersecurity* (pp. 111–121). Springer. doi:10.1007/978-3-319-41932-9_10

Wikipedia. (2019). *Investing online*. Retrieved from https://en.wikipedia.org/wiki/Investing_online

Xu, Z. A. (2017). Malware detection using machine learning based analysis of virtual memory access patterns. In *Proceedings of the Conference on Design, Automation and Test in Europe* (pp. 169--174). European Design and Automation Association. 10.23919/DATE.2017.7926977

Yang, T. T. (2015). Automated detection and analysis for android ransomware. In *17th IEEE International Conference on High Performance Computing and Communications (HPCC)* (pp. 1338-1343). IEEE.

Yen, T.-F. A. (2013). *Beehive: Large-scale log analysis for detecting suspicious activity in enterprise networks*. ACM. doi:10.1145/2523649.2523670

Yujuan, Z. A. (2015). Malware detection based on Android permission information. *Jisuanji Yingyong Yanjiu*, 3036–3040.

Yun'an, C. A. (2017). An Andriod Malware Detection Algorithm based on Permissions count. *Computer Applications and Software*, 55.

Zeng, E. A. (2017). End user security & privacy concerns with smart homes. *Symposium on Usable Privacy and Security (SOUPS)*.

Zhang, C., Sun, J., Zhu, X., & Fang, Y. (2010). Privacy and security for online social networks: Challenges and opportunities. *IEEE Network*, *24*(4), 13–18. doi:10.1109/MNET.2010.5510913

Zhang, M., Wang, L., Jajodia, S., Singhal, A., & Albanese, M. (2016). Network diNetwork dversity: A security metric for evaluating the resilience of networks against zero-day attacks. *IEEE Transactions on Information Forensics and Security*, *11*(5), 1071–1086. doi:10.1109/TIFS.2016.2516916

Zhang, Y. J. (2014). Cross-tenant side-channel attacks in paas clouds. In *Proceedings of the 2014 ACM SIGSAC Conference on Computer and Communications Security* (pp. 990 - 1003). ACM. 10.1145/2660267.2660356

Zhang, Y. L. (2017). *QoS Prediction in Cloud and Service Computing*. Springer Briefs in Computer Science. doi:10.1007/978-981-10-5278-1

Chapter 4
Security and Privacy Challenges in Big Data

Dharmpal Singh
JISCE, India

Ira Nath
JISCE, India

Pawan Kumar Singh
Honeywell Labs, India

ABSTRACT

Big data refers to enormous amount of information which may be in planned and unplanned form. The huge capacity of data creates impracticable situation to handle with conventional database and traditional software skills. Thousands of servers are needed for its processing purpose. Big data gathers and examines huge capacity of data from various resources to determine exceptional novel awareness and recognizing the technical and commercial circumstances. However, big data discloses the endeavor to several data safety threats. Various challenges are there to maintain the privacy and security in big data. Protection of confidential and susceptible data from attackers is a vital issue. Therefore, the goal of this chapter is to discuss how to maintain security in big data to keep your organization robust, operational, flexible, and high performance, preserving its digital transformation and obtaining the complete benefit of big data, which is safe and secure.

INTRODUCTION

BIG DATA is a term used for a collection of data sets so large and complex that it is difficult to process using traditional applications/tools. It is the data exceeding Terabytes in size. Because of the variety of data that it encompasses, big data always brings a number of challenges relating to its volume and complexity. A recent survey says that 80% of the data created in the world are unstructured. One chal-

DOI: 10.4018/978-1-5225-9742-1.ch004

lenge is how these unstructured data can be structured, before we attempt to understand and capture the most important data. Another challenge is how we can store it. Here are the top tools used to store and analyze Big Data. We can categorize them into two (storage and Querying/Analysis).

Big data is often characterized by the 3Vs: the extreme *volume* of data, the wide *variety* of data types and the *velocity* at which the data must be processed. Those characteristics were first identified by Gartner analyst Doug Laney in a report published in 2001. More recently, several other Vs have been added to descriptions of big data, including *veracity*, *value* and *variability*. Although big data doesn't equate to any specific volume of data, the term is often used to describe terabytes, petabytes and even exabytes of data captured over time.

Such voluminous data can come from myriad different sources, such as business transaction systems, customer databases, medical records, internet clickstream logs, mobile applications, social networks, the collected results of scientific experiments, machine-generated data and real-time data sensors used in internet of things (IoT) environments. Data may be left in its raw form or preprocessed using data mining tools or data preparation software before it's analyzed.

Big data is a collection of data from various sources ranging from well-defined to loosely defined, derived from human or machine sources.

Big data also encompasses a wide variety of data types, including structured data in SQL databases and data warehouses, unstructured data, such as text and document files held in Hadoop clusters, or NoSQL systems, and semi-structured data, such as web server logs or streaming data from sensors. Further, big data includes multiple, simultaneous data sources, which may not otherwise be integrated. For example, a big data analytics project may attempt to gauge a product's success and future sales by correlating past sales data, return data and online buyer review data for that product.

Velocity refers to the speed at which big data is generated and must be processed and analyzed. In many cases, sets of big data are updated on a real- or near-real-time basis, compared with daily, weekly or monthly updates in many traditional data warehouses. Big data analytics projects ingest, correlate and analyze the incoming data, and then render an answer or result based on an overarching query. This means data scientists and other data analysts must have a detailed understanding of the available data and possess some sense of what answers they're looking for to make sure the information they get is valid and up to date. Velocity is also important as big data analysis expands into fields like machine learning and artificial intelligence (AI), where analytical processes automatically find patterns in the collected data and use them to generate insights.

A.P.Plageras et al (2018) describes how Internet of Things (IoT) supplies to everybody with latest types of services with the aim of development in our day by day living. With this innovative skill, other currently constructed technologies such as Big Data, Cloud Computing, and careful observing could be accomplished. In this work, we study the aforesaid technologies for searching their common functions, and merging their operations, in order to have advantageous situations of their usage. Instead of the boarder perception of a smart city, we will attempt to explore new systems for gathering and controlling sensors' information in a smart building which functions in IoT domain. For the proposed work, a cloud server could provide the service for gathering the information that generated from each sensor in the smart building. This information is not very hard to be controlled from distance, by a distant (mobile) device working on a network arrangement in IoT technology. As an outcome, the proposed results for gathering and controlling sensors 'information in a smart building could move us to an energy efficient green smart building.

The authors have an enormous reference for the concept and exercise of computer security (Gupta, 2018). Inclusive in all type of possibilities, this writing covers applied and practical fields, concept, and the explanations for the construction of applications and safety measures. It covers the administration and the engineering domain together for computer safety and security. It supplies outstanding examples of thoughts and methods that explain how different procedures and principles are merged together in enormously utilized schemes. This text is commended for its clear aim and objective, strong and eloquent writing, and its integration of concept and practical details with actual systems, technologies, procedures, and strategies.

The authors explain the Internet usage has grown to be an essential part of everyday life, particularly as more technical progress has prepared it easier to attach to the web from virtually anywhere in the developed world (Gupta, Agrawal & Yamaguchi, 2016). However, with this large volume of usage appears a sensitive hazard for safety issues within digital environments. This book recognizes emerging research and procedures being used in the area of cryptology and cyber security hazard anticipation. This book can give us the future direction for further research to all who are eager for finding about the attacks and hazards within digital domain and try to solve it.

The authors have shown the Mobile Cloud Computing is a recent technology which indicates to an architecture where both information storage and data processing performs exterior to the mobile device (Stergiou et al., 2018). Another new technology is Internet of Things (IoT). IoT is a recent skill which is developing very quickly in the area of telecommunications. More particularly, IoT is connected with wireless telecommunications. The vital objective of communication and collaboration between things and objects which sent through the wireless networks is to accomplish the aim to fix them as a joined individual. Additionally, there is a swift progress of both technologies, Cloud computing and Internet of Things, regard the field of wireless communications. In this paper, we table a survey of IoT and Cloud Computing with a target on the safety measures of both skills. Specially, we join the two above-mentioned skills (i.e. Cloud Computing and IoT) for investigating the familiar characteristics, and for finding out the advantages of their combination. At last we table the contribution of Cloud Computing to the IoT technology. So, it displays how the Cloud Computing technology develops the responsibility of the IoT. Last of all, we study the safety issues of the combination of IoT and Cloud Computing.

The authors have shown the Internet technology is extremely persistent today (Adat & Gupta, 2018). The number of devices associated to the Internet, those with a digital identity, is growing day by day. With the growth in the technology, Internet of Things (IoT) turns into essential part of human life. However, it is not defined properly and safe at all. Now, different safety measures are thought about as vital problem for a full-fledged IoT domain. A huge number of safety issues are present with the proposed heuristics and which creates the backbone of the IoT. Few essential safety measures have been grown for safety of the IoT atmosphere. Hence, the challenges are still growing and the resolutions have to be forever advancing. Therefore, the main objective of this paper is to talk about the history, literature survey, statistics of IoT and safety based study of IoT architecture. Additionally, we will supply taxonomy of safety issues in IoT atmosphere and taxonomy of different resistance procedures. We conclude our paper talking over different security challenges that will survive in future, which provides improved understanding of the problem, present solution space, and future research directions to guard IoT against various assaults.

The authors have shown the Internet of Things (IoT) is a growing architecture which joins several devices to Internet for interaction or obtaining up to date information from a cloud or a server (Tewari & Gupta, 2018). In future, the number of these attached devices will enhance enormously creating them a vital part of our daily lives. Even though these devices build our lives more relaxed, they also locate our own data at danger. Therefore, safety of these devices is a vital problem today too. In this paper, we suggest an ultra-lightweight shared authentication protocol which utilizes only bitwise operation and hence is extremely competent in terms of storage and interaction expenditure. Additionally, the calculation hazard is very little. We have also measured the performance of our proposed work with the already existing heuristics which checks the potential of our protocol, as received outcomes are auspicious. A concise cryptanalysis of our heuristic that assures unruliness is tabled too.

The authors have shown the Big Data (BD) is of enormous significance particularly in the area of wireless telecommunications (Stergios et al., 2018). Social Networking (SNg) is one further rapidly-increasing skill that permits consumers to construct their profile and could be illustrated as web applications. Both of them conflict with confidentiality and safety problems. In this paper, we study SNg, BD and Cloud Computing (CC) skills and their fundamental features by focusing on the safety concerns of those skills. Particularly, we intend for merging the performance of these two technologies (i.e. Big Data and Social Networking) in a CC domain, so that we can evaluate the general characters and determine the benefits of their combination associated with safety problems. During this investigation, we table an innovative system-framework-network in CC domain using which clients of different Social Networks (SNs) will be capable to swap data and information, and mostly large-scale information (Big Data). With our proposed scheme, we can accomplish significant development of the interaction of SN users, and thus grow to be additional security and accurate in a Cloud environment. More significantly, this scheme could be recognized as an intermediary communication node that could be used with the aim of progress the safety of SNg's clients in the course of the utilize of heuristics that can supply further privacy in the information connected with BD skill. In this effort, we table few dimensions and outcome related with our proposed scheme utilization too. At last the chance to construct a database during which every client can observe the statistics of his interaction with the SNg is conversed additionally.

Application of Big Data

As per the market strategy, companies who miss big data opportunities of today will miss the next frontier of innovation, competition, and productivity. Big Data tools and Technologies help the companies to interpret the huge amount of data very faster which helps to boost production efficiency and also to develop new data-driven products and services. So, big data applications are creating a new era in every industry. The below Figure 1 shows examples of Big Data applications in different type in industries.

BIG DATA ANALYSIS TECHNIQUES

Big data analysis techniques are mix of traditional statistical data analysis techniques and modern computational analysis techniques. Statistical analysis are used when data of entire population is available before and we want to get the results from it while computation analysis is best suited when stream of data is flowing in dataset over a time.

Figure 1. Big data Application in different industries

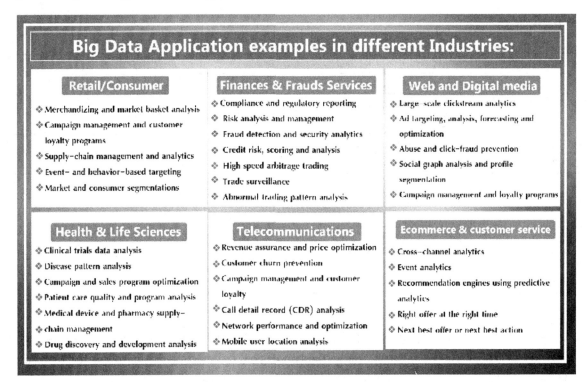

Association Rule Learning

Association rule learning is a technique of data analysis where data is analysed to find some interesting association between item sets. Say for example in a grocery store when people buy meat they often buy beer or if a customer buy milk then they often buy bread. These behaviours of people are observed from data a grocery store has gathered. Similarly, interesting observation could be found like people who often go to a movie theatre they tend to visit a nearby restaurant or a person like action movie might like superhero movie too. In ARL or Association Rule Learning the data is analysed to find such relations between two or more items and they are defined as rules.

Basic Concepts of Association Rules

A rule in ARL is a relationship between various items. The rule could be strong or weak but every item-set eventually has some relationship. There are several techniques to find out the relationship between two item sets.

From the above table we can quickly find out that Burger and French Fries has been purchased 5 times together, similarly Vegetables and fruits are purchased 4 times together. If we keep analyzing this way we will be able to find that these items are purchased often and hence they hold strong relationship. On the other hand, Vegetable and Burger has been purchased only once together while separately they have been purchased more than 5 times. That means people don't like to buy these items together and hence these items have weaker association.

Table 1. Grocery shop billing data

Transaction ID	Product
324576	Burgers, French Fries, Vegetables
347158	Burgers, French Fries, Ketchup
354931	Bread, Fruits, Vegetables
378270	Pasta, Fruits, Butter, Vegetables
421046	Burgers, Pasta, French Fries
440175	Fruits, Orange Juice, Vegetables
451217	Burgers, French Fries, Ketchup, Mayo
469837	Vegetables, Fruits
483673	Milk, Bread, Butter
512780	Burger, French Fries, Mayo
528563	Bread, Eggs, Milk
549470	Vegetable, Bread, Milk
589479	Bread, Ketchup, Pasta

Many algorithms for finding the relationship between dataset or association rule has been proposed such as Apriori, Eclat and FP Growth. These algorithms find out the frequent itemsets and then rules are generated based on the relative association between various itemsets.

Apriori Algorithm

Apriori algorithm has 3 parts: support, confidence and lift

Support is defined as the likelihood of presence of any item i in the whole dataset. It is calculated as the probability of item i in the dataset and expressed as the mathematical formula:

$$support(i) = \frac{No. \, of \, itemset \, containing \, an \, item \, i}{total \, number \, of \, itemsets}$$

Confidence is defined as likelihood of presence of item i and j together in all itemset when item i is present.

$$confidence(i \rightarrow j) = \frac{total \, number \, of \, itemset \, containing \, an \, item \, i \, and \, j}{total \, number \, of \, items \, sets \, containing \, item \, i \, and \, j \, together}$$

Lift is defined as the improvement in the prediction.

$$\frac{confidence(i \rightarrow j)}{support(j)}$$

Table 2. Record of Tennis playing weather conditions

Humidity	Wind	Outlook	Played
High	Normal	Sunny	No
High	Strong	Rain	No
Normal	Weak	Sunny	Yes
Normal	Strong	Overcast	No
High	Weak	Overcast	Yes
Normal	Weak	Rain	Yes
High	Weak	Rain	Yes
High	Strong	Overcast	Yes
Normal	Weak	Rain	No
High	Strong	Sunny	No

Step 1: Set a minimum support and confidence

Step 2: Take all the subsets in transaction having higher support than minimum support

Step 3: Take all the rules of these subsets having higher confidence than minimum confidence

Step 4: Sort the rule by decreasing lift

Application of Association rule learning: These learning techniques can be used in various area where we are interested to find out correlation among various items while following applications are often seen using association rule learning:

- **Basket Data Analysis**: Supermarkets, online stores, grocery shop etc could analyse the association of purchased items in a single purchase and promote user to buy likely product which user might want to buy.
- **Cross Marketing**: Various brands (product companies) can analyse data and find out their association with another product from other brand. Using such associated items they could use design their market strategies together. For example a car company and a tyre company can promote their products together.
- **Catalog Design**: The selection of items can be designed to complement certain product in such a way that buying one item could lead to buying another item. Sometime it may be possible to use weak relationship to promote products together with heavy discount to clear off stock or another time strongly related product could be offered in bundle to accelerate the sell.

Classification Tree Analysis

Classification tree analysis or decision tree analysis are the technique based on the creation of tree like data partitioning techniques. Classification tree has non-leaf nodes which represent the decision-making attribute and leaf nodes which represent the data related to a class, classified based on all the decision criteria from root to its parent.

The above table is the record of a Tennis club which shows whether the games were played or not played due to various weather conditions. Using this data we can try to find out a relationship for future events if certain weather condition will be suitable to play Tennis or not? If we analyse the table we find very interesting fact that whenever the Outlook attribute has value as Overcast, the games were played. Figure 2 is the classification tree drawn from the above dataset.

Algorithms such as CART (Classification and Regression Tree), ID3 (Iterative Dichotomiser 3), C4.5, AID (Automatic Interaction Detection), THAID (Theta-AID), CHAID (Chisquare – AID) are very well known and used to create classification tree.

Entropy: Entropy is the measure of impurity. Higher the impurity lower the value of entropy.

$$e\left(S\right) = \sum_{i=1}^{c} p_i log_2 p_i \ where\ p_i\ is\ the\ probability\ of\ class\ i$$

In a binary classification tree entropy is 0 if all the items are in single class and it is 1 if items are equally divided in two classes.

Information Gain: Information gain is impurity-based criterion which is the measure of difference in entropy on node S before split and after split on attribute A. It is measure of decrease in entropy.

$$Information\ gain\left(A,S\right) = entropy\left(S\right) - entropy\left(S,A\right)$$

Gini Index: Gini Index is used in CART algorithm an it is criterion to minimize the probability of misclassification

$$Gini\left(S\right) = 1 - \sum_{i=1}^{c} p_i^2 \ where\ p_i\ is\ the\ probability\ of\ class\ i$$

Misclassification Error:

$$Classification\ Error\left(S\right) = max\left(p_i\right) where\ p_i\ is\ the\ probability\ of\ class\ i$$

Figure 2. Classification tree for tennis playing weather condition

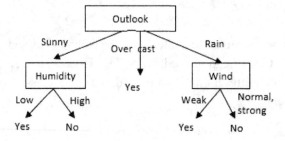

Figure 3. Probability vs entropy graph

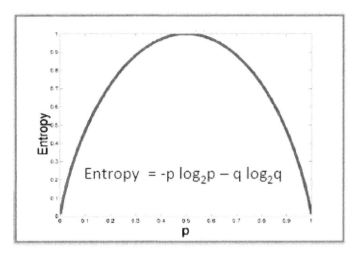

$$Entropy = -0.5 \log_2 0.5 - 0.5 \log_2 0.5 = 1$$

ID3 uses entropy and information gain calculation to create a classification tree. It begins with single node and adds children at every level to split the data set based on best attribute where information gain is high and entropy is less.

Genetic Algorithm

Genetic algorithms are based on natural selection and inheritance of natural evolution theory. It is adaptive heuristic search which begins with creation of potential solutions called parents. These initial set of potential solutions make the population. All these potential solutions are called parents and they are assigned with fitness score. Based on the fitness score, fittest solutions among the mare selected at random to form offspring. After selection of parents, they are passed to crossover state where attributes of solution are selected to create new solutions as offspring. This crossover product is then undergoes the mutation state where random rules (usually swapping of attributes) are applied to create better offspring. The offspring created are included in next generation population and all the steps are repeated over and over to reach towards an optimal solution. In every step, individual solutions(parents) are assigned fitness score then selected at random from current population and passed on to crossover and mutation stages to create children of next generation.

Genetic algorithms can be applied to solve various optimization problems which may not be suitable for standard optimization problem. It can also be used to find highly optimized searching problems.

Genetic algorithms were presented by John Holland in 1960 based on the concept of Darwin's theory of evolution and later on in 1989 Goldberg; student of John Holland extended it.

Let us try understanding GA with an example of shortest route problem of travelling salesman. A salesman has to travel to 5 cities and he needs to find out the optimal route of traveling to save time and money both.

Step 1: Population generation by randomly selecting cities in order and create several routes.

Route1: City1 → City2 → City3 → City4 → City5

Route2: City2 → City1 → City3 → City5 → City4

Route3: City3 → City5 → City1 → City4 → City2

Route4: City4 → City2 → City3 → City1 → City5

Route5: City5 → City2 → City4 → City3 → City1

We have created some potential routes and these will be calculated to create optimal routes using genetic algorithm.

Step 2: We will select two chromosomes at random. For simplicity we are assuming all these routes are considered after fitness assignment and they are fit by assuming the cost of travelling using all these routes falls under the maximum budget. We have selected route1 and route4.

Step 3: Now we will pass these selected routes to crossover function which will return new route (offspring).

Route1: City1 → City2 → City3 → City4 → City5

Route4: City4 → City2 → City3 → City1 → City5

Offspring: City4→City2→ City3→ City1→ City5

At random we have selected City2 → City3 from route 1 and rest of the cities we have taken in order from route 4.

Step 4: We will now pass the offspring route through mutation function which will swap cities based on probability. It may or may not change the offspring if probability of swapping cities does not fall under the tolerance range. In this example we will swap city2 and city5 and hence final offspring after first iteration is –

City4 →City5 → City3 → City1 → City2

Now the algorithm can repeat step 2 through step 4 multiple times in order to find optimal route.

Basic Terminologies

- **Population**: Entire set of potential solutions in a search space is called population. Population is created with all the randomly generated potential solutions of search space which fulfils the fitness criteria.
- **Chromosomes**: Individual solution in population is known a chromosome. Chromosomes are strings in a finite alphabet usually binary alphabet.
- **Gene**: A particular location in chromosome alphabet is known as gene.
- **Allele**: Allele is the value of the gene in the chromosome.

- **Initialization**: In initialization, all the potential solutions or chromosomes are created by randomly selecting items and assigned in the population array. Same chromosome can appear multiple time in the population.

Figure 4. Flowchart of GA algorithm

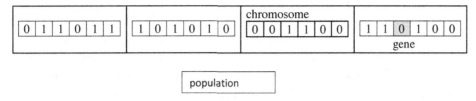

population

Concept of GA algorithm has be given below as flowchart

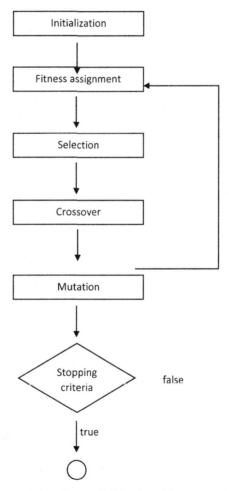

Flowchart of GA algorithm

- **Fitness Assignment**: The fitness function is the function that we want to optimize.It is a computation that evaluates the quality of the chromosome as a solution to a particular problem in a population.

- **Selection**: The selection component of a GA is designed to use fitness to guide the evolution of chromosomes by selective pressure. Chromosomes are therefore selected for recombination on the basis of fitness. Those with higher fitness should have a greater chance of selection than those with lower fitness, thus creating a selective pressure towards more highly fit solutions.

- **Crossover**: Crossover is the process by which chromosomes selected from a source population are recombined to form members of a successor population. The idea is to simulate the mixing of genetic material that can occur when organisms reproduce. The crossover operator represents the mixing of genetic material from two selected parent chromosomes to produce one or two child chromosomes. After two parent chromosomes have been selected for recombination, a random number in the interval [0,1] is generated with uniform probability and compared to a pre-determined "crossover rate". If the random number is greater than the crossover rate, no crossover occurs and one or both parents pass unchanged on to the next stage or recombination. If the crossover rate is greater than or equal to the random number, then the crossover operator is applied.

- **Mutation**: Mutation operators act on an individual chromosome to flip one or more allele values. In the case of bit-string chromosomes, the normal mutation operator is applied to each position in the chromosome. A random number in the interval [0,1] is generated with uniform probability and compared to a pre-determined "mutation rate". If the random number is greater than the mutation rate, no mutation is applied at that position. If the mutation rate is greater than or equal to the random number, then the allele value is flipped from 0 to 1 or vice versa. Mutation rates are typically very small (e.g., 0.001).

Application of Genetic Algorithm

GA can be used in several areas and few of them are listed down below.

1. **Trip, Traffic and Shipment Routing:** Applications such as "Traveling Salesman Problem" or TSP which needs to plan the most efficient routes and scheduling for travel planners, traffic routers, shipping companies could use GA. The shortest distance, best timing to avoid traffic tie-ups and rush hours, most efficient use of transport for shipping including pickup loads and deliveries along the way could benefit from GA.

2. **Gene Expression Profiling:** The 'snapshots' of the genes in a cell or group of cells using microarray technology are passed through GAs to make analysis of gene expression profiles has made the process much quicker and easier. This helps to classify what genes play a part in various diseases, and further can help to identify genetic causes for the development of diseases. Quicker and efficient analysis will allow researchers to focus on individual patients' unique genetic and gene expression profiles and it could enable "personalized medicine".

3. **Engineering Design:** GA could be used in engineering design and analysis of complex aircraft parts, automobile parts, high riser building architecture design, powerplant design etc and then it can further be used to analyse the weakness of design and point stress of failure etc.

Machine Learning

Humans are limited by the natural capability to process huge amount of data and but they are good at finding out some interesting patterns and rules if data is processed by some computing devices. For example human can predict whether it will rain or not tomorrow based on the data collected from various sources like - satellites, radars, radiosondes etc and analysed by the supercomputers at meteorology department.

Machines can process large amount of data very quickly given the how to process it. Human are good to quickly figure out how to process data (finding correct data analysis algorithm) and machines are good at processing colossal dataset. These model are known as machine learning model.

There are various algorithm which can be used to analyse data and find out some learning pattern. These patterns can help predict future results based on input like predicting whether a patient is having cancer or not, calculating price of a house, etc.

Machine learning algorithms are broadly categorized as follows -

Classification

Classification is a supervised learning technique using which data is classified in relevant groups of previously learned classes. For example a tumour is malign or benign is learned by medical practitioner and researchers over several decade in past and when they see new cases of tumour cell they use the past learning experience and could be able to classify this in relevant group based on past data. In another example, when a customer applies for loan, the bank investigate the probable new customer's credibility to return the loan based on several parameter such as age, occupation, earning, expenses, existing loan, dependents, liability, assets, past record of loan repayment (if any) etc to classify the customer as good customer or bad customer.

In classification learning following steps are taken –

1. Past data which has correct label/class or every item is given to a chosen machine learning algorithm to generate a model.
2. Model generated in step 1 is used to mark new unlabelled items to correct class based on the similarities the item is having with a class of similar item set.

Algorithms: There are several well-known machine learning algorithms for classification problem such as SVM (Support vector machine), ANN (Artificial Neural Network), KNN (K nearest neighbours), Naïve Bayes etc.

Binary and Multiclass Classifier

Classification algorithm could be binary classification or multiclass classification. Binary classification algorithm has two categories of data while multiclass classification algorithms get data which has multiple categories. For example a simple binary classifier model to find whether a tumor is benign or malign is a binary classification problem while finding the mood of a person from him facial expression is multiclass classification problem.

Figure 5. Classification of tumour cell based on size and age of patient

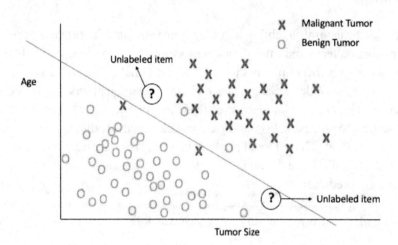

In many situation binary classifier models are used for multiclass classification problem and the strategy used is one vs all. In this strategy an item is checked for all the classes one by one and whatever it is more similar, it is labelled as that category.

Clustering

Clustering is an unsupervised learning technique in which data is clustered using similar properties. There is no prior knowledge of similarity available or no criteria of similarity is set beforehand rather the clusters created after grouping of items are labelled afterwards. For example when population of a city is surveyed and measurement for clothes of each individual are taken. Using these measurement data set we might come up with size of t-shirt group and can be labelled as S, M, L, X, XL, XXL, XXL etc or simply S, M, L, XL. In another example we can see that all known creature were grouped based of similarity and this similarity wasn't known before studying their properties such as habitat, food behaviour, physical measurement, manoeuvre behaviour etc.

Well known clustering algorithms are K-Means, DBSCAN (Density based spatial clustering application with noise), EM (Expectation minimization), HAC (Hierarchical agglomerative clustering). All these algorithms uses different correlation logic to find the similarity between the items and group them based on the similarity index usually called cluster distance.

Outlier Detection

Outlier detection is a process comprising a set of techniques to find out a data item which is significantly different or inconsistent with the rest of data population. For example a military surveillance system could use such model to find out intrusion on the border or a bank can use these techniques to find out fraudulent credit card transaction for its customers.

Usually outlier detection learning techniques falls under semi-supervised learning category but it could be supervised classification analysis or unsupervised cluster analysis. Usually It employees a set of classification and clustering model to find out anomalous or outlier item.

Figure 6. Cluster of credit card user based on their transactions

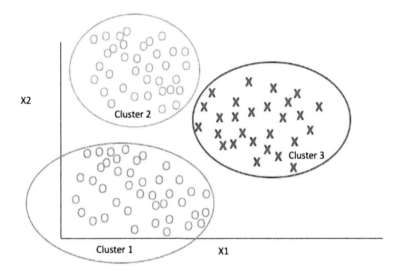

Filtering

Filtering techniques are used to find the similar relevant items from a set of items. Usually used by ecommerce or online content provider companies, these techniques are used for developing recommender system. For example an ecommerce company can analyse user's past purchase record and recommend them some new product to buy or even recommend same product which was bought in past and user may need them again as it could have been consumed. An online video provider can recommend videos to its user if the video is trending and user might have seen and liked similar videos in past. A social network site might promote some content in similar fashion.

Figure 7. Outlier customers based on their irregular credit card transaction and payment

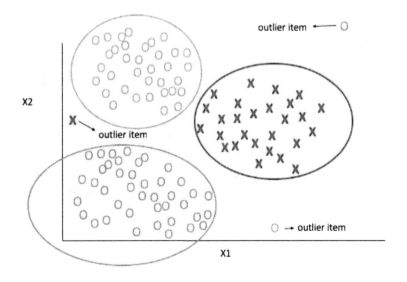

In filtering techniques, Items can be filtered either based on a user's own past behaviour or by matching the behaviour of multiple users. Filtering is generally applied based on the following two approaches:

- Collaborative filtering
- Content-based filtering

Collaborative Filtering

Collaborative filtering is a technique where data of similar group of users are analysed to establish relationship between users behaviour. It is based on the assumption that a similar group of user likes or does similar things like a young tech savvy user like to buy latest gadget while a new parent might be interested to buy stuffs which would be helpful for their new born kid.

In collaborative filtering method large amount of data is collected and analysed to extract the user's behaviour and activity such as past purchased product, liked/disliked items, reviews, ratings, products added in wish list, products added in cart but not purchased, product browsed etc. Based on relevant information and user groups a recommendation engine can use some classification algorithm such as KNN (K-Nearest neighbour) or Pearson Correlation algorithm to create the list of items which a target user may like.

Content-Based Filtering

It is an item filtering technique based on a description of the item and a profile of the user's preferences. A user profile is created based on that user's past behavior, for example, their likes, ratings and purchase history. The similarities identified between the user profile and the attributes of various items lead to items being filtered for the user. Contrary to collaborative filtering, content-based filtering is solely dedicated to individual user's preferences and does not require data about other users.

Application of filtering techniques:

1. **Business:** E-Commerce websites, retail stores, stock brokerage companies, investment institutions, restaurant and online food delivery platforms, hospitals etc can use filtering techniques to sell certain product, stock, mutual fund, food or preventive healthcare test etc based on the past record of user and similar users.
2. **Content Providers and Social Networking:** Online content providers such as video, news, story can promote and recommend new or interesting content which user might like. Dating app or social networking sites can recommend partners or friends.
3. **Marketing Agency:** Marketing agencies can use filtering techniques to come up with products which can be like by its users or they can promote the right kind of product to potential individual users by sending email, social media posts.
4. **Cross Selling** opportunities could also be realized by business for example a bank may tie up with a car company to provide loan and promote it to target user who might have visited online car sell portal and checked the same car.

Table 3. Area vs price

Area (in sq ft)	Price (in dollar)
400	16000
700	28000
580	23200
820	32800
980	39200
640	25600
760	30400
1020	40800
550	22000
950	38000

Figure 8.

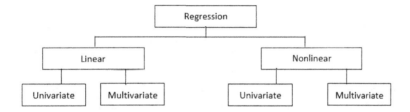

REGRESSION ANALYSIS

Regression analysis is type of analysis in which a relationship between the dependent attribute and independent attribute is established. Say for example in a table if prices of homes are given based on area then the relationship between area and home is established through regression analysis. The relationship could be linear or nonlinear.

Example: Below we have a table which has prices of homes of different size. Now if we try to analyse this dataset we could quickly come up with a relationship between these two attributes. Now if someone wants to know per square foot price of any home then we can easily say it is $40 per square foot.

This graph is very simple and it is a straight line passing through all the data points. Sometime there may not be possible to draw a simple straight line which passes through all the item point then we can draw the best fit straight line which has minimum average of errors for all data points.

Types of Regression Analysis

Linear Regression

Linear regression represents the relationship between independent and dependent variable as a straight line. It means the relationship of values of dependent and independent variables are always fixed. For example, the price of house vs area is drawn above as a straight line and this is linear regression.

It can be represented by a simple mathematical equation as y = ax + b where x is dependent variable; y is dependent variable; a and b are constant values. In our previous example if you notice the value of a is 40 and value of b is 0.

Mathematical equation: $y_i = \beta_0 + \beta_1 x_i + \varepsilon_i$

where i denotes the ith item set and ε_i denotes the error in ith item set.

Nonlinear Regression

Nonlinear or polynomial regression is a kind of relationship between independent and dependent variable which can't be expressed using a straight line and it can only be expressed by some n degree polynomial equation. In this kind of relationship, the relationship of values of dependent and independent variables is not fixed. A very simple example of such relationship would be exponential or logarithmic relationship.

It can be represented by a simple mathematical equation as y = ax^2 + bx + c where x is dependent variable; y is dependent variable; a, b and c are constant values.

Univariate Regression

If there is only one dependent variable (attribute) available then such relationships are called univariate relationship. For example, in our table above we have only one dependent variable i.e, price of the house (variable x) and area of the house (variable y).

Mathematical equation for univariate linear regression:

$$y_i = \beta_0 + \beta_1 x_i + \varepsilon_i$$

Mathematical equation for univariate nonlinear regression:

$$y_i = \beta_0 + \beta_1 x_i + \beta_2 x_i^2 + \dots + \beta_n x_i^n + \varepsilon_i$$

Above equation represents n-th degree polynomial equation having single dependent variable.

Multivariate Regression

If there are more than one dependent variables (attributes) available then such relationships are multivariate relationship. For example, in our table below we have 4 dependent variable i.e, no of bedrooms (variable x_0), no of bathroom (variable x_1), kitchen availability (variable x_2), and garden availability (variable x_3) and one independent variable i.e,price of the house (variable y).

Mathematical equation for multivariate linear equation:

$$y_i = \beta_0 1 + \beta_1 x_{i1} + \beta_2 x_{i2} + \ldots + \varepsilon_i$$

Mathematical equation for multivariate nonlinear equation:

$$y_i = \beta_0 1 + \beta_1 x_{i1} + \beta_2 x_{i2}^2 + \ldots + \beta_n x_{in}^n + \varepsilon_i$$

SENTIMENT ANALYSIS

Sentiment analysis or opinion analysis or emotion AI all are referred to data analysis and learning technique which deals with substantial amount of text analysis to find out the emotions, sentiment or opinion about the subject.

For example all the reviews given for a restaurant by its customers can be analysed to find out the public opinion about its services, food, beverages, best or worst desert etc. In another example, a book could be analysed to understand its genre whether it is sci-fi, romance, political, science, technology, travel etc.

Examples:

1. Food is good but ice-cream is great.
2. Ambiance is great, food is nice but not great.
3. Nice food and great desert options.
4. Amazing mouth-watering food but slow service.
5. Food is great, service is not so great and ambiance is nice.

From these five reviews we can find out that food and ambiance is liked by most of the people while service is not.

Sentiment analysis is subdomain of natural language processing. Sentiment analysis are widely used by marketing agencies to find out the sentiments of public using the publicly available social media data, reviews, survey responses etc and accordingly they might plan their marketing campaigns like discounts, improve customer services or promote some special offers.

Generally, a binary opposition in opinion is assumed for analysis such as like/dislike, good/bad, angry/happy, satisfied/dissatisfied etc and binary classification of data are done around these factors. In some cases the polarity of given textual document are also considered to analyse such as {"positive", "negative", "neutral"} or {"angry", "sad", "happy"}.

Algorithms

Existing sentiment analysis approaches can be grouped into three main categories: knowledge-based techniques, statistical methods, and hybrid approaches.

Knowledge-based techniques classify text by affect categories based on the presence of unambiguous affect words such as happy, sad, afraid, and bored. It makes use of publicly available resources, to extract the semantic and affective information associated with natural language concepts.

Statistical methods leverage elements from machine learning such as latent semantic analysis, support vector machines, "bag of words", "Pointwise Mutual Information" for Semantic Orientation, and deep learning. More sophisticated methods try to detect the person who is expressing his/hersentiment and entity about which it was expressed. To establish the opinion in a context and get the feature about which the speaker has opined, the grammatical relationships of words are used by deep parsing of the text.

Hybrid approaches leverage both machine learning and elements from knowledge representation such as ontologies and semantic networks in order to detect semantics that are expressed in a subtle manner, e.g., through the analysis of concepts that do not explicitly convey relevant information, but which are implicitly linked to other concepts that do so.

Challenges

Computer systems will make very different errors than human assessors. For instance, a computer system will have trouble with negations, exaggerations, jokes, or sarcasm, which typically are easy to handle for a human reader.It is harder for computer system to analyse data in context and it becomes really hard when multiple context (present, past and future) are used in conversation.

Application areas of sentiment analysis:

- **Business**: The marketing agencies can identify using such analysis where they need to improve and what is their best service/product?
- **Political**: Before elections a political party can try to understand what are the best or bad part of their or oppositions governance agenda or weakness are and they can take corrective measures or campaign against the current government.
- **Sociology**: Sociologist can use various data to understand the social economical aspects of society, happiness indices, job satisfaction, educational pressure, inclination towards some propagandist ideology etc.
- **Healthcare**: Medical practitioner and researcher can use such techniques to understand the patients sentiment or psychological reaction when certain drug or procedure is applied. Medical guidelines could be affected with such study. For example, a certain drug produces anxiety or patient is not satisfied with the doctor's treatment etc.

- **Governance**: Government implements many social welfare policies and they want to understand how much satisfied citizens are or how much they have liked the certain policies, they can use such techniques.

BIG DATA TOOLS

Big Data analytics is an essential part of any business workflow nowadays. To make the most of it, we recommend using these popular open source Big Data solutions for each stage of data processing.

Why opting for open source Big Data tools and not for proprietary solutions, you might ask? The reason became obvious over the last decade—open sourcing the software is the way to make it popular.

Developers prefer to avoid vendor lock-in and tend to use free tools for the sake of versatility, as well as due to the possibility to contribute to the evolvement of their beloved platform. Open source products boast the same, if not better level of documentation depth, along with a much more dedicated support from the community, who are also the product developers and Big Data practitioners, who know what they need from a product. Thus said, this is the list of 8 hot Big Data tool to use in 2018, based on popularity, feature richness and usefulness.

Apache Hadoop

This one is well-known for its capabilities for huge-scale data processing. This open source Big Data framework can run on-prem or in the cloud and has quite low hardware requirements. The main Hadoop benefits and features are as follows: HDFS—Hadoop Distributed File System, oriented at working with huge-scale bandwidth, MapReduce—a highly configurable model for Big Data processing, YARN—a resource scheduler for Hadoop resource management, Hadoop Libraries—the needed glue for enabling third party modules to work with Hadoop

Apache Spark

Apache Spark is the alternative—and in many aspects the successor—of Apache Hadoop. Spark was built to address the shortcomings of Hadoop and it does this incredibly well. For example, it can process both batch data and real-time data, and operates 100 times faster than MapReduce. Spark provides the in-memory data processing capabilities, which is way faster than disk processing leveraged by MapReduce. In addition, Spark works with HDFS, OpenStack and Apache Cassandra, both in the cloud and on-prem, adding another layer of versatility to big data operations for your business.

Apache Storm

Storm is another Apache product, a real-time framework for data stream processing, which supports any programming language. Storm scheduler balances the workload between multiple nodes based on topology configuration and works well with Hadoop HDFS. Apache Storm has the following benefits:

Great horizontal scalability, Built-in fault-tolerance, Auto-restart on crashes, Clojure-written, Works with Direct Acyclic Graph(DAG) topology, Output files are in JSON format

Apache Cassandra

Apache Cassandra is one of the pillars behind Facebook's massive success, as it allows to process structured data sets distributed across huge number of nodes across the globe. It works well under heavy workloads due to its architecture without single points of failure and boasts unique capabilities no other NoSQL or relational DB has, such as: Great liner scalability, Simplicity of operations due to a simple query language used, Constant replication across nodes, Simple adding and removal of nodes from a running cluster, High fault tolerance, Built-in high-availability

MongoDB

MongoDB is another great example of an open source NoSQL database with rich features, which is cross-platform compatible with many programming languages. IT Svit uses MongoDB in a variety of cloud computing and monitoring solutions, and we specifically developed a module for automated MongoDB backups using Terraform. The most prominent MongoDB features are:

Stores any type of data, from text and integer to strings, arrays, dates and Boolean, Cloud-native deployment and great flexibility of configuration. Data partitioning across multiple nodes and data centers. Significant cost savings, as dynamic schemas enable data processing on the go

SECURITY ISSUES AND PRIVACY CHALLENGES IN BIG DATA

Recently, the accessibility of Big Data keeps more potential to use the supremacy of abundant data sets and translate that power into alterations and developments in science, technology, health care, education, and financial progress. Although guaranteeing information security and privacy challenges still continue to proper utilization of these gigantic data sets in big data. These challenges are like vulnerabilities to false data generation, protective measures contrary to security gaps and data outflow etc. The safety and confidentiality of huge amount of data becomes more challenging for utilization of an energetic, distributed situation and tracing and controlling data entrée. In this section the various security issues and privacy challenges related to Big Data have been described.

Security Issues in Big Data

The huge amount of data which is growing rapidly and consistently is required to be safe and secure. This is a major challenge to manage and process this huge amount of data in a dynamic and distributed environment. In this section we have described eight major security issues related with big data in real life.

Vulnerability to Fake Data Generation

The false data generation is a major issue for security challenges in big data. The false data can be generated by the cyber hackers and can be mixed with the huge amount of original data. A good example can be sited for this purpose. Suppose, our industry utilizes the sensor data to distinguish the out of order products. Cyber hackers can go through our system and influence our sensor to produce faulty results. Before occurring notified damage, an alarming notice can be unsuccessful and the advantage of getting solution prior to severe scratch is occurred. Such problems can be resolved through concerning fake discovery approach.

Potential Presence of Untrusted Mappers

Parallel processing is required after accumulation of our big data. One of the techniques is known as MapReduce scheme. If huge amount of data is divided into several sizes, a mapper is required for processing and assigning to individual memory. The settings of the existing mappers can be modified if any stranger has right to entry into our mappers' code. The stranger can acquire admission to perceptive data. As Big data do not have any extra security layer for secure its data, the intruder can get admission very easily also. They usually tend to rely on perimeter security systems. But if those are imperfect, our big data turn out to be a small hanging fruit.

Troubles of Cryptographic Protection

Encryption is a method to transmit challenging data securely and safely in a familiar manner. In big data security challenges, it plays a vital role. In reality the challenging data is accumulated in the cloud without any encryption. To take the challenge of cryptograpy handling with huge amount of data is making the system slow in real world which significantly lessen the preliminary advantage of Big data i.e speed.

Possibility of Sensitive Information Mining

For securing huge amount of sensitive information in big data perimeter-based security is the best choice now a days. The perimeter-based security implies the security in every end points of the system. The huge amount of data may be polluted with dishonest IT professionals inside the border for fulfilling their personal needs. So related company can be suffered from a massive damage due to passing the private information from the company such as new product or service launch, the financial information of the company etc. For this vital reason, additional border is required for more security of sensitive data. Our company's safety could assist from without identification. So, if the personal data without any name is being stolen then their bad intention will not be fulfilled.

Struggles of Granular Access Control

It may happen often that some data are partially visible from all the users and the private information inside the data are hidden from every one. Partial information of those hidden item may be supportive for some other users without any entrance to the private part. From here the journey of granular access begins. So, the interested persons can use the required information but with limited access. This type of permission for restricted entrée is troublesome for allowance in big data as preliminary, this technology is not built for this purpose. The parts of required data sets which can be claimed by the user are stored in a distinct big data warehouse and delivered to specific user groups. We can site the medical research as an example. All the information related with any particular disease are copied without the personal details of the patients. In this way the volume of the big data is being increased very quickly which can provide direct bad impact for the company's performance and maintenance.

Data Provenance Difficulties

It is very difficult problem for preserving the historical records of big data. Big data is basically the collection of a huge amount of metadata which is formed by the operations accomplished upon it. So, keeping all the records about the sources of data are extremely complicated task in big data. But at the view point of safety, storing the historical details of the big data is essential. Mainly two reasons are there. Firstly, the illegal modification of metadata can motivate us to select the inaccurate data sets which will misguide us to search required data. Secondly, undetectable origins of data can be an enormous impairment to searching the origins of safety holes and false information creation scenarios.

High Speed of NoSQL Databases' Evolution and Lack of Security Focus

This is a major concern in big data. Now a days, NoSQL databases are a familiar and widespread trend in big data technology. Its familiarity creates massive problems. New characteristics are being added always with NoSQL databases hampering the safety of big data. So, it is required to handle the safety measures of big data from outside whenever the new features are being added in the NoSQL database.

Absent Security Audits

Big data security audits support companies to achieve the consciousness of their security breaches. In spite of the guide to execute it in regular interval, it is performed hardly in the real scenario. Now a days, the security audits becomes impractical in the companies due to deficiency of time, funds, skilled peoples there. So, among all security challenges and concerns in big data, audit is one of them.

Privacy Challenges in Big Data

This section describes the challenges elevated by big data in privacy-preserving data managing. First, we investigate the issues related with big data with respect to already existing ideas of private data management.Most of the organizations are facing tremendous problem for maintaining privacy in their huge amount of collected data. We have described here the nine major privacy challenges related with big data.

Protecting Transaction Logs and Data

A multi-layered stock media is required to collect the data and transaction logs. The motion of data among the various layers provides the IT professionals a mastery to know what data is shifted and when. The huge amount of information set is expanding rapidly, continuously. These huge amounts of data set are required auto-tiering for proper management. Actually, the proper path is not maintained by Auto-tiering solutions to find out the original position of data storage. This creates novel contests to safe information storing. The original methods are imperious to prevent illegal access and sustain accessibility always.

Validation and Filtration of End-Point Inputs

From many resources such as end-point devices, a huge amount of data is accumulated in enterprise settings. The input validation process of huge amount of accumulated data is a major issue. Three questions are related with validation of data. Firstly, how can we belief the collected information? Secondly, how can we assure that resources of the input information are not malignant. Thirdly, how can we separate the malignant input from our accumulated data? Validation of input and separating the actual data from malignant one is an intimidating trouble created by the unauthorized resources.

Securing Distributed Framework Calculations and Other Processes

The parallelism in calculation and repository to process a huge amount of information is required for distributed, secured programming frameworks. MapReduce framework is a suitable sample which divides an input file into several lumps. In the first stage of MapReduce, a mapper for every lump goes through the information. Then few calculations are executed. Finally, the list of keys is generated. After that, a Reducer amalgamated the values owned by each well-defined key and the results is generated. Two attack prohibition steps are present. The first one can save the mappers and other can save the information in the existence of an unauthorized mapper.

Securing and Protecting Data in Real Time

The safety alarms created by security devices are really a major issue for real-time safety supervising system. With increasing amount of data, the real-time safety monitoring system becomes more problematic. Big data technologies must also supply an advantage for which it permits for quick managing and analytics of various types of information. So, the real-time abnormality identification can be supplied based on extensible safety measures.

Protecting Access Control Method Communication and Encryption

The encryption and decryption of data is required for assuring end-to-end safety and prevent the data from access of unauthorized unit. The Attribute-Based Encryption (ABE) has enriched more in the research area of this field. The cryptography-based data transmission is required to be executed to guarantee authentication and a safety communication among the scattered entities.

Data Provenance

In big data applications, the provenance metadata will be enlarged in size for huge origin graphs created from source-authorized programming domain. Analyse of such huge source-enabled graphs to identify metadata determination for safety and privacy approaches is rationally concentrated.

Granular Audits

At present situation, we want to identify an ambush with real-time safety measures. The data for audit is required to receive failed ambush. This is required to realize what occurred and what went inaccurate. Auditing is not a new thing but the opportunity and granularity might be separated. So many data objects are handled which possibly are scattered.

Granular Access Control

The privacy of data can be maintained by stopping the access of data from mankind. The trouble with course-grained access policies are that information that could otherwise be distributed which sometimes transferred into a more secure region to assure sound safety. Granular access control provides the ability to the data administrations to allot sufficient amount of data without hampering security and privacy.

Privacy Protection for Non-Rational Data Stores

The NoSQL database i.e. non-rational data stores are developing gradually with respect to safety foundation. Every NoSQL DBs were constructed to handle various challenges imposed by the rational world. So, safety was not at all a portion of the model at any point of its developing phase. The founders using NoSQL database usually implant safety in the middleware. NoSQL database do not supply any help for implementing it directly in the database. However, clustering features of NoSQL databases imposes extra provocations to the steadiness of such safety applications.

METHODS TO OVERCOME THE BIG DATA SECURITY ISSUES AND PRIVACY CHALLENGES

The epoch of big data is building a massive amount of data producing larger intuitions that motivate us for provoking research, improved business choices, and in many ways, superior worth for clients. To accomplish these results, companies are required to be capable to maintain it competently, rapidly, and because frequently this data will contain sensitive message with safety in large scale. Many companies woefully vacillate for looking at safety specially in encryption when it meets to big data solutions because they are worried about arranging at large scale or upcoming analytics tools that prepare these solutions so treasured.

Big Data Encryption and Key Management Enterprises Trust

For safety measures of big data of the clients, Gemalto's SafeNet portfolio of data protection solutions is used nowadays without identifying their database whether it's a Hadoop set-up or a non-relational (NoSQL) database such as MongoDB or Couchbase. Also, it is not very important to obtain the procedure that the analytics tools are procuring to create these solutions. Moreover, Gemalto combines the above-mentioned solution and a whole system of companion encryption solutions beyond a consolidated encryption key managing application.

Hadoop Encryption Solutions

In Hadoop architecture, the SafeNet data protection portfolio can safe information at several point at distinct nodes in the data stream. The client can choose any one of the following three options. Firstly, customer can get safety measures of the big data by integrating application-level security through APIs instead of hampering their database structure. Secondly, a column-level solution can be selected for Hive that allows typical interrogating. Thirdly, a file system level solution can be selected which allows a vigorous policy-based admission regulator. The whole data encryption solution by Hadoop is totally clear to the customers and they will be profited by the analytics tools that attract more attention for rapidly increasing data sets.

NoSQL Database Encryption Solutions

Non-relational or NoSQL databases are multiskilled database solutions those are fit for accommodating with a huge amount of diverse data sets as they cover more than conventional database tables instead of a dissimilar method for big data safety. Clients can nowadays shield data in any NoSQL database with all other foremost database vendors such as MongoDB, Cassandra, Couchbase, and HBase. The application-level big data encryption solutions added seafty straight to the information before it constantly stored into the NoSQL schema. The procedures persist clear to the customers while the database remembers its capability to regulate queries and distribute data without suppressing achievements.

CONCLUSION

Big data can be used in many location and it also provide the good solution to achieve the many goal of real life but it also have the some security issue that required proper management. In this book chapter, the security and challenges of the big data has been discussed and how to overcome the challenge is also discussed for better result. The concept and technologies of big data and usage of of big data is the main part of this book chapter. The concept of big data with cloud computing will be presented in the next book chapter.

REFERENCES

Adat, V., & Gupta, B. B. (2018). Security in Internet of Things: Issues, challenges, taxonomy, and architecture. *Telecommunication Systems*, *67*(3), 423–441. doi:10.100711235-017-0345-9

Gupta, B. B. (2018). *Computer and cyber security: Principles, algorithm, applications, and perspectives*. Auerbach Publications.

Gupta, B. B., Agrawal, D. P., & Yamaguchi, S. (2016). *Handbook of Research on Modern Cryptographic Solutions for Computer and Cyber Security*. Hershey, PA: IGI Global. doi:10.4018/978-1-5225-0105-3

Plageras, A. A., Psannis, K. E., Stergiou, C., Wang, H., & Gupta, B. B. (2018). Efficient IoT-based sensor BIG Data collection–processing and analysis in smart buildings. *Future Generation Computer Systems*, *82*, 349–357. doi:10.1016/j.future.2017.09.082

Stergiou, C., Psannis, K. E., Kim, B.-G., & Gupta, B. B. (2018). Secure integration of IoT and cloud computing. *Future Generation Computer Systems*, *78*(3), 964–975. doi:10.1016/j.future.2016.11.031

Stergiou, C., Psannis, K. E., Xifilidis, T., Plageras, A. P., & Gupta, B. B. (2018) Security and privacy of big data for social networking services in cloud. *IEEE INFOCOM 2018*.

Tewari, A., & Gupta, B. B. (2017). Cryptanalysis of a novel ultra-lightweight mutual authentication protocol for IoT devices using RFID tags. *The Journal of Supercomputing*, *73*(3), 1085–1102. doi:10.100711227-016-1849-x

ADDITIONAL READING

McCall, J. (2005, December 1). Genetic algorithms for modelling and optimisation. *Journal of Computational and Applied Mathematics*, *184*(1), 205–222. doi:10.1016/j.cam.2004.07.034

Statsoft. (n.d.) How to predict membership, classification trees. *Statsoft*. Retrieved from: http://www.statsoft.com/textbook/classification-trees https://www.cise.ufl.edu/~ddd/cap6635/Fall-97/Short-papers/2.htm https://in.mathworks.com/help/gads/what-is-the-genetic-algorithm.html https://en.wikipedia.org/wiki/Genetic_algorithm https://www.doc.ic.ac.uk/~nd/surprise_96/journal/vol1/hmw/article1.html https://towardsdatascience.com/introduction-to-genetic-algorithms-including-example-code-e396e98d8bf3 https://www.analyticsvidhya.com/blog/2017/07/introduction-to-genetic-algorithm/ https://www.irjet.net/archives/V4/i7/IRJET-V4I7187.pdf

Chapter 5
Cloud–Centric Blockchain Public Key Infrastructure for Big Data Applications

Brian Tuan Khieu
San Jose State University, USA

Melody Moh
https://orcid.org/0000-0002-8313-6645
San Jose State University, USA

ABSTRACT

A cloud-based public key infrastructure (PKI) utilizing blockchain technology is proposed. Big data ecosystems have scalable and resilient needs that current PKI cannot satisfy. Enhancements include using blockchains to establish persistent access to certificate data and certificate revocation lists, decoupling of data from certificate authority, and hosting it on a cloud provider to tap into its traffic security measures. Instead of holding data within the transaction data fields, certificate data and status were embedded into smart contracts. The tests revealed a significant performance increase over that of both traditional and the version that stored data within blocks. The proposed method reduced the mining data size, and lowered the mining time to 6.6% of the time used for the block data storage method. Also, the mining gas cost per certificate was consequently cut by 87%. In summary, completely decoupling the certificate authority portion of a PKI and storing certificate data inside smart contracts yields a sizable performance boost while decreasing the attack surface.

INTRODUCTION

Verification of one's identity continues to be the cornerstone upon which any interactions or transactions between two parties lie. One key method of verifying one's identity is through using public and private keys, which are cryptographically related strings that can be used to lock and unlock files. If a public key is used to lock a file, only its corresponding private key can be used to unlock it and vice-versa. People

DOI: 10.4018/978-1-5225-9742-1.ch005

could use a public key to lock or encrypt a file, and they would be sure that the only person who could unlock it would be whoever held the matching private key. However, the issue after the establishment of public and private keys was identifying whether or not someone's private key and persona were appropriately matched. Malicious actors could claim to be another party and attempt to associate their own public key with the false persona in an attempt to redirect and steal sensitive information. Thus, public key infrastructure (PKI) was born in order to properly associate online identities with the correct public keys so that any online communication could be trusted to involve the correct parties.

However, with the pervasiveness and expansion of the Internet of Things, there comes new challenges for securing and authenticating the heavy flow of data generated by IoT devices. PKI's age has shown, and it has been unable to keep up with the demands of the IoT and Big Data era (Claeys, Rousseau, & Tourancheau, 2017). Big Data ecosystems require solutions that are scalable and resilient, two attributes that fail to be applied to traditional PKIs. Thus, in order to further secure the internet, a new method for identity verification over the web needs to be realized. The main issue with the currently outdated PKI lies with the Certificate Authority (CA) portion of the PKI (Doukas, Maglogiannis, Koufi, Malamateniou, & Vassilacopoulos, 2012; Gupta & Garg, 2015). CAs are the authorizing parties within a PKI; they validate and associate online personas with public keys by distributing and revoking digital certificates. These digital certificates act as ID cards for anyone that communicates over the internet, and they give a degree of assurance that the party one is communicating with is actually who they say they are. As of now, these CAs are the main points of failure within a PKI system; once any one CA is compromised, the whole PKI crumbles (Zhou, Cao, Dong, &Vasilakos, 2017). Furthermore, it is currently extremely difficult for a traditional CA to revoke an old identity. However, there are newer iterations of PKI that attempt to overcome these shortcomings; one of which is called Web of Trust (WoT). Another promising new solution marries the traditional PKI system with that of cloud and blockchain technology to overcome the weaknesses of the past (Tewari, Hughes, Weber, & Barry, 2018). Both of these systems are new ways of verifying identities that can pave the way towards a safer and more secure internet.

In this chapter, we explore the current state of PKI and its new incarnations that attempt to address the limitations of traditional systems. By doing so, we aim to answer the following questions: "How can new technologies such as blockchain be leveraged to improve traditional PKIs" and "What are the pros and cons of using one new solution over another". This chapter is extended from a conference paper which reported preliminary results (Khieu & Moh, 2019).

This chapter is organized in the following manner. First, it will establish background information surrounding the project and then cover research related to this area with a specific focus on other implementations of different PKIs. Afterwards, the methodology and reasoning behind our solution to the issues with the PKI model will be detailed. Subsequently, the chapter will cover the test results and performance comparisons between the different PKI models including our solution. Finally, the chapter will conclude with a summary and areas for future work.

RESEARCH OBJECTIVE

The objective of this research is to test and implement a Cloud-based blockchain PKI system, CBPKI, to provide Big Data applications with a scalable and persistent identity management system. In addition, the goal is to determine whether such a system can outperform traditional PKI models using metrics such as complete revocation time.

PUBLIC KEY INFRASTRUCTURE

A public and private key are two mathematically and cryptographically linked strings of characters. The two of them together form a key pair; an operation conducted using one can be reversed using the other half of the key pair. In practice, encrypting a document with a public key ensures that the only feasible method of decrypting said document is by using the corresponding private key. As their names imply, a public key is the public portion of a key pair while the private key is the private portion. Key pairs help ensure the privacy and integrity of online communications.

A public key infrastructure is a system that authenticates devices and handles digital certificates; digital certificates are essentially virtual ID cards designated by the PKI to associate an identity with a public key. By relying on a public key infrastructure, users trust that any party with a digital certificate distributed by the PKI is accurate. Once a certificate is retired or deemed to be compromised, the public key infrastructure will revoke that certificate to protect other users from communicating with anything that tries to use the revoked certificate. Currently, PKIs revolve around a Certificate authority (CA) to administer and revoke certificates using the X.509 standard.

Certificate authorities certify and issue these certificates to requesting users. Since they are central to the security provided by PKIs, they often must endure more attacks. Once a certificate authority is compromised, the integrity and authenticity of every certificate within the ecosystem comes under question.

WEB OF TRUST

As Chen, Le and Wei (2009) explain, WoT is a new system that attempts to validate one's identity and corresponding public key in a different way from how traditional PKI systems do. In order to avoid the single point of failure of PKIs, it mimics human society and its network of authenticating statements by the individuals; trust between parties is generated through past interactions with other parties. Certificate Authorities are not needed or used by WoT systems since they disperse the role of authenticator and validator to all of the user in the system. The basis for WoT is comprised of three rules: When two parties interact, they generate "trust information" (Chen et al., 2009). Secondly, every party knows what information belongs to them. And finally, every party must provide "trust" feedback to everyone else. These tenets form a model in which users are able to make decisions on whether to trust others.

In the research conducted by Bakar, Ismail, Ahmad and Manan (2010), it is stressed that WoT relies on a decentralized nature of authenticating users and they push for a trust scoring process for WoTs. The researchers postulate that this decentralization property allows the systems to overcome the past issues of traditional PKIs. With users providing trust scores for each other, there is no longer a need for a CA to dispense certificates. Instead, each user acts as a fraction of a CA, and only when enough pieces are put together is something allowed to be verified and used. Thus, according to the research by Bakar et al. (2010), the single point of failure in PKIs, the CA, is completely removed as a factor in WoT systems. However, this avoidance of a need for a CA comes at a cost as stated by the two papers referenced above.

While WoT systems lack the weak spot that traditional PKIs possess, the study conducted by Alexopoulos, Daubert, Mühlhäuser, and Habib (2017) criticizes the WoT model and conclude that the decentralized nature of the model negatively impacts its ease of setup and limits its applicable areas. By its very nature, WoT systems require further assistance in the setup phase than other PKIs (Alexopoulos et al., 2017). Not only does it require a sizable amount of users to be effective, it also needs enough of a history of interactions to generate meaningful trust scores. Furthermore, this process is not automatable, because the system is based on activity from real users. WoT complicates the initial setup, because it requires a number of real people to manually validate other real people until it can successfully run on its own. In addition to the effects on its setup, WoT cannot be applied to every use case due to its decentralized nature (Bakar et al., 2010). For example, systems that require a strict hierarchy of users, e.g. government agencies, do not have time for nor wish for the trust building process. If a system cannot handle the initial setup requirement of having enough users validate both each other and enough new users, then WoT should not be applied to it. In the case of Big Data applications and ecosystems, the Web of Trust model fails to properly meet the needs of the two. The setup requirements are too burdensome, and while WoT can eventually scale properly, the need for cross-verification would be another bottleneck on the ecosystem,

BLOCKCHAIN PKI

Blockchain technology is a relatively new invention; it revolves around the usage of a public immutable ledger called a blockchain. Multiple parties on a network encode transactions into this ledger after going conducting a verification process. In a blockchain network, every party holds essentially the same power to verify new transactions that wish to be recorded onto the public ledger. The whole system is decentralized, and the users act as a self-policing force to ensure the integrity of every transaction that is embedded into the public ledger.

Within a blockchain network, miners, nodes that hold a current version of the ledger, compete with one another in an attempt to be the first to mine a new block on the ledger. They do so to receive transaction fees for their services rendered. Once a block has been mined, the data will be publicly accessible on the blockchain network.

Closely associated with blockchains, smart contracts are digital contracts typically hosted on an electronic public ledger. It comprises of an agreement between two parties and facilitates the completion of said agreement. The smart contract allows money to be deposited within it for holding and future disbursement upon successful completion of the aforementioned agreement between both parties. If a party does not abide by the terms, the money the contract holds will automatically refund the held deposit and self-terminate. Smart contracts are self-executing and can be used in a large variety of applications from legal processes to residential leases.

Tewari et al. (2018) emphasized the viability of integrating current iterations of both PKIs and blockchains. In order to shore up the current weakness of PKIs, the group implemented a blockchain PKI management framework by developing a hybrid x.509 certificate that included details such as the blockchain name and hashing algorithm used. The system relied upon a Restful service as a communication medium; users could request certificates or certificate revocation lists (CRL) from the framework. Upon receiving a request for a new certificate, the framework would generate a hybrid certificate, send the requesting user a copy of it, and finally embed the certificate into a smart contract for storage in the Ethereum blockchain (Tewari et al., 2018). This approach fused many aspects of both blockchain technology and traditional PKIs; this lends itself an increased ease of usage and compatibility due to the usage of pre-existing technologies.

Along similar lines, Alexopoulos, Daubert, Mühlhäuser, and Habib (2017) highlighted the importance of establishing perpetual access to the new PKI framework in order to avoid certain attacks. In their study, they also utilized blockchain technologies to circumvent the issues with CAs. The authors note that the CAs of old could be blocked by Denial of Service (DOS) attacks that would prevent the distribution of CRLs (Alexopoulos et al., 2017). Since internet entities rely on checking these CRLs for whether a given certificate is still valid, the denial of access to them would allow faulty or compromised certificates to be accepted. Because of the decentralized and immutable nature of blockchain ledgers, they can be used to easily distribute the lists of certificates a Certificate Authority has created as well as its CRL. This makes DOS attacks ineffective versus this new PKI model; there will also be ensured access to the PKI due to the distributed nature of the blockchain (Tewari et al., 2018; Alexopoulos et al., 2017). However, these benefits of integrated blockchain PKIs come at the cost of limitations created through integration; one such limit is that CRLs can often exceed the size of a block which poses an issue for access to said CRLs.

Conversely to the previous approach by the two groups, Chen, Yao, Yuan, He, Ji, and Du (2018) decided to completely overhaul the PKI model and developed a service that heavily utilizes blockchain technology and concepts. CertChain is a new PKI scheme that aims to overcome the issues with past implementations of blockchain based PKIs. Specifically, past implementations possessed three issues: Centralized nodes could overpower other nodes and thus control a larger share of the blockchain. When checking the history of operations on a certificate, the entire blockchain would need to be traversed in order to find said info. And finally, block size limits would often break up CRLs whose size could reach 76MB. Unfortunately, for each of these issues, Tewari et al. and Alexopolous et al. chose to leave these issues as future concerns and did not implement safe guards versus them (Tewari et al., 2018; Alexopoulos et al., 2017).

Throughout their study, Chen et al. (2018) develop solutions for the problems with the integrated approach taken by Tewari et al. (2018) and Alexopolous et al. (2017) in order to create a more robust blockchain PKI. J. Chen et al. addresses the first issue of centralization through dispersing the trust within the system by use of a distributed dependability-rank based protocol (Chen et al., 2018). Essentially, an incentive mechanism was put in place to determine whether or not a CA would be made leader of a block like that of a centralized node in typical blockchains. Each CA would be given a dependability rank that would move up or down depending on the CA's good or bad behavior. On the other hand, the approach Tewari et al. and Alexopolous et al. took relies on the infeasibility of aggregating that much control over the network of nodes (Tewari et al., 2018; Alexopoulos et al., 2017). Rather than build in a safeguard like how J. Chen et al. does, they prefer to pay the sacrifice of provable security for the convenience of integration (Tewari et al., 2018; Alexopoulos et al., 2017; Chen et al., 2018). Regarding the second issue of traversal, this was solved through the proposal and development of a new data structure called CertOper while this issue goes unaddressed by Tewari et al. and Alexopolous et al. (Tewari et al., 2018; Alexopoulos et al., 2017). This data structure would be stored in a block and allow for operations such as efficient query and forward traceability (Chen et al. 2018). And finally, the issue of block size limits for CRLs was solved through the usage of Dual counting bloom filter, a method that efficiently stores data space wise and eliminates false positives that may come up during queries (Chen et al., 2018). And in regards to the existing integrated versions of blockchain PKIs, they also fail to address this issue (Tewari et al., 2018; Alexopoulos et al., 2017). CertChain builds upon the idea of blockchain based PKIs by overhauling previous hybridized systems in order to overcome the inherent issues with the fusion approach. Unfortunately, while it is faster and more robust in its security, it will be quite expensive to implement and maintain. The second problem, the issue of traversal, places an unnecessary bottleneck on the verification process of a certificate; this hindrance prevents blockchain PKIs from fully addressing the needs of Big Data applications and ecosystems.

REAL WORLD STATUS OF PKI

Current traditional PKIs are unable to keep up with the demands of new applications; in one survey, over 60% of respondents stated that their current PKI system was unable to handle new apps regardless of what the software was based in (Grimm 2016). Some companies have already taken steps towards basing their PKI in the cloud; others use newer versions such as the Web of Trust (WoT) approach. However, the WoT version generally lacks speed due to its manual nature of authenticating new users even though it is quite strong in its security.

The literature notes that WoT systems are currently used in several applications when they fit the use case, but blockchain based PKIs lack the same amount of adoption. Bakar et al. notes that while WoT is not applicable to every situation, it lends itself well to systems that are also decentralized in nature and can tolerate the manual addition and validation of new users. Currently, WoT is used in Peer to Peer (P2P) file-sharing networks and is embedded in some email clients (Bakar et al., 2010). Despite its manual nature, WoT has been adopted by some niche applications, but this manual nature and large setup requirements hold it back from being properly applied to Big Data applications. Blockchain based PKIs have not been as widely adopted primarily due to the lack of commercial offerings. This new iteration of a PKI has not fully left the research and development phase of its life cycle. However, it has further reaching consequences than that of WoT systems; it possesses more viability in replacing traditional PKIs than WoT systems do (Alexopoulos et al., 2017). And while there may not be any commercially available blockchain based PKIs available, Tewari et al. stresses that they can be implemented if one is willing to bear both the cost of development as well as that of encoding certificates into a blockchain (Tewari et al., 2018).

SECURITY OF CLOUD AND IOT

Past work in the area of cloud computing and IoT note the inherent security issues with both and attempt to rectify them in a variety of manners. In regards to IoT, these problems result from the computing limitations of the devices which prevents full-fledged security solutions from being applied to them. Stergiou, Psannis, Kim, and Gupta (2018) surveyed the literature surrounding cloud and IoT technology and identified limitations such as that regarding the security of a cloud service provider to customer relationship. The customer must surrender any potentially sensitive and damaging information to the provider by use of the service and trust that the provider has undertaken proper measures to protect said information. With the integration of cloud and IoT, issues arise regarding the storage location of sensitive data and lack of trust in service-level agreements. The group developed a new hybridized Advanced Encryption Standard (AES) platform composed of both IoT and cloud technologies to rectify some of these limitations (Stergiou et al., 2018). Similarly, Tewari and Gupta addressed the security issues regarding IoT resulting from the limited resources of its devices (2016). Their approach differed by use of an ultra-lightweight solution consisting of only bitwise operations for mutual authenitication between RFID tags and readers. Due to lack of computationally intensive operations, this method would be more readily usuable directly by the IoT sensors themselves.

Furthermore, the literature highlights the need for a proper management system in IoT and Big Data ecosystems and proposes several solutions. In one paper, the authors proposed that all data from IoT devices in a smart building be relayed to a cloud server with the additional ability to control such sensors remotely (Plageras, Psannis, Stergiou, Wang, & Gupta, 2017). This system aimed to provide proper monitoring of sensors and optimization of energy efficiency within a cloud environment. Contrastingly, another approach took techniques applied to Wireless Sensor Networks (WSN) to develop a new solution, an Efficient Algorithm for Media-based Surveillance Systems (EAMSuS) to provide privacy and security for IoT networks (Memos, Psannis, Ishibashi, Kim, & Gupta, 2017). WSN techniques were paired with High Efficiency Video Encoding (HEVC) compression and one-time pads in order to cover the privacy and security weaknesses of a one-to-one adaptation of WSN techniques to IoT ecosystems.

SUMMARY OF THE LITERATURE

The literature identifies that researchers have developed two key methods for solving the issues with traditional PKIs. D. Chen et al. and Bakar et al. developed and tested WoT systems; these systems avoid incorporating the CAs, the single point of failure of past PKIs, by offloading the validation and addition of new users through a community based trust model (Chen et al., 2009; Bakar et al., 2010). Alternatively, Tewari et al. (2018) developed a blockchain based PKI that demonstrated its practicality and compatibility with current technologies while also improving and protecting CAs. Chen et al. (2018) took the scheme further and developed a new system that overcomes the issues plaguing existing blockchain based PKI models. In summary, while PKIs have become outdated, there are two models that improve upon and may ultimately replace traditional PKIs to pave the way for a safer, more secure internet. However, there are still areas that require more development and research to increase the viability of replacing traditional PKIs. And even then, both solutions do not completely satisfy the needs of current Big Data applications in terms of scalability and persistence.

Additionally, the literature notes the inherent weaknesses in the security of IoT environments due to the computational limitations of the sensor devices. Stergiou et al. developed a hybrid cloud and IoT AES system to address the weaknesses of both cloud and IoT systems with the strengths of the other (2018). Conversely, another approach minimized the need for heavy computation through simplifying authentication down to bitwise operations (Tewari & Gupta, 2017). Several management systems were also proposed for IoT and Big Data environments. One revolved around the use of a cloud server to provide remote monitoring and control of sensors (Plageras et al., 2017). Another proposed the usage of WSN techniques paired with HEVC and one-time pads for proper application to IoT networks (Memos et al., 2017).

RELATED RESEARCH

Several other public key infrastructure models also utilize blockchain technology. These other models do closely resemble our proposed model, but we have made significant departures from their approaches.

X509Cloud, the model proposed by Tewari et al. (2018) emphasized the storage, retrieval, and revocation of certificates. In order to circumvent the associated maintenance costs of verifying identities, the model aims for mutual authentication between users and the organizations. The framework connects a cloud service to a Bitcoin inspired blockchain protocol that is used to store in newly created certificates. This approach differs from CBPKI in that instead of storing the entire certificate itself within a blockchain, mine holds all relevant certificate data within a smart contract.

A paper authored by Alexopolous et al. (2017) analyzed the merits of integrating open distributed ledgers (ODLs). Alexopolous et al. (2017) developed a formally defined trust management model for use with ODLs; these ODLs are the ledgers that blockchain technologies have implemented and center around. The paper also provided an analysis of common attacks versus typical trust management systems and detailed how the use of ODLs assisted in mitigating or even preventing the harm. This mathematical model was used in part as a blueprint for the implementation of CBPKI. It also inspired further modifications in an effort to circumvent the common denial-of-Service attack.

Conversely, to the previous approach by the two groups, Chen et al. (2018) overhauled the PKI model and developed a service that heavily utilizes blockchain technology and concepts. The proposed model, CertChain, does not simply embed certificates inside of a blockchain. Instead, CertChain uses a newly created data structure, CertOper, to aid in both the storage of certificates within a blockchain and traversal along a blockchain. Also, it modified certificate authorities into miners belonging to the CertChain blockchain network. CBPKI does not go as far as CertChain does in terms of using a newly developed blockchain system specifically designed to fix the power centralization and block traversal issues. Rather, CBPKI uses the pre-existing blockchain Ethereum to store certificate data. However, CertChain directly inspired the use of smart contracts to store certificate data to address the traversal issue, and the usage of smart contracts is addressed in section 10.1.1.

These projects inspired CBPKI, but they differ from it in some significant aspects. While CBPKI utilizes blockchain technology to store data, it does not store the certificate itself; rather, it holds certificate data such its validity and expiration date within a blockchain. In addition, our proposed model altered the certificate authority portion of a PKI by hosting it as a stateless web app on a cloud provider.

PROPOSED SOLUTION AND METHODOLOGY

The following sections detail our newly proposed model for a PKI system that utilizes blockchain and cloud technologies, and they are organized as follows. Firstly, the model itself and the enhancements are explained in the next section. Afterwards, implementation details are covered, and the final section discusses the differences CBPKI possesses compare to models from related works.

Model

CBPKI consists of a stateless certificate authority that stores certificate data on the Ethereum network, a blockchain network that allows unlimited processing potential for smart contracts. The certificate authority is implemented as a Restful API; upon receiving a certificate service request posted to it, the CA generates a new certificate. Shortly following, the new certificate is embedded into a blockchain whose address is listed on the certificate itself. A python script is used to check for the certificate's appearance within the blockchain. Upon revocation of a certificate, the certificate is similarly embedded within a different blockchain for further verification purposes. Figure 1 below displays the overall flow of the generation and verification of a certificate using CBPKI.

Enhancements

One specific enhancements over past PKI models is the transformation of the certificate authority into a stateless web service hosted on the cloud. The conversion of the certificate authority into a stateless protocol hosted on a cloud platform significantly reduces the size of the viable attack surface. Since coveted data is no longer stored within the CA itself, it also lowers the value of targeting the certificate authority for attacks. In addition, stateless web services are more conducive to relying on the protections offered by cloud platforms. For example, Amazon offers a web traffic monitoring service named AWS Shield to secure stateless web services. In addition, hosting the CA on a cloud platform with auto-scaling mitigates the common Denial-of-Service attack; with auto-scaling, more resources are automatically provisioned to the certificate authority so it can handle the flood of requests during a DOS attack.

The second enhancement made by CBPKI is the use of smart contracts as a storage device on the blockchain network. In general, the use of blockchains in PKI systems allows persistent certificate revocation list access and further circumvention of DOS attacks. Using smart contracts to store certificate

Figure 1. CBPKI process of certificate generation and verification

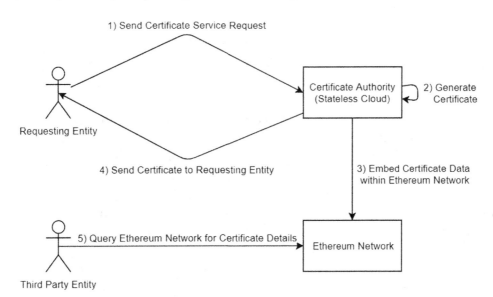

data instead of using block transaction data fields yields the additional benefits of lowered mining times and operating costs. Also, CBPKI removes the need for CRLs due to the storage of certificate validity within the smart contracts. This allows for direct verification of a certificate as opposed to traversing a blockchain for a certificate's status thus making our solution better fit the needs of Big Data applications.

Implementation

As noted earlier, CBPKI builds on the works of Tewari et al. (2018), Alexopolous et al. (2017), and Chen et al. (2018). Three different PKIs were built for testing and comparison purposes: a traditional PKI and two Cloud Based PKIs utilizing blockchain technology. Both the traditional PKI and the Cloud PKIs used a remote CA in order to standardize the experiment. The overarching approach is as follows:

1. Implement a Restful API using Python and Django to act as a CA. Allow for the traditional CA to service queries for its certificate revocation lists (CRL).
2. Connect the Certificate Authority to the Ethereum Test Net Ropsten. Associate a cryptocurrency wallet with the CA in order to pay for the associated cost of embedding a certificate
3. For one of the blockchain PKIs, hash a X.509 certificate and embed it into the transaction data field of a block and send it to be mined in Ropsten. Similarly for the new approach, set up a smart contract in which to embed the hash of an X.509 certificate and send it to be mined in Ropsten. In both cases, the X.509 certificate requires the address of where it is stored within Ethereum.
4. Implement certificate verification methods for the Blockchain PKIs. This involves searching for the hash of a certificate within a blockchain or pulling certificate information from the smart contract.

Distinct Features

The modifications to the approach created by Tewari et al. (2018) and Alexopolous et al. (2017) center around the hosting of the CA on the cloud as well as the embedding of certificate data in smart contracts. Both research groups utilized a Restful API implementation of a CA in order to accept and service requests for certificates. However, they did not host the CA in the Cloud; conversely, CBPKI's hosting of the CA within a cloud service such as Amazon Web Services (AWS) allows for some added security benefits. For one, AWS offers web traffic monitoring and filtering of requests to a web app. In addition, Denial of Service attacks are mitigated since AWS with its auto-scaling feature will simply continue to provision more resources in order to meet the increased demand. This change allows for CBPKI to scale properly with any changes in demand by Big Data applications.

CBPKI also drew upon the hybridized certificate implementation from Tewari et al. (2018) and Alexopolous et al. (2017); the modified certificates possess information regarding where pertinent certificate or CA information is stored in the blockchain network. In addition to the hosting of the CA on a cloud service, our proposed solution differs from the two referenced papers' approach in how certificate data is stored within the blockchain network. Instead of storing the revocation list data within a block's transaction data field, our new approach stores said data within smart contracts. This has the added benefit of lower gas cost to be mined as well as quicker mining speed as opposed to the block approach. Also of note is that this method addresses the traversal issue with the approach of Tewari et al. (2018) and Alexopolous et al. (2017) as put forth by Chen et al. (2018). Instead of having to traverse the blockchain in search of a revoked certificate, the certificate itself would contain the direct address of where to access the smart contract that contains all of the relevant data regarding said certificate. Since smart contracts can update its data fields, the CA can simply update the status of a certificate to revoked; this removes the need for CRLs and eliminates the traversal issue certificate data will be directly accessible. Note that in order to use this PKI system, one needs to simply implement a quick verification script that matches the hash of the certificate on hand with that stored within the smart contract. This use of smart contracts helps our solution better fit the needs of Big Data applications in both terms of scalability and persistence. For one, it avoids the need for a traversal along the blockchain in order to verify the certificate. And secondly, there should be minimal persistent access issues to the data required for verification since said data is being held in a distributed network with no single point of failure.

PERFORMANCE AND RESULTS

This section consists of the performance and results from the experiments conducted on the CBPKI model. Three different models were used for testing, and these models consisted of one traditional PKI and two variants of the CBPKI model. The section is organized as follows. First, the experimental settings subsection details the environment and testing methods used for each model. Then, the results subsection summarizes the outcomes of the tests. And finally, the last subsection evaluates each model's level of security compared to one another.

Experimental Settings

The experiments conducted on our proposed work revolved around access times and the costs associated with operating different models. Our proposed model utilized many different software tools, and two different variants were used alongside one another for the tests. As mentioned earlier, three models in total were subjected to the same conditions, and their performance was evaluated based on three metrics relating to speed, time, and cost where applicable.

Implementation and Resources

The following software resources are required for the implementation of our project: Python Programming language, Python Packages Cryptography, Hashlib, and Web3.py, Heroku, Django web framework, Django API TastyPie, Solidity Smart Contract programming language, X.509 certificates, Ethereum Test Net Ropsten, MetaMask, Ethereum IDE Remix, Etherscan, and the Infura Ethereum API. Django and the API Tastypie were used to implement the CA as a Restful API; these two technologies were available at no cost. Django web apps can be hosted by use of Heroku, a cloud platform as a service, and Heroku could also be used at no cost by use of its free tier. The Solidity smart contract programming language is available at solidity.readthedocs.io. In addition, the Python programming language is also available at python.org, and the X.509 certificates being used can be imported by installing the pyca/cryptography package for python with pip. Also, the Hashlib python package, which is used to hash certificates, and Web3.py, which handles connections to the Ethereum network, are available through pip. Ethereum Test Net Ropsten is a test blockchain network for the cryptocurrency Ethereum. MetaMask is a free Ethereum wallet which is used to pay for the gas required to mine blocks or smart contracts. Ethereum IDE Remix is a free IDE for Ethereum smart contracts used to create and deploy said smart contracts.

Also, Etherscan is a website that can monitor transactions, smart contracts, and wallets. Finally, Infura is a blockchain API that allows a connection between the Ethereum network and a python script. Below in Table 1 is a compilation of all software tools used along with their associated costs.

Experimental Settings

Every test run used the same settings amongst each model; fifty runs were conducted for each model type. Across different models, the most similar conditions as possible to one another were used; each PKI model would be loaded with the same initial dataset of a 2 MB large certificate history list. This history list consisted of details regarding old certificates the CA had distributed in the past. Each model was also paired with a certificate revocation list that was 1MB big; this CRL comprised of half of the distributed certificates within the certificate history list. The traditional model stored the both the history and revocation lists within cloud platform. Instead, the CBPKI block storage version held the data from both lists within two separate blockchains while the smart contract version used smart contracts as storage devices.

Experimental Settings

The metrics used for judgment of both the traditional PKI and the CBPKIs will be revocation status access time. Certificate revocation status time within this chapter is defined as the time it takes for a given certificate's status to be verified. In addition, the two CBPKIs will have additional metrics regarding mining time of certificate data and gas costs of mining certificate data in their different storage methods. Mining time is the time it takes for the data storage method to be mined and thus publicly accessible

Table 1. Software tools used and associated costs

Software Tool	Cost
Python Programing Language	Free
Python Package: Cryptography	Free
Python Package: Hashlib	Free
Python Package:Web3.py	Free
Heroku Cloud Platform	Free Tier Used
Django Web Framework	Free
Django API: TastyPie	Free
X.509 Certificates	Free
Ethereum Test Net Ropsten	Free
Ethereum IDE Remix	Free
Etherscan	Free
Infura Blockchain API	Free
Solidity Smart Contract Programming Language	Free

on the blockchain network. Mining gas costs are the amount of gas or money required in order to pay miners to service the mining request.

PKI Models

During the experiments, three PKI models were used; these models were the traditional version, CBPKI block storage version, and the CBPKI smart contract version. The traditional version is hosted on a cloud service to limit variables, but it still holds all certificate data and certificate revocation lists together with its certificate authority. The two CBPKI models instead use a stateless CA hosted in the cloud while holding certificate data within the Ethereum blockchain network. However, they differ distinctly in how they store said data. The block storage version stores the certificate itself within the transaction data field while the smart contract version merely stores a hash of the certificate along with key certificate data inside smart contracts.

Results

Overall, there is a notable improvement in each area for the Cloud PKI implementation using smart contracts to store certificate data. While both CBPKIs allow for faster CRL retrieval than that of the traditional PKI, Table 2 shows that the smart contract version is faster than the block storage version. This is mostly likely due to how the block storage version requires a traversal across the blockchain in order to find the specific certificate while the smart contract version simply pulls the relevant validity data directly from the smart contract.

Regarding the mining times, there is a significant speedup when using smart contracts as displayed in Table 3. Smart contracts are smaller and thus do not need as many resources to complete mining when compared to blocks. According to the monitoring done by Etherscan, most of the time used for mining the block was spent waiting to be serviced. Mining times are highly dependent on network congestion which helps explain the variance between different run times.

Table 2. Certificate revocation status access times (ms)

Model	Mean
Traditional	208.52
Block Storage	142.97
Smart Contract	129.34

Table 3. Mining timings per certificate (ms)

Model	Mean
Block Storage	325.60
Smart Contract	21.36

The final category of tests centered on the mining gas cost to embed certificate data into the Ethereum network. As the Table 4 shows, the average cost of mining a smart contract is greatly reduced in comparison to that of an entire block. This average reduction of about $5 gives significant savings in the operational costs of a PKI utilizing blockchain technology. However, it pales in comparison to the traditional PKI since there is a negligible cost associated with storing a certificate in a database.

Security Analysis and Qualitative Comparison

The various public key infrastructure models covered in this chapter possess clear benefits and tradeoffs. Traditional models retain the discussed failings of certificate authorities; their large attack surface size makes them vulnerable and a target for infiltration and disruption. The weaknesses of these traditional models are well known which thus makes them quite susceptible to any attacks launched by malicious actors. However, they are cheap to operate in terms of issuing certificates, and apart from hosting and electricity costs, there is a negligible cost per certificate issuance. The CBPKIs both decrease this attack surface size significantly, and by making the CA stateless, they are able to piggyback on a cloud platform's security measures. But as noted in table 5 below, this comes at a significant operating cost.

Using blockchain technology as a storage device for certificates and certificate data does not come for free. Amongst the two CBPKI models, the smart contract variant outperformed the corresponding block storage version in every metric used. The smart contract version has the additional benefit of not requiring CRLs which has resulted in measurable performance boosts over the block storage version. Table 6 highlights the inherent tradeoffs between the two approaches. It is important to note that the

Table 4. Mining gas cost per certificate ($)

Model	Mean
Block Storage	5.97
Smart Contract	0.79

Table 5. Qualitative comparison of PKI models

PKI Model	Certificate Issuance Cost	CA Attack Surface Size
Traditional	Low	High
CBPKI Block Storage	High	Low
CBPKI Smart Contract	Medium	Low

Table 6. Qualitative comparison of CBPKI variants

PKI Model	CRL Size	Immutable Records
Block Storage	High	Yes
Smart Contract	Low	No

smart contract version does not necessarily possess immutability. Depending on the implementation, the smart contract data fields could be subject to malicious alteration. While the code behind the smart contract itself is immutable, the data it holds does not possess this attribute. Thus, even though the block storage method may be more costly and slower to use than the smart contract CBPKI model, the block storage model is more secure since its records are immutable. Another thing of note is that one must be careful in programming a smart contract; since the code itself is immutable, a bugged smart contract can run forever on the network.

CONCLUSION

Traditional PKIs contain issues regarding its certificate authorities that inhibit their ability to properly meet the demands of Big Data ecosystems. These issues can be addressed by usage of integrating current PKIs with existing blockchain and cloud technologies. Offloading the certificate authority to the cloud allows the PKI to tap into existing security measures against common attacks such as Denial of Service. In addition, storing certificate data in the blockchain enables persistent CRL and certificate data access while avoiding potential caching issues and DOS attacks. The aforementioned qualities provide an advantage for our CBPKI model over past models in fitting the needs, scalability and availability, of Big Data applications and ecosystems.

The results of the conducted tests reflect a significant performance increase of blockchain PKIs over traditional PKIs. Furthermore, the proposed solution of storing certificate data in smart contracts also outperformed the block storage version in terms of CRL access time, mining speed, and mining cost. However, this mining cost is a large source of the operational costs associated with blockchain PKIs, something that traditional PKIs don't possess.

Areas for further research are based on the study conducted by Chen et al. (2018). As noted earlier, the group of researchers highlighted three specific issues regarding the approach taken by Tewari et al. (2018) and Alexopolous et al. (2017). Additional study could be conducted in trying to resolve these issues without having to completely overhaul the PKI system as done by Chen et al. (2018). In addition, since there is a significant operating cost associated with storing certificate data on a blockchain network, further study in the reduction of this cost is also warranted.

Additional areas for future work involve the cloud portion of the CBPKI model. Routing requests for certificates through a cloud service opens up a plethora of possibilities for the application of cloud and alternative services. One such possibility is to further merge the CBPKI model with a machine learning model to automatically verify and revoke faulty certificates, potentially before the certificate has even been issued.

REFERENCES

Alexopoulos, N., Daubert, J., Mühlhäuser, M., & Habib, S. M. (2017). Beyond the Hype: On Using Blockchains in Trust Management for Authentication. *2017 IEEE Trustcom/BigDataSE/ICESS*.

Bakar, A. A., Ismail, R., Ahmad, A. R., & Manan, J. A. (2010). Trust Formation Based on Subjective Logic and PGP Web-of-Trust for Information Sharing in Mobile Ad Hoc Networks. *2010 IEEE Second International Conference on Social Computing*. 10.1109/SocialCom.2010.149

Chen, D., Le, J., & Wei, J. (2009). A Peer-to-Peer Access Control Management Based on Web of Trust. *2009 International Conference on Future Computer and Communication*. 10.1109/ICFCC.2009.77

Chen, J., Yao, S., Yuan, Q., He, K., Ji, S., & Du, R. (2018). CertChain: Public and Efficient Certificate Audit Based on Blockchain for TLS Connections. *IEEE INFOCOM 2018*.

Claeys, T., Rousseau, F., & Tourancheau, B. (2017). Securing Complex IoT Platforms with Token Based Access Control and Authenticated Key Establishment. *2017 International Workshop on Secure Internet of Things (SIoT)*. 10.1109/SIoT.2017.00006

Doukas, C., Maglogiannis, I., Koufi, V., Malamateniou, F., & Vassilacopoulos, G. (2012). Enabling data protection through PKI encryption in IoT m-Health devices. *2012 IEEE 12th International Conference on Bioinformatics & Bioengineering (BIBE)*.

Grimm, J. (2016). PKI: Crumbling under the pressure. *Network Security, 2016*(5), 5–7. doi:10.1016/S1353-4858(16)30046-0

Gupta, R., & Garg, R. (2015). Mobile Applications Modelling and Security Handling in Cloud-Centric Internet of Things. *2015 Second International Conference on Advances in Computing and Communication Engineering*.

Tewari, H., Hughes, A., Weber, S., & Barry, T. (2018). A blockchain-based PKI management framework. *NOMS 2018 - 2018 IEEE/IFIP Network Operations and Management Symposium*.

Zhou, J., Cao, Z., Dong, X., & Vasilakos, A. V. (2017, January). Security and Privacy for Cloud-Based IoT:Challenges. *IEEE Communications Magazine, 55*(1), 26–33. doi:10.1109/MCOM.2017.1600363CM

Chapter 6
Security Vulnerabilities, Threats, and Attacks in IoT and Big Data:
Challenges and Solutions

Prabha Selvaraj
https://orcid.org/0000-0002-0820-9146
VIT-AP University, India

Sumathi Doraikannan
https://orcid.org/0000-0003-2920-4640
VIT-AP University, India

Vijay Kumar Burugari
https://orcid.org/0000-0002-7871-2396
KL University, India

ABSTRACT

Big data and IoT has its impact on various areas like science, health, engineering, medicine, finance, business, and mainly, the society. Due to the growth in security intelligence, there is a requirement for new techniques which need big data and big data analytics. IoT security does not alone deal with the security of the device, but it also has to care about the web interfaces, cloud services, and other devices that interact with it. There are many techniques used for addressing challenges like privacy of individuals, inference, and aggregation, which makes it possible to re-identify individuals' even though they are removed from a dataset. It is understood that a few security vulnerabilities could lead to insecure web interface. This chapter discusses the challenges in security and how big data can be used for it. It also analyzes the various attacks and threat modeling in detail. Two case studies in two different areas are also discussed.

DOI: 10.4018/978-1-5225-9742-1.ch006

INTRODUCTION

The main usage of Big Data is identify and optimize the processes in business, financial trading, enhancing and optimizing smart cities and nations, better relationship management of customers, enhancing healthcare, sports, transport services etc. IoT refers to the connection of a huge number of physical devices that are located all around the world are now connected to the internet in such a way that data could be collected and shared. Nowadays, IoT make sure that the environment which we live in could be made as smart i.e. makes our homes, offices and vehicles to be smarter and chattier. In addition, a few sensors play a vital role in assessing the noise present in the environment, pollution in the environment. A variety of techniques are used by IoT devices in order to connect with other devices for data sharing. Technologies like Standard Wi-Fi, Bluetooth low energy, Local Terminal Equipment (LTE), satellite connections are used for connecting several devices at various levels. Low Power Wide Area Networks (LPWAN) initiated its deployment of IoT devices with Sigfox, LORa and recently LTE Cat-M, Narrow Band IoT (NB-IOT) as discussed by Usman Raza et al (2017) are used and a comparison is given below in the Figure 1.

Recently enterprises augment the dependency of IoT devices which leads to more focus in security of these devices. IoT security does not alone deals with the security of the device but it also has to care about the web interfaces, cloud services and other devices that interact with it. Hence enterprise IoT systems must be free from vulnerabilities M Mowbray (2017). Therefore, many researchers put their attention on detection and countermeasures of security attacks in IoT systems.

Challenges and Issues in Big Data

Big data challenges and issues are discussed below:

- **Privacy**: The large of volume of data need to be safeguarded in order to prevent the misuse of these big data stores.
- **Veracity**: Data must meet the trustworthiness.
- **Volume**: Large volume of data need to be stored and processed in case of big data but RDBMS tools cannot be used to store or process it. So the traditional SQL based queries are not used to solve this challenge, instead compression technology can be used to compress the data at rest and also in memory.

Figure 1. Comparison of LPWAN technologies

S.No.	Sigfox	LoRa	NB-IOT
1	Entire city is covered by a single base station.	Data rates are very low	Network coverage is good and it works well in indoors and dense urban areas
2	Low bidirectional latency	Latency time is very long	QoS is good and response time is fast
3	Small amount of data is sent very slowly	Depending on the device class, device has the restrictions on receiving the data	Sending a huge amount of data down to a device is hard
4	Mobility is difficult	It works well when the devices are in movement. Hence it keeps good track of assets on the move.	It suits for primarily static assets due to the issues like network and tower hand-offs

- **Analysis**: The huge data generated are from different types of sites and in different structure so analyzing such data will take lot of resource and time so scaled out architecture can be used for processing. Data can be splitted into small pieces and processed in different computers available in network, and then it can be aggregated.
- **Limitations of Traditional Encryption Approaches**: It is difficult to secure configuration information and log files with the encryption in big data.
- **Up to Date Transaction State**: Updating the state and data logs is very significant because we are handling with sensitive data so they need to be monitored.
- **Intrusion From the End Devices**: It is necessary to secure data not only in the route it ravels but also at the destination to which data is sent.
- **Real Time Data Consideration and Protection**: Many companies are handling real time data but they don't have periodic check so it is equally important to protect like maintaining historical transaction log.
- Securing the Storage Medium: It is necessary and important to secure data in storage as well as during transmission. So encryption plays an important role here.
- **Data Provenance**: Identification of data origin is another security measure is important in order to find the issues related to authentication and authorization and prevent it from attacks.

BIG DATA SECURITY ANALYTICS

The biggest risk of Big Data is privacy and security issues. The challenge is the personal data or the unauthorized data are getting tweaked by analytics engineers to produce erroneous results. The Big Data is a collection of large volume of interrelated data set which needs its own security from unauthorized access. The main motive of Big Data security analytics (BDSA) is to provide a complete and up-to-date IT activities which leads to security analytics in time and for data-driven decisions making. IT helps in improving security intelligence and provides way for security and intelligence agencies.

The main purpose of BDSA is to association and clustering for criminal analysis, criminal network analysis, Spatial-temporal analysis and visualization, providing security by using multilingual text analytics and Sentiment and affect analysis and analyzing cyber attacks.

Big Data Analytics is helpful in providing security in network as follows

- It helps in identifying the hidden abnormality by finding and predicting whether sources and destinations are malicious and suspicious, also analyzes network traffic pattern abnormality.
- It is used in detecting and predicting abnormality in access pattern of user especially when they access critical resources or activities, usage pattern, sudden change of server configuration and its abnormal behavior. It is also be used to improve access control mechanism.

The major network security methods are Anomaly and Misuse Detection. The anomaly detection is a challenging issue while detecting anomaly from giant data. The misuse of resource is a well-known and it slows down the system instead of directly affecting the system.

WHY BIG DATA ANALYTICS FOR SECURITY?

Big data analysis can transform security analytics in the following ways: In order to make a consolidated view of the required data it accumulates data from various internal organizational sources as well as external sources called as a vulnerability database. It helps to uncover unique patterns which are a source of many security issues to perform an in-depth analytics on the data using security intelligence. It provides a one dimensional view of all the related information, real time analysis of streaming data and uses previous results as a feedback to the system as a whole. In order to extract knowledge from huge volume of data collected, to manage threats efficiently, decision making using security intelligence they need to take big data approach for security management. To do this big data driven security system must provide infrastructure, analytical and visual tools, threat intelligence, reduce repetitive tasks, map the monitored data, high risk activity detection, etc.

HOW BIG DATA CAN HELP IN CYBER SECURITY?

- To enhance the security due to high risk and vulnerabilities in mining large amount of data.
- Big data tools support is needed to analyze cyber security and efficient handling of IP Network and its complexity. Handling structured/unstructured data and identifying anomalies is easier using it.
- The abnormal behavior can be discovered by classification and prediction using various machine learning algorithms. The probability to make correct assessment and classification by a model is more when there is more variability of data.
- Iterate through huge data quickly, adaptive model building, quick visual analysis, collection and storage of huge volume of data is made easier using commodity hardware and Hadoop framework and then breaches and malware are identified by applying analytic techniques. Also it eases the analysis of millions of data by cyber security analysis.
- The data models should have high predictive power to differentiate and analyze normal and abnormal network traffic automatically so that it can identify an active malware infection or a cyber attack.

VULNERABILITY

The term vulnerability refers to the weakness in a system or a design that allows an attacker to access unauthorized data so as to reduce a system's information assurance. It is considered as the combination of three components namely a system flaw, an intruder who accesses the flaw and the intruder's capability to utilize the flaw. Weaknesses might prevail in system hardware or software, policies and procedures used in the systems as discussed by Bertino et al (2010). Users also might be a weakness to the system. IoT systems comprise of two components namely hardware and software. Flaws might exist in both of these components during the design stage. Vulnerabilities could be categorized into three categories namely hardware vulnerabilities, software vulnerabilities and technical vulnerabilities.

Hardware Vulnerability

Vulnerabilities that occur in hardware components could be very hard and tricky. It is not possible to identify due to the compatibility of hardware and interoperability. Fixing it after the identification is not -so easy.

Software Vulnerability

The vulnerabilities that occur in operating systems, application software, communication protocols and device drivers are termed as software vulnerabilities. Certain factors such as human factors, software complexity etc contributes to the software design flaws.

Technical Vulnerability

Human behavior results in technical vulnerabilities.

Several vulnerabilities are shown in the below figure 2 and countermeasures have been explored in this section.

Insecure Web Interface

A control panel that fits between the users and software running on a web server is considered as a web interface and it is shown in the below figure 3. Web interfaces are very easy to build and modify. Security considerations have to be seen during the designing of web interfaces that are built into IoT devices since user interacts with the device. During this session, chances may be there for the attacker to gain an unauthorized access to the device.

From the above Figure 3, it is understood that few security vulnerabilities that could lead to the insecure web interface are

Figure 2. Vulnerabilities

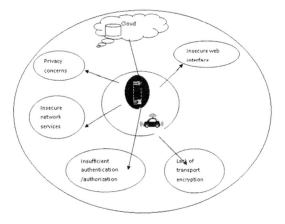

Figure 3. Insecure web interface

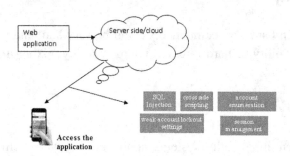

- **SQL Injection**: It is an application security weakness. Application's database is considered as a victim and it is done by attackers. They try to access or modify the data, alter an application's data-driven behavior. This action is performed by inserting unexpected SQL commands by hoaxing the application.
- **Credentials Exposed in Network Traffic**: User credentials such as passwords, access keys might be stored in default manner without the user's knowledge.
- **Account Enumeration**: This is one type of authentication process. In this process, the user is given information whether the user possess a valid account identifier or not.
- **Weak Default Credentials**: Users might use standard credentials such as default passwords which are easy to guess.
- **Cross-Site Scripting (XSS):** It is a client-side code injection attack. Malicious scripts could be executed into a legitimate website or web application.
- **Session Management:** Attackers try to steal the sessions and there is no need for authentication.
- **Weak Account Lockout Settings**: Account Lockout must be strong so as to lessen brute force password guessing attacks. A self-service unlock mechanism might be available only after a pre-determined period of time when the account gets locked after 3 to 5 unsuccessful login attempts. A relation must be maintained between the protection of account from unauthorized users and from being denied authorized access.

Certain countermeasures to be followed in order to protect against the threats that have been specified above are:

- Make sure that the strong passwords are needed.
- Ensure granular access control is in place when necessary.
- Make certain that credentials are protected properly.
- Deploy two-factor/three factor authentication wherever necessary.
- Employ secured password recovery mechanisms.
- Implement re-authentication process for sensitive features.
- Make use of options that are available for configuring password controls.

Inadequate Authentication/ Authorization

Mechanisms are found to be in futile. Authorization mechanisms are not much effective since the user could be able to access the data which is being secured. Authentication could be either in terms of username and password credentials or biometrics or user access card with photo and it is illustrated in the following Figure 4.

Certain security vulnerabilities that could lead to this issue are listed below:

- **Ineffective Mechanism of Two factor Authentication**: Implement Two factor Authentication Mechanisms.
- **Lack of Password Complexity:** Requires strong passwords.
- **Credentials are Not Protected Properly**: Granular access control is positioned whenever necessary.
- **Password Recovery is Not Proper:** Secured password recovery mechanisms have to be implemented.
- **An Increase in Privileges**: Need of ensuring re-authentication mechanisms.
- **Role Based Access Control:** Framing of proper privileges for accessing the account.
- Different methods of checking of insufficient authentication include.
- Need to monitor the network traffic for identifying the proper transmission of credentials.
- Assess whether the process needs re-authentication, since sensitive features might be used in the context.
- Evaluate the requirements when the new user sets the password. When the user is about to set the password, it has to check for factors like password complexity, previous history of password, expiry period of the password and password reset.
- Prior checking of the interface is needed in order to identify the possibility of various interfaces for the separation of roles.
- Analyze the features and categorize according to the roles.
- Examine the access controls and perform the testing process in order to modify the privileges if required.

Figure 4. Authentication factors

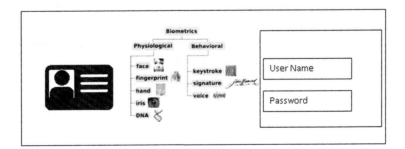

Insecure Network Services

Certain vulnerabilities that prevailed in the network during the time of accessing the IoT devices might lead to the chance of permitting the intruder to gain unauthorized access.

This might lead to certain vulnerabilities. They have been listed below:

- Denial-of-Service
- Vulnerable Services.
- Buffer Overflow.
- Open Ports through UPnP.
- Utilizable UDP Services.
- DOS through Network Device Fuzzing.

Some countermeasures that have to be followed against the threat are

- The network ports or services must be ensured in such a way that they must not be accessed from the internet through UPnP.
- Buffer overflow and futzing attacks could be overcome by providing proper secured services.
- Ports that are necessary only must be shown and made available.
- Certain services that are not vulnerable to DoS attacks might affect the devices as well as users on the network or other networks.

Inefficient Transmission Due to Not Encryption Data

When the data gets exchanged between IoT devices is not in encrypted form, intruder gets the chance of sniffing the data. Intruder tries to capture the data or the device gets compromised itself.

Certain vulnerabilities that raise the issue of inefficient transport encryption are

- Services those are unencrypted through the Internet and Local Network.
- Poor implementation of SSL/TLS.
- Improper configuration of SSL/TLS.

Few countermeasures that have to be implemented so as to prevent from the above mentioned threats are

- Encryption techniques could be applied for data with the help of SSL and TSL protocols during the transmission.
- Other industry standard encryption techniques have been applied for data encryption during the transmission in absence of SSL and TSL protocols.
- Proprietary encryption protocols must be avoided and usage of accepted encryption standards are applicable.

Privacy Concerns

User privacy is influenced when the features like confidentiality and integrity are considered as false provision and this leads to the accessing of sensitive data by the malicious parties. This occurs due to the following activities

- Improper protection of data that raised along with the privacy concerns.
- Review of data has to be done after the data collection. During this review, issues related to privacy might arise.
- Availability of automated tools so as to check for particular data patterns. This might specify the personal data or sensitive data collection.
- Vulnerabilities that could lead to the privacy concerns comprises of unnecessary personal information collection. Some counter measures that have to be implemented against the threats are data that has been collected has to be protected with proper encryption methods.
- Device and all its components have to be implemented properly to provide protection for personal information.
- The collected data has to prove for its sensitivity.
- Criticalness to the data has to be given and ensured.
- Ensuring that the data that has been collected is anonymous or could not be identified properly.
- Authorized individuals might be given access to collect personal information.
- Retention limits are allotted for the collected data.
- Providing the end users with the option "Notice and Choice" when the data collected is more than the expectations.
- Privacy by design could be addressed as a solution which supports the user for dynamic control, storage and sharing of data. Request that has been posted by the user must be analyzed in order to grant access for the data.
- Transparency could be provided so that users must know the corresponding persons those who manage and use the data.
- Necessity for data type, identification of the owner of the data, limit in accessing the data could be enforced in terms of policies
- A privacy broker could be implemented which is made to act as a proxy between the user and the network.

Insecure Cloud Interface

Security issues related to the cloud interface which is used to communicate with the IoT device. Authentication mechanisms are poor and data transmission is in unencrypted format that makes the device as accessible by the attacker. Certain vulnerabilities that lead to the issues are

- Exposure of credentials in the network traffic.
- Account lockout will not occur.
- Maintenance of Account details.

Few suggestions regarding the countermeasures towards the protection of threats are given below:

- A change in default username and password which is provided during the initial setup.
- A lock in the account must occur when there is failure in login attempts and this must happen when the attempts are 3 -5 in number.
- Recapitulation of user accounts could not be done with the help of password reset mechanisms.
- Make sure that the cloud-based web interface is not vulnerable to XSS, SQLi or CSRF.

Insecure Mobile Interface

An attacker might have a chance to access the device or the data of an IoT device due to the weak authentication or unencrypted data channels. Definite security vulnerabilities that might lead to this issue comprises of

- Security credentials are exposed in the network traffic.
- No Account lockout.
- Account Enumeration.

Few counter measures that could be implemented so as to protect threats are mentioned as below:

- During initial setup, default username and passwords would be given. This must be changed.
- Remuneration of account could be enhanced by providing various mechanisms such as password reset, security questions etc.
- The account gets locked automatically after 3-5 failed login attempts.
- Two/Three factor authentication could be made possible.
- Ensuring security credentials not to be shown when the system is open to wireless networks.

Insufficient Security Configurability

This issue prevails once when the users of the device are unable to modify the security controls. When the web interface does not have strong web interface, then this issue arises. Specific security vulnerabilities that leads to this issue are

- Password security options are missing
- Monitoring the security lacks and there is no security logging.
- Granular Permission model lacks.

The countermeasures that could be followed to protect against the threats are given below:

- Strong password policies to be maintained.
- Data at transit and data at rest must be encrypted.
- Distinguish of normal users and administrative users.
- Notification could be sent to users about the security events.

Insecure Software/Firmware

Whenever the device encounters the vulnerabilities, it should have the ability to get updated by it. There may be chances of insecure firmware/software due to the automatic updates of files and as well as the network connection might be prone to attackers. It is also observed that the software/firmware is insecure when it contains hardcoded sensitive data. Definite security vulnerabilities that lead to this issue involves

- Encryption is done for the updated file.
- To fetch updates, encryption is not used.
- Verification of updates before uploading is missing.
- Firmware consists of sensitive information.
- Update functionality is not clear.

Certain countermeasures have been recommended in order to protect against the threats are

- Make sure that the server that has been updated is secure.
- The file that has been updated must be transmitted through an encrypted connection.
- The device must have the ability to get updated and this is the most important factor.
- Before the uploading process, make sure that the update has to be signed and verified.

Poor Physical Security

Physical weaknesses are present when the device is ready to access the storage medium and as well as when USB ports or other external ports could be used to access the device. This might lead to unauthorized access to the device or the data. Vulnerabilities that could lead to this issue are listed below:

- Software could be accessed from USB ports.
- Storage media is removed.

Dos Attacks on L1-L3 Communication Protocol

The adversary target layer 1 or layer 3 and tries to send unnecessary data in bulk over the medium to interrupt wireless communication. On Medium Access Control layer, collusion is been created with legitimate packets in order to stop the proper communication. Certain IoT routing protocols like RIP, BGP, OSPF etc are open to security attacks such as spoofing attacks, impersonate attacks, falsification of routing packets or selective forwarding.

Generic Attacks

The upper layer protocols are prone to attacks and it grabs the attention of the adversaries. Using intelligent firewall system, IDS etc upper layer protocols could not be secured due to inadequate of low resources. Hence a robust security scheme is required to protect upper layer protocols.

Redirection Attack

Few perilous attacks that aim to interrupt communication protocols stack are ICMP redirect, ARP poisoning, DNS poisoning attack. In this type of attack, the adversary's aim is to first organize the communication packets then the data is changed or modified or bogus data is injected so as to wreck both the sender and receiver.

Recommendations for the users to follow certain countermeasures so as to protect against the threats are

- Storage data is encrypted at rest.
- Device could not be easily disassembled.
- Storage medium could not be removed easily.
- To access the device maliciously, USB ports or other external ports could not be used.

Issues With Interoperability

To avail the full prospective of the connected experience through various sensors or devices, an IoT ecosystem needs the most important attribute-interoperability so that the seamless programmability could be achieved. Hence, IoT is need of certain standards to facilitate a communicable, operable and programmable platform across various devices irrespective of model, manufacturer or industry. Therefore, a universal framework has to enable the interoperability across devices, applications and operating systems for the consumers so that IoT applications have been created as an adaptable, plug and play. Through this framework, flexibility and adaptability to the system could be provided in a small amount which in turn allows the interoperable attributes arise from the same source framework.

THREATS

Normally a threat is defined as an action that usually takes advantage of security weaknesses. It could be categorized as human threats and nature threats as per the discussions done by Dahbur et al (2011) and Rainer et al (2010). Certain threats that are common and pertain to any kind of applications are

- **Big Data on Threat:** Data could be collected from so many devices in the IoT. Hence there is a need for the vulnerability management solution and a threat detection solution.
- **IoT Encryption:** standard cryptographic algorithms are used to encrypt data at rest and in transit in order to maintain data integrity and data sniffing could be prevented from hackers. Several IoT devices and hardware profiles confines the ability to follow standard encryption processes and protocols.
- **IoT Network Security:** Network that connects IoT devices to back-end systems has to be protected and secured. A set of communication protocols and standards have been maintained to protect and secure the network. Features such as firewalls, intrusion prevention, intrusion detection systems S Raza et al (2013), antivirus and anti malware etc are considered to be the endpoint security features.

- **IoT Public Key Infrastructure:** This is the process of issuing a complete X.509 digital certificate and cryptographic key functionalities such as public/private key generation, key distribution, key management and key revocation facilities. Digital certificates could be loaded onto IoT devices during the manufacturing period. These certificates get enabled by third party PKI software suites.
- **IoT API Security:** API security is most important factor for maintaining data integrity. Data that flows between edge devices and back-end systems has to be secured and only authorized devices, developers and apps communicates with APIs.
- **IoT Security Analytics:** Specific attacks and intrusions could be detected. Definite solutions that include machine learning techniques, artificial intelligence and big data techniques could be provided for predictive modeling and anomaly detection. Security must be provided to data that has been collected and as well as aggregated from various IoT devices and provides alerts on specific activities or when activities fail in establishing policies. Machine learning is used along with a neural network-based framework for authentication of wireless nodes by analyzing the variations in RF properties. The hybrid prediction model consists of clustering-based outlier detection and a machine learning-based classification model

Privacy and security threats in IoT could be classified based on the four features and it is shown below in Figure 5.

Threats pertained to Cloud are listed as follows:

- In-Cloud data leaks.
- SQL Injection.
- Attacks on unsecure Cloud Interface
- Poorly configured SSL/TSL.
- Out of date legacy devices.

Threats related to hardware are listed as follows:

- Unauthorized access.
- Lack of security.
- Malicious software updates.
- Expired legacy devices.

Figure 5. Threats in IoT

Cloud	Cloud/Web Insecurity SQL Injection, In-cloud data leaks, Poor configuration of SSL/TSL, Cross-site scripting
Application	Unsecured Mobile apps, no device lock out, weak / improper credentials, Lack of Multifactor Authentication
Communication	Denial of service, Buffer overflow, Lack of security configuration
Device and Hardware	Physical insecurity, personal information is collected unnecessarily

Definite threats that arise during the communication process are given below:

- Lack of transport encryption.
- DDoS attacks.
- Vulnerable services over unsecure network.

Application threats that occurs in IoT are given below

- No role based access.
- Application or password lockouts are disabled.
- Unnecessary personal data is collected and shared over the network.
- Password recovery mechanisms might not be proper.
- Attacks on unsecure mobile/PC and applications.

Privacy Threats

Identification: This is one kind of threat in associating an identifier with data about him. The threat thus leads to associating an identity to a privacy violating context and thus it leads to aggravation and enabling of other threats like combination of different data sources or profiling and tracking of individuals. This identification threat is the most prevailing threat in the information processing phase since huge amount of information is focused in a central place outside of the subject's control.

Localization and tracking

This determines and records the person's location through time and space. Tracking is the process of identifying and binding continuous localizations to one individual. Nowadays, tracking is done with the help of various means such as internet traffic, cell phone location or GPS stalking which has been referred in Voelcker J. (2006). Various privacy violations like leakage of private information such as an illness are being let out as mentioned by Chow CY and Mokbel MF (2009). This type of information leakage is treated as a violation since they don't have control over their location information. In addition, it might be unaware of its disclosure or the information might be used and joined in an unsuitable context. In the instantaneous physical immediacy, violations might not arise due to the localization and tracking. Conventionally this approach seems to be a threat in the information processing segment. Therefore, due to this evolution of IoT, threat might be changed and intensified in three ways:

- When data collection process seems to be inert, more persistent and less meddling, users turn out to be unaware of tracing and the risks involved in that.
- Due to this development of IoT, the location-based services could be improved much and the progress is seen in accuracy and these services get expanded to indoor environments too.
- Data trails occur during the interaction of system with smart devices. Hence, the user is at their risk due to this service.

The threat of this service occurs in the communication phase. In this scenario, the subject is traced in various situations in which the subject might erroneously distinguish the physical separation from others either by obstacles like wall or door, as privacy.

- Privacy-violating interface and presentation

Ziegeldorf et al (2014) discussed that this deals with the process of dissemination of private and secured information through the public medium or revealing the information to an unsolicited audience. This could be drafted as shoulder surfing. Various IoT applications such as healthcare, medical, transportation etc needs proper communication with the user. In certain scenarios, chances are there for the information required by the user might be displayed with the help of smart devices which is considered to be as threat. For example, recommender systems store the information that brings out the interest of an individual when posted in social networking sites. Due to the close connection of interaction and presentation mechanisms, threat seems to occur in the homonymous phases of our reference model. There are two challenges that have to be addressed.

Automatic detection of privacy-sensitive content must be solved. For example, when the sender wants to share the information with the receiver, the information must be shared through the medium that could be either public or private. Scoping should be identified. One has to identify the scope of the presentation medium since the information has to be shared among the specific subgroup of recipients or through a specified physical area. The development of platform with highly innovative and scalable service by the integration of cloud computing and advances in IoT to provide security and privacy.

Profiling

Threat occurs during the compilation of information that gets recorded about each individual so as to find out interests by associating with other data and profiles. This is mainly used in various recommender systems, newsletter and as well as in optimization of customer demographics and interests. Profiling leads to various privacy violations such as display of advertisements, social engineering, erroneous automatic decisions etc. Nowadays the profiles that have been stored are given to several marketplaces which are a privacy violation. Threat in profiling occurs in the propagation phase. When the information is broadcasted to third parties or towards the subject itself threats might occur. This IoT development leads to the data sources outburst as more and more things get connected. Data collection increases tremendously both by qualitatively and quantitatively. Moreover, location and tracking threats further stimulates the potential for profiling and danger from uncertain data-selling business. Various approaches that have been followed to preserve privacy could also be implemented for IoT devices. This needs substantial efforts for revision of metrics and redesign of algorithms.

Inventory Attacks

The information about the subsistence and the features of personal things that has been collected in an unauthorized manner could be referred as the inventory attacks. When the legitimate users are in the process of responding to the posted information, chances are there for the non-legitimate parties to exploit this information and compile a set of things and present it on the medium. Specific features such as communication speeds, reaction times and other unique features etc could be used to identify the legitimate users from illegitimate users. Various attacks like fingerprinting; modifying the information shall be mounted submissively. Due to the tremendous development in communication facilities of things, threats occur in the information collection phase. With the advent of new technologies, the brunt on this type of threat is not clear. Due to the diversified new technologies in the IoT, more smart devices become smart and in addition, fingerprinting attack becomes more dangerous. The advent in new technologies results in various configurations of web browsers too. Due to this, the standards for communication and interaction must be improved in order to ignore such type of differences. Privacy violations based on inventory attacks might happen. A comprehensive inventory attack could be used to profile the anti burglar system down to each last sensor. Law enforcement and other authorities could use the attack to conduct searches. Private information is revealed by the possession of special information such as health, interests etc. Certain efforts for industrial surveillance could be complemented through an inventory attack. The attack vector could be improved by increasing propagation of wireless communications, end-to-end connectivity and more complicated queries. Definite ways that could be followed to prevent the inventory attacks are

- Smart devices must be able to authenticate queries and response to those queries could be done by legitimate parties.
- Mechanisms that make sure about robustness against fingerprinting might be required to put off passive inventory attacks.

Few inventory attacks might certainly be difficult to defy. Privacy enabled technologies ensured to protect privacy, makes fingerprinting easier, leaved hiding in the ample presently as the most feasible but a very clear suboptimal solution. But, an IoT system that reveals inclusive information about its owner's possessions is not likely to gain acceptance.

Lifecycle Transitions

When smart devices disclose private information, privacy issues occur. Issues might arise during the transmission of photos, videos found in cameras or smart phones. Threats occur during the information collection and storage phase. Certain issues aggravates due to the two developments in the IoT.

Information gets accumulated in product history logs when the smart device gets interacted with a number of persons, systems and other devices etc. But this type of storage could be exposed to threat since the personal information such as location; name etc might reveal the lifestyle of the person. A need might arise for the implementation of a convenient privacy lifecycle management mechanism when there is an automatic detection of lifecycle transitions of a smart thing. Few examples such as automatic cleaning of all items includes the deletion of private information such as medicine prescription in a smart rubbish bin, borrowing a smart device from others needs to lock the private information provisionally and once when it is returned to the owner, the information has to be unlocked so that the user can use it impeccably.

Linkage

When data sources from different systems are linked together to form the data in such a way that the subject did not reveal to the previously isolated sources. Privacy violations arise during the bypassing privacy protection mechanisms, when the risks of unauthorized access and leaks of private information also increases as systems collaborate to combine data sources. The common approach of privacy protection is that it works on anonymized data only, however the task of merging various sets of anonymous data might facilitate re-identification through unforeseen effects. Threats get propagated due to the innovations in the IoT field for two reasons.

Horizontal integration will ultimately connect systems from various companies and manufacturers so as to form a heterogeneous distributed system of systems that distributes new services that no single system could provide on its own. Successful cooperation needs the exchange of data and controls between the parties. Local data flows more in horizontal integration rather than vertical integration. The linkage of systems might provide data collection in the IoT even less clear than what is expected from the forecasted passive and unobtrusive data collection by smart devices.

Three technical challenges for privacy enhanced systems-of-systems have been identified. Information sharing between the systems needs transparency so as to gain user acceptance. Permission models and access control must be adapted to stakeholders that combine various systems. Data anonymization techniques must work on combined systems and be robust against combination of many different sets of data.

- **Attacks in IoT:** It could be categorized into three categories and they are discussed below.
- **Attacks Against IoT Devices:** Any device that is been connected in the network is treated as a target for a potential attacker.
- **Attacks Against Communications**: In this process, messages that pass between the source and destination could be exposed for attacks. This type of attack is considered to be very dangerous since the messages could be captured and manipulated. Hence, all these threats put the trust at risk during the transmission of data and information.

UNAUTHENTICATED COMMUNICATION

Few IoT devices provide software updates automatically. Without authentication and encryption, this approach is inadequate because the update mechanism could be disabled. Moreover, many IoT devices might not use the process of authentication in the communication process.

Unencrypted Communications: Plain text is used for communication purpose instead of encrypted text. The adversary would have keen interest in observing the communication process.

Lack of Mutual Authentication and Authorization: A device that permits an unidentified party to modify its code or to access the data is treated as a threat. The device could identify that the owner is present or absent, make possible the installation process or cause its core IoT function to be compromised.

Network Isolation is missing: IoT devices are prone to risks and attacks inside the home since the devices in the home network might get connected with other devices on the same network. This might create a great impact on behavior of unrelated devices.

- **Date Leaks:** There are chances of leakage of data in cloud and IoT devices as suggested by Mirza Abdur Razzaq et al (2017).
- **Leaks From the Cloud:** Data breach occurs due to an external attack or an insider threat. Moreover, if users work on weak authentication or encryption methods, data gets compromised.

- **Leaks From and Between Devices**: Data such as the names of people in a home, the geographical location of a home or the products that a consumer purchases might be observed from other devices or devices on the same network.
- **Attacks Against the Masters**: The responsibility of a master is to issue and manage devices. Masters could be either service providers, manufacturers or IoT solution providers. Their responsibility is to keep the data safe and secure.

Attacks might arise with the following categories:

- **Authentication**: This is the process of checking for mutually in order to share the information and in addition to assure the data that is to be shared among the peers originates from the trusted source.
- **Access Control**: Unauthorized nodes are prevented.
- **Confidentiality**: information is protected particularly when it is shared over a medium which is public.
- **Integrity**: This works on data protection and ensures that there are no modifications in the data.
- **Availability**: During this process, data is made available on demand or request of users.

Attacks could be on IoT devices has been discussed by Abomhara and Køien (2015) and it has been illustrated as shown in the below Figure 6.

PHYSICAL ATTACKS

This tampers the hardware and other components. Tamper resistance is the need for the security requirement. Various examples are layout reconstruction, micro probing attacks etc.

Micro probing attacks: Microscopic needles could be attached on to the internal wiring of a chip. These needles are used for finding out the secrets that are intended to leave the chip or it could be used for fault attacks.

Knockoff Smart Devices

Manufacturers could consider smart device knockoffs for cloning. Such type of cloning lacks in many functionalities. Users should be aware of apprehensive manufacturers because they might change the functionality's of the device to steal, eavesdrop and the user's activity is monitored.

Figure 6. Attacks in IoT devices

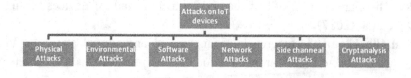

Firmware replacement attack: A malicious piece of software has been installed by the user to download. The drive which has been infected could be reflashed.

DIRECT PHYSICAL INFORMATION EXTRACTION

Devices could be physically accessed with the help of extracting security credentials. This kind of breach is mainly done by an employee who worked in the institution and left the organization. IoT device could be exposed to the environment could be vulnerable and this could be handled by making a strong and transparent SLA between the consumer and service provider.

SOFTWARE ATTACKS

The communication interface is used to exploit the vulnerabilities through this attack. It could be presented as below: They are

- Virus
- Trojan Horse
- Logic Bombs
- Worms
- Denial of service

NETWORK ATTACKS

The different types of network attacks are discussed below

- **Eavesdropping:** There is a possibility for an adversary to get the secret key that has been used for data encryption over the network. The network protocol identification or VPN connection type could provide the adversary to conduct an attack.
- **Man-in-the-Middle Attack:** When the data is transmitted from the source to destination, this attack takes place. The key that has been shared between the sender and received is retrieved by the attacker and it is used to create a bogus data. Broadcasting of data could make the server to authenticate the packet. The attack that happens at a particular instant reveals the network parameters so that the network topology could be revealed.
- **Routing Attacks:** The network adversary might have a keen interest in gathering the knowledge about the router used in the network. Routers usually share the information and hence it becomes the target for the attackers. Strong security measures have to be deployed among the borders, since the network consists of heterogeneous components and protocols. Since the VPN connections are not secure enough between the provider and the consumer, then the Generic Routing Encapsulation channel established to transmit and receive packets are vulnerable to routing attacks.
- **Distributed DOS Attacks:** An attacker conducts the Denial of service or Distributed Denial of Service attack (DoS/DDoS) would make all the resources to be consumed. In this, attacker

obtains the unused legitimate IP address. A large number of network packets have been sent by the attacker by masquerading behind the legitimate source IP address for further processing. The authenticity of each packet has to be verified and this process has to be done by the network server. But this network server might be little busy in verifying the network resources. Due to this, traffic increases tremendously and services might be waiting to get serviced by the server. This is known as Denial of Service (DoS). If such type of attacks occurs in distributed network due to load balancing and elastic nature, a distributed Dos attack might take place in the system.

This type of attack makes the system to shut down completely by consuming the resources. These attacks might lead the entire home network to risk and the network could be seized.

- **Node Outage Attack:** This attack occurs due to the stopping of functionality of components of IoT devices. This attack usually prevails in the physical layer and the network layer. This attacks creates a great impact on node services such as reading, gathering and launching the functions. The effects of this attack are stopping the node services such as reading, gathering and launching the functions.
- **Cryptanalysis Attacks**: In this attack, the encryption key is used to obtain the plaintext. This attack is focused on the cipher text. Examples of cryptanalysis attacks include cipher text only attack, known-plaintext attack, chosen-plaintext attack, man-in-the-middle attack, etc.
- **Node Subversion:** This one kind of active attack where the attacker could get the cryptographic keys from a capture node. Extracting the information is possible only when the device is first captured.
- **Traffic Analysis:** It is treated as a high level attack. The data is been intercepted and examined during the encryption process which therefore could not be decrypted.
- **Camouflage:** The attacker introduces a fake edge node or attacks an unauthorized node to hide at the edge level. Traffic is analyzed in order to obtain and manipulate packets.
- **Node Replication Attacks:** Network performance is degraded and the attacker could easily be corrupted or packets diverted that arrives at the replicated node. A new node is inserted to an existing node through duplicating node's ID number. Certain attacks that are common to conventional network are also applicable in IoT.

They could be listed as

- **Sinkhole Attack:** The traffic is been decoyed from an area through a node that has been compromised in which selective forwarding could follow with the attacker and it is been decided the type of data that must be allowed through.
- **Sybil Attack:** Attackers might exist in various places in such a way that a single node possesses multiple identities to others in the network.
- **Wormhole Attack:** The messages that are received in one part of the network over a low latency link have to be replayed to other parts of the network and this process is done by the adversary.
- **Hello Flood:** The attacker makes every node to spot it as their parent. The nodes are out of range and due to this, a lot of packets get lost. In addition, routing loops could be set up through spoofing routing updates, with two nodes being attacked and packets are redirected to each other.

- **Acknowledgement Spoofing:** In this attack, the network links is either strengthened or weakened by the attacker so that packets get lost from a node. This is mainly used for a selective forwarding attack.
- **Side Channel Attacks:** When the side channel information could be retrieved from the encryption device, there exists a side channel attack. In this case neither the cipher text nor the plain text is encrypted. Various parameters such as radiation of various sorts, power consumption and timing information etc are produced by the encryption devices. The key that has been used in the device might be recovered with the help of this attack. Few attacks such as fault analysis attacks, electromagnetic attacks, timing attacks, power analysis attacks etc are classified under this category.
- **Timing Attack:** User's private information is obtained by vigilantly determining the time it takes for the user to carry out cryptographic operations.

The basic assumptions of timing analysis are

- Run time of a cryptographic operation and key are dependent to some extent.
- Noise injection approach is used to make the timing attack less feasible.
- Branch equalization i.e., the computation could be done in two branches might take the same amount of time and to do this, software approaches are utilized.
- Large numbers of encryptions are carried out, in which the key does not change. To perform the timing attacks, challenge response protocol seems to be a perfect approach.
- Time could be measured with the known error. The smaller the error, then the fewer measurements is needed.

Countermeasures for timing attacks could be framed and there are two approaches that are currently in use. They are noise injection and branch equalization. Noise injection approach is used to weaken the power of timing attack, but it does not defeat it whereas the branch equalization defeats the attack.

Fault Attacks: This is one of the predominant and effective attacks that are performed against the cryptographic hardware devices such as smart cards. This attack provides many opportunities to attack a cryptosystem. The probability of a fault attack and the adversary capabilities are dependent. Normally, a fault model should at least identify the following aspects:

- The time and location on which the fault occurs during the execution of a cryptographic module could be attained by an attacker.
- The length of the data is affected by a fault.
- The perseverance of the fault is identified; the fault might be transient or permanent.
- The type of the fault is determined.

There are two major kinds of fault side channels.

- Channels might be made by computational faults that occur during the cryptographic computation in an attacked module. These faults could be either intentional or random.
- Channels might be induced by sending an intentionally corrupted input data to the attacked module.
- A fault attack is considered to a successful when the cryptographic modules or devices need two steps namely the fault injection and the fault exploitation. This is illustrated in the below figure

Fault Injection Step: A fault is been injected at the appropriate time during the process. It depends on the devices' hardware. When the smart card is put in abnormal conditions then faults could be induced in a smart card. Few parameters could be listed as

- Abnormal and abrupt low or high voltage
- Clock
- Temperature
- Radiations
- Light

Fault Exploitation Step: This procedure exploits the erroneous result or unexpected behavior. It depends on the software design and implementation. When a product has to be designed and specified, fault attacks are considered to be real and big threats for any secure token. Both hardware and software approaches were designed for creating countermeasures and protection mechanisms against fault attacks. The strength of countermeasures has been deployed and they are used to devise and analyze fault attacks.

Electromagnetic Attacks: Electro Magnetic Analysis (EMA) attacks can also be separated into two main categories: Simple Electro Magnetic Analysis (SEMA) and Differential Electro Magnetic Analysis (DEMA)

Power Analysis Attack: This attack is particularly effective and successful in attacking smart cards. This is treated as the most powerful attacks for straightforward implementation of symmetric and public key ciphers. This attack is divided into simple and differential power analysis. The main objective of the simple power analysis is to deduce from the power trace in which a specific instruction is being executed at a certain time and identify the input and output of this process. As a result of this, the adversary must possess a deep knowledge in the implementation procedure to mount such an attack. But, on the other hand differential power analysis does not require any knowledge of the implementation process. This attack is one of the most powerful attacks and it requires very little resources for mounting.

COUNTERMEASURES COULD BE CLASSIFIED INTO TWO BROAD CATEGORIES

Signal Strength Reduction: Certain techniques include the redesign of circuit so as to reduce accidental emanations. The strength of compromising signals could be reduced with the help of shield and physical secured zones.

Signal Information Reduction: Definite techniques were implemented for randomization and/or regular key refreshing within the computation in order to reduce the efficiency of statistical attacks. Several common cyber attacks and how the threats rise to an extraordinary level with the potential of IoT have been given below.

Botnet: It is defined as a group of systems that is joined together with the idea of remotely taking control and issues malware. Botnet operators take over the control with the help of Command-and-Control-Servers. Criminals all over the world use this, so as to expose online banking data, filch private information, DDoS attacks or for spam and phishing emails. Due to this threat, many devices are found to be in a dangerous situation. Thing bots and botnets have two main features in common:

Both are connected through internet and data transfer is done automatically

By applying anti-spam technology it is easy to identify the device that sends thousands of similar emails, but however, it is very difficult to speck all the devices that sends the emails since these devices belong to the botnet.

Main-in-the-Middle Attack: The aim of the adversary is to intercept and intrude the communications between two separate systems. This is considered to be a hazardous attack since the two parties might be in a belief that they gets communicated directly each other. Yet, both the parties might be in an illusion that the messages are legitimate messages. Examples of this attacks could be devices that exists in industries like machinery, tools or vehicles to safe connected objects such as smart TV's or garage door openers.

Data and Identity Theft: Hackers try to access the data and money with their knowledge on various hacking techniques.

Internet connected devices such as mobile phone, iPad, laptop etc might be in the hands of malicious thieves to access the private data that is kept confidentially.

Social Engineering: Through this method, cybercriminals found the way of human-to-human interaction to facilitate the user to disclose the sensitive information. Criminals deceive the user by accessing the personal information from the computer by installing malicious software. Due to this, the control would be given to the criminals. Phishing email is done in order to access the information through these social engineering hacks. The other way of attacks is the redirection of websites like banking or shopping sites that looks similar to the legitimate websites so as to access and store the personal details of the user.

Denial of Service: This attack occurs when a request put forth by the user is not services due to the unavailability. Usually unavailability refers to infrastructure that cannot be managed due to the overload of the capacity. In a Distributed Denial of Service (DDoS) attack, a large number of systems maliciously attack one target. This could be done with the help of a botnet, in which many devices could be implemented in order to post the request for the service at the same time. This attack leads to the loss of reputation for the company since it still cost a lot of time and money. Due to this issue, customers might switch to a competitor. Often a DoS attack provides itself to crusader and blackmailers.

CASE STUDY

Challenges of IoT in "Industrial Automation"

Connecting the sensors at the basic level to the internet in order to bring the industrial devices all at one place is a challenging task (Tomas Lennvall et al) 2017. Several challenges that arise in Industrial Automation that drew more attention of researchers are

- Normally there exists the internet connection at the highest level, and firewall is used for protection. More focus is required while looking into the connection of IoT devices since chances might be there for the new security threats that affect the whole industrial system Pal Varga et al (2017).
- How to protect privacy and create a secure environment within the industrial automation?
- Installation of IP cameras creates the denial of service attacks, smart appliances that leaks WiFi passwords, unauthorized control of the automated vehicle used inside the industry and unauthenticated use of TV streaming devices.

- A crucial and critical core functionality of the automation system is the maximum availability of the plant during the minimal downtime. This high availability facility is needed from the bottom most level of the automation system i.e right from the sensors and actuators.
- It is also significant to be clear with the process of different protocol layers. Therefore, the major challenging task is to make sure of reliability and in addition to perform the end-to-end congestion control in the transport layer. It is observed that the Transmission Control Protocol (TCP) is inadequate for IoT for various reasons and in addition a considerable amount of latency is also produced.

The following Figure 7 illustrates the attacks that might happen in each layer of industrial automation systems.

Case Study: Smart Homes- Attacks, Threats and Countermeasures

It is observed that an additional comfort, security and enhanced ecological sustainability could be obtained through the deployment of smart home. For example, smart devices used in the smart homes make use of sensors and intelligent operating decisions could be made with the help of web-based data source Jacob Wurm et al (2014). When the attacker tries to open the door in order to steal, the attacker might block the alarm that could be raised during the opening of door. Sensors implanted in the lights, fans, air conditioning systems predict the occupancy of humans by tracking their temperature, location so that the comfort level is obtained by saving the energy. The predominant factor is that the smart home could assist the independent living for the aged people. Attacks, threats and countermeasures are shown in the below Figure 8.

Certain scenarios might happen due to the introduction of a product in the market by IoT startups might move out of business or discard the support extended. Those devices are treated as "zombie devices "since it will remain in the network without any support during the patches of security and safety.

Figure 7. Attacks in industrial automation systems

Layers	Attacks	Countermeasures
Application	System integrity, Communication channel might be disrupted	Frequent integrity checking could be done by applying security algorithms and communication channel could be monitored
Data Processing and Storage	Exhaustion type of attacks	A novel Prevention system could be designed
Network Layer	Issues related to data transfer	Strong security could be applied onto the data during transit and storage
Smart sensors, actuators	Denial of Service, Tampering , Eavesdropping	Prevention mechanism must be made stronger.

Figure 8. Smart home

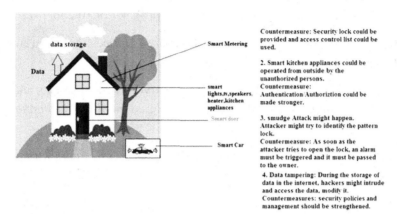

There might be a possibility of interaction with these devices from the external world and that has to be monitored and the other way is to disable these types of devices remotely by the manufacturers when it is found that the device has no support. Smart health in the home could be managed mainly for the old age people by the wearable sensors in order to monitor their health after surgery. The data thus collected might be a backdoor vulnerability for the hospital. The data thus collected might help the patients when their health conditions triggers to critical conditions. Data thus collected might be exposing to intruders for further modifications. Intruders also found their way to identify the devices that are connected with the help of search engines that are exclusively for the internet connected devices.

CONCLUSION

A number of challenges, security, threats and attacks have been recognized in IoT and Big Data. This chapter gives an overview of challenges, issues and security threats. The countermeasures against security threats from the prevention of any smash to IoT network have been also discussed in detail. In addition, a simple case study on industrial automation system has been discussed.

REFERENCES

Abomhara, M., & Køien, G. M. (2015). Cyber Security and the Internet of Things: Vulnerabilities, Threats, Intruders and Attack. *Journal of Cyber Security*, *4*, 65–88. doi:10.13052/jcsm2245-1439.414

Adat & Gupta. (2018). Security in Internet of Things: issues, challenges, taxonomy, and architecture. *Telecommunication Systems: Modeling, Analysis, Design and Management, 67*(3-4), 423-441.

Bertino, E., Martino, L. D., Paci, F., & Squicciarini, A. C. (2010). Web services threats, vulnerabilities, and countermeasures. In Security for Web Services and Service-Oriented Architectures. Springer.

Chatterjee, Das, Maity, & Sen. (2019). *RF-PUF: Enhancing IoT Security Through Authentication of Wireless Nodes Using In-Situ Machine Learning*. Academic Press.

Chen, H., Chiang, R. H., & Storey, V. C. (2012). Business intelligence and analytics: From big data to big impact. *Management Information Systems Quarterly, 36*(4), 4. doi:10.2307/41703503

Chow, C. Y., & Mokbel, M. F. (2009). Privacy in location based services: A system architecture perspective. *SIGSPATIAL Special, 1*(2), 23–27. doi:10.1145/1567253.1567258

Dahbur, K., Mohammad, B., & Tarakji, A. B. (2011). A survey of risks, threats and vulnerabilities in cloud computing. In *Proceedings of International conference on intelligent semantic Web-services and applications.* ACM.

Jindal, Jamar, & Churi. (2018). Future and Challenges Of Internet Of Thing. *International Journal of Computer Science & Information Technology, 10*(2). doi:10.1145/1980822.1980834

Khan, R., Khan, S. U., Zaheer, R., & Khan, S. (2012). Future Internet: The Internet of Things architecture, possible applications and key challenges. *Proc. IEEE 10th Int. Conf. Frontiers of Information Technology*, 257–260.

Lafuente, G. (2015). The big data security challenge. *Network Security, 2015*(1), 12–14. doi:10.1016/S1353-4858(15)70009-7

Lennvall, Gidlund, & Akerberg. (2017). Challenges when bringing IoT into Industrial Automation. *IEEE Africon Proceedings.*

Mahmood, T., & Afzal, U. (2013). Security analytics: Big data analytics for cybersecurity: A review of trends, techniques and tools. *2nd National Conference on Information Assurance (NCIA)*, 129–134. 10.1109/NCIA.2013.6725337

Mowbray, M. (2017). *Detecting Security Attacks on the Enterprise Internet of Things: an Overview.* Hewlett Packard Enterprise Development LP.

Nia, A. M., & Jha, N. K. (2016). A Comprehensive Study of Security of Internet-of-Things. *IEEE Transactions on Emerging Topics in Computing.*

R Cloud Security Alliance Big data Analytics for Security Intelligence. (n.d.). Retrieved from http://cloudsecurityalliance.org/research/bigdata

Rainer, R. K., & Cegielski, C. G. (2010). *Introduction to information systems: Enabling and transforming business.* John Wiley & Sons.

Raza, S., Wallgren, L., & Voigt, T. (2013). SVELTE: Real-time intrusion detection in the Internet of Things. *Ad Hoc Networks, 11*(8), 2661–2674. doi:10.1016/j.adhoc.2013.04.014

Raza, U., Kulkarni, P., & Sooriyabandara, M. (2017). *Low Power Wide Area Networks: An Overview.* Retrieved from https://arxiv.org/pdf/1606.07360.pdf

Razzaq, M. A., Qureshi, M. A., Gill, S. H., & Ullah, S. (2017). Security Issues in the Internet of Things (IoT): A Comprehensive Study. *International Journal of Advanced Computer Science and Applications, 8*(6), 383–388.

Stergioua, C. (2018). Secure integration of IoT and Cloud Computing. *Future Generation Computer Systems, 78*, 964–975. doi:10.1016/j.future.2016.11.031

Varga, P., Plosz, S., Soos, G., & Hegedus, C. (2017). Security Threats and Issues in Automation IoT. *Proc. IEEE 13th International Workshop on Factory Communication Systems (WFCS)*. 10.1109/WFCS.2017.7991968

Voelcker, J. (2006). Stalked by satellite - an alarming rise in GPS-enabled harassment. *IEEE Spectrum, 43*(7), 15–16. doi:. doi:10.1109/MSPEC.2006.1652998

Wurm, J. (2014). Security Analysis on Consumer and Industrial IoT Devices. Academic Press.

Yin, C., Zhang, S., Xi, J., & Wang, J. (2017). An improved anonymity model for big data security based on clustering algorithm. *Concurrency and Computation, 29*(7), 3902–3904. doi:10.1002/cpe.3902

Zhang, C., Shen, X., Pei, X., & Yao, Y. (2016). Applying big data analytics into network security: Challenges, techniques and outlooks. *IEEE International Conference on Smart Cloud (SmartCloud)*, 325–329. 10.1109/SmartCloud.2016.62

Ziegeldorf, J. H., Morchon, O. G., & Wehrle, K. (2014). Privacy in the Internet of Things: Threats and Challenges. *Security and Communication Networks, 7*(12), 2728–2742. doi:10.1002ec.795

Chapter 7
Threat Hunting in Windows Using Big Security Log Data

Mohammad Rasool Fatemi
University of New Brunswick, Canada

Ali A. Ghorbani
University of New Brunswick, Canada

ABSTRACT

System logs are one of the most important sources of information for anomaly and intrusion detection systems. In a general log-based anomaly detection system, network, devices, and host logs are all collected and used together for analysis and the detection of anomalies. However, the ever-increasing volume of logs remains as one of the main challenges that anomaly detection tools face. Based on Sysmon, this chapter proposes a host-based log analysis system that detects anomalies without using network logs to reduce the volume and to show the importance of host-based logs. The authors implement a Sysmon parser to parse and extract features from the logs and use them to perform detection methods on the data. The valuable information is successfully retained after two extensive volume reduction steps. An anomaly detection system is proposed and performed on five different datasets with up to 55,000 events which detects the attacks using the preserved logs. The analysis results demonstrate the significance of host-based logs in auditing, security monitoring, and intrusion detection systems.

INTRODUCTION

One of the results of the continually growing number of devices connected to the Internet is the production of vast amounts of logs and other data. This ever-increasing volume of data, especially security logs, should be stored and can be analyzed for different proposes. Whether it be an attack or a malicious activity, with an excellent and in-depth analysis of the right log data, we can find it. Also, event pattern discovery, one of the most critical tasks in security log management and analysis, can be used to build security log file profiles thus anomalous lines in the log files can be identified. Based on recent researches, despite having notable progress, there are several remaining challenges in log analysis, and there is still a long way to go when it comes to security analysis of big data. Having more than 75% of the share of

DOI: 10.4018/978-1-5225-9742-1.ch007

desktop operating systems (Statista, 2019), Windows is considered as the most widely used desktop operating system worldwide, and hence, there is a massive number of logs generated by Windows-operated workstations and laptops every day. Network log analysis has come a long way so far, but system log analysis seems to have been undervalued compared to that. Sysmon could be one possible way to help solve this issue. As a good start, security researchers at Microsoft developed Sysmon to help with Windows auditing process. This logging tool can help address several above issues if properly configured and deployed. There are many system information and event management software (SIEM) that can help with the analysis of these logs and other logs from different sources. In this chapter, the authors aim to show the importance of host-based logs for security analysis. They also list an address related challenges and discuss potential solutions. This chapter will demonstrate how an enormous amount of security logs can be handled and used as the sole source of information for anomaly detection.

Here, the researchers propose a set of tools to help detect anomalies in Windows workstations. The goal of the chapter is to provide a set of simple and easy-to-deploy tools that can be used to track and hunt malicious activities and help with the response after an attack. To achieve this, authors focus on host-based logs generated by Sysmon and aim to show their importance and demonstrate that they can be used as an exclusive source of information for anomaly detection. The researchers take a two-step procedure to reduce the size of the logs produced by Sysmon. First, they define several rules to include relevant information and exclude network logs as well as less informative and noisy events like empty key retraction processes. They create several datasets in two different virtual environments using the two most common versions of Windows. The authors implement a fast and highly configurable Sysmon parser that can clean and parse Sysmon logs which also extracts features based on its configuration. The second step in data reduction is done after parsing. Using clustering techniques, they detect outliers to reduce the size of the data extensively. The outliers are analyzed and flagged in the anomaly detection engine. Here logs are analyzed by all engines available in VirusTotal where the malicious ones are normally detected. A human analyst then checks the few remaining logs that are flagged as *suspicious* or *unknown* in the previous step. All attacks are detected successfully at the end. In summary, the following are the chapter's contributions:

- Implementation of a comprehensive highly configurable Sysmon parser for parsing and extracting features from the logs.
- Proposal of a hierarchical approach to considerably reduce the volume of Windows generated Sysmon logs while preserving actionable intelligence.
- Introduction of an anomaly detection engine that successfully detects attacks and malware on different datasets.
- Creation of 15 different Sysmon events datasets with no modification or anonymization.

The remainder of this chapter is organized as follows. Log-based anomaly detection systems, log clustering, and log parsing tools are discussed in Section Background. After that, challenges in the area are reviewed in the next section. In Section Log Analysis, the authors provide a detailed description of Sysmon and some of its capabilities. The next section discusses the datasets along with the malware and the environment used to create them. Subsequently, details of deploying the system and the proposed anomaly detection engine's architecture are described, followed by the analysis process. Results of the analysis are presented in the next section. The conclusion and potential future work are discussed in the last section.

BACKGROUND

Logs can be used to get a glimpse into every change and state of a computer system. There are different types of logs with various content and formats that are used in particular use cases. Along with log analysis applications, the work by (Oliner, 2012) reviews some of the advances in log analysis in the recent decade as well as observing the remaining challenges in the area. But in general, we review log analysis and big data from 4 different aspects mainly log-based anomaly detection, big data for anomaly detection, log clustering, and log parsing.

Log Based Anomaly Detection

Logs can become massive and noisy. But they contain so much information that makes them a valuable and essential source of data to address different security problems such as detecting attackers on a network. In work by (Yen, 2013), authors designed and implemented a system that automatically analyzes the logs and mines useful information from them to enhance the security of an enterprise network. The experiment was extended by (Oprea, 2015) who proposed a complementary tool to detect early-stage enterprise network infections. The focus of the paper is on high-risk attacks with a potential financial loss. The idea is followed in other work as well. A signal come from the analysis result of network audit logs can become a low-cost security solution for an enterprise network which can cooperate with their current antivirus and other security software to provide a more secure network (Berlin, 2015). However, not all log-based anomaly detection systems rely on network logs. Some works even rely on host-based audit logs as the only source of data for threat hunting. One highly valuable resource to take part in a more extensive security audit process is Windows event logs collection. The users working on workstations are one of the main targets of the cyberwar that is going on today and sometimes they are the first place where the attacks start from (Anthony, 2013). As an example, the threat detection system suggested by (Mavroeidis, 2018) uses Sysmon logs to present an automatic threat detection and classification system. Threats are classified into different levels based on their characteristics identified through the analysis of the logs. Similarly, host-based logs are used for security enhancement purposes in different applications. Monitoring audit logs are not limited to small applications such as anomaly detection, but sometimes they are used for prediction. As suggested by (Fu, 2009), in large distributed systems, analysis of unstructured logs can be used to detect anomalies inside future generated log files. These logs are also used to help identify insider threats (Ambre, 2015). Console logs and mobile device generated events can be considered as other types of host-based logs which are used for security analysis and threat detection. Most applications and software contain enough information to detect anomalies by extracting unusual patterns from their console logs (Bao, 2018). On mobile devices, the analysis of system logs can help detect mobile threats such as smishing and backdoor attacks (Kim, 2018). Lastly, in (Vaarandi R. a., 2014), the authors discussed the security metrics that can be collected with the use of security logs. They reviewed several scenarios for security metrics collection based on different common security log types. Also, a framework was described that can help with the collection and report process and is implemented based on open-source technologies for log management.

Big Data for Anomaly Detection

Processing of real-time big data is one of the critical aspects of every log-based anomaly detection system. Gathering and preprocessing massive data constantly generated by components of a network is difficult and hence is usually done using big data techniques. In a work by (McNeil, 2016), the authors analyzed several tools to detect mobile devices malware. They mostly lacked sufficient user profiling abilities and therefore failed to automate the process of dynamic analysis of big data for malware detection. Large scale testing of their proposed real-time mobile malware detection framework reveals the need for performance optimization which can be addressed using machine learning algorithms optimized for big data. As another example, in (Terzi, 2017), the authors used Azure HDInsight and Apache Spark to handle and analyze NetFlow data for anomaly detection. Some highly efficient big data algorithms in other areas such as intelligent cloud systems were significantly improved in recent studies (Psannis, 2019). Efficient streaming algorithms designed for cloud steaming can be used to handle big log data streams. Also, privacy-preserving big data frameworks designed for IoT and Social Networks (Stergiou, 2018) can help address privacy issues related to data collection tasks to safely gather, transfer and exchange required data for anomaly detection.

Log Clustering and Mining

Several different approaches can be employed to capture insightful data from the logs. One of the main methods is clustering. Starting with (Vaarandi R., 2003), the author proposed SLCT, a data clustering algorithm that is capable of mining and extracting interesting patterns from different types of event logs as well as finding the outliers. Most of the shortcomings of the work were then addressed in (Vaarandi R. a., 2015) where the authors propose an approach that fixes wildcards detection issues along with word shifting sensitivity and delimiter noise. Researchers in (Heikkinen, 2015) suggested a generic log clustering framework named LOGDIG. The framework relies on temporal data (time-stamps) and data related explicitly to the system (e.g., data associated with moving objects). The state-machine-based behavior mining searches for the states and aims to find desired event messages and uses meta-data interpretation for input data. The output of the system is a human-friendly behavioral knowledge report. In one work by (Makanju, 2009), authors introduce IPLoM which is an algorithm for the mining of clusters from event logs. They take a hierarchical 3-step partitioning process which they call iterative partitioning mining. Descriptions of the clusters are presented as the results. The algorithm outperforms both (Makanju, 2009) and (Vaarandi R. a., 2015) in terms of precision and performance. Another approach to log mining is log abstraction. Log abstraction is a technique to convert the messages hidden inside the log files to different event types. In a complementary work by (Zhuge, 2017) the same clustering algorithm namely LogCluster was implemented in C which greatly improved the speed and efficiency. It was originally written in Perl which is significantly slower than C. This implementation took the crown once again for LogCluster algorithm and was also extended to work with stream mining scenarios. Another example of log abstraction is (Nagappan, 2010) in which authors presented a comprehensive and straightforward approach to log file abstraction that is similar to the SLCT log clustering tool. They have clustered similar frequency words in each line and abstracted it to event types.

Log Parsing

Automated methods for parsing logs are critical when it comes to knowledge extraction and anomaly detection from any log (Abbott, 2015). Authors of (He P. a., 2016) study four different log parsers and parsing packages to provide a better understanding of the advantages of parsers and their impact on log mining. Their insightful findings substantiate the significance of the information that is obtainable from logs. Their work is further extended by (He P. a., 2017) who implement an online parser for web service management techniques. Later, it was updated to function in a streaming manner with dynamic parsing rules (He P. a., 2018). In certain scenarios, having a dedicated parser for each type of log could be a better approach. There are tools available that help with the field retrieval process from different logs. Microsoft came up with a SQL based log parsing tool for logs generated by their services, mainly Windows logs. They discussed the necessity of it and why having a parser is essential for mining data from logs (Giuseppini, 2005). However, by the time of this writing, the tool is more than 14 years old and does not work properly with newer types of logs including Sysmon logs. The alternatives to most of these parsers are commercial SIEMs. They usually have a user interface and can help with log parsing as well as the analysis and mining process. Nonetheless, their parsing system is generally basic and log messages are mostly treated like text values with no specific structure. In most cases, the end users themselves need to define the parser using regular expressions which requires extensive knowledge of logs and is a time-consuming task (Du, 2018).

Motivation and Challenges

Although significant progress has been made in the area, several challenges make the detection and response process more difficult, and some of them are still fully open. As an example, built-in Windows logging and auditing tools while useful, are for the most part not informative enough to address these security issues. First off, the information provided by these tools is limited especially for sensitive files like DLLs and for some critical events such as process creation. Moreover, network logging in Windows is too limited, messy, and often obscure. These limitations make it hard to track and capture the attackers' behavior (Yen, 2013). Therefore, several other complementary tools have been developed to address these issues. The following are some of the challenges we face in log analysis-based security solutions.

- **Data Sources:** The first challenge is sources of the logs which is the process of choosing the right logging tool to capture events. Logging tools have their advantages and disadvantages regarding accuracy, dependability, configurability, and performance impact. The tools of choice must meet some minimum requirements to be useful. The importance of having the right data to analyze and get the correct result is undeniable. Having several different tools and software and hundreds of ways of configuration and deployment make this process time consuming and difficult.
- **Data Generation:** Logging process and producing security logs need extensive management and effort. Data must be accurate, comprehensive and dependable. It also must give a good enough representation of what is happening in the system. We need to make sure the data is first large enough and second, covers different types of activities so that we can make sure we will have a complete package of raw log data to analyze on. These include size, content, realism, and accuracy.

Figure 1. ELK Stack architecture (Berman, 2018)

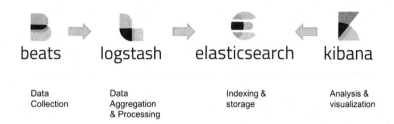

- **Data Preprocessing:** Security-relevant logs in a large enterprise can grow by terabytes per day. Handling, cleaning, and processing this massive volume of security log files remains one of the main challenges. Moreover, parsing this data adds another problem. While there are tools that can help with this part, depending on the type of logs, it could be challenging to find the right parser. In some cases, a parser is not provided so we will have to implement our parser to be able to extract meaningful data and features out of the raw logs.
- **Analysis Process:** The last challenge is providing actionable insights from mining large quantities of security log data and finding anomalous behaviors from it. Statistical techniques could be helpful, but they do not explain what we can do about the malicious pattern that is found and where to go from there. Also, a subjective interpretation of the analysis result, as well as metrics to validate the informativeness of the results, could become complicated.

LOG ANALYSIS

A tool such as Sysmon is still far from being widely used mainly because of the lack of support by analysis software and parsing tools. System Information and Event Management agents (SIEMs) are one of the most common destinations of Sysmon logs. They provide insights from the logs and analyze them in real-time. The main idea of having a SIEM is to aggregate similar logs and events from various sources and combine and manage all of them together to extract meaningful insights and detect possible deviations.

SIEMs are also used as the security control center and monitoring and can usually be configured to generate an alert when something suspicious happens. There exist a lot of similar software. Here is a brief overview of 3 of the most commonly used SIEMs worldwide.

Elastic Stack

As an open source data processing pipeline, Logstash is a server-side tool that can gather data from several sources simultaneously. The data is then transformed and sent to the analysis module. In this case, the analyzer is Elasticsearch which is a search engine that provides meaningful information and queries from the input data which can be used to detect threats and generate alerts.

Figure 2. The Elastic Stack is a set of open-sources software and tools for data analysis. ELK gathers logs from different distributed sources. It can index and store events to help the user query and visualize the logs. Figure above shows a Kibana environment, the visualization engine implemented to visualize Elasticsearch data.

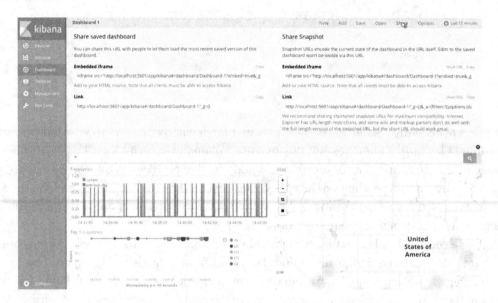

Splunk

Splunk is a software platform that can search, analyze, and visualize various types of logs and other machine-generated data. Splunk supports several different sources of input data streams and can provide analytical insights from them. Splunk's add-on for Microsoft Sysmon helps import Sysmon data and extract relevant fields from the logs, which makes it a common destination for Sysmon logs for the analysis and threat detection.

QRadar

QRadar is a SIEM and a platform that provides an all-around overview of an organization's security systems. It is used to monitor and detect security threats and suspicious behaviors and report them. QRadar normalizes all the incoming events from various log sources and based on the configuration and the pre-defined rules, correlates the data and make them ready for analysis. QRadar's Sysmon integration is a content extension that can help detect threats on Windows workstations using Sysmon endpoint logs.

The complicated process of choosing the right software aside, analysis and identification of malicious activities using SIEMs could become costly. They need much effort to implement, install, and properly configure. Also, the costs of running a SIEM could be high and based on the scale and the quantity of the data it is processing, it could easily become a reason for companies to ignore it as a not cost-effective security solution (Horisberger, 2013). Even after proper configuration, using a SIEM to analyze logs is not a simple process. It normally requires prior knowledge as well as time and practice.

Figure 3. Sysmon architecture (Russinovich, 2017)

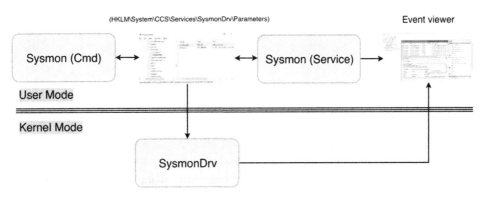

Sysmon

Sysmon is a sophisticated logging tool designed for Windows workstations by Microsoft. It is a device driver and is run as a Windows service that records system's activities and events.

The logs are stored in the Windows event log application. Logs generated by Sysmon, in general, contain more information and details than the ones generated using built-in Windows audit logging system.

Sysmon logs provide information about process creations, file access and modification, network access logs and several other types of events. Some of Sysmon's capabilities are as follows: Logging the process creation with full command line level details, recording multiple hashes of process image files at the same time, process and session global IDs, logging driver loads and DLLs along with their hashes, file creation events with their accurate and real modification time and several other types of events. Table 1 is a complete list of events that Sysmon can record. Also, since Sysmon is highly configurable, the administrator can specify what events to be logged. This way, not only the user can reduce the number of logs generated but also can add or remove different types of logs based on their usefulness.

Table 1. Sysmon event ID for each category

Category	ID	Category	ID
Sysmon Service Status Changed	0	Process Access	10
Process Create	1	File Create	11
File Creation Time Changed	2	Registry Object Create Delete	12
Network Connection	3	Registry Value Create	13
Sysmon Service State Change	4	Registry Object Rename	14
Process Terminated	5	File Create Stream Hash	15
Driver Loaded	6	Sysmon Configuration Changed	16
Image Loaded	7	Pipe Created	17
Create Remote Thread	8	Pipe Connected	18
Raw Access Read	9	Error	255

Figure 4. Example rules in the configuration file

```
<ProcessAccess onmatch="include">
    <TargetImage condition="is">C:\Windows\system32\lsass.exe</TargetImage>
    <TargetImage condition="is">C:\Windows\system32\winlogon.exe</TargetImage>
    <TargetImage condition="is">C:\Windows\system32\explorer.exe</TargetImage>
</ProcessAccess>
```

Sysmon Configuration

The first contribution of this chapter is proposing a safe way to reduce the enormous volume of Windows generated log data while preserving the interesting information inside them. To monitor and trace the events using Sysmon, while not necessary, it is highly recommended to have a configuration based on the use case. Filtering abilities of Sysmon are a part of what makes it a more sophisticated tool than the built-in Windows tools for auditing. Based on the configuration suggested by (SwiftOnSecurity, 2018), the researchers made a configuration file that carefully filters events that are probably not malicious or do not help with the security investigations process. Network traffic was also filtered as the main idea of the project was to focus on host-based logs.

Furthermore, the logs generated by the virtual environment (AWS and VirtualBox) were also filtered as they are not present in a real-world physical machine. It is worth noting that as suggested in the base configuration, some of the highly sensitive network logs were not filtered as they might be needed in the investigation process and for the future work. It is expected that any malicious activity and behavior would be detected at its early stages of running on the machine.

After deploying the configuration, the number of logs generated is hugely reduced and, in some cases, the reduction can be close to 95% compared to the time when having Sysmon log every action that is performed on the system. Also, compared to the built-in Windows logging system which stores the logs in different sections, when combined, the result is outstanding, and it is kept above 90% reduction in volume all the time. This is the first step of a two-step volume reduction process. The second step is explained in the analysis section.

Dataset CReation

Environment

Windows, as the most widely used desktop operating system, is one of the main targets of attackers (Delasko, 2018). Motivated by this and the fact that Sysmon is a tool written specifically for Windows, authors decided to gather and analyze host-based logs which are for the most part different for every operating system. To achieve this goal, they created five different datasets, three of which contain malicious activity and the other two are benign. For each dataset, either AWS or VirtualBox was used as a host to install the operating system. One of the two benign datasets was created using VirtualBox and the other one was an AWS based virtual machine so that a ground truth to know what normal activities in each environment would look like was created. In order to create the log data, the researchers prepared a Windows environment that was as close to a real-world scenario as possible. Since one of the main

Table 2. Datasets description

Dataset	Platform	Environment	Total Events	Total Lines	Days of Run
CoinMiner	Amazon Web Services	Windows 10	33793	777151	16
Kuaizip	Oracle VM VirtualBox	Windows 7	12728	292647	8
WannaCry	Oracle VM VirtualBox	Windows 10	45156	1038488	5
Benign	Amazon Web Services	Windows 10	34697	797345	17
Benign	Oracle VM VirtualBox	Windows 10	30024	690478	10

targets of attackers is enterprise workstations, the test Windows environments were fully equipped with normal day-to-day office tools and applications like Acrobat Reader, Microsoft Office, Slack, Google Chrome, Spotify etc. As for the version of Windows operating system, Windows 10 was used for 4 datasets and Windows 7 was used to create the last one.

Logging Process

The logging process for each dataset was slightly different in terms of system usage, applications, and the duration of running the operating system. However, all datasets were generated using similar behaviors and baselines. The final datasets have tens of thousands of events each of which normally contains more than 20 lines of information.

The systems were run from a few days to a couple of weeks until they were crashed by the malware or stopped manually. The systems were constantly turned on and off daily like in normal use and some cases, were kept on for several days. In the end, some reached more than 45,000 events and over a million lines of logs. Thanks to the configuration, authors managed to hugely shrink the log data to a relatively small set while keeping useful events. Some datasets are slightly smaller than others. More than 20 sets of data were generated in 6 months, 5 of which were chosen for the experiments. Datasets are not modified or anonymized.

Primary Dataset

To test the malware detection engine, authors needed to run malware on some of the datasets. Some of the most well-known malware were chosen for the experiments. A ransomware, a trojan and an adware were selected, which are explained in the following.

WannaCry: Ransomware is a computer malware that locks the user's file data using encryption techniques and then holds the entire or some of the device data hostage until the user pays the ransom to the attacker. The attacker then might give the decryption key to the user so that they can recover the files. Ransomware is one the most common types of malware these days and WannaCry attack was one of the most destructive ransomware ever known (Mohurle, 2017).

Kuaizip: As an adware, Kuaizip is bundled with several free but potentially unwanted programs that are usually installed on users' computers without them asking for it and in some case without users' knowledge. But while in most cases they can do what they were advertised for, they might also collect the victim's online and offline activities and perform unwanted actions. Kuaizip is a free-to-download software that claims to be a highly effective file archiver application. Autostarts with Windows, online

Figure 5. The Sysmon log event in XML format related to Kuaizip adware

```
<EventID>1</EventID>
<TimeCreated SystemTime='2018-10-11T21:56:47.330914000Z'/>
<EventRecordID>17836</EventRecordID>
<Execution ProcessID='1964' ThreadID='2068'/>
<Channel>Microsoft-Windows-Sysmon/Operational</Channel>
<Computer>test-PC</Computer>
<Security UserID='S-1-5-18'/>
<EventData>
<Data Name='RuleName'></Data>
<Data Name='UtcTime'>2018-10-11 21:56:47.315</Data>
<Data Name='ProcessGuid'>{3904188F-C71F-5BBF-0000-00100EA60B00}</Data>
<Data Name='ProcessId'>3016</Data>
<Data Name='Image'>C:\Program Files\KuaiZip\Update.exe</Data>
<Data Name='FileVersion'>1, 0, 0, 1</Data>
<Data Name='Description'>kuaizip</Data>
<Data Name='Product'>Kuaizip automatic updates application</Data>
<Data Name='Company'>Suzhou Shijie Software Co., LTD</Data>
<Data Name='CommandLine'>"C:\Program Files\KuaiZip\Update.exe" -ke 1</Data>
<Data Name='CurrentDirectory'>C:\Windows\system32\</Data>
<Data Name='User'>test-PC\test</Data>
<Data Name='LogonGuid'>{3904188F-C637-5BBF-0000-00209B240100}</Data>
<Data Name='LogonId'>0x1249b</Data>
<Data Name='TerminalSessionId'>1</Data>
<Data Name='IntegrityLevel'>Medium</Data>
<Data Name='Hashes'>MD5=960055F63557F450EBDA9F8CC293D659,
          SHA256=233D809EE5756E1AB2FD9B552E154DE772A83A83031A24E791778601AB2A676B</Data>
<Data Name='ParentProcessGuid'>{3904188F-C71F-5BBF-0000-0010E39A0B00}</Data>
<Data Name='ParentProcessId'>3036</Data>
<Data Name='ParentImage'>C:\Program Files\KuaiZip\KZMount.exe</Data>
<Data Name='ParentCommandLine'>"C:\Program Files\KuaiZip\KZMount.exe" -ke</Data>
</EventData>
```

activity tracking, adding unknown background services, injecting advertising banners on visited web pages, turning random web pages texts into malicious URLs and installing other unwanted programs are some of the malicious activities of this adware.

CoinMiner: With the recent rise in cryptocurrency prices, dozens of unwanted malicious software that mine cryptocurrencies have been developed by attackers. These programs while in most cases do not threat the users and their data, are run on the victim's machines and use their resources to mine cryptocurrencies for the attacker. CoinMiner which is a Bitcoin miner trojan was chosen for the experiments. This sophisticated malware hides and automatically terminates when the user tries to check the system's resources. It will appear neither in task manager nor any other user-accessible application. The trojan then relaunches after the task manager is closed which makes it hard to detect by the user.

Secondary Malware Data

Unlike the primary data, in this part, authors create 10 different malware datasets with a different approach. This time, instead of trying to mimic a real user's behavior, the researchers only ran the malware for a short period of time on a clean installed Windows 10 with no third-party application installed except Sysmon and the pre-installed system applications. The running time of all datasets was approximately the same to make sure that the difference in the datasets is minimal besides the changes caused by the malware that is run on the system. Furthermore, even highly sensitive network logs were ignored, and the machine had no network connection. This helps to identify the nature of the malware before it is triggered by an external actor. Malware chosen for this part were selected based on the top 10 Window malware in 2017/2018 reported by (AV-TEST, 2019). Table below represents the list of malware along with their share of Windows malware.

Table 3. Top 10 Windows malware in 2017 (AV-TEST, 2019)

Rank	Malware	Share
1	Ramnit	21.54%
2	Agent	13.78%
3	Virut	6.37%
4	Virlock	6.25%
5	Allaple	4.69%
6	VB	3.98%
7	Sivis	2.39%
8	Upatre	2.03%
9	Injector	2.00%
10	Kryptik	2.00%

The primary goal of gathering this set of malware and creating this dataset was to understand the exact changes the malware makes to the operating system and also to find the exact differences between and clean installation of Windows 10 before and after infection by malware. This way, distinguishing the changes solely caused by malware is easier. The findings of this part were mostly used in the analysis, design and implementation of the main anomaly detection engine.

Parsing SYSMON Logs

As another contribution, the researchers implemented a flexible Sysmon parsing tool to manage, process, and extract features from the logs. This is to the best of our knowledge, the first independent publicly available tool for parsing and processing Sysmon generated log data. There is no publicly available configurable parser for Sysmon other than Microsoft's own Log Parser 2.2, which is a general-purpose parsing tool for different types of text-based Windows logs and data. Since Log Parser is almost 14 years old and was not designed to support Sysmon logs, its output is not anything close to what it should have been, so an independent parser was implemented to parse the logs.

The proposed parser is a highly configurable and powerful tool written in Python that collects, parses, and saves the output as a CSV file that is ready for the analysis. It can parse more than 50,000 events in less than a fraction of a second. It is a very versatile and flexible tool that can be configured for different types of analysis.

There are many fields and features that you can specify and select from and then configure the parser for what you need. The features can be chosen from 'UTC Time and Date', 'Sequence Number, 'Event's Rule', 'Executable file's Hash (SHA-256 or MD5 or both), 'File Version', 'Description', 'Product', 'Company', 'User', 'Current Directory', 'Process ID', 'Process GUID', 'Parent Process ID', 'Parent Process GUID', 'Logon ID', 'Logon GUID', 'Image', 'Parent Image', 'Terminal Session ID', 'Integrity Level', and 'Process Command Line', 'Parent Process Command Line'. Not all events have every field. So, in some cases, the value of 'Null' is returned if they do not exist. Limiting the number of events, filtering the events by type or the code, and exporting the output in vertical or horizontal shapes are some other abilities of this parser.

Figure 6. Raw log messages of a WannaCry-related event (top) and structured logs after parsing (bottom). Events are stored sequentially without any particular separator. The separation of the events is done by the parser. The fields are randomly selected but in various analysis scenarios fields can be chosen based on the application

```
 1 Information,8/23/2018 12:15:04 PM,Microsoft-Windows-Sysmon,1,Process Create (rule: ProcessCreate),"Process Create:
 2 RuleName:
 3 UtcTime: 2018-08-23 19:15:04.632
 4 ProcessGuid: {5C081F1E-07B8-5B7F-0000-0010F3AE2103}
 5 ProcessId: 3140
 6 Image: C:\Users\SysmonTestPC\Downloads\@WanaDecryptor@.exe
 7 FileVersion: 6.1.7600.16385 (win7_rtm.090713-1255)
 8 Description: Load PerfMon Counters
 9 Product: Microsoft® Windows® Operating System
10 Company: Microsoft Corporation
11 CommandLine: @WanaDecryptor@.exe
12 CurrentDirectory: C:\Users\SysmonTestPC\Downloads\
13 User: DESKTOP-GOCAJKD\SysmonTestPC
14 LogonGuid: {5C081F1E-BD70-5B7D-0000-002095130600}
15 LogonId: 0x61395
16 TerminalSessionId: 1
17 IntegrityLevel: Medium
18 Hashes: MD5=7BF2B57F2A20576875SC07F238FB32CC,SHA256=B9C5D4339809E0AD9A00D4D3DD26FDF44A32819A54ABF846BB9B560D81391C25
19 ParentProcessGuid: {5C081F1E-F79F-5B7E-0000-00103CE88A02}
20 ParentProcessId: 9100
21 ParentImage: C:\Users\SysmonTestPC\Downloads\WannaCry.EXE
22 ParentCommandLine: ""C:\Users\SysmonTestPC\Downloads\WannaCry.EXE"" "
```

PROPOSED APPROACH

The last contribution of this chapter is a new anomaly detection system. While there are different anomaly detection software and tools available, many of them are too complicated to use and require many different sources of data to detect malicious activities. In this study, the focus has been strictly on host-based Windows logs without taking advantage of information in the network and firewall logs.

The results show that many types of malicious activities are easily detectable solely using host-based logs generated by the system. This is interesting in several ways. One is that it reveals the potential of the host-based logs and the amount of information that can be extracted from them without relying on network and firewall logs. Another reason is that it provides useful information that traps many malicious activities before they destroy or cause damage to the files. And finally, the comprehensibility of the output will help the analyst detect and analyze malicious events that have happened before, which is very difficult when doing it on raw log messages.

System Architecture

The system includes several components that can cooperate to detect malware or malicious activities. The output of the system is the security analysis of the workstation logs. First off, activities of different users are distinguishable based on the logon ID so any action performed by a user will be logged with their own identity. This way, if malicious activity is performed on a multi-user workstation, the user responsible for that action can easily be identified. Furthermore, the logs produced by the Windows machines are gathered and stored in 3 different formats of EVTX, XML, and CSV. This adds more flexibility if the logs are taken to other tools and software for further investigations.

In this work, only the CSV files are used. The XML and EVTX versions are stored but not used. Next, the logs are passed to Parsing and Feature Extraction Engine to extract useful features for analysis. The extracted information is then stored in the database to prevent reprocessing in the future. Ultimately, the

Figure 7. Architecture of the anomaly detection system

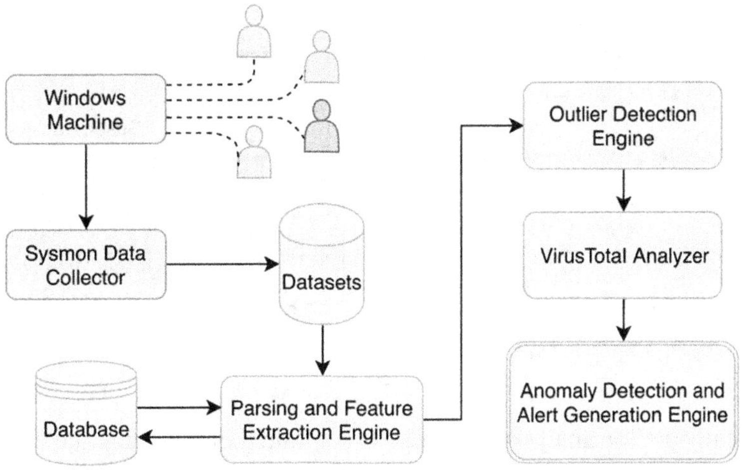

features are passed to the Outlier Detection Engine, the VirusTotal Analyzer, and the Human Analyst respectively to extract knowledge and interesting activities from them.

The Analysis Process

In this section, the analysis steps are briefly introduced and explained. When logs from a properly configured workstation are exported, they are sent to the parser for the parsing process. Based on its configuration, the parser generates the output as a CSV file. The following is a description of how the output file is thoroughly analyzed in 3 steps.

Step 1: Outlier Detection Process

Due to VirusTotal's free API limitations and also to further ease processing the events, authors decided to perform the second step of volume reduction. Therefore, the events that are more likely to be interesting are identified. To achieve this, 7 attributes namely 'Time', 'Date', 'Event Type', 'MD5 Hash', 'Process GUID', 'Parent Process GUID', and 'Logon GUID' were selected. The attributes are selected on an experimental basis mostly based on their availability, correlation, and robustness. The outliers are detected using Weka (Hall, 2009) which is an open-source knowledge analysis and data mining software. The result is several hundreds of events that have been detected as outliers. These events are then sent to the VirusTotal Analyzer for analysis.

Step 2: VirusTotal Analyzer

VirusTotal has one of the largest malware databases in the world. It is also equipped with over 70 antivirus products and other malware scanning engines. One can submit several types of information online on the website to get the analysis results of the submitted file or data. It gives a thorough examination of the data to the user. The request can be a file, URL, IP address, domain, or a hash. Using the API,

Figure 8. Architecture of VirusTotal analyzer

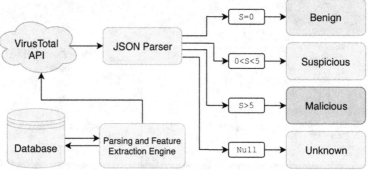

a user can automatically get the analysis result of the submitted data in their application. The analyzer uses the Sysmon parser to extract MD5 hash of previously detected outliers and then stores them in a set container to prevent duplicates. The result set of hashes is then automatically sent to VirusTotal for analysis. Once ready, the results are sent back to the user as a JSON file for each hash. A simple parser was implemented to parse the output JSON results, capture the required information, and report them as the output. The outputs are then classified in the following four classes:

- **Benign:** This is the expected output for most of the hashes. A hash is considered clean when the output of VirusTotal indicates that zero engines have detected the hash as malicious.
- **Malicious:** This happens if the VirusTotal's output is a non-zero number which is usually higher than 20. This means that for example, more than 20 engines have confirmed that the hash belongs to a malicious file.
- **Suspicious:** In some rare cases, the output for some hashes is a small non-zero number, normally between 1 to 5. While most engines consider the file to be benign, it is flagged it as a suspicious file that needs further investigations.
- **Unknown:** The last case is where the returned result of VirusTotal shows the executable file has not been uploaded thus not analyzed by anyone yet. This type of output is unusual because many new or unknown malware are in this category. Another possible scenario is that the file is benign but so new or so unknown that nobody has tried uploading it yet. Either way, this type of output should be treated very carefully since it can be dangerous. In the case of new malware, it will probably get caught by the analyst at its early stages of activities.

Figure 8 shows the analysis process using VirusTotal's API as well as the thresholds used in the flagging process. When an event is flagged as *unknown* or *suspicious* by the VirusTotal analyzer, it is sent to a human analyst for further investigations.

Step 3: Analysis

Most malicious activities and attackers' attempts are traced and detected at the previous stages automatically. However, there are some events that are considered suspicious or unknown which require more analysis. In this step, a human analyst analyzes suspicious activities. Hereupon, since the events

Table 4. Analysis results of each dataset (number of events per category)

Category Dataset	Total	Analyzed	Malicious	Suspicious	Unknown
CoinMiner	33793	86	1	2	5
Kuaizip	12728	117	5	2	3
WannaCry	45156	107	6	1	12
Benign AWS	34697	69	0	3	3
Benign VBox	30024	124	0	2	9

are normally limited to a dozen, a human analyst can do the analysis easier, faster, and more accurately. Table 3 shows that on average, less than 0.01% of events need to be analyzed by the human analyst.

Results

Out of the five primary datasets, three were infected, and two were benign. In the first case, the dataset was infected by a trojan called CoinMiner. The second one was infected by WannaCry and the last one by an adware called Kuaizip. In all the 3 malware datasets, the malicious files were all detected at the VirusTotal stage in less than five seconds of analysis started.

The results show that in two cases, malware was detected in one or more file creation processes before they are run. This shows that an effective logging procedure for file creation and file modification processes can help easily detect known malware instantly right after they are downloaded and before they are even run on the system. In all three cases, there is a significant time gap between the malware download time and the time when the infected file was run on the system which can help take necessary actions before they cause damage to the system. However, even if they are not detected at the download stage, all of them are detected as soon as their executables run on the system. This especially helps with malware like CoinMiner as they are completely hidden while running. In the two benign cases, 17 suspicious and unknown files turned out to be either false positives by some antivirus engines or some other benign software like new device drivers.

Table 3.

Field	Value
Event ID	1
Event Type	Process Create
Time	19:15:04.632
Date	2018-08-23
MD5 Hash	7BF2B57F2A205768755C07F238FB32CC
Process GUID	5C081F1E-07B8-5B7F-0000-0010F3AE2103
Parent Process GUID	5C081F1E-F79F-5B7E-0000-00103CE88A02
Logon ID	0x61395
Logon GUID	5C081F1E-BD70-5B7D-0000-002095130600
Image	C:\Users\SysmonTestPC\Downloads\@WanaDecryptor@.exe
Command Line	@WanaDecryptor@.exe
Parent Command Line	C:\Users\SysmonTestPC\Downloads\WannaCry.EXE

Table 3 shows the massive reduction in volume while preserving the important events. In all cases, every component of the malware was detected.

In CoinMiner, malware was a single executable which was successfully detected while running. In WannaCry and Kuaizip cases, malware and all its components, including the ones that were installed later by the malware were successfully detected both at download and running stages.

Another important point to derive from the results is that despite the noticeable difference in the size of the datasets, the number of remaining events is relatively similar and close to each other. This shows that the detection engine selects certain events that are known to be more important and the number of these events normally remain consistent in different datasets.

Figure 9 shows the number of raw events divided by 100 compared to the ones that are picked for analysis by the anomaly detection engine. Looking closer, we can see that despite the remarkable difference between Kuaizip and WannaCry raw events, the number of final events is close and even slightly higher for Kuaizip. The average number of selected events is around 100 which is a reasonably small number for a human analyst to perform the necessary and immediate investigation on the data to find the potential threats.

In terms of speed and efficiency, there are three main stages that should be considered to evaluate the performance of the proposed method. The first stage is the preprocessing and parsing of the logs. Even the largest datasets were run in a fraction of a second. Despite being so fast, since the parser is written in Python, the performance can even further improve if implemented in some other languages such as C or C++. The second stage is analysis by the VirusTotal analyzer. This is the bottle neck of the system and is limited by the limitations of the free API. However, when the premium and unlimited API is used, and since the number of analyzed events is so limited, it can be done very fast and even in real-time. The last part is the clustering part which again, runs under a second. Overall, due to heavy preprocessing on the data the performance is fast mostly because the remaining data is always very limited. Moreover, with minor optimization and improvements, the system can run in real-time on very large scales.

Figure 9. Ratio of the number of total and analyzed events

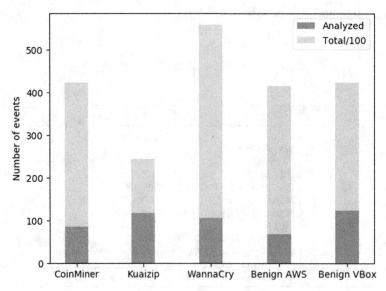

Table 5. Secondary dataset results analyzed by VirusTotal analyzer only. The number of unique executables followed by the number of malicious executables detected by VirusTotal engine.

Malware	Total events	Unique Executables	Malicious Detected
Baseline (benign)	826	38	0
Ramnit	1169	46	0
Agent	1501	46	0
Virut	1066	47	1
Virlock	2771	52	3
Allaple	1483	46	0
VB	1249	50	1
Sivis	1463	47	1
Upatre	1106	47	0
Injector	1648	47	1
Kryptik	1157	45	0

The secondary set of data were mostly intended to be used for the implementation of the actual anomaly detection engine and also for differential analysis of the logs which makes distinguishing the malware logs from the malicious logs much easier by comparing different datasets to each other and to a baseline. Consequently, authors compared the data to a benign baseline, separated new logs from the remaining logs, and flagged them as malicious activity. The results show that in most cases, the malware-related logs are perfectly separated. However, some malware like the HTML-based variant of Ramnit used to create one of the datasets, which mostly depends on the services and since the suggested configuration does not monitor all services activities, it bypasses the logging process and thus is never detected by the system before it is completely activated. However, in a more realistic environment, it will be detected before causing harm to any component of the system, merely because all executable, important services such as Local Security Authority Subsystem Service (LSASS), and file modifications are monitored.

Even though the substantial differences in number of events is the result of activities by the specific malware run on the machine, in 50% of the datasets, the malware remains completely undetected by the VirusTotal analyzer. This further proves that signature-based malware detection methods are limited when it comes to detection capabilities. Furthermore, since the volume of the data is low, and the malware was only run for a certain and limited amount of time, there is not enough data to properly feed and train the main anomaly detection algorithm.

Sysmon is a relatively new tool and is fully dependent on its configuration, there is a few works and datasets available to compare the method to. This is due to the nature of the tool which can be configured differently in various environments and based on the application the output log can largely vary which makes it difficult to compare different datasets to each other. Also, compared to general log analysis systems, not many works strictly focus on host-based logs and even then, they use vastly different sources of logs and data to do the analysis. Therefore, having a useful comparative analysis in this new domain is still impractical.

CONCLUSION AND FUTURE RESEARCH DIRECTIONS

Host-based logs are a rich source of information that can help to detect intrusions and anomalies and to understand attackers' behavior and tools. These logs can be used to trace and hunt malicious activities as well as for forensics and incident response. The logs, however, can become so large that sometimes need several extensive preprocessing and size reduction steps before we can use them for analysis. The retention of useful information is one of the most important factors in the preprocessing stage.

This chapter discussed the use of Windows generated logs data, mainly Sysmon logs, to trace and hunt attackers on Windows hosts and how to prepare the data for investigations and incident response. A log-based anomaly detection approach was proposed, and the use of different tools and related essential software and solutions were presented. Future trends include the online analysis of big log data which will be helpful to profile and capture different behaviors on the host and to use them to detect anomalies and attackers and improve the security of the system. Furthermore, the possible privacy issues that come with the gathering of a large amount of log data from users' workstations and how to conform to the related laws like GDPR can be discussed. Furthermore, the work presented here could be extended to other popular operating systems like GNU/Linux or Mac OS X or even mobile operating systems like Android.

REFERENCES

Abbott, R. G., McClain, J., Anderson, B., Nauer, K., Silva, A., & Forsythe, C. (2015). Log analysis of cyber security training exercises. *Procedia Manufacturing*, *3*, 5088–5094. doi:10.1016/j.promfg.2015.07.523

Ambre, A., & Shekokar, N. (2015). Insider threat detection using log analysis and event correlation. *Procedia Computer Science*, *45*, 436–445. doi:10.1016/j.procs.2015.03.175

Anthony, R. (2013). *Detecting security incidents using windows workstation event logs.* SANS Institute, InfoSec Reading Room Paper.

Bao, L., Li, Q., Lu, P., Lu, J., Ruan, T., & Zhang, K. (2018). Execution anomaly detection in large-scale systems through console log analysis. *Journal of Systems and Software*, *143*, 172–186. doi:10.1016/j.jss.2018.05.016

Berlin, K. a. (2015). Malicious behavior detection using windows audit logs. In *Proceedings of the 8th ACM Workshop on Artificial Intelligence and Security* (pp. 35-44). ACM. 10.1145/2808769.2808773

Berman, D. (2018). *The Complete Guide to the ELK Stack.* Retrieved 2 5, 2019, from logz.io: https://logz.io/learn/complete-guide-elk-stack/

Delasko, S. A. (2018). Operating Systems of Choice for Professional Hackers. *ICCWS 2018 13th International Conference on Cyber Warfare and Security.*

Du, M., & Li, F. (2018). Spell: Online Streaming Parsing of Large Unstructured System Logs. *IEEE Transactions on Knowledge and Data Engineering*, 1. doi:10.1109/TKDE.2018.2875442

Fu, Q. G. (2009). Execution anomaly detection in distributed systems through unstructured log analysis. In *Data Mining, 2009. ICDM'09. Ninth IEEE International Conference on* (pp. 149-158). IEEE.

Giuseppini, G. A. (2005). *Microsoft Log Parser Toolkit: A complete toolkit for Microsoft's undocumented log analysis tool*. Elsevier.

Hall, M. A. (2009). The WEKA data mining software: an update. *ACM SIGKDD Explorations Newsletter, 11*, 10-18.

He, P. A. (2016). An evaluation study on log parsing and its use in log mining. In *46th Annual IEEE/IFIP International Conference on Dependable Systems and Networks (DSN)* (pp. 654-661). IEEE. 10.1109/DSN.2016.66

He, P. A. (2017). Drain: An online log parsing approach with fixed depth tree. In *International Conference on Web Services (ICWS)* (pp. 33-40). IEEE. 10.1109/ICWS.2017.13

He, P. A. (2018). *A Directed Acyclic Graph Approach to Online Log Parsing*. CoRR, arXiv preprint arXiv:1806.04356

Heikkinen, E. (2015). LOGDIG Log File Analyzer for Mining Expected Behavior from Log Files. *14th Symposium on Programming Languages and Software Tools*.

Horisberger, M. (2013). *Centeractive AG: When SIEM is too much*. Retrieved 10 18, 2018, from Retrospective: https://retrospective.centeractive.com/blog_retrospective_whenSIEM.html

Kim, D. H. (2018). Attack Detection Application with Attack Tree for Mobile System using Log Analysis. *Mobile Networks and Applications*, 1–9.

Makanju, A. A.-H. (2009). Clustering event logs using iterative partitioning. In *Proceedings of the 15th ACM SIGKDD international conference on Knowledge discovery and data mining* (pp. 1255-1264). ACM.

Mavroeidis, V. A. (2018). Data-Driven Threat Hunting Using Sysmon. *2018 International Conference on Cryptography, Security and Privacy (ICCSP)*. 10.1145/3199478.3199490

Mohurle, S. A. (2017). A brief study of wannacry threat: Ransomware attack 2017. *International Journal of Advanced Research in Computer Science, 8*.

Nagappan, M. A. (2010). Abstracting log lines to log event types for mining software system logs. In *7th IEEE Working Conference on Mining Software Repositories (MSR)* (pp. 114-117). IEEE. 10.1109/MSR.2010.5463281

Oliner, A., Ganapathi, A., & Xu, W. (2012). Advances and challenges in log analysis. *Communications of the ACM, 55*(2), 55–61. doi:10.1145/2076450.2076466

Oprea, A. F. (2015). Detection of early-stage enterprise infection by mining large-scale log data. In *Dependable Systems and Networks (DSN), 2015 45th Annual IEEE/IFIP International Conference on* (pp. 45-56). IEEE.

Russinovich, M. (2017). How to Go from Responding to Hunting with Sysinternals Sysmon. *RSA Conference*.

Statista. (2019, January). *Global market share held by operating systems for desktop PCs, from January 2013 to January 2019*. Retrieved from Statista: https://www.statista.com/statistics/218089/global-market-share-of-windows-7/

Vaarandi, R. (2003). A data clustering algorithm for mining patterns from event logs. In *IP Operations & Management, 2003.(IPOM 2003). 3rd IEEE Workshop on* (pp. 119-126). IEEE.

Vaarandi, R. A. (2014). Using Security Logs for Collecting and Reporting Technical Security Metrics. In *Military Communications Conference (MILCOM)* (pp. 294--299). IEEE. 10.1109/MILCOM.2014.53

Vaarandi, R. A. (2015). LogCluster - A data clustering and pattern mining algorithm for event logs. In *11th International Conference on Network and Service Management (CNSM)* (pp. 1-7). IEEE. 10.1109/CNSM.2015.7367331

Yen, T.-F. A. (2013). Beehive: Large-scale log analysis for detecting suspicious activity in enterprise networks. In *Proceedings of the 29th Annual Computer Security Applications Conference* (pp. 199-208). ACM. 10.1145/2523649.2523670

Zhuge, C. A. (2017). Efficient Event Log Mining with LogClusterC. In *Big Data Security on Cloud (BigDataSecurity), IEEE International Conference on High Performance and Smart Computing (HPSC), and IEEE International Conference on Intelligent Data and Security (IDS)* (pp. 261-266). IEEE.

Chapter 8
Nature–Inspired Techniques for Data Security in Big Data

S. R. Mani Sekhar
Ramaiah Institute of Technology (MSRIT), India

Siddesh G. M.
Ramaiah Institute of Technology (MSRIT), India

Shaswat Anand
Ramaiah Institute of Technology (MSRIT), India

D. Laxmi
Ramaiah Institute of Technology (MSRIT), India

ABSTRACT

Inspired computing is based on biomimcry of natural occurrences. It is a discipline in which problems are solved using computer models which derive their abstractions from real-world living organisms and their social behavior. It is a branch of machine learning that is very closely related to artificial intelligence. This form of computing can be effectively used for data security, feature extraction, etc. It can easily be integrated with different areas such as big data, IoT, cloud computing, edge computing, and fog computing for data security. The chapter discusses some of the most popular biologically-inspired computation algorithms which can be used to create secured framework for data security in big data like ant colony optimization, artificial bee colony, bacterial foraging optimization to name a few. Explanation of these algorithms and scope of its application are given. Furthermore, case studies are presented to help the reader understand the application of these techniques for security in big data.

INTRODUCTION

Biologically inspired computing, better known as Bio-inspired computing is a discipline in which problems are solved using computer models which derive their abstractions from real-world living organisms and their social behavior. It can be considered a branch of Machine Learning which is very closely related to artificial intelligence. Its foundation is based upon the subjects of Computer Science, Biology

DOI: 10.4018/978-1-5225-9742-1.ch008

and Mathematics. Thus, Bio-inspired computing can go a long way in studying the diverse patterns and variations found among living beings which can be used to build better computer systems for solving complex problems in the future.

This form of computing can be effectively used for extracting a limited number of distinguishing features for a set of data which may have many irrelevant data features. It is also helpful in situations where the Classical Methods of Computation can be put to limited use only, like in cases involving pattern recognition in a data set which may have incomplete or vague information. It is also has an edge over the Classical Methods of Computation where the system needs to adapt itself to changes and variations over a period of time. In other words, it is more adaptive compared to its rather rule-bound counterpart (Sekhar, Bysani, & Kiranmai, 2018), Bio Inspired computing is a sub branch of machine learning can be implement using various languages. (Sekhar, & Siddesh, 2018).

Some of the most popular Biologically inspired Computation algorithms covered under this section involve methods like Neural Networks, Artificial Bee Colony, Genetic Algorithm, Particle Swarm Optimization, Ant Colony Optimization, Bacterial Foraging Optimization, Cuckoo Search, Firefly Algorithm, Leaping Frog Algorithm, Bat Algorithm, Flower Pollination Algorithm and Artificial Plant Optimization. The chapter presents the working of and drawbacks of each algorithm. Further the applications of the algorithms in big data security are discussed with the help of case studies.

Types of Bio-inspired Computing Algorithms

Some of the algorithms discussed in the chapter are:

- Artificial Bee Colony Algorithm
- Bacterial Foraging Algorithm
- Cuckoo Search Algorithm
- Leaping Frog Algorithm
- Bat Algorithm
- Flower Pollination Algorithm
- Firefly Algorithm

Artificial Bee Colony Algorithm

Introduction

Areas like Engineering, Economy and Management are prone to certain Optimization Problems. To tackle such Optimization problems, there is a need for some effective and efficient Optimization Algorithms. These algorithms are divided into two categories -Evolution-categories (Fogel, 2000) and Swarm Intelligence categories (Eberhart Kennedy., 2001) optimization algorithms. Over the past few years many Swarm Intelligence based optimization algorithms have been put forward which on analyzing the demeanor of insects, birds or fishes concepts can be helped in solving numerical optimization complexities in various scientific domains.

One such Optimization methodology is the Artificial Bee Colony (ABC) also known as the ABC Algorithm. The ABC technique was introduced by Karaboga in 2005, he used the base concept of honeybees while trying to obtain a valuable meal (Karaboga, 2005). The swarm of honey-bees possesses numerous qualities like intercommunicating information within the hive, storing such information and then arriving at a decision based on this information. The word information here means the quality; availability of its bread. There are basically three different types of bees in the swarm- employed bees which gather information about their food source, onlooker bees which reside in the beehive and analyze the quality of the food based on the data gathered by the employed bees and the scout bee which is an employed bee searching for a new meal after its previous meal is exhausted (Karaboga, & Akay, 2009). This sort of peer-to-peer connection among swarms of bees forms the basis for the ABC algorithm.

Working Principle

The Artificial Bee Colony algorithm comprises of a cycle of four different phases based on the type of bees in the colony. Firstly the initialization phase, trailed by the employed bees level, onlooker bees level and lastly, the scout bees level. A detailed description of each of these phases is described below:

1. Initialization Phase

In this phase the ABC methodology creates a randomly distributed population of SN results (food origins) where SN represents the size of the swarm. For each value of $x0_i$ (i = 1, 2, 3, ...,SN) is consider as a D - dimensional vector.

Meanwhile the total no. of variables in the optimization concept is represented as a D and x_i represents the i th food source. An individual employed bee generates a new food source by considering random variable, direction and distance.

2. Employed Bees Phase

This phase involves the employed bees deciding between the existing solution and the new solution on the basis of the nectar amount or fitness value of the latest solution. If the nectar variable of the latest solution (food source) is greater than the previous value, the honey bee changes its location to the new food position and disposes the old one.

3. Onlooker Bees Phase

In this third stage, each of the employed bees share with the onlooker bees at the hive, information regarding the nectar available at the food sources that is, the updated solutions and the new positions of the food sources. This sort of information is called fitness information. The onlooker bees scrutinize this evidence and choose a best solution having a probability pi correlated to its ability. Subsequently probability will be calculated. If the ability is greater than that of the previous one, subsequently the bees learn the updated location and leave the previous result.

4. Scout Bees Phase

This phase begins when the location of a food resource has not been revised for a fixed number of cycles, i.e the food source is assumed to be redundant. In this case, the bee with the abandoned meal is called the scout bee and that old abandoned meal will be replaced with a new randomly selected meal within a search space. The predetermined number of cycles here is called the boundary for rejection. Consider that the unrestricted value is x_i then the scout bee changes this location value with new value.

The efficiency of the algorithm depends on the initial swarm size. The effectiveness decreases after a certain limit of the swarm size. The efficiency also depends on the parameter limits.

Literature Survey

- Optimization of clustering approach in big data (Ilango, Vimal & Kaliappan, 2018) - Big data growth rate is estimated to be 40%. To manage huge amounts of data, clustering is done in order to group datasets into similar characteristics. ABC is used here for effective clustering. ABC carries out both local and global search by employed and onlooker bees respectively. Programming of ABC is done using Hadoop environment using a map/reduce. Based on minimum time execution, the optimal cluster is found. The success rate of the proposed methodology is determined by a series of experiments.
- Optimization of feature selection in big data (Ahmad et el., 2018) – A system architecture is presented which performs selection of features with the help ABC. The efficiency of processing is improved by ABC. Implementation is done using Hadoop and map reducer. The efficiency of proposed system is evaluated by processing various databases.

Applications

- **Used in the Computation of Set Covering Problematic (Crawford, Soto, Cuesta & Pareses, 2014):** The ABC algorithm is used to decipher the Non-Unicost Set Covering Problem. The set covering Problematic is a legal function for various practical optimization condition where the aim is to select a group of columns of least cost that covers each row.
- **Texture Feature Identification in Image Data (Chandrakala & Sumitha, 2014):** A demanding problem in the world of data mining today is to derive useful data from the massive images being generated by grouping the images into different categories. The traditional method of penetrating through the huge collections of images in the database by matching a keyword and image caption has a huge drawback for the user as he has to remember the exact caption and keywords to obtain the desired image. Alternatively, the Artificial Bee Colony Algorithm uses the technique of merging the similarity score based on the color and texture features of an image, thereby attaining good result in minimal time.

Advantages and Disadvantages

Advantages

- Implementation of the algorithm is easy.
- Has a wide range of applications as it can be applied to complex functions, which use continuous, discrete or mixed variables.(Gerhardt &Gomes, 2012)
- It has the ability to explore local solutions.
- Time can be saved by using this algorithm as the structure of the algorithm allows parallel processing.

- The simplicity, robustness and flexibility of the algorithm allow adjustments to be made by observing nature.
- The objective function need not be differentiable or continuous.

Disadvantages

- The secondary information about the problem is not used.
- In order to improve performance, the new algorithm parameters need to go through some new fitness tests.(Gerhardt et al., 2012)
- When there is a need to obtain accurate solutions, the process slows down.
- Have a huge number of objective function evaluations?
- Some information about the behavior of the function might be lost, thus some more optimization is necessary.

CASE STUDIES

Intrusion Detection

Introduction

Intrusion detection system (IDS) is a security model which makes use of machine learning for automatic detection of attack behavior. The action taken through an analysis of various parameters in the system. It is a hotspot for research in network security.

Proposed Solution

Modifies naive Bayes algorithm for Intrusion detection (Yang,Ye,Yan, Gu & Wang) have used ABC. Naive Bayes classifier is a widely used for classification. A modified naive based classifier (MNBC) is proposed for IDS. In MNBC, weights are assigned to the network. Weights are real numbers in the range of [0,2]. The classification accuracy of MNBC is assigned as fitness value for ABC. Public test data are used to test the proposed algorithm.

Bacterial Foraging Optimization Algorithm

Introduction

Bacterial foraging algorithm created by passino in 2002 belongs to a family of Bacterial optimization and swarm optimization algorithms. The inception of this algorithm came from the foraging behavior of E.coli bacteria. The foraging behavior can be classified into four processes namely reproduction, chemotaxis, swarming, and elimination and dispersal.

Working Principle

The foraging strategy is to maximize the energy intake per unit time. This involves four processes namely:

- **Chemotaxis**: The E-coli cell moves by swimming and tumbling using a flagella. The motility of the bacterium depends on the alteration of these two modes wh ich helps it to search for nutrients. It can swim in one direction or it can tumble for its entire lifetime.
- **Swarming:** A particular group behavior is exhibited by E-coli where it forms stable patterns(swarms) while searching for nutrients. The cells release attraction signals so that they can swarm together.
- **Reproduction**: It takes place when a Healthy bacterium divides itself into two or more bacteria and is placed in the same region. This keeps the size of the population constant. Whereas the least healthy ones don't survive.
- **Elimination and Dispersion**: Each bacterium is eliminated and dispersed so as to keep the population constant. If one bacterium is eliminated, then another is dispersed in another location in the optimization domain.

The bacterial foraging algorithm (Passino, 2002) is explained as follows:

- The parameters initialized are population size, number of chemotactic steps, maximum step size, number of steps in reproduction process, number of steps in elimination-dispersion, probability of elimination-dispersion, step size.
- Position of each bacterium must be initialized.
- Loop for elimination and dispersal: $c=c+1$
- Loop for reproduction: $b=b+1$
- Loop for chemotaxis: $a = a+1$

The chemotaxis loop:

- Calculate the fitness function of each bacterium, save this value.
- For the tumbling, a random vector is generated.
- The bacteria move in the direction of tumble according to the defined step size.
- New fitness value is calculated for the bacteria with updated position.
- For swim, initialize a counter c. While c is less than the maximum number of steps increment the value of the counter.
- If the value of the new fitness is less than the previous fitness value, then update the position and record the new fitness. Stop when counter is equal to the maximum number of steps. End of chemotactic loop.
- In reproduction step, compute the health of each bacteria. The bacteria with lowest health do not survive and the ones with high health split and are replicated at the same position. End of reproduction loop.
- Eliminate and disperse each bacteria according to their probability. End of elimination-dispersion loop.

The bacteria foraging algorithm deals with calculating the fitness function value at each iterative step value of the fitness is inversely proportional to the cost function. At each step, the parameters represent the coordinates of the bacteria. These parameters are to be optimized

The value of these parameters is discrete in the desired range. The bacteria move to new positions at each iterative step and the value of cost function is estimated. Finally, the bacteria reach to a position with optimal fitness value.

For optimization, there are challenges in choosing the values of these parameters. They are as follows:

- The Size of population of the bacteria St. With an increase in value of St, the computational complexity of the algorithm increases. If the value of S is very large then the population can be distributed randomly. This gives a possibility that some bacteria can start near the optimum point. Over time there will be increase in population at that point due to chemotaxis and reproduction.

- The basic chemotactic step $D(i)$ denotes the step size taken by the bacteria. If the value of $D(i)$ is very large then there is possibility of missing the local minima. I the value of the $D(i)$ is small then the process of finding local minima becomes slow.

- The cell to cell attractant function T^i_{cc} defines the nature of swarming. If the width of the attractant is high and very deep then the tendency to swarm is high. Otherwise, if the width of the attractant is small and shallow then the tendency to swarm is low.

- Large values of M_c ensures more number of chemotactic steps with increase in probability of optimization followed by increasing computational complexities. There is a reliance on chance and reproduction when value of M_c chosen is small.

- If small values of M_{re} are chosen then the algorithm might remain in the local minima itself. Alternatively if the values are high then then complexity of computation increases.

Literature Review

- Chen and Lin (2009) have introduced a novel approach to the BFO algorithm called iBFO in order to improve the classical approach of BFO. Here, the scope of search and the chemotaxis steps are varied dynamically accelerating precision of search and convergence. In order to find healthy bacteria for reproduction, the improvement proposed here is to locate those bacteria whose position is closer to the global minima as opposed to the number of chemotaxis steps taken in its lifetime. This reduces the time for computation. Another improvement suggested is to narrow down the search scope in order to accelerate convergence and increase accuracy. Benchmark functions used to test and provide analysis of iBFO are Sphere, Rosenbrock, Rastrigin and Griewank. NARMAX (nonlinear autoregressive moving average with exogenous) model has been used for parameter estimation.

- Personal information collected by various organizations is present on public domains. Data mining can be applied on them to obtain useful characteristics. At the same time mining on such data can leak private information about individuals. Privacy preserving data mining (Lindell & Pinkas, 2002). A novel clustering algorithm based on fractional calculus(Bhaladhare & Jinwala, 2014) has been proposed in data mining to improve convergence and optimization. l- diversity cryptographic method is used for privacy protection of an individual. Through experiments, the proposed clustering technique showed less loss of information.

Applications

- Task scheduling in cloud computing (Verma, Sobhanayak, Sharma, Turuk & Sahoo, 2017) have proposed an improved bacteria foraging algorithm iBFO to effectively schedule resource allocation in cloud computing environment.
- Control of Servo Motors (Lin, Leu & Lu, 2012) has applied bacterial foraging algorithm to fuzzy model to improve its parameters. This model is utilized in designing controllers for servo motors.
- Fingerprint recognition (Brar & Singh, 2014) have used BFO and support vector machine(SVM). It is used improve efficiency of classification of fingerprint dataset and provide accurate result.

Advantages and Disadvantages

Advantages

- It is a high performance optimization algorithm.
- Convergence is achieved faster due to its global search technique.
- It can handle multiple objective function.
- The computation time is less.

Disadvantages

- A bacterium which is near the optimal position may get dispersed or eliminated, hence the efficiency of convergence reduces.
- Large search space decreases the rate of conversion.
- The effects of cell to cell attractant and repellent are crucial to algorithm. High value of attractant produces swarming effect, however the increases the computation time of the algorithm. On the other hand, high value of repellant will cause oscillations.

CASE STUDIES

Implementation of Bacterial Foraging in Data Clustering

Introduction

Clustering is a technique to classify unsupervised patterns into groups (Jain, Murty & Flynn, 1999). Data clustering is a prominently used technique in data mining. Issues faced in clustering are efficiency and accuracy. To address these issues various nature inspired algorithms and techniques have been applied in recent years. Multi objective clustering analysis using particle swarm optimization (Armano & Farmani, 2016) to obtain optimal number of clusters. Big data service provided in mobile networking (Hossain, Moniruzzaman, Muhammad, Ghoneim & Alamri, 2016) have given an algorithm combining the features of PSO and k-means clustering.

Proposed Solution

Problem of Data Clustering (Mahapatra & Banerjee, 2015) have given a solution using bacterial foraging. The solution is given by providing an object oriented design of the BFO.

This design consists of three classes namely Environment System class, Bacterium class, and Bacteria System class. It provides a computational structure. Each of these classes contain private and public member function, UML diagrams are also given. By this method, adaptive reproduction is introduced.

The benchmark algorithm used here are k-means, BCO, GA based technique, and PSO-based algorithm. It is used to draw comparisons between the results obtained from performing object oriented BFS clustering on some artificial data sets and real life datasets.

Cuckoo Search Algorithm

Introduction

Xin-She Yang and Suash Deb proposed the Cuckoo Search algorithm in 2009.The Cuckoo Search algorithm also known as CSA, inspired by the parasitic nature of particular cuckoo kind anywhere they lay their eggs in the nests of other birds. This algorithm is further enhanced by lévy flights. If the host bird discovers these alien eggs, it either pushes them out of the nest or abandon the nest itself. There is a specific pattern in which these cuckoos choose their host nest. Some cuckoos chooses the host where eggs have been just layed . Often cuckoo eggs hatch prior then their host eggs. The first hatched cuckoo chick often evicts the other eggs in order to remove competition for food.

Working Principle

The Cuckoo Search algorithm (Yang & Deb, 2009) comprises of three ideal rules.

- A cuckoo bird lays only one egg at a time and allots it to a nest of a host bird chosen randomly.
- High quality of eggs from best nests is proceeding to the next generation.
- There is a limited count of host nests available. $p_b[0,1]$ denotes the probability of cuckoo's eggs being discovered. Moreover, the host bird removes the egg or abandons its nest.

Consider that each nest contains a single egg. Let's say a cuckoo j,performs a Lévy flight . The new solution $x_j^{(h)}$ can be represented as follows:

$$x_j^{(h)} = x_j^{(h-1)} + \beta \oplus L(\lambda)$$

Here $\beta > 0$, denotes the step size whose value depends on the problem type. The product $\oplus$ denotes entry wise multiplications. The above equation describes a random walk. A random walk is represented by a Markov chain in which the new position depends on the current position and the probability of transition between them.

CSA steps:

- Define an objective function which is to be maximized.
- Form an initial populace of host nests.
- While the value of the iterator is less than that of the maximum iterator, perform Lévy flight to pick a cuckoo. Calculate its fitness value.
- A nest is chosen randomly, if its fitness value is less than that of the cuckoo's then it is replaced with new solution.
- Some of the worst nests are abandoned represented by fraction p_b and new are built.
- The best solution proceeds to the next generation.
- The solutions are sorted and best one is chosen at that time.

The values of parameters p_a and β are fixed initially. When a small value is fixed for and high value for β then the algorithm efficiency decreases and computational complexities increases. If a high value is fixed for p_a and β value is small then convergence rate increases but the algorithm may miss the optimal solution. To overcome these challenges an improved CSA (Valian, Mohanna, & Tavakoli, 2011) has been introduced.

Literature Review

- Ranjani and Sridhar in 2017 have proposed a hybrid algorithm by the combining CS and PSO. It has been applied to solve the problem of scalability in big data clustering. Performance of this algorithm has been tested using test functions. The results have shown that the speed of convergence is fast.
- Cuckoo search with deep search (Zefan & Xiaodong, 2017) is based on opposition based learning (OBL). OBL is used to improve local and global search. OB-swarm is generated and selection is applied. At the end of each generation, local search is done close to the global optima in the direction of the evolution. Results of the simulation have yielded better global search ability, increase in convergence speed and the overall precision of the algorithms is improved.
- Big data retrieval (Prasanth & Gunasekaran, 2019) makes use of deep learning modified neural network (DLMN) to overcome the shortcomings of pre-existing methods of document retrieval. The first step involves feature extraction and pre-processing of data. Weight of the frequently occurring data item is found. The parameters related to the weight of the DLMN are optimized using CSA.

Applications

- Image processing of 2D images (Woźniak & Połap, 2014) use CSA – Here key points in an examined 2D image are found. Some natural features are efficiently searched for without the use of complicated mathematical operations.
- For the Clustering Problem (Girsang, Yunanto & Aslamiah, 2017) have developed a hybrid algorithm by combining CS and the K-Means algorithm to form FSCA. CS algorithm is used for initialization and K-means is used for clustering problem.

- To solve traveling Salesman Problem (Laha, 2015) have combined quantum and CS algorithm to form a novel algorithm.

Advantages and Disadvantages

Advantages

- The CS algorithm has the capability to perform both global and local search as search space is more efficiently explored.
- It is advantageous due to its simplicity and efficiency in highly non-linear, optimization problems in real-world, engineering problems.
- It uses Lévy flights as global search strategy.
- It meets the global convergence requirements.

Disadvantages

- Convergence to the optimal solution is not possible when dealing with high dimensional complex problems.
- Generally parameter values are kept constant, eventually decreasing its efficiency.
- The search speed and accuracy is low optimization of functions.

CASE STUDIES

Medical Text Data Security

Introduction

The advancement in healthcare technology has led to generation of huge number of medical data which is referred to as Medical Big Data (MBD). Huge amount of sensitive information is present in public domain and maintaining it becomes challenging. Security is crucial in such systems. The securities of medical text data (Thangavel & Adam, 2018) have used CSA to identify strong key in AES algorithm.

Proposed Solution

Using CSA to generate strong key. CSA is used for optimization. It is assumed that each egg laid is a key. The best nest with strong quality of eggs that is strong key proceeds forward to next generation. Here java is used for CSA implementation. The best solution obtained is a shared secret key and is used in AES algorithm. In AES algorithm, the shared key is used for encryption and decryption. Its operation is symmetric.Key generation using CSA is implemented in jdk 8.1 compiler. Encryption and Decryption is applied and the performance is evaluated on the basis of loss of information and time.

Leaping Frog Algorithm

Introduction

A new meta-heuristic algorithm was developed by the combination of concepts of Shuffled complex evolution(SCE) algorithm and Particle swarm optimization (PSO) called the Shuffled Leaping frog algorithm. It was proposed by Eunuff and Lansey in 2003. It is inspired from the concept of mematics. A meme is an idea that duplicates by parasitically transferring them to human being or living being minds to cause behavioral changes which is further propagated. In SFLA, the individuals are defined by introducing a model called virtual population. A swamp area consisting of a set of frogs leaping is considered. The swamp has a number of stones at different locations .The frogs leap from one stone to another in order to get the maximum food source. To improve the quality of the meme carried by each frog, they communicate among themselves and exchange their information. SFLA has been successful implemented to find solutions to combinatorial optimization problem by performing a heuristic search with the help of some heuristic functions.

Working Principle

The algorithm starts with a populace of frogs spread across a swamp area. The populaces of the frogs are divided into different sub-groups known as memeplexes and the frogs belonging to them can conduct independent searches. In each memeplex, frogs infect each with memes leading to memetic evolution. To ensure effective evolution, frogs with better memes are selected rather than those with poor memes. This selection is done through a triangular probability distribution. The quality of the memes is further improved through shuffling process. It is done mixing different memeplexes.

The algorithm (Eusuff, Lansey & Pasha,2006) can be explained through the following steps:

- A virtual population of F frogs is initialized in feasible space. Each frog represents a vector, with d dimension.

$$V = \{v1, v2, \ldots, v_d\}$$

- The fitness value $f(i)$ of each frog is calculated. F frogs are arranged in decreasing of their fitness. The location of the frog with finest ability among the entire populace is denoted as V_g.
- The frogs are alloted to M memeplexes. Each memeplex contains b number of frogs. The initial (first) frog is allocated to the first memeplex, subsequently second frog is assigned to the second memeplex and so on I^{th} frog assigned to I^{th} memeplex. $I+1^{th}$ assigned to the first memeplex and so on.
- Within each memeplex, a procedure of evolution takes place through a local search. K is the number of evolution steps taken within each memeplex.

A sub memeplex is constructed in which frogs with high value of fitness are given higher weights and those with lower values of fitness, lower weights. These weights are allocated by using triangular probability distribution. The frogs in sub memeplex are arranged in decreasing order of their suitability values. The list of frog in each sub memeplex is p.

The location of the frog with best suitability is denoted as V_b and the location of the frog with least fitness is denoted as V_w.

The position of the frog with worst fitness is updated as

$$Y = \min\{int[rand(V_b - V_w)], Y_{max}\} \text{ for positive step}$$

$$= \max\{int[rand(V_b - V_w)], -Y_{max}\} \text{ for negative step}$$

$$V_w' = V_w + Y$$

Here Y is the step size and rand() is a function having value between 0 and 1.

If updation doesn't produce a better fitness value then that frog has a solution in the global range. Y_{max} is the maximum step size.

1. The memeplexes are shuffled after a set of evolution steps. The frogs are rearranged in decreasing order of their fitness and the location of the finest frog of the whole populace is updated.
2. The condition for convergence is checked. If it is satisfied then the process stops otherwise partition and updation is repeated until convergence is achieved.

The performance of the algorithm depends on the choice of parameters. It has been observed that different set parameters are chosen depending on the problem type.

Challenges in optimization are as follows:

*   Parameters involved in SFLA are
    a : count of memeplexes
    b : count of frogs in respectively memeplex
    p : count of frogs in respectively sub memeplex
    K : count of evolution steps
    F : size of the population
    Y_{max}: maximum step size.
*   F is given as F = M * n. Increasing the population size, increases the computational complexity. Also the chances of losing the optimum value are high.
*   When n value is too small, it leads to the failure of memetic evolution.
*   For a small p value, the process of infection becomes slow.
*   Unwanted ideas are propagated when there too many frogs, that is if higher value of n is chosen.
*   Shuffling process becomes frequent when the value of K is small. This reduces the propagation of memes locally. When K value is high, memeplex tend to remain in their local optimum.
*   If the value of Y_{max} is small then the exploration of the frogs is reduced to local search. The actual optimum can be missed when the value of Y_{max} is high.

Literature Review

- Feature selection in high dimensional bio-medical data (Hu et al., 2018). Bio-medical data set contain huge number of features most of which are unnecessary. In this paper improved SFLA is proposed to optimize the accuracy of feature prediction by performing search operations on sub-groups and also to minimize the unwanted features. The effectiveness of the model is checked by performing a comparative analysis using k-nearest neighbor method.
- In order to ensure security in scheduling of resources in Cloud computing (Hu, 2015) have proposed a resource dispatching model which uses adaptive optimization SFLA. Here the learning ability is improved and the continuity of the update process is also maintained. The original algorithm had the tendency to confine itself in the local optima. Local search capability is improved by using Cauchy mutation operator. This new model showed better convergence after a series of simulations was performed.
- Classification of tweets based on crowd sentiment (Yuvaraj & Sabari, 2017) . In this paper, a new algorithm is proposed to classify tweets using a new method for feature selection. The feature vectors are expressed as binary encoding. SFLA is used in transfer function in order to flip the encoding bits.

Applications

- A modified shuffled leaping frog algorithm (MSFLA) for a face recognition system (Torkhani, Ladgham, Sakly, & Mansouri, 2017).
- Distributed generation placement in distributed systems (Suresh & Edward, 2017). In this paper, SFLA is used for efficient placement of distributed generation (DG). The position and size of DG is determined.

Advantages and Disadvantages

Advantages

- It is a robust meta-heuristic algorithm
- It is used to solve combinatorial problems.
- It can be further extended to solve problems related to mixed-integer.
- It can be applied in parallelization.
- The algorithm consists of few parameters and has high speed.
- It is simple and easy to implement.

Disadvantages

- The initial distribution of the population is non-uniform due to which diversity and search capability of the population is decreased.
- During the updating process, only the location of the frog with less fitness rate is updated and best fitness ones remain the same.

- In the process of updating, the number of updating is not noted. This eventually slows down the convergence.

CASE STUDIES

Privacy Protection in Social Network Using Clustering and SFLA

Introduction

In recent times, social networking has become popular on the Internet. Social networks provide various services to people like connecting with friends, forming groups online and sharing information online. These platforms allow users to enter their personal information. With a huge amount of personal information being available on these networks, privacy protection and security of these data becomes crucial. Privacy protection in social media (Gazalian & Safi, 2018) have used k-clustering and SFLA.

Proposed Solution

Social network is denoted by graph $G = \{V,E\}$, where V is the vertex of the graph denoting a user in the network. E is the edge of the graph which denotes the connection between users. In this paper, k-degree anonymity (Liu & Terzi, 2008) is used for the graph. The distance between users in the network is measured by closeness centrality.

To preserve user privacy, k-anonymity is proposed by applying graph clustering and SFLA.The approach has been formulated into three steps. The first step is clustering of graph. It is done to get k-degree anonymity. Each cluster has k vertices and equal degree. The second step is to apply SFLA in order to get k-anonymity. Vertices with equal degree are anonymized and the rest are anonymized through addition and deletion of vertices and edges. SFLA is applied to achieve equal degree for each vertex. The fitness function is minimized in this case. The parameters considered for SFLA are edges and vertices. Here the fitness is the difference of sum of degree of vertices in the cluster. The fitness is calculated for each addition of vertex or edge and deletion of edge. The third step is graph modification, where a necessary modification in the graph is carried out in order to reach anonymity. The proposed model is tested on different data sets.

Network Security: Intrusion Detection

Intrusion detection is a network security model which senses network attack automatically.

Intrusion detection system (Yang & Li, 2014) makes use of shuffled leaping frog algorithm. By using KD99 data set, Classification rules are formed by SFLA. These rules are applied for detection.

Bat Algorithm

Introduction

The Bat Algorithm uses a meta-heuristic procedure which was implemented by Xin-She Yang in 2010 (Yang, 2010). The algorithm is built upon the process of echolocation techniques used by bats to detect their prey which may be very small, through the use of loud ultrasonic waves. These waves are generated at regular intervals depending upon the proximity between the bat and its prey.

Working Principle

There are various components used in this methodology like wavelength, velocity, occurrence, and loudness. As mentioned earlier, the loudness of the sound wave differs rendering to the space between the bat and its prey. The algorithm involves some basic assumptions, which are as follows:-

- The bats gauge the space of the prey using echolocation and they have the skill to distinguish between an object and a prey.
- They generate a random values called as velocity (vel_i) and is at a location position p_i, with a fixed frequency $freq_{min}$. Whereas wavelength (λ) and loudness (lod_0) used for prey search. Subsequently customized along with the proportion of pulse emission $r \in [0, 1]$, dependent on the nearness to their goal.
- The loudness signal can differs in numerous conducts but the system assume it to vary between a huge (positive) A_0 to a lowest fixed value A_{min}.

Literature Review

- Classification of malicious URLs (Bansal, 2017) have used bat algorithm to select features from a list of URLs. Further SVM classifier is used to classify these URLs as malign or benign.
- In cloud computing environment, to ensure data security and its integrity (Punitha & Indumathi, 2018) have introduced a new framework. This framework utilizes cryptographic techniques for the system. Here the generation of key is done using bat algorithm.

Applications

- Used in microelectronic devices by Topology Optimization (Yang, Karamanoglu & Fong, 2012).
- For Multispectral Satellite Image Classification (Senthilnath, Kulkarni, Benediktsson & Yang,2016).
- Full Model Selection (Bansal & Sahoo,2015).
- For Scheduling Workflow Applications in Cloud (Raghavan, Sarwesh, Marimuthu,& Chandrasekaran,2015) have used bat algorithm for optimal use of resources and minimization of cost incurred.

Advantages and Disadvantages

Advantages

- The rate of convergence of the algorithm is fast initially.
- The frequency parameter can be fine-tuned.
- There is transfer from the process of exploration to exploitation in order to strategically look for solutions locally.

Disadvantages

- Chances of falling into local optima are high.
- The precision of the optimal solution depends on the selection of parameter values, which requires series of tests and its analysis.

CASE STUDIES

Full Model Selection Using Bat Algorithm

Full Model Selection (FMS) is used to select the optimal combination of pre-processing procedure, and learning methodology in command to generate the least classification error for a given value.

In order to implement FMS by incorporating bat algorithm (BFMS), the author uses a adapted Bat Algorithm (Bansal, & Sahoo, 2015). The traditional bats methodology is altered to integrate the binary programmed bats values. Moreover, the suitability of every bat is computed in a hierarchical process.

The FMS use the following process:

- Consider binary vector size as two.
- Generate bat for each feature selection binary numbers.
- Map index value equivalent to selected feature, else state is as 0 (not selected).
- Update itself and subsequently generate real values. next assign values to Gaussian transfer function (between 0 and 1).
- Define fitness function(fit_fun) and subsequently reduce classification error(CE) and also decrease feature vector measurement.

fit_fun= ran1 * CE + ran2*(NoFe / TF)

here, ran1 and ran2 are random values (sum of given value is 1)

TF: total features

NoFe: number of feature

Scheduling Workflow Applications in Cloud

In a cloud, the Bat algorithm can be used to schedule workflow with the help of binary bats. In particular, this method is used for the mapping of tasks and resources. To decrease the total cost of the workflow we should select the ideal resources. We exactly focus on the task of resource mapping. Thus, our key goal is to efficiently map the resources with reduced cost. The following scheduling algorithm is used:- (Raghavan, et al.,2015)

- Set or fix the cost of various compute resources.
- Compute the value of every job (Ti) on each compute resource Rj.
- For various possible mappings Ti X Rj need to be generate.
- Find the negligible cost for the job on various resources corresponding to Bat method.
- Based on the above results, assign the tasks.
- Generate the final minimal value

Flower Pollination Algorithm

Introduction

The Flower Pollination Algorithm (FPA) plants which is essential for their reproduction and survival. Pollination can do through either biotic or abiotic means. Biotic pollination means transfer of pollens through pollinators like insects, bees, etc. while abiotic pollination includes other factors like wind. Pollination can also happen within the same flower which is referred to as Self-pollination and can also occur between different flowers, which are known as Cross-pollination. Flower constancy is maintained when a pollinator visits the same type of flowers, thus maximizing pollen transfer among the same flower species.

Working Principle

The flower pollination algorithm is based upon certain rules which are listed below: -

- Global pollination generated from cross-pollination and biotic where the pollinators are considered to be having a Levy flight (Pavlyukevich, 2007) behavior.
- Local pollination consists of abiotic and self-pollination.
- Flower constancy is correspondent to the probability of reproduction which is related to the resemblance of two flowers.
- Local pollination and international pollination is exact by a probability of switch $p \in [0, 1]$ which may be slightly inclined towards local pollination.

The solution $x0_i^t$, read as solution x_i at iteration t for the worldwide pollination is given by the following equation $x0_i^{t+1} = x0_i^t + LP(x0_i^t - g_*)$, where g_* is the present finest solution and LP is the parameter representing the strength of pollination.

Similarly, the solution for local pollination can be represented as $x0_i^{t+1} = x0_i^t + \epsilon (x0_j^t - x0_k^t)$, where $x0_j^t$ and $x0_k^t$ are pollens from dissimilar flowers belonging to the similar species and ϵ is uniform distribution [0,1].

The pseudo code for the Flower Pollination Algorithm can be summarized as below:-

- Compute minimum function and maximum function
- Set the total value of flower population using random values
- Compute the finest result i.e. g*
- Calculate switch probability
- Repeat the process until you find the best value in the given population
- Compute the current finest value i.e g_*
- Display the result

Literature Review

- Medical images contain sensitive information and its presence on public networks raises security concerns. To address these, (Avudaiappan et al., 2018) have provided a two-step encryption procedure. First step uses blowfish encryption to encrypt the original image. Opposition base flower pollination algorithm has been used to strengthen the key generation.
- In recent times, there is a potential for using electroencephalogram (EEG) signals for biometric authentication. (Alyasseri, Khader, Al-Betar, Papa & Alomari,2018) have proposed a new technique where multi-objective flower pollination algorithm has been used to obtain important features from denoised signals. Comparisons are drawn against standard datasets of EEG signals.

Applications

- For Parameter Identification of DC Motor Model (Puangdownreong, Hlungnamtip, Thammarat, & Nawikavatan, 2017). In this paper, FPA along with levy distribution is used to reach global optima efficiently.
- For scheduling problem using disparity count process (Phuang, 2017).
- Feature selection in review spam detection (Rajamohana, Umamaheswari, & Abirami, 2017).
- In computation of Graph Coloring Problem (Bensouyad & Saidouni, 2015).

Advantages and Disadvantages

Advantages

- The algorithm is simple to implement and offers flexibility.
- The convergence of the algorithm is exponential in nature.
- It is efficient to solve problems of multi-objective type.

Disadvantages

- The performance of the algorithm be enhanced by fine tuning its parameters.

CASE STUDIES

Graph Colouring Problem

Assume *G = (Vx, Ex)* be a graph where *Vx = {v1, v2,..., vn}* consist of fixed set of vertices and *Ex ⊆ V × V* is a fixed set of edges. A solution for the Graph Colouring Problem is one in which a maximum of 'k' colors are used such that no two neighboring vertices have the same color. Mathematically, this can be represented as a function C: $V \rightarrow$ {1,…,} such that *C* (*u*) ≠ *C* (*v*) for some (*u, v*) ∈ *E*, where *C* (*u*) is the color of the vertex 'u'. Conflicting vertices are those pair of adjacent vertices which have the same color, while the edge connecting them is known as a conflicting edge.

The solution to the above problem can be proposed through the following algorithm:- (Bensouyad & Saidouni,2015)

- Provide input graph G=(Vx, Ex)
- Set total population count or size for the flowers
- Set No. number of iteration with respect to highest degree in graph and color as k
- With random value adjust a population of No. flowers
- Compute efficient result and subsequently state probability of switch (0,1)
- Make finite number of iteration with the help of random number and draw vector or uniform distribution.
- Compute distribution
- Generate integer value using round function.
- If found best solution store the result otherwise Repeat the above step

Spam Detection

In the current world, where people are becoming increasingly dependent on product reviews, it becomes essential to select features depending upon which spam reviews can be detected (Sekhar, Matt, Manvi & Gopalalyengar, 2019). Since feature selection is a binary classification, thus we represent 1 to represent if a feature is selected or else 0 otherwise. S variables represent the features of a flower as $Fi_-(fi_1, fi_2..., fi_n)$. In this Binary Flower Pollination Algorithm (Rajamohana, et al.,2017), the following sigmoid function is used to restrict the values in the range of [0.0 to 0.1]. $S(xi_j(t))=1/(1+e^{-xi_j(t)})$. The two equations in the flower pollination algorithm is thus replaced by the following equation:-

$$x_i^j\left(t\right) = \{1, \wedge if S\left(x_i^j\left(t\right)\right) > \sigma 0, \wedge otherwise$$

where $x_i^j\left(t\right)$ shows the latest pollen result i with j^{th} feature value at iteration t and $\sigma \cup \left(0,1\right)$.

Firefly Algorithm

Introduction

The Firefly algorithm is yet another algorithm developed by (Yang, 2010) belonging to the class of meta-heuristic algorithms. It is based upon those flashing characteristics of fireflies which are considered to be ideal.

Working Principle

The ideal characteristics of flashing fireflies are listed below:-

- Every firefly gets involved in another firefly regardless of its sex, implying that all fireflies are unisex.
- The charm character of a firefly is related to its glow which means that a less bright one gets attracted towards the more brighter one. The more attractive firefly moves randomly. Also, the attractiveness and brightness vary inversely with distance.
- The light intensity or brightness of a firefly depends upon the scenery of the impartial purpose to be optimized.

For an expansion problem, the illumination can be relative to the impartial function whereas it can be inversely proportional to the impartial method for a minimization problem.

Below step illustrate the process of computation using fireflies:

- Set the Impartial function
- Initialize the fireflies populace.
- Set interest coefficient of light
- For each fireflies compute the intensity of light with respect to the distance and move to a particular direction
- Repeat the process until you get new solution and subsequently update light intensity
- Rank the fireflies and compute the best result subsequently visualize.

Literature Review

- With the help of big data analytics, (Raj & Babu, 2015) have given a firefly inspired algorithm to form new connections over social networks.
- To solve big data optimization problems, (Wang et al., 2018) have proposed a hybrid algorithm based on firefly algorithm.

Applications

- Image Segmentation using Firefly Algorithm (Sharma & Sehgal, 2016).
- Software Modularization Using the Modified Firefly Algorithm (Mamaghani & Hajizadeh, 2014).
- For Resolving Economic Dispatch issues (Sulaiman, Mustafa, Zakaria, Aliman & Rahim, 2012).
- For Solving issues related to Schemes of Nonlinear Equations (Wang,& Zhou,2014).

Advantages and Disadvantages

Advantages

- The population is divided into small groups. The search takes place within these groups.
- It is applied for multi modal optimum problems.
- The rate of convergence increases with fine tuning of parameters.

Disadvantages

- The algorithm may contain to local optima.
- Hybridization of this algorithm can be used to solve non-linear multi modal optimization problems.

CASE STUDIES

Economic Dispatch Problem

One of the challenging difficulties of power technique is the Economic Dispatch(ED) as it is very challenging task to generate the optimum scheduling result subsequently to meet the specific load request with the less fuel cost and transmission loss.

The Firefly algorithm proposed (Sulaiman et al., 2012) to generate the ideal result of ED is mainly focus on the assessment of load flow platform. The variables of the optimal ED are coded as follow: $x= x_1 x_2 x_3,...,x_{ng}$ where n_g is the sum of producer plant in the system.

Mainly, the ED program incorporated with the Firefly Algorithm to generate the most favorable ED values. These values are incorporated in the statistics of load flow subsequently the load flow value is used to generate the final loss of the application meanwhile the total cost function value is computed. The system should run iterative so the optimal result can be generated.

Solving Systems of Nonlinear Equations

Solving systems of linear equations is an essential part of computation in engineering and scientific research. The traditional algorithms are susceptible to poor convergence and high compassion to initial guess of the result. The computation precision can be improved by using the Firefly algorithm integrated with pattern examine strategy.

Hooke and Jeeves proposed a shortest technique for resolving the unconstrained optimization problem which makes axial move and style move alternately. The main objective of axial route step is to explore the improved way of decrease while that of the style change is to accelerate decrease along a favorable way. This approach combined with the Firefly algorithm is listed using the following steps:- (Wang & Zhou,2014)

Below section illustrate the different steps:

- Set the different parameter like population of fireflies, light intensity, light absorption coefficient & times.
- Initialize positions of firefly.
- Calculate maximum brightness of firefly and also set relative brightness
- Set direction and position.
- Generate better result using pattern search method.
- Repeat the above steps utile you get the optimization solution.

CONCLUSION AND FUTURE WORK

This chapter presents the work in the area of bioinformatics and big data. Subsequently it also illustrates the working of various bio-inspired algorithms and addresses its drawbacks. A variety of applications of these algorithms are also provided. The author discusses the different issues faced in big data security such as privacy protection, access control and secured storage. This chapter provides how bio-inspired techniques have been integrated with data encryption, network security and distributed storage to form a security framework with the help of case studies. The different case study proves that bio-inspired computing can be a better solution for security in big data. Although there is a scarcity of literature in this field, bio-inspired computing has future research scope. The applications of bio-inspired computing in medical data security, intrusion detection system (Stergiou, Psannis, Kim & Gupta,2018) and privacy protection (Gupta,Yamaguchi & Agrawal,2018) discusses its scope in the lines of big data security. Future work in bio-inspired computing has potential to solve problems faced with big data and its security counterpart.

REFERENCES

Ahmad, A., Khan, M., Paul, A., Din, S., Rathore, M. M., Jeon, G., & Choi, G. S. (2018). Toward modeling and optimization of features selection in Big Data based social Internet of Things. 2018. *Future Generation Computer Systems*, *82*, 715–726. doi:10.1016/j.future.2017.09.028

Alyasseri, Z. A. A., Khader, A. T., Al-Betar, M. A., & Papa, J. P., & ahmad Alomari, O. (2018, July). EEG-based person authentication using multi-objective flower pollination algorithm. In *2018 IEEE Congress on Evolutionary Computation (CEC)*, (pp. 1-8). IEEE. 10.1109/CEC.2018.8477895

Armano, G., & Farmani, M. R. (2016). Multiobjective clustering analysis using particle swarm optimization. *Expert Systems with Applications*, *55*, 184–193. doi:10.1016/j.eswa.2016.02.009

Avudaiappan, T., Balasubramanian, R., Pandiyan, S. S., Saravanan, M., Lakshmanaprabu, S. K., & Shankar, K. (2018). Medical image security using dual encryption with oppositional based optimization algorithm. *Journal of Medical Systems*, *42*(11), 208. doi:10.100710916-018-1053-z PMID:30244385

Bansal, A. (2017). *Malicious Web URL Classification using Evolutionary Algorithm*. Academic Press.

Bansal, B., & Sahoo, A. (2015). Full Model Selection Using Bat Algorithm. *Cognitive Computing and Information Processing (CCIP), 2015 International Conference on*, 1-4. 10.1109/CCIP.2015.7100693

Bensouyad, M., & Saidouni, D. (2015). A discrete flower pollination algorithm for graph coloring problem. *Cybernetics (CYBCONF), 2015 IEEE 2nd International Conference on*, 151-155. 10.1109/CYBConf.2015.7175923

Bhaladhare, P. R., & Jinwala, D. C. (2014). *A Clustering Approach for the -Diversity Model in Privacy Preserving Data Mining Using Fractional Calculus-Bacterial Foraging Optimization Algorithm*. Advances in Computer Engineering. doi:10.1155/2014/396529

Brar, H. S., & Singh, V. P. (2014, September). Fingerprint recognition password scheme using BFO. In *2014 International Conference on Advances in Computing, Communications and Informatics (ICACCI)* (pp. 1942-1946). IEEE. 10.1109/ICACCI.2014.6968600

Chandrakala, D., & Sumathi, S. (2014). Image classification based on color and texture features using frbfn network with artificial bee colony optimization algorithm. *International Journal of Computers and Applications*, *98*(14).

Chen, Y., & Lin, W. (2009, December). An improved bacterial foraging optimization. In *Robotics and Biomimetics (ROBIO), 2009 IEEE International Conference on* (pp. 2057-2062). IEEE. 10.1109/ROBIO.2009.5420524

Crawford, B., Soto, R., Cuesta, R., & Paredes, F. (2014). Application of the artificial bee colony algorithm for solving the set covering problem. *The Scientific World Journal*, *2014*, 1–8. doi:10.1155/2014/189164 PMID:24883356

Edla, D. R., Lipare, A., Cheruku, R., & Kuppili, V. (2017). An efficient load balancing of gateways using improved shuffled frog leaping algorithm and novel fitness function for WSNs. *IEEE Sensors Journal*, *17*(20), 6724–6733. doi:10.1109/JSEN.2017.2750696

Eusuff, M., Lansey, K., & Pasha, F. (2006). Shuffled frog-leaping algorithm: A memetic meta-heuristic for discrete optimization. *Engineering Optimization*, *38*(2), 129–154. doi:10.1080/03052150500384759

Eusuff, M. M., & Lansey, K. E. (2003). Optimization of water distribution network design using the shuffled frog leaping algorithm. *Journal of Water Resources Planning and Management*, *129*(3), 210–225. doi:10.1061/(ASCE)0733-9496(2003)129:3(210)

Gazalian, P., & Safi, S. M. (2018). Presentation of a method for privacy preserving of people in social networks according to the clustering and sfla. *International Journal of Computer Science and Network Solutions*, *6*(1), 1–9.

Gerhardt, E., & Gomes, H. M. (2012). Artificial bee colony (ABC) algorithm for engineering optimization problems. *International Conference on Engineering Optimization*, 1-11.

Girsang, A. S., Yunanto, A., & Aslamiah, A. H. (2017, August). A hybrid cuckoo search and K-means for clustering problem. In *2017 International Conference on Electrical Engineering and Computer Science (ICECOS)* (pp. 120-124). IEEE. 10.1109/ICECOS.2017.8167117

Gupta, B. B., Yamaguchi, S., & Agrawal, D. P. (2018). Advances in security and privacy of multimedia big data in mobile and cloud computing. *Multimedia Tools and Applications, 77*(7), 9203–9208. doi:10.100711042-017-5301-x

Hossain, M. S., Moniruzzaman, M., Muhammad, G., Ghoneim, A., & Alamri, A. (2016). Big data-driven service composition using parallel clustered particle swarm optimization in mobile environment. *IEEE Transactions on Services Computing, 5*(5), 806–817. doi:10.1109/TSC.2016.2598335

Hu, B., Dai, Y., Su, Y., Moore, P., Zhang, X., Mao, C., ... Xu, L. (2016). Feature selection for optimized high-dimensional biomedical data using the improved shuffled frog leaping algorithm. *IEEE/ACM Transactions on Computational Biology and Bioinformatics*. PMID:28113635

Hu, X. (2015). Adaptive optimization of cloud security resource dispatching SFLA algorithm. *International Journal of Engineering Science, 4*(3), 39–43.

Jain, A. K., Murty, M. N., & Flynn, P. J. (1999). Data clustering: A review. *ACM Computing Surveys, 31*(3), 264–323. doi:10.1145/331499.331504

Karaboga, D. (2005). *An idea based on honey bee swarm for numerical optimization* (Vol. 200). Technical report-tr06. Erciyes University, Engineering Faculty, Computer Engineering Department.

Karaboga, D., & Akay, B. (2009). A comparative study of artificial bee colony algorithm. *Applied Mathematics and Computation, 214*(1), 108–132. doi:10.1016/j.amc.2009.03.090

Laha, S. (2015, December). A quantum-inspired cuckoo search algorithm for the travelling salesman problem. In *Computing, Communication and Security (ICCCS), 2015 International Conference on*. IEEE. 10.1109/CCCS.2015.7374201

Li, J. Q., Xie, S. X., Pan, Q. K., & Wang, S. (2011). A hybrid artificial bee colony algorithm for flexible job shop scheduling problems. *International Journal of Computers, Communications & Control, 6*(2), 286–296. doi:10.15837/ijccc.2011.2.2177

Lin, Y. S., Leu, Y. G., & Lu, W. C. (2012, November). Fuzzy bacterial foraging system and its applications in control of servo motors. In *Fuzzy Theory and it's Applications (iFUZZY), 2012 International Conference on* (pp. 203-207). IEEE. 10.1109/iFUZZY.2012.6409701

Liu, K., & Terzi, E. (2008, June). Towards identity anonymization on graphs. *Proceedings of the 2008 ACM SIGMOD international conference on Management of data*, 93-106. 10.1145/1376616.1376629

Mahapatra, G., & Banerjee, S. (2015, October). An object-oriented implementation of bacteria foraging system for data clustering application. In *2015 International Conference and Workshop on Computing and Communication (IEMCON)*. IEEE. 10.1109/IEMCON.2015.7344430

Mamaghani, A. S., & Hajizadeh, M. (2014). Software Modularization Using the Modified Firefly Algorithm. *Software Engineering Conference (MySEC), 2014 8th Malaysia*, 321-324. 10.1109/MySec.2014.6986037

Passino, K. M. (2002). Biomimicry of bacterial foraging for distributed optimization and control. *IEEE Control Systems, 22*(3), 52-67.

Pavlyukevich, I. (2007). Lévy flights, non-local search and simulated annealing. *Journal of Computational Physics*, *226*(2), 1830–1844. doi:10.1016/j.jcp.2007.06.008

Phuang, A. (2017). The flower pollination algorithm with disparity count process for scheduling problem. *Information Technology and Electrical Engineering (ICITEE), 2017 9th International Conference on*, 1-5. 10.1109/ICITEED.2017.8250497

Prasanth, T., & Gunasekaran, M. (2019). Effective Big Data Retrieval Using Deep Learning Modified Neural Networks. *Mobile Networks and Applications*, 1–13.

Puangdownreong, D., Hlungnamtip, S., Thammarat, C., & Nawikavatan, A. (2017). Application of flower pollination algorithm to parameter identification of DC motor model. *Electrical Engineering Congress (iEECON), 2017 International*, 1-4. 10.1109/IEECON.2017.8075889

Punitha, A. A. A., & Indumathi, G. (2018). Centralized cloud information accountability with bat key generation algorithm (CCIA-BKGA) framework in cloud computing environment. *Cluster Computing*, 1–12.

Raghavan, S., Sarwesh, P., Marimuthu, C., & Chandrasekaran, K. (2015). Bat Algorithm for Scheduling Workflow Applications in Cloud. *Electronic Design, Computer Networks & Automated Verification (EDCAV), 2015 International Conference on*, 139-144. 10.1109/EDCAV.2015.7060555

Raj, E. D., & Babu, L. D. (2015). A firefly swarm approach for establishing new connections in social networks based on big data analytics. *International Journal of Communication Networks and Distributed Systems*, *15*(2-3), 130–148. doi:10.1504/IJCNDS.2015.070968

Rajamohana, S. P., Umamaheswari, K., & Abirami, B. (2017). Adaptive binary flower pollination algorithm for feature selection in review spam detection. *Innovations in Green Energy and Healthcare Technologies (IGEHT), 2017 International Conference on*, 1-4. 10.1109/IGEHT.2017.8094094

Ranjani, A. C., & Sridhar, D. M. (2017). *A Proportional Study of Issues in Big Data clustering Algorithm with Hybrid Cs / Pso Algorithm. SSRG International Journal of Electronics and Communication Engineering*.

Sekhar, Bysani, & Kiranmai. (2018). Security and Privacy Issues in IoT: A Platform for Fog Computing. In *The Rise of Fog Computing in the Digital Era*. IGI Global.

Sekhar, M., Sivagnanam, R., Matt, S. G., Manvi, S. S., & Gopalalyengar, S. K. (2019). Identification of Essential Proteins in Yeast Using Mean Weighted Average and Recursive Feature Elimination. *Recent Patents on Computer Science*, *12*(1), 5–10. doi:10.2174/2213275911666180918155521

Sekhar, S. M., & Siddesh, G. M. (2018). *Introduction and Implementation of Machine Learning Algorithms in R. In Sentiment Analysis and Knowledge Discovery in Contemporary Business*. IGI Global.

Senthilnath, J., Kulkarni, S., Benediktsson, J. A., & Yang, X. S. (2016). A novel approach for multispectral satellite image classification based on the bat algorithm. *IEEE Geoscience and Remote Sensing Letters*, *13*(4), 599–603. doi:10.1109/LGRS.2016.2530724

Sharma, A., & Sehgal, S. (2016). Image Segmentation using Firefly Algorithm. *Information Technology (InCITe)-The Next Generation IT Summit on the Theme-Internet of Things: Connect your Worlds, International Conference on*, 99-102. 10.1109/INCITE.2016.7857598

Stergiou, C., Psannis, K. E., Kim, B. G., & Gupta, B. (2018). Secure integration of IoT and cloud computing. *Future Generation Computer Systems*, *78*, 964–975. doi:10.1016/j.future.2016.11.031

Sulaiman, M. H., Mustafa, M. W., Zakaria, Z. N., Aliman, O., & Rahim, S. R. A. (2012). Firefly Algorithm Technique for Solving Economic Dispatch Problem. *Power Engineering and Optimization Conference (PEDCO) Melaka, Malaysia, 2012 IEEE International*, 90-95. 10.1109/PEOCO.2012.6230841

Suresh, M. C. V., & Belwin Edward, J. (2017). Optimal Placement Of Distributed Generation In Distribution Systems By Using Shuffled Frog Leaping Algorithm. *Journal of Engineering and Applied Sciences (Asian Research Publishing Network)*, *12*(3).

Thangavel, G., & Adam, T. (2018). Securing Medical Text Data using Cuckoo Search based Advanced Encryption Standard (AES). *IOSR Journal of Computer Engineering*, 35-40.

Torkhani, G., Ladgham, A., Sakly, A., & Mansouri, M. N. (2017). A novel optimised face recognition application based on modified shuffled frog leaping algorithm. *International Journal of Applied Pattern Recognition*, *4*(1), 27–43. doi:10.1504/IJAPR.2017.082653

Valian, E., Mohanna, S., & Tavakoli, S. (2011). Improved cuckoo search algorithm for global optimization. *International Journal of Communications and Information Technology*, *1*(1), 31–44.

Verma, J., Sobhanayak, S., Sharma, S., Turuk, A. K., & Sahoo, B. (2017, May). Bacteria foraging based task scheduling algorithm in cloud computing environment. In *2017 International Conference on Computing, Communication and Automation (ICCCA)*, (pp. 777-782). IEEE. 10.1109/CCAA.2017.8229901

Wang, H., Wang, W., Cui, L., Sun, H., Zhao, J., Wang, Y., & Xue, Y. (2018). A hybrid multi-objective firefly algorithm for big data optimization. *Applied Soft Computing*, *69*, 806–815. doi:10.1016/j.asoc.2017.06.029

Wang, X., & Zhou, N. (2014).Pattern Search Firefly Algorithm for Solving Systems of Nonlinear Equations. *Computational Intelligence and Design (ISCID), 2014 Seventh International Symposium on*, 228-231. 10.1109/ISCID.2014.222

Woźniak, M., & Połap, D. (2014, August). Basic concept of cuckoo search algorithm for 2D images processing with some research results: An idea to apply cuckoo search algorithm in 2d images key-points search. In *Signal Processing and Multimedia Applications (SIGMAP), 2014 International Conference on*. IEEE.

Yang, H. D., & Li, Y. (2014). An Intrusion Detection Method Based on Shuffle Frog Leaping Algorithm. In Advanced Materials Research. Trans Tech Publications. doi:10.4028/www.scientific.net/AMR.1030-1032.1646

Yang, J., Ye, Z., Yan, L., Gu, W., & Wang, R. (2018, September). Modified Naive Bayes Algorithm for Network Intrusion Detection based on Artificial Bee Colony Algorithm. In *2018 IEEE 4th International Symposium on Wireless Systems within the International Conferences on Intelligent Data Acquisition and Advanced Computing Systems (IDAACS-SWS)*, (pp. 35-40). IEEE. 10.1109/IDAACS-SWS.2018.8525758

Yang, X. S. (2010). A new metaheuristic bat-inspired algorithm. In *Nature inspired cooperative strategies for optimization (NICSO 2010)* (pp. 65–74). Berlin: Springer. doi:10.1007/978-3-642-12538-6_6

Yang, X. S. (2010). *Firefly algorithm, stochastic test functions and design optimisation.* arXiv preprint arXiv:1003.1409

Yang, X. S. (2012, September). Flower pollination algorithm for global optimization. In *International conference on unconventional computing and natural computation* (pp. 240-249). Springer. 10.1007/978-3-642-32894-7_27

Yang, X. S., & Deb, S. (2009, December). Cuckoo search via Lévy flights. *2009 World Congress on Nature & Biologically Inspired Computing (NaBIC)*, 210-214. 10.1109/NABIC.2009.5393690

Yang, X. S., Karamanoglu, M., & Fong, S. (2012). Bat algorithm for topology optimization in microelectronic applications. *Future Generation Communication Technology (FGCT), 2012 International Conference on*, 150-155. 10.1109/FGCT.2012.6476566

Yuvaraj, N., & Sabari, A. (2017). Twitter sentiment classification using binary shuffled frog algorithm. *Intelligent Automation & Soft Computing*, 23(2), 373–381. doi:10.1080/10798587.2016.1231479

Zefan, C., & Xiaodong, Y. (2017, December). Cuckoo search algorithm with deep search. In *2017 3rd IEEE International Conference on Computer and Communications (ICCC)* (pp. 2241-2246). IEEE. 10.1109/CompComm.2017.8322934

KEY TERMS AND DEFINITIONS

Artificial Intelligence: A system's capability of impersonating human intelligence.

Big Data: Refers to large volumes of data, dealing with the computational techniques to manage them.

Bio-Inspired Computing: Computational method of solving problems using algorithms inspired from biological processes.

Cloud Computing: Distribution of system resources across the internet.

Machine Learning: Field of study of algorithms and statistical models which enables the computer to perform tasks without being specifically programmed.

Security: Protection of data from possible threats and mismanagement.

Chapter 9
Bootstrapping Urban Planning:
Addressing Big Data Issues in Smart Cities

Ankur Lohachab
https://orcid.org/0000-0002-5291-7860
Kurukshetra University, India

ABSTRACT

Rapid growth of embedded devices and population density in IoT-based smart cities provides great potential for business and opportunities in urban planning. For addressing the current and future needs of living, smart cities have to revitalize the potential of big data analytics. However, a colossal amount of sensitive information invites various computational challenges. Moreover, big data generated by the IoT paradigm acquires different characteristics as compared to traditional big data because it contains heterogeneous unstructured data. Despite various challenges in big data, enterprises are trying to utilize its true potential for providing proactive applications to the citizens. In this chapter, the author finds the possibilities of the role of big data in the efficient management of smart cities. Representative applications of big data, along with advantages and disadvantages, are also discussed. By delving into the ongoing research approaches in securing and providing privacy to big data, this chapter is concluded by highlighting the open research issues in the domain.

INTRODUCTION

IoT envisages enormous number of smart devices and embedded systems which empowers physical objects with pervasive sensing, seeing, hearing, and communication with each other. As a result, IoT can be considered as a big outlook for future Internet which provides a new scope of opportunities. The promise of Smart Cities ensures the transformation in various areas of human life including transportation, education, health, and energy. Smart Cities led to the concept of smart communities in which distinct electronic devices are inter-connected with each other and generally produce high-quality two-way interactive multimedia content. This multimedia content along with colossal amount of incommensurable types of datasets generated by heterogeneous IoT devices are collectively termed as Big Data. As compared with traditional data, Big Data contains more unstructured data that also require

DOI: 10.4018/978-1-5225-9742-1.ch009

real-time analysis. Mainly, three aspects are used for characterizing Big Data: (a) it cannot be classified into regular relational database, (b) it is in enormous amount, and (c) it is captured, processed, and generated expeditiously. An observation from McKinsey & Company suggests that Big Data create productive, competitive, and economic value in the five core sectors. Record creation of data due to its deep detailing is eliciting attention of everyone.

Along with IoT, Cloud Computing is a major breakthrough technology which is used as an alternative for providing dedicated storage space, software, and even expensive hardware to the users according to their uses and needs. The reason for adoption of Cloud Computing among common users is that it minimizes infrastructure cost by providing virtual resources and parallel processing with anytime, anywhere user access, and efficient management (Bhushan & Gupta, 2018; Chen, Mao, & Liu, 2014; Bhushan & Gupta, 2017). The said advantages motivate organizations for using the virtualized environment in the Smart Cities scenario. The increasing popularity of IoT devices and personal digital assistants has taken the Cloud Computing concept to prominence peak due to their limited storage capacity, processing capability, and constrained energy resources. The concepts of Cloud Computing, IoT, and Big Data are coalescing as IoT provides users the convenience to interact with their physical objects, Cloud Computing provides the fundamental engine through the use of virtualization, and Big Data provides users the capability of using commodity computing for processing their queries in a timely and efficient manner.

Despite the fact that these smart connected objects are used for reducing traffic congestion, fighting crime, making local decisions more open, and foster economic development, they are creating the Big Data that require excessive amount of energy which is also responsible for increasing greenhouse gases. Researchers and industrialists see Big Data as an opportunity for developing new solutions and analyzing new problems. Big Data can be seen as one of the driving technology for drastic increase in development of machine learning algorithms (Labrinidis & Jagadish, 2012). For enhancement of Smart City services, Big Data is mined, processed, and stored efficiently in order to help managers for taking right decisions in real-time according to the provided information (Caragliu, Bo, & Nijkamp, 2011). Although analyzing datasets of network flows, logs, and system events is always considered as a problem, nevertheless this Big Data driven information security is utilized for forensics and intrusion detection.

The field of security and privacy has many standards and regulations, but the unprecedented value of Big Data exposes it to various security and privacy risks. In various authentication protocols, anonymized information is primarily used for hiding critical information, but recent studies show that this anonymized information can be easily breached by attackers in terms of privacy (Lohachab & Karambir, 2019). Usually in the process of data anonymization, removal of obvious identifiers is done, but attackers easily re-identify the information using spatial-temporal points in the processed datasets. Although cryptography is a powerful technique for privacy protection, various attacks motivate us to rethink the exact meaning of identification (Gupta & Quamara, 2018). Accordingly, communication privacy should also be explored in terms of Big Data. Privacy protection mechanisms can be classified into two major categories: content and interaction privacy.

Along with security and privacy issues, various issues regarding to Big Data including scalability, availability, transformation, data quality, heterogeneity, regulatory, governance, and data integrity should be addressed. Computational intelligence algorithms and Quality of Service (QoS) for maintaining the scalable, reliable, fault tolerant, and flexible Big Data are still facing many challenges. According to the growing demands of Big Data analysis for the development of new Smart City, services should be

Figure 1. Impact of big data and IoT in rise of smart cities ecosystem

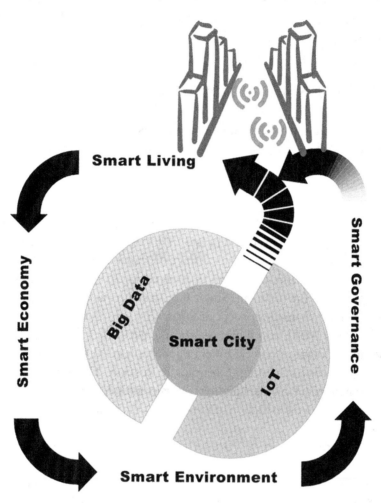

managed well for addressing the technological adoption of applications among common users. Figure 1 shows how Big Data and IoT collectively focus towards Smart Cities and their various services. Although, the age of Big Data also opens us to digital forensics investigation, but due to heterogeneous datasets, it is still considered as a challenging task (Cárdenas, Manadhata, & Rajan, 2013). Knowledge of this hype of Big Data analysis provides fine-grained, real-time control, and analysis for the governing bodies of the Smart Cities.

In this chapter, in depth analysis is done on the role of Big Data in Smart Cities. This chapter investigates the advantages of Big Data analysis in context of Smart Cities. Thereafter, it reviews the state-of-the-art of Big Data, and general background of the related technologies of Big Data. This chapter also examines the representative applications of Big Data including IoT, Smart Cities, Cloud Computing, and collective intelligence for presenting the big-picture to readers of this area. This chapter not only explores advantages of Big Data in relation to Cloud Computing and IoT, but also discusses various security and privacy challenges faced by the evolution of Big Data. This chapter also looks into the possibilities of Big Data forensics using secure data provenance mechanisms. How the issues like security and privacy of Big Data is affecting the use of widespread adoption of Big Data is also discussed. By delving into the on-going research approaches in securing and providing privacy to Big Data, this chapter concludes by highlighting the open research issues of Big Data and Smart City.

EVOLUTION, STATISTICS, AND MOTIVATION

This section summarizes evolutionary aspects of Smart Cities and Big Data and discusses their various aspects with the help of statistics along with motivation to work in the domain.

Historical Background

Although the synergic inter-connections between Smart Cities and Big Data are recognized by the recent developments made by IoT, their origin started in late 1990s after demands of smart growth. Since after its first appearance, the concept of Smart Cities springs its remarkable effects into various dimensions of our day-to-day lives (Zanella, Bui, Castellani, & Vangelista, 2014). The objectives of Smart Cities include Smart Mobility, Smart Environment, Smart Infrastructure, and Smart Utilities to their citizens. From an early understanding where the concept of Smart City gives emphasis only on Information and Communication Technology (ICT), now it also realizes the needs for connected physical infrastructure which assures better utilization of resources. Emerging technologies like Big Data and IoT make Smart Cities a responsive and effective inhabitant (Lazaroiua & Rosciab, 2012). Therefore, by reviewing the past events, it is more complacent for understanding their current state of importance. Table 1 summarizes the major events associated with the evolution of Smart Cities along with Big Data and IoT technologies.

Statistical Assessment

Most organizations and professionals believe that for making a plan more successful, data analytics plays a role of new frontier. Hence, during urban planning which is considered as the fundamental unit of Smart Cities, analysis of Big Data provides deeper insights. Big Data analysis can be done based on various requirements and levels. According to Intel research report in which they collected a broad range of data from top organizations for analyzing different types of data, they found that documents are still considered as the topmost data analytics source. Figure 2 summarizes the percentage of different kinds of sources that have been asked for analysis (Big Data Analytics, 2012).

It can be clearly seen from the Figure 2 that considerable amount of data has been asked for analysis. But in case of Smart Cities, these different kinds of data are collectively analyzed, since Smart City itself consists of various sources of data. Along with these heterogeneous types of data, various different sub-projects contribute their shares to Smart Cities. According to the Statista report 2017, various major sectors that represent the share in Smart Cities are shown in Figure 3 (IoT: smart cities projects share breakdown, 2017). Besides these sub-projects, comprehensive detail is given in Figure 4 which presents the number of installed IoT devices, particularly in Smart Cities within a time period from 2015 to 2018 (Smart cities total installed base of connected things 2015-2018, 2018).

Table 1. Unfolding progress in the field of smart cities and the concept of Big Data

Year	Events
1949	Claude Shannon did research on punch cards and photographic data storage capacity and largest item stored was Library of Congress sized 100 trillion bits in Claude Shannon's list of items.
1980	Formulation of Parkinson's Law of Data
1986	1st Municipal open data provided by Greater London Council, Intelligent and Research Services.
1989	Business intelligence appears after an acceleration in Enterprise Resource Planning (ERP) systems.
1992	Agenda of "Smart Growth" discussed in United Nations (UN) Conference on Environment and Development, Rio.
1994	First digital city practice started in Amsterdam.
1997	Two NASA researchers David Ellsworth and Michael Cox used the term "Big Data" for the first time in their research paper.
1997	Concept of Smart communities" introduced in Global Forum World Foundation for Smart Communities and first literature evidence of virtual Smart Cities had recorded.
1999	First actual practice of Smart City started in Dubai.
1999	An approximate quantified report of data presented by Hal R. Varian and Peter Lyman and it tells that 1.5 Exabyte's of Information exists in the world. At the same time the term "IoT" was termed by Kevin Ashton.
2005	For processing large amount of unstructured datasets, Mike Cafarella and Doug Cutting introduced an open source solution namely "Hadoop".
2005	First literature evidence for eco city and also first ubiquitous city practice started in Dongtan, Hwaseong, South Korea.
2007	First European Smart City group is announced.
2008	CPU's around the world processed almost 9.57 trillion gigabytes of data, in which Google alone processed 20 petabytes of data on a single day.
2009	A report given by McKinsey estimates that, US company with an average of 1000 employees stores more than 200 TB of information and also UN Habitat Agenda Urban Indicators are declared.
2011	In few seconds, 4TB of data is analyzed by IBM's supercomputer Watson and first U.S Smart City group is introduced.
2013	Several Smart City standards are introduced and Dell EMC studies finds out that only 22% of the actual collected data contains semantic value.
2014	Gartner finds out that almost 4.9 billion connected things present in our surroundings.
2015	IEEE declares its first Smart City group and also every day in the world approximately 2.5 quintillion bytes of data is produced, of which google processes 3.5 billion requests every day.

Apart from general processing of information, enterprises use Big Data for security analytics. Security strategies adopted by enterprises are still not sufficient to prevent insider threats or hackers. There are various reasons that are responsible for these types of attacks including weak security infrastructure, malware, and many others. Hence, there are various companies who believe that re-designing the whole infrastructure is not an effective idea. Instead, if they implement preventive and defensive strategies based on the data analysis, then it would be a better option. Hence, to do this effectively, enterprises rely on various kinds of real-time and historical data for identifying various types of illegitimate behavior. Although this approach is not new, but the organizations still believe that this is an efficient way. Various kinds of data with their share that can be considered for security analysis are shown in Figure 5 (Balaganski & Sebastian, 2016).

Figure 2. Various sources for data analysis in organizations

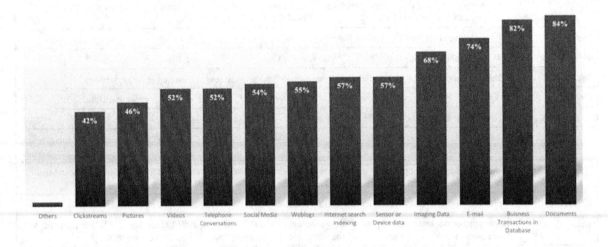

Total % ask to analyze

Figure 3. Contribution of various sub-projects that collaboratively constitute smart cities

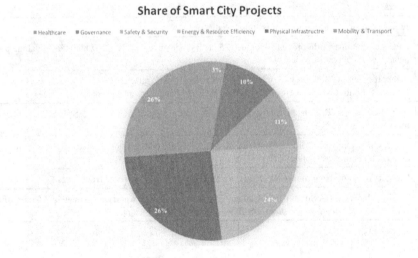

Share of Smart City Projects

According to KuppingerCole report, 85% of the log data is used for security analysis despite the fact that the primary reason for keeping these files are auditing and compliance. Ponemon Institute conducted a survey on more than 750 organizations and found that various technologies are generally combined with Big Data analytics for detecting potential threats to their organizations and betterment of their security, as shown in Figure 6 (Big Data Analytics in Cyber Defense, 2013).

Figure 4. IoT devices installed within smart cities

Connected Things (in billions)
Connected Things (in billions)
3.5
3
2.5
2
1.5
1
0.5
0
2014.5
2015
2015.5
2016
2016.5
2017
2017.5
2018
2018.5
2015, 1.18
2016, 1.64
2017, 2.33
2018, 3.33

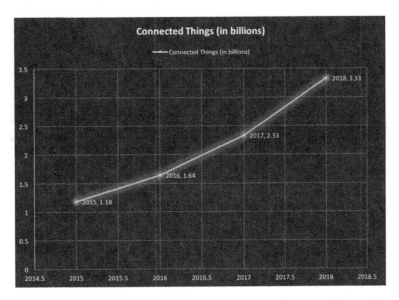

Figure 5. Various kinds of raw data used for security analysis

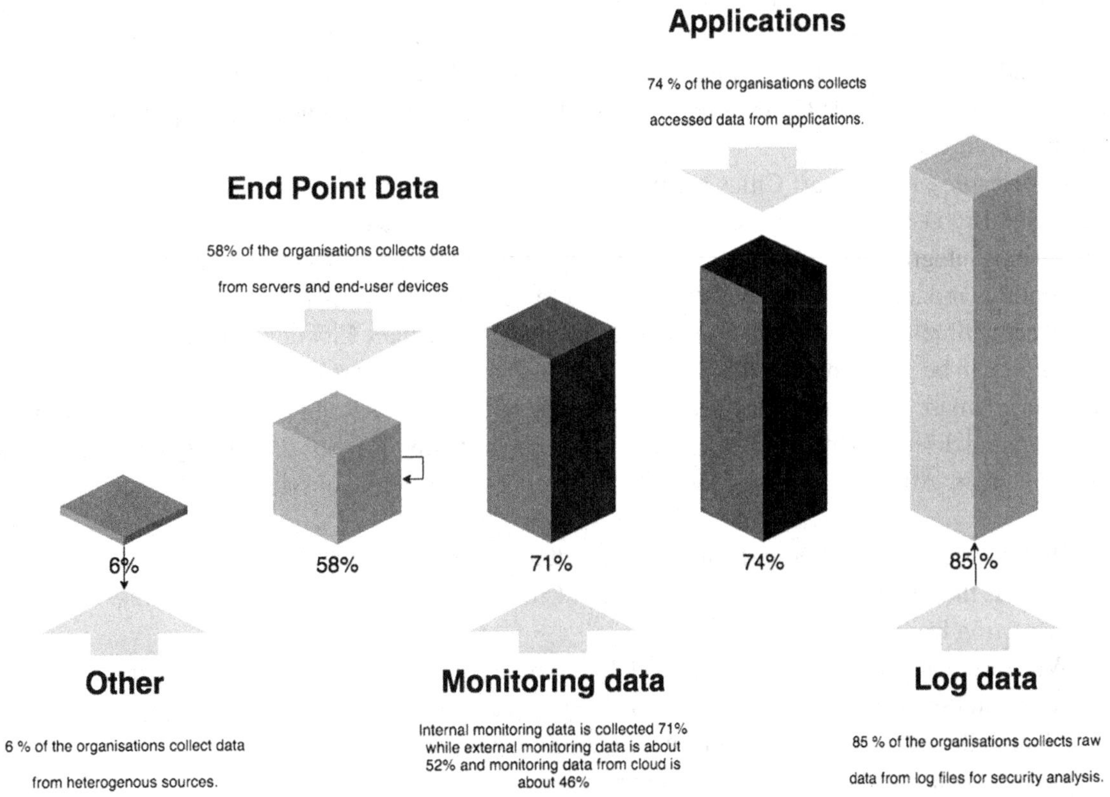

Applications
74 % of the organisations collects accessed data from applications.
End Point Data
58% of the organisations collects data from servers and end-user devices
6%
58%
71%
74%
85%
Other
6 % of the organisations collect data from heterogenous sources.
Monitoring data
Internal monitoring data is collected 71% while external monitoring data is about 52% and monitoring data from cloud is about 46%
Log data
85 % of the organisations collects raw data from log files for security analysis.

Figure 6. Various technologies integrated with big data analytics for security betterment

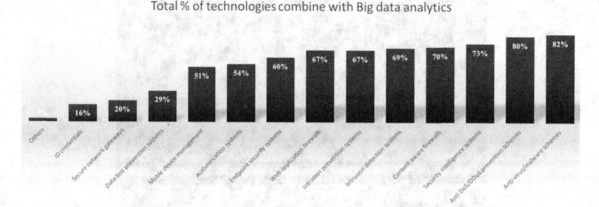

Total % of technologies combine with Big data analytics

Motivation

As Smart Cities are equipped with various IoT and traditional digital devices, so due to the embellished nature of digital devices, Smart Cities produce enormous amount of data. For providing value added services, various applications take initiatives to integrate with IoT devices, such as street cameras, sensors, actuators, and so forth. The majority of these applications have the facility to provide real-time sensing and actions, resulting in voluminous data being produced. By considering this, a formal definition and structure for Smart Cities is required, so that a significant amount of development can be seen in the near future.

The structure of the Smart Cities requires all the capabilities for efficient urban planning. Despite the fact that Big Data analysis prescribes the best environment suited for taking decisive actions, it also faces various integration challenges with the Smart City. This is also a fact that huge portion of the Big Data contains redundant and noisy data that need to be converted into a fruitful state. Both Big Data and IoT capabilities help in the process of urban planning and Smart City development, so accordingly, smart cities can be grouped into various component areas. These Smart City components include smart governance, smart economy, smart healthcare, smart people, and so on. Thus, this chapter comes up with a detailed discussion of Big Data, its impact on Smart Cities, various Smart City components, and their challenges. After reading this chapter, the readers will be able to answer the following questions:

- How can Big Data and Smart City be conceptualized and defined?
- What is the roadmap for Big Data and Smart Cities development according to the historical documentation from literature?
- What are the significant impacts of collaboration Big Data analysis with Smart Cities?
- How can the process of Big Data and Smart City be classified?
- What is the meta-architecture for Smart Cities from Big Data point of view?
- What are the current concerns for Big Data and Smart Cities?

SMART CITIES AND BIG DATA: AN OVERVIEW

In this section, basic concepts of Smart Cities and Big Data are illustrated for providing more appropriate understanding of these concepts.

Concept of Smart Cities

The paradigm of Smart Cities has gained more popularity among international policies and scientific literature in the last two decades. Hence, to understand the concept of Smart Cities, there is a need to understand that why the concept of cities achieves so much concern and why it is believed to be the primary element for the future (Angelidou, 2015). 21st century witnesses a global trend of shifting of citizens towards cities, and this maneuver is making cities denser and large. From the perspective of enterprises, these large and dense cities increase demands for innovative, productive, and desirable solutions for overwhelming the demands of their citizens and hence, enterprises believe that they can increase their revenues by lavishing these cities with solutions (Letaifa, 2015). Along with the various advantages these cities bring, the expeditious increase of new citizens creates new challenges for the Governments in various aspects including traffic congestion, informal development, waste management, and crime. This scenario looks for a way to find out the best possible scenario to tackle these challenges. In this context, global cities start looking for the solutions that will provide high-quality services by making deep-rooted effects on the economy (Osman, 2019). The approach to smart urban planning based on astonishing technologies focuses towards the concept of Smart Cities. The concept of the term Smart City is not just limited to the applications related to cities. In fact, this concept proliferates itself in many areas, but with no settlement on unanimous definition. Although various definitions of the Smart Cities exist in the literature, with conceptual variants accomplished by replacing "smart" with "digital" or "intelligent". This suggests that Smart City is a fuzzy concept, as single framing of definition cannot fit all templates of its applications (Piro, Cianci, Grieco, Boggia, & Camarda, 2014). Despite the fact that the current ongoing discussion does not settle down on a single definition of Smart City, but Smart Cities can be generally defined as a conceptual development model which makes collective use of humans and technology for the expansion of collaborative urban development. Anthopoulos and Fitsilis discusses various other alternative definitions of Smart Cities based on their classes by doing an analysis over 34 Smart City projects (Winters, 2010). Although their classes are not exactly reflecting the representative definition of Smart City, but some of the useful classes and also new classes along with their representative cities are summarized in Table 2. As per Table 2, it can be seen that various representative cities come under different categories.

Architecture of Smart Cities

Smart Cities architecture contemplates various technological aspects and design principles including facilitating smart services, smart governance, smart infrastructure, smart environment, and smart living (Cardullo & Kitchin, 2018). This chapter proposes an architecture which defines the structure of the layers and relationship among them. The main significance of this proposed architecture is that it takes Big Data and IoT into account during its definition of layers. Along with this, the fundamental concept

Table 2. Representative smart cities on the basis of different categories

Initiative Year	Categories	Representative Cities
2005	Ubiquitous City	Helsinki, Arabianranta, Finland
2005	Ubiquitous City	Dongtan, South Korea
2008	Ubiquitous City	Masdar, United Arab Emirates
2008	Ubiquitous City	Osaka, Japan
2008	Ubiquitous City	New Sondgo, South Korea
2010	Ubiquitous City	Manhattan Harbour, Kentucky, U.S.A.
1999	Smart City	Dubai, U.A.E
2000	Smart City	Barcelona, Spain
2004	Smart City	Taipei, Taiwan
2004	Smart City	Brisbane, Australia
2004	Smart City	Kochi, India
2007	Smart City	Tianjin, China
2007	Smart City	Malta
1995	Digital City	Austin, U.S.A.
1995	Digital City	Knowledge Based Cities, Portugal
2000	Digital City	Cape Town, South Africa
2000	Digital City	Hull, U.K
2003	Digital City	Trikala, Greece
2003	Digital City	Tampere, Finland
1996	Virtual/Web City	Kyoto, Japan
1997	Virtual/Web City	Bristol, U.S.A.
1997	Virtual/Web City	Amsterdam, Netherlands
1997	Virtual/Web City	America-On-Line (AOL) Cities
1994	Connected City	New York, U.S.A
1994	Connected City	Geneva-MAN, Switzerland
1995	Connected City	Helsinki, Finland
1995	Connected City	Antwerp, Belgium
1997	Connected City	Seoul, South Korea
1999	Connected City	Beijing, China
2002	Connected City	Kista Science City/Stockholm
2006	Connected City	Florence, Italy

upon which this Smart City architecture design relies is that it apparently separates the layers according to their functionalities (Mohanty, Choppali, & Kougianos, 2016), (Pan, Qi, Zhang, Li, Wu, & Yang, 2013).

The purpose of designing a Smart City architecture is somewhat similar to various other architectures that it also provides end-users with refined and comprehensible structure of collection of different functionalities and components (Walravens & Ballon, 2013). Moreover, various other features that are provided by defining the architecture of the Smart City concept are as follows:

- A single "platform" is defined by the architecture.
- Various functional aspects are also described by the architecture.
- It also focuses on the description of the structure of the Smart City environment.
- It describes the inter and intra-relationships among various components of the prescribed layers.

Hence, in this regard, layers from left to right constitute the meta multi-layered architecture for the Smart Cities as shown in Figure 7.

- **IoT Devices Layer:** From the Smart Cities view, the main functionality of this layer is to collect information, object control, and perception. Since Smart Cities need a physical infrastructure which is able to provide smart and efficient services. Hence, for fulfilling these requirements, IoT devices are deployed all over the city according to the functionalities needed by the end-users. Various devices like Radio Frequency Identification (RFID), sensors, actuators, and many others are used in the IoT devices so as to provide connectivity along with smartness (Kohler & Specht, 2019).
- **Networking Layer:** Now after the successful deployment of the physical infrastructure, Smart Cities need ubiquitous networks which will be able to connect the end-user and service provider anytime and anywhere. It includes the core network, transport layer functionalities, and edge computing nodes. Core network is the basic network which provides access to the IoT devices accord-

Figure 7. Multilayer meta-architecture for the smart cities

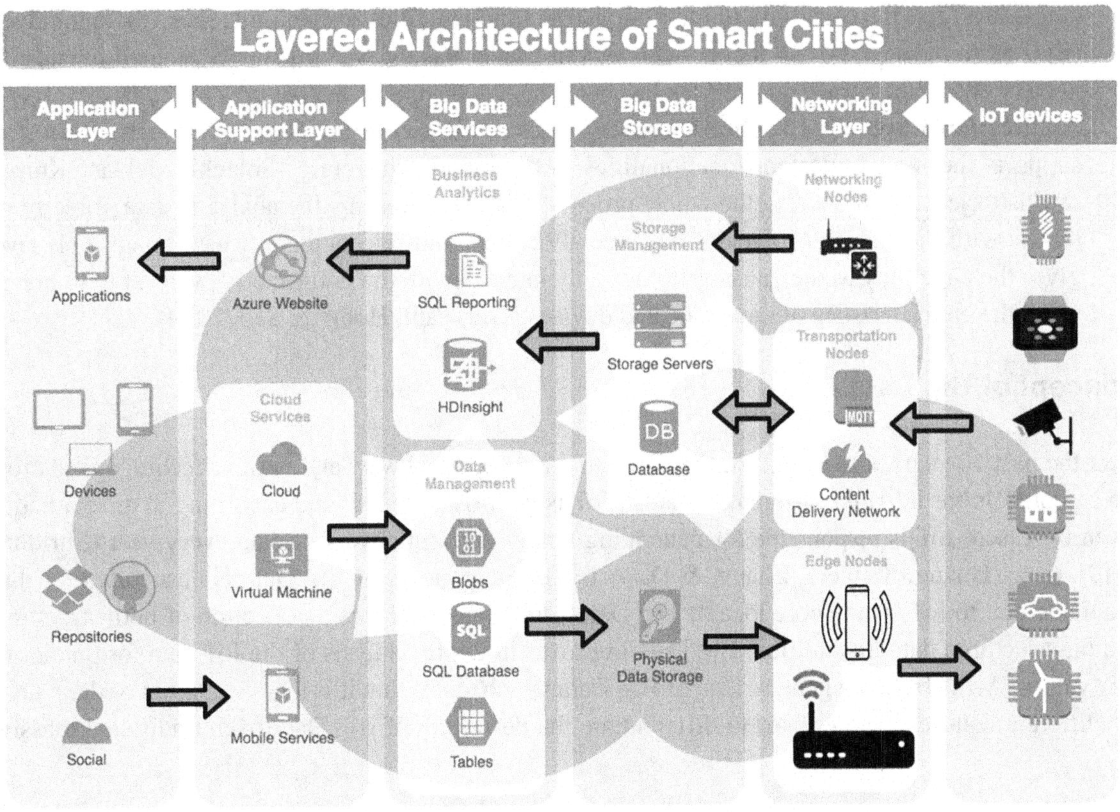

ing to the structure of the network. The reason of the integration of the edge nodes is that they are able to process the information locally and hence, decrease the latency in the network. They are also able to provide real-time processing in a much faster way and also reduce the load of the Cloud infrastructure. Moreover, the transport layer nodes are also integrated in this layer for resolving interoperability issues in the network (Muhammad, Lloret, & Baik, 2019). Heterogeneous protocol integration at this layer provides not only the reliability, but also provides energy efficient solutions to the IoT nodes.

- **Big Data Storage Layer:** Since the traditional database technologies are not reliable in case of Big Data storage, so in order for Smart Cities to incorporate the collected large scale data, Big Data storage mechanisms have to be promoted for the development of better and scalable infrastructure (Wang & Mao, 2019). Hence, according to the requirement of databases, file systems, and programming models, this layer provide the features.

- **Big Data Services Layer:** After successful storage of Big Data, now comes the challenge of managing and analysis of Big Data. Hence, this layer supports the analysis and management of the Big Data (Yu, Yang, & Sinnott, 2018). The data collected from the IoT devices are managed by this layer.

- **Application Support Layer:** This is an advanced layer which collectively provides Big Data storage, management, and analysis in a cost efficient way. Basically, the need of this layer is that some enterprises build their own local Big Data infrastructure for storage and analysis purpose. But now-a-days, various organizations are shifting their data to the Cloud (Doku & Rawat, 2019). Hence, this layer supports the functionalities of Cloud Computing and various mechanisms are also included in this layer. So when Smart Cities based on the Cloud Computing are designed, this single layer has the capability to incorporate the functionalities of the immediate two right layers (Ejaz & Anpalagan, 2018). It concludes that this layer has the functionality which eliminates the need of Big Data storage and service layers as this layer support the features of the both.

- **Application Layer:** The application layer comes at the end of the Smart City architecture, but supports the most important functionalities in the meta-architecture (Solanki, Makkar, Kumar, & Chatterjee, 2018). During the whole process, this layer presents the analyzed data, directly interacts with the end-users, decides resource allocation, and selects the processed data. This layer gives the capability to the end-user to not only interact with the connected devices, but to understand the characteristics of the connected devices (Din, Paul, Hong, & Seo, 2019).

Concept of Big Data

Over the past 10 years, size of data has risen in an unprecedented way, and various technological areas are responsible for it. Amid different domains, IoT is the primary area, and according to an estimation given by Cisco, IoT is responsible for generating nearly 500 Zettabytes of data every year (Shridhar, 2019), (Luo, Huang, Kanhere, Zhang, & Das, 2019). The concept of Big Data is best suited for data generated due to IoT, as the core idea of Big Data itself states that it is a collection of both structured and un-structured data. In addition, Big Data improves in-depth analysis of the IoT data for predicting new values. Apart from the general idea of Big Data which states that it is a huge amount of data, there are different features that are used to differentiate the definition of Big Data from traditional massive data. Technical practitioners, data analysts, technological enterprises, research and scientific scholars, have their different opinions about the definition of Big Data according to their concerns and applications. But their definitions focus on the general idea of Big Data which explores the definition of Big Data in a profound manner and states that Big Data is collection of datasets that could not be acquired, processed, perceived, and managed by traditional hardware and software tools within a specific time. A similar definition in the context of Big Data is given by McKinsey & Company (global consulting company), which also believes that volumetric datasets are not the only criterion for defining Big Data, but it also includes that managing growing scale of data that cannot be handled by traditional technologies. Research departments of IBM, Microsoft, Gartner, and many other enterprises use "3Vs" (Volume, Velocity, and Variety) model for describing Big Data (Berry & Johnston, 2019), (Romanowski, 2019), (Fahmideh & Beydoun, 2019). Here, Volume refers to the increasing amount of enormous data, Velocity refers to timely maximizing the commercial value of Big Data by conducting rapid analysis of collected data, and Variety refers to the heterogeneous types of structured, semi-structured, and un-structured data ranging from sensor data and text to videos.

Value Chain in Big Data

By considering Big Data as raw material, the process of Big Data is categorized into four phases: (1) data generation (2) data acquisition (3) data storage, and (4) data analytics, in which data acquisition and data generation can be seen as exploitation processes, whereas data analysis can be considered as a production process, and data storage as a storage process, as shown in Figure 8.

Data Generation

In the process of Big Data, first step is generation of the data. Taking the example of IoT data, enormous amount of data is generated from the sensors, actuators, IoT smart devices, applications, and communication (Du, Wang, Xia, & Zhang, 2018). A close substantial connection between this generated data and people's daily lives has been found which includes low density and high value features of this data. Moreover, this generated data appends more characteristics when it comes from IoT based Smart Cities, as the data consists of medical care, industry, public departments, smart communities, agriculture, and transport. Due to heterogeneity of IoT devices, generated data possess various distinctive characteristics that are discussed below:

- **Correlation Between Space and Time:** In a broader manner, IoT devices that are responsible for acquisition of data are placed at distinct geographic locations. Since every packet of data has its own timestamp, that is why, space and time correlation are inter-related and important dimensions for statistical analysis of data.
- **Heterogeneity and Large Scale:** IoT acquisition devices collect heterogeneous forms of data from distributed sources and due to this, sometimes there is a need of large scale of data to be acquired for different kinds of analysis. Moreover, sometimes historical data has to be recalled for analysis in real-time. Hence, this historical data has to be stored in a certain amount of time, and due to this, real-time and historical data collectively needs huge amount of data storage.

Figure 8. Various processes involved in big data leading towards building smart cities

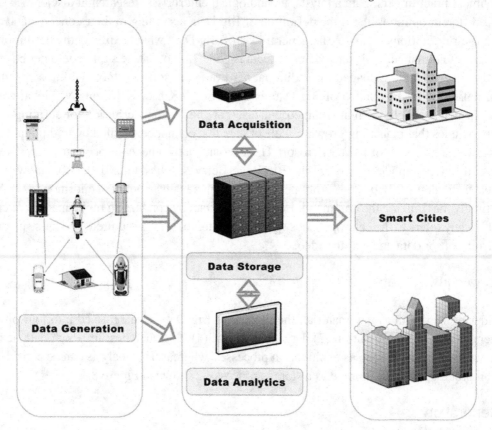

- **Effective Data:** During the process of data generation and collection, various kinds of noises get intermixed with IoT data. This suggests that only a small portion of the original collected data is significant and rest of the data falls under the category of invaluable data. For instance, during the process of video capturing of traffic, only a few data are useful during its whole lifetime and the rest of the collected data is not useful at all.

Data Acquisition

After successful generation of Big Data, it needs to be collected, transmitted, and pre-processed in an efficient manner, and all these come under the data acquisition phase (Pang, Yang, Khedri, & Zhang, 2018). This phase of data acquisition consists of various processes for efficient transmission and storage. These processes have their own significance and are discussed below:

- **Data Collection:** The generated data needs to be collected in an appropriate manner, and this collection of data needs specific tools and techniques. One such way of collecting data is in the form of log files, that are record files and are automatically generated by the source digital device. These different file format recorded activities are used for subsequent analysis (Lohachab & Bidhan, 2018). Most popular use of log files is for stock indication and network monitoring. Sensory data (temperature, voice, automobile, weather, chemical, current, pressure, vibration) are collected at data collection point from the deployed IoT sensors by sending requests through wired or wireless medium to the base station. The IoT network data is collected using specific technology including zero-copy packet capture technology and Libpcap-based packet capture technology. IoT application data based on web pages is accomplished by the combination of index, task, and word segmentation system.

- **Data Transportation:** For processing and analysis of collected raw data, it should be transferred to storage infrastructure (Mohammadi, Fuqaha, Sorour, & Guizani, 2018). In case of Big Data, generally the infrastructure used for data storage are data centers. Hence, there is need for adjustment of data layout for facilitating hardware maintenance and improving computing efficiency. Data centers also facilitate internal transmission of data in two phases: Intra-DCN transmissions, and Inter-DCN transmissions. In the Intra-DCN transmissions, flow of data communication happens within the data centers. Communication mechanism (protocols, network architectures of data centers, internal memories, physical connection chips) are responsible for Intra-DCN transmissions. A typical data center contains various integrated server racks inter-connected by their internal networks (i.e., three-layer or two-layer structures, fat-tree). While on the other hand, inter-DCN transmissions utilize the physical network infrastructure for communicating data between data source and data center. The existing cost-effective, high rate, and volume optic fiber systems are able to fulfil the demands of rapidly increasing network traffic.

- Data pre-processing: During the process of data collection and transportation under some circumstances, data becomes redundant and noisy. For improving data quality and better data analysis, this meaningless data should be converted to useful data (Li, He, & Li, 2019). Pre-processing of data not only reduces expenses of storage, but also enhances analytical accuracy of analysis methods. Data cleaning, integration and redundancy elimination are some of the common methods of data pre-processing. In the current state of art, process of data integration acts as a keystone in commercial informatics. It provides consistent view of data to the end-users irrespective of the heterogeneity of data.

Data Storage

After the successful exploitation of data, now comes the challenge of how to store this enormous amount of data. In this storage phase, we focus on the storage of explosive amount of data. The concept of Big Data storage refers to the stricter requirements on management and storage of large-scale data by accomplishing the goals of reliability and availability. Unlike the traditional equipment of data storage where servers used structured Relational Database Management Systems (RDBMs) to store, lookup, manage, and analyze the stored data, various distinctive technologies are used for massive data storage management. These technologies can be categorized as Network storage, and Direct Attached Storage (DAS) (Aazam, Huh, & Hilaire, 2016). In the DAS storage peripheral equipment, generally hard disks and servers are directly connected for providing server-centric approach. This server-centric approach of managing data is good enough to inter-connect servers only at a mini scale where peripheral devices utilize definite number of input/output resources and are managed by distinctive application software. In general scenario of Smart Cities, DAS is insufficient to provide desirable results due to its limited scalability, expandability, and upgradeability. Storage Area Network (SAN) and Network Attached Storage (NAS) can be categorized under network storage. The basic concept behind network storage is that it utilizes network for providing storage to the end-users and it also provides consolidated interface for data sharing and access. NAS can be considered as an auxiliary storage device which is connected with network through switch or hub by using TCP/IP protocols. Although NAS is network-oriented service, but for providing specific services like scalability and bandwidth, SAN would be a preferable option for intensive networks. Basically, SAN provides independent data storage management by utilizing multipath based data switching among local area network (Mihovska & Sarkar, 2017).

Data Analysis

Most important and final phase in the process of Big Data is the analysis of Big Data which mainly involves providing analytical structure, methods, and software for Big Data. By the intention of extracting valuable records, contributing decisions, and suggestions, Big Data generates heterogeneous potential values of datasets. Data analysis creates a colossal impact on the development of various plans for Smart Cities as it helps to understand end-user's demands (Ferraro, King, & Shorten, 2018). Although there are various traditional data analysis methods that are rigorous in nature when dealing with Smart City data analysis, but Big Data analysis methods provide methods for Smart City data analysis that are much more helpful and precise. In the traditional data analysis methods, statistical methods are used for analyzing bulky data and to extract valuable data from hidden datasets. Cluster, correlation, factor, and regression analysis are some of the ways that are used in the traditional data analysis. Bucket testing and data mining algorithms are used as data extracting techniques in the traditional data analysis. Big Data analysis not only requires statistical analysis, but also various additional features that are provided by specific Big Data analysis methods. Some of the Big Data analysis/ processing methods are discussed as follows:

1. **Trie:** It is also called Triel, digital tree, prefix tree, or radix tree, and is mainly used for calculating word frequency statistics, and also makes retrieval process expeditious which makes it more suitable for Big Data. The basic concept of Trie is that it is considered as a kind of search tree which uses ordered data structure for storing associative array or dynamic sets where strings are usually used as the keys for reducing comparison between strings and improving query efficiency (Ghasemi, Yousefi, Shin, & Zhang, 2019).
2. **Bloom Filter:** It can be seen as an alternative to various hashing techniques that use standard hash tables. These tables resolve collision by using open addressing. However, in bloom filter, arbitrary number of elements are represented by fixed size. The main principle behind bloom filter is that it uses series of hash functions and stores hash values by using a bit array (Luo, Guo, Ma, Rottenstreich, & Luo, 2018). Despite the fact that it has several disadvantages, (i.e., deletion and misrecognition) it has several features that are suitable for Big Data such as fast query processing and highly space efficient.
3. **Parallel Computing:** As compared to the traditional computing where complete resources are given for computing one task at a time, in parallel computing paradigm, simultaneous utilization of resources takes place for completing any number of given computing tasks. Basically, there are various mechanisms that are used in the parallel computing, but the fundamental concept remains the same (i.e., allocate distinctive processes to different tasks for their completion) (Gong, Wang, Zhang, & Fu, 2019). Hence, for accomplishing co-processing, some of the various classical models are discussed in Table 3 along with their comparison.

Table 3. Feature comparison of DRYAD, MPI, and MapReduce

Models → Features ↓	DRYAD	Message Passing Interface (MPI)	MapReduce
Deployment	In the same node Computing and data storage is arranged	Storage of data is separate from computing node	In the same node Computing and data storage is arranged
Programming	DryadLINQ, Dryad API, Scope	MPI API	MapReduce API, Pig, Hive, Jaql
Data Storage	NTFS, Cosmos DFS	NFS, Local file system	GFS (google), HDFS(Hadoop), KFS, Amazon S3
Task Partitioning	Automation	User manually partition the tasks	Automation
Communication	FIFOs, Shared-memory, TCP Pipes, Files	Remote memory access, Messaging	Files(Local FS, DFS)
Fault-Tolerant	Task re-execute	Checkpoint	Task re-execute

Big Data Open Source Tools

To accomplish the competitive nature of Big Data market, selecting the tools for data analysis and processing by considering the effectiveness and cost is always a primary concern. Along with these factors, multiple other aspects are also considered. For instance, what kind of analysis is required, quantity of data sets, quality of data, and so forth. Although there are various categories of tools that are available in the market for fulfilling the heterogeneous needs of organizations, this sub-section discusses the open source tools that have a possible future for adoption in the market. These are given are as follows:

- **Apache Hadoop:** Hadoop has created pronounce effect in the Big Data market with its colossal capability of processing large scale datasets efficiently. It is an open source tool which can run on an existing hardware or even on Cloud infrastructure.
- **Apache Spark:** This is also an open source tool which has created its image in the industry by fulfilling the concerns of Hadoop. It processes the data in a much faster manner, and is able to handle both real-time and batch data. It also provides flexibility to run on a single local system while working with various kinds of data formats.
- **Apache Storm:** For processing the data stream using the real-time distributed framework, Storm is useful. This tool supports various kinds of programming languages. It can also work with Hadoop's HDFS which makes it more useful in case of interoperability.
- **Apache Cassandra:** It provides distributed database which does not follow master-slave architecture. With no single point of failure, it is considered as the best open source tool for dealing with structured datasets.
- **MongoDB:** It is an open source tool which has built-in feature of interoperability among various platforms and hence, is ideal for providing real-time data processing with data-driven experiences.
- **RapidMiner:** It is an open source tool written in Java programming language and follows a client/server model for providing advanced analytical solutions.

Table 4. Taxonomy of smart city component features and affected sectors

Functionalities	Affected Sectors	Features Exploited
Smart Living	Quality and Security	Ease in cultural facilities
		Ease in Health monitoring
		Personal safety
		Increase in housing quality
		Social cohesion
		Education facilities and tourist attraction
Smart Environment	Sustainability and Efficiency	Better prediction of natural environment
		Better management of pollution
		Better management of natural resources
		Enhance protection of environment
		Flexibility in internal factors
		Smart disaster detection
Smart Mobility	Infrastructure and Mobility	Smart accessibility
		Innovation traffic system
		Safe international accessibility
		Safety in transportation
		Flexibility in travelling
		Sustainable mobility solutions
Smart Governance	Planning and Decision Making	Ease of public participation
		Transparency in governance
		Better political perspectives
		Flexibility in social services
		Ease in public services
		Electronic government
Smart People	Education standards	Increase in education qualifications
		Increase creativity
		Open minded people
		Increase in public engagement
		Flexibility in decisions
		Increase in learning
Smart Economy	Industry and Consumers	Entrepreneurship
		Increase in productivity
		Flexibility in markets
		Better lifestyle of labors
		Ability to transform
		International trademarks

STATE-OF-THE-ART OF BIG DATA FOR PLANNING IN SMART CITIES

After a detailed discussion about various aspects of Smart Cities and Big Data, this section will review the specific role of Big Data in Smart Cities. The main application of Big Data in Smart Cities is to improve the QoS in almost all characteristics related to Smart Cities. Different characteristics of Smart Cities along with their impact in urban living are summarized in Table 4.

Effective functioning of a Smart City requires persuasive communication, integration, coordination, and coupling among infrastructure and the services. Therefore, this needs new methods of database technology, new integration software, and many other things, so that Smart Cities are able to effectively balance equality by improving citizen's standards. There is quest going on for mastering the complexity of Big Data process for Smart Cities, and this quest suggests that there is a need for building a comprehensive system for data mining, acquisition, and querying (Mohammadi & Fuqaha, 2018). The process of Big Data analytics plays a major role in creating productive services for the Smart Cities, so it will have to support the following features:

- Dealing with Big Data by using distributed and incremental mining strategies for improving scalability.
- For exploring the behavior of models and patterns, resulting analytics have to be shown through visualization.
- Management and integration of heterogeneous data streams will be done into an intelligible database.
- Supports data transformation, and new definitions for observing relevant information.
- Management of distributed network analytics for seamless analysis of extracted patterns.
- Evaluation tools will have the quality of extracting patterns and models.

According to space and time complexity, there are various ways in which Big Data is analyzed in Smart Cities. So by considering this, two main categories for Big Data analysis are discussed as follows:

1. **Offline and Real-time Analysis (on the Basis of Timeliness Requirements):** From the security point of view, offline analysis is recommended as in this, by utilization of precise machine learning and recommendation algorithms, statistical analysis is performed. Through data acquisition, logs can be imported for conducting offline analysis based on which security measures can be taken into account (Lv, Song, Val, Steed, & Jo, 2017). In the context of social connections and online marketing, various Hadoop based Big Data analysis tools (like Scribe from Facebook, Kafka from LinkedIn, Timetunnel from Taobao) are used for better analysis of various connected nodes in order to increase efficiency of their products. Although these offline mechanisms meet the demand of data analysis with hundreds of MB per second, still these analysis methods are not well suitable for applications with requirements of fast response time. Along with offline data analysis, online data analysis also plays a crucial role in Smart Cities. The main feature of online analysis is that it does real-time analysis within a very short amount of time. HANA from SAP and Greenplum from EMC are two popular real-time analysis platforms that are capable for doing rapid data analysis (Faerber, Dees, Weidner, Baeuerle, & Lehner, 2015). In Smart Cities, since smart economy is seen as the major component, so by doing real data time analysis, better understanding of the finance data can be provided.

2. **Memory-Level, Massive, and Business Intelligent Analysis (on the Basis of Different Levels):** The memory-level analysis is best suited for the cases where volume of total memory of a cluster is larger than the total acquired data. It can be seen as an internal database analysis technique, as it believes that the crucial data still resides in the memory. With the recent developments in the Solid-State Drive technology, this memory-level architecture is best suited for real-time analysis and its representative architecture is MongoDB (Colombo & Ferrari, 2015). Massive analysis is used in the case where the capacity of data totally surpasses the existing relational database technology. According to the processing time of this analysis, it comes under the category of offline analysis (e.g., Map Reduce). Business intelligence analysis is used in the middle of both these cases, where data is not much bulky, but enough for analysis for making strategic decisions. This kind of analysis comes under the category of both offline and online analysis as in some cases, collected data demands immediate decisions (e.g., in finance sector) and sometimes data can be analyzed in an offline mode where data has to be analyzed deeply (online marketing) (Peng, Wang, & Xie, 2016).

Moreover, beyond this general categorization of Big Data analysis, there are various kinds of data that need to analyzed in a Smart City scenario for fulfilling the requirements of Smart City components. Hence, the various types of data fields that need to be analyzed are discussed below:

- **Personal Digital Assistant (PDA) Data Analysis**: With the massive growth of PDAs among users, now they are being used for building social communities, controlling devices, geographical coordination, and many other things. There are abundant number of applications that are specifically designed for every purpose, resulting of which generates PetaBytes (PB) amount of raw data. Considering as whole raw data of PDAs, analysis of data should be done for removing redundancy and noise. Mobile phones and smart watches are popular among other PDAs, since they support rich interactions among individuals or communities anywhere and anytime (Sarikaya, 2017). In fact, recent progress of IoT devices, specifically wireless sensors, enable end-users to create Body Area Network (BAN) for real-time monitoring of their health. Hence, analysis of medical data in context to smart health component of Smart Cities helps organizations to understand the physiological relations, time, and other health related features (He, Zeadally, Kumar, & Lee, 2016).
- **Smart City Network Data Analysis:** It involves quantitative analysis, sensors data analysis, and sociological network data analysis. Many Smart City network services include IoT devices, social networking, and enterprises network data. For detecting the behavior of network topology, peer nodes, and illegitimate behavior of network, concept of capturing the network data can be utilized. Recommendation, marketing, advertisement, security, and many other features are provided by the qualitative and quantitative analysis of network data (Jin, Wah, Cheng, & Wanga, 2015) .
- **Multimedia Data Analysis:** In the context of smart people component in Smart Cities, multimedia data analysis plays an important role for deciding the quality and content of data that is to be presented. Generally, it includes images, video, and audio from which richer information needs to extracted. But the process of analysis and extraction of data is not that simple, since it contains heterogeneous data with semantic differences (Zhu, Cui, Wang, & Hua, 2015). Hence, by considering this scenario in multimedia analysis, there are different sub-processes including multimedia annotation, multimedia summarization, multimedia suggestion, multimedia retrieval and indexing, and multimedia event detection. Extraction of embossed phrases and words is done during the

process of audio data analysis for processing useful information. Both static and dynamic analysis can be performed during the video data analysis for finding the most adumbrative video sequence. In the multimedia annotation, labels are inserted for describing the contents of both video and audio at both semantic and syntax level. For conveniently providing assistance and description regarding information to the end users, multimedia indexing use five procedures. Now, the multimedia analysis after performing all sub-procedures looks forward for fulfilling its primary goal which is to recommend a specific content to the users according to their interests (Tous, Torres, & Ayguadé, 2015). The main benefit of this process is that citizens in the Smart Cities are able to personalize their services in an effective way. Collaborative-filtering based system and content based systems are the two existing systems that are popular among video data analysis.

- **Web Data Analysis:** For discovering fruitful knowledge from web documents, web data analysis can be seen as an effective field. Web usage mining, web content mining, and web structure mining are the persuasive fields of web data analysis. During the productive interaction with the web, the generated data including device and user registration data, proxy servers, queries, sessions, access logs, and other kinds of data are mined during the process of web usage mining (Mongeon & Hus, 2015). Web content mining includes the database and information retrieval methods in which structured and unstructured data is mined and then knowledgeable data is extracted. For finding the various correlations and similarities between services, web structure mining is used. For instance, in case of websites, CLEVER and PageRank are used for finding relevant description and information regarding web pages (Riedy, 2016).

- **Structured and Text Data Analysis:** Although the structure and text data analysis is not very useful in the context to IoT devices, but regarding the Smart Cities, it plays an important role, specifically in the smart economy as it analyzes various text data documents along with structured data for making competitive economy (Chen, Hao, Hwang, Wang, & Wang, 2017). Powerful statistical mathematical algorithms are used for exploiting data flows, time, and space to make better interpretations. Natural Language Processing (NLP) is the powerful process when it comes to analyze text, and its method includes probabilistic context free grammar, lexical acquisition, part-of-speech tagging, and word sense disambiguation. For energy control and anomaly detection, structured data analysis provides knowledge structures driven by process mining.

Big Data Application in Smart Cities

Smart city services can be enhanced by processing information from data storage. Big Data applications are efficiently managing the Smart City data by helping decision makers during development of Smart City resources and services. For effective and efficient analysis of Smart City data, Big Data needs advance methods and tools to achieve its goals. Some of the involved tools and methods in the Big Data mechanism have been discussed in the above sections. Now, based on the methods and tools, various applications of Big Data in Smart Cities are discussed in this section. Table 5 summarizes various applications of Big Data in the Smart City scenarios that are discussed as follows –

- **Smart Economy:** Traditional economy refers to the way in which goods are produced and consumed in order to increase wealth and resources. In addition to all this, smart economy includes new way for increasing entrepreneurship, trademarks, innovations, productivity, and international markets. Hence, for increasing new and existing talents to come up with new solutions, there is

Table 5. Various Big Data applications in smart cities

Applications	Utilization	Involved IoT Devices	Possible Communication Technologies	Advantages	Limitations
Smart Economy	Digitalization of financial services	Smart phones, RFID cards, Sensors, Actuators	Wi-Fi, Bluetooth, ZigBee, MQTT, CoAP, and many others	Easy monitoring of financial activities, reduction in paper work	Security threats, dis-connectivity
Smart Grid	Manage power supply	Smart readers, Smart meters	Wi-Fi, Z-wave, ZigBee, 5G, MQTT, CoAP, and many others	Efficient power supply, Efficient manage of energy market	Currently costly, Security threats
Smart Healthcare	Flexible health monitoring	RFID cards, Cameras, smart wearable devices, sensors, smart vehicles	ZigBee, Bluetooth, 5G, CoAP, MQTT, and many others	Early diagnosis of diseases, easy monitoring, effective remote treatment	Lack of precision, Patients trust, Security Threats
Smart Governance	Smart, efficient and flexible policies	Cameras, Transportation, Smart phones, Sensors, Actuators	LoRaWAN, LTE-A, Bluetooth, WiMAX, Wi-Fi, LTE, and many others	Easy fulfillment of the needs of citizens	Heterogeneous data to be analyzed, security threats
Smart Transportation	Efficient traffic management	Smart vehicles, cameras, smart phones	5G, 4G, 3G, RFID and many others	Effective management of routes	Dis-connectivity, Security Threats
Information security	Protection against various advance threats and attacks	Various IoT sensors and actuators	Wi-Fi, Bluetooth, ZigBee, MQTT, CoAP, and many others	Effective actions for strengthening security	Big Data availability and integration

need of the existing and real-time data analysis (Boes, Buhalis, & Inversini, 2014). Dealing with the labor and managing funds also need efficient and effective Big Data analysis methods.

- **Smart Grids:** For optimized consumption, supply, and generation of electric energy, the concept of smart grids integrate the traditional energy networks with next generation grids that are enabled with remote automation, communication, and computation. Big Data in smart grids is generated from various resources, such as (i) maintenance, management, and control data of power generation equipment's and devices, (ii) Financial data of energy market, (iii) energy consumption data collected by smart meters, and (iv) end-user's habits of power utilization. Hence, in this regard, Big Data analysis is used for efficient management of electricity to fulfill the supply demands of the end-users. Furthermore, collected Big Data from smart grids help decision makers for making specific objectives while deciding the pricing plans (Deng, Yang, Chow, & Chen, 2015).

- **Smart Healthcare:** Rapidly growing complex medical and healthcare data is potentially handled by the Big Data methods. In fact, the growth in the business of healthcare is profoundly influenced by the applications of healthcare Big Data. Big Data related to the healthcare sector facilitates the decisions behind the changes in the delivery system of medical services. Smart gadgets, homes, and vehicles constitute for providing the best medical facilities in order to cure diseases and predicting epidemics. By analyzing the patient's data along with preventable measures, it helps to understand the patient's behavior during their health issues. The primary purpose of the healthcare

Big Data is to save lives as many as possible by detecting, curing, and taking preventive measures for the serious diseases (Hossain, 2016).

- **Smart Governance:** Every city has its own needs for managing its internal and external policies in order to fulfill the goals. Smart Cities need specific governance policies that are dynamic in nature. Hence, for making dynamic policies and finding the common goals of their citizens, Big Data analytics has the potential to lead forward for enabling smart governance (Lin, Zhang, & Geertman, 2015). Big Data analytics implements satisfactory development with collaboration between governing policies. Since Governments are already aware of the needs of their citizens in terms of employment, medical, education, and so forth, Big Data helps them in increasing the success ratio.

- **Smart Transportation:** In the traditional transportation system, governing parties are aware of the situations like traffic jam, but unable to take strict actions. The simple reason behind this is that they collect the raw data, but are unaware of what to do with the collected data. Big Data methods help transportation systems in the way that they predict patterns from the enormous amount of collected raw data. These patterns help to analyze the current situation for taking the decisive actions, such as suggesting alternative routes in order to minimize the traffic congestion. Moreover, various factors like finding the cause of any mishaps happened during movement of vehicles are recommended by Big Data analysis that certainly reduce number of accidents. Smart transportation also includes facilities like tracking of shipments. Hence, in order to reduce wastage of supply chain, Big Data improves the experience of end-users by suggesting more appropriate factors.

- **Information Security:** Along with various general purpose applications in Smart Cities, Big Data also brings efficient development in the information security mechanisms in Smart Cities. Big Data analysis helps to discover various potential security threats, and system loopholes. After analysis of the log files of the various connected devices, it develops specific intrusion detection systems. It can also easily identify various characteristics of attacks, loopholes, viruses, and characterizes them accordingly into various levels of security threats.

CONCERNS OF BIG DATA AND SMART CITIES

Despite the fact that age of Big Data made a significant impact on the concept of new value creation in Smart Cities, it has also opened various multi-dimensional challenges that can possibly require interdisciplinary perspectives to get addressed properly. Both Big Data and Smart Cities needs a comprehensive and holistic definition, structural model, and formal description of their integration. From commercial to academic research point of view, there is a need for scientific research than speculations (Lohachab, 2019). Big Data and Smart Cities confront various individual and combined challenges. However, ongoing research efforts done by organizations and researchers are also creating a significant impact in the domains. In the remainder of this section, current challenges of Big Data and ongoing research efforts are summarized.

- **Smart City Planning:** In the business model of Smart Cities, growing market of IoT and Big Data has gained attention for the future developments. In the planning of the Smart Cities, challenges are encountered in the form of building the combined control methodologies and master planning

Big Data and IoT for the Smart Cities. To understand how Big Data can be used for designing the best model and guidelines for Smart Cities at minimal cost is still a challenge.

- **Sustainable Smart Cities:** How to establish communication and interaction with Big Data and IoT in a sustainable and resilient way with their full potential is still a challenge. Moreover, how to integrate the power of Big Data and IoT in Smart Cities for making them self-sustainable is still considered as a complex task. Scarcity of available resources in Smart Cities points towards lack of planning. Hence, to make a sustainable city by planning with the help of Big Data regarding IoT resources should be precise.

- **Smart City Costs and Sources:** Diversity in technologies can help the organizations for accelerating the process of services. However, on the other side, this diversity introduces challenges for consumers and markets. For instance, if a user utilizes various applications on daily basis, organizations face many difficulties in finding their interests. Another challenge for adoption of these heterogeneous technologies in a Smart City is that integration of different standards or components of these technologies will certainly increase the cost of infrastructure. Although there are various open standards that are able to provide robust integration mechanisms through facilitating collaboration among different services, devices, products, and applications, these open standards have not been adopted in a comprehensive way.

- **Big Data Standardization:** For increasing computational efficiency of the collected data, there should be an improvement in the process of data analytics and evaluation. However, to increase these features, a unified benchmark for standardizing the process is required. To effectively evaluate the quality of data, process of screening and processing the data should be simplified. Another important characteristic of Big Data is that it is collected from diverse and heterogeneous data sources, which makes the conversion of data format more complex. Certainly if these data conversions can be more reliable and easier, the applications of Big Data can be increased in context of Smart Cities.

- **Performance of Big Data:** The performance of Big Data transfer involves Big Data storage, acquisition, and generation that arise new problems as compared to the traditional data analysis. High performance of Big Data has incurred higher costs, which coercion its use in a limited way. Moreover, real-time processing of Big Data requires vast amount of resources which limits its capabilities in resource-constrained environment (e.g., IoT environment). Hence, if effective utilization of the processes involved in Big Data is done during building real-time computation models in the Smart Cities, it will influence the overall development scenario.

- **Big Data Provenance:** The concept of data provenance is used from the data generation till its evolution in order to investigate the data. Since the value of an individual dataset is much lower than comprehensive Big Datasets, the process of data provenance faces more challenges in Big Data. Because the process of data provenance not only has to track the data generation and evolution, but the integration of various heterogeneous datasets is also to be tracked. However, the process of data provenance in Big Datasets helps in understanding the concept of Smart Cities more effectively as it gathers the integrated information from various datasets of different standards. Moreover, Big Data provenance suggests various security measures in accordance for taking decisive actions against various data security threats and attacks (Wang, Crawl, Purawat, Nguyen, & Altintas, 2015).

- **Big Data Privacy and Security:** The era of Big Data is confronted by two primary concerns which includes security and privacy of data. Although various traditional mechanisms are available for data protection, they are inefficient while dealing with Big Data security concerns. Privacy in Big Data may be breached in two aspects – first, privacy may be violated during acquisition of data, and second, violation of privacy may be done during storage, usage, and transmission of data. Big Data analysis provides seamless useful information. But at the same time, it opens challenges for its management. For instance, during the process of analysis, it mines sensitive information which if breached can lead to user's privacy at stake. In addition to the privacy challenges, Big Data also faces various security challenges. Mechanism of encryption in traditional dataset can be easily implemented. However, it faces challenges due to high diversity and large scale of Big Datasets. By looking into the performance of the traditional encryption methods on datasets, it can be seen that there is a need for developing effective Big Data encryption techniques. Goals of security including authentication, availability, and confidentiality should be implemented in unstructured datasets in an efficient manner (Lohachab & Karambir, 2019) .

CONCLUSION

In this chapter, in-depth analysis is done over the role of Big Data for efficient urban planning in Smart Cities. The chapter investigated the concepts of Big Data analysis including how it exploits the opportunities in Smart Cities, and also discussed the various possible applications of Smart Cities. The chapter also tried to find out the possible architecture of Smart Cities by integrating Big Data technology with it. The process of Big Data is also summarized along with the various components of the Smart Cities. Finally, the chapter is concluded by exploring the on-going research challenges faced by Smart Cities and Big Data.

REFERENCES

Bhushan, K., & Gupta, B. B. (2017). Network flow analysis for detection and mitigation of Fraudulent Resource Consumption (FRC) attacks in multimedia cloud computing. *Multimedia Tools and Applications*, *78*(4), 4267–4298. doi:10.100711042-017-5522-z

Boes, K., Buhalis, D., & Inversini, A. (2014, December 27). Conceptualising Smart Tourism Destination Dimensions. *Information and Communication Technologies in Tourism*, 391-403.

Caragliu, A., Bo, D. C., & Nijkamp, P. (2011). Smart Cities in Europe. *Journal of Urban Technology*, *18*(2), 65–82. doi:10.1080/10630732.2011.601117

Cárdenas, A. A., Manadhata, K. P., & Rajan, P. S. (2013). Big Data Analytics for Security. *IEEE Security and Privacy*, *11*(6), 74–76. doi:10.1109/MSP.2013.138

Cardullo, P., & Kitchin, R. (2018). Being a 'citizen' in the Smart City: Up and down the scaffold of smart citizen participation in Dublin, Ireland. *GeoJournal*, *84*(1), 1–13. doi:10.100710708-018-9845-8

Chen, M., Hao, Y., Hwang, K., Wang, L., & Wang, L. (2017). Disease Prediction by Machine Learning Over Big Data from Healthcare Communities. *IEEE Access: Practical Innovations, Open Solutions*, *5*, 8869–8879. doi:10.1109/ACCESS.2017.2694446

Chen, M., Mao, S., & Liu, Y. (2014). Big Data: A Survey. *Mobile Networks and Applications*, *19*(2), 171–209. doi:10.100711036-013-0489-0

Colombo, P., & Ferrari, E. (2015). Enhancing MongoDB with Purpose-Based Access Control. *IEEE Transactions on Dependable and Secure Computing*, *14*(6), 591–604. doi:10.1109/TDSC.2015.2497680

Deng, R., Yang, Z., Chow, Y. M., & Chen, J. (2015). A Survey on Demand Response in Smart Grids: Mathematical Models and Approaches. *IEEE Transactions on Industrial Informatics*, *11*(3), 570–582. doi:10.1109/TII.2015.2414719

Din, S., Paul, A., Hong, H. W., & Seo, H. (2019). Constrained application for mobility management using embedded devices in the Internet of Things based urban planning in Smart Cities. *Sustainable Cities and Society*, *44*, 144–151. doi:10.1016/j.scs.2018.07.017

Doku, R., & Rawat, B. D. (2019). Big Data in Cybersecurity for Smart City Applications. *Smart Cities Cybersecurity and Privacy*, 103-112.

Du, M., Wang, K., Xia, Z., & Zhang, Y. (2018, April 24). Differential Privacy Preserving of Training Model in Wireless Big Data with Edge Computing. *IEEE Transactions on Big Data*.

Ejaz, W., & Anpalagan, A. (2018, October 13). Dimension Reduction for Big Data Analytics in Internet of Things. *Internet of Things for Smart Cities*, 31-37.

Faerber, F., Dees, J., Weidner, M., Baeuerle, S., & Lehner, W. (2015). Towards a web-scale data management ecosystem demonstrated by SAP HANA. In *2015 IEEE 31st International Conference on Data Engineering* (pp. 1259-1267). Seoul, South Korea: IEEE.

Fahmideh, M., & Beydoun, G. (2019). Big data analytics architecture design—An application in manufacturing systems. *Computers & Industrial Engineering*, *128*, 948–963. doi:10.1016/j.cie.2018.08.004

Ferraro, P., King, C., & Shorten, R. (2018). Distributed Ledger Technology for Smart Cities, the Sharing Economy, and Social Compliance. *IEEE Access: Practical Innovations, Open Solutions*, *6*, 62728–62746. doi:10.1109/ACCESS.2018.2876766

Ghasemi, C., Yousefi, H., Shin, G. K., & Zhang, B. (2019). On the Granularity of Trie-Based Data Structures for Name Lookups and Updates. *IEEE/ACM Transactions on Networking*, *27*(2), 777–789. doi:10.1109/TNET.2019.2901487

Gong, L., Wang, C., Zhang, C., & Fu, Y. (2019). High-Performance Computing Based Fully Parallel Security-Constrained Unit Commitment with Dispatchable Transmission Network. *IEEE Power & Energy Society*, *34*(2), 931–941.

Gupta, B. B., & Quamara, M. (2018). Multi-layered Cloud and Fog based Secure Integrated Transmission and Storage Framework for IoT based Applications. In *2018 5th International Conference on Signal Processing and Integrated Networks (SPIN)* (pp. 462-467). Noida, India: IEEE.

He, D., Zeadally, S., Kumar, N., & Lee, H. J. (2016). Anonymous Authentication for Wireless Body Area Networks with Provable Security. *IEEE Systems Journal*, *11*(4), 2590–2601. doi:10.1109/JSYST.2016.2544805

Hossain, S. M. (2016). Patient State Recognition System for Healthcare Using Speech and Facial Expressions. *Journal of Medical Systems*, *40*(12), 272. doi:10.100710916-016-0627-x PMID:27757715

IoT: Smart Cities projects share breakdown 2017, by type. (2017). Retrieved February 27, 2019, from The Statistics Portal: https://www.statista.com/statistics/784331/internet-of-things-smart-Cities-projects-by-type/

Jin, X., Wah, B. W., Cheng, X., & Wanga, Y. (2015). Significance and Challenges of Big Data Research. *Big Data Research*, *2*(2), 59–64. doi:10.1016/j.bdr.2015.01.006

Kohler, J., & Specht, T. (2019). Towards a Secure, Distributed, and Reliable Cloud-Based Reference Architecture for Big Data in Smart Cities. *Big Data Analytics for Smart and Connected Cities*, 38-70.

Labrinidis, A., & Jagadish, V. H. (2012). Challenges and opportunities with big data. *Proceedings of the VLDB Endowment International Conference on Very Large Data Bases*, *5*(12), 2032–2033. doi:10.14778/2367502.2367572

Lazaroiua, C. G., & Rosciab, M. (2012). Definition methodology for the Smart Cities model. *Energy*, *47*(1), 326–332. doi:10.1016/j.energy.2012.09.028

Letaifa, B. S. (2015). How to strategize Smart Cities: Revealing the SMART model. *Journal of Business Research*, *68*(7), 1414–1419. doi:10.1016/j.jbusres.2015.01.024

Li, S., He, H., & Li, J. (2019). Big data driven lithium-ion battery modeling method based on SDAE-ELM algorithm and data pre-processing technology. *Applied Energy*, *242*, 1259–1273. doi:10.1016/j.apenergy.2019.03.154

Lin, Y., Zhang, X., & Geertman, S. (2015). Toward smart governance and social sustainability for Chinese migrant communities. *Journal of Cleaner Production*, *107*, 389–399. doi:10.1016/j.jclepro.2014.12.074

Lohachab, A. (2019). A Perspective on Using Blockchain for Ensuring Security in Smart Card Systems. In B. B. Gupta & P. D. Agrawal (Eds.), *Handbook of Research on Cloud Computing and Big Data Applications in IoT* (pp. 418–447). IGI Global. doi:10.4018/978-1-5225-8407-0.ch019

Lohachab, A., & Karambir. (2019). ECC based inter-device authentication and authorization scheme using MQTT for IoT networks. *Journal of Information Security and Applications, 46*.

Lohachab, A., & Karambir. (2019). Next Generation Computing: Enabling Multilevel Centralized Access Control using UCON and CapBAC Model for securing IoT Networks. In *2018 International Conference on Communication, Computing and Internet of Things (IC3IoT)* (pp. 159-164). Chennai, India: IEEE.

Lohachab, A., & Bidhan, K. (2018). Critical Analysis of DDoS—An Emerging Security Threat over IoT Networks. *Journal of Communications and Information Networks*, *3*(3), 57–78. doi:10.100741650-018-0022-5

Luo, L., Guo, D., Ma, B. T., Rottenstreich, O., & Luo, X. (2018, December 24). Optimizing Bloom Filter: Challenges, Solutions, and Comparisons. *IEEE Communications Surveys and Tutorials*.

Luo, T., Huang, J., Kanhere, S. S., Zhang, J., & Das, K. S. (2019, March 13). Improving IoT Data Quality in Mobile Crowd Sensing: A Cross Validation Approach. *IEEE Internet of Things Journal*.

Lv, Z., Song, H., Val, B. P., Steed, A., & Jo, M. (2017). Next-Generation Big Data Analytics: State of the Art, Challenges, and Future Research Topics. *IEEE Transactions on Industrial Informatics*, *13*(4), 1891–1899. doi:10.1109/TII.2017.2650204

Mihovska, A., & Sarkar, M. (2017). Smart Connectivity for Internet of Things (IoT) Applications. *New Advances in the Internet of Things*, *715*, 105–118.

Mohammadi, M., & Fuqaha, A. A. (2018). Enabling Cognitive Smart Cities Using Big Data and Machine Learning: Approaches and Challenges. *IEEE Communications Magazine*, *56*(2), 94–101. doi:10.1109/MCOM.2018.1700298

Mohammadi, M., Fuqaha, A. A., Sorour, S., & Guizani, M. (2018). Deep Learning for IoT Big Data and Streaming Analytics: A Survey. *IEEE Communications Surveys and Tutorials*, *20*(6), 2923–2960. doi:10.1109/COMST.2018.2844341

Mohanty, P. S., Choppali, U., & Kougianos, E. (2016). Everything you wanted to know about Smart Cities: The Internet of things is the backbone. *IEEE Consumer Electronics Magazine*, *5*(3), 60–70. doi:10.1109/MCE.2016.2556879

Mongeon, P., & Hus, P. A. (2015). The journal coverage of Web of Science and Scopus: A comparative analysis. *Scientometrics*, *106*(1), 213–228. doi:10.100711192-015-1765-5 PMID:25821280

Muhammad, K., Lloret, J., & Baik, W. S. (2019). Intelligent and Energy-Efficient Data Prioritization in Green Smart Cities: Current Challenges and Future Directions. *IEEE Communications Magazine*, *57*(2), 60–65. doi:10.1109/MCOM.2018.1800371

Osman, S. M. (2019). A novel big data analytics framework for Smart Cities. *Future Generation Computer Systems*, *91*, 620–633. doi:10.1016/j.future.2018.06.046

Pan, G., Qi, G., Zhang, W., Li, S., Wu, Z., & Yang, T. L. (2013). Trace analysis and mining for Smart Cities: Issues, methods, and applications. *IEEE Communications Magazine*, *51*(6), 120–126. doi:10.1109/MCOM.2013.6525604

Pang, Z., Yang, G., Khedri, R., & Zhang, T. Y. (2018). Introduction to the Special Section: Convergence of Automation Technology, Biomedical Engineering, and Health Informatics Toward the Healthcare 4.0. *IEEE Reviews in Biomedical Engineering*, *11*, 249–259. doi:10.1109/RBME.2018.2848518

Peng, S., Wang, G., & Xie, D. (2016). Social Influence Analysis in Social Networking Big Data: Opportunities and Challenges. *IEEE Network*, *31*(1), 11–17. doi:10.1109/MNET.2016.1500104NM

Piro, G., Cianci, I., Grieco, A., Boggia, G., & Camarda, P. (2014). Information centric services in Smart Cities. *Journal of Systems and Software*, *88*, 169–188. doi:10.1016/j.jss.2013.10.029

Riedy, J. (2016). Updating PageRank for Streaming Graphs. In *2016 IEEE International Parallel and Distributed Processing Symposium Workshops (IPDPSW)* (pp. 877-884). Chicago, IL: IEEE. 10.1109/IPDPSW.2016.22

Romanowski, A. (2019). Big Data-Driven Contextual Processing Methods for Electrical Capacitance Tomography. *IEEE Transactions on Industrial Informatics*, *15*(3), 1609–1618. doi:10.1109/TII.2018.2855200

Sarikaya, R. (2017). The Technology Behind Personal Digital Assistants: An overview of the system architecture and key components. *IEEE Signal Processing Magazine, 34*(1), 67–81. doi:10.1109/MSP.2016.2617341

Shridhar, S. V. (2019). The India of Things: Tata Communications' countrywide IoT network aims to improve traffic, manufacturing, and health care. *IEEE Spectrum, 56*(2), 42–47. doi:10.1109/MSPEC.2019.8635816

Smart Cities total installed base of connected things 2015-2018. (2018). Retrieved February 25, 2019, from The Statistics Portal: https://www.statista.com/statistics/422886/smart-Cities-connected-things-installed-base/

Solanki, K. V., Makkar, S., Kumar, R., & Chatterjee, M. J. (2018, December 31). Theoretical Analysis of Big Data for Smart Scenarios. *Internet of Things and Big Data Analytics for Smart Generation*, 1-12.

Tous, R., Torres, J., & Ayguadé, E. (2015). Multimedia Big Data Computing for In-Depth Event Analysis. In *2015 IEEE International Conference on Multimedia Big Data* (pp. 144-147). Beijing, China: IEEE. 10.1109/BigMM.2015.39

Walravens, N., & Ballon, P. (2013). Platform business models for Smart Cities: From control and value to governance and public value. *IEEE Communications Magazine, 51*(6), 72–79. doi:10.1109/MCOM.2013.6525598

Wang, J., Crawl, D., Purawat, S., Nguyen, M., & Altintas, I. (2015). Big data provenance: Challenges, state of the art and opportunities. In *2015 IEEE International Conference on Big Data (Big Data)* (pp. 2509-2516). Santa Clara, CA: IEEE. 10.1109/BigData.2015.7364047

Wang, N., & Mao, B. (2019). The Research on the Problems of Smart Old-Age Care in the Background of Smart City Construction. In *International Conference on Intelligent Transportation, Big Data & Smart City (ICITBS)* (pp. 151-154). Changsha, China: IEEE. 10.1109/ICITBS.2019.00043

Winters, V. J. (2010). Why are smart cities growing? who moves and who stays. *Journal of Regional Science, 51*(2), 253–270. doi:10.1111/j.1467-9787.2010.00693.x

Yu, H., Yang, Z., & Sinnott, O. R. (2018). Decentralized Big Data Auditing for Smart City Environments Leveraging Blockchain Technology. *IEEE Access: Practical Innovations, Open Solutions, 7*, 6288–6296. doi:10.1109/ACCESS.2018.2888940

Zanella, A., Bui, N., Castellani, A., Vangelista, L. Z., & Zorzi, M. (2014). Internet of Things for Smart Cities. *IEEE Internet of Things Journal, 1*(1), 22–32. doi:10.1109/JIOT.2014.2306328

Zhu, W., Cui, P., Wang, Z., & Hua, G. (2015). Multimedia Big Data Computing. *IEEE MultiMedia, 22*(3), 96–c3. doi:10.1109/MMUL.2015.66

ADDITIONAL READING

Cheng, B., Longo, S., Cirillo, F., Bauer, M., & Kovacs, E. (2015, June). Building a big data platform for smart cities: Experience and lessons from santander. In *2015 IEEE International Congress on Big Data* (pp. 592-599). IEEE. 10.1109/BigDataCongress.2015.91

Hashem, I. A. T., Chang, V., Anuar, N. B., Adewole, K., Yaqoob, I., Gani, A., ... Chiroma, H. (2016). The role of big data in smart city. *International Journal of Information Management*, *36*(5), 748–758. doi:10.1016/j.ijinfomgt.2016.05.002

Sun, Y., Song, H., Jara, A. J., & Bie, R. (2016). Internet of things and big data analytics for smart and connected communities. *IEEE Access: Practical Innovations, Open Solutions*, *4*, 766–773. doi:10.1109/ACCESS.2016.2529723

KEY TERMS AND DEFINITIONS

Big Data: Big data is collection of datasets that could not be acquired, processed, perceived, and managed by traditional hardware and software tools within a specific time.

Data Provenance: Data provenance is associated with the records of the inputs, systems, entities, and processes that influence the data of interest, and provide historical records of the data and its origins.

Internet of Things (IoT): IoT can be defined as the idea of envisaging enormous number of smart devices and embedded systems which empowers physical objects with pervasive sensing, seeing, hearing, and communication with each other.

Smart Cities: Smart cities can be generally defined as a conceptual development model which makes collective use of humans and technology for the expansion of collaborative urban development.

Smart Governance: Smart governance is about the use of technology and innovation for facilitating and supporting enhanced decision making and planning. It is associated with improving the democratic processes and transforming the ways that public services are delivered.

Smart Grid: For optimized consumption, supply, and generation of electric energy, the concept of smart grids integrates the traditional energy networks with next generation grids that are enabled with remote automation, communication, and computation.

Smart Healthcare: Smart healthcare can be defined as an integration of patients and doctors onto a common platform for intelligent health monitoring by analyzing day-to-day human activities.

Smart Transportation: Smart transportation is defined as the integration of modern technologies, innovations, and management strategies in transportation systems, that aim to provide enhanced services associated with different modes of transport and traffic management, and enable users to be actively informed regarding safe and smarter use of transport networks.

Urban Planning: Urban planning may be described as a specialized technical and political procedure which is concerned with the design and development of land usage and the built environment, which includes air, water, and the physical and virtual infrastructure passing into and out of urban zones, such as communication, transportation, and dissemination networks.

Chapter 10
Securing Online Bank's Big Data Through Block Chain Technology:
Cross–Border Transactions Security and Tracking

Kommu Narendra
National Institute of Technology Puducherry, India

G. Aghila
National Institute of Technology Puducherry, India

ABSTRACT

Many sectors and fields are being computerized to make the work paperless, more transparent, and efficient. Banking is one such sector that has undergone enormous changes. Any amount from any part to any corner of the world is now possible around the clock. The dependency on technology for providing the services necessitates security, and the additional risks involved in cross-border nature of transactions of banks poses new challenges for banking regulators and supervisors. Many types of research are going in this area of banks big data processing, data analytics, and providing security for cross-border payments to mitigate the risks. Block chain is one such advancement for addressing the challenges in financial services. This chapter provides a brief overview of block chain usage, addressing the traditional issues and challenges for cross-border transactions.

INTRODUCTION

A small historic word called Usury meaning "lending at interest or excessive interest" the ancient historical records show the proof, that it has been practiced in various parts of the world. Subsequently changed its form substantially due to change in various traditions, institutions and social reforms on moral, ethical, religious and legal grounds. The Vedic texts of Ancient India (2000-1400BC), has the earliest of such

DOI: 10.4018/978-1-5225-9742-1.ch010

record. The Indian religious manuscript of Jain (1929) period records the oldest known references to usury and gives an outstanding summary on Indigenous Banking in India(Visser & Mcintosh, 1998). Since then there were many constitutional changes, amalgamations and various recommendations of Committees(RBI, 1998) and Commissions(Reserve Bank of India, 2017) drawn by the Reserve Bank of India (RBI) right from its establishment("Reserve Bank of India - History," 2019) on March 6, 1934. The transformation of banking from a primitive stage to the latest modern trends in India has no parallel in world history. India got its long history of having both public and private banking("Chapter - 5 Recent Developments in Banking Sector in India," 2007). The tremendous increase in the tempo of economic activities paved the path in the growth of the volume and complexity of banking activity. The Banks in India have established themselves by taking new tasks in expanding their geographical presence, functional heterogeneity, and personal portfolio services thus making them transformed from 'Class banks to Mass banks'. This has been realized by Computerization which is as an indispensable tool for improving the efficiency of the work environment in a better way and in ensuring the faster customer service, with better control systems. Innovations such as telephone lines, credit card systems, the internet, and mobile technologies have promoted the convenience, speed, and efficiency of transactions while shortening or even eliminating the distance between the customers and banks. Over 80% of the funds flowing through banks which are the most dominant segment of the financial sector, requires the following primary functions: (i) Operation of a payment and settlement system, (ii) Mobilization of savings and (iii) Allocation of savings to investment projects. The growth of the economy as a whole depends on the smooth functioning of financial markets, individual remittances, financial inclusion which is an integral part of Payment and settlement systems(Chaum, 1983). The oversight of payment and settlement systems over the years has often been as a critical function of the central bank contributing to the overall financial stability, along with prudential supervision (which indeed a function of an independent bank or its supervisory authority). Worldwide, the trend has been to recognize and strengthen the role of the central banks in ensuring financial stability. Reserve Bank of India (RBI), as a regulator and under its powers vested by the Payment and Settlement Systems Act, 2007 (PSS Act) sets the necessary framework through an advisory committee in order to regulate, and to ensure the safe, secure and efficient operations of different types of payment system operators to meet the varied social needs(RBI, 2018). All these wide networks of operators under payment systems in the country are strengthened by technological infrastructure such as electronic funds transfer, centralized funds management system, structured financial messaging solution, and negotiated dealing system with a move towards Real Time Gross Settlement (RTGS). Payment Systems in India have grown in a manner which is characterized by a few operators like National Payments Corporation of India (NPCI) – National Financial Switch (NFS), Cheque Truncation System (CTS(Delhi, 2014)), Immediate Payment Service (IMPS), Unified Payments Interface (UPI)-including Bharat Interface for Money (BHIM), National Unified USSD (Unstructured Supplementary Service Data) Platform (NUUP), National Automated Clearing House (NACH), Aadhaar Enabled Payment System (AePS) doing a wide array of payments and settlements(RBI, 2018).

In spite of these advancements, many business transactions still remain costly, vulnerable and inefficient may be due to the following hurdles(Schaechter, 2002):

- Physical cash is being used in local transactions and for relatively small amounts
- The duration for transactions and its settlement may be long
- Limited transparency and inconsistent information in the transactions hindering the efficient movements of funds

- Possible risk of frauds, cyber-attacks(technology, 2016); and even simple small mistakes leading to increasing the cost and complexity of the business
- The need for third parties verification and validations and/or the presence of intermediaries adding to the inefficiencies

The growth of e-commerce, digital banking(previously referred to as e-banking or online banking, with more focus on customer experience, which mostly falls within the boundary of retail banking as an industry), and in-app purchases, coupled with the increasing mobility of people around the world, has increased the growth of transaction volumes. The rate of growth of these voluminous transactions is exploding with the rise of Internet of Things (IoT). In other words, the volumes of transactions throughout the world are growing exponentially affecting the cost of existing transactions systems.

To address these issues and other challenges, the world needs better and faster payment networks, building a system providing a mechanism of trust(Batlin, Przewloka, & Williams, 2016) without no further specialized or additional equipment's. Apart from this, the system should support minimal or no fees along with good backtracking and record keeping for all the transactions carried out. Among the technologies available, this chapter explores the role of the emerging technology "Blockchain" in addressing these issues.

WHY GO FOR NEW TECHNOLOGY

In general, banking operations performed are as classified as daily / periodic transactions or non-daily / aperiodic transactions by numerous stakeholders such as customers, debtors, employees of the bank and other external entities. Here the transactions means involving money either in physical form or in terms of orders given by the stake holders to the banks for doing transactions on their behalf in the form of electronic transactions (e-transactions) i.e. e-data information exchange of bits and bytes on which these operations rely on. These are the vital enablers of business operations and are identified as "information assets". As banks being the purveyors of the money in any form, safeguarding this information is even more vital for them.

The fundamental principle is how good this information is provided by the stakeholders? Is the information provided is sufficient to do the transaction has been verified right from initial stage till the completion of transaction by the system. Providing inadequate or insufficient low quality data is like allowing errors to creep in any day to day operations, thus a specified set of standard procedures and disciplines with respect to fundamental attributes have been identified to set up for ensuring accuracy, integrity, timeliness validity, completeness of information, consistency, accessibility, usability and auditability. This standard of data quality depends upon how good the information is built upon by the business organizations.

Every organization again have their own set of standards laid down as per their requirements called the 'Organizational Asset'. This asset again requires high levels of protection as it involves corresponding business events and cycles of their day to day dealings. Over time these events may unfold the possibilities of those events being malicious in nature, random mistakes done by employees or due to an inevitable complex circumstance that goes beyond the control. This necessitates constant monitoring as neither bank nor the stake holder nor business organization can roll back,affecting the business adversely.

Early detection of errors in these assets as mentioned above be it information asset or organization asset will significantly ameliorate potential ill-effects, and in some cases actively prevent them from occurring too. Literature survey, clearly indicates 'Blockchain' technology may take a major role in addressing these issues.

This section of the chapter highlights the benefits to the banking sector by adopting Block Chain Technology; to provide better customer service, operational efficiency, and cost optimization. This switchover(CAPGEMINI, 2015) of technology is possible by the works done by several individual entities, institutes, and organizations across the globe. While on one hand advancements in the fields of computer, communication, and other relevant technologies carried out in the research works of academic institutions; on the other hand, the employees of the banks and other financial-technological companies are working together for the betterment of banking by newer technologies.

THE BLOCKCHAIN: HISTORY AND OVERVIEW

The age-old traditional methods for recording the transactions, keeping a track on the assets are generally, participants maintaining their own ledgers and other records. But the traditional methods are expensive, partially due to the involvement of intermediaries, who will charge heavily for their services. Also it is inefficient due to delays in executing agreements and the duplication of effort required in maintaining numerous ledgers without linking the corresponding services. It is vulnerable because if a central system (for example, a bank) is compromised due to fraud, cyber-attack, or a simple mistake, the entire business network will be affected.

Blockchain has been making a buzz for quite some time now in different fields as shown in fig (1) such as (i) government administration, (ii) health care industry, (iii) education sector, (iv) supply chain management, (v) legal purposes and record keeping, (vi) retail markets, (vii) travel information, (viii) music, (ix) movies and entertainment of film industry, (x) communication sector, (xi) real estate, (xii) insurance companies, (xiii) power sector, (xiv) internet of things(IoT) (xv) banking and finance sector.

As mentioned earlier, in all the above mentioned fields, major concerns are delays and vulnerability during transactions. Hence the concept of 'distributed ledger blockchain' are widely scrutinized / considered by Banking and finance sectors to tackle these issues.

To address the nucleus of these issues, participants should be given the ability to share a ledger that is updated through peer-to-peer replication each time a transaction occurs. Peer-to-peer replication means that each participant (also called a node) in the network acts as both a publisher (transaction originator) and a subscriber (participant in the network). As, the blockchain architecture inherently possesses this ability to handle, this chapter throws a open view of various possibilities.

The participants on both ends of the transaction systems of the network are the same. The noted change from the traditional way is how the transaction record has been shared and available to all parties. As far as block chain technology is considered,each participanting nodes can receive or send transactions to other nodes in the network called the blockchain network. In this, the data has to be synchronized across the network when it is transferred.

Generally,the blockchain network is economical(Microsoft, 2018) and efficient since it eliminates duplication of effort and reduces the need for intermediaries. It is also less vulnerable because it uses a consensus model for validating the information. Use of this technology builds, a secure, authenticated, and verifiable transaction system.

Figure 1. Fields and areas of block chain technology

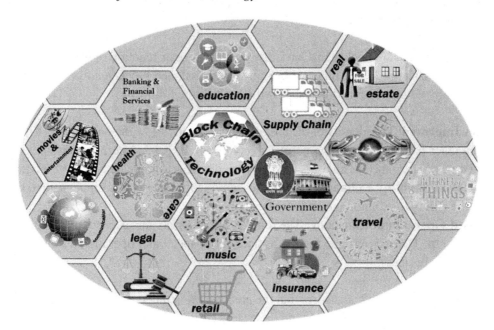

In a nutshell, use of blockchain network has the following key characteristics:

- **Consensus**: All participants of the network must agree upon, for a transaction to be validity(Schwartz, Youngs, & Britto, 2014).
- **Provenance**: Participants of the transaction are aware of where the asset came and how the ownership changed over a time period.
- **Immutability**: Tamper proof transaction i.e.no participant can change a transaction after it has been recorded in the ledger. And if under any situation any error occurs in the transaction, only a new transaction is used to reverse it, so that in the network both the transactions are visible.
- **Finality**: A single, shared ledger provides a one-stop solution place to determine the ownership of an asset on the completion of a transaction.

In addition, Blockchain has the following specific benefits:

- **Time Saver**: The reduction or change of time from days to hours or even to minutes for a complex transaction, multi-party interactions are seen. Thus make the settlement of transaction much faster as it doesn't require verification by a central authority.
- **Cost Minimizer**: A blockchain network further reduces expenses in quite a few different ways:
  - Less oversight is required, due to self-policed framework done by network participants, all of whom are known in the network they are working.
  - Intermediaries called the middlemen are reduced as the participants can directly exchange the items or do their transactions at their ease.
  - Since all the participants are connected to a shared ledged the duplication of data is eliminated over the network.

- **Hard Security**: Blockchain's security features protect the data against tampering, fraudulent transaction, and cybercrime.

It is not necessary that all blockchains have the same purpose or function of their intended building. Some may be permissioned, while others may not. A permissioned blockchain network is critical for business, especially within regulated industries which offers the following:

- **Privacy Improved**: The identity of the user and permissions allow the participants to have control over the other participants and the permissions to view. Expanded Permissions are given for the special type of users such as auditors who may need access to more detailed transactions.
- **Financial Auditablitiy Enhanced**: Having a shared ledger serves as a single source of truth improves the ability to monitor and audit transactions.
- **Increased Operational Efficiency**: The digitization of assets makes a streamline for transfer of the ownership. Transactions are done at a much more speed and operational efficiency with the pace of doing business.

If a network is permissioned, it ensures that the creation of members-on the network with proof that the members are the ones who they claim and the exact goods or assets being traded.

Categories of Blockchain

There are various (often conflicting) categorizations of blockchain types, such as access to the blockchain data itself is public or private. The first categorization:

- Permissionless blockchains, where anyone can participate in the verification process, i.e. no prior authorization is needed or required and a user is allowed to contribute his/her computational skills and analytical power, usually in exchange for a monetary benefit or a reward.
- Permissioned blockchains, where verification nodes are preselected by a central authority, Regulators or consortium.

The Second categorization:

- Public blockchains (Figure 2) are the one where anyone in the network can read, write and submit transactions to the blockchain.

- Private blockchains (Figure 3) are those which restricts the permission to users within an organization or group of organizations

Services Offered by Block Chain

The following are the high usage services (Froystad & Holm, 2015) of the blockchain(Banking & Sector, 2017) beyond the primary distributed ledger functionalities, implementations in their technical details and capabilities. Few are mentioned below

Figure 2. Public block chain

Figure 3. Private block chain

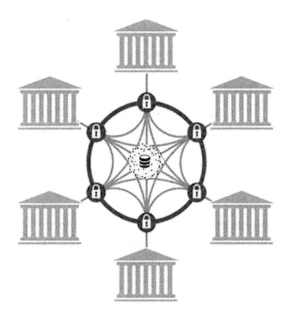

- Financial Services
- Trade finance
- Post-trade clearing and settlement
- Trusted digital identity
- Multinational Policy Management
- Cross-border transactions

- IoT (Internet of Things) (Memos, Psannis, Ishibashi, Kim, & Gupta, 2018)
- Smart City Environments (Plageras, Psannis, Stergiou, Wang, & Gupta, 2018)

Implementations of the technology differs based on the mechanisms enforced and the consensus used, and the role of programming language used as it defines the capabilities and determines who is allowed to participate and who is not allowed (Beck & Müller-Bloch, 2017; Yli-Huumo, Ko, Choi, Park, & Smolander, 2016)

Recent reviews on blockchain shows that majority of the work has focused on improvements of protocols apart from cryptocurrencies in general and bitcoin in particular.

The reader may note that this chapter restricts its view to only the cross-border transactions and payments.

What is a Cross-Border Transaction?

A cross-border payment is a transaction involving individuals or organizations operating in at least two different nations. A person or an individual can be a payee or payer doing the transaction. A cross border transaction can be of following cases: (i) Transaction can be between a person/ individual to any other person/ individual doing an international remittance either to his family or friends having accounts in same banks of different countries or different banks in different countries. A Remittance is a fund-transfer transaction wherein funds are moved from one account to another account within the same or any other financial institution. (ii) Any business organization may do remittance to get goods from a foreign supplier or a government entity may do remittance for paying salaries or pensions of their employees, again with same banks in different countries or different banks in different countries. Below Table 1 details the matrix of the types of cross-border transactions.

For doing a cross-border transaction a network has been established in 1973 called ***SWIFT SCRL*** (Society for Worldwide Interbank Financial Telecommunication). This is a financial messaging platform that brings together 10,500 financial institutions and corporations across 215 countries, has been built on the base of varied financial applications, high business intelligence, reference data and most recently compliance services. The SWIFT INDIA("What is the purpose of SWIFT India? | SWIFT India," 2019) network got more than 22 million payments, securities, trade finance and treasury messages daily on an average and its members exchange these messages in a highly reliable, secure and resilient manner.

In India, we call it as SWIFT India Domestic Services Pvt Ltd ("SWIFT India"-in Figure 4 image courtesy: refer websites). A SWIFT network can be visualized as a bit like traveling from one airport to another. It is not always possible to take a direct flight, which means it is necessary to travel from one city

Table 1. Types of cross-border transactions

Payee/Payer	Person/Individual	Business organization/ Government	Type/Category
Person/Individual	international remittance to family/friends	payments for e-commerce purchase from abroad	same (or) different banks in different countries
Business organization/ Government	salaries/pensions to employees working abroad	supply chain payments to foreign suppliers	same (or) different banks in different countries

Figure 4. SWIFT INDIA services

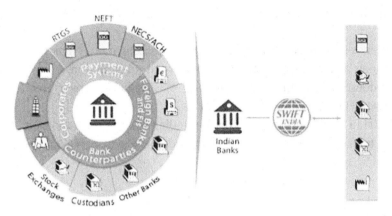

to another via several connecting flights. SWIFT works logically the same way. The money will travel from one country to another, but to do that there are often intermediary/correspondent banks involved.

The operation of SWIFT is as follows: The SWIFT network doesn't actually involve in the transfer of funds directly, but instead, it sends an order of payment requests made between institutions' accounts, using SWIFT codes. It is SWIFT that uses a standardized IBAN (International Bank Account Numbers) and specified BIC (Bank Identifier Codes) formats. SWIFT organization has full rights which acknowledge and governs the BIC system, meaning that it can quickly identify a bank and send a payment securely. In a cross-border payment, the movement of messages along with the payment chain is ensured only by SWIFT which in turn informs the corresponding banks that are involved in original or actual transfer for the debits and credits across accounts based on the request (or) ordered message by which the value is passed to the final beneficiary.

A scenario is explained with an example in Figure 5:

Figure 5. Payment flow- Bank P sending Indian Rupees to Banks S in US

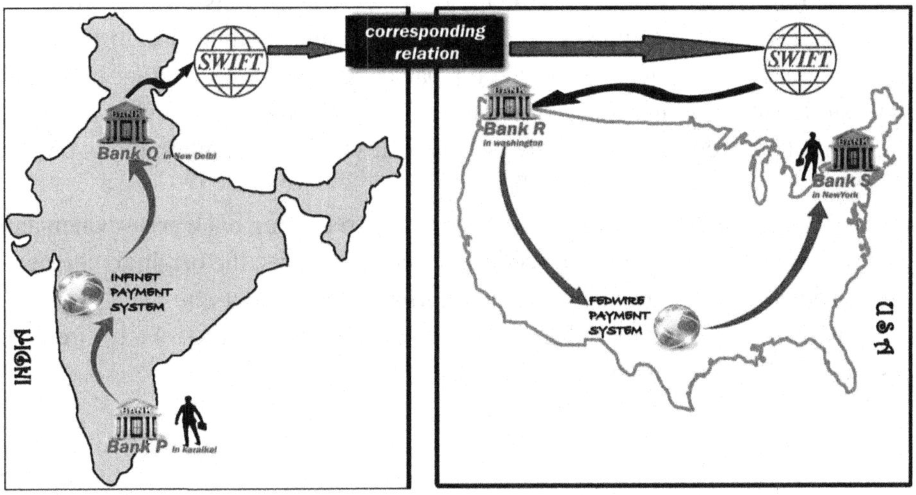

- A person Mr.X in Karaikal, India through Bank P is sending Indian Rupees to his friend Mr.Y in NewYork, US having an account in Bank S. The workflow is given below:

  ◦ Bank P sends the payment request to its corresponding bank, Bank Q via INFINET wire and accompanies a debit/credit instruction for onward transmission.
  ◦ Bank Q does the adjustments and sends a message to its correspondent bank, Bank R in Washington via the SWIFT network.
  ◦ An MT103 (a SWIFT message format) in Indian Rupees is sent to Bank R in the US.
  ◦ Bank R transmits the value via Single Fedwire Payments Area (FedPA) to Bank S in NewYork.
  ◦ Bank S credits Mr.Y's account in US dollar $.

In order to transmit these messages among the corresponding banks, a charge is levied by SWIFT which subsequently adds up to the rise in cost. The ledgers here are local to banks where the debit entries are made. In other words,one bank's ledger is communicated to the other bank for pass/ post of the corresponding credit entry side of its ledger. As the number of payment message increased in the chain of payment messages, the corresponding commission or fees charged on SWIFT messages also increases.

The process for an international remittance of funds in the current ongoing system with the corresponding banks inclusion has got the following drawbacks:

- No correspondent banks can confirm a transaction based on their own ledger entry until SWIFT came into the light to guarantee and confirm these message transmissions for both the banks. The central bank or the regulatory bank act only as an agency just to the guarantee of the operated settlement of payments without actual involvement.
- Irrespective of the kind of correspondent bank either as sending bank or receiving a bank of the instruction, SWIFT charges both banks for processing the payment orders or messages.
- Initiating one single cross-border payment will have to pass through different correspondent banks involving many activities like gathering, verifying, and netting of payment messages before a messaged is retransmitting by confirmations/denials to the respective banks which maximizes the settlement time.
- A trustworthy third-party organization or middlemen company has been given powers to overwrite and overturn ledger activities if needed during any unavoidable circumstances.
- A Nostro account is one such account which a bank maintains with another bank and should always have sufficient funds in order to do the foreign exchange transactions. These accounts are under the central bank control, which always mandates them to maintain funds becoming typical to banks.
- A concern related to data protection and security at the receiving bank arises when any cross-border payment is sent from the group of accounts of certain banks, the original message is modified and resent to complete the transaction, by an internal bank account number.
- Since the payment moves across INFINET to SWIFT and then through Fed Wire Payment Area, the messages involved are varied and different.

How Block Chain Can Help to Facilitate Cross-Border Money Transfers

The blockchain is a universal ledger present in a distributed network which is accessible to everybody in the network. Every participating node of the blockchain network have a replica of the entire database or ledger, further to this, any modifications and updates done to data block are permitted only when all the other nodes/participants of the network validate and agree upon the changes done. So a consensus of nodes is required for validating the state of the ledger. This underlying distributed ledger concept empowers the banks to have a visible, immutable and bilateral transfer of funds, without any fear of manual manipulations and intervention by intermediaries or correspondent banks at any point of time thereby delivering instant funds transfer directly to the receiver.

As shown in Figure 6.Blockchain brings in the following benefits:

- The transaction becomes a bilateral agreement between the participants making it a trustworthy environment for processing the cross-border payments directly thereby smoothly eliminating the necessity of intermediaries like third-party organizations, central agencies or the correspondent banks from the picture.
- Initiating one single cross-border payment one has to pay charges or commissions to various corresponding banks for the activities like gathering, verifying, and netting of payment messages before a message is retransmitted by confirmations/denials,in addition to the SWIFT charges if the transactions are routing through it. These charges are reduced with minimal or no charges along the payment.
- As mentioned above there is no need for the intermediaries like third-party organizations, central agencies or the correspondent banks, the turnaround time for settlement of funds reduces.
- Verification of funds of Nostro accounts becomes easy, as each participating bank will have a copy of the distributed ledger with the balances of their account maintained with other banks. Thus central banks mandatory control for ensuring sufficient funds are totally being eliminated.
- The details of the transactions are hidden by means of encryption and hashing thus making it very hard to modify the data.

Figure 6. Money transfer from bank P to bank S through blockchain eliminating the 3rd party players

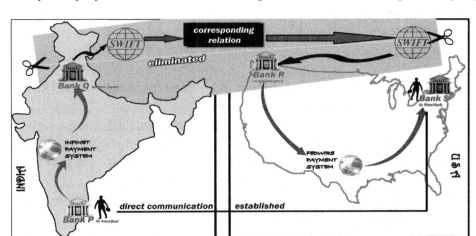

- The task of making standardized messages while transmitting any payments used earlier are minimized.
- The sender and receiving participants will have increased transparency with respect to their payment transactions and settlements, as the nodes in the network posses the distributed ledger.
- With the help of private(consortium) or permissioned category of blockchain one can address the challenges roaming around the data privacy and security, as it becomes difficult for the intruders to anonymously jump and become a node in the blockchain network

Now the challenge comes to RBI as a regulator in maintaining the compliance of banks big data and its regulatory control over the banks ensuring the data protection and privacy in a private blockchain environment.

The authors now wanted the reader's attention to a topic called big data-what, why and how it is linked or collaborated with blockchain(Bataev, 2018).

A simple answer to the question of what is big data? Big data is the designation of structured and unstructured data of huge volumes and having different presentation formats that are processed. In a broad sense, "big data" is said to be a socio-economic phenomenon associated with the emergence of technological capabilities to analyze huge amounts of data, in some problem areas and the resulting transformative effects.

What characteristics do big data (Figure 7) possess?

- Following are the characteristics:
  - **Volume**: As a value of physical volume;
  - **Velocity**: In terms of both the rate of increase and the need for high-speed processing and obtaining results;
  - **Variety**: As the possibility of simultaneous processing of different types, structured and semi-structured data
- Technologies of big data:
  - Clustering
  - Text Analytics
  - Neural networks
  - Link analysis
  - Survival or event analysis
  - Decision trees
  - Random trees

The volume here relates to the Large amounts of data related to customers KYC(Know Your Customer), from datasets with sizes of terabytes to zettabyte.

The speed at which the data grows is given by velocity of big data i.e. Large amounts of data from transactions with high refresh rate dynamically resulting in data streams coming at great speed and the time to act on the basis of these data streams will often be very short. There is a shift from batch processing to real time streaming or real time gross settlements of the payments.

The data may be from different heterogenous sources and in general they may be from banks internal request or external third party data source requests. More importantly, the data may be in different formats such as transaction or log data from various applications may be in different format, structured data

Figure 7. Big data characteristics collabration with block chain

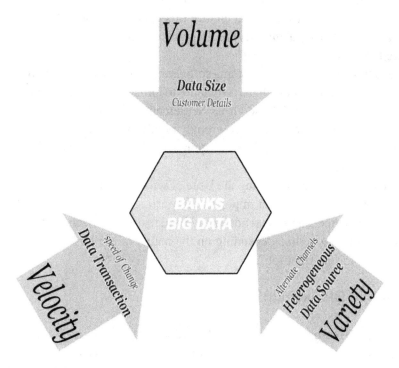

such as database tables, semi-structured data such as XML data, unstructured data such as photographs and other images and more. There is a shift from sole structured data to increasingly more unstructured data or the combination of the two.

The data that we are talking about the banks as an organization have a tradition of capturing transactional data. Apart from that, banks nowadays are capturing additional data from its operational environment at an increasingly fast speed. Some example are listed here.

- Web data. Customer level web behaviour data such as page views, searches, reading reviews, purchasing, can be captured. They can enhance performance in areas such as next best offer, churn modelling, customer segmentation and targeted advertisement.
- Text data (email,documents, etc) is one of the biggest and most widely applicable types of big data. The focus is typically on extracting key facts from the text and then use the facts as inputs to other analytic process (for example, automatically classify insurance claims or a loan application with respect to bank as fraudulent or not.)
- Time and location data. GPS and mobile phone as well as Wi-Fi connection makes time and location information a growing source of data. At an individual level, many organizations come to realize the power of knowing when their customers are at which location. Equally important is to look at time and location data at an aggregated level. As more individuals open up their time and location data more publicly, lots of interesting applications start to emerge. Time and location data is one of the most privacy-sensitive types of big data and should be treated with great caution.

Traditionally, this can be done, but the accuracy was far less impressive with the given limited time and source of data. But significantly Big data change this equation. Fast and actionable insight means that whatever we get out of the data analysis has an impact on the business process and preferable the impact is embedded in the process.

For instance, an automated remainder systems software observes a customers trend of daily transactions and automatically generate personalized remainder to him for purchase of material from a company (e.g. Daily funds transfer using Real Time Gross Settlement(RTGS) done by customer A to some X company for his raw material,the software may wrongly predict and recommend something different by observing the old patterns than what exactly the requirement is on that particular day) is of the concern for that current days transaction.

The role of big data comes here in solving the issue of wrong prediction using data analytics. This is not to say that descriptive analytics is not important. Reporting has been and will still be an important part of business life. In practice, one should not be rigid and insisting on only a specific type of analytics. What yields most benefit is of course depending on the nature of the business question and thereafter choosing "the right tool for the right job".

How is it Related to Blockchain?

The blockchain uses the Tree-based technology of big data and it is believed that it has the capacity to support the big data characteristics to maintain the compliance of splitted data, which are arranged using hash functions for every transaction duly partitioned by region, country, and date to track the transactions. Hash functions are extensively used in blockchain for the integrity of data/transactions. It also used in organizing and linking data/transactions with blocks. The linking is done through the hashing of various elements in the block header containing a hash of previous block, timestamp, and some miscellaneous information. While linking(Mukkamala, Vatrapu, Ray, Sengupta, & Halder, 2018),(Fig.8) each transaction is hashed, then the resulting hash of each transaction is hashed to build a tree structure until the top node known as the Merkle root is obtained. A successful hash function has the following characteristics:

Figure 8. Tree structure of block in blockchain

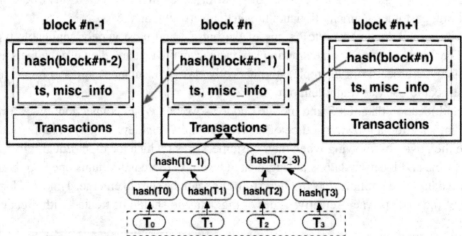

deterministic - the same input always creates the same output, efficient - output is computed in a timely manner, distributed - evenly spread across the output range. Care should be taken while distribution, since similar data may correlate to similar hashes. This ensures tracking by giving the conventional input details and looking at the tail end output and vice versa. Different big data technologies are introduced in many areas of banking right from mobile banking, revealing the signs of fraudulent happenings in internet banking, to the management of cash. These technologies contribute to a higher level of automation.

The Collaboration of Blockchain and Big Data in Cross-Border Transactions

The handshake between blockchain and big data technology improves the bank in efficient ways and developing the financial sector of the country to grow in different dimensions. These new opportunities entitle the enterprises, research institutes, and other sectors to collaborate with banks for all types of tasks. These technologies help the banks to more efficiently manage a variety of tasks like customer/client, account, disposition, pay orders, transactions, loans, credit card, demographic data etc..

The main areas of introduction and use of big data with banks is related to its static information (e.g. Date of creation of an account, name, and address of the customer, address of the branch) that deals with basic information and dynamic information (payments credited or debited, balances) about transactional information.

This static data of the customer of a particular bank may be entered at the time of registering or creating an account into a permissioned blockchain environment as in Fig.6. The regulatory authority may assign privileges for interaction among the banks involved in the transactions. The dynamic data details related to the transactions, of a particular user of a bank, is then clubbed together with a hash function making it hash transaction data.

Similarly, at the receiving end, the static data is matched with the details to that of other bank customer entered in blockchain and finally adjusting the ledgers for the current transactions. The distributed ledger should contain the corresponding details of credit and debit entries.

This ensures the settlement of the cross-border payment done as the ledger is updated at both ends. Any manual interving in modifying the data leads to change in the static hashed data which makes the total block to become void. This feature ensures the security of cross border transactions.

CONCLUSION

In this chapter, we discuss blockchain, its categories and how efficient and useful it becomes to banks in India on migrating to this blockchain technology. The discussion is restricted to cross-border transactions of banking with the alliance of big data and blockchain. The main focus being security and backtracking by which how the regular transaction costs, commissions charges are reduced or even eliminated in the cross border transaction. Blockchain for banks big data will not only allow banks to help their clients but also in planning their expenses by offering them faster services and other privileges. Since the research on blockchain is still a nascent stage, the scope may be further extended to customer payments need in domestic payments environment within the country between different banks, and further the identified areas are still more to be explored in the banking sector and data management it can also be extended in the data analytics field of big data.

REFERENCES

Banking, T. O., & Sector, F. (2017). *Institute for Development and Research in Banking Technology Applications of Block Chain Technology to Banking and Financial Sector in India.* Retrieved from http://www.idrbt.ac.in/assets/publications/Best Practices/BCT.pdf

Bataev, A. V. (2018). Analysis of the Application of Big Data Technologies in the Financial Sphere. *2018 IEEE International Conference "Quality Management, Transport and Information Security, Information Technologies" (IT&QM&IS)*, 568–572. 10.1109/ITMQIS.2018.8525121

Batlin, A., Przewloka, A., & Williams, S. (2016). *Building the trust Engine- How the block chain could transform (and the world) by Hyder Jaffrey Strategic Investment & Fintech Innovation.* UBS Investment Bank Christopher Murphy Global Co-Head of FX, Rates and Credit, UBS Investment Bank-white paper.

Beck, R., & Müller-Bloch, C. (2017). Blockchain as Radical Innovation: A Framework for Engaging with Distributed Ledgers as Incumbent Organization. *Proceedings of the 50th Hawaii International Conference on System Sciences*, 5390–5399. 10.24251/HICSS.2017.653

CAPGEMINI. (2015). *What You Need to Know About Blockchain and How to Assess the Opportunity Blockchain: A Fundamental Shift for Financial Services Institutions.* Author.

Chaum, D. (1983). *Blind Signatures for Untraceable Payments.* Advances in Cryptology; doi:10.1007/978-1-4757-0602-4_18

Delhi, B. C. H. N. (2014). *Bankers' Clearing House at New Delhi (BCHND) Procedural Guidelines for Cheque Truncation System (CTS).* Author.

Froystad, P., & Holm, J. (2015). Blockchain: Powering the Internet of Value. *Whitepaper*, *50*. doi:10.3141/2411-03

Institute for Development and Research in Banking Technology. (2016). Cyber Security Checklist. Institute for Development and Research in Banking Technology.

Memos, V. A., Psannis, K. E., Ishibashi, Y., Kim, B. G., & Gupta, B. B. (2018). An Efficient Algorithm for Media-based Surveillance System (EAMSuS) in IoT Smart City Framework. *Future Generation Computer Systems*, *83*, 619–628. doi:10.1016/j.future.2017.04.039

Microsoft. (2018). *Five ways blockchain is transforming financial services.* Author.

Mukkamala, R. R., Vatrapu, R., Ray, P. K., Sengupta, G., & Halder, S. (2018). Converging Blockchain and Social Business for Socio-Economic Development. *2018 IEEE International Conference on Big Data (Big Data)*, 3039–3048. 10.1109/BigData.2018.8622238

Plageras, A. P., Psannis, K. E., Stergiou, C., Wang, H., & Gupta, B. B. (2018). Efficient IoT-based sensor BIG Data collection–processing and analysis in smart buildings. *Future Generation Computer Systems*, *82*, 349–357. doi:10.1016/j.future.2017.09.082

RBI. (1998). *Committees on Computerisation.* Retrieved from https://www.rbi.org.in/scripts/PublicationsView.aspx?id=162

RBI. (2018). *Authorisation of New Retail Payment Systems.* Reserve Bank of India Department of Payment and Settlement Systems Central Office, Mumbai.

Reserve Bank of India. (2017). *Guidelines on Information security, Electronic Banking, Technology risk management and cyber frauds.* Department of Banking Supervision.

Reserve Bank of India - History. (2019). Retrieved February 20, 2019, from https://www.rbi.org.in/Scripts/Project1.aspx

Schaechter, A. (2002). *Issues in Electronic Banking: An Overview.* International Monetary Fund.

Schwartz, D., Youngs, N., & Britto, A. (2014). *The Ripple protocol consensus algorithm.* Ripple Labs Inc White Paper. Retrieved from http://www.naation.com/ripple-consensus-whitepaper.pdf

Visser, W. A. M., & Mcintosh, A. (1998). A short review of the historical critique of usury. *Accounting Business & Financial History*, *8*(2), 175–189. doi:10.1080/095852098330503

What is the purpose of SWIFT India? (2019). Retrieved February 20, 2019, from https://www.swiftindia.org.in/what-purpose-swift-india

Yli-Huumo, J., Ko, D., Choi, S., Park, S., & Smolander, K. (2016). Where Is Current Research on Blockchain Technology?-A Systematic Review. *PLoS One*, *11*(10), e0163477. doi:10.1371/journal.pone.0163477 PMID:27695049

Chapter 11
Enhance Data Security and Privacy in Cloud

Hicham Amellal
 https://orcid.org/0000-0002-7344-3246
University Mohamed V, Morocco

Abdelmajid Meslouhi
University Mohamed V, Morocco

Abderahim El Allati
Abdelmalek Essaadi University, Morocco

Annas El Haddadi
ENSA El-Hoceima, Morocco

ABSTRACT

With the advancement of communication and information technology, the internet has become used as a platform for computing and not only a way of communications networks. Accordingly, the large spread of cloud computing led to the emergence of different privacy implications and data security complexities. In order to enhance data security in the cloud, the authors propose in this chapter the use of an encryption box, which includes different cryptosystems. In fact, this step gives the user the opportunities to encrypt data with an unknown algorithm and makes a private key before the storage of data in the host company servers. Moreover, to manage the encryption database, the authors propose a quantum approach in search based on Grover's algorithm.

INTRODUCTION

In general terms, the cloud computing refers to the ability to access and manipulate, the stored data and the computer applications run somewhere else's in the servers of the host companies via the internet, using any internet-enabled platform, including smart phones. The cloud computing is used by companies in all industries and for different services this includes: Web-based email services such as Yahoo and

DOI: 10.4018/978-1-5225-9742-1.ch011

Microsoft Hotmail, Photo storing services such as Googleis Picassa, spreadsheet applications such as Zoho, online computer backup services such as Mozy, Applications associated with social networking sites such as Face book and much others. This technology, allows companies to buy IT resources as a service, in the same way that they consume electricity, instead of having to build and maintain internal IT infrastructures (Gupta & Agrawal, 2016; Papazoglou & van der Heuval, 2007). Also, the cloud computing offers several advantages and benefits for users such as self-service provisioning which allows users to access any on-demand computing resource, elasticity offers the opportunity to increase or decrease the consumption of resources according to the needs of the company and pay per use allows companies to pay only for the resources consumed (Papazoglou & van der Heuval, 2007). At the same time, the cloud is a multifaceted challenge includes technical and laws, obstacles this includes trust the operators, the question of intellectual property. Therefore, we must be found the achievement of a balanced relationship that guarantees the user rights and the economic return of the company. Recently, the scandal Facebook-Cambridge Analytica showed how the host companies reckless the user privacy. Therefore, the user in his relationship with the company has been always in a weak position, because he cannot verify compliance with the security mechanisms declared as security requirements. Accordingly, the cloud is represented a black box for the user. In order to give the users more control of data and more trust we propose in this paper to protect the privacy in the cloud via encryption box which includesvdifferent classical cryptosystems (Amellal et al., 2018; Armbrust et al., 2009).

The paper is organized as follows: In Sec. II, The complexities of privacy in cloud computing. In Sec. III, Cloud computing services. In Sec.IV, our proposition to protect data and privacy in cloud. Finally, conclusion is drawn in the last section.

THE COMPLEXITIES OF PRIVACY IN CLOUD COMPUTING

The privacy implications of cloud computing services introduce a number of unidentified parameters in the management, which makes the relation between the service providers and users are unclear. When customers store their data on host companies' servers, they lose a degree of control over their sensitive information. Accordingly, the responsibility of data security against all menaces including hackers and internal data breaches then falls into the hands of the hosting company rather than the individual user. Moreover, different companies could even readily sale the user's sensitive information with marketing firms. Therefore, there is a big risk in putting our data in someone else's hands (Taylor & Francis, 2018). Therefore; many internet users believe that the safest approach is to maintain sensitive information under your own control. One of the problems with cloud computing is that technology is frequently light years ahead of the law. There are many questions about privacy that need to be answered such as:

- Who are the interferers in cloud computing?
- Does the user or cloud computing own the data?
- What are their limits, roles and responsibilities?
- Can the host deny a user access to their own data?
- Where is the data reserved?
- How is the data replicated?
- What are the relevant legal rules for data processing?
- How will the host companies meet the expected level of data security and privacy?

- If the host company goes out of business, what happens to the users' data it holds?

With the spread of relying on cloud computing by companies and individuals, the services proposed by the host companies are evolving, and the challenges of data security and privacy are increased. This is what we will discuss in the next parts of this work.

THE CLOUD COMPUTING SERVICES

The cloud provider proposes different services for creating and storing data or using computer applications online, as well as strategies for where and how to consume them. These solutions are used to set up virtual infrastructures for small and large organizations, to host specific applications or functions, and a place to develop and test new features. In addition, they include on-demand services and products (hardware, software, and networks) and solutions that you can buy to install in your environment. There are many cloud solutions, each offering different functions, and services. Cloud functions and services for compute and storage are combined to enable the implementation of software as-a-service (SaaS), Platform-as-a-service (PaaS) and Infrastructure-as-a-service (IaaS) in public and private cloud solutions (see Figure 1).

1. **Infrastructure as a Service (IaaS):** Give the customer the opportunity to use the vital web architecture, this includes: storage space, servers, and connections, without needing of purchasing and managing this internet infrastructure themselves.
2. **Platform as a Service (PaaS):** A model in which the host company delivers hardware and software tools to users over the internet.
3. **Software as a Service (SaaS):** A software distribution model in which a third party provider hosts the applications and makes them available to its customers via the internet.

These features can be provided as a service, product, or bundled solution, also known as (ITaaS) (Reese, 2009). Here are some of the common adjectives and expressions used to describe cloud solutions:

- **Optimized**: Align resources with service level goals to meet service level agreements
- **Flexible**: Support growth without increasing complexity

Figure 1. Services of cloud computing

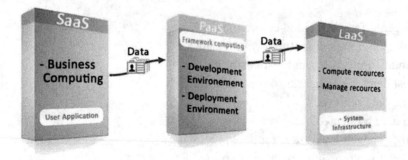

Figure 2. Cloud types

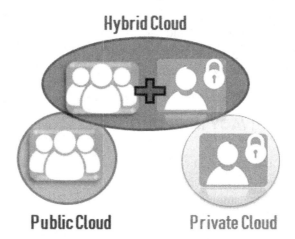

- **Dynamic**: Adapt to changing needs while remaining available
- **Automatic Provisioning**: Quickly Access Resources and Services
- **Measured and Managed**: Metrics for reporting, analytic and service management

Generally, the cloud service includes:

- **Public Cloud**: This service is provided by a third party, via the internet.

These services are sold on request usually in the minute or hour following the request.

- **Private Cloud:** An infrastructure entirely dedicated to a single enterprise, which can be managed internally or by a third party and hosted internally or externally. This model offers business versatility while maintaining management, control and security.
- **Hybrid Cloud:** The cross between the public cloud and the private cloud. For example, organizations can perform very large tasks or sensitive applications on the private cloud, and use the public cloud for tasks requiring scalability of resources

Despite all the advantages of cloud storage, there are some serious drawbacks such as:

- **Trust the Operators:** This is the main criticism of the cloud. Telecoms, media companies control access. Fully trusting the cloud also means believing in continuous access to data without any long-term problems. Such comfort is conceivable, but its cost is high. In addition, this price will continue to increase as cloud providers find a way to charge more by, for example, measuring usage of the service. The rate increases proportionally to the bandwidth used.
- **The Question of Privacy:** it is indeed difficult to determine who owns and access the data stored on the internet. One example is the many controversies surrounding changes to the terms of use of cloud-based sites like Face book or Instagram. These social networks create controversy by granting rights to photos stored on their platforms. There is also a difference between the data uploaded

and the data created directly within the cloud. A supplier could easily claim ownership of the latter. Property is a factor to consider. No central authority governs the use of the cloud for storage and services. The Institute of Electrical and Electronics Engineers (IEEE) is trying to become this regulatory controller especially in the field of business. For now, the rules are still unclear and problems are resolved on a case by case basis.

DATA SECURITY AND PRIVACY IN CLOUD

To analyze the data security and privacy in cloud in order to increase the protection level of sensitive information, we propose in Figure 3 a new scheme of cloud computing, which include a third part responsible for data encryption before the storage in the provide servers. Before talking about data encrypting in the cloud, it should be noted that there is no classical algorithm which can search in cipher-Text, for that we propose a quantum approach based on Grover's algorithm (Buyya, Yeo & Venugopal, 2008; Dirac, 1947; Wang et al., 2000; Kollmitzer & Pivk, 2010).

The Proposed Encryption Box

Since antiquity, the cryptography is considered as a very effective way to secure data. In fact, many cryptosystems have been developed such as: Caesar Cipher Encryption, Vigenere Cipher, Data Encryption Standard (DES), Advanced Encryption Standard (AES), cryptosystem RSA and much other (McMahon, 2007; Menezes et al., 1996; Diffie & Hellman, 1976; Rivest Hamir & Adleman, 1978). The cryptography has passed through different generations and classified according to several categories. Generally, we can adopt the classification in three types: artisanal cryptography, technical cryptography and scientific cryptography. In fact, the scientific cryptography represents the current generation of cryptography, where the cryptosystems used are more complex, but the philosophy remains the same. The big difference is that the modern algorithms directly manipulate the bits, unlike the old methods that operated on alphabetic characters. In other words, this is only a change of representation, since we use more than two elements instead of the 26 letters of the alphabet (English). In fact, the implemented cryptography is composed of two main concepts: symmetric and asymmetric cryptography (Rivest

Figure 3. Data Security scheme using encryption box

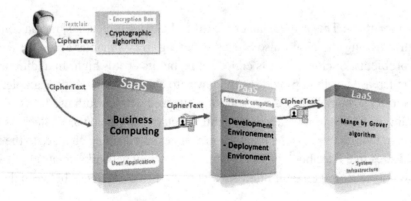

Hamir & Adleman, 1978). One of the most powerful ways to protect the privacy in cloud is giving the customer the possibility to participate in the security steps of cloud. In the some context, we propose an encryption box which including different cryptosystems controlled by the customer. The proposed encryption box give the opportunity to the user to chose an encryption cryptosystem and chose a private encrypted key. In the following we study some famous encryption algorithms which could be part of the proposed protection system.

Advanced Encryption System

AES is a symmetric block cipher algorithm on hardware and software to protect sensitive data. AES was invented by Rijmen and Deamen in 1997 for the National Institute of Standards and Technology (NIST), which was looking for a strong solution to replace the Data Encryption Standard (DES) algorithm, aging and increasingly vulnerable to brute force attacks. However the AES should respect the next specifications:

- General security;
- The cost in terms of calculations (speed);
- The simplicity of the algorithm and its ease of implementation;
- An easy reading of the algorithm, since it is intended to be made public;
- Resistance to known attacks;
- Flexibility & Portability: the algorithm to replace the DES, it is intended to serve as well in smart cards, low-bit 8-bit processors, as in specialized processors to encrypt thousands of telecommunications on the fly;
- Technically, the encryption must be in blocks of 128 bits, keys with 128, 192 or 256 bits.

In each round, four transformations are applied:

1. Byte substitution in the state table (see Figure 4);
2. Row offset in the state table;
3. Moving columns in the status table (except in the last round);
4. Addition of a "round key" that varies with each round.

The following scheme briefly describes the encryption process:

1. **SubBytes:** A non-linear function that operates independently on each block from the substitution table (Figure 4).
2. **ShiftRows:** A function operating offsets. Typically it takes the input in 4 pieces of 4 bytes and operates offsets to the left of 0, 1, 2 and 3 bytes for pieces 1, 2, 3 and 4 respectively.
3. **MixColumns:** A function that transforms each input byte into a linear combination of input bytes.

Decryption consists of applying reverse operations, in reverse order and with sub keys also in reverse order. The following scheme briefly describes the decryption process:

In real implementation, we use a programming language to generate the keys for example we propose in the following a script of AES written by C++:

Figure 4. The state table of AES

	0	1	2	3	4	5	6	7	8	9	A	B	C	D	E	F
0	63	7C	77	7B	F2	6B	6F	C5	30	01	67	2B	FE	D7	AB	76
1	CA	82	C9	7D	FA	59	47	F0	AD	D4	A2	AF	9C	A4	72	C0
2	B7	FD	93	26	36	3F	F7	CC	34	A5	E5	F1	71	D8	31	15
3	04	C7	23	C3	18	96	05	9A	07	12	80	E2	EB	27	B2	75
4	09	83	2C	1A	1B	6E	5A	A0	52	3B	D	B3	29	E3	2F	84
5	53	D1	00	ED	20	FC	B1	5B	6A	CB	BE	39	4A	4C	58	CF
6	D0	EF	AA	FB	43	4D	33	85	45	F9	02	7F	50	3C	9F	A8
7	51	A3	40	8F	92	9D	38	F5	BC	B6	DA	21	10	FF	F3	D2
8	CD	0C	13	EC	5F	97	44	17	C4	A7	7E	3D	64	5D	19	73
9	60	81	4F	DC	22	2A	90	88	46	EE	B8	14	DE	5E	0B	DB
A	E0	32	3A	0A	49	06	24	5	2	D3	AC	62	91	95	E4	79
B	E7	C8	37	6D	8D	D5	4E	A9	6C	56	F4	AE	65	7A	AE	08
C	BA	78	25	2E	1C	A6	B4	C6	E8	DD	74	1F	4B	BD	8B	8A
D	70	3E	B5	66	48	03	F6	0E	61	35	57	B9	86	C1	1D	9E
E	E1	F8	98	11	69	D9	8E	94	9B	IE	87	E9	CE	55	28	DF
F	8C	A1	89	9D	BF	E6	42	68	41	99	2D	9F	B0	54	BB	16

Figure 5. Encryption process of AES

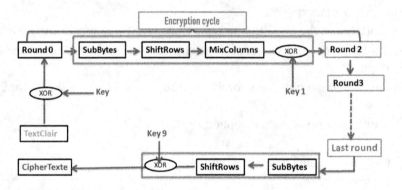

Figure 6. Decryption process of ASE

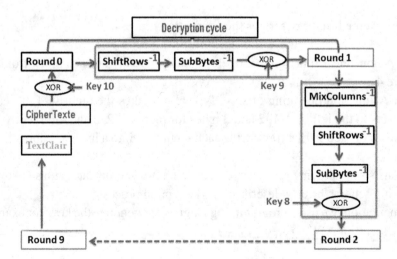

```cpp
#ifndef AES_HPP
#define AES_HPP
#include <cstring>
#include <array>
#include <iostream>
#include <vector>
#include <BlockCipher/BlockCipher.hpp>
#include <Util/Types.hpp>
#include <Util/Util.hpp>
namespace Crypto
{
class AES: public BlockCipher
{
private:
constexpr static uint8 S_BOX [256] =
{
0x63, 0x7C, 0x77, 0x7B, 0xF2, 0x6B, 0x6F, 0xC5, 0x30, 0x01, 0x67, 0x2B, 0xFE,
0xD7, 0xAB, 0x76,0xCA, 0x82, 0xC9, 0x7D, 0xFA, 0x59, 0x47, 0xF0, 0xAD, 0xD4,
0xA2, 0xAF, 0x9C, 0xA4, 0x72, 0xC0,0xB7, 0xFD, 0x93, 0x26, 0x36, 0x3F, 0xF7,
0xCC, 0x34, 0xA5, 0xE5, 0xF1, 0x71, 0xD8, 0x31, 0x15,0x04, 0xC7, 0x23, 0xC3,
0x18, 0x96, 0x05, 0x9A, 0x07, 0x12, 0x80, 0xE2, 0xEB, 0x27, 0xB2, 0x75,0x09,
0x83, 0x2C, 0x1A, 0x1B, 0x6E, 0x5A, 0xA0, 0x52, 0x3B, 0xD6, 0xB3, 0x29, 0xE3,
0x2F, 0x84,0x53, 0xD1, 0x00, 0xED, 0x20, 0xFC, 0xB1, 0x5B, 0x6A, 0xCB, 0xBE,
0x39, 0x4A, 0x4C, 0x58, 0xCF,0xD0, 0xEF, 0xAA, 0xFB, 0x43, 0x4D, 0x33, 0x85,
0x45, 0xF9, 0x02, 0x7F, 0x50, 0x3C, 0x9F, 0xA8, 0x51, 0xA3, 0x40, 0x8F, 0x92,
0x9D, 0x38, 0xF5, 0xBC, 0xB6, 0xDA, 0x21, 0x10, 0xFF, 0xF3, 0xD2,0xCD, 0x0C,
0x13, 0xEC, 0x5F, 0x97, 0x44, 0x17, 0xC4, 0xA7, 0x7E, 0x3D, 0x64, 0x5D, 0x19,
0x73,0x60, 0x81, 0x4F, 0xDC, 0x22, 0x2A, 0x90, 0x88, 0x46, 0xEE, 0xB8, 0x14,
0xDE, 0x5E, 0x0B, 0xDB,0xE0, 0x32, 0x3A, 0x0A, 0x49, 0x06, 0x24, 0x5C, 0xC2,
0xD3, 0xAC, 0x62, 0x91, 0x95, 0xE4, 0x79,0xE7, 0xC8, 0x37, 0x6D, 0x8D, 0xD5,
0x4E, 0xA9, 0x6C, 0x56, 0xF4, 0xEA, 0x65, 0x7A, 0xAE, 0x08,0xBA, 0x78, 0x25,
0x2E, 0x1C, 0xA6, 0xB4, 0xC6, 0xE8, 0xDD, 0x74, 0x1F, 0x4B, 0xBD, 0x8B, 0x8A,
0x70, 0x3E, 0xB5, 0x66, 0x48, 0x03, 0xF6, 0x0E, 0x61, 0x35, 0x57, 0xB9, 0x86,
0xC1, 0x1D, 0x9E, 0xE1, 0xF8, 0x98, 0x11, 0x69, 0xD9, 0x8E, 0x94, 0x9B, 0x1E,
0x87, 0xE9,0xCE, 0x55,0x28, 0xDF,0x8C,0xA1, 0x89, 0x0D, 0xBF, 0xE6,0x42,0x68,
0x41, 0x99, 0x2D, 0x0F,0xB0, 0x54, 0xBB, 0x16
};
constexpr static uint8 INV_S_BOX [256] =
{
0x52, 0x09, 0x6A, 0xD5, 0x30, 0x36, 0xA5, 0x38, 0xBF, 0x40, 0xA3, 0x9E, 0x81,
0xF3,0xD7, 0xFB,0x7C, 0xE3, 0x39, 0x82, 0x9B, 0x2F, 0xFF, 0x87, 0x34, 0x8E,
0x43, 0x44,0xC4, 0xDE, 0xE9, 0xCB,0x54, 0x7B, 0x94, 0x32, 0xA6, 0xC2, 0x23,
0x3D, 0xEE, 0x4C,0x95, 0x0B, 0x42, 0xFA,0xC3, 0x4E,0x08, 0x2E, 0xA1, 0x66,
0x28, 0xD9, 0x24, 0xB2,0x76, 0x5B, 0xA2, 0x49, 0x6D, 0x8B, 0xD1, 0x25,0x72,
```

```
0xF8, 0xF6, 0x64, 0x86, 0x68,0x98, 0x16, 0xD4, 0xA4, 0x5C, 0xCC, 0x5D, 0x65,
0xB6, 0x92,0x6C, 0x70, 0x48, 0x50,0xFD, 0xED, 0xB9, 0xDA, 0x5E, 0x15, 0x46,
0x57, 0xA7, 0x8D, 0x9D, 0x84,0x90, 0xD8,0xAB, 0x00, 0x8C, 0xBC, 0xD3, 0x0A,
0xF7, 0xE4, 0x58, 0x05, 0xB8, 0xB3, 0x45, 0x06,0xD0, 0x2C, 0x1E, 0x8F, 0xCA,
0x3F, 0x0F, 0x02, 0xC1, 0xAF, 0xBD, 0x03, 0x01, 0x13,0x8A, 0x6B,0x3A, 0x91,
0x11, 0x41, 0x4F, 0x67, 0xDC, 0xEA, 0x97, 0xF2, 0xCF, 0xCE,0xF0, 0xB4, 0xE6,
0x73,0x96, 0xAC, 0x74, 0x22, 0xE7, 0xAD, 0x35, 0x85, 0xE2, 0xF9,0x37, 0xE8,
0x1C, 0x75, 0xDF, 0x6E,0x47, 0xF1, 0x1A, 0x71, 0x1D, 0x29, 0xC5, 0x89,0x6F,
0xB7, 0x62, 0x0E, 0xAA, 0x18, 0xBE, 0x1B,0xFC, 0x56, 0x3E, 0x4B, 0xC6, 0xD2,
0x79, 0x20, 0x9A, 0xDB, 0xC0, 0xFE, 0x78, 0xCD, 0x5A, 0xF4,0x1F, 0xDD, 0xA8,
0x33,0x88, 0x07, 0xC7, 0x31, 0xB1, 0x12, 0x10, 0x59, 0x27, 0x80,0xEC, 0x5F,
0x60, 0x51,0x7F, 0xA9, 0x19, 0xB5, 0x4A, 0x0D, 0x2D, 0xE5, 0x7A, 0x9F, 0x93,
0xC9, 0x9C, 0xEF,0xA0, 0xE0, 0x3B, 0x4D, 0xAE, 0x2A, 0xF5, 0xB0, 0xC8, 0xEB,
0xBB, 0x3C, 0x83, 0x53,0x99, 0x61,0x17, 0x2B, 0x04, 0x7E, 0xBA, 0x77, 0xD6,
0x26, 0xE1, 0x69, 0x14, 0x63,0x55, 0x21, 0x0C, 0x7D
};
constexpr static uint8 RCON [11] = {0x8d, 0x01, 0x02, 0x04, 0x08, 0x10, 0x20,
0x40,
0x80, 0x1b, 0x36};
void KeyExpansion(const uint8 key [], uint8 expandedKey[]) const;
static void KeyScheduleCore (uint8 roundNumber, const uint8 keyIn[4], uint8
keyOut[4]);
static void AddRoundKey (uint8 state[4][4], const uint8 roundKey[4][4]);
static void SubBytes (uint8 state[4][4]);
static void ShiftRows (uint8 state[4][4]);
static void MixColumns (uint8 state[4][4]);
static void InvSubBytes (uint8 state[4][4]);
static void InvShiftRows (uint8 state[4][4]);
static void InvMixColumns (uint8 state[4][4]);
public:
AES () = delete;
explicit AES (uint16 keyLen);
explicit AES (const BlockCipher& blockCipher);
explicit AES (const AES& aes);
void encrypt(const uint8 input[], const uint8 key[], uint8 output[]) const
override;
void decrypt(const uint8 input[], const uint8 key[], uint8 output[]) const
override;
};
}
```

RSA Encryption

RSA was invented by three mathematicians: Ron Rivest, Adi Shamir and Len Adleman, in 1977 (We find the acronym RSA in the names of the inventors). The RSA encryption system is a powerful way to encrypt personal data. Today, he surrounds us without even knowing it. It is in our bank cards, our transactions, our courier, our software. To encrypt a message we start by transforming it into one-or-several numbers. The encryption and decryption processes use several concepts:

1. We choose two primes p and q that we keep secret and we put $n = p \times q$. The principle being that even knowing n it is very difficult to find p and q (which are numbers with hundreds of digits).
2. The secret key and the public key are calculated using Euclid's algorithm and Bezout coefficients.
3. The encryption calculations will be modulo n,
4. Decryption step based on Fermat's small theorem.

The asymmetric systems use two keys the first to encrypt and the second to decrypt. The key used to encrypt and private key the key used to decrypt is called public key. In fact, the public key is visible to everyone in a kind of directory that associates each person's public key. However, the private key is visible and known only by its owner. Under no circumstances should anyone other than the owner be in possession of it. For example, we chose tow prime numbers $p = 101$ and $q = 103$. Therefore, we can calculate n and $f(n)$ as the following:

$$n = p \times q = 10403 \tag{1}$$

and

$$f(n) = (p - 1) \times (q - 1) = 10200 \tag{2}$$

- Alice chooses an exponent e where the GCD *(e, f(n)) = 1*;
- She calculates the inverse d of module $e\ f(n)$: $d \times e = 1 \bmod f(n)$. This calculation is done by the extended Euclidean algorithm;
- Alice chooses for example $e = 7$. Therefore, we have *GCD $(n; f(n)) = (7; 10200) = 1$*. Know it's easy to calculate the private key $d = 8743$.

In the following a script of RAS written by C++:

```
#include <iostream>
using namespace std;
int main()
{
int i, x;
char str[100];
cout << "Please enter a string:\t";
cin >> str;
```

```
cout << "\n Please choose following options:\n";
cout << "1 = Encrypt the string.\n";
cout << "2 = Decrypt the string.\n";
cin >> x;
switch(x)
{
case 1:
for(i = 0; (i < 100 && str[i] != '\0'); i++)
str[i] = str[i] + 2;
cout << "\n Encrypt via RSA cryptosystem: " << str << endl;
break;
case 2:
for(i = 0; (i < 100 && str[i] != '\0'); i++)
str[i] = str[i] - 2;
cout << "\n Decrypted via RSA cryptosystem: " << str << endl;
break;
default:
cout << "\n You give a invalid Input !!!\n";
}
return 0;
}
```

Actually exist different cryptographic algorithms and solutions that we trust, such as AES, RSA, ECDSA and SHA-2 and others. Moreover, we understand how to implement and apply these algorithms to provide a level of security

that, when used correctly, no-one can break with today's technology. But in our days is not impossible to search in encrypted databases, for that we propose a theoretical study based quantum algorithms which may be used in the future.

Searching in Encryption Data Via Grover's Algorithm

Grover's algorithm is a quantum algorithm for searching in NoSQL databases was proposed by Lov Grover in 1996 [9{12] .Classically, searching an unsorted database requires a linear search, which is $O(N)$ in time. Contrary, Grover's algorithm takes $\sqrt{N}$ steps to find the marked element with high probability using $O(\log N)$ storage space. Mathematically Grover's algorithm solves the problem search in unstructured list. We consider that the database include items represented by numbers from 0 through N-1 forming a set $\beta = \left\{ a_0, a_1, ..., a_{N-1} \right\}$, and given a Boolean function f: $\beta \rightarrow \{0,1\}$ The key will be represented by a function that is zero on all N numbers, with the exception of one, for which it is 1, on condition that:

$$\exists_{a \in \{0,1,..N-1\}} f_a(a) = 1 \text{ and } \forall_{a \in \{0,1,..N-1\} \in x \neq a} f_a(x) = 0 \tag{3}$$

Unstructured data is frequently given as a database search problem in which we are defined a database and we want to find an entity that respects the critters search. For example, taking into consideration a database of N elements, we might want to find where a specific element in our database. Grover's algorithm begins with a quantum register of n qubits, where n is the quantity of qubits necessary to form the search space of size $2^n=N$, all initialized to $|0\rangle$:

$$|0\rangle^{\oplus n} = |0\rangle \tag{4}$$

The first step is applying the Hadamard transform $H^{\oplus n}$ where $O(\log N)=O(\log 2^2)=O(n)$:

$$|\varphi\rangle = H^{\oplus n}|0\rangle = \frac{1}{\sqrt{2^n}}\sum_{\beta=0}^{2^n-1}|\beta\rangle \tag{5}$$

For realize the optimal probability to find the correct state, we want the overall rotation of the phase to be $\frac{\pi}{4}$ radians. Therefore, the Grover's iteration is $\frac{\pi}{4}\sqrt{2^n}$. The first step in

Grover iteration is a call to a quantum oracle O, which resemble to black-box function, which can observe and modify the system without failing it to a classical state, which we identify if the system is in the correct state. The oracle's effect on $|\beta\rangle$ may be written simply:

$$|\beta\rangle \xrightarrow{\quad O \quad} (-1)^{f(a)}|\beta\rangle \tag{6}$$

where $f(a)=1$ is the correct state, and $f(a)=0$ is the false state

We can resume the Grover's algorithm by the flowing steps:

Inputs:

- Define quantum oracle which realize: $|\beta\rangle \xrightarrow{\quad O \quad} (-1)^{f(a)}|\beta\rangle$
- $n$qubits initialized to the state $|0\rangle$.

Outputs:

- initial state: $|0\rangle^{\oplus n} = |0\rangle$
- Apply the Hadamard transform to all qubits:

$$|\varphi\rangle = H^{\oplus n}|0\rangle = \frac{1}{\sqrt{2^n}}\sum_{\beta=0}^{2^n-1}|\beta\rangle \tag{7}$$

- Apply the Grover iteration $t \approx \frac{\pi}{4}\sqrt{2^n}$:

$$[(2|\varphi\rangle\langle\varphi| - I)O]^t \approx |\beta_0\rangle \tag{8}$$

To prove the effectiveness of the algorithm, we examine a data base consisting of states $N=8=2^3$ (elements) and we make search to find one element from the list. For example we try to find a state $|\beta_0\rangle$ which is represented by the bit string $|101\rangle$. To illustrate this system, $n=3$ qubits are necessary, represented as:

$$|\beta\rangle = a_0|000\rangle + a_1|001\rangle + a_2|010\rangle + a_3|011\rangle + a_4|100\rangle + a_5|101\rangle + a_6|110\rangle + a_7|111\rangle \tag{9}$$

where a_i is the amplitude of the state $|i\rangle$.

Grover's algorithm begins with a system initialized to 0: $|000\rangle$ Applying the Hadamard transformation.

For $n=3$ we have $\dfrac{1}{\sqrt{n}} = \dfrac{1}{8} = \dfrac{1}{2\sqrt{2}}$, therefore:

$$H^3|000\rangle = \frac{1}{2\sqrt{2}}|000\rangle + ... + \frac{1}{2\sqrt{2}}|111\rangle = \frac{1}{2\sqrt{2}}\sum_{\beta=0}^{7}|\beta\rangle = |\varphi\rangle \tag{10}$$

Applying a rotation $\dfrac{\pi}{4}$:

$$\frac{\pi}{4}\sqrt{N} = \frac{\pi}{4}\sqrt{8} \approx 2,22 \tag{11}$$

Therefore, we should iterate almost 2 times. In each iteration, we should call again the quantum oracle O, The oracle query will negate the amplitude of the state $|\beta_0\rangle = |101\rangle$:

$$|\beta\rangle = \frac{1}{2\sqrt{2}}|000\rangle + \frac{1}{2\sqrt{2}}|001\rangle + \frac{1}{2\sqrt{2}}|010\rangle + \frac{1}{2\sqrt{2}}|011\rangle + \frac{1}{2\sqrt{2}}|100\rangle - \frac{1}{2\sqrt{2}}|101\rangle + \frac{1}{2\sqrt{2}}|110\rangle + \frac{1}{2\sqrt{2}}|111\rangle \tag{12}$$

Next step is performing the diffusion transform:

$$[(2|\varphi\rangle\langle\varphi| - I)]|\beta\rangle = [(2|\varphi\rangle\langle\varphi| - I)]\left[|\varphi\rangle - \frac{2}{2\sqrt{2}}|101\rangle\right] = \frac{1}{2}|\varphi\rangle + \frac{1}{2\sqrt{2}}|101\rangle \tag{13}$$

We replace the state $|\varphi\rangle$ by the value motioned above:

$$[(2|\varphi\rangle\langle\varphi| - I)]|\beta\rangle = \frac{1}{2}\left[\frac{1}{2\sqrt{2}}\sum_{\beta=0,\beta\ne3}^{7}|\beta\rangle\right] + \frac{1}{\sqrt{2}}|101\rangle = \frac{1}{4\sqrt{2}}\sum_{\beta=0,\beta\ne3}^{7}|\beta\rangle + \frac{5}{4\sqrt{2}}|101\rangle \tag{14}$$

Consequently, after the first iteration we have:

$$|\beta\rangle = \frac{1}{4\sqrt{2}}|000\rangle + \frac{1}{4\sqrt{2}}|001\rangle + \frac{1}{4\sqrt{2}}|010\rangle + \frac{1}{4\sqrt{2}}|011\rangle + \frac{1}{4\sqrt{2}}|100\rangle + \frac{5}{4\sqrt{2}}|101\rangle + \frac{1}{4\sqrt{2}}|110\rangle + \frac{1}{4\sqrt{2}}|111\rangle \tag{15}$$

We apply the same two transformations in the second iteration:

$$|\beta\rangle = \frac{1}{4\sqrt{2}}|000\rangle + \frac{1}{4\sqrt{2}}|001\rangle + \frac{1}{4\sqrt{2}}|010\rangle + \frac{1}{4\sqrt{2}}|011\rangle + \frac{1}{4\sqrt{2}}|100\rangle - \frac{5}{4\sqrt{2}}|101\rangle + \frac{1}{4\sqrt{2}}|110\rangle$$

$$+ \frac{1}{4\sqrt{2}}|111\rangle = \frac{1}{4\sqrt{2}}\sum_{\beta=0,\beta\ne3}^{7}|\beta\rangle - \frac{5}{4\sqrt{2}}|101\rangle = \frac{1}{2}|\varphi\rangle - \frac{3}{2\sqrt{2}}|101\rangle \tag{16}$$

Finally:

$$[2|\varphi\rangle\langle\varphi| - I]\left[\frac{1}{2}|\varphi\rangle - \frac{3}{2\sqrt{2}}|101\rangle\right] = \frac{-1}{4}|\varphi\rangle + \frac{3}{2\sqrt{2}}|101\rangle = \frac{-1}{8\sqrt{2}}\sum_{\beta=0,\beta\ne3}^{7}|\beta\rangle + \frac{11}{8\sqrt{2}}|101\rangle \tag{17}$$

To determine the success rate for the search, we calculate the probabilities, where we consider $P_{|101\rangle}$ the success probability to find the correct element and P_{Error} the probability of error.

$$P_{|101\rangle} = \left|\frac{11}{8\sqrt{2}}\right|^{2} = 0{,}9453 \approx 94{,}53\% \tag{18}$$

By analogy

$$P_{Error} = 1 - P|101\rangle = 0{,}0546 \approx 5{,}46\% \tag{19}$$

We remark that the value of success probability is much larger than the probability of error for a list of 8 elements. Although Grover's algorithm is probabilistic, which makes the probability of error becomes negligible with higher number of items N, contrary to success probability which increase with big N. Accordingly, Grover's algorithm is very promising solution to search in Big data.

Figure 7. Implementation scheme of Grover's algorithm in cloud

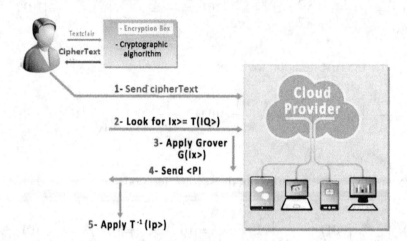

Using Grover's Algorithm in Encryption Database

To protect the privacy of users we propose a new scheme based on encryption of data before saving it in the host server (see Figure 3). We summarize the proposed scheme by the following steps:

- The user sent a plaintext to the box encryption
- The user chose a cryptographic algorithm in the encryption box,
- The user chose a private key to encrypt data,
- The user receive the cipher-Tex from the box encryption,
- Finally, the user saves the cipher-Text in the cloud server.

CONCLUSION

In this work we propose a new scheme to enhance data security and privacy in cloud computing based an encryption box. The idea is encrypting data before the storage in the host servers may ensure to some extent the user's privacy. Accordingly, we add to the standard cloud architecture scheme an encryption box, which includes different cryptographic algorithms to give a large chose to the user to encrypt data with a private key before stored it the in the host server. Therefore, the user can have an access to the data security process by choosing one of the cryptosystems proposed in the encryption box and make a private key, knowing that the provided has no relation with the encryption box, which makes the stored data in cloud is just a cipher-Text whit out knowing any information about the encryption phase. Moreover, we propose to manage the encryption database based on a quantum approach in search by using Grover's algorithm. In fact, the storage of cipher Text in cloud will in general increase the level of data security against different menaces and more particularly will complicate any attempt by the host company to exploit the user's information and because the company has no relationship with the encryption box.

REFERENCES

Amellal, H., Meslouhi, A., El Allati, A., & ElHaddadi, A. (2018). Protect the privacy in cloud via data encryption. *The IEEE International Symposium on Advanced Electrical and Communication Technologies*. doi: 10.1109/ISAECT.2018.8618834

Armbrust, M., Fox, A., Griffith, A., Joseph, A., Katz, A., & Konwinski, A. (2009). *Technical Report No. UCB/EECS-2009-28 Above the clouds: a Berkeley view of cloud computing*. University of California at Berkeley.

Buyya, R., Yeo, C. S., & Venugopal, S. (2008). Market oriented cloud computing: vision, hype, and reality for delivering IT services as computing utilities. In *Proceedings of the tenth conference on high performance computing and communications (HPCC)*. IEEE Press. 10.1109/HPCC.2008.172

Diffie, W., & Hellman, M. (1976). New directions in cryptography. *IEEE Transactions on Information Theory*, *22*(6), 644654. doi:10.1109/TIT.1976.1055638

Dirac, P. A. M. (1947). The Principles of Quantum Mechanics (3rd ed.). Oxford, UK: Clarendon Press.

Gupta, B. B., & Agrawal, P. (2016). *Handbook of research on modern cryptographic solutions for computer and cyber security*. Hershey, PA: IGI Global. doi:10.4018/978-1-5225-0105-3

Kollmitzer, C., & Pivk, M. (2010). *Applied quantum cryptography*. Springer.

McMahon, D. (2007). *Quantum computing explained*. Wiley Interscience.

Menezes, A. J., Van Oorschot, P. C., & Vanstone, S. A. (1996). Handbook of applied cryptography. CRC Press.

Papazoglou, M. P., & van den Heuvel, W.-J. (2007). Service-Oriented Architecture: Approaches, Technologies, and Research Issues. *Very Large Data Bases*, *16*(3), 389–415.

Reese, G. (2009). *Cloud application architectures: building applications and infrastructure in the cloud*. Sebastopol, CA: OReilly Media Inc.

Rivest, R. L., Hamir, A., & Adleman, L. (1978). Method for obtaining digital signatures and public-key cryptosystems. *Communications of the ACM*, *21*(2), 120-126. doi:10.1145/359340.359342

Taylor & Francis. (2018). Computer and Cyber Security: Principles, Algorithm, Applications, and Perspectives. CRC Press.

Wang, X., Sanders, B. C., & Pan, S. H. (2000). Entangled coherent states for systems with *SU* (2) and *SU* (1,1) symmetries. *Journal of Physics. A, Mathematical and General*, *33*(41), 7451–7467. doi:10.1088/0305-4470/33/41/312

Chapter 12
The Unheard Story of Organizational Motivations Towards User Privacy

Awanthika Senarath
University of New South Wales, Australia

Nalin Asanka Gamagedara Arachchilage
The University of New South Wales, Australia

ABSTRACT

There could be numerous reasons that drive organizations to provide privacy protections to end users in the applications they develop and maintain. Organizational motivations towards privacy affects the quality of privacy received by end users. Understanding these motivations and the approaches taken by organizations towards privacy protection would assist the policymakers and regulators to define effective frameworks encouraging organizational privacy practices. This study focuses on understanding the motivations behind organizational decisions and the approaches they take to embed privacy into the software applications. The authors analyzed 40 organizations different in size, scope, scale of operation, nature of data used, and revenue. they identified four groups of organizations characterized by the approach taken to provide privacy protection to their users. The taxonomy contributes to the organizational perspective of privacy. The knowledge presented here would help addressing the challenges in the domain of user privacy in software applications and services.

INTRODUCTION

With the pervasiveness of information technology, connected applications that continuously collect user data have become indispensable in modern life (Shapiro, 2016). Users heavily depend on organizations that develop and publish software applications to protect an enormous amount of personal data disclosed, such as locations, personal schedules, identification and financial information and even blood types and

DOI: 10.4018/978-1-5225-9742-1.ch012

glucose levels (Ginosar & Ariel, 2017). This impose a huge responsibility and risk on the organizations that collect, store and process user data in their businesses to uphold the trust extended by end users on their data practices.

Privacy experts and privacy-concerned users are continuously demanding for better privacy through ubiquitous systems such as on-line sales, banking, social networking applications, mobile phones and telecommunication services (Sarvas & Frohlich, 2011). Research community in the field of privacy and security are implementing methodologies for organizations to follow, in embedding privacy into the systems they develop (Langheinrich, 2001) (Wright & De Hert, 2012). Governments and legal authorities are pushing organizations to comply with rules and regulations defined to protect end user privacy (Fromholz, 2000). However, for the success of all of the aforementioned attempts this research aims to address the following research questions,

- What motivate organizations, to embed privacy into the software systems they develop and on-line services they provide?
- Driven by these motivations, what are the approaches taken by organizations to embed privacy into the systems they develop and maintain?

Organizations that deal with personal information of users differ significantly in size, scope, scale of operation, field of operation, nature of data stored and used, and by the revenue they make. It is estimated that the volume of user data stored in Facebook would be measured in zeta-bytes by 2020 (Anthonysamy, Rashid, & Chitchyan, 2017), which cannot even compare to the amount of data handled by small-scale companies. Anecdotal evidence suggest that such differences in organizational structures and backgrounds, affect their approach towards end user privacy. Nevertheless, Ginosar and Ariel (Ginosar & Ariel, 2017) emphasize that an interpretation of privacy from an organizational aspect has been missing from the privacy research approaches taken so far. Understanding this gap is critical because, as Brunton and Nissen (Brunton & Nissen, 2017) claim, "In the digital economy, the real power is not held by individual consumers and citizens using their smart-phones and laptops to navigate the twists and turns of their lives, but by the large government and corporate entities who monitor them".

Driven by these motivations, we scrutinized 40 organizations that deal with user data. Our study revealed interesting aspects as to how different organizations see and perceive user privacy within their business practices. Further, we define a taxonomy of privacy protection approaches adopted by organizations based on the motivation they have towards end user privacy. Based on our taxonomy we provide implications for businesses, governments and researchers to consider in establishing privacy frameworks, regulations and policies.

Our work contributes to the knowledge of organizational perspective on privacy in the governing and regulating authorities that define and enforce privacy regulations. Findings of this study would also help the research community to identify how to communicate their research and proposals on privacy methodologies, and guidelines effectively to target organizations. Through this work we invite the research community and national and sectoral bodies (Ginosar & Ariel, 2017) to focus on providing tailor made privacy solutions for businesses operating on different types of personal data for different business motives and purposes, in different scales and business models.

The paper is structured as below. The related work extensively elaborate on work done so far in identifying organizational characteristics pertaining to their decisions and approaches towards privacy. Research methodology section contains information on our study approach followed by the results. In the Discussion section, we have extensively discussed our proposed taxonomy based on previous work done, not only in the field of privacy, but also in the fields of business studies and organizational motivations. Finally, we have provided our conclusions and the future directions in the Conclusion section.

RELATED WORK

The inherent desire in humans to be known and to interact is found to be the driving factor for most people to voluntarily disclose their personal information in the event they know they have an audience (Waters & Ackerman, 2011). Furthermore, Mendel and Toch (Mendel & Toch, 2017) has shown that the intention to adopt privacy practices is correlated with the intention to further influence other people. However, the motivations and intentions that drive organizations, the entity with more controlling power in determining the extent to which privacy is provided in ubiquitous applications, has not received adequate attention of the research community.

Ginosar and Ariel (Ginosar & Ariel, 2017) identified web-site owners and management (essentially organizations) as an important stakeholder whose ideas, concerns efforts and views has been missing from privacy research. In their analysis of how websites shape their privacy policies in communicating with end users, they claim that organizations are driven to create privacy policies either as a response to external pressure, according to institutional theory, or as a resource-base view, by identifying user information as an important resource to gain competitive advantage in their business. Ginosar's claim is in-line with our taxonomy. However, we have gone beyond that to investigate and understand the motives, efforts; concerns and attitudes organizations have towards, providing privacy policies and privacy protection to end users.

Anthonysamy et al. (Anthonysamy et al., 2017) have identified four approaches towards privacy implementation in systems from an engineering perspective, namely Compliance, Access Control, Verification and Usability. The classification in this study however, comes into play even before an organization define privacy as an engineering requirement into their systems. We attempt to identify what drives organizations to consider privacy in their business model in the first place. This motivation in organizations to implement privacy is what defines the organization's policies and practices on privacy. Understanding this motivation is important because the organizational policies and the culture within an organization is said to have a significant impact in the behavior of individual developers actions in implementing privacy in systems (Hadar et al., 2018).

Notario et al (Notario et al., 2015) have identified two approaches to implement privacy protection during a software development process, as risk based and goal oriented. They identify risk-based method as identifying threats to the system that might compromise the privacy of its end users and take measures to mitigate those risks in the development stage of the system. The goal-oriented approach is defining principles through regulations that the system must fulfill to provide data protection. Notario et al (Notario et al., 2015) state that *both aim to provide an understanding of what the system has to do in order to comply with the privacy principles by means of a set of privacy requirements*. However, our work attempts to understand the motivations organizations have towards providing privacy protection and differentiating the approaches taken based on these motivations. We believe that our work provides a more complete and a reliable picture on the context.

Stuart et al. (Schwaig, Kane, & Storey, 2006) conducted study to investigate the compliance to Fair Information Practices by the top 500 largest US corporations by total revenue. They have found out that larger organization are more likely to take serious measures to adhere to privacy regulations and declare commitment to user privacy. Their analysis conclude that out of 361 customer oriented websites, only 2/3rd displayed a privacy policy and out of that 2/3 only 14% reflected compliance with Fair Information Practices (FIP) in the privacy policy. However, even though FIP is an accepted principle for providing end user privacy, we believe, to be fully committed towards end user privacy there are additional aspects that should be considered. Some of these aspects are transparency, accountability (Pearson & Charlesworth, 2009) and agency (Xu & Jia, 2015). Hence, the actual percentage of organizations that cover end user privacy with genuine commitment could be far less than the above figures. Their study also revealed that only 9% of the companies in the experiment ensured consistency with the policy they displayed. 1/4th of the companies that displayed policies only used it for public relation purposes. Interestingly they discovered that IT, software and telecommunication industries are more likely to adopt privacy sealing programs. However, their conclusion was that different companies adopted different approaches in choosing the type of privacy protection they would provide for their customers. This implies that self-regulation may not be sufficient in ensuring end user privacy. Our work attempts to investigate the causes behind these different approaches taken by organizations towards privacy, to facilitate deep understanding on motivations organizations have towards privacy.

Van et al. (Van Blarkom, Borking, & Olk, 2003), in chapter 7 of their Handbook for Privacy and Privacy Enhancing Technologies, mention two categories which could motivate organizations to perform privacy auditing. Their categorization is economic motive and social motive. Both economic motive and social motive are extrinsic motivations where an organization is sensitive to the economy, society and its requirements in which the business operates. We conducted our study to understand and interpret extrinsic and intrinsic characteristics of organizations that drive them to embed privacy into their business practices.

In contrast to previous work, our work includes an analysis of organizational policies, reports, and declared commitment towards privacy in understanding their motivation towards privacy. We did not have any prejudice as to how we believe organizations would frame their privacy strategies. Our taxonomy is solely based on empirical evidence, which in fact verified some of the previous conceptual classifications claimed in literature. We have also used work done in the field of psychology, law and business studies to interpret and reflect on the findings.

STUDY DESIGN

Selection of Organizations

As a preliminary step for the study, we first identified categories of organizations that heavily deal with personal information of users as follows.

- Electronic and Software Development Organizations (Social Networking and Mobile applications, and Mobile Phones and Computer Hardware Manufacturers)
- Telecommunication Industry

- Banking and Insurance Organizations
- Organizations involved in On-line Sales and Services
- Government Service Oriented Organizations

This list was compiled following an extensive study on recent (last 5 years) data breaching incidents. Organizations in above categories appeared commonly in breaching incidents probably due to their heavy dependency on personal information of users. For the study, we selected 40 organizations that differ significantly in organizational structure (open source, board controlled, privately owned and proprietary), scale (very large scale, locally based) and revenue (based on Forbes list of companies against their net worth) that belongs to the above categories aiming to increase the validity and credibility of our taxonomy. We considered the availability of data, ease of access of data and public interest when selecting organizations.

STUDY APPROACH

In the first step of the study, we used mixed data-collection method with newspaper clippings, field notes, administrative records, on-line resources, government reports and interviews published in the internet and newspapers. This approach is known as content analysis (Small, 2011), and is considered a very effective technique in social science research. Using primary and secondary sources helped us looking at the company from within and outside. We collected newspaper articles (available on-line) within the last 10 years concerning privacy incidents of the selected organizations. The content and the presentation of the privacy policy, public reports and scholarly articles published by the organizations related to their privacy strategies was our main resource on which the classification is based. Further, we also used interviews previously given by the organizations with related to strategies taken by them towards privacy, newspaper articles, government reports and independent reports by third parties to understand the organizations motivation and approaches towards privacy. Triangulation method (verification of primary result through a separate source) (Small, 2011) in qualitative research was used in the experiment to ensure the development of a rich, robust, comprehensive and a well-developed taxonomy from the study. Based on all these information, we listed down characteristics on each organization that define their approach towards privacy, which was followed by the classification based on the characteristics.

We primarily used the public policy declarations and privacy policy of each organization to be fair in the categorization. We eliminated 5 organizations from our initial list of 45 due to unavailability of adequate data such as the privacy policy. The study consisted of three phases as shown in Figure 01. As

Figure 1. Study process

a further explorative step following the basic investigation, exclusive interviews with technical personnel from the companies were used from 17.5% of the companies used in the study to identify their transparent motivations towards privacy. In-depth interviews are always identified as a reliable source in research, especially in understanding companies and businesses (Brashear, Granot, Brashear, & Ce- sar Motta, 2012; Yin, 2013). Making use of different data types from different sources contributed to a remarkably comprehensive picture, uncovering many aspects and hence supporting a holistic taxonomy (Small, 2011).

We selectively sent email invitations for interviews to 15 higher-level (security, privacy, technical and legal) managers of the organizations through university contacts, of which 7 responded with expression of interest. We conducted interviews over the phone, and the interviewees were guaranteed that neither their personal profile, nor their company profile would be revealed in presentation of data gathered. The interviewees were not compensated in any way for their participation, other than a verbal appreciation for their input as a professional in the field. Each interview lasted for about 20 minutes in average.

Ethical Conduct of the Study

The complete study design was approved by the ethic committee of the University X. In the interviews, the participants were informed of the motivation of the study and the modes of use of the information gathered and presented. Following the expression of interest received by the participants through email/phone, we sent them emails with the basic questionnaire outlined for the interview for their agreement. Three of the candidates who expressed interest for the interviews, dropped off after receiving extensive details about the questions asked in the interview. Actual phone interviews took place following the consent of the participants for their participation in the interviews. Participants were given the choice to opt-out of recording the phone interview, in which case the conductor used speakerphone and noted important information during the interview. 2 out of the 7 interview participants opted out of recording their interview conversations.

We could observe that most participants were reluctant to disclose their organization's internal strategies and information concerning privacy practices. This was mostly observed in banking and financial organizations. Some participants responded saying, "I'm sorry, this is not something I'm comfortable talking about". This showed that some organizations had specific restrictions disclosing their internal regulations and strategies towards end user privacy, and that privacy is generally considered a sensitive topic.

STUDY RESULTS

In this section, we have descriptively depicted the results we obtained through the study. The next section contains direct answers to our research questions based on the findings followed by a description on the findings that lead to define the "taxonomy of privacy protection approaches demonstrated by application development and maintenance organizations". The following sections demonstrates categorized results we obtained throughout the study.

Answers to Our Research Questions

What Motivate Organizations to Provide Privacy Protection to Users Who Use the Software Systems They Develop and On-Line Services They Provide?

We identified the main categories of motivation for organizations to consider privacy in their business to be risk based extrinsic motivation and voluntary based intrinsic motivation. Both these motivations are driven by organizational requirement to sustain in their business. Furthermore, we identified four different approaches taken by organizations, to embed privacy into their business under these two main categories with distinct characteristics

What are the Approach Taken by the Organizations to Embed Privacy Into Systems They Develop and Maintain?

The field they operate in, the nature of their business (financial, on-line applications) and the scale of their business seem to affect the way organizations consider privacy. We could observe that risk induced compliance based organizations mainly focus on giving policy based privacy to users adhering to laws in breaching incidents. However, voluntary based organizations invest more time on privacy research, education, defining self-regulations implementing protocols and also understanding and manipulating general perception on privacy.

Taxonomy of Privacy Protection Approaches

Based on our analysis, we were able to categorize the organizations investigated to have two distinctly identifiable motivations behind their attempts to embed privacy into their business strategies. We named these two branches as *Risk Induced Motivation* and *Voluntary Motivation* towards Privacy.

A significantly large portion of organizations was motivated to consider privacy based on their concern towards organizational risk. This risk element had various aspects such as legal risks, economical risks, and ethical risks. As a preventive strategy against such potential risks, organizations were observed to pay attention towards end user privacy in their business. On the other hand, voluntary motivation was induced mainly through an inherent characteristic within the organization, followed by the knowledge, that providing privacy protection to their users is the *right thing to do*. The voluntary approach for privacy protection in organizations happens mainly for business reasons, to attract a niche area of customers through declaration of privacy commitment, to promote the brand name and protect the market shares. This could also be regarded as self-regulation for benefits. These organizations publicly declare their commitment towards end user privacy, and use it as a marketing tool. They recruit and maintain special staff members to maintain and evaluate privacy decisions taken within the organization. As Asghari et al. claim, (Asghari, Guerses, Mahieu, & van Eeten, 2016) this motivation is driven by the market demand for privacy rather than risk. Further, organizations motivated towards privacy in this way were observed to be more experimental and direct about their privacy strategies. Rather than limiting themselves to achieve a particular goal through providing privacy protection to their customers, they were more inclined to experiment with general notion on user privacy. They had an inherent need to provide privacy to their customers, in a way they believed would benefit their business.

Through further investigations as to how these motivations encourage the approach an organization takes towards privacy, we identified that an organization driven by risk could take two main approaches, with the resulting privacy to the end user having minute differences. One category (RISK-REG) was observed to be restricting their privacy protection approach strictly according to government policies and regulations. Most of these organizations openly declared in their privacy policies, and web sites that they are in compliant with relevant government regulations in providing privacy protection to their users. The other category (RISK-SELF) was observed to be complying with self-made regulations. These organizational regulations were mostly going beyond government regulations. However, at times there were organizations that had compiled self-regulations based on a selective set of government regulations and industry standards set up by their competitors. Banking and insurance industry provides a good example as to how competition among peers set industry standards in defining an organization's approach towards privacy. Almost all banks that operate studied demonstrated similar concerns towards privacy with subtle differences in their approach.

Consequently, Voluntary motivation, driven by economical and ethical reasons, induce organizations to adopt privacy either through user interaction (VOL-USER) that address what users demand from them, or through education (VOL-EDU) and knowledge of privacy and their perception that it is the *right thing to do*. The result of both these approaches was a self-made regulation or a company policy to achieve their intentional goal of providing privacy protection towards end users.

Table 1 gives the overview of our classification, as to how the organizations included in the study demonstrated their approach towards end user privacy. Table 2 gives a comprehensive list of common characteristics for organizations that belong to the categories in our taxonomy. The complete taxonomy based on these categorizations is available in Figure 02.

Most organizations displayed a risk induced motivation towards incorporating privacy into their business (62.5%). Within the risk-induced category, compliance towards government regulation (RISK-REG) branch identifies the benchmark of privacy protection an organization should provide to an end user. A significant portion of organizations analyzed falls into this category (37.5%) which implies that most organizations are motivated to provide users with privacy to enable them to operate their business in a country or a region.

37.5% of the organizations studied fall into the voluntary based privacy implementation category. However, 87% of those were social networking software providers. Voluntary based user interactive approach (VOL-USER) towards privacy was observed to be practiced only by social networking software providers in the study group, possibly due to their wide interaction with billions of users and large-scale operations with funds to conduct user interactive surveys. 75% of these companies had over US $7 Billion quarterly revenues declared. Following sub sections, describe the extensive analysis we performed based on the organizational characteristics.

Table 1. Results overview

Approach	No. of Organizations	%
Risk Induced Govt. Regulation Compliance (RISK-REG)	15	37.5%
Risk Induced Self-Regulation Compliance (RISK-SELF)	10	25%
Voluntary Education Motivation (VOL-EDU)	7	17.5%
Voluntary User Focus Motivation (VOL-USER)	8	20%

Figure 2. Privacy protection approaches: Taxonomy

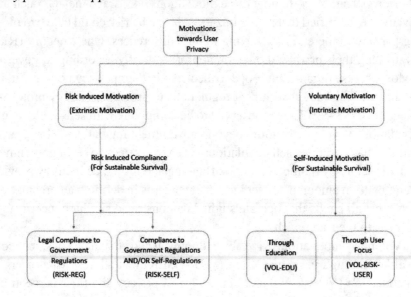

Table 2. Characteristics of taxonomy categories

RISK-REG	RISK-SELF	VOL-EDU	VOL-USER
Investigate about government regulations due to potential risks on the survival of their business.	Declare their privacy policy with focus on potential privacy risks imposed on the organization	Organizations that implement privacy because they think it is the right thing to do.	These organizations provide end users with privacy they believe that fits best with user requirements.
Generally implement privacy according to govt. regulations through consultation and security and legal measures.	In addition to the laws in the region and country they operate, adhere to some best practices recommended by third parties due to the risk factor	Their privacy policies are mostly incomplete and complex and are not reflected in practice.	Their privacy policies are well versed and readable, comprehensive to a normal user.
Mention that they are considering privacy as a part of government requirements.	Obtain privacy certifications and participated in sealing programs to display commitment.	Generally, large organizations that operate globally, and have their own research and development in privacy.	They may always change and modify their privacy policies and release products to change customer perception on privacy.
Always disclose privacy breaching incidents according to regulations.	Mindful of how their competitors are adopting privacy and attempt to provide the same or better to their customers	The solutions they come up with may or may not adhere completely to the rules declared by governments and authorities.	Conduct their own studies to figure out end user requirements, or define user requirements through their experience, which may or may not reflect actual user requirements.
Companies are more dependent on the region and country they operate in.	Define their own organizational policies and regulations towards privacy, which may be less than, equal to, greater than government laws.		Generally software development companies that build their business around with sensitive user information.
Most privacy incidents happen due to unintentional mistakes and malpractices	Whilst complying to government regulations they conduct employee training and adhering to self-made regulations.		May get into arguments with governments on dis- closure requests on customer information.

Field of Business Against Privacy Motivation

Our study shows a significant relationship between the field of business of an organization, and the way they are motivated to consider privacy. All of the social networking related software-manufacturing organizations included in the study were observed to have a voluntary based motivation towards privacy.

This could be because they are capable of implementing privacy tools and features directly in to their products. They are capable of going beyond policy-based privacy and hence it is meaningful for them to conduct their own research and experiments on privacy. Financial institutions, on the other hand were observed to display a risk induced regulation adherence approach due to their dependence on the government policies. Further, all telecommunication companies and service-providing companies too seemed to consider privacy as a risk induced compliance. Figure 03 shows the graphical representation of our results.

Business Model Against Privacy Motivation

In Figure 4, we can observe that almost all the proprietary organizations in our study group that provided their online applications on a monetary payment had a tendency to have compliance-based motivation towards privacy (75%). Only 16% of organizations motivated by risk were providing free services. Majority of the organizations providing their services free had a voluntary motivation towards privacy (67%).

To interpret the results of our study against the organizational net worth in the year 2016, we used the Forbes list of companies and their net worth as the source for financial information about the organizations (*ForbesThe World's Biggest Public Companies*, n.d.).

There was no strong correlation with the organizational net worth against them being motivated to user privacy voluntarily (r=0.05). Irrespective of the organizational worth, all financial corporations and service providing industries investigated were observed to approach privacy due to risk. This could be due to their dependence on the governments of different countries and the regional investments and infrastructures they had. All software manufacturing organizations, developing applications for end users for social networking and gaming were observed to be voluntarily induced towards user privacy through user focus irrespective of their organizational worth (r=0.61). The plot [Figure 6] represents the trend of adopting privacy in organizations depending on their net worth.

Figure 3. Privacy protection approaches: Organization type vs motivation

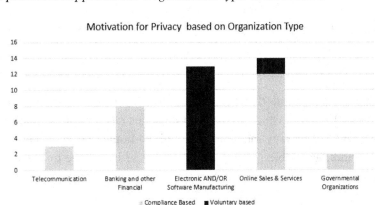

Figure 4. Privacy protection approaches: Business model vs motivationOrganizational Net Worth Against Privacy Motivation

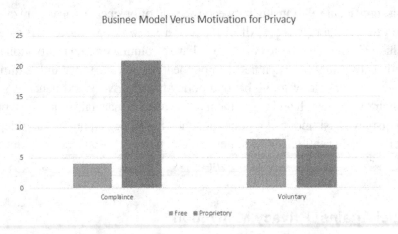

Figure 5. Privacy protection approaches: Organizations net worth vs motivation

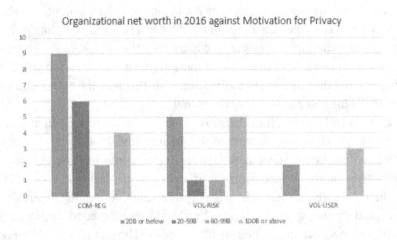

However, if we considered all organizations, the trend of organizations with lower net worth adopting compliance based motivation was observed to be significant (r=0.8). Lower net worth implied that they had limited resources to invest on privacy. They were more concerned on the risks imposed on their organizations by privacy incidents and adopted the regulations to address those risks.

Privacy Incident Study

We could observe that all organizations that were considered, except for 3 had had at least one breaching incident during the past 10 years. In studying privacy breaches faced by the organizations we studied, we could observe two types of privacy incidents, one unintentional data breaches due to hacking and employee negligence, other, avoidable privacy disasters due to ignorance of privacy requirements in innovative product releases.

Figure 6. Trend: Organizations net worth vs motivation

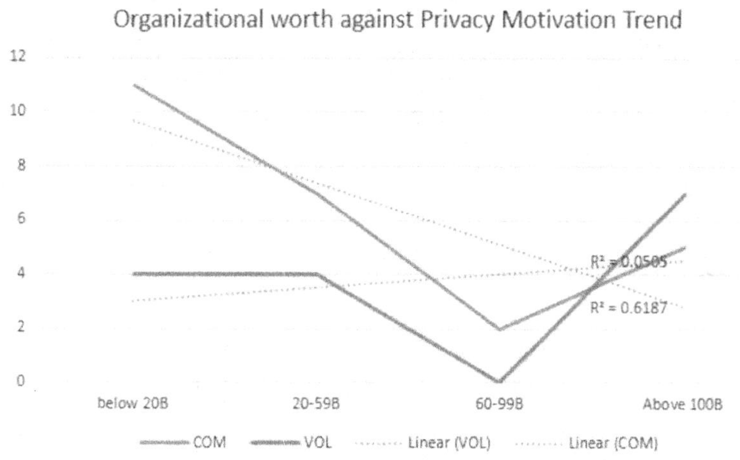

Table 3. Interview participants

Experience 2 up-to 5 years	2
Experience 5 up-to10 years	1
Experience 10 years or more	4

Interestingly, most compliance-based organizations had breaches due to negligence, caused by manual errors (mis-sending emails and mails with customer information) or hackers leaking customer personal data (*The Sydney Morning Herald,* 2016.). Compliance based organizations were observed to have taken instant measures in disclosing the breach to affected customers and taking preventive actions with very few exceptions (*The Sydney Morning Herald,* 2015.). However, their interest towards taking proactive actions to avoid such incidents were minimal. Almost all telco, banking and insurance organizations are observed to adhere to strict regulations imposed by the governments and follow their recommendations and not beyond that.

Software and Hardware manufacturing organizations on the other hand appeared to be having privacy incidents due to their business policies, experiments and motives of making revenue out of data. Many tech companies, even with declared user privacy interests were observed to be failing to meet users' privacy expectations (*Think Tank Ranking Digital Rights*, n.d.), (Kumar, 2016). For example, Google Street View project had to remove many of its images taken during their car mapping, as they lost the court case against the USA government (*Electronic Privacy Information Center,* 2016). Their approach towards privacy by removing images was reactive and remedial (*George Jepsen Attorney General, State of Cennecticut*, n.d.). Their product was privacy invasive and the company lacked privacy concerned product designing approach. Similarly, Google Buzz and Facebook beacon are two examples for projects that had to be called off due to concerns raised by privacy experts (Rubinstein & Good, 2012).

Table 4. Qualitative analysis of interviews

Managers	Government Organizations		Private Organizations	
	Yes	No	Yes	No
Work done by the gvt. In the field of privacy is sufficient.	2	1	2	2
Technology advancements (e.g. Big data) should be controlled through regulations	3	0	0	4

Interview Outcomes

We sent interview requests to 15 security managers in selected organizations, of which 7 responded. We interviewed 7 managerial level personnel (approx. 25%) in the industry who can influence organizations decisions especially with respect to privacy, risk management and security. The interviewees had industry experience from a range of 2.5 years (startup owners) to 20 years.

We Interviewed two senior managers from small scale startup companies that heavily depend with personal information of users, one manager from a privacy and security consultation firm, two security and privacy managers from a large scale application development organization that use personal information, and two managers from government organizations.

The less-experienced managers were not much aware of the legal frameworks and compliance requirements about privacy. They were more concerned about user requirements. They mentioned that they could observe a significant improvement in their user base after integrating privacy concerns into their products, which motivated them to pay attention to privacy continuously. They also mentioned notifications and interactive messages to be more effective in communicating their privacy commitment to users, whereas the more experienced managers only favored privacy policies.

Overall, this suggests a gap in the knowledge of organizational management on data protection regulations. This suggests a need for communicating the legal requirements in enabling user privacy for organizations in order to ensure that they are aware of the compliance requirements.

Managers stated that the government should focus on educating the industries on the regulations and compliance requirements in addition to establishing the laws. A senior manager that provides consultation on privacy and security implementations to other companies further emphasized this. He mentioned that most of the clients they receive contact them because they believe it is the *right thing to do*. He also mentioned that following a huge security or privacy incident similar to the *panama papers* (Tuttle & Hilary, 2016) results in a hike in the number of clients they receive. This confirms our classification

Table 5. Qualitative analysis of interviews

	2-5 years	5-10 years	10 years or more
Methods used to communicate Privacy commitment to end users	Notifications, messages, pop-ups and privacy policies	Privacy policies	Privacy policies
Work done by government in the field of privacy is sufficient	No (100%)	No (100%)	Yes (50%) and No (50%)

that organizations are either voluntarily motivated to privacy due to education, or due to risk to adhere to compliance requirements.

Government policy makers were confident that they are in the right direction even though they accepted that further regulations were required. When it comes to big data analytics, the government managers mentioned that regulations and monitoring compliance adherence is required to control organizations. However, more experienced managers in the industry expressed their concerns on better policies to allow technological advancements where both users and organizations could gain through sharing of data in a controlled environment. Further, the managers expressed their concerns on some aspects of privacy regulations. One manager suggested the government regulate the laws concerning the resale of client data for analytical purposes, as it would enable businesses to better perform as well as act as a deterrent to black market sales of user data. These concerns organizations have and their suggestions could help better defining privacy with shared responsibility and are important in deciding the future approach governments and researchers should take towards a privacy-preserving world.

Interestingly none of the managers interviewed were confident in saying they were 100% positive that their expressed privacy commitment is reflected in their business practices. They mentioned that "we are getting there, I believe so" and even one mentioned, "We are not sure, we are making progress, but we are not there yet". This is due to the fact the there are no proactive strategies established to monitor compliance. Until a privacy incident happens, the compliance of employees to organizational strategies or data protection requirements is not measurable.

Limitations

Our study analyzed 40 organizations, which we believe might not be sufficient to provide a comprehensive statistical analysis of the results. We believe that analyzing a large number of organizations would further broaden the results revealing more trends. It would also enable us to come up with a statistical model for interpreting organizations behavior in providing privacy protection to their customers based on its characteristics. Furthermore, all the organizations we studies are international level organizations. Even small-scale organizations we studied had a net worth close to 1B USD. Studying more organizations with low revenues and smaller in size with diverse business models, could perhaps reveal more branches in our initial taxonomy.

DISCUSSION

Matrix of Privacy Protection Approaches

According to this matrix [Figure 7], the more independent an organization is on regional infrastructure, state policies and regulations (banking, telecommunication) more inclined it is towards adhering to government regulations on privacy. On the other hand, organizations such as social networking companies, software and hardware manufacturers operating on a global scale, heavily dependent on user data were more inclined towards adopting a user-focus privacy strategy. The services these companies provide are more privacy invasive and impose a huge risk on the users. Therefore, they have a tendency to take more proactive measures and transparently convince their users about the privacy practices they have. This may be because users are now gaining more knowledge on the business model of free networking service

Figure 7. Privacy protection approaches: Matrix against organizational business model

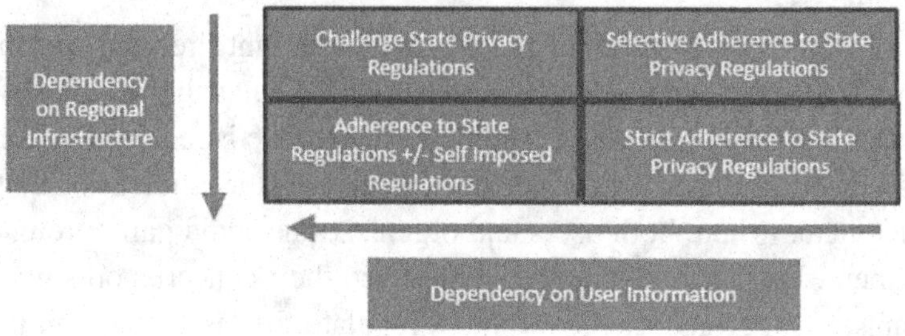

providers and realizing that *if you are not paying for it, you are not the customer, you are the product* (Goodson, 2012). Hence, merely complying with government regulations on data breaching prevention and disclosure is not adequate for them to convince their customers about the privacy protection they get. These organizations sometimes go to an extent to challenge government pressure to corporate with requirements in data acquisition and disclosure (Rubinstein & Good, 2012) as their large operational scale and higher revenues make the penalties and fines appear minute.

Principles such as privacy by design (Cavoukian, 2012), propose that privacy should be an initial consideration in application development, and that proactive measures are necessary. However, our results suggest that until organizations can interpret such principles in the context of organizational risk or as a common user requirement, they would not be motivated to consider privacy within their business strategies. Therefore, interpretation of privacy either as a risk, or as a user requirement may encourage organizations.

Interpreting Privacy as Risk

European Union enforces privacy regulations on companies that handle personal data (Wagner & Benecke, 2016). They define many guidelines for organizations that deal with user data to follow, to ensure that they take substantial measures to prevent potential data breaches and act on the best interest of the end users in case of data breaches. However, Gurses and Alomo. (Gürses & del Alamo, 2016) points out that privacy is far more complex and vast than mere data breaching, which is the focus of many regulative entities. Design flaws, lack of concern on privacy during business decision making could bring consequences, which have a higher impact on the end user privacy concerns than in data breaching incidents. Therefore, it is critical that such regulating bodies pay attention on how such unforeseen risks are conveyed to organizations.

Some legal frameworks encourage risk-based compliance, which we believe to be the correct approach that should be taken by lawmakers. For example, the latest General Data Protection Regulation of the European Union, (Voss, 2017) enforces a risk based compliance model to organizations, to implement and maintain privacy protection in their business. The GDPR (General Data Protection Regulation), also has clauses which exempts organizations from the requirement of notifying affected users on data breach in the event where the company could prove that they have taken sufficient steps to prevent the impact of data breaching risks to a satisfactory level (Wagner & Benecke, 2016), thereby reducing risk through compliance. Our results revealed that a significant portion of organizations is motivated to embed privacy into their systems through risk. Some organizations even go beyond government regulations to define organizational policies and governance frameworks to better control their risks. Therefore, national and sectoral bodies that define, and enforce privacy related regulations should further improve their approach in the direction of highlighting privacy risks to induce motivation in organizations to understand the importance of compliance.

Organizational Approach Towards Risk Based Privacy

Risk based approach is driven by stakeholder interests and competitor behaviors (Dusuki & Yusof, 2016). Some organizations that had risk-induced privacy were observed to conduct risk identification processes to identify potential privacy impacts on stakeholders (Wright & De Hert, 2012). Based on the identified risks they take measures to mitigate identified privacy risks. We believe that this approach involves a deep understanding of the system, its impacts on the end users and end user requirements in privacy. However, the risks the organization perceive could mismatch the actual risks perceived by the end users of a system. It has been shown that many developers feel that communicating with end users of a system is not necessary as they know what users want from a system (Caputo et al., 2016), which could hinder an organization's capability to identify real user risks. This may lead to mis-prioritization of risks and hence not delivering adequate protection to the privacy of end users.

Further to that, the results of our study also shows that providing partial protection to user privacy through regulations is not at all sufficient. If it is legally mandatory to provide a privacy policy, organizations would provide a privacy policy and not be consistent with it in practice. If it is legally mandatory to conduct privacy sealing to comply with the privacy policy they will carefully word the privacy policy and conduct sealing that they are consistent without genuine commitment. A pure legal solution will not work in ensuring end user privacy in cyber context, due to the complex nature of privacy. Therefore, the regulations imposed should be practical and realistic for the industry to adopt and practice in the industrial environment. For example, Privacy Impact Assessment (PIA), a procedure that could be adopted to evaluate the impact of a system to the privacy of the stakeholders is a regulatory requirement in many regions in the world. The European Commission has embedded PIAs into the new regulation proposal for legal data protection (Oetzel & Spiekermann, 2014) to ensure that organization conduct PIAs before system design. After proven privacy breaching incidents, the Federal Trade Commission has required both Google and Facebook to regularly conduct PIAs for the next 20 years (Oetzel & Spiekermann, 2014). Ideally, this should encourage other private organizations that deal with personal data to adopt PIAs voluntarily, which rarely happens due to the complexity of PIA procedure. Oetzel et al. (Oetzel & Spiekermann, 2014) has proposed a systematic approach for PIA to enable its wide adoption. We need similar procedures with engineering realizations to encourage self-regulation of organizations as much as possible and our work provides the basis and platform for such pragmatic realizations.

Anthonysamy et al. (Anthonysamy et al., 2017), in their study on approaches to privacy in systems, list down strengths and weaknesses of the compliance base solutions for privacy, which we identified as risk induced motivation. Their analysis is more limited towards the approach as an implementation directive rather than a motivation for initiation. However, the strengths and weaknesses identified by them are also valid for our taxonomy. They claim that *consideration of privacy only being an early stage task*, and *the element of regulation and accountability* to be positives of the compliance based approach. *Compliance being limited to government legal documents, lack of concern for third party imposed risk on privacy*, and *non-adherence to the continuous changes in privacy requirements and functionalities* are identified as weaknesses. Our study further revealed *the disjoint nature of privacy risk analysis and policy declaration from the technological and development practices* to be a weakness visible in many organizations motivated for privacy through compliance. Furthermore, the extrinsic nature of the motivation driving the organization to limit their contribution strictly to the legal documents depicted by governments is another weakness in compliance-based approach towards privacy.

An Analysis From a Psychological Perspective

According to psychological studies, the basic categories of motivation to be intrinsic motivation and extrinsic motivation (Ryan & Deci, 2000). Intrinsic motivation is defined as *doing of an activity for its inherent satisfactions rather than for some separable consequence*. Extrinsic motivation is the complete opposite of intrinsic motivation and is defined as *doing an activity in order to attain some separable outcome, or to avoid a penalty*. We could observe that the risk-induced motivation identified in our taxonomy remonstrated characteristics similar to that of extrinsic motivation, while voluntary motivation was closely related to intrinsic motivation (Carroll, 1979). Ryan et al. state that intrinsic motivation is better in motivating a person towards a task compared to extrinsic motivation because the former is out of choice towards personal endorsement whereas the latter is a compliance with an external control, which is non-autonomous (Ryan & Deci, 2000). Therefore, the latter would always be done with the minimum possible effort to reach a pre-defined level of expectation (Olafsen, Halvari, Forest, & Deci, 2015). On this basis, the limited scope on privacy observed in risk induced organizations, focusing on data breaching and compensations (Fromholz, 2000), neglecting the risks imposed by design flaws, lack of concern on privacy in business decisions could be interpreted as a result of the extrinsic nature of the motivation. However, this should be further investigated through studies focusing on more in-depth evaluation of risk based motivation towards privacy.

Privacy, Because Users Want It?

Interactive approach with users towards privacy, which was first coined by Gurses and Alomo (Gürses & del Alamo, 2016), is defined as *the methodology of capturing privacy matters that arise between peers or in a workplace due to the introduction of information systems, and improve user's agency with respect to privacy through socio-technical designs*. We have identified this approach as VOL-USER category in our taxonomy. However, when it comes to organizational motives, users wanting privacy is not the main reason for user interactive approach towards privacy. It is that users concerned about privacy, being reluctant to disclose their information. This is further strengthened through observations where organizations, with user interactive privacy approach conducting research and experiments to not only understand user needs, but to manipulate public perception on privacy. For example, Zuckerberg introduced new privacy settings in Facebook in 2010, stating that social norms towards privacy would evolve with time. In addition to this, in 2010 Google CEO stated that he hoped young people in future generations would be able to change their name, and disown their past stored on web if they wanted privacy. Such experiments demonstrate the overall perspective social networking organizations in general have about user privacy expectations.

Voluntary Motivation Towards Privacy

In voluntary motivation, it is very difficult to estimate whether the declaration of commitment towards end user privacy is genuine, and whether the commitment is reflected in their system development practices. In the event where voluntary motivation encourage self-regulation, the organization may or may not adhere to the complete regulations depending on their business motives. Our investigation on the breaching incidents showed, that in organizations, which declared voluntary commitment towards privacy, irrespective of the declarations, their business models itself are serious threats to end user privacy. In such cases, organizational intentions towards privacy are manipulated by their business interests.

The main weaknesses in the voluntary based approach is the lack of criteria to evaluate the commitment declared. The organizations may declare commitment and not adhere to what they claim. Furthermore, they could use their declaration of commitment as an incentive to encourage users disclose more information when dealing with their systems. Nevertheless, the intrinsic nature of this motivation implies that these organizations are having an interest of comprehending user requirements in privacy, to be more user centered than relying on government regulations in providing privacy. This motivation, if properly monitored, could be used to shape the future of privacy research and development. We believe that governments and the research community, rather than attempting to bring such organizations into legal frameworks in cases of privacy incidents, should focus on making use of the motivation they have together with their resources to redefine privacy to address both their business motives and user interests. Our interviews revealed that these organizations believed the existing laws to be outdated or non-considerate concerning their business models and requirements. This is critical mainly because fines imposed and legal frameworks enforced on these organizations appear minute compared to the scale of their operations. Additionally, continuous monitoring of organizational behavior towards privacy is required with governments working together with large-scale organizations that have the capacity to conduct research and development in the area of end user privacy. With the monetary value of personal information use in marketing and targeted advertising rising, the demand for mechanisms to control large organizations compromising user privacy against business motives is critical (Mai, 2016). Privacy by Design (PbD) in their fourth principle state *Full functionality – positive-sum, not zero-sum*, which encourage organizations to consider privacy and business goals as mutual goals without compromising each other (Cavoukian, Taylor, & Abrams, 2010). Such principles should be adopted in the industry and new technologies and business motives should complement privacy rather than compromising. PbD 2.0 proposed by Cavoukian (Cavoukian, 2012), which is a technology driven methodology for storing user data in a privacy preserving authorization model in the cloud, could be identified as a step in this direction.

Voluntary Motivation in the Ground Level

Interestingly, a common characteristic that was evident in all motivational approaches we identified was that they are all top-down induced motivations. This essentially means that even though the organization motive could be either voluntary or compliance towards privacy, for the ground level staff it is always compliance or obligation. It is identified that for better privacy implementation the top management should have the need and motivation to do so (Cavoukian et al., 2010). For example, Alge et al. (Alge, Ballinger, Tangirala, & Oakley, 2006) state that organizations are continuously monitoring employees who may (un/willingly) manipulate the privacy practices exercised by a company. The recent incident at Uber, where employees were accused of spying on celebrity travel information in their systems (The-

Guardian, Alex Hern Uber employees 'spied on ex-partners, politicians and Beyonce, n.d.) is a good example of the need for such strict measures. However, we believe that if we can induce motivation for the ground level staff, service providing personnel, development teams and quality assurance and legal teams to have voluntary motivation, the prevailing burdensome attitude towards privacy within an organization's staff could be changed (Senarath, 2017). For example, technical organizations are moving towards flat hierarchical team based management strategies to encourage technological breakthroughs from ground level staff, by giving them opportunity and authority (Brem & Wolfram, 2017). We believe that applying the same for privacy practices could nudge ground level staff for better privacy practices. In contrast to the voluntary motivation discussed in our taxonomy above, here the voluntary motivation is expected to be generated from all levels of an organization.

Voluntary motivation, which is a form of intrinsic motivation is expected to be effective against extrinsic motivation in encouraging people to perform tasks (Deci, 1972). Voluntary attitude towards privacy should be cultivated in the designers and developers of systems in organizations. Recent developments in Privacy Engineering (Senarath, 2017; Wurster & van Oorschot, 2009) suggest that rather than educating and burdening the developers and designers with complex theories and concepts in privacy, they should be provided with support to easily comprehend and embed privacy in their tasks. However, an engineering framework for embedding privacy into systems would only be successful when engineers with genuine concerns and interests practice it.

STUDY IMPLICATIONS

Organizations, most of the time consider user privacy as an additional cost that they have to incur in order to comply with government regulations. A Microsoft representative once stated that privacy is a responsibility an organization takes up when they make a decision to use personal information in their business (*Julia Allen, Kim Howell, 2009*). An organization would always implement their company policies around these obligations. Organizations are legally bound by law in the regions they operate, to adopt recommended privacy practices. Failing to do so results in lawsuits and heavy fines. For example, due to their negligence of privacy regulations, Google and Facebook have gone through many privacy lawsuits (Young & Quan-Haase, 2009). According to news, during the period of 2012-2014 alone, Facebook has paid more than US $30 million to settle lawsuits relating to privacy (*ABC news, 2014.*). Therefore organizations have a compliance based motivation, at the very least to embed privacy into systems (Fromholz, 2000). However, such legal penalties and guidelines proposed by researchers and regulatory bodies have not been 100% effective in serving their purpose due to ineffective communication and lack of understanding of the organizations and their business models (Davies, 2010). If the research community and authorities that regulate privacy could understand their target sector of organizations in proposing privacy guidelines, they could mold their proposals in such a way that the organizations would adopt the proposals. The findings of this research contribute to this gap by exposing the required underpinning knowledge to understand organizations, for which the privacy regulations and guidelines are aimed at, and the factors that motivate those organizations to adopt privacy. Following are the guidelines we propose, based on our research.

- Governments should make it a priority to regulate privacy policies and laws: Since more than half of the organizations studied were observed to be motivated to consider privacy in their business model due to compliance.
- Research community should engage with organizations to develop engineering methodologies, understanding the motivations that drive organizations towards privacy: Even though the rules and regulations were observed to be setting the standards of privacy,
- Organizations should be guided to have risk/voluntary motivation at all levels of employment to provide privacy protection to their customers.
- Authorities should respect the business model organizations have, and enforce regulations to ensure win-win situation for both organizations and users, by providing privacy protection to users: Not understanding the business models organizations have, and attempting to frame them towards a "one solution fits all" (Gürses & del Alamo, 2016) model would only result in organizations not adhering to privacy regulations.
- Research community, authorities, and regulatory bodies should interpret privacy as a user requirement, or as an organizational risk to encourage organizational attention towards privacy.

CONCLUSION AND FUTURE WORK

In this work, we have analyzed existing motivational factors for organizations, from a business perspective to embed privacy into the systems they develop and use. We have provided a comprehensive taxonomy based on our study of 40 international scale organizations based on their declarations, public reports, government reports and third party interviews. We also made use of exclusive interviews to further explore and reflect on our findings. Our results revealed voluntary motivation and risk based motivation as the primary motivations that drive organizations towards privacy. Further, we identified four distinct categories of approaches taken by organizations to provide privacy protection to the users of their applications. The different approaches demonstrated by organizations to provide privacy protection to their end users affected significantly to the quality and nature of privacy available in the applications they developed and maintained. Based on these findings, we invite the research community and the governments to consider providing customized privacy regulations and frameworks for organizations, because privacy should be achieved as a mutual goal, without compromising the potential technological advancements.

REFERENCES

ABC News. (n.d.). *Pat McGrath facebook alleged to have sold information in users' private messages.* Retrieved from http://www.abc.net.au/news/2014-01-03/facebook-sued-for-selling-information-in-users-private-messages/51839041

Alge, B. J., Ballinger, G. A., Tangirala, S., & Oakley, J. L. (2006). Information privacy in organizations: Empowering creative and extrarole performance. *The Journal of Applied Psychology, 91*(1), 221–232. doi:10.1037/0021-9010.91.1.221 PMID:16435952

Allen, J., & Howell, K. (n.d.). *Ralph Hood integrating privacy practices into the software development life cycle.* Retrieved from http://resources.sei.cmu.edu/asset_files/Podcast/2009_016_100_47206.pdf

Anthonysamy, P., Rashid, A., & Chitchyan, R. (2017). *Privacy requirements: present and future*. Academic Press.

Asghari, H., Guerses, S. F., Mahieu, R., & van Eeten, M. (2016). *Can markets deliver privacy enhanced services on scale?* Academic Press.

Brashear, T., Granot, E., Brashear, T. G., & Cesar Motta, P. (2012). A structural guide to in-depth interviewing in business and industrial marketing research. *Journal of Business and Industrial Marketing*, *27*(7), 547–553. doi:10.1108/08858621211257310

Brem, A., & Wolfram, P. (2017). Organisation of new product development in asia and europe: Re- sults from western multinationals r&d sites in germany, india, and china. *Review of Managerial Science*, *11*(1), 159–190. doi:10.100711846-015-0183-7

Brunton, F., & Nissen, H. (2017, February). Privacy's trust gap: A review. *The Yale Law Journal*, *126*(4), 908–1241.

Caputo, D. D., Pfleeger, S. L., Sasse, M. A., Ammann, P., Offutt, J., & Deng, L. (2016). Barriers to usable security? three organizational case studies. *IEEE Security and Privacy*, *14*(5), 22–32. doi:10.1109/MSP.2016.95

Carroll, A. B. (1979). A three-dimensional conceptual model of corporate performance. *Academy of Management Review*, *4*(4), 497–505. doi:10.5465/amr.1979.4498296

Cavoukian, A. (2012). Privacy by design. *IEEE Technology and Society Magazine*, *31*(4), 18–19. doi:10.1109/MTS.2012.2225459

Cavoukian, A., Taylor, S., & Abrams, M. E. (2010). Privacy by design: Essential for organizational accountability and strong business practices. *Identity in the Information Society*, *3*(2), 405–413. doi:10.100712394-010-0053-z

Davies, S. (2010). *Why privacy by design is the next crucial step for privacy protection*. Academic Press.

Deci, E. L. (1972). Intrinsic motivation, extrinsic reinforcement, and inequity. *Journal of Personality and Social Psychology*, *22*(1), 113–120. doi:10.1037/h0032355

Dusuki, A. W., & Yusof, T. F. M. T. M. (2016). The pyramid of corporate social responsibility model: Empirical evidence from Malaysian stakeholder perspective. *Malaysian Accounting Review, 7*(2).

Electronic Privacy Information Center (EPIC). (n.d.). *USA investigations of Google street view*. Retrieved from https://epic.org/privacy/streetview/

Forbesthe world's biggest public companies. (n.d.). Retrieved from https://www.forbes.com/global2000/

Fromholz, J. M. (2000). The European Union data privacy directive. *Berk. Tech. LJ*, *15*, 461.

George Jepsen attorney general, state of Connecticut. (n.d.). Retrieved from http://www.ct.gov/ag/cwp/view .asp?Q=520518&A=2341

Ginosar, A., & Ariel, Y. (2017). An analytical framework for online privacy research: What is missing? *Information & Management*, *54*(7), 948–957. doi:10.1016/j.im.2017.02.004

Goodson, S. (2012). *If you're not paying for it, you become the product.* Forbes.com.

Gürses, S., & del Alamo, J. M. (2016). Privacy engineering: Shaping an emerging field of research and practice. *IEEE Security and Privacy, 14*(2), 40–46. doi:10.1109/MSP.2016.37

Hadar, I., Hasson, T., Ayalon, O., Toch, E., Birnhack, M., Sherman, S., & Balissa, A. (2018). Privacy by designers: Software developers' privacy mindset. *Empirical Software Engineering, 23*(1), 259–289. doi:10.100710664-017-9517-1

Kumar, P. (2016). Ranking digital rights: Pushing ict companies to respect users' privacy. In Chi '16 workshop: Bridging the gap between privacy by design and privacy in practice (p. 15). ACM.

Langheinrich, M. (2001). Privacy by design—principles of privacy-aware ubiquitous systems. In *International conference on ubiquitous computing* (pp. 273–291). Academic Press. 10.1007/3-540-45427-6_23

Mai, J.-E. (2016). Big data privacy: The datafication of personal information. *The Information Society, 32*(3), 192–199. doi:10.1080/01972243.2016.1153010

Mendel, T., & Toch, E. (2017). Susceptibility to social influence of privacy behaviors: Peer versus authoritative sources. In *Proceedings of the 2017 ACM conference on computer supported cooper- ative work and social computing* (pp. 581–593). ACM. 10.1145/2998181.2998323

Notario, N., Crespo, A., Martín, Y.-S., Del Alamo, J. M., Le Métayer, D., Antignac, T., . . . Wright, D. (2015). Pripare: Integrating privacy best practices into a privacy engineering methodology. In Security and privacy workshops (SPW), 2015 IEEE (pp. 151–158). IEEE.

Oetzel, M. C., & Spiekermann, S. (2014). A systematic methodology for privacy impact assessments: A design science approach. *European Journal of Information Systems, 23*(2), 126–150. doi:10.1057/ejis.2013.18

Olafsen, A. H., Halvari, H., Forest, J., & Deci, E. L. (2015). Show them the money? the role of pay, managerial need support, and justice in a self-determination theory model of intrinsic work motivation. *Scandinavian Journal of Psychology, 56*(4), 447–457. doi:10.1111jop.12211 PMID:25810152

Pearson, S., & Charlesworth, A. (2009). Accountability as a way forward for privacy protection in the cloud. In IEEE international conference on cloud computing (pp. 131–144). IEEE. doi:10.1007/978-3-642-10665-1_12

Rubinstein, I., & Good, N. (2012). *Privacy by design: A counterfactual analysis of Google and Facebook privacy incidents.* Academic Press.

Ryan, R. M., & Deci, E. L. (2000). Intrinsic and extrinsic motivations: Classic definitions and new directions. *Contemporary Educational Psychology, 25*(1), 54–67. doi:10.1006/ceps.1999.1020 PMID:10620381

Sarvas, R., & Frohlich, D. M. (2011). *From snapshots to social media-the changing picture of domestic photography.* Springer Science & Business Media. doi:10.1007/978-0-85729-247-6

Schwaig, K. S., Kane, G. C., & Storey, V. C. (2006). Compliance to the fair information practices: How are the fortune 500 handling online privacy disclosures? *Information & Management, 43*(7), 805–820. doi:10.1016/j.im.2006.07.003

Senarath, A., Arachchilage, N. A., & Slay, J. (2017). Designing Privacy for You: A Practical Approach for User-Centric Privacy. In *International Conference on Human Aspects of Information Security, Privacy, and Trust* (pp. 739-752). Springer. 10.1007/978-3-319-58460-7_50

Shapiro, S. S. (2016). Privacy risk analysis based on system control structures: Adapting system- theoretic process analysis for privacy engineering. In Security and privacy workshops (SPW), 2016 IEEE (pp. 17–24). IEEE.

Small, M. L. (2011). How to conduct a mixed methods study: Recent trends in a rapidly growing literature. *Annual Review of Sociology*, *37*(1), 57–86. doi:10.1146/annurev.soc.012809.102657

The Guardian. (n.d.). *Michael Macegoogle logic: why google does the things it does the way it does.* Retrieved from https://www.theguardian.com/technology/2013/jul/09/google-android-reader-why

The Guardian. (n.d.). *Alex Hern uber employees 'spied on ex-partners, politicians and Beyonce.* Retrieved from https://www.theguardian.com/technology/2016/dec/13/uber-employees-spying-ex-partners-politicians-beyonce

The Sydney Morning Herald. (n.d.a). *Adam Turner malware hijacks big four australian banks' apps, steals two-factor SMS codes.* Retrieved from http://www.smh.com.au/technology/ consumer-security/malware-hijacks-big-four-australian-banks-apps-steals-twofactor-sms-codes-20160309-gnf528.html

The Sydney Morning Herald. (n.d.b). *Clancy Yeates nab scandal reveals shortcomings with breach re- porting.* Retrieved from http://www.smh.com.au/business/banking-and-finance/nab-scandal-reveals-shortcomings-with-breach-reporting-20150226-13pslp.htmll

Think Tank Ranking Digital Rights. (n.d.). Retrieved from https://rankingdigitalrights.org/ index2015/

Tuttle, H. (2016). Data deluge: what the Panama Papers leak means for business. *Risk Management*, *63*(6), 22.

Van Blarkom, G., Borking, J., & Olk, J. (2003). *Handbook of privacy and privacy-enhancing technologies. Privacy Incorporated Software Agent (PISA).* The Hague: Consortium.

Voss, W. G. (2017). European union data privacy law reform: General data protection regulation, privacy shield, and the right to delisting. *Business Lawyer*, *72*(1), 221–233.

Wagner, J., & Benecke, A. (2016). National legislation within the framework of the gdpr. *European Data Protection Law Review*, *2*(3), 353–361. doi:10.21552/EDPL/2016/3/10

Waters, S., & Ackerman, J. (2011). Exploring privacy management on facebook: Motivations and perceived consequences of voluntary disclosure. *Journal of Computer-Mediated Communication*, *17*(1), 101–115. doi:10.1111/j.1083-6101.2011.01559.x

Wood, D. J., & Logsdon, J. M. (2016). Social issues in management as a distinct field: Corporate social responsibility and performance. *Business & Society*.

Wright, D., & De Hert, P. (2012). Introduction to privacy impact assessment. In *Privacy impact assessment* (pp. 3–32). Springer. doi:10.1007/978-94-007-2543-0_1

Wurster, G., & van Oorschot, P. C. (2009). The developer is the enemy. In *Proceedings of the 2008 workshop on new security paradigms* (pp. 89–97). Academic Press.

Xu, H., & Jia, H. (2015). Privacy in a networked world: New challenges and opportunities for privacy research. *Washington Academy of Sciences. Journal of the Washington Academy of Sciences, 101*(3), 73.

Yin, R. K. (2013). *Case study research: Design and methods.* Sage Publications.

Young, A. L., & Quan-Haase, A. (2009). Information revelation and internet privacy concerns on social network sites: a case study of Facebook. In *Proceedings of the fourth international conference on communities and technologies* (pp. 265–274). Academic Press. 10.1145/1556460.1556499

Chapter 13
Botnet and Internet of Things (IoTs):
A Definition, Taxonomy, Challenges, and Future Directions

Kamal Alieyan
Universiti Sains Malaysia, Malaysia

Ammar Almomani
Al-Balqa Applied University, Jordan

Rosni Abdullah
Universiti Sains Malaysia, Malaysia

Badr Almutairi
Majmaah University, Saudi Arabia

Mohammad Alauthman
Zarqa University, Jordan

ABSTRACT

In today's internet world the internet of things (IoT) is becoming the most significant and developing technology. The primary goal behind the IoT is enabling more secure existence along with the improvement of risks at various life levels. With the arrival of IoT botnets, the perspective towards IoT products has transformed from enhanced living enabler into the internet of vulnerabilities for cybercriminals. Of all the several types of malware, botnet is considered as really a serious risk that often happens in cybercrimes and cyber-attacks. Botnet performs some predefined jobs and that too in some automated fashion. These attacks mostly occur in situations like phishing against any critical targets. Files sharing channel information are moved to DDoS attacks. IoT botnets have subjected two distinct problems, firstly, on the public internet. Most of the IoT devices are easily accessible. Secondly, in the architecture of most of the IoT units, security is usually a reconsideration. This particular chapter discusses IoT, botnet in IoT, and various botnet detection techniques available in IoT.

DOI: 10.4018/978-1-5225-9742-1.ch013

INTRODUCTION

In this digital world where everything is connected through the internet, the Internet of Things (IoT) plays a major role. Most of the people get attracted towards this innovative approach which helps the people to enjoy their life in their hectic routine. For instance, just imagine if refrigerators will be able to monitor their content and can place the order to a retailer shop if any food item is running out or imagine if you would be able to order your Sunday breakfast from your bed through a gesture or a voice command like the intelligent assistants Google Assistant, Apple Siri or Amazon Alexa. All these thoughts are not only some science fiction story but is now becoming a reality just because with use of smart devices such as Google Home, Amazon echoes with Alexa, etc., smart television, smart phones, etc. (Engrish, 2017).

In 1999, the concept of IoT was proposed by Kevin Ashton. IoT was refereed as the objects that are interoperable and exclusively identifiable and are connected with radio-frequency identification technology. Though, IoT is defined by in many forms by the various researchers as (Ray, 2018):

- ''A global infrastructure for the information society enabling advanced services by interconnecting (physical and virtual) things based on, existing and evolving, interoperable information and communication technologies'' (ICTP Workshop, 2015).
- ''3A concept: anytime, anywhere and any media, resulting into sustained ratio between radio and man around 1:1'' (Srivastava, 2006).
- ''a dynamic global network infrastructure with self-configuring capabilities based on standard and interoperable communication protocols where physical and virtual 'Things' have identities, physical attributes, and virtual personalities and use intelligent interfaces, and are seamlessly integrated into the information network'' (Kranenburg, 2008).

Evolution of Internet of Things (IoT)

As shown in Figure 1 that is how the Internet of Things actually evolved with the advent of time. At the era of pre-internet, which is also known as "H2H" or "Human-to-Human" era, people had the fixed or mobile telephony. Except that one of the primary ways of communication was through SMS services. After that with the incorporation of smart networks when the internet came into existence, the "www" or "world wide web" era the communication as well as information and entertainment etc. gets better through the internet. Furthermore, smart IT platforms and services were added to "www" that results in "web 2.0" era that totally converts everything into digital transformation like e-productivity, e-commerce, etc.

Figure 1. Evolution of IoT

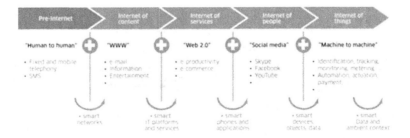

Next era is considered to bean era of "social media" that is Skype, Facebook, YouTube, etc. which involves the smart phones and applications. Moreover, currently, we live in "M2M" or "Machine-to-Machine" era that is possible because of the Internet of Things and with smart devices, objects, and data. Here we can easily identify, trace, monitor things with smart devices as well as automation, actuation and payment are also possible through IoT.

Generic Architecture of IoT

Basically, the Internet of Things architecture consists of smart things that may be devices, objects or data that are connected to one another through internet and all the data that is shared among them is stored at a cloud with the help of Big Data and these things are further managed, analyzed and visualized by the various units that are used to provide the services to a cloud.

The simplest architecture of the Internet of Things is shown in Figure 2. Where things may be any smart device, data or object and all these things are connected to the cloud through a gateway mostly internet. Many individual units like device management, analytics, visualization, etc. are used for managing the data with the help of Big Data that is used to store this data.

BOTNETS WITH IOT

The risks to the IoT units are an essential problem since they are difficult to repair and resolve. These can be easily affected by the attackers. The presence of IoT botnets was recognized after 2008. Nevertheless, the scope of risk presented by them was not recognized until 2016 (Engrish, 2017). Generally, the infected end-hosts (called bots) network is defined by the botnets, and these networks are actually controlled by a human being which is called Botmaster. Susceptible models are recruited by botnets using strategies that are employed by other malware classes (e.g., social engineering, applications vulnerabilities that are exploited remotely, etc.) (Li, Jiang & Zou, 2010), such devices establish a command and control (C&C) infrastructure among them so that they will be able to implement the malicious activities. Therefore, Botmaster receives the following services from the bots (Wang, Sparks & Zou, 2010):

- Botmaster provides easy recovery and monitoring
- Each bot has limited botnet exposure

Figure 2. Generic architecture of IoT

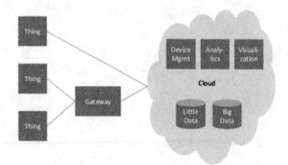

- Distinct control traffic dispersion as well as encryption
- Robust network connectivity

Components of Botnet

Command and Control (C&C) Server

It is a centralized system which can receive the information and sends the instructions to the bots residing in that particular network. This infrastructure comprises of many technical parts along with many servers. Many botnets make use of a client server-structure, but several botnets use peer-to-peer (P2P) architecture consisting of botnets that are having the C&C functionality.

Peer-to-Peer (P2P) Botnet

For providing additional security against the takedowns a decentralized bot network is used that is called P2P botnet. While P2P botnets can have a C&C server, they might additionally run without this and also be organized arbitrarily to additional obscure the botnet and its goal. While P2P botnets are not as likely being revealed, the botmaster cannot quickly supervise command distribution as well as there exist complex implementation of it.

Botmaster

It is also known as a bot herder or botnet controller, the botmaster performs the botnets operator function. A botnet is regulated by issuing the commands to specific botnets as well as C&C server within the system by the remote botmaster. To prevent the law enforcement prosecution and identification of botmaster, the location, and name of botmaster are kept obscured.

Bot

It is defined as the device that is connected to the internet within a botnet network. Mostly computer system is used as a bot, but with the advent of the technology an IoT device, a smartphone can also be used as botnet part. Operational instruction is sent to the botnets either from the bots of the same network or from the botmaster directly or from a C&C server.

Zombie

Zombie is nothing just another synonym for a bot. As an external person or a computing device is used to control the bot; therefore, a bot is called as 'zombie' and botnet is called a "zombie army."

Botnet Attack

- A botmaster gets a botnet by distributing bot malware to infect PCs and additional systems. He might also lease a current botnet from an additional criminal.
- The botnet's C&C is reported by a newly harvested bot or "zombies."

- These bots are now controlled by C&C, and potential victim address lists, email templates, and executable malware files are distributed by the bots as per C&C instructions.
- Many potential victims then receive the malware containing email messages from the infected bots on the order of botmaster.

BOTNET DETECTION TECHNIQUES BASED ON IOT ENVIRONMENT

Typically, Botnet detection, as well as monitoring, is a significant investigation subject in recent years as a result of a boost in the malicious activity. Because of the existence of malicious activity (Botnet) from a while, till currently few proper researches has analyzed the Botnet issue. Therefore, various bot detection methods were proposed by researchers as discussed in the next section.

Related Work and Taxonomy of Botnet Detection Techniques

Figure 3 shows the taxonomy of botnet detection techniques. There are two main categories of botnet detection techniques (Liu et al., 2008), Intrusion Detection Systems (IDSs) and HoneyNets (Stinson & Mitchell, 2007; Provos, 2004).

Honeynet

Usually Honeypot and Honeywell collectively make the Honeynet based method (Zang et al., 2011). In terms of security, Honeypot is considered as a computer system which helps to lure the attackers so that the attacker will attack on a specific computer system. This honeypot is supposed to be an end host. It can be compromised in a small time and is much more susceptible to malicious attacks whereas honeywall consists of software through which the traffic through the honeypot is monitored, collected, controlled

Figure 3. Botnet detection technique taxonomy (Ahmad et al., 2014)

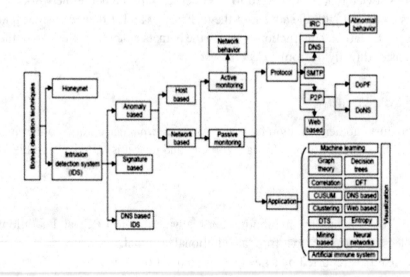

as well as modified, e.g., Snort (Schaffer, 2006). The computer systems that are used as Honeypots do not possess any kind of production value. Based on this particular principle, most interactions among other systems and honeypot are distrustful or suspicious and should be examined. For instance, in your network, you could install a honeypot web server in a particular location. Since it is a honeypot and it does not have some productive tasks, therefore any interaction with this particular web server is actually an unauthorized entry or a malicious task. A comparable Honeynet was built (Zeidanloo et al., 2010), where Honeywell component shall be in a position to examine as well as capture all of the site traffic payloads to access information related to Botnet like the DNS/IP address of the C&C server with the corresponding port number as well as the authentically data required to sign up for the C&C channel and also able to isolating the Honeypots from various other devices in the area community by obstructing outgoing contacts that contain distrustful key phrases connected to potential malicious pursuits.

Therefore in order to record the detailed steps of the Botnets, Rajab et al. (2006) have built a distributed and multifaceted measurement infrastructure by merging Honeynets with an altered version of the nepenthes platform.

IDS

IDSs are used to report the managing website when system policies are violated, system services are monitored for malicious activities or there are any other violations. These IDS can be either a hardware machine or a software application. The benefit of an IDS detection feature (Wurzinger et al., 2009; Kugisaki et al., 2007; Goebel & Holz, 2007) is that it has signatures of a selection of recognized botnets. Nevertheless, the main disadvantages of such methods are: firstly, the primary reason why there is an increase in anomaly is because of the small refresh rate of IDS signature updates. Secondly, for detecting the freshly activated botnets, the signature knowledge base repository needs to be refreshed frequently (Kugisaki et al., 2007). Further, these detection methods are categorized into signature based, anomaly based and DNS-based IDSs (Stalmans & Irwin, 2011).

Signature-Based Detection

In this particular method according to the accessible information as well as the signature of the current bot is adequate to trap the bots. To identify the botnets, a library of particular Botnet function names as well as instructions is collected that may be included and summarized in the IDS that are proposed by various researchers. After the IDS located corresponding search phrases while examining the content of payload, it can cause the alert and take additional steps from the Botnet though this particular method is restricted to identify just the recognized Botnets. For instance, Snort (Roesch, 1999) is a wide open source IDS which monitors network traffic to locate indications of intrusion by looking matches depending on the predefined set of signature as well as guidelines.

Anomaly-Based Detection

This method detects risk, malicious risk by looking for irregular or abnormal actions of the system. Here "abnormal" action usually means bots detection as a variation from "normal" action that is already defined appropriately by some guidelines. Sigh and Binkley (2006) proposed a good TCP based anomaly detection method with IRC tokenization as well as IRC message statistics to identify Botnet customers and also expose Botnet servers. Initially, an IRC parsing component is implemented in this particular anomaly based method that collects the TCP packet information as well as determines the IRC channel. Further, the scanning activities are performed on a large sampled data set which is correlated with the IRC channel traffics (Dagon et al., 2007). Moreover, finally, the IRC routes with good checking matter will be stamped as the attainable Botnet stations. A 3-metrics based measurement is proposed by Akiyama et al. (2007) that helps in detecting the behaviors of abnormal Botnets. It was assumed that all the bots would show some similar synchronization, response, and relationship that belongs to the same Botnet. BotHunter, a Botnet detection system was proposed by Gu et al. (2007). This detection system by using user-defined bot infection life cycle model runs a correlation algorithm that helps in recognizing the bot infection phase.

DNS-Based Detection

This detection method is a hybrid of data-mining based and behavior based methods that are used on the DNS traffic. In general, a Botmaster can easily hide and maintain its bots, therefore, think about the factors DNS queries are applied in several Botnet phases, like C&C server update, malicious attack initiation, and rallying process after infection that is a benefit of the strategy.

Bot Net Attacks

Attacking BotNet occurs when a bot is infected with an internet-connected device. A botnet is therefore also part of an infected device web which is monitored by a single attacker or group. Often Botnets are called Computer Worms or Zombie Armies, and bot masters or bot herders are their owners.

Command and Control (C&C)

Botnet C&Cs are unique and will probably not change between botnets and variants. In addition to supporting an operating, efficient botnet the botnet C&C is essential. The C&Cs are also believed to be the weakest link in the operational dimension of botnets-if we manage to disrupt an active C&C or simply cause communication disruption-botmasters cannot connect too many bots or initiate large, coordinated attacks. In order to combat botnets, therefore, it is important to understand the C&C function in botnets. This is how C&C operates a C&C server. Usually, an IRC server is created by Botmaster. If a host is infected by a bot virus, it will return to a server in C&C to wait on command of the botmaster. The bot joins a specific IRC channel in a typical IRC botnet to read messages from its master.

Rallying Mechanisms

The rallying mechanisms for botnets are another feature studied. Mechanisms for rallying botnets to find and rally new bots under their botmasters are crucial. Following are discussed the most commonly used rallying mechanisms.

Hard-Coded IP Address

This is the most common procedure used to rally new bots: A bot has C&C server IP addresses that are hard-coded in its database. If the bot initially infects a computer, the IP address of the hardcoded server contained within the binary code can be used to connect back to the C&C server.

Dynamic DNS Domain Name

Hard-coded domain names are frequently given by dynamic DNS providers in the bots today. The benefit of dynamic DNS is to allow botmasters to easily resume control by creating a new C&C server and by updating the IP address in the corresponded dynamic DNS input if a C&C server is shut down by authorities. The bots will make DNS queries and be sent back to the new C&C server when connections to the old C&C server fail.

Distributed DNS Service

Many of the newest botnet breeds operate in locations outside the reach of the law enforcement authorities their own distributed DNS service. Bots include the DNS server's addresses and communicate with them to solve the C&C server's IP addresses. In order to avoid detection by security devices on gateways, these services are often used at large port numbers.

Communication Protocols

The communication protocols used in botnets are among the main botnet characteristics. In this respect, as with many other software tools that rely on a network to communicate, bots communicate in certain well-defined network protocols with each other and their botmasters. Botnets generally do not create new communication network protocols. They use existing communication protocols that are implemented by software tools that are publicly available.

DISCUSSION AND OPEN CHALLENGE

The standard botnet is made up of computers that have been remotely accessed without knowledge of the owner and set up to forward transmissions to other computers on the Internet. The IoT is generally consisted of not only dedicated computers but also mechanical sensors, automobiles, industrial and household appliances, cardiac implant monitors and various other devices that are equipped by IP addresses and can also transmit data over a network. In the IoT context, these are known as things. Generally, the infected end-hosts (called bots) network is defined by the botnets, and these networks are actually controlled by a human being which is called Botmaster. Susceptible models are recruited by botnets using strategies that are employed by other malware groups.

Botnets have turned out to be a worldwide phenomenon as well as the botmaster is responsible for recording a huge number of insecure hosts that are present in domains throughout the world. There are many issues which encircle the analysis of botnets as well as detection of a botnet. The primary issues regarding botnet detection over a broad scale are as follows:

Among the key elements in finally identifying the intensity of botnet, risks are assessing the impacted botnet span. Pre-existing detection techniques typically do not have precision in computing the dimensions of botnets, and also the figures produced are appropriate only for a small range.

The applicability of assured detection, as well as mitigation techniques, is restricted through particular conflicts involving the laws that provide secure IT services operation as well as some data protection laws (Plohmann, Gerhard-Padilla & Leder, 2011). Researchers face difficulty in evaluating the outcomes of theirs with earlier published benchmarks, as the datasets to a complete level are not readily available for the researcher group. It is tough to get actual traces, whereas scientists need contents for analyzing the functionality of the methods of theirs on small data traces sets that is a difficult job since heterogeneity (differences in hardware, software, architectural design, etc.) on the web is not clearly identified for many datasets. Another threat that is becoming extremely terrifying in this particular area may be the botnet phenomenon in devices that are mobile and the detection of its that is caused due to the increasing expansion of Internet use and computing proficiencies (e.g., GPRS, 3G, and Wi-Fi) for mobile devices like hand-held devices and smartphones. Further, there are many restrictions in botnet detection mechanism that are caused by various factors namely; (i) private IP addresses (ii) tracking other mobile devices (iii) SMS messages (iv) GPS data (v) saturated phone service (vi) limited bandwidth (vii) limited battery power.

When it is decided to use a botnet with hundreds or perhaps thousands of products, most with their very own unique IP addresses, the hacker causes it to be nearly impossible to quit the attack or even differentiate genuine owners from a bunch of fake ones. Today, botnets are not brand new. Since as earlier as 2000, hackers have already been by using botnets by increasing entry to unsecured products (usually computer systems then) to be able to produce the DDoS attacks. Though the Internet of Things makes the issue significantly more terrible. The market place was flooded with affordable products - webcams, baby monitors, thermostats, moreover, of course, even yoga mats as well as fry pans - that connects on the Internet, each one of that has the own IP address of its. Though the gadgets have minimal or maybe no integrated protection, and also whenever they do, subscribers frequently fail to actually consider the fundamental stage of setting a password for them. Which permits them to be very easy goals for online hackers desiring to develop as well as make use of a botnet.

An integral Internet infrastructure supplier, Dyn, was partly offline with a botnet of approximately 100,000 unsecured IoT devices in 2016. This led to a short period of departure from the Internet for many high profile and traffic websites. This botnet was made with Mirai malware which automates the co-opting of these unsecured devices— and it is available to the public. In other words, it was not a genius hacker who wrote new and innovative code, but someone who puts what is existing in new ways. Such DDoS attacks are not the only way hackers can use botnets. They can be used for clicking fraud, avoiding spam filters, speeding up password guessing, anything else, which would require a huge network of computers working together. They can be used to perpetrate fraudulent clicks. It is actually an open secret for criminal organizations to rent time on a botnet for any task they want.

The best solution would be to make sure all IoT devices work with safe software, but the probability is slim. Most IoT devices are not security-constructed, and no way to add additional security is patched. Moreover, millions of devices are already in use, produced and sold. The problem of botnets is also likely to grow since the use and fabrication of IoT devices is expected to exponentially increase over the next few years. Moreover, the security measures we have against the attackers will soon be overwritten and outmoded, or at least somewhat effective.

CONCLUSION AND FUTURE WORK

As in 2007, the first Botnet workshop was organized and after that various researchers proposed the different Botnet detection techniques and depending on some of these techniques some systems were implemented with actual bot detection methods. One of the most difficult issues is the Botnet detection. Therefore, this particular paper described a total Botnet detection methods survey. Further, Botnet detection strategies are classified in 2 primary types: establishing honeynets as well as Intrusion Detection System (IDS), and also other detection techniques in particular category are discussed.

The future directions hope for the innovation of new technologies for IoT because if in the coming years there is similar development in technology then it is obvious that the IoT will not be able to provide the same services in terms of addressability, scalability, concurrency, interoperability, and flexibility. Because of such issues the botnets may also become more prominent in such networks and may harm users. So there will be a need for some techniques that will help in overcoming these issues.

REFERENCES

Akiyama, M., Kawamoto, T., Shimamura, M., Yokoyama, T., Kadobayashi, Y., & Yamaguchi, S. (2007). A proposal of metrics for botnet detection based on its cooperative behaviour. *Applications and the Internet Workshops, 2007. SAINT Workshops in 2007. International Symposium on*, 82–82.

Bailey, M., Cooke, E., Jahanian, F., Xu, Y., & Karir, M. (2009). *A survey of botnet technology and defenses*. IEEE Cybersecurity Applications & Technology Conf. for Homeland Security. doi:10.1109/CATCH.2009.40

Bailey, M., Cooke, E., Jahanian, F., Xu, Y., & Karir, M. (2009). A survey of botnet technology and defenses. In *Proceedings of the 2009 Cybersecurity Applications & Technology Conference for Homeland Security*. Washington, DC: IEEE Computer Society. 10.1109/CATCH.2009.40

Barford, P., & Yagneswaran, V. (2006). An Inside Look at Botnets. In *Special Workshop on Malware Detection, Advances in Information Security*. Springer.

Binkley, J., & Singh, S. (2006). An algorithm for anomaly-based botnet detection. *Proceedings of USENIX Steps to Reducing Unwanted Traffic on the Internet Workshop (SRUTI)*, 43–48.

Binkley, J. R., & Singh, S. (2006). An algorithm for anomaly based botnet detection. *Proc. USENIX Steps to Reducing Unwanted Traffic on the Internet Workshop*, 43-48.

Cai, T., & Zou, F. (2012). Detecting HTTP botnet with clustering network traffic. *IEEE 8th Int. Conf. on Wireless Communications, Networking and Mobile Computing*, 1-7. 10.1109/WiCOM.2012.6478491

Chang, S., & Daniels, T. E. (2009). P2P botnet detection using behavior clustering & statistical tests. *Proc. 2nd ACM Workshop on Security and Artificial Intelligence*, 23-30. doi:10.1145/1654988.1654996

Choo, K. K. R. (2007). *Zombies and Botnets. Trends and issues in crime and criminal justice, no.333*. Canberra: Australian Institute of Criminology.

Coskun, B., Dietrich, S., & Memon, N. (2010). Friends of an enemy: identifying local members of peer-to-peer botnets using mutual contacts. *Proc. 26th Annual Computer Security Applications Conf.*, 131-140. 10.1145/1920261.1920283

Cremonini, M., & Riccardi, M. (2009). The Dorothy project: an open botnet analysis framework for automatic tracking and activity visualization. *IEEE European Conf. on Computer Network Defense*, 52-54. 10.1109/EC2ND.2009.15

Dagon, D., Gu, G., Lee, C. P., & Lee, W. (2007). A Taxonomy of Botnet Structures. *Proc. 23rd Annual Computer Security Applications Conference (ACSAC 2007)*, 325-339.

Dagon, D., Gu, G., Lee, C. P., & Lee, W. (2007). A taxonomy of botnet structures. *IEEE 23rd Annual Computer Security Applications Conf.*, 325-339. 10.1109/ACSAC.2007.44

Engrish, K. (2017). *Turning internet of things (not) into the internet of vulnerabilities (Nov): It botnets.* Retrieved from: https://arxiv.org/pdf/1702.03681.pdf

Ezhilarasi, M., & Krishnaveni, V. (2018). *A Survey on Wireless Sensor Network: Energy and Lifetime Perspective* (Vol. 14). Taga Journal of Graphic Technology.

Ezhilarasi, M., & Krishnaveni, V. (2019). An evolutionary multipath energy-efficient routing protocol (EMEER) for network lifetime enhancement in wireless sensor networks. *Soft Computing*, 1–11. doi:10.100700500-019-03928-1

Feily, M., Shahrestani, A., & Ramadass, S. (2009). A survey of the botnet and botnet detection. *3rd Int. Conf. on Emerging Security Information, Systems, and Technologies*, 268-273. 10.1109/SECURWARE.2009.48

Freiling, F., Holz, T., & Wicherski, G. (2005). Botnet Tracking: Exploring a Root-cause Methodology to Prevent Denial of Service Attacks. *Proceedings of 10th European Symposium on Research in Computer Security (ESORICS'05)*. 10.1007/11555827_19

Ge, L., Liu, H., & Zhang, D. (2012). On effective sampling techniques for host-based Intrusion detection in MANET. *IEEE Military Communications Conf.*, 1-6. 10.1109/MILCOM.2012.6415605

Goebel, J., & Holz, T. (2007). Rishi: identify contaminated bot hosts by IRC nickname evaluation. *Proc. 1st Conf. on 1st Workshop on Hot Topics in Understanding Botnets*, 1-12.

Gu, G., Porras, P., Yegneswaran, V., Fong, M., & Lee, W. (2007). BotHunter: Detecting malware infection through ids-driven dialog correlation. *Proceedings of the 16th USENIX Security Symposium*, 167–182.

Gu, G., Porras, P., Yegneswaran, V., Fong, M., & Lee, W. (2007). BotHunter: Detecting Malware Infection through ids-driven dialog correlation. *Proceedings of the 16th USENIX Security Symposium (Security'07)*.

Jian, G., Zheng, K., Yang, Y., & Niu, X. (2012). An evaluation model of botnet based on peer to peer. *IEEE 4th Int. Conf. on Computational Intelligence and Communication Networks*, 925-929. 10.1109/CICN.2012.46

Karim, A., Bin Salleh, R., Shiraz, M., Shah, S. A. A., Awan, I., & Anuar, N. B. (2014). Botnet detection techniques: Review, future trends, and issues. *Journal of Zhejiang University Science C, 15*(11), 943–983. doi:10.1631/jzus.C1300242

Kranenburg, R.V. (2008). The Internet of Things: A Critique of Ambient Technology and the All-Seeing Network of RFID, Institute of Network Cultures. ITU work on Internet of things, 2015. *ICTP Workshop.*

Kugisaki, Y., Kasahara, Y., Hori, Y., & Sarkurai, K. (2007). Bot detection based on traffic analysis. *IEEE Int. Conf. on Intelligent Pervasive Computing*, 303-306.

Li, C., Jiang, W., & Zou, X. (2009). Botnet: Survey and case study. *4th International Conference on Innovative Computing, Information and Control.*

Liu, L., Chen, S., Yan, G., & Zhang, Z. (2008) BotTracer: execution based bot-like malware detection. *International Conference on Information Security*, 97-113. 10.1007/978-3-540-85886-7_7

Nagarajan, M., & Karthikeyan, S. (2012) *A New Approach to Increase the Life Time and Efficiency of Wireless Sensor Network*. IEEE. doi:10.1109/ICPRIME.2012.6208349

Plohmann, D., Gerhard-Padilla, E., & Leder, F. (2011). *Botnets: Detection, Measurement, Disinfection & Defence.* ENISA.

Provos, N. (2004). A virtual honeypot framework. *USENIX Security Symp.*

Rajab, M., Zarfoss, J., Monrose, F., & Terzis, A. (2006). *A multifaceted approach to understanding the botnet phenomenon.* Retrieved October 31, 2009, from http://www.imconf.net/imc- 2006/papers/p4-rajab.pdf

Rajab, M., Zarfoss, J., Monrose, F., & Terzis, A. (2007). My botnet is bigger than yours (maybe, better than yours): Why size estimates remain challenging. *USENIX Workshop on Hot Topics in Understanding Botnet.*

Rajab, M. A., Zarfoss, J., Monrose, F., & Terzis, A. (2007). My Botnet is Bigger than Yours (Maybe, Better than Yours): why size estimates remain challenging. *First Workshop on Hot Topics in Understanding Botnets (HotBots'07).*

Ray, P. P. (2018). A survey on the Internet of Things architectures. *Journal of King Saud University-Computer and Information Sciences, 30*(3), 291–319. doi:10.1016/j.jksuci.2016.10.003

Roesch, M. (1999). Snort-lightweight intrusion detection for networks. *Proceedings of the 13th USENIX conference on System administration*, 229–238.

Sable, N. A., & Datar, D. S. (2013). A review-botnet detection and suppression in clouds. *Journal of Information Engineering and Applications, 3*(12), 1–7.

Saha, B., & Gairola, A. (2005). *Botnet: An overview.* CERT-In White PaperCIWP-2005-05.

Schaffer, G. (2006). Worms and Viruses and Botnets, Oh My: Rational Responses to Emerging Internet Threats. *IEEE Security and Privacy, 4*(3), 52–58. doi:10.1109/MSP.2006.83

Shanmughapriya, M., Sumathi, G., & Aarthi, K. C. (2018). Bot Net of Things – A Survey. *International Journal of Engineering and Computer Science, 7*(5), 23926–23930.

Srivastava, L. (2006). Pervasive, ambient, ubiquitous: the magic of radio. *Proceedings of European Commission Conference From RFID to the Internet of Things.*

Stalmans, E., & Irwin, B. (2011). *A framework for DNS based detection and mitigation of malware infections on a network.* IEEE Information Security South Africa. doi:10.1109/ISSA.2011.6027531

Stevanovic, M., & Pedersen, J. (2014). An efficient flow-based botnet detection using supervised machine learning. *International Conference on Computing, Networking, and Communications (ICNC),* 797 – 801. 10.1109/ICCNC.2014.6785439

Stinson, E., & Mitchell, J. C. (2007). Characterizing bots' remote control behavior. In *Detection of Intrusions and Malware, and Vulnerability Assessment* (pp. 89–108). Springer. doi:10.1007/978-3-540-73614-1_6

Stinson, E., & Mitchell, J. C. (2007). Characterizing bots' remote control behaviour. *Proceedings of the 4th GI International Conference on Detection of Intrusions and Malware, and Vulnerability Assessment (DMV A'07).*

Tyagi, A. K., & Aghila, G. (2011). A wide-scale survey on a botnet. *International Journal of Computers and Applications, 34*(9), 10–23.

Villamarin-Salomon, R., & Brustoloni, J. C. (2008). Identifying Botnets Using Anomaly Detection Techniques Applied to DNS Traffic. *Proc. 5th IEEE Consumer Communications and Networking Conference (CCNC2008),* 476-481. 10.1109/ccnc08.2007.112

Wang, P., Sparks, S., & Zou, C. C. (2010). An advanced hybrid peer-to-peer botnet. *Proc. in Workshop on Hot Topics in Understanding Botnets.*

Whitmore, A., Agarwal, A., & Xu, L. D. (2015). The Internet of Things—A survey of topics and trends. *Information Systems Frontiers, 17*(2), 261–274. doi:10.100710796-014-9489-2

Wurzinger, P., Bilge, L., Holz, T., Goebel, J., Kruegel, C., & Kirda, E. (2009). *Automatically generating models for botnet detection.* Computer Security ESORICS.

Zang, X., Tangpong, A., Kesidis, G., & Miller, D.J. (2011). *CSE Dept Technical Report on "Botnet Detection through Fine Flow Classification."* Report No. CSE11-001.

Zeidanloo, H. R., & Manaf, A. A. (2010). Botnet Detection by Monitoring Similar Communication Patterns. *International Journal of Computer Science and Information Security, 7*(3).

Zeidanloo, H.R., Manaf, A.B., Vahdani, P., Tabatabaei, F., & Zamani, M. (2010). Botnet Detection Based on Traffic Monitoring. *IEEE Transaction.*

Chapter 14
A Conceptual Model for the Organizational Adoption of Information System Security Innovations

Mumtaz Abdul Hameed
Technovation Consulting and Training (Private) Limited, Maldives

Nalin Asanka Gamagedara Arachchilage
University of New South Wales, Australia

ABSTRACT

Information system (IS) security threats are still a major concern for many organizations. However, most organizations fall short in achieving a successful adoption and implementation of IS security measures. In this chapter, the authors developed a theoretical model for the adoption process of IS security innovations in organizations. The model was derived by combining four theoretical models of innovation adoption, namely diffusion of innovation theory (DOI), the technology acceptance model (TAM), the theory of planned behavior (TPB), and the technology-organisation-environment (TOE) framework. The model depicts IS security innovation adoption in organizations, as two decision proceedings. The adoption process from the initiation stage until the acquisition of innovation is considered as a decision made by organisation while the process of innovation assimilation is assumed as a result of the user acceptance of innovation within the organization.

INTRODUCTION

Information and computer resources (hardware, software, database, networks, etc.) collectively be referred as Information System (IS) assets (Alshboul, 2010) that need to be protected against malicious attacks such as unauthorised access and improper use. Thus, safeguards of IS assets is a widespread concern for individuals and organisations (Stergioua et al., 2016; Zhang et al., 2016). Research on the preservation of IS assets falls under the theme of IS Security. There are numerous technical measures

DOI: 10.4018/978-1-5225-9742-1.ch014

(software and hardware tools) and non-technical safeguards (physical defences and security procedure) available that provides protection for IS assets. Nevertheless, organisations are still struggling to keep up with threats to their IS assets and security breach incidents that have cost them tens of thousands of dollars in loss (Kaspersky lab, 2015). Previous scholarly contributions have constantly argued that the weakest link in any security plan is the computer users themselves (Almomani et al. 2013a; Almomani et al. 2013b; Arachchilage, 2016; Arachchilage et al., 2016; Gross and Mary, 2007; Wynn et al., 2012). As a matter of fact, computer security education needs to be considered as a means to combat against IS threats (Arachchilage, 2016; Arachchilage and Love, 2013; Arachchilage & Love, 2014; Arachchilage et al., 2016; Ben-Asher & Gonzalez, 2015, Gupta et al., 2016; Gupta et al., 2018; Tewari & Gupta, 2017).

The main focus of IS security is to deploy strategies to protect and safeguard IS assets from vulnerabilities (Alshboul, 2010). However, adoption and implementation of IS security measures in an organisation are a complex process (Hameed & Arachchilage, 2016). Besides, adoption of IS security measures by the individuals and organisations is exceptionally low, considering the efforts put in for developing and implementing such systems (Lee & Kozar, 2008; Tuncalp, 2014). Hence, it is critically important to understand what causes the users accept or reject the organisations IS security measures (Jones et al., 2010). As far as we can tell from the IS security literature that there is no model that fully explains the IS security adoption in organisations. Nonetheless, research on IS innovation has introduced models, theories and frameworks related to the adoption and implementation of IS innovations in organisations (Hameed et al., 2012a). IS scholars define innovation as an idea, a method, a product, a program or a technology that is new to the adopting unit (Damanpour, 1991; Hameed et al., 2012a). Hence, the measures of IS security, undoubtedly, be considered as an IS innovation and the theories based on innovation adoption may obviously be applied in an empirical study on IS security adoption process.

In this research, we aimed to theoretically construct a model for IS security innovation adoption process in organisations, which includes organisational adoption process and the user acceptance of innovation. To this end, we explore the past literature on the stages of innovation adoption, theories of innovation adoption, models of technology acceptance and popular frameworks developed by researchers for organisational adoption, with factors considered to influence IS innovation adoption. This study, then utilised the most suitable concepts and relationships of prominent IS innovation adoption theories and user acceptance models, to explain the process of adoption of IS security innovations in organisations. In addition, this study suggests a number of factors from different context that would either assist or inhibit the process of IS security innovation adoption.

The current study focuses on IS security adoption in organisations. The research makes several contributions to the theory and practice of IS security and innovation adoption research. First, it draws upon and synthesizes the rich literature in IS innovation adoption theories and applied it in the context of IS security innovations. The IS security innovation adoption model proposed is based on the theoretical perspective of four innovation adoption theories. The integrated illustration of these models could methodically be used to examine the adoption process and user acceptance of IS security innovations in organisations. Secondly, the proposed IS security adoption model encompasses both the organisational adoption process and user acceptance of innovation. It is evident from the literature that previous scholarly IS security adoption contributions have on no account addressed organisational adoption process and user acceptance of innovation in a single investigation. Past studies on IS security adoption either examine the processes of adoption of IS security innovation until the acquisition of innovation with no assessment on whether the innovation grows to be part of their regular practice (Lee & Kozar, 2005; Safa et al., 2015). On the other hand, studies on user acceptance have only examined the behaviour and attitude of individuals accepting an IS security innovation (Li, 2015; Salleh et al., 2015). Combining the organisational adoption process and user acceptance of innovation in a single model allows illustrating the overall adoption process more comprehensively compare to any of the past IS security adoption frameworks. Thirdly, the proposed model has introduced several determinants that could possibly influence IS security adoption in organisations. The suggested association, the study draws between various technological, organisational, environmental, and user acceptance characteristics for IS security adoption provide an abundant opportunity for potential future research. Furthermore, the IS security adoption model proposed in this study provides important practical implications for organisations and academia.

THEORETICAL BACKGROUND

IS security is, unquestionably, a major concern for most organisations and the risk of computer crimes has become an increasing threat for many companies (Chatterjee et al., 2015; Memos et al., 2017; Tewari et al., 2016). As organisations depend more on IS to succeed in their businesses, the management is obliged to invest more on improving their IS reliability (Hameed and Arachchilage, 2016). ISs need to be secure if they are to be reliable (Kim et al., 2013). Safeguard and the management of Confidentiality, Integrity and Availability (CIA) of information are the most important IS security concerns for an organisation (Feruza & Kim, 2007).

Security of IS encompasses both technical and non-technical concerns for safeguarding IS assets against a variety of threats such as phishing, botnet, virus, worms, Trojans, etc. As a safeguard measure, organisations are required to implement policies, practices and technologies that protect against unauthorized access, use, disclosure, disruption, modification or destruction of information (Feruza & Kim, 2007). Although there is no such a standard mechanism to completely safeguard all of the IS assets of an organisation, a handful of measures can be put in practice to limit the number of attacks (Albuquerque-Junior & Santos, 2015). Recent developments have created new tools and techniques that help organisations effectively secure their IS assets.

A comprehensive range of security measures in the form of physical controls, procedural controls and technical controls would thwart almost all forms of security breaches to ensure CIA of information in an organisation (Feruza and Kim, 2007). A wide range physical, procedural and technical security controls can be used to provide security in a number of different ways in an organisation. Any physical, procedural or technical security control put in place in an organisation to protect information and computer resources may possibly be characterized as IS security innovation. As previously outlined, an innovation is the possession of ideas, systems, practices, products or technologies that are new to the adopting organisation. What's more, adoption of innovation is a process that results in the introduction and use of products, processes, or practices that are new to the adopting organisation (Damanpour & Wischnevsky, 2006; Hameed et al., 2012a). Damanpour (1991) defines adoption of innovation as the initiation, development and implementation of new initiatives. Hence, implementation and the use of physical, procedural or technical security control may be considered as the adoption of IS security innovation in an organisation.

Correct IS security measures in organisations have long been recognized, however, the empirical research in this area is still at its early stage (Arachchilage & Martin, 2014; Arachchilage et al., 2013). Although there are a number of IS security innovations available, an organisation can only benefit if those innovations are adopted and implemented properly. The main hindrance for organisations from attaining a successful implementation of IS security innovation is the lack of appropriate models of IS security adoption. Therefore, this research attempts to examine IS security adoption process in organisations.

METHODOLOGY

The study involved identifying from literature the relevant models and frameworks that could be employed to frame the components that will be used to assess the adoption process of IS security innovations in organisations. Hence, we initially performed a literature search to identify theoretical models utilised in examining adoption and user acceptance of IS innovations. Based on this search result, the study, then identified the most commonly used innovation adoption and user acceptance models. The IS security adoption studies that used IS innovation adoption models in their empirical investigations were then selected. The IS security literature extracted includes studies conducted for both individual and organisational contexts. The most prominent innovation adoption models used in IS security adoption were then drawn together, to synthesize the conceptual model presented in this study. In addition, we extracted the factors from different categories that were examined in the IS security adoption literature.

MODELS AND PROCESSES OF IS INNOVATION ADOPTION

A significant amount of research has been conducted in examining the process and the factors influencing the adoption and user acceptance of innovations in organisations (Hameed & Counsell, 2014a, 2014b; Hameed et al., 2012b). However, there is no organisational innovation adoption theory that is in existence for researchers to utilise (Hameed et al., 2012a). Up till now, researchers have been utilising theories and theoretical models from other subjects appropriate to explain the adopter's attitude and innovation adoption behaviour of IS innovation adoption. In addition, innovation adoption research has tailored theories from disciplines such as psychology, sociology and organisational behaviour propose several theoretical models related to the adoption and user acceptance of IS innovations in organisations (Hameed et al., 2012a).

The most common theoretical models used to examine adoption and user acceptance of innovation are Diffusion of Innovation Theory [DOI] (Rogers, 1983), Perceived Characteristics of Innovation [PCI] (Moore & Benbasat, 1991), Theory of Reasoned Action [TRA] (Fishbein & Ajzen, 1975), Theory of Planned Behaviour [TPB] (Ajzen, 1991), Technology Acceptance Model [TAM] (Davis, 1989), Technology Acceptance Model 2 [TAM2] (Venkatesh and Davis, 2000), Technology Acceptance Model 3 [TAM3] (Venkatesh & Bala, 2008), Technology, Organisation, Environment [TOE] Model (Tornatzky & Fleischer, 1990) and the Unified Theory of Acceptance and Use of Technology [UTAUT] model (Venkatesh et al., 2003). Amongst all of these models, DOI, TAM, TRA, TPB and TOE have been widely used in innovation adoption research (Hameed et al., 2012a). DOI, TAM, TRA and TPB are primarily utilised in examining the user behaviour of innovation adoption and TOE framework has widely been exploited in organisational level studies of IS innovation adoption.

Innovation adoption processes in an organisation are considered to be successful only if the innovation is implemented in the organisation and individuals continue to use the innovation over a period of time (Gopalakrishnan & Damanpour, 1997; Hameed et al., 2012a). Based on this perception, the model presented by Hameed et al. (2012a) for IT innovation adoption for organisations considered both organisational level analysis and individual level assessment.

Researchers have described the process of adoption of innovation into a number of sequences of stages. According to Hameed et al. (2012a), the cycle of stages illustrated by different research falls more or less into the initiation, adoption-decision and implementation stage. These three phases of initiation, adoption-decision and implementation are more often referred to as pre-adoption, adoption-decision and post-adoption in the IS literature.

SECURITY INNOVATION ADOPTION MODEL

This study seeks to develop a conceptual model for IS security adoption that includes the process of adoption and user acceptance of IS security innovations in organisations. A search in literature confirmed that there was hardly any distinct theoretical model with the aim of explaining IS security adoption. IS security research generally utilised IS innovation adoption and user acceptance models (Claar & Johnson, 2012; Lee & Kozar, 2005). In addition, researchers have applied models from other disciplines such as health belief model to examine user behaviour of IS security adoption (Claar & Johnson, 2010; Ng et al., 2009).

Meanwhile, innovation adoption literature suggests that researchers have been utilising several theories and theoretical models that explain the adopter's attitude and organisational innovation adoption's behaviour to examine different types of innovation such as IS security. As a result, a suitable model or a combination of models of IS spectrum that are general enough may perhaps be sufficient to explain IS security adoption in organisations. Indeed, a number of studies have introduced adoption and user acceptance models in the organisational context for various other innovations (Hameed & Counsell, 2014a; Hameed et al., 2012b).

Innovation Adoption Models Relevant for IS Security

Most of the research on innovation adoption of organisational surrounding conducts their analysis by integrating innovation adoption and user acceptance theories with frameworks that consists of determinants that are relevant to the study context. For example, Teo et al. (2009) empirically examined adopters and non-adopters of e-procurement in Singaporean organisations, incorporating two innovation adoption theories and a framework consisting determinant of TOE model. Moreover, Hameed et al. (2012a) proposed a more general IS innovation adoption model for organisations by combining innovation adoption and user acceptance theories, and major frameworks used in IS innovation studies. Their model is a combination of DOI, TRA, TAM, TPB and a framework that consists of determinants of TOE and CEO characteristics. The model exploited DOI model and the TOE framework with CEO characteristics to illustrate the organisational adoption process until the acquisition of innovation and TRA, TAM and TPB were utilised to construct user acceptance of innovation. Here, TOE framework takes account of the various determinants relevant to IS innovation adoption in organisations.

Consistent with extant research on IS security, we developed the IS Security adoption model by replicating the theories of IS innovation adoption. Based on innovation adoption literature, the study draws together a conceptual model for IS security innovation adoption by integrating multiple theoretical depictions of innovation adoption and user acceptance of IS with popular frameworks. The model is a combination of DOI, TAM, TPB models together with the TOE framework.

Diffusion of Innovation (DOI)

DOI model introduced by Rogers (1983) is the most commonly used theoretical foundations to study innovation adoption. According to Rogers (1983), diffusion is a process by which an innovation is communicated through certain channels over a period of time among the members of a group. The DOI theory explains how the individuals or groups adopt innovations and the process involves in their decision towards it. DOI model suggests a number of attributes of innovation that were perceived to assist the diffusion of technological innovation. Rogers (1995) suggests that relative advantage, compatibility, complexity, trialability and observability of the innovation plays a key role in an individual's attitudes towards innovation adoption.

The literature shows that the DOI has a solid theoretical basis and the five characteristics suggested in DOI have successfully explained a number of IS adoption behaviours (Premkumar & Roberts, 1999). As for the IS security studies, Lee and Kozar (2008) applied DOI to empirically investigate the anti-spyware adoption of computer users of the United States of America.

Nevertheless, Hameed et al. (2012a) identified two major limitations of the DOI, in its application for organisational innovation adoption. First, the model mainly focuses on the behaviour and attitude of individuals in the adoption of innovation. Another obvious drawback of DOI which Hameed et al. (2012a) suggested was its inability to address the full innovation adoption process. Hence, the DOI model is inadequate to fully explain IS adoption in organisations. Lee and Kozar (2008) argued that DOI model does not clearly explain how an attitude is formed, how it leads to adoption intention and to actual adoption. Nevertheless, the DOI can explain the individual level adoption process in the pre-adoption and adoption-decision stages of innovation adoption. In addition, some researchers have integrated DOI with other theories allowing it to address the interaction between attitude, intention and behaviour (Premkumar & Roberts, 1999; Quaddus & Hofmeyer, 2007).

Technology Acceptance Model (TAM)

TAM is a persuasive extension or modification of TRA introduced by (Davis, 1989) that aims to explain and predict user acceptance of IS. TAM posits that two cognitive attributes, namely: 'perceived usefulness' and 'perceived ease of use' influence the actual use of IS innovations (Davis, 1989; Davis et al., 1989). According to Davis (1989), perceived usefulness is 'the degree to which a person believes that using a particular system would enhance his or her job performance' and perceived ease of use is 'the degree to which a person believes that using a particular system would be free of effort'. Furthermore, TAM articulates that perceived usefulness and perceived ease of use affect a user's attitude towards using an IS and a user's attitude directly relates to a user's intention which eventually determines the system usage of an IS. Among the different models that have been proposed, the TAM appears to be the most widely accepted innovation adoption model among IS researchers (Hameed & Counsell, 2014b; Wang et al., 2003). Significantly, TAM has consistently outperformed the TRA in terms of explaining variances across many studies (Davis et al., 1989; Venkatesh et al., 2003). In addition, TAM has been validated as a powerful and parsimonious framework for explaining user acceptance of IS innovations (Davis, 1989; Davis et al., 1989). Notably, as far as this study is concerned, TAM may possibly be utilized to investigate IS security implementation. Meanwhile, in a research to examine the factors that influence employee acceptance of IS security measures, Jones et al. (2010) extended the TAM.

While IS researchers have investigated and replicated TAM, and agreed that it is suitable in predicting the individual acceptance of IS innovations, the TAM's fundamental constructs do not fully unveil the influence of contextual factors that may affect the users' acceptance of IS innovation (Hameed et al., 2012a). Further, Legris et al. (2003) argued that TAM needed to be integrated into a larger model that includes technological and social factors to enhance its analytical capability to predict innovation acceptance of IS innovations. One of the shortcomings of TAM is that it only considers the individual level acceptance and neglects group level aspects of decision making (Hameed et al., 2012a). Another limitation of TAM is that; it theorises user's adoption decision based purely on voluntary situations, neglecting users' judgement influenced by their peers or in response to social pressure. To overcome these limitations, researchers have incorporated TAM with other IS adoption models to examine organisational adoption process (Quaddus & Hofmeyer, 2007; Teo et al., 2009).

Theory of Planned Behaviour (TPB)

TRA envisaged that the individual acceptance behaviour was purely voluntary, however, many decisions by an individual does not appear fully volitional. Hence, to address the non-voluntary actions of user acceptance behaviour, Ajzen (1991) revised TRA by adding a new component to develop an improved replica known as the TPB. According to TPB, human action is guided by three kinds of thoughts: (1) behavioural beliefs - one's opinions about the likely consequence of the behaviour (2) normative beliefs - one's perception about the normative expectation of others and (3) control beliefs - one's judgments about the presence of factors that may facilitate or impede the performance of the behaviour. TPB's behavioural belief intends to produce a favourable or unfavourable attitude towards the behaviour and normative belief is the result of perceived social pressure or subjective norm to perform the action. In addition, TPB's control beliefs, namely Perceived Behavioural Control (PBC), foresees the decisions regarding the absence or presence of factors that might facilitate or impede the performance of the behaviour (Ajzen, 1991).

TPB proposes that a combination of attitude toward the behaviour, subjective norm, and PBC may lead to the formation of a behavioural intention to perform the behaviour. TPB suggests that PBC affects behaviour directly or indirectly through behavioural intention. Ajzen (1991) argued that in conditions where behavioural intention has minimal effect on the actual behaviour, PBC alone can be used to predict the behaviour. Armitage and Conner (2001) showed that PBC was a significant factor in the prediction of behavioural intention and actual behaviour in TPB, regardless of the effects of attitude toward the behaviour and subjective norm.

In a meta-analytic review of TPB, Armitage and Connor (2001) concluded that the theory is an effective model to validate user acceptance of innovation and the three antecedents of TPB model directly and indirectly predict individual behaviour for a number of innovations. TPB has been used in numerous IS innovation adoption contexts to predict and explain individual behavioural intentions as well as the actual use of innovation (Brown & Venkatesh, 2005; Venkatesh et al., 2003).

TPB model has also been used to examine IS security innovation adoption studies. For example, Lee and Kozar (2005) used TPB model to identify the factors influencing the user adoption of anti-spyware systems. The research examines the influence of three constructs of TPB i.e. attitude, social influence and Perceived Behavioural Control (PBC) for anti-spyware adoption of individuals. Similarly, in a review to observe the user behaviour to conscious care behaviour in the domain of information security, Safa et al. (2015) utilised TPB model. Lee and Kozar (2008) applied DOI and TPB model for an empirical investigation of anti-spyware adoption of computer users. The study investigates the attributes of DOI and TPB for user's anti-spyware adoption intention.

Like all other innovation adoption models discussed above, TPB has certain limitations, which needs to be considered when applied in the innovation adoption research. Albeit TPB considers normative influences, it still does not take into account the influence of environmental or organisational factors that may influence the innovation adoption. As a result, researchers extend TPB by combining its constructs with the components from other contextual frameworks such as TOE.

TOE Model

Tornatzky and Fleischer (1990) synthesized a structure for organisational innovation adoption based on the Contingency Theory of Organisations. The framework identified determinants of technology, organisation and environment as three dimensions of a firm that affects organisational adoption. Hence, the framework was named as "TOE" framework. In this framework, the technological context relates to both internal and external technologies available to an organisation. Its main focus is on how the existing technologies within the organisation as well as the available innovations external to the firm influences the innovation adoption process. The organisational context describes the impact of the characteristics of firms on innovation adoption process. Common organisation characteristics include firm size, degree of centralization and formalization, the complexity of its management structure, the quality of its human resources, and the number of slack resources available internally. The external environmental context is the arena, in which an organisation conducts its business (Tornatzky & Fleischer, 1990). This includes the industry, competitors, regulations, and relationships with the government.

TOE framework unravels the limitations of other innovation adoption and user acceptance models to predict innovation adoption in organisations. TOE model describes the impact of specific attributes in the three contextual domains of organisations towards the innovation adoption process. TOE framework can be combined with other theories to better explain IS innovation adoption in organisations.

Synthesizing IS Security Innovation Adoption Model

The model for the adoption of IS security innovation in organisations we presented in this study consists of a combination of innovation adoption and user acceptance theories jointly with contextual frameworks of IT innovation adoption. It is evident from the literature that previous scholarly IS security adoption contributions have on no account addressed organisational adoption process and user acceptance of innovation in a single investigation. By and large, IS security adoption studies have examined individual attitudes and behaviour towards innovation (Jones et al., 2010; Lee & Kozar, 2008; Safa et al., 2015). Research on IS security rarely considers the adoption process at the organisational level.

IS Security Innovation Adoption Process

Establishing the views of IS innovation literature and consistent with the model presented by Hameed et al. (2012a), the model we presented in this study discusses IS security innovation adoption for organisations as a two level adoption process, an organisational level analysis and individual or user level evaluation. The developments the organisations undergo from the introduction of the IS security innovation until the actual acquisition of the innovation is regarded as an organisational level adoption process. Following that, the user acceptance of innovation and the continuous use of the innovation as an IS security application within the organisation is classified as an individual level adoption process.

To concur with the basics of much of the previous research in IS innovation adoption (Hameed et al., 2012a; Pierce, and Delbecq, 1977; Rogers, 1995) this study considered IS security innovation adoption process in organisations as a three stage process of pre-adoption, adoption-decision and post-adoption. The study deems that the pre-adoption stage consisting of activities related to recognizing a need, acquiring knowledge or awareness, forming an attitude towards the innovation and proposing innovation for adoption (Gopalakrishnan & Damanpour, 1997; Rogers, 1995). The adoption-decision stage described by Hameed et al. (2012a) reflects the decision to accept the idea and evaluates the proposed ideas from a technical, financial and strategic perspective, together with the allocation of resources for its acquisition and implementation. The study also considered the post-adoption stage, which involves the acquisition of innovation, preparing the organisation for the use of the innovation, performing a trial for confirmation of innovation, acceptance of the innovation by users and continued actual use of the innovation (Rogers, 1995).

Integrating Innovation Adoption Models

The study synthesized the conceptual model for IS security innovation adoption in organisations by integrating four theoretical replicas of innovation adoption and user acceptance of IS. The model is an integrated combination of DOI, TAM, TPB models together with the TOE framework. DOI is the most generally accepted model for identifying the main characteristics of IS innovation adoption (Hameed et al., 2012a; Premkumar & Roberts, 1999; Thong et al., 1996). However, the model cannot be used to explain full IS security innovation adoption process as it does not include the post-adoption behaviour of the innovation adoption. In addition, DOI only explicates the individual level adoption process which inhibits the model to utilise in explaining IS security innovation adoption in organisations. Combining DOI with TAM and TPB helps us to derive a model that reflects pre-adoption, adoption-decision and post-adoption stages of IS security innovation adoption. TAM and TPB have been used in empirical investigations to predict and explain user acceptance of IS innovation (Hameed & Counsell, 2014b). TPB complements TAM's constructs at the same time TPB explanatory and predictive power enhances further by integrating with TAM (Awa et al., 2014). Furthermore, TAM combined with TPB constructs would allow predicting user acceptance of innovations for both volitional and non-volitional conditions (Hameed et al., 2012a). DOI, TAM and TPB models have been successfully exploited and effectively been used in explaining and predicting either the adoption or user acceptance of IS innovations by individuals (Hameed et al., 2012a). In order for our IS security adoption model to address organisational level adoption process, integrative illustration of DOI, TAM and TPB have to be combined with a contextual framework. The TOE model has been extensively adapted for the studies of IS adoption in organisations (Premkumar & Roberts, 1999; Quaddus & Hofmeyer, 2007; Teo et al., 2009). Thus, an integrative model consisting of DOI, TAM, TPB and TOE would fully explain IS security innovation adoption in organisations.

Use of DOI and TOE in the proposed model could successfully explicate the adoption process at organisation perspective. In light of the technology, organisation and environment attributes that facilitate the adoption, both DOI and TOE competently elucidate pre-adoption and adoption-decision stages of IS security adoption in organisations. The proposed model uses the constructs of TAM and TPB to account for the user acceptance of IS security innovation. Hence, the user acceptance attributes of TAM and TPB affect the IS security adoption process at the post-adoption stage. TPB has been a particularly useful model to predict user acceptance of IS innovations in organisations, where the use of IS is not entirely under the volitional control of the user.

Proposed Model of IS Security Innovation in Organisation

Figure 1 illustrates our proposed conceptual model for the IS security innovation adoption in organisations.

DETERMINANTS OF SECURITY INNOVATION ADOPTION

For the IS security adoption model shown in the Figure 1, we considered technology, organisation, environment and user acceptance attributes that were examined in the past IS innovation adoption literature. In addition, each of the factors included in proposed model have been examined and found to have a significant influence on IS security innovation adoption research.

Figure 1. Model for the adoption of information system security innovation in organisations

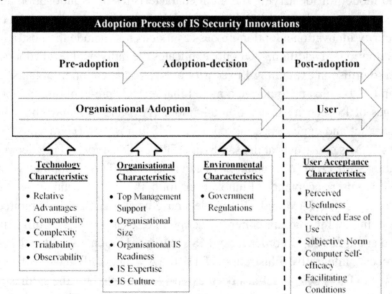

Technology Characteristics

Technological context of TOE model outlines a number of attributes of technologies inside the organisation and the innovations available outside the firm. The importance of technology attributes for the adoption and implementation of IS and the perception of innovations influencing the pre-adoption and adoption-decisions have been documented in the IS literature (Rogers, 1983). Specific characteristics of innovation are examined as factors that explain innovation adoption in organisations. DOI theory provides a set of innovation attributes that may affect the adoption decision (Rogers, 1995).

For this study, we considered the relative advantage, compatibility, complexity, trialability and observability in terms of technology characteristics. Lee and Kozar (2005) and Lee and Kozar (2008) examined anti-spyware software adoption and found that relative advantage, compatibility, trialability and visibility (observability) as important determinants. Salleh et al. (2015) suggests that perceived complexity and perceived compatibility of innovation are important attributes of big data security solutions adoption.

Relative Advantage

Relative Advantage is the degree to which the innovation is perceived as better than the idea it supersedes (Hameed & Counsell, 2014a). Relative advantage refers to the degree to which the innovation is more productive, costs saving, less maintenance, efficient compared to the existing practices (Rogers, 1995). Indeed, relative advantage is one of the key determinants that would influence a person or an organisation to adopt an IS innovation (Hameed & Counsell, 2014a; Moore & Benbasat, 1991). Hence, we suggest that organisations are more likely to adopt IS security innovation when they perceive that it is a valuable and effective means of protecting their IS assets.

Compatibility

Compatibility is the degree to which an innovation is perceived as being consistent with the existing values, past experiences and needs of the users (Hameed & Counsell, 2014a; Rogers, 1995). An innovation must be considered generally acceptable if it is to be implemented successfully. The more compatible the new innovation is with the existing processes and systems, the more easily the innovation gets implemented and integrated into the organisation (Hameed & Counsell, 2014a). According to Lee and Kozar (2005), if the IS security innovation is compatible with the current system, the less resistance the organisation will experience accepting the innovation. Hence, compatibility of an IS security innovation is positively related to adoption and implementation within the organisation.

Complexity

Complexity is the degree to which the innovation is perceived as difficult to understand and use (Rogers, 1995). Innovations that are simple to comprehend are more likely to be adopted by organisations. The complexity of an innovation is expected to negatively influence for the adoption of IS innovations in organisations (Hameed & Counsell, 2014a; Tornatzky & Klein, 1982). Hence, less complex IS security innovations are believed to adopt faster and propagates a smooth implementation process, thereby achieving the anticipated efficiency.

Trialability

Rogers (1995) defines "trialibility" as the degree to which the innovation may be experimented with. Hence, IS innovations are likely to be adopted if they can be tried out on a temporary basis. Being able to try an innovation before adoption reduces the uncertainty of potential adopters (Tornatzky & Klein, 1982). Trialability is important in the initiation stages of innovation adoption, however, its implication will affect the usage of the innovation. The literature suggests a positive relationship between trialability and innovation adoption (Hameed & Counsell, 2014a; Rogers, 1995). In this model, we assume that the better exposure one gets to a particular IS security innovation, the more likely that it will be adopted and used in an organisation.

Observability

Observability is the degree to which the results and the advantages of an innovation are visible to others (Rogers, 1995). Hence, observability is sometimes referred to as "visibility." Lee and Kozar (2008) investigated the adoption of anti-spyware software and found that observability has a significant impact on the probability of adoption. The more visible or observable the usage and the outcome of an IS security innovation, the more likely the innovation will be adopted and implemented in an organisation. Observability is expected to have a positive relationship with adoption of innovations (Rogers, 1995).

Organisational Characteristics

The organisational context of TOE model has been the most frequently examined attributes in adoption of IS innovations in organisations. The attributes of organisational context address the facilitating and inhibiting factors in the area of operations in a firm. Researchers have advocated the primary importance of organisational determinants compared to other contexts as predictors for innovation adoption (Damanpour, 1991; Hameed et al., 2012b). Organisations are adopting innovations in response to an external demand or to achieve an advantage of an environmental opportunity (Hameed & Counsell, 2012). For this study, we propose top management support, organisational size, organisational IS readiness, IS expertise and IS culture as organisational attributes that influence IS security adoption.

To verify IS conscious care behaviour formation in organisations, Safa et al. (2015) found IS awareness, IS experience and organisation policy as important factors. IS awareness and IS experience described by Safa et al. (2015) is often described as a single attribute in the IS literature, namely: IS expertise (Hameed et al., 2012b). Hence, for the proposed model of IS security adoption, we refer IS expertise that takes account of the organisational awareness and experience of the innovation. Li (2015) verified that the size of the organisations impacted on online security performance in organisations. Salleh et al. (2015) utilised the TOE framework to explore top management support, IS culture and organisational learning culture as security determinants of big data solutions. According to Leidner and Kayworth (2006), IS culture is a variable that explains how social groups interacts with IS in the development, adoption, use and its management. Hence, IS policy suggested by Safa et al. (2015) and IS learning culture described by Salleh et al. (2015) could simply be classified under IS culture. In our proposed model, we included IS culture as a determinant that accounts the perception of IS policy and IS learning culture. Lee and

Kozar (2005) and Lee and Kozar (2008) found that computing capacity of the organisation significantly influence anti-spyware systems adoption. In the IS literature, computing capacity is termed as IS readiness and we adopt this terminology in our model.

Top Management Support

A recurring, organisational factor studied by IS researchers is top management support. Top management support is one of the consistently found and a highly critical factor that influence IS implementation (Thong et al,. 1996). It is commonly believed that top management support plays a vital role in all stages of adoption of IS (Hameed et al., 2012b). There is also evidence in the innovation literature that suggests top management support is positively related to the adoption of new technologies in organisations (Tornatzky & Klein, 1982). For IS security adoption, top management's role in allocating the required resource to safeguard IS asserts and to provide a supportive climate in the user acceptance of innovations is vital.

Organisational Size

Organisational size has been the most frequently examined factor in the study of organisational innovation adoption (Premkumar & Roberts, 1999). Organisational size is the most important factor influencing IS adoption, since, the size of an organisation determines other organisational aspects, particularly slack resources, decision making and organisational structure (Rogers, 1995). As the size of the organisation gives a good indication of the slack resources available, we suggest that organisational size has a positive influence on the adoption of IS security innovation.

Organisational IS Readiness

Organisational IS readiness is defined as the degree to which an organisation has the knowledge, resources, commitment and governance to adopt IS innovations (Hameed et al., 2012b). Adoption of IS has often been positively associated with organisational IS readiness. IS infrastructure and computing resources are essential to successfully implement and gain advantages from any IS adoption (Premkumar & Ramamurthy, 1995). Prior studies revealed a positive association between the existence of IS readiness and adoption of IS (Hameed et al., 2012b). We suggest that the existence of IS infrastructure and the availability of financial and technological resources within an organisation influence the adoption of IS security innovations.

IS Expertise

In an organisation, knowledge of IT is a major factor in the adoption of new technologies (Fichman & Kemerer, 1997). An organisation with existing knowledge of new innovation makes adoption effortless and retains knowledge of innovation adoption (Lertwongsatien & Wongpinunwatana, 2003). For the study, firm's possession of the awareness of IS security and expertise of IS security threats within an organisation helps the adoption of IS security innovations.

IS Culture

Introduction of a new IS fundamentally changes the way the organisation solves problems and this process results in the creation of a new IS culture. Organisational culture has also been shown to play a significant role in IS management policies (Cabrera et al., 2001). Organisational culture can support IS adoption and can thus be a critical success factor for the development and implementation of IS innovations.

Furnell and Thomson (2009) investigated IS culture and found to have a positive effect on IS security adoption. We propose that organisational beliefs and values regarding IS security and the existing IS security policies play an important role in the IS behaviour of an organisation.

Environmental Characteristics

IS has not only been used for internal needs; instead, organisations often communicate with customers, suppliers and other trading partners (Hameed & Counsell, 2012). Hence, environmental factors are increasingly being studied in innovation adoption studies. The recommended attribute of this study in terms of environmental context is government regulation (Hameed & Counsell, 2012; Jeon et al., 2006). Li (2015) verified that the existence of government regulation significantly influenced online security adoption in organisations.

Government Regulations

The regulatory environment and governmental institutions enforce policies on taxes, trade, investment, patents, product liability, consumer protection and human resources that may have a powerful effect on technology adoption. Numerous researchers have highlighted the role of government regulations on the adoption decision of IS innovation (Hameed & Counsell, 2012). This study suggests that government's support and regulatory policies may have a huge impact on IS security adoption and implementation.

User Acceptance Characteristics

Constructs of TAM and TPB contribute most towards user acceptance attributes. The two attributes of TAM, perceived usefulness and perceived ease of use were key determinants of user IS acceptance (Hameed & Counsell, 2014b). The constructs of TPB namely: attitude, subjective norm and PBC were also key determinants of user acceptance of IS innovations (Armitage & Conner, 2001). Furthermore, two sub-constructs of PBC, computer self-efficacy and facilitating conditions which predicts the non-volitional behaviours were also found to be important characteristics (Hameed & Counsell, 2014b).

Lee and Kozar (2005) found that user acceptance attributes of attitude, social influence and PBC significantly influence anti-spyware systems adoption. Lee and Kozar (2008) examined anti-spyware software adoption and found that user acceptance attributes of attitude, subjective norm and self-efficacy are important determinants. Jones et al. (2010) examined TAM attributes and found perceived usefulness; perceived ease of use and subjective norm had a significant impact on user intention to use IS security measures. To verify IS conscious care behaviour formation in organisations, Safa et al. (2015) found an important relationship with user attitude, subjective norm and self-efficacy.

As our proposed model uses the constructs of TAM and TPB to account for the user acceptance of IS security innovation, the factors included were perceived usefulness, perceived ease of use, subjective norm, computer self-efficacy and facilitating condition. Venkatesh and Davis (2000) and Hameed and Counsell (2014b) also considered these five characteristics to determine user acceptance of IS innovation.

Perceived Usefulness

Perceived usefulness is defined as "the degree to which a person believes that using a particular system would enhance his or her job performance (Davis, 1989). Perceived usefulness is a major determinant of intention to use the innovation and was found to have a direct effect on the usage behaviour. Much of the previous research has investigated TAM, and confirmed that perceived usefulness is the strongest predictor of an individual's intention to use an innovation (Venkatesh & Davis, 2000; Venkatesh et al., 2003). In our proposed model, we define perceived usefulness as the degree which as an individual believes that the use of IS security innovation will virtually secure his or her IS assets.

Perceived Ease of Use

Perceived ease of use is "the degree to which a person believes that using a particular system would be free of effort (Davis, 1989). TAM suggests that perceived ease of use has a significant influence on perceived usefulness, behavioural attitude, intention, and actual use of an innovation (Davis et al., 1989). In this research, we define perceived ease of use as the extent to which an individual perceives that the interaction with the IS security innovations is effortless.

Subjective Norms

Fishbein and Ajzen (1975) described subjective norms as the pressure enforces on individuals by people or organisations important to them, to perform or not to perform a particular behaviour. For our proposed model, subjective norms is the social pressure on the employee of an organisation by the management, supervisor, head of department and colleagues to accept or reject an IS security innovation. This pressure affects the employee's acceptance decision and the use of IS security innovations.

Computer Self-Efficacy

Computer self-efficacy is defined as an individual's self-confidence in one's ability to perform a behaviour (Hameed & Counsell, 2014b). In the context of IS security adoption, the dimension of self-efficacy is defined as an individual's beliefs about their ability to proficiently implement preventive security behaviours and use preventive security tools (Wynn et al., 2012). In the information security adoption literature, self-efficacy has been found to be significantly associated with both intentions (Liang & Xue, 2010) and use (Ng et al., 2009) of IS security innovations. Hence, it is expected that higher levels of computer self-efficacy will cause higher levels of PBC, thus with increased intentions to use IS security innovation.

Facilitating Condition

Facilitating conditions is the degree to which an individual believes that an organisational and technical infrastructure exists to support the use of the innovation (Venkatesh et al., 2003). IS security requires preventive software and tools in addition to technical supports to the user (Wynn et al., 2012). This study suggests that the more support services available to the users, the better chance that the users accept and trust the IS security innovation.

CONCLUSION AND FUTURE RESEARCH

In this study, we developed and proposed a model for the process of IS security innovation adoption in organisations. The study considered the IS security innovation adoption process to be successful only if the innovation is accepted and integrated into the organisation and the individual users continue using the innovation. The study described IS innovation adoption process as a two level decision proceeding: an organisational level adoption judgement followed by the verdict of the users regarding the innovation. Thus, the model exemplifies a two level of evaluation, i.e. from the initiation stage until the acquisition of innovation was assessed as organisational process and the process of user acceptance of the innovation is analysed in terms of the behaviour of the individuals within the organisation. Furthermore, the proposed model portrayed the IS security adoption process, as progressing in three distinct phases, from pre-adoption through adoption-decision and then post-adoption stages.

The basis of the model is derived by replicating theories and models used in the studies of innovation adoption and user acceptance of IS innovation. The study integrated perspectives from DOI, TAM, TPB and TOE to depict IS security innovation adoption process in organisations. The model exploited DOI model and TOE framework to characterize the organisational adoption process until the acquisition of innovation and the constructs of TAM and TPB explains the user acceptance of IS security innovation. The model also included several factors from different contexts that is perceived to impact IS security innovation adoption in organisations. The study suggests that relative advantage, compatibility, complexity, trialability and observability of the innovation influences the IS security adoption in an organisation. In terms of organisational characteristics, the study proposes top management support, the size of the firm, IS readiness, IS expertise and IS culture to impact IS security innovation adoption process. In addition, the study advocates that government regulations are key to the adoption decision of IS security adoption in organisations. The study suggests that perceived usefulness, perceived ease of use, subjective norm, computer self-efficacy and facilitating conditions are factors that enables users to accept IS security innovations.

The proposed model presented has considerable significance in understanding the process involved in the adoption of IS security innovation in organisations. Also, it allows highlighting the key steps to navigate to achieve a successful adoption of IS security innovations. Equally, the study provides researchers and practitioners with a set of factors that affect the adoption of IS security in organisations. It serves as a guideline for practitioners to identify and address the facilitating and inhibiting issues in the context of technology, organisation, environment and user acceptance attributes in the process of IS security adoption. Managers need to consider these issues when embarking on IS security adoption in their organisations.

The contribution of the study includes an enhancement of our understanding of IS security adoption and implementation process in organisations. It draws upon and merged from the rich literature in IS innovation adoption theories and applies it in the context of IS security where, it has seldom been examined. To overcome the shortcomings of individual IS innovation adoption models such as the DOI and TAM; the proposed model combined a number of innovation adoption models. Combining different innovation adoption models allows the individual model to complement each other, strengthening the analytical ability of the proposed model. Another important contribution of this research is that the proposed IS security model considers both the organisational adoption process and the user acceptance of innovation in a single illustration. Incorporating the organisational adoption process and the user acceptance of innovation in a single representation allows to explain IS security innovation adoption process more thoroughly. In addition, the proposed model introduces several determinants from technology, organisation, environment and user acceptance characteristics that may influence IS security adoption in organisations.

The IS security adoption model proposed in this study provides important implications for practice as well as for further research. This study has a number of implications for managers and IS researchers. Managers can draw up this model and assess the condition of the IS security adoption process and possible factors that would lead to a successful adoption of IS security innovations in their organisations. In addition, managers can utilise the model to plan and prepare for the adoption process and establish smooth conditions for the user acceptance in the IS security implementation process. In addition, the model is of great interest to academics because it provides them new literature with an approach to IS security adoption and benefits from the point of view of the development of industrial IS security applications. Also, IT practitioners may utilise this model to investigate the factors influencing the adoption of IS security innovations in various demographic settings; the model could be tested by organisations from different sectors and different countries. We believe that the model will serve as a useful conceptual tool for further research on the IS security adoption behaviour.

The study has some limitations that need to be considered when interpreting the results. First, as this is a theoretical model, unavailability of any empirical insights of the model limits us to draw causal implications of the findings. Second, the methodology used and the methodological screening imposed for the inclusion and exclusion of studies may limit interpretation of the results. This is one of the limitations of our research that was unavoidable as the number studies that examined IS security adoption is very scarce. Third, limitation may be publication bias. As for any literature study, the review of studies may have been subjected to publication bias. However, with every effort to cover all the literature on IS security innovation adoption; the study may not be completely immune to publication bias. Another limitation is that this research obtained technology, organisation, environment and user acceptance attributes from a small number of studies. This could result in a narrow scope that does not adequately capture all determinants relating to IS security adoption.

In terms of future research, the proposed model may be empirically tested to verify the effectiveness in predicting IS security adoption in organisations. Another obvious addition to this study would be to experimentally examine the impact of the attributes identified in the proposed model. As the model gives no indication of the significance of each factor for different stages of IS security adoption, the researchers could extend this study by analysing the interaction between different characteristics at different stages of the IS security adoption process.

REFERENCES

Ajzen, I. (1991). The Theory of Planned Behaviour. *Organizational Behavior and Human Decision Processes, 50*(2), 179–211. doi:10.1016/0749-5978(91)90020-T

Albuquerque-Junior, A. E., & Santos, E. M. (2015). Adoption of Information Security Measures in Public Research Institutes. *Journal of Information Systems and Technology Management, 12*(2), 289–316. doi:10.4301/S1807-17752015000200006

Almomani, A., Gupta, B. B., Atawneh, S., Meulenberg, A., & Almomani, E. (2013a). A Survey of Phishing Email Filtering Techniques. *IEEE Communications Surveys and Tutorials, 15*(4), 2070–2090. doi:10.1109/SURV.2013.030713.00020

Almomani, A., Gupta, B. B., Wan, T., & Altaher, A. (2013b). Phishing Dynamic Evolving Neural Fuzzy Framework for Online Detection Zero-day Phishing Email. *Indian Journal of Science and Technology, 6*(1), 122–126.

Alshboul, A. (2010). Information Systems Security Measures and Countermeasures: Protecting Organisational Assets from Malicious Attacks. Communications of the IBIMA, 9.

Arachchilage, N. A. G. (2016). *Serious Games for Cyber Security Education*. LAP Lambert Academic Publishing. Retrieved from https://arxiv.org/abs/1610.09511

Arachchilage, N. A. G., & Love, S. (2013). A Game Design Framework for Avoiding Phishing Attack. *Computers in Human Behavior, 29*(3), 706–714. doi:10.1016/j.chb.2012.12.018

Arachchilage, N. A. G., & Love, S. (2014). Security Awareness of Computer Users: A Phishing Threat Avoidance Perspective. *Computers in Human Behavior, 38*, 304–312. doi:10.1016/j.chb.2014.05.046

Arachchilage, N. A. G., Love, S., & Beznosov, K. (2016). Phishing Threat Avoidance Behaviour: An Empirical Investigation. *Computers in Human Behavior, 60*, 185–197. doi:10.1016/j.chb.2016.02.065

Arachchilage, N. A. G., & Martin, A. (2014). *A Trust Domains Taxonomy for Securely Sharing Information: A Preliminary Investigation*. HAISA.

Arachchilage, N. A. G., Namiluko, C., & Martin, A. (2013). A Taxonomy for Securely Sharing Information among Others in a Trust Domain. In *Internet Technology and Secured Transactions (ICITST). 8th International Conference for 2013*. IEEE.

Armitage, C. J., & Conner, M. (2001). Efficacy of the Theory of Planned Behaviour: A Meta-analysis Review. *British Journal of Social Psychology, 40*(4), 471–499. doi:10.1348/014466601164939 PMID:11795063

Awa, H. O., Ojiabo, O. U., & Emecheta, B. C. (2014). Integrating TAM, TPB and TOE Frameworks and Expanding their Characteristic Constructs for E-commerce Adoption by SMEs. *Journal of Science and Technology Policy Management, 6*(1), 76–94. doi:10.1108/JSTPM-04-2014-0012

Ben-Asher, N., & Gonzalez, C. (2015). Effects of cyber security knowledge on attack detection. *Computers in Human Behavior, 48*, 51–61. doi:10.1016/j.chb.2015.01.039

Brown, S. A., & Venkatesh, V. (2005). A Model of Adoption of Technology in the Household: A Baseline Model Test and Extension Incorporating Household Life Cycle. *Management Information Systems Quarterly, 29*(3), 399–426. doi:10.2307/25148690

Cabrera, A., Cabrera, E. F., & Barajas, S. (2001). The Key Role of Organizational Culture in a Multi-System View of Technology-Driven Change. *International Journal of Information Management, 21*(3), 245–261. doi:10.1016/S0268-4012(01)00013-5

Chatterjee, S., Sarker, S., & Valacich, J. S. (2015). The Behavioral Roots of Information Systems Security: Exploring Key Factors Related to Unethical IT Use. *Journal of Management Information Systems, 31*(4), 49–87. doi:10.1080/07421222.2014.1001257

Claar, C. L., & Johnson, J. (2010). Analyzing the Adoption of Computer Security Utilizing the Health Belief Model. *Issues in Information Systems, 11*(1), 286–291.

Claar, C. L., & Johnson, J. (2012). Analyzing Home PC Security Adoption Behaviour. *Journal of Computer Information Systems, 52*(4), 20–29.

Damanpour, F. (1991). Organisational Innovation: A Meta-analysis of Effects of Determinants and Moderators. *Academy of Management Journal, 34*(3), 555–590.

Damanpour, F., & Wischnevsky, J. D. (2006). Research on Organisational Innovation: Distinguishing Innovation-Generating from Innovation-Adopting Organisations. *Journal of Engineering and Technology Management, 23*(4), 269–291. doi:10.1016/j.jengtecman.2006.08.002

Davis, F. D. (1989). Perceived Usefulness, Perceived Ease of Use, Acceptance of Information Technology. *Management Information Systems Quarterly, 13*(3), 319–340. doi:10.2307/249008

Davis, F. D., Bagozzi, R. P., & Warshaw, P. R. (1989). User Acceptance of Computer Technology: A Comparison of Two Theoretical Models. *Management Science, 35*(8), 982–1003. doi:10.1287/mnsc.35.8.982

Feruza, Y. S., & Kim, T. (2007). IT Security Review: Privacy, Protection, Access Control, Assurance and System Security. *International Journal of Multimedia and Ubiquitous Engineering, 2*(2), 17–32.

Fichman, R. G., & Kemerer, C. F. (1997). The Assimilation of Software Process Innovations: An Organizational Learning Perspective. *Management Science, 43*(1), 1345–1363. doi:10.1287/mnsc.43.10.1345

Fishbein, M., & Ajzen, I. (1975). *Belief, Attitude, Intention and Behaviour: An Introduction to Theory and Research*. Addison-Wesley.

Furnell, S. M., & Thompson, K. L. (2009). From Culture to Disobedience: Recognising the Varying User Acceptance of IT Security. *Computer Fraud & Security, 2009*(2), 5–10. doi:10.1016/S1361-3723(09)70019-3

Gopalakrishnan, S., & Damanpour, F. (1997). A Review of Innovation Research in Economics, Sociology and Technology Management. *Omega, International Journal of Management Science, 25*(1), 15–28.

Gross, J. B., & Mary, B. R. (2007). Looking for trouble: understanding end-user security management. In *Proc. The 2007 Symposium on Computer Human interaction For the Management of information Technology*. ACM. 10.1145/1234772.1234786

Gupta, B. B., Agrawal, D. P., & Yamaguchi, S. (2016). *Handbook of Research on Modern Cryptographic Solutions for Computer and Cyber Security*. IGI Global. doi:10.4018/978-1-5225-0105-3

Gupta, B. B., Arachchilage, N. A. G., & Psannis, K. E. (2018). (2018) Defending against Phishing Attacks: Taxonomy of Methods, Current Issues and Future Directions. *Telecommunication Systems*, *67*(2), 247–267. doi:10.100711235-017-0334-z

Hameed, M. A., & Arachchilage, N. A. G. (2016). A Model for the Adoption Process of Information System Security Innovations in Organisations: A Theoretical Perspective. In *Proc. the 27th Australasian Conference on Information Systems*. ACIS. Retrieved from https://arxiv.org/abs/1609.07911

Hameed, M. A., & Counsell, S. (2012). Assessing the Influence of Environmental and CEO Characteristics for Adoption of Information Technology in Organizations. *Journal of Technology Management & Innovation*, *7*(1), 64–84. doi:10.4067/S0718-27242012000100005

Hameed, M. A., & Counsell, S. (2014a). Establishing Relationship between Innovation Characteristics and IT Innovation Adoption in Organisations: A Meta-analysis Approach. *International Journal of Innovation Management*, *18*(1), 41. doi:10.1142/S1363919614500078

Hameed, M. A., & Counsell, S. (2014b). User Acceptance Determinants of Information Technology Innovation in Organisations. *International Journal of Innovation and Technology Management*, *11*(5), 7. doi:10.1142/S0219877014500333

Hameed, M. A., Counsell, S., & Swift, S. (2012a). A Conceptual Model for the Process of IT Innovation Adoption in Organisations. *Journal of Engineering and Technology Management*, *29*(3), 358–390. doi:10.1016/j.jengtecman.2012.03.007

Hameed, M. A., Counsell, S., & Swift, S. (2012b). A Meta-analysis of Relationships between Organisational Characteristics and IT Innovation Adoption in Organisations. *Information & Management*, *49*(5), 218–232. doi:10.1016/j.im.2012.05.002

Jeon, B. N., Han, K. S., & Lee, M. J. (2006). Determining Factors for the Adoption of E-Business: The Case of SMEs in Korea. *Applied Economics*, *38*(16), 1905–1916. doi:10.1080/00036840500427262

Jones, C. M., McCarthy, R. V., Halawi, L., & Mujtaba, B. (2010). Utilizing the Technology Acceptance Model to Access the Employee Adoption of Information System Security Measures. *Issues in Information Systems*, *11*(1), 9–16.

Kaspersky lab. (2015). *Damage Control: The Cost of Security Breaches*. Retrieved from https://media.kaspersky.com/pdf/it-risks-survey-report-cost-of-security-breaches.pdf

Kim, H., Lee, D., & Ham, S. (2013). Impact of Hotel Information Security on System Reliability. *International Journal of Hospitality Management*, *35*, 369–379. doi:10.1016/j.ijhm.2012.06.002

Lee, Y., & Kozar, K. A. (2005). Investigating Factors Affecting Adoption of Anti-spyware Systems. *Communications of the ACM*, *48*(8), 72–77. doi:10.1145/1076211.1076243

Lee, Y., & Kozar, K. A. (2008). An Empirical Investigation of Anti-spyware Software Adoption: A Multi-theoretical Perspective. *Information & Management*, *45*(2), 109–119. doi:10.1016/j.im.2008.01.002

Legris, P., Ingham, J., & Collerette, P. (2003). Why do People Use Information Technology? A Critical Review of the Technology Acceptance Model. *Information & Management*, *40*(3), 191–204. doi:10.1016/S0378-7206(01)00143-4

Leidner, D. E., & Kayworth, T. (2006). Review: A Review of Culture in Information Systems Research: Towards a Theory of Information Technology Culture Conflict. *Management Information Systems Quarterly*, *30*(2), 357–399. doi:10.2307/25148735

Lertwongsatien, C., & Wongpinunwatana, N. (2003). E-commerce Adoption in Thailand: An Empirical Study of Small and Medium Enterprises (SMEs). *Journal of Global Information Technology Management*, *6*(3), 67–83. doi:10.1080/1097198X.2003.10856356

Li, D. C. (2015). Online Security Performances and Information Security Disclosures. *Journal of Computer Information Systems*, *55*(2), 20–28. doi:10.1080/08874417.2015.11645753

Liang, H., & Xue, Y. (2010). Understanding Security Behaviours in Personal Computer Usage: A Threat Avoidance Perspective. *Journal of the Association for Information Systems*, *11*(7), 394–413. doi:10.17705/1jais.00232

Memos, V. A., Psannis, K. E., Ishibashi, Y., Kim, B., & Gupta, B. B. (2017). An Efficient Algorithm for Media-based Surveillance System (EAMSuS) in IoT Smart City Framework. In Future Generation Computer Systems. Elsevier.

Moore, G. C., & Benbasat, I. (1991). Development of an Instrument to Measure the Perceptions of Adopting an Information Technology Innovation. *Information Systems Research*, *2*(3), 173–191. doi:10.1287/isre.2.3.192

Ng, B. Y., Kankanhalli, A., & Xu, Y. C. (2009). Studying Users' Computer Security Behavior: A Health Belief Perspective. *Decision Support Systems*, *46*(4), 815–825. doi:10.1016/j.dss.2008.11.010

Pierce, J. L., & Delbecq, A. L. (1977). Organisation Structure, Individual Attitudes and Innovation. *Academy of Management Review*, *2*(1), 27–37. doi:10.5465/amr.1977.4409154

Premkumar, G., & Ramamurthy, K. (1995). The Role of Inter-organizational and Organizational Factors on the Decision Mode for the Adoption of Inter-organizational Systems. *Decision Sciences*, *26*(3), 303–336. doi:10.1111/j.1540-5915.1995.tb01431.x

Premkumar, G., & Roberts, M. (1999). Adoption of New Information Technologies in Rural Small Businesses. *Journal of Management Science*, *27*(4), 467–484.

Quaddus, M., & Hofmeyer, G. (2007). An Investigation into the Factors Influencing the Adoption of B2B Trading Exchanges in Small Businesses. *European Journal of Information Systems*, *16*(3), 202–215. doi:10.1057/palgrave.ejis.3000671

Rogers, E. M. (1983). *Diffusion of Innovations* (3rd ed.). New York: The Free Press.

Rogers, E. M. (1995). *Diffusion of Innovations*. New York: The Free Press.

Safa, N. S., Sookhak, M., Solms, R. V., Furnell, S., Abdul-Ghani, N., & Herawam, T. (2015). Information Security Conscious Care Behaviour Formation in Organisations. *Computers & Security, 53*, 65–78. doi:10.1016/j.cose.2015.05.012

Salleh, K. A., Janczewski, L., & Beltran, F. (2015). SEC-TOE Framework: Exploring Security: Determinants in Big Data Solutions Adoption. *Proc, of the Pacific Asia Conference on Information Systems (PACIS)*, 203.

Stergioua, C., Psannisa, K. E., & Gupta, B.B. (2016). Secure Integration of IoT and Cloud Computing. In Future Generation Computer Systems. Elsevier.

Teo, T. S. H., Lin, S., & Lai, K. (2009). Adopters and Non-adopters of E-Procurement in Singapore: An Empirical Study. *Omega. International Journal of Management Sciences, 37*(5), 972–987.

Tewari, A., & Gupta, B. B. (2017). Cryptanalysis of a Novel Ultra-lightweight Mutual Authentication Protocol for IoT Devices using RFID Tags. *The Journal of Supercomputing, 73*(3), 1085–1102. doi:10.100711227-016-1849-x

Tewari, A., Jain, A., & Gupta, B. B. (2016). Recent Survey of Various Defense Mechanisms against Phishing Attacks. *Journal of Information Privacy and Security, 12*(1), 3–13. doi:10.1080/15536548.2016.1139423

Thong, J. Y. L., Yap, C., & Raman, K. S. (1996). Top Management Support, External Expertise and Information Systems Implementation in Small Businesses. *Information Systems Research, 7*(2), 248–267. doi:10.1287/isre.7.2.248

Tornatzky, L. G., & Fleischer, M. (1990). The Process of Technological Innovation. Lexington Books.

Tornatzky, L. G., & Klein, K. J. (1982). Innovation Characteristics and Innovation Adoption Implementation: A Meta-analysis of Findings. *IEEE Transactions on Engineering Management, 29*(1), 28–45. doi:10.1109/TEM.1982.6447463

Tuncalp, D. (2014). Diffusion and Adoption of Information Security Management Standards across Countries and Industries. *Journal of Global Information Technology Management, 17*(4), 221–227. doi:10.1080/1097198X.2014.982454

Venkatesh, V., & Bala, H. (2008). Technology Acceptance Model 3 and a Research Agenda on Interventions. *Decision Sciences, 39*(2), 273–315. doi:10.1111/j.1540-5915.2008.00192.x

Venkatesh, V., & Davis, F. D. (2000). A Theoretical Extension of the Technology Acceptance Model: Four Longitudinal Field Studies. *Management Science, 46*(2), 186–204. doi:10.1287/mnsc.46.2.186.11926

Venkatesh, V., Morris, M. G., Davis, G. B., & Davis, F. D. (2003). User Acceptance of Information Technology: Toward a Unified View. *Management Information Systems Quarterly, 27*(3), 425–478. doi:10.2307/30036540

Wang, Y., Wang, Y., Lin, H., & Tang, T. (2003). Determinants of User Acceptance of Internet Banking: An Empirical Study. *International Journal of Service Industry Management, 14*(5), 501–519. doi:10.1108/09564230310500192

Wynn, D. Jr, Karahanna, E., Williams, C. K., & Madupalli, R. (2012). Preventive Adoption of Information Security Behaviours. *Proc. the 33rd International Conference on Information Systems.*

Zhang, Z., Sun, R., & Zhao, C., Wang, J., Chang, C.K., & Gupta, B.B. (2016). CyVOD: A Novel Trinity Multimedia Social Network Scheme. *Multimedia Tools and Applications*, 1–17.

Chapter 15

Theoretical Foundations of Deep Resonance Interference Network:
Towards Intuitive Learning as a Wave Field Phenomenon

Christophe Thovex
LAFMIA (UMI 3175), France & Mexico

ABSTRACT

Digital processes for banks, insurances, or public services generate big data. Hidden networks and weak signals from frauds activities are sometimes statistically undetectable in the endogenous data respective to processes. The organic intelligence of human experts is able to reverse-engineer new fraud scenarios without statistically significant characteristics, but machine learning usually needs to be taught about them or fails to this task. Deep resonance interference network is a multidisciplinary attempt in probabilistic machine learning inspired from waves temporal reversal in finite space, introduced for big data analysis and hidden data mining. It proposes a theoretical alternative to artificial neural networks for deep learning. It is presented along with experimental outcomes related to fraudulent processes generating data statistically similar to legal endogenous data. Results show particular findings probably due to the systemic nature of the model, which appears closer to reasoning and intuition processes than to the perception processes mainly simulated in deep learning.

INTRODUCTION

Intelligence is not what we know, but what we do when we do not know. This statement is commonly attributed to the well-known psychologist JEAN PIAGET, biologist and epistemologist who agreed with the importance of communication and social interactions for the development of language and of human intelligence, as the philosopher H. PUTNAM (Putnam, 1975). According to the historical experimentation supposed to have been led by the roman emperor FREDERICK II HOHENSTAUFEN (1197-1250), when

DOI: 10.4018/978-1-5225-9742-1.ch015

babies cannot communicate with other babies and adults, after a few years they have no cognitive ability to learn language then they cannot acquire normal intellectual capabilities. Hence, human learning is social, and social learning - the action of learning aided by social networks, which are not necessarily digitized - is essential to foster or accelerate the development of intelligence (Balystok & Poarch, 2014). This forms a first statement.

Nevertheless, according to Corballis (2003), babies start to communicate by signs before being physically able to talk and verbalize thoughts with adults. Babies and animals such as dolphins and primates fail to the Turing's test, an imitation game designed to test the existence of thought in computing machinery (Turing, 1950). Obviously, the Turing's test fails to detect thought but estimates the ability of computing machinery to interact with natural language skills. It shows how much *computing machinery only performs what we know how to order it to perform*, as stated by ADA OF LOVELACE and quoted in Turing (1950). This forms a second statement.

Unifying the first and second statements, we may accept the eventuality of an intelligence to be developed with computing machinery without interpreted and outer evidence of its existence - *i.e.*, *Absence of evidence is not evidence of absence*. However, in 2018 we were still unable to say a machine how to play the imitation game and handle the Turing's test more than a few minutes, while adult humans cannot fail to the test, at least in their native language[1]. Anyway, it reminds us how fair was the conclusion of ALAN TURING about thinking machines: "We can only see a short distance ahead, but we can see plenty there that needs to be done" (Turing, 1950).

Since precursor works such as presented in Pitrat (1990), the hypothesis of a self-programming machine offers the promise of an Artificial Intelligence (AI), *i.e.* a genuine AI *doing when it does not know*, according to Piaget's definition of intelligence and performing what we do not know how to order it to perform. J. PITRAT and its general problems solver CAIA opened the Pandora's box providing mathematical solutions to some specialized problems that were never coded, thanks to meta-knowledge (Pitrat, 2010). Because the machine still does not develop itself but does nothing without human programming, it entails there could be no AI in machine learning, just artificial knowledge, finally.

Talking machines (*i.e.,* chatbots) process patterns in textual representations for performing operations on natural language. Computer vision processes patterns in images, video or 3D representations for objects classification. Both systems can collaborate but chatbots "ignore" everything of what computer vision "sees" and conversely. This is where the first and second statements are recalled for theoretical opening - *i.e.*, (1) human learning is social and (2) machine only performs what we know how to order it to perform.

Indeed, human intelligence feeds forward knowledge and knowledge feeds backward human intelligence. Conversely, propagation and back-propagation processes defined in Convolutional Neural Networks (CNN) inherit from human intelligence and feed forward artificial knowledge to data and human knowledge, in deep learning models (Dimitrakakis & C.A., 2012; Krizhevsky, Sutskever, & Hinton, 2012; Lecun, Bottou, Bengio, & Haffner, 1998). They do not feed backward any intelligence, because the intelligence feeding machine is human and there is no integrated body feeding backward human intelligence with artificial knowledge, only hardware interfaces adapted to human perception. Brain implants of silicon chips would not change this, they could augment senses and perception but would remain separated components still not forming a single body with the grey matter, organic intelligence and brain plasticity (Galván, 2010). Nevertheless, the diversity of models offered by deep networks structures and neuronal plasticity remain largely unexplored in computer science. This, could be a reason why we still satisfy uncertain problems such as weak signal detection and social opinion mining with exploratory models aiding human experts to decision-making, and probabilistic machine learning (Chen & Qi, 2011; Ghahramani, 2015).

There were the conceptual roots of the presented work, which aims at learning structural knowledge from big data and social context as human intelligence does for social learning, hoping to foster or accelerate the development of artificial knowledge - *i.e.*, *Analytic Intelligence* so as to mislead nobody about the nature and results of analytic algorithms and brute force.

Fraud detection is a classical example of complex task requiring human expertise, with the risk of errors it also represents when processing large and complex data. The Facsimile case represents a recurrent problem concerning fraud detection. There is apparently no formalization of such a case as a problem or a class of problems. A proper definition is introduced prior to the presented work.

A facsimile is a conform copy of a document, literally. Extending this notion to any kind of support and information enables to define a class of issues in fraud detection, the facsimile problem. It concerns all cases of successful frauds based on the conformity of the fraud process with the normal process, turning both processes statistically similar and so undetectable by common models in machine learning. As an example, a fake banknote that would be perfectly conform to a genuine banknote with the same identification code (*i.e.*, a *facsimile*) would not allow to say which one is official and which one is fake based on their physical comparison. Thus, making such a fake banknote would ensure a 100% successful fraud process - an infinite loss potential -, given the unique dataset that would represent the physical characteristics of both banknotes - *i.e.*, endogenous data. As an example, in 1999 a reduction of 2.5% of credit card fraud triggered a saving of one million dollar per year (Brause, Langsdorf, & Hepp, 1999).

To detect a facsimile fraud process would necessarily require exogenous data - *i.e.*, data tied to the banknotes and external to their intrinsic form - such as owners history or geographical tracks forming distinctive datasets, respectively to each banknote. Without exogenous data, facsimile issues remain insolvable. In real life, exogenous data are not often available with endogenous data and fakes are never perfect, but can be so close to the original that they mislead experts and detection algorithms as facsimile could do. Consequently, tackling some of the most efficient fraud processes depends on solutions to facsimile or pseudo-facsimile problems.

This work introduces a deep network structure of supervised learning for the detection of fraud process close to facsimile in business data. The next section (Background) presents previous works providing theoretical foundations and technical bases to the presented work. Then, the following section proposes a model as a structural and probabilistic alternative of deep network inspired from the time reversal phenomena, for signal interference in finite spaces as a solution to the facsimile problem. Solutions and recommendations are argued thanks to offline experimentations of the proposed model based on different datasets built from business process databases and simulations, including training and test datasets. Interactions between people and/or actions/items stored in the data define the topology of a deep network built from user-defined sequences of variables. Lastly, outcomes and additional observations resulting from the experimentation are discussed with future research directions and applications perspectives, before to conclude the chapter.

Background

Artificial neural networks are hierarchical networks inspired from the observation of biological neurons solicited for vision (Hubel & Wiesel, 1962; Lecun et al., 1998). Defined as Graph Transformer Networks (GTN), they allow supervised machine learning from a sample of labeled or selected data (texts, pictures, audio), thanks to back-propagation process and are able to minimize the output error rate in a multi-layers comparative process of samples and sub-samples. In Lecun et al. (1998), Convolutional Neural Networks (CNN) combine an optimizing method such as gradient descent with sub-sampling layers to find the optimal response path for an input, regarding learned features, samples scales and parameters. For pictures or handwriting recognition, the analytic redundancy produced by deep multi-scales layers (up to 20 layers) organized in CNN provide lower error rates and high performances with low memory space, compared with models integrating individual and multiple modules, according to Krizhevsky et al. (2012) or Lecun et al. (1998). GTN and CNN remind us the efficiency of biomimetics in computer vision (Hubel & Wiesel, 1962; Lecun et al., 1998), then in other applications of computer science requiring pattern-recognition such as fault detection in power systems (Wang, 2009).

Neuronal structures in biological bodies are not only processing vision, pattern recognition and similarity-based classification problems such as do CNN in computer vision. Therefore, dealing with rules discovery or semantics for problems solving - *i.e*, machine reasoning - could require different heuristics, neuronal processes and structures than those usually found in deep learning. As an example, Generative Adversarial Networks (GAN) seek for a "MinMax" solution in a zero-sum game while CNN processes to parallel optimization (Goodfellow et al., 2014; Von Neumann, 1944). Reinforcement learning also extracts new application perspectives from the game theory, enabling the dynamic optimization or retrieval of intrinsic causes from small groups interactions (Dimitrakakis & C.A., 2012). Based on the biomimetic metaphor, many more different approaches of neural networks might be defined for other problems than parallel optimization problems. One must imagine how far artificial neuronal networks remain from the biological brain, only simulating energy distribution through static and predefined networks while the brain permanently reconfigure billions of synaptic connections in-between neurons, submitted to the influence of glial cells that is still not well understood (Petrelli, Pucci, & Bezzi, 2016). Furthermore, some inferential approaches in knowledge management, constraints satisfaction problems or other research domains provide significant results without bio-mimetic approach (Pitrat, 2010).

Inverse problems enable to retrieve original state from a derived state in a data space - *e.g.* picture, signal. In Starck, Murtagh F, & J. (2015), wavelets processing as an inverse problem enhances images from large astronomical instruments. Solutions are generally based on statistics or probabilistic estimators or optimizers such as least squares or Bayesian models (Dimitrakakis & C.A., 2012; Mosegaard & Tarantola, 2002; Tarantola & Valette, 1982). Due to chaotic phenomena, retrieving the accurate location of an original signal in a complex and finite space is not satisfied with enough accuracy and confidence as a linear inverse problem, but in a wave-defined space the specific approach defined as time-reversal enables to locate and reproduce the original signal with reliable results (Fink, 1992). It presents a particular robustness to complex data systems and uncertainty for retrieving the original characteristics of weak and/or complex signals in finite data spaces. Such a property might be propitious to retrieve and locate undefined features conjunctions within deep and/or social networks structures, regarding the facsimile problem.

Graph models remain theoretical tools relevant in numerous domains. They are unavoidable in knowledge and information retrieval from/for the World Wide Web (Brin & Page, 1998; Yessad, Faron, Dieng, & Laskri, 2008). Since the introduction of sociograms in social psychology by Moreno (1934), social networks analysis and mining is mostly based on graph models (Freeman, Bloomberg, Koff, Sunshine, & Fararo, 1960; Freeman, White, & Romney, 1989; Thovex, Le Grand, Cervantes, Sánchez, & Trichet, 2017) and regularly borrowing to physics, such as advocated in Koppal (2008) and Newman (2004). Artificial neural networks present obvious similarities, but also divergences with Markovian networks detailed in Wilinski, Solaiman, Hillion, & Czarnecki (1998). Based on Mukhanov (2008), Bayesian networks produce interesting results in fraud detection but are not appropriated for statistically insignificant data characterizing the facsimile problem. Probabilistic propagations in social networks for risk analysis is also introduced in Pearson & West (2003).

Cyber Security became a main issue with the generalization of web services. Certain principles and applications are detailed in Gupta (2018). In order to keep track with the rapid changes of organized attacks and patterns of credit card fraud, automatic learning fraud models are needed instead of pre-defined rules-based expert systems (Brause et al., 1999). Time reversal in wave-defined spaces meets this requirement (Fink, 1992). However, in large and/or deep networks, complexity and computing costs induced by Markov chains with memory entail a fine tuning or alternative models alleviating complex processes such as stochastic propagation by simpler ones (Saul & Jordan, 1999). In Koppal (2008), paired neural networks with antagonist rules avoid the Markov chains for training, using exact propagation instead of stochastic approximation. While deep learning remains greedy in time and space (CPU and RAM), online algorithms for the surveillance of massive data streams must frequently have recourse to distributed approaches such as defined in Memos, Psannis, Ishibashi, Kim, & Gupta (2018).

Considering deep neural networks as energy models, such as also stated in Lecun et al. (1998), one must admit biochemical electricity as a natural phenomemon, observable and measurable as an immanation of the law of physics. Brain and its oscillatory activity might so be seen as a finite space in which electrochemical phenomena resulting from its biological structure generate a wave field, measurable in frequency and amplitude (tension and intensity). Considering brain as a wave field in a finite space while observing the backward-forward paradigm common to most of the deep learning models, the works of Fink pave the way towards new openings in artificial intelligence. Indeed, time reversal of wave fields such as defined in Fink (1992) exploits forward-backward propagation of waves as an inverse problem, particularly resistant to chaotic phenomena. This particularity enables to produce accurate representations of complex signals and sources in finite space, which is appreciated for applications such as IRM and Radars. Consequently, it appears relevant to retain time reversal as an alternative to common approaches in deep learning, convenient for applications in detection of weak signals and of fraudulent process close to facsimile or pseudo-facsimile problems. However, regarding the causality of brain composition and its oscillatory activity, one must note a reciprocity demonstrated in recent works (Vitali et al., 2018).

The deep network model presented next must be attached to Network Science, a multidisciplinary branch of Data Science defined since 2005 by the United States National Research Council as "the study of network representations of physical, biological, and social phenomena leading to predictive models of these phenomena" (Council, 2005).

DEEP RESONANCE INTERFERENCE NETWORK: DRIN

Issues, Controversies, Problems

In Brause et al. (1999), the proposal shorten raw association rules learned from symbolic data (transactions data, 38 fields, 11 700 rows) into generalizations for detecting misuses with neural data mining. A strong interaction is observed in the results between confidence/precision and fraud discovery/recall. Even combining a credit network with a time network, raising recall results in the heavy reduction of precision, down to 1%. A trade-off of about 80% of confidence for about 100% recall is finally obtained but necessitates two different rules-based expert systems for training, which is not compliant with the initial concerns about the rapid changes of organized attacks and patterns.

Based on current observations, the presented proposal results from a multidisciplinary study leading to a disruptive approach defining a model of Deep Resonance Interference Network (DRIN). It is designed for big data (thousands of columns and billions of rows), but convenient for smaller data sets. It aims at providing a solution for facsimile problems and fraud detection that is not affected by the rapid changes of organized attacks and patterns (rules-free system) and let the experts focus on visual frauds cases and/or risks, instead of chasing unknown and local rules in perpetual change, which are sometimes in conflict at global scale.

In large data sets, the variety of variables and values induces the loss of subtle local characteristics in the mass of information. It entails a phenomenon that presents a conceptual similarity with the chaotic phenomenon tackled thanks to the wave-based model for time reversal defined in Fink (1992). The time reversal model also presents an interesting conceptual similarity with CNN as both approaches are based on feed-forward and back-propagation processes. Basically, these conceptual observations supply the foundations of an hypothesis by which appear a possible solution for the detection of fraud cases related to facsimile or pseudo-facsimile problems.

Learning and discriminating features in scales and samples from stochastic gradient descent, CNNs are described as optimizers in Goodfellow et al. (2014). Deep Resonance Interference Network is not a large combinatorial optimizer but a *correlator*. Its purpose is not to classify an input based on trained features, but to correlate unknown features based on some training instances of a unique feature. Such as with the separated processes presented in Saul & Jordan (1999), DRIN enables to mine huge data spaces as separated data sub-spaces and to retrieve undefined features conjunctions, as well within as across separated sub-spaces. As for GAN, it avoids stochastic approximation for training large data sets in affordable execution costs in time and space (Goodfellow et al., 2014).

Solutions and Recommendations

DRIN first defines a trivial function to propagate exact values in a multidimensional way instead of a hierarchical way through the multiple layers as a training signal, to be compared with a discrete snapshot of a pure wave in the data space. The training values are based on a certified training set and the discrete signal representation is stored in nodes. Then the propagation process pushes the signal in a hierarchical way as a probabilistic relationship, simulating interferences and resonances across the whole data space. Interferences and resonances represent an energy model emanating through nodes within a dense network structure. Local divergences in-between nodes and flows resulting from the two-phases propagation process within the simulated waves field are smoothed as average probabilities, trivially making the model globally coherent with the energy propagation rules in networks - *e.g.*, node and mesh method (Gottling, 1995). Then DRIN triggers a back-propagation process strictly reversing the hierarchical propagation process through the coherent global state obtained, resulting in a second and globally coherent state. Back-propagation generates here a coherent amplification of the variance in interferences and resonances within the discrete wave field simulated, avoiding any global energy loss or amplification along the probabilistic paths of the deep network structure. As a result, unknown features and features conjunctions correlated with the instances of the training set are expressed in probabilistic values such as $p \in [0; 1]$, unveiling the risk of facsimile fraud case within the whole data space and sub-spaces, with {T} set of certified instances of a known fraud feature.

The basic design of the model is formalized for a large dataset in next subsection - *Basic design of Drin*.

The implementation of DRIN core concept is then detailed - subsection *Core concept of DRIN*. It was implemented and experimented as a solution to the facsimile problem with a large institutional dataset (hundreds of test variables), then experimented with a simulated dataset (10 test variables). However, as a combinatorial correlator it should find other applications in analytic intelligence, might be for machine reasoning with epistemic properties and inferences such as introduced in Bottou (2014), Rosenschein & Pack Kaelbling (1986) and Thovex & Trichet (2013).

Basic Design of DRIN

Let v a variable in a big data set {DS} such as {DS} is a superset of m subsets {D} and each {D} is a subset of relations $r\left(v_k, v_{k+1}\right)$ in which all $\left(v_k, v_{k+1}\right)$ are unique in {D} and in {DS}. There exists a subset {S} of sequences s such as $s\left(r_{k=1}\left(v_k, v_{k+1}\right), r_{k+1}\left(v_k, v_{k+1}\right), ..., r_n\left(v_{n-1}, v_n\right)\right)$ with $1 < n < +\infty$, in {DS}.

This defines a NOSQL[2] and generic scheme of database for big data applications - *i.e.*, a nondescript relational scheme for large heterogeneous databases without normalization and integrity constraints.

Let {DS} represent a complex business process such as found in trading, client relationship management, companies accountancy etc. Let v be the root variable on which we focus for frauds detection related to facsimile cases - *e.g.*, v might represent products, categories, people, accounts, quantities, modalities etc. To facilitate understanding, the root variable might be compared with the root value in the Erdos-Renyi algorithm (Erd & Rényi, 1959).

Let a sequence be $uds\left(r_{k=1}\left(v_k, v_{k+1}\right), r_{k+1}\left(v_k, v_{k+1}\right), ..., r_n\left(v_n, v_{n+1}\right)\right)$ in {DS}. It is user-defined such as $v = v_k$ in $r_{k=1}\left(v_k, v_{k+1}\right)$ of *uds* - *i.e.*, the root variable is at the first rank in *uds*. The length of *uds* enables users to control the trade-off between computing costs and results completeness/relevance. With *uds* including all relations $r\left(v1, v2\right)$ in {D}, computing costs are maximal for {DS}.

For each user-defined sequence *uds*, DRIN builds a highly connected networks, persistent or in-memory depending on the chosen implementation, and returns the set of bipartite graphs represented by *uds*, fully valued with probabilistic weights resulting from a feed-forward and back-propagation process detailed later in this section. For instance, with $uds = \left(r_1\left(v_1, v_2\right), r_2\left(v_2, v_3\right)\right)$, the directed and virtually symmetric graph returned is valued and persistent. It is defined as $OG(N,A)$, with N,A respectively sets of nodes and of arcs such as:

$$N : \forall v_x \in v_1 \bigcup v_2 \bigcup v_3 \exists n \in N : n = v_x, v = v_1$$
$$A : \forall a(n, n') \in A \text{ with } n \in N \wedge n' \in N$$
$$\exists (n, n') : n = v_1 \wedge n' = v_2 \wedge \exists r_1(n, n') \qquad (1)$$
$$\vee (n, n') : v_2 \wedge n' = v_3 \wedge \exists r_2(n, n')$$
$$\vee \exists va(n', n) \in A$$

Equation (1) defines a complete virtually symmetric network $G(N,A)$ representing all possible sequences $s = \left(v1, v2, v3 \right)$ such as the root variable v is at the first rank and there virtually exists $vs = (v3, v2, v1)$. Virtual arcs $va\left(n', n \right)$ are not added in A as they are temporarily processed as abstract objects for computing enhanced variances during the back-propagation process, such as explained beforehand.

Core Concept of DRIN

The core concept of DRIN inherits from the physical modeling of multidimensional waves resonance and interference in finite space, developed for time reversal applications by Fink. The basic design of DRIN projects this heuristic within a multidimensional and deep network structure, appearing as a promising approach for tackling problems such as facsimile and undetected fraud cases in big data sets. Related works on Markov chains with graphs, focused on mixed memory models and on conceptual similarities and differences between neural and Markovian networks, compared with antagonist models avoiding stochastic approximations appeared helpful for converging towards such a multidisciplinary approach (Goodfellow et al., 2014; Pearson & West, 2003; Saul & Jordan, 1999; Wilinski et al., 1998).

DRIN defines a probabilistic feed-forward and back-propagation process, inspired from the quotations above and mimicking time reversal within deep heterogeneous networks. It covers the finite and discrete space of the superset $\{DS\}$ with a deep heterogeneous graph, then implements a mixed form of Bayesian network for the artificial propagation of probability values from a uniform training set. As a result, it makes appear the local amplification/absorption of conjugated probabilities as a signal for fraud risks, mapped onto the nodes and arcs of the output network $OG(N,A)$. In *Figure 1*, physical interference pattern with two sources is presented for illustration[3]. Resonance is symbolized by dark dots (maximum intensity) and interference by light dots (phase cancellation).

While *Figure 1* illustrates the combinatorial width of a two-sources and two-dimensions data space (wave amplitude being a hidden dimension), one must imagine the phenomenon simulated with DRIN in a Big Data space of hundreds or thousands of columns and millions of rows or more, each root value in the training set behaving like a source. Given a dataset $\{DS\}$, a root variable v and a user-defined

Figure 1. Two sources physical correlation pattern

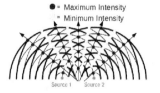

sequence *uds* such as previously defined, DRIN builds an intermediate graph *IG(N,A)* covering the sub-space of {*DS*} constrained with *uds*.

Let {*T*} be the training dataset for *IG(N,A)* with {*T*} representing the same object class than *v* - *e.g.*, company, place, date, client, product name, purchased quantity etc. Given {*V*} the set of modalities/values of *v*, $\{T\}\cap\{V\}=\varnothing$. At the initial state of the DRIN process, *IG(N,A)* is an open network with {*N*}={*V*} and {*A*}=$\varnothing$. An element of {*N*} have no proper weight value.

Propagation Stage

The first stage of the DRIN process consists in populating $rc\left(r_{k=1}, r_{k=2}, ..., r_k\right)$ with valued elements, depending on *uds*. Given the relation $r_{k=1}\left(v_k, v_{k+1}\right)$ in *uds*,

$$\forall v_k : \exists v_k \in \{T\}, P\left(v_k\right)=1$$
$$P\left(r_{k=1}\left(v_k, v_{k+1}\right)\right)=P\left(v_k\right) \qquad (2)$$

In step 1, DRIN initializes the values of all pairs of variables $\left(v, v_k\right)$, with a relational probability value $P\left(v_k\right)$, assuming the root value *P(v)*=1 for the certified positive found within the training dataset It means the root variable in *uds* takes *P(v)*=1 when it exists into *T* and $P\left(v_k\right)$ is the probability of a *v* positive for each v_k within the relation (v, v_k), with $P\left(v, v_k\right)=P\left(v\right)/\left|\left(v, v_k\right)\right|$. An illustration of the relational probability value at Step 1 of DRIN is presented in *Figure 2* for better understanding.

The root variable v_0 (assuming $v=v_0$) simulates a source diffusing a signal into a discrete plane. Then the process propagates the root probability v_0 from $v_k=1$ towards v_n .within the arcs $a\left(v_k, v_{k+1}\right)$ .representing all relation/bipartite graphs $r_{k=1}\left(v_k, v_{k+1}\right)$ .in *uds*.

Figure 2. Relational probability value during Step 1 - DRIN

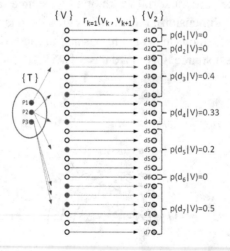

Given the relations chain $rc\left(r_{k=1}, r_{k=2}, ..., r_k\right)$. with $r_k\left(v_k, v_{k+1}\right)$ .and $k>1$. the initial value of $P\left(v_k\right)$ .is calculated from $rc\left(r_{k=1}, r_{k=2}, ..., r_k\right)$ .and the initial value of $P\left(v_{k+1}\right)$ .s calculated from $rc\left(r_{k=1}, r_{k=2}, ..., r_{k+1}\right)$ ..
In such a relations chain rc. there is no continuous orthogonality from r_k .to r_{k+1}. As a consequence, rc.cannot represent a continuous and discrete plane but a set of distinct and discrete planes coherent one-to-one. It means that rc.represents a single multidimensional and discrete space.

Let $f\left(n_k, p\right)$ .be a function returning the initial probability of a node n_k .from $IG(N,A)$ .in $r_k\left(v_k, v_{k+1}\right)$. such as $f\left(v_k, 1\right)$ .calculates

$$\frac{\left| rc\left(r_{k=1}, r_{k=2}, ..., r_k\right) : P\left(v_k \in r_{k=1}\left(v_k, v_{k+1}\right)\right) = p = 1\right|}{\left| rc\left(r_{k=1}, r_{k=2}, ..., r_k\right)\right|} \tag{3}$$

$f\left(n_k, p\right)$ returns the proportion of true positive of same object nature than the root variable in indirect relation with any variable across the relations chain $rc\left(r_{k=1}, r_{k=2}, ..., r_k\right)$. This value is named initial risk index, $niri\left(n_k\right)$. It simulates the punctual sample of a wave field resulting from the propagated signal (training set) within the represented space.

In step 2, DRIN sets all nodes n of $IG\left(N, A\right) : n \notin \{V\}$ (not root nodes) with an initial risk index $niri\left(n_k\right)$ thanks to $f\left(n_k\right)$. It ensures a trivial and reliable state for the following steps.

In step 3, DRIN sets the arcs of $IG\left(N, A\right) : \forall a\left(n, n'\right) \in A\, n \notin \{V\}$ with an initial index named mean probability of propagation (*mpp*). This index is based on the initial risk index and incoming chains of n. Given $r_{k>1}\left(v_k, v_{k+1}\right)$, it is defined as follows:

$$mpp\left(r_{k>1}\right) = \left(\frac{\sum P\left(r_{k-1}\left(v_k, v_{k+1}\right)\right)}{\left| r_{k-1}\left(v_k, v_{k+1}\right)\right|} + niri\left(v_k\right)\right) / 2 \tag{4}$$

.Equation (4) defines the mean probability from $P\left(v_k, v_{k+1}\right) \mid P\left(v_{k-1}, v_k\right)$ and $niri\left(v_k\right)$. It propagates the incoming signals from a variable of order k - 1 towards a variable of order $k+1$ depending on the relations chains of order k and $k+1$. The signal is smoothed by the transition variable of order k (Eq. 4) and propagated within the entire space of *uds* (user-defined sequence), or in the entire space of {*DS*} when *uds* includes all relations $r\left(v1, v2\right)$ of all subsets {*D*}. It results in a complete network simulating a discrete wave field and local resonances or interferences, within the represented space.

In step 4, DRIN replaces the initial risk index, having ensured a reliable state for the first steps, with a transition probability. The goal is to avoid punctual incoherence in nodes within the simulated wave field before to process it with back-propagation. It is achieved thanks to a couple of new values named local transition probability (*ltp*) and conditional propagation probability (*cpp*). Local transition probability represents a local probability of signal transmission for a node $n_k : k>1$, based on its local context known thanks to the previous steps. The parametric function $f\left(n_k, p\right)$ (Eq. 3) is already defined for that, in a way that when $p=0$ it returns:

$$P\left(vk \in r_{k=1}\left(v_k, v_{k+1}\right)\right) > 0 \text{ .instead of } P\left(vk \in r_{k=1}\left(v_k, v_{k+1}\right)\right) = 1.$$

So $f\left(v_k, 0\right)$ returns the proportion of positive elements of {V} in relation to v_k across the relations chain $rc\left(r_{k=1}, r_{k=2}, \ldots, r_k\right)$ (with $rk = r_k\left(v_k, v_{k+1}\right)$). In case there exists no v_{k+1} it does not fail or return incoherent values, and, for improved reading, it is trivially defined in Equation (5).

$$\frac{\left| rc\left(r_{k=1}, r_{k=2}, \ldots, r_k\right) : P\left(v_k \in r_{k=1}\left(v_k, v_{k+1}\right)\right) \rangle 0 \right|}{rc\left(r_{k=1}, r_{k=2}, \ldots, r_k\right)}. \tag{6}$$

Conditional propagation probability is trivially defined as - Eq. (6):

$$cpp\left(v_k\right) = \left(niri\left(v_k\right) + f\left(v_k, 0\right)\right) / 2 \tag{6}$$

.Equation (6) smoothes propagation chains for alleviating the bias that results from the initial risk index of nodes n_k, needed as a bootstrap in DRIN.

It is important to notice that the relations chain $rc\left(r_{k=1}, r_{k=2}, \ldots, r_k\right)$ does not lose path information in DRIN. By the way, rc stores full end-to-end paths for each chain $(v_k = 1, \ldots v_{k-1}, v_k)$, so that there can be several $n \in \{N\}$ having the same label (value) in *IG(N,A)*. This particularity enables to conserve a maximal probability density from $f\left(v_k, 0\right)$, in the space of representation exposed by *us*d as in {*DS*}. Such as with time reversal and wave-based models able to deal with chaotic phenomena, it is essential for avoiding the degradation of original signal, being amplification or energy loss.

At the end of the propagation stage, *IG(N,A)* still comprises all $n : n \in \{T\}$ and the relations chains starting from these nodes. It means {V} the set of root values still contains at least one element of the training dataset {*T*}. This is obviously useless when the purpose is to detect fraud cases and we later exclude all training elements from *IG(N,A)* (intermediate graph) to ensure its relevance. DRIN offers the choice to delete all elements remaining from the training dataset in the output network *OG(N,A)*, in order to focus on the detection of new fraud cases without disturbing the estimations of recall and precision for experimentation (*fmeasure*). Nevertheless, for certain use cases they remain useful to the domain experts for the exploratory analysis, visualization and understanding of endogenous data related to facsimile or pseudo-facsimile problems.

Back-Propagation Stage

The propagation stage of DRIN simulates a discrete waves field and resonances or interferences from a training signal in a multidimensional and coherent space. The back-propagation stage simulates a reversal as an echo of the training signal within the wave field, for a better separation of resonances and interferences in final representations resulting from the model.

The multidisciplinary heuristic that DRIN aims at implementing is mostly defined in the propagation stage, which can be thought as a probabilistic signals propagation in a finite and discrete space without degradation of spatial distribution and signal-to-noise ratio[4]. Therefore, in order not to introduce bias in $IG(N,A)$, which state at the end of propagation stage is coherent, the back-propagation process must faithfully reverse the propagation process. However, the bootstrap step (step 1 of DRIN) may not be avoided for a regular interference generation before to focus the signals reversal onto the chosen root variable. As a result, the back-propagation process in DRIN is fast to define, even though its execution remains greedy.

In step 5, DRIN returns the signals represented by risk probability values across the relations chains exposed by *usd*, from r_k to r_{k+1}. Based on Equation (4), the reversal of mean probability of propagation is defined in Eq. (7). In case there exists no v_{k+1} it does not fail, but for improved reading it is trivially defined as - Eq. (7):

$$rmpp\left(r_k\right)=\left(\frac{\sum P\left(r_k\left(v_k,v_{k+1}\right)\right)}{\left|r_k\left(v_k,v_{k+1}\right)\right|}+cpp\left(v_k\right)\right)/2\,. \tag{7}$$

For better understanding, it is reminded that $k+1$ is the highest order value in *uds* when starting the back-propagation process. Equation (7) defines the reversed mean probability from $\left(v_{k-1},v_k\right)\mid P\left(v_k,v_{k+1}\right)$ and $cpp\left(v_k\right)$. It propagates the incoming signals from a variable of order $k+1$ towards a variable of order k-1 depending on the relations chains of order k and k-1.

As with Eq. (5), a reversal function $f\left(n_k,p\right)$ is defined as follows:

$$\frac{\mid rc\left(r_k,r_{k-1},\,...,r_{k=1}\right):P\left(v_k\in r_{k=1}\left(v_{k-1},v_k\right)\right)\langle 1\mid}{rc\left(r_k,r_{k-1},\,...,r_{k=1}\right)}\,. \tag{8}$$

Equation (8) slightly improves the dispersion of probability values, due to the fact it excludes all maximal values $p\left(v_k\right)=1$ in *rc* from the final state of $IG(N,A)$.

In facsimile or pseudo-facsimile problems, an item and its facsimile have no quantitative/qualitative differences. As a consequence, there is no interest in discerning their properties and all items of the same type can be considered as atoms. In such a case, information related to each item can be thought as endogenous information, *i.e*, a probable and unique way to discern original items from facsimiles, as previously stated. These theoretical considerations are fully assumed in DRIN, which projects a physical model into a big data set and deep learning network for detecting fraud cases related to facsimile problems. Experiments and results are presented in the following sections.

Offline Experimentation for Big Data

Before to return an output graph $OG(N,A)$, DRIN builds $IG(N,A)$, a probabilistic and discrete representation of a finite space of n dimensions, with $n=\max(k)$ from the user-defined sequence *uds*. Each different *uds* returns a new and persistent $OG(N,A)$. As a result, $OG(N,A)$ is the local network related to *uds* as a local exposition of $\{DS\}$. Due to the way DRIN defines deep networks from large heterogeneous data sets without requiring direct root variable-to-root variable relationship stored into $\{DS\}$, $OG(N,A)$ may also be thought as a hidden network of root values.

Conversely with the directed and symmetric graphs $IG(N,A)$, in $OG(N,A)$ there exists only one node per distinct label (value) from $\{DS\}$ and one arc per distinct pair of nodes $\left(n,n'\right)$. It enables to merge different stored $OG(N,A)$ into a single global network so as to provide an overview of several concomitant spaces and to explore them as distinct communities, thanks to social networks analysis methods and tools (Freeman et al., 1960, 1989; Newman, 2004; Thovex et al., 2017). As concepts and neuronal activity are commonly associated with network representations, it points up a possible use of these methods and tools in cognitive psychology and may be neuroscience, for a better understanding of the brain activity with data resulting from tomography, for instance. An example of such a multidimensional network visualized for exploratory analysis is illustrated, in *Figure 3*.

The composite network $CG(N,A)$ illustrated (*Figure 3*) merges six $OG(N,A)$ of 2 to 19 dimensions. It enables to mine deep hidden networks on small hardware clusters, instead of defining a single $OG(N,A)$ from a maximal user-defined sequence *uds* covering $\{DS\}$, which could require an important comput-

Figure 3. Composite network merging several OG(N,A) - DRIN

ing cost. An illustration of hidden network structure found by filtering $CG(N,A)$ on its DRIN values is presented in *Figure 4*.

DRIN works after-the-fact (offline) with previously stored data sets[5]. However, large in-memory graph models being propitious to network-computing and parallel processing, it appears relevant to take advantage of DRIN offline processing in order to trigger real-time alerts from an online process standing on the theoretical basements provided[6].

DRIN was experimented with several databases from about 1 to 100 GB, including data sets up to 1 000 variables mapped onto 1 billion rows. Temporary data sets of about 5 billion rows were observed, with up to 34 dimensions. The experimental datasets were collected from real activities by large organizations or simulated for academic purposes, such as the Paysim dataset simulating mobile transactions in accordance with the method presented in Lopez-Rojas, Elmir, & Axelsson (2016).

Outcomes and Observations

Deep learning models generally require large training sets before to ensure satisfying recall and precision measures. In Brause et al. (1999), the training dataset is more than half the test dataset, for about 100% recall and 80% precision. As an example, the CNN LeNet-5 requires about 20 passes on a training set of 60 000 patterns before to reach a stable performance (Lecun et al., 1998). However, these examples are not necessarily to be compared with DRIN as purposes, heuristics, contexts are different for each model, even though they present certain conceptual similarities. DRIN is more a deep correlator than a network-based optimizer, thus it should produce different reactions than commonly observed with feed-forward and back-propagation models for classification.

DRIN is a recurrent learning model which can improve its performance adding new positives in the training set from previous results, such as in reinforcement learning (Dimitrakakis & C.A., 2012). Anyway in a context as sensible as frauds tracking, the domain experts have to carefully check and label new positives before the training set could be updated.

Figure 4. Mining hidden networks by filtering CG(N,A) - DRIN

Experiment #1

With an institutional dataset, a small training dataset representing 1.3% of the distinct root values in the dataset was tested in order to evaluate the initialization performance. The test dataset was reduced to 60 000 values containing 0.0001% of positive values, representing real transactions. The arbitrarily chosen dimension of $IG(N,A)$ was 7. After empirical and quick tuning of thresholds parameters, DRIN reached 100% recall. Precision could be about 40% if all candidates found out of the training set were checked as false positives, but as the goal is first to detect and rank unknown positives with a risk value, and as it was too expensive for experts in terms of time and money, precision measurements were replaced with a double-blind test.

Falloffs of about 20% in recall were observed with larger test datasets of about 6 million values. A significant effect of parameters tuning was observed too, which makes difficult to ensure that the best setting was found. Increasing the training set to 70% of the distinct root values, no significant changes in recall were noticed but the minimal precision raised up to 55%, supposing all proposed candidates out of the training set were false positives, what was not demonstrated, with a quick empirical tuning that might be enhanced. These statistical observations show a remarkable resistance of DRIN to initialization with a tiny training dataset.

As noticed, one must be careful with the relevance of precision measurements in line with the concerned application purpose, such as for weak signals and fraud detection or the detection of unexpected and/or unknown events. The well-known F-score/F-measure (precision and recall) compares retrieved patterns or properties with experts-defined labeled objects. By the way, it does not take into account undefined/unknown objects and turns irrelevant with training sets in which true positives are missing and costly to check from calculated results - case for which DRIN was properly defined. Therefore, it is not convenient for measuring the detection of unknown patterns in properties and values. It is the reason why a double-blind protocol was necessary for experimentation.

The most important observation to retain, in accordance with the main goal of DRIN, comes from the double-blind test realized. A few positives, presenting a rare particularity for the domain experts, were deleted from the training dataset/hidden to the system while their related data, initially not quantified with any weights as all initial data, were left intact in the test dataset. The research team ignored it. DRIN being a continuous correlator, it ranks every elements with a risk probability in $OG(N,A)$. With several couples $[usd; OG(N,A)]$, DRIN found the same Top 3 ranked identifiers. This particularity having called the researcher team attention, the domain experts were solicited and revealed the anomaly. These identifiers were known to be critical by the experts who had chosen to delete them first from the training set for this test.

Despite of endogenous data tied to the missing positives had not been highly ranked as it is for known positives, these particular missing positives were detected as a principal risk without appearing in the training dataset. Statistical hypothesis testing appears not reliable to proof and explain such a case. No understanding of this results is demonstrated. May be due to the epistemic foundations of DRIN, the missing positives might have been estimated as a systemic anomaly (*i.e.*, a physical aberration or irregularity) acting as a sort of "black hole" in the data space, having triggered a ranking alert.

Experiment #2

Further experiments were processed with a sample from the Paysim dataset, simulated as defined in (Lopez-Rojas et al., 2016). The sample size is 480 MB for 8 variables and 6.36 million rows, simulating random mobile transactions (no null values) [7]. Two variables, *name of origine* (nameOrig) and *name of destination* (nameDest), were aimed as root variables for successive experiments. The training set is defined by the *isFraud* variable (8 213 known positives), containing 16 specific rows for large amount transactions, identified by *isFlaggedFraud*. As presented in *Table 1*, the repartition is insignificant with variable 1(max card/value = 3), while variable 2 appears better for statistical or probabilistic learning.

The training set it copied from the data set based on the variable 3 - *Table 1*. On will notice the maximal cardinality by value of 2 for the training variable, meaning only certain destination names are implied in more than 1 fraudulous transaction. It produced 26 risk values above 1, among 125 distinct values for the aimed variable and a 100% recall.

The distribution of risk values above 1 for v1 is illustrated in *Figure 5*. Two main values appear, about 12.6 for 7 921 distinct names of origin and 8.45, for 98 other ones and a total of 8 019 or 97.6% of the training set. At this point, one might notice a set of 2 risk values above 50.

In *Figure 6*, illustrating the risk values above 1 for all v1 included within the training set, one might notice no value superior to 12.6, while it is the main and maximal value resulting from DRIN for all true positives. This main risk value alone represents 96.44% of the training set, while values below 1 represent about 1% of the training set.

In this experiment, the domain experts might be first interested in investigating about the two names of destination surprisingly ranked with a risk value 4 times higher than the maximal one from the training set. At this point, one will have noticed the difference advocated between DRIN and deep networks for pattern recognition, which were not originally designed for detecting higher ranks out of the learning sets.

Table 1. Description of the experimented variables: Paysim

	Distinct values	Min card/value	Max card/value	Positive values	isFlaggedFraud
1. NameOrig	53 307	1	3	8169	16
2. NameDest	22 362	1	113	8213	16
3. IsFraud	8213	1	(nameDest) 2	8213	16

Figure 5. Risk values above 1 - variable v1

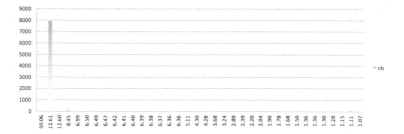

Lastly, for simple checking and observation, known positives were left within the test set at *Step 2* of DRIN. As expected, the training values got a 100 (maximal) risk index. The other v1 values were still ranked from 50.6 (2 values) to about 0.1 with a rank above 1 for about 860 values.

Experiment #3

In a last experiment with Paysim, positives from the training set were hidden to DRIN for the training phase, as defined in *Step 2* of the process. As a result, DRIN was supposed to be "blind" to true positives. The test was processed with v2, of which distribution was more propitious to learning in such conditions.

DRIN produced a suggestion of 356 candidates, all ranked with a risk index above 1. As illustrated in *Figure 7*, their distribution followed a long tail curve from the lowest value to the highest value (about 26). 41 values - about 11% - were found between 5 and 26.

This experiment demonstrated the importance of the conceptual origin of DRIN. Indeed, the model have learnt a root variable from the context/data space *uds* being artificially "blind" to learn this variable. Although the produced results might appear poor to the pragmatism of domain experts, they must be thought as a resurgence of a hidden signal in a discrete wave field simulated within the user-defined data space. Therefore, such an observation sounds interesting regarding the theoretical foundations of DRIN.

Figure 6. Risk values above 1 for positives - variable v1

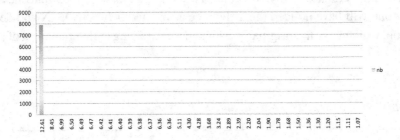

Figure 7. Distribution of NameDest in experiment #3

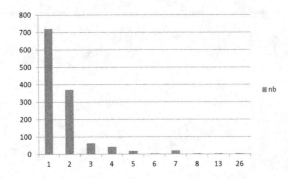

FUTURE RESEARCH DIRECTIONS

DRIN offered two thresholds parameters for filtering the suspicious conjunctions of variables and values (candidate subnets) in its first version, so as to allow users to act on the level of recall and precision. There were no automatic setting of the best parameters. It might be achieved from convex optimization or other methods defined in the literature (Bubeck & Eldan, 2016). Next versions should fulfill the lack, however empirical tuning is easy and quick for common uses with small or middle-size hardware - *e.g.*, 80 GB-16 cores.

Deep Resonance Interference Network proposes an alternative in the field of deep networks and machine learning. Neuronal networks - *e.g.* ANN, Perceptron, CNN - are deep networks structures historically anchored in the biological observation of visual cortex (Hubel & Wiesel, 1962; Lecun et al., 1998). Based on deep networks and on a principle of *optimization-separation* for classification, the resulting applications gravitate around the recognition of patterns in images, texts or streams and more generally, around perception. Due to its theoretical anchorage, DRIN appears to introduce a novel principle of *correlation-unification* in deep networks, closer to reasoning and intuition than to perception. Instead of recognizing known patterns from multiple features learned from numerous data, it enables to detect unknown patterns from a unique feature learned from sparse data. It might open a large spectrum of novel applications in "artificial intelligence" that should be observed as a main future research direction. It might be relevant to experiment its theoretical foundations in neuroscience, too.

CONCLUSION

Deep Resonance Interference Network (DRIN) results from a multidisciplinary study. It defines deep probabilistic networks aiming at the simulation of time reversal in a discrete and finite space (Fink, 1992) to provide a solution for frauds detection related to the facsimile problem - introduced beforehand - in Big Data.

The proposed model is not affected by the rapid changes of organized attacks and patterns (rules-free system) and let the experts focus on visual frauds cases and/or risks instead of chasing unknown rules in perpetual change. It concerns Network Science, a multidisciplinary branch of Data Science defined since 2005 by the United States National Research Council (Council, 2005).

DRIN defines a probabilistic feed-forward and back-propagation process inspired from wave-based time reversal within deep heterogeneous networks. It generates artificial probability values·within a coherent and multidimensional data space without global attenuation or amplification. As a result, it makes appear deep local amplification/absorption of conjugated probabilities as a signal focused on subtle fraud cases invisible to the domains experts, which are by nature the most efficient ones. The propagation stage of DRIN simulates a discrete wave field and resonances or interferences from a training signal in a multidimensional and coherent space. The back-propagation stage simulates a reversal as an echo of the training signal within the wave field, for a better separation of resonances and interferences in final representations resulting from the model.

Successive experiments were realized since the first stages, with several databases from about 1 to 100 GB including data sets up to 1 000 variables mapped onto 1 billion rows. Concomitant spaces were explored as distinct communities, thanks to social networks analysis and mining (Freeman et al., 1960, 1989; Newman, 2004; Thovex et al., 2017).

Statistical observations show a remarkable resistance to initialization from a tiny training dataset - *e.g.*, 1.3% of distinct test values reach 100% recall. Supposing all proposed candidates were false positives, which was not proofed as the goal is to detect unknown positives, mean precision would be observable with large test datasets (55% for 6 million rows), depending on of filtering parameters. However, interesting but not measurable outcomes were observed in an double-blind experiment.

Coherent results were found with two different datasets. Particular positives known as critical have been detected as a major risk, without appearing in the training dataset of the experiment #1. There is still no clear demonstration of such a finding. It might be due to the multidisciplinary foundations of DRIN from which missing positives should be estimated as a systemic anomaly - *i.e.*, a physical aberration/irregularity within the simulated wave field.

DRIN works on small hardware clusters with small/big data sets. The first future works should be focused on optimizing multiple parameters online, for automatic tuning related to user-defined choices, and on the perspective of triggering real-time alerts to support the domain experts.

Finally, neuronal networks models such as ANN, GTN, CNN, RNN are all deep networks structures stemming from optimization and separation functions. Their biomimetic inspiration, historically anchored in the biological observation of visual cortex, shows through their resulting applications that gravitate around the recognition of visual patterns in images, text or streams and around perception - *cf.* Perceptron.

A first alternative in deep learning recently appeared with adversarial networks and their applications in imagery and artistic creation. Deep Resonance Interference Network proposes another alternative in the field of deep networks and machine learning, modifying the principle *optimizer-separator*, inherent to the current models in deep learning, into a novel principle *correlator-unifier*, toward an applicative field closer to reasoning and intuition than to perception. Instead of recognizing known patterns from multiple features learned from numerous data, it enables to detect unknown patterns from a unique feature learned from sparse data. As a result, it might open a new track in artificial intelligence for discovering linked features in big data such as exposed from data collectors for neuroscience (*e.g.*, tomography, IRM). Later applications from the social and semantic web might also let foresee artificial intelligence as a *digital implementation of social learning* for society and governance (Thovex, 2018).

However, by now and even though these perspectives were confirmed in future research works, one must remember again the sentence of conclusion of Turing (1950): "We can only see a short distance ahead, but we can see plenty there that needs to be done".

ACKNOWLEDGMENT

Special thanks are first addressed to the team, public/private partners and stakeholders for supporting these research works, as well as the French government for its financial helps to private research, development and innovation. Academic researchers and members of the international research unit LAFMIA (UMI CNRS 3175) are warmly thanked for their welcome and support since years.

REFERENCES

Balystok, E., & Poarch, G. (2014). *Language Experience Changes Language and Cognitive Ability.* Zeitschrift Fur Erziehungswissenschaft; doi:10.100711618-014-0491-8

Bottou, L. (2014). From Machine Learning to Machine Reasoning. *Machine Learning, 94*(2), 133–149. doi:10.100710994-013-5335-x

Brause, R., Langsdorf, T., & Hepp, M. (1999). *Neural Data Mining for Credit Card Fraud Detection. In Proceedings of the 11th IEEE International Conference on Tools with Artificial Intelligence, ICTAI '99* (p. 103). Washington, DC: IEEE Computer Society. Retrieved from http://dl.acm.org/citation.cfm?id=850950.853684

Brin, S., & Page, L. (1998). The Anatomy of a Large-Scale Hypertextual Web Search Engine. *Proceedings of the seventh International Conference on the World Wide Web (WWW1998)*, 107–117. 10.1016/S0169-7552(98)00110-X

Bubeck, S., & Eldan, R. (2016). *Multi-scale exploration of convex functions and bandit convex optimization.* Conference On Learning Theory - COLT.

Chen, L., & Qi, L. (2011). Social opinion mining for supporting buyer's complex decision making: Exploratory user study and algorithm comparison. *Social Network Analysis and Mining Journal, 1*(4), 301–320. doi:10.100713278-011-0023-y

Corballis, M. (2003). *From mouth to hand: Gesture, speech, and the evolution of right-handedness.* Academic Press. doi:10.1017/S0140525X03000062

Council, U. S. N. R. (2005). *Network Science.* Washington, DC: The National Academies Press. doi:10.17226/11516

Dimitrakakis, C., & C.A., R. (2012). Bayesian Multitask Inverse Reinforcement Learning. In H. M. Sanner S. (Ed.), *Recent Advances in Reinforcement Learning. EWRL 2011., Lecture Notes in Computer Science* (Vol. 7188). Springer.

Erd, P., & Rényi, A. (1959). On random graphs. *Publicationes Mathematicae, 6*, 290–297.

Fink, M. (1992). Time reversal of ultrasonic fields. I. Basic principles. *IEEE Transactions on Ultrasonics, Ferroelectrics, and Frequency Control, 39*(5), 555–566. doi:10.1109/58.156174 PMID:18267667

Freeman, L. C., Bloomberg, W., Koff, S. P., Sunshine, M. H., & Fararo, T. J. (1960). *Local Community Leadership.* Syracuse.

Freeman, L. C., White, D. R., & Romney, A. K. (1989). *Research methods in social network analysis.* George Mason University Press.

Galván, A. (2010). Neural plasticity of development and learning. *Human Brain Mapping, 31*(6), 879–890. doi:10.1002/hbm.21029 PMID:20496379

Ghahramani, Z. (2015). Probabilistic machine learning and artificial intelligence. *Nature, 521*(7553), 452–459. doi:10.1038/nature14541 PMID:26017444

Goodfellow, I., Pouget-Abadie, J., Mirza, M., Xu, B., Warde-Farley, D., Ozair, S., & ... . (2014). Generative Adversarial Nets. In Z. Ghahramani, M. Welling, C. Cortes, N. D. Lawrence, & K. Q. Weinberger (Eds.), Advances in Neural Information Processing Systems (Vol. 27, pp. 2672–2680). Curran Associates, Inc. Retrieved from http://papers.nips.cc/paper/5423-generative-adversarial-nets.pdf

Gottling, J. G. (1995). Node and Mesh Analysis by Inspection. *IEEE Transactions on Education*, *38*(4), 312–316. doi:10.1109/13.473148

Gupta, B. B. (Ed.). (2018). *Computer and Cyber Security: Principles, Algorithm, Applications, and Perspectives*. CRC Press, Taylor & Francis.

Hubel, D., & Wiesel, T. (1962). Receptive fields, binocular interaction and functional architecture in the cat's visual cortex. *The Journal of Physiology*, *1*(160), 106–154. doi:10.1113/jphysiol.1962.sp006837 PMID:14449617

Koppal, A. (2008, April). *The Ising Model and Percolation on Graphs*. Retrieved from http://www1.cs.columbia.edu/ coms6998/Notes/lecture22.pdf

Krizhevsky, A., Sutskever, I., & Hinton, G. E. (2012). ImageNet Classification with Deep Convolutional Neural Networks. In *Advances in Neural Information Processing Systems 25: 26th Annual Conference on Neural Information Processing Systems 2012. Lake Tahoe, Nevada, United States* (pp. 1106–1114). Academic Press.

Lecun, Y., Bottou, L., Bengio, Y., & Haffner, P. (1998). Gradient-based learning applied to document recognition. *Proceedings of the IEEE*, 2278–2324.

Lopez-Rojas, E. A., Elmir, A., & Axelsson, S. (2016). PaySim: A financial mobile money simulator for fraud detection. *The 28th European Modeling and Simulation Symposium-EMSS, Larnaca, Cyprus*, 174–179. Retrieved from http://www.scopus.com/record/display.url?origin=inward&partnerID=40&eid=2-s2.0-85002406569

Memos, V. A., Psannis, K. E., Ishibashi, Y., Kim, B.-G., & Gupta, B. B. (2018). An efficient algorithm for media-based surveillance system (EAMSuS) in IoT smart city framework. *Future Generation Computer Systems*, *83*, 619–628. doi:10.1016/j.future.2017.04.039

Moreno, J. L. (1934). *Who Shall Survive: A New Approach to the Problem of Human Interrelations*. Nervous and Mental Disease Publishing Co. doi:10.1037/10648-000

Mosegaard, K., & Tarantola, A. (2002). Probabilistic Approach to Inverse Problems. In International Handbook of Earthquake & Engineering Seismology (pp. 237–265). Academic Press.

Mukhanov, L. E. (2008). *Using Bayesian Belief Networks for Credit Card Fraud Detection. In Proceedings of the 26th IASTED International Conference on Artificial Intelligence and Applications* (pp. 221–225). Innsbruck, Austria: ACTA Press. Retrieved from http://dl.acm.org/citation.cfm?id=1712759.1712801

Newman, M. E. J. (2004). Detecting community structure in networks. *European Physical Journal. B, Condensed Matter and Complex Systems*, *38*(2), 321–330. doi:10.1140/epjb/e2004-00124-y PMID:15244693

Pearson, M., & West, P. (2003). Drifting smoke rings: social network analysis and Markov processes in a longitudinal study of friendship groups and risk taking. *Connections: bulletin of the International Network for Social Network Analysis, 25*(2), 59–76. Retrieved from http://eprints.gla.ac.uk/2701/

Petrelli, F., Pucci, L., & Bezzi, P. (2016). Astrocytes and Microglia and Their Potential Link with Autism Spectrum Disorders. *Frontiers in Cellular Neuroscience, 10*, 21. doi:10.3389/fncel.2016.00021 PMID:26903806

Pitrat, J. (1990). Métaconnaissance: Futur de l'intelligence artificielle. *Hermes.*

Pitrat, J. (2010). *Artificial Beings: The Conscience of a Conscious Machine.* Wiley.

Putnam, H. (1975). Mind, Language and Reality. Cambridge University Press. doi:10.1017/CBO9780511625251

Rosenschein, J. S., & Pack Kaelbling, L. (1986). The Synthesis of Digital Machines with Provable Epistemic Properties. In J. Halpern (Ed.), *Proceedings of the Conference on Theoretical Aspects of Reasoning About Knowledge* (pp. 83–98). Morgan Kaufmann. 10.1016/B978-0-934613-04-0.50009-0

Saul, L. K., & Jordan, M. I. (1999). Mixed Memory Markov Models: Decomposing Complex Stochastic Processes as Mixtures of Simpler Ones. *Machine Learning, 37*(1), 75–87. doi:10.1023/A:1007649326333

Starck, J.-L., Murtagh F., & J., F. (2015). *Sparse Image and Signal Processing: Wavelets and Related Geometric Multiscale Analysis.* Cambridge University Press.

Tarantola, A., & Valette, B. (1982). Generalized nonlinear inverse problems solved using the least squares criterion. *Reviews of Geophysics, 20*(2), 219–232. doi:10.1029/RG020i002p00219

Thovex, C. (2018). Social Network and Surveillance for Society. In T. Özyer, S. Bakshi, & R. Alhajj (Eds.), *Social Network and Surveillance for Society* (pp. 101–113). Springer International Publishing.

Thovex, C., Le Grand, B., Cervantes, O., Sánchez, A. J., & Trichet, F. (2017). Encyclopedia of Social Network Analysis and Mining. In R. Alhajj & J. Rokne (Eds.), Encyclopedia of Social Network Analysis and Mining (pp. 1–12). New York, NY: Springer. doi:10.1007/978-1-4614-7163-9_381-1

Thovex, C., & Trichet, F. (2013). An Epistemic Equivalence for Predictive Social Networks Analysis. *Lecture Notes in Computer Science, 7652*, 201–214. doi:10.1007/978-3-642-38333-5_21

Turing, A. M. (1950). Computing Machinery and Intelligence. (O. Academic, Ed.) Mind, 59(236), 433–460. doi:https://doi.org/10.1093/mind/LIX.236.433

Vitali, I., Fièvre, S., Telley, L., Oberst, P., Bariselli, S., Frangeul, L., ... Jabaudon, D. (2018). Progenitor Hyperpolarization Regulates the Sequential Generation of Neuronal Subtypes in the Developing Neocortex. *Cell, 174*(5), 1264–1276. doi:10.1016/j.cell.2018.06.036 PMID:30057116

Von Neumann, J. (1944). *Theory of Games and Economic Behavior.* Princeton University Press.

Wang, Q. (2009). Artificial Neural Network and Hidden Space SVM for Fault Detection in Power System. In *ISNN 2009: Proceedings of the 6th International Symposium on Neural Networks.* Springer Verlag. 10.1007/978-3-642-01510-6_45

Wilinski, P., Solaiman, B., Hillion, A., & Czarnecki, W. (1998). Toward the Border Between Neural and Markovian Paradigms. *IEEE Trans. Systems, Man, and Cybernetics. Part B*, *28*(2), 146–159. doi:10.1109/3477.662756

Yessad, A., Faron, C., Dieng, R., & Laskri, T. (2008). Ontology-Driven Adaptive Course Generation for Web-based Education. *ED-MEDIA 2008*.

KEY TERMS AND DEFINITIONS

Bootstrap: Statistical method for creating samples from a population or to small part of code for starting a computer. Derived expression for the initialization phase of analytic algorithms.

Convex Optimization: Based on convex functions in mathematics (i.e., functions defining optimal value/set of values) convex optimization enables to find parameters in a linear progression for which loss is minimal.

Epistemic: From *epistēmē*, Greek for "knowledge." That Greek word is from the verb *epistanai*, meaning "to know or understand," a word formed from the prefix *epi-* (meaning "upon" or "attached to") and *histanai* (meaning "to cause to stand"). The study of the nature and grounds of knowledge is called *epistemology*, and one who engages in such study is an epistemologist.

Greedy Algorithm: An algorithm which explore the whole combinatory for solving a problem, instead of other approach such as random walk, for instance.

Hidden Variable/Network: Variables and/or networks that are not directly visible but acts in the results of a calculus, a computing process or a network structure.

Interference: The weakening and degradation of a wave with another wave in opposite phase.

Orthogonality: Perpendicular reference to a plane or a geometric object. Various object defined within an orthogonal frame belong to a continuous orthogonality.

Resonance: The intensification and enriching of a wave in phase with another wave-phase conjunction.

Sparse Data: Available data partially representing objects in a data space.

Threshold: Parameter defining minimal or maximal values beyond which data are filtered.

ENDNOTES

[1] Human fails at the Turing's test invalidate the test.
[2] Acronym for Not Only SQL, databases without integrity constraints.
[3] Source. https://astarmathsandphysics.com/ib-physics-notes/waves-and-oscillations/1492-the-two-source-interference-pattern.html
[4] Simulating a discrete wave field entails the existence of noise and signal-to-noise ratio within the network representations $IG(N,A)$ and $OG(N,A)$.
[5] Batch layer in Lambda architecture.
[6] Speed layer in Lambda architecture.
[7] Download from https://www.kaggle.com/ntnu-testimon/paysim1

Chapter 16
Malware Threat in Internet of Things and Its Mitigation Analysis

Shingo Yamaguchi
Yamaguchi University, Japan

Brij Gupta
National Institute of Technology Kurukshetra, India

ABSTRACT

This chapter introduces malware's threat in the internet of things (IoT) and then analyzes the mitigation methods against the threat. In September 2016, Brian Krebs' web site "Krebs on Security" came under a massive distributed denial of service (DDoS) attack. It reached twice the size of the largest attack in history. This attack was caused by a new type of malware called Mirai. Mirai primarily targets IoT devices such as security cameras and wireless routers. IoT devices have some properties which make them malware attack's targets such as large volume, pervasiveness, and high vulnerability. As a result, a DDoS attack launched by infected IoT devices tends to become massive and disruptive. Thus, the threat of Mirai is an extremely important issue. Mirai has been attracting a great deal of attention since its birth. This resulted in a lot of information related to IoT malware. Most of them came from not academia but industry represented by antivirus software makers. This chapter summarizes such information.

INTRODUCTION

In September 2016, Brian Krebs' web site "Krebs on Security" came under a massive DDoS attack (Krebs, 2016). This attack was caused by a new type of malware called Mirai. Mirai primarily targets IoT devices such as security cameras and wireless routers. This is because IoT devices feature large volume, pervasiveness, and high vulnerability (Kolias, Kambourakis, Stavrou, &Voas, 2017). As a result, a DDoS attack raised from infected IoT devices tends to become massive and disruptive. Thus, the threat of Mirai is an extremely important issue.

DOI: 10.4018/978-1-5225-9742-1.ch016

This chapter introduces malware's threat in IoT and then analyzes the mitigation methods against the threat. It consists of two parts. In the former part, we describe Mirai's threat, attack, mechanism, and mitigation methods. In the beginning, we trace the history from Mirai's birth. Next, we illustrate the mechanism of Mirai's infection and attack. Against the threat, there are some mitigation methods such as rebooting infected devices and using an IoT worm called as Hajime which blocks Mirai. In the latter part, we present a mathematical model of the infection phenomenon of Mirai. We regard the infection phenomenon as a multi-agent system and express it with agent-oriented Petri net called as Petri nets in a Petri net (PN^2 for short). Intuitively, a PN^2 is a Petri net in which each token is a Petri net again. PN^2 is not only as a graphical and mathematical modeling tool but also useful as a simulation tool. We reflect the mitigation methods into the PN^2 model and evaluate the methods of the model. We illustrate the dynamic behavior of the mitigation methods with the simulation of the model. We finally conclude this chapter by summarizing our key points and give future research directions.

MALWARE IN INTERNET OF THINGS: MIRAI

Threat and Attack

Mirai (means "future" in Japanese) is a malware which changes IoT devices into malicious bots and creates the network of bots called botnet. The botnets can be used to perform large-scale network attacks typified by DDoS attacks. We shall trace Mirai's history to show its threat and attack.

- **Discovery (August 31, 2016):** A malware research group MalwareMustDie reported the discovery of Mirai. See [MalwareMustDie. (2016)].
- **Early Major Attacks (September 2016):** The first attack came on September 18, 2016. It targeted a French cloud hosting company OVH [Bonderud, D. (2016)]. At about the same time as the first attack, another attack fell on Brian Krebs' website "Krebs on Security" [Krebs, B. (2016)]. It reached 620 Gbps that means twice the size of the largest attack in history. In addition, a United States Domain Name System provider Dyn was exposed to attacks on October 21, 2016 [York, K. (2016)]. Major internet services such as Amazon and Twitter were made unavailable. These massive and disruptive attacks and threats made Mirai well-known.
- **Source Code Released (September 30, 2016):** The author of Mirai "Anna-senpai" posted the source code of Mirai on Hack Forums as open source [Statt, N. (2016)]. Later, it was removed by the administrator of Hack Forums. For the academic purpose, it has also been archived to Github: https://github.com/jgamblin/Mirai-Source-Code.
- **Variant (December 2017):** The released source code enabled anyone not only to implement Mirai but also to evolve Mirai into new variants. In December 2017 researchers discovered a variant of Mirai called "Satori" [360 netlab. (2017)]. Satori has higher infectivity than Mirai by using vulnerabilities in IoT devices. In the following month, a variant of Satori called "Okiru" was found. Okiru becomes able to target more architectures like ARC [Arzamendi, P., Bing, M. & Soluk, K. (2018)]. Following Satori and Okiru, more than ten variants of Mirai have been discovered. That number of variants will continue to increase.

Mirai infected over 300,000 IoT devices in 164 countries (Devry, 2016). Figure 1 illustrates the difference in countries possessing the infected IoT devices before and after the outbreak of Mirai (Nakao, 2018). Before the outbreak, the top 5 countries were China (14.1%), Brazil (10.5%), India (8.6%), Vietnam (6.6%), and Taiwan (4.7%). After the outbreak, the top 5 countries were changed to Vietnam (15.3%), Brazil (15.3%), Taiwan (8.1%), Turkey (7.6%), and India (8.6%). This means that malware activity was moving to emerging markets and developing countries.

Mechanism

A Mirai botnet is composed of three major components: bots, command and control (C&C) server, and loader. In Sinaović and Mrdovic (2017), the authors analyzed the source code for Mirai.

- **Bot:** Runs on an infected device. It consists of three modules: scanner, killer, and attack. Scanner module uses telnet and looks for other vulnerable IoT devices. Killer module kills the processes that use ports 22, 23 and 80 and reserves those ports. Attack module executes the command issued by attackers.
- **C&C Server:** Used by attackers to maintain a botnet and to send malicious commands to the botnet.
- **Loader:** Turns a discovered vulnerable IoT device into a new bot. After logging in, the loader downloads and executes an architecture-dependent malicious binary code.

Mirai takes the following operational steps (See Figure 2):

- **Infection Phase**
  Step 1: An IoT device infected by Mirai, i.e. bot, searches for another IoT device which uses port 23 or 2323. If discovering such a device, the bot attempts to log-in with the list of easy-to-guess username and password pairs.

Figure 1. Countries possessing the infected IoT devices before and after the outbreak of Mirai (Nakao, 2018)

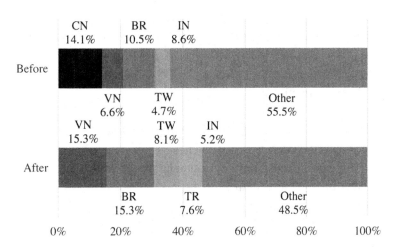

Figure 2. Sequence chart of Mirai's operation

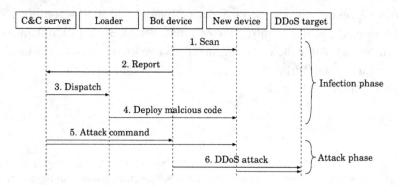

Step 2:   If logging in successfully, the bot sends the discovered device's information to the C&C server.

Step 3:   The C&C server checks the information and orders the loader to turn the device into a new bot.

Step 4:   After logging in, the loader downloads and executes an architecture-dependent malicious binary code.

- **Attack Phase**

Step 5:   Once attackers issue a malicious command like a DDoS command, the C&C server relays it to the bots.

Step 6:   All the bots begin to attack the target server in unison.

Mitigation

The US Computer Emergency Readiness Team (US-CERT) gave the following steps to remove Mirai from an infected IoT device in US-CERT. (2016)., Bertino and Islam (2017):

Step 1: Disconnect the device from the network.
Step 2: Perform a reboot. It clears Mirai from the device.
Step 3: If the password is easy-to-guess, change it to a strong password.
Step 4: Should reconnect to the network only after rebooting and changing the password. If the device is reconnected before changing the password, it could be shortly reinfected by Mirai.

In addition, in order to prevent Mirai's infection, the US-CERT recommends the users and administrators to take the following precautions:

- Ensure that all default passwords are changed to strong passwords
- Update IoT devices with the latest security patches
- Disable Universal Plug and Play (UPnP) on routers unless it is absolutely necessary
- Purchase IoT devices from secure companies

- Allow devices to operate only on a home network with a secured Wi-Fi router.
- Monitor ports 23 and 2323. Mirai attempts illegal login by using telnet.
- Look for suspicious traffic on port 48101. Infected devices often attempt to spread Mirai by using this port.

In Nakao (2018), the author has proposed to make use of darknet, honeypot, and sandbox for the proactive response of cyber security. Darknet monitoring is simple and useful for monitoring wider networks. Honeypot and sandbox can be used to emulate vulnerable IoT devices to capture malware and analyze them in detail. He has pointed out that IoT malware problem is already too big to be solved with only manufacturers' effort.

In October 2016, a new type of worm called *Hajime* (means "beginning" in Japanese) was reported by the Security Research Group at Rapidity Networks, Inc. (Edwards & Profetis, 2016) Just like Mirai, Hajime infects IoT devices. The crucial difference from Mirai is that Hajime has neither DDoS capabilities nor attacking code except for the propagation module. Instead, it displays a message which warns the user of the risk of malware (Grange, 2017). In addition, Hajime blocks ports which Mirai uses to infect a device. Hajime is an unethical way but has practically mitigated the threat of Mirai. Thus we can consider Hajime as one of the mitigation methods against the threat of Mirai.

MITIGATION ANALYSIS

Modeling of Mirai's Infection Phenomenon

In Tanaka and Yamaguchi (2017), the authors regarded Mirai's infection phenomenon as a multi-agent system and expressed it with PN^2. The mapping among Mirai's infection phenomenon, multi-agent system, and PN^2 is shown in Table 1. Since Mirai and IoT devices respectively have objectives and behave autonomously to achieve the objectives, they are regarded as autonomous agents. An IoT network enables them to interact with each other, thus it is considered as an environment.

PN^2 is a Petri net-based mathematical tool for modeling and analysis of multi-agent systems. This chapter assumes that the readers have some knowledge about Petri net and preferably even know PN^2. For the formal definitions and analysis techniques, the readers are referred to Yamaguchi, Bin Ahmadon, and Ge, (2016) and Hiraishi (2001). A PN^2, as its name suggests, is a Petri net (called an *environment net*) in which each token is a Petri net (called an *agent net*) again. Each agent net represents an autonomous agent. It has a state which can be changed by the fire of its transition. The environment net represents an environment in which agents interact and move. Each transition in the environment net is synchronized with the transitions in one or more agent nets. The synchronization is decided through dynamic binding by label. In Nakahori and Yamaguchi (2017), the authors have developed a software tool called

Table 1. Mapping among Mirai's infection phenomenon, multi-agent system, and PN^2

Mirai's Infection Phenomenon	Multi-Agent System	PN^2
Mirai, IoT device	Autonomous agent	Agent net
IoT network	Environment	Environment net

PN2Simulator for editing and simulating PN². Figure 3 shows a screenshot of PN2Simulator. The left-side of PN2Simulator shows an environment net, while the right-side shows agent nets. A user can edit those nets through direct manipulation and can execute them by playing a token game interactively. PN2Simulator can highlight which transitions are enabled.

Mirai repeatedly infects IoT devices. This behavior can be modeled as the agent net N_{mirai} shown in Figure 4. Transition t1 represents an infection action by Mirai. An IoT device is initially normal. Once a device is infected by Mirai, it becomes a bot. This behavior can be modeled as the agent net N_{device} shown in Figure 5. Transition t1 represents an infection action by the infected device. An IoT network consists of nodes. A node may or may not connect to another node directly. Figure 6 shows an environment net N_{net} which represents a line topology network consisting of three nodes. Each transition of the environment net represents that Mirai infects a device. For example, transition T1 represents that Mirai of place P1 infects the device of place P2.

Tokens are used to represent a state. An agent net N have zero or more tokens at each place. The state with one token only at place p is denoted by [p]. $(N, [p])$ denotes N with [p]. For agent nets N_{mirai} and N_{device}, the initial state is [p1]. Environment N_{net} has zero or more $(N_{mirai}, [p1])$ and/or $(N_{device}, [p1])$ in

Figure 3. Screenshot of PN2Simulator

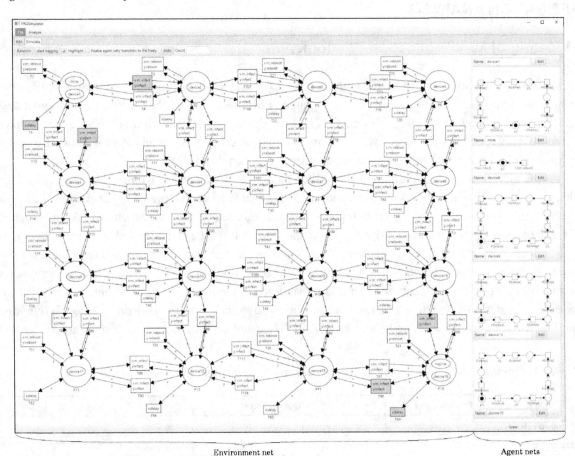

Environment net   Agent nets

Figure 4. Agent net N_{mirai} which represents Mirai

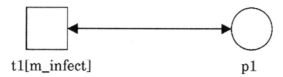

Figure 5. Agent net N_{device} which represents an IoT device

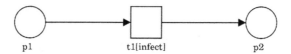

Figure 6. Environment net N_{net} which represents a line topology network consisting of three nodes

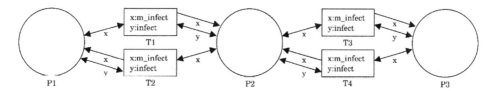

each place as tokens. A token game on N_{net} enables us to simulate Mirai's infection phenomenon. Figure 7 shows a state transition of N_{net} with the following initial state:

Node 1: The device device1 has already been infected by Mirai and is a bot, which is represented as $(N_{device1}, [p2])$ and $(N_{mirai}, [p1])$ at place P1;

Node 2: The device device2 is normal, which is represented as $(N_{device2}, [p1])$ at place P2; and

Node 3: The device device3 is normal, which is represented as $(N_{device3}, [p1])$ at place P3.

This initial state s_0 is illustrated in Figure 7 (a). In s_0, transition T1 is enabled. This means that Mirai attempts to infect device2. The occurrence of T1 in s_0 results in a new state s_1 shown in Figure 7 (b). Mirai is characterized by self-reproduction. Mirai at place P1 produces a copy of itself at place P2, and the copy infects device2. In s_1, transition T3 is enabled. This means that Mirai attempts to infect device3. The occurrence of T2 in s_1 results in a new state s_2 shown in Figure 7 (c). In s_2, all the devices have been infected by Mirai. In this state, there is no longer a transition that can occur.

Modeling of Mitigation Methods

In Yamaguchi and Tanaka (2018), to evaluate mitigation methods against Mirai, the authors reflected them into the PN² model. The analysis was focused on two methods: rebooting and the use of Hajime.

One method is to reboot infected devices. Mirai stays only on the dynamic memory of an infected device, so it could be removed if the device is rebooted. Figure 8 shows an agent net N_{mirai}' of Mirai that is removed by rebooting. This is an extension of N_{mirai} of Figure 4. Transition t2 represents a reboot ac-

Figure 7. A state transition of N_{net} from the initial state with one Mirai

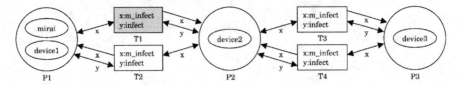

(a) The initial state s₀. Mirai has already infected `device1` *and attempts to infect* `device2`.

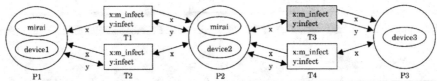

(b) The state s₁ just after Mirai infected `device2`. *Mirai attempts to infect* `device3`.

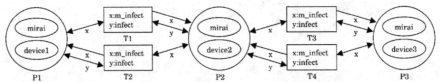

(c) The state s₂ just after Mirai infected `device3`. *There is no longer device which Mirai can infect.*

Figure 8. Agent net N_{mirai}' of Mirai that is removed by rebooting. This also means agent net N_{hajime}'

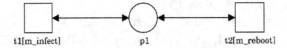

tion by Mirai. This method is simple but carries the risk of reinfection if the device is not updated. Even though an IoT device became a bot, it can be returned to normal by rebooting. However, the device is not always rebooted immediately after the infection. Therefore some delay would be introduced until the reboot. Figure 9 shows an agent net N_{device}' of IoT device that is returned to normal by rebooting after some delay. This is an extension of N_{device} of Figure 5. Transitions t2 and t3 respectively represent a delay action and a reboot action by the infected device.

The other method is to use Hajime. Hajime has the same infection capability as Mirai. Once Hajime infects a device, it protects the device against Mirai. Unfortunately, if the infected device was rebooted, Hajime and its effect would be lost. This behavior is considered to be the same as that of Mirai. Therefore, Hajime was modeled as an agent net N_{hajime}' which has the same structure as N_{mirai}'.

Figure 9. Agent net N_{device}' of IoT device is returned to normal by rebooting after some delay

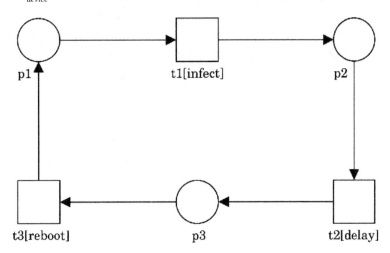

Figure 10 shows an environment net N_{net}' which includes rebooting devices after some delay. This is an extension of N_{net} of Figure 6. As an example, for agents at place P1, transitions t5 and t6 respectively represent a reboot action and a delay action.

Figure 11 shows a state transition of N_{net}' with the following initial state.

Node 1: Device1 has already been infected by Mirai, which is represented as ($N_{device1}$', [p2]) and (N_{mirai}', [p1]) at place P1;

Node 2: Device2 is normal, which is represented as ($N_{device2}$', [p1]) at place P2; and

Node 3: Device3 has already been infected by Hajime, which is represented as ($N_{device3}$', [p2]) and (N_{hajime}', [p1]) at place P3.

Figure 10. Environment net N_{net}' which includes rebooting devices after some delay

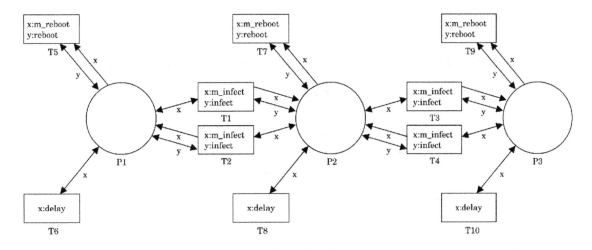

This initial state s_0' is illustrated in Figure 11 (a). In s_0', transitions T1 and T4 are enabled. This means that Mirai and Hajime attempt to infect device2. Transitions T6 and T10 are also enabled. This means time elapses as delay. The occurrence of T4 in s_0' results in a new state s_1' shown in Figure 11 (b). Hajime at place P3 produces a copy of itself at place P2, and the copy infects device2. At this time, Mirai cannot infect device2 any longer. That is, Hajime protects the device against Mirai. After transition T6 occurs in s_1', the occurrence of transition T5 results in a new state s_2' shown in Figure 11 (c). In s_2', since device1 was rebooted after some delay, Mirai exists no more in place P1.

Figure 11. A state transition of N_{net}' from the initial state with one Mirai and one Hajime

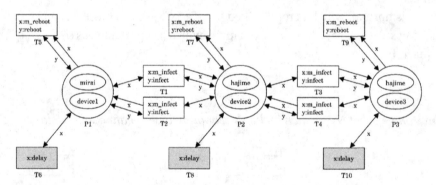

(a) *The initial state s_0'. Mirai and Hajime have respectively infected* `device1` *and* `device3`, *and they attempt to infect* `device2`.

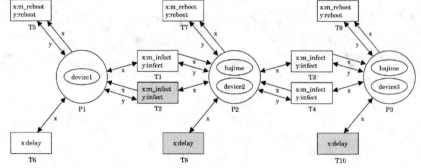

(b) *The state s_1' just after Hajime infected* `device2`. *At this time, Mirai cannot infect it any longer.*

(c) *The state s_2' just after* `device1` *was rebooted after some delay. Mirai exists no more in place* `P1`.

Evaluation of Mitigation Methods

In Yamaguchi, Tanaka, and Bin Ahmadon (in press), the authors evaluated the effect of the mitigation methods against Mirai through two simulation experiments of the PN^2 model.

In the first experiment, they used a grid network composed of 16 nodes. It is illustrated in Figure 12. They measured the infection rate of Mirai (= the number of devices infected by Mirai / the total number of devices) after 1,000 steps under the following condition:

- The delay of rebooting is 0, 1, 2, 3, 4, or 5 steps;
- The initial number n of Hajime is 0, 1, 2, or 3; and
- In the initial state, one Mirai is put at node 1 and n Hajime are put as follows: The first, the second, and the third are respectively at nodes 6, 11, and 16.

Table 2 shows the result of the experiment. It is illustrated in Figure 13. The horizontal axis is the delay of rebooting. The vertical axis is the mean of Mirai's infection rate for 1,000 trials. Let us first consider the case of only rebooting. Rebooting reduced the infection rate to 23.4% when the delay is zero. However, the infection rate steeply increased with the increase in the delay. Even when the delay is one step, the infection rate became 70.3%. Next, let us consider the case of using both of rebooting and Hajime. Hajime reduced Mirai's infection rate to less than 50% without depending on the delay of rebooting. The infection rate decreased with the increase in the initial number of Hajime. However, the reduction rate gradually decreased. The reason is that the network became saturated with Hajime.

Figure 12. The grid network used in the first experiment

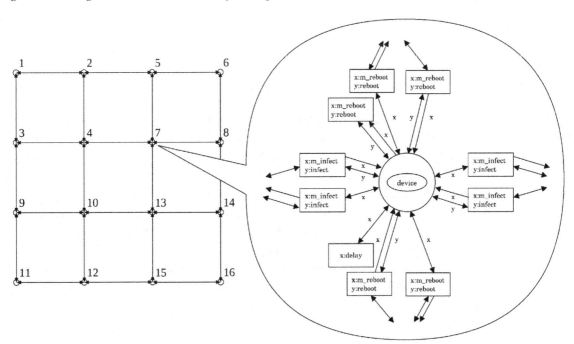

Table 2. Result of the experiment for the grid network

Initial Number of Hajime	Delay of Rebooting [Steps]					
	0	**1**	**2**	**3**	**4**	**5**
0	23.4%	70.3%	83.5%	89.0%	92.0%	93.5%
1	17.7%	40.5%	44.7%	44.5%	45.2%	46.2%
2	13.8%	26.6%	29.8%	30.7%	33.9%	33.1%
3	13.1%	20.7%	22.1%	24.0%	24.2%	24.8%

Figure 13. Effect of rebooting and Hajime to Mirai's infection in the grid network

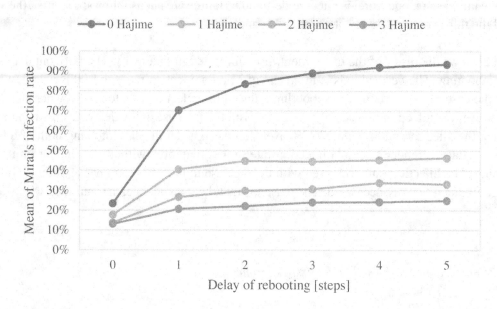

In the second experiment, they used a hierarchy network composed of 16 nodes, which is a ring network of ring networks. It is illustrated in Figure 14. They measured the infection rate of Mirai under the same condition as the first experiment.

Table 3 shows the result of the experiment for the hierarchy network. It is illustrated in Figure 15. The horizontal and vertical axes respectively have the same meaning as those of Figure 13. Let us first consider the case of only rebooting. Rebooting reduced Mirai's infection rate to 4.9% when the delay is zero. The hierarchy network could reduce more the infection rate than the grid network because of the restriction of network structure. However, the infection rate steeply increased with the increase in the delay. Even when the delay is one step, the infection rate became 61.4%. Next, let us consider the case of using both of rebooting and Hajime. Hajime showed higher effect than the case of the grid network because of the same reason as the case of only rebooting.

In addition, the authors of this chapter conducted a simulation experiment to investigate the relationship between the size (the number of nodes) of grid network and the effect of the mitigation methods. They measured the infection rate of Mirai after 1,000 steps under the following condition:

Figure 14. The hierarchy network used in the second experiment

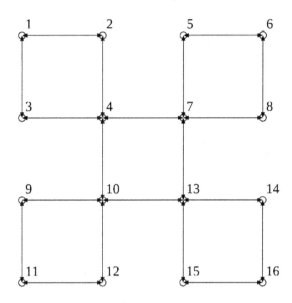

- The size (the number of nodes) of grid network is 9 (=3×. 3), 16 (=4×. 4), or 25 (=5×5);
- The delay of rebooting is 3 steps;
- The initial number *n* of Hajime is 0, 1, 2, or 3; and
- In the initial state, one Mirai is put at node 1 and *n* Hajime are put as follows: The first, the second, and the third are respectively at the lower-right, the lower-left, and the upper-right corner nodes.

Table 4 shows the result of the experiment. It is illustrated in Figure 16. The horizontal axis is the size of grid network. The vertical axis is the mean of Mirai's infection rate for 1,000 trials. Even though the size of grid network varied, Mirai's infection rate did not almost change. The influence of network size is smaller than that of network topology. This suggests that the network topology should be emphasized rather than size.

Table 3. Result of the experiment for the hierarchy network

Initial Number of Hajime	Delay of Rebooting [Steps]					
	0	**1**	**2**	**3**	**4**	**5**
0	4.9%	61.4%	79.3%	86.2%	90.7%	92.0%
1	4.9%	38.8%	42.9%	45.0%	47.4%	47.1%
2	3.3%	25.2%	28.7%	29.0%	33.1%	31.2%
3	3.3%	19.1%	18.9%	21.3%	21.9%	22.1%

Figure 15. Effect of rebooting and Hajime to Mirai's infection in the hierarchy network

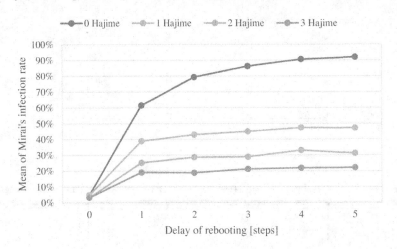

Table 4. Result of the experiment in the case of varying the size of grid network

Size of Grid Network	Initial Number of Hajime			
	0	1	2	3
9	86.8%	46.6%	33.2%	22.7%
16	89.0%	44.5%	30.7%	24.0%
25	89.2%	46.7%	32.2%	22.9%

Figure 16. Relationship between the size of grid network and the effect of the mitigation methods

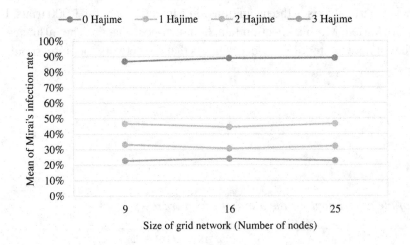

CONCLUSION

This chapter presented IoT malware Mirai's threat and then analyzed the mitigation methods against the threat. They were written in two parts. At the former part, we first traced Mirai's history to show its threat and attack. Next, we revealed Mirai's mechanism from both the static structure and dynamic behavior. Then, we described mitigation methods against the threat. At the latter part, we first explained a PN^2 model of Mirai's infection phenomenon. Next, we reflected the mitigation methods into the PN^2 model. Then, we evaluated the methods through the simulation of the model. The evaluation result shows:

- **Rebooting:** Drastically reduces Mirai's infection rate when the delay is zero. The effect, however, is rapidly lost with the increase in the delay
- **Hajime:** Reduces Mirai's infection rate to less than half without depending on the delay of rebooting. The reduction rate, however, gradually decreases with the increase in the initial number of Hajime.

Is Hajime a "white worm"? Hajime continues to stay at the infected device even though completing the protection against Mirai. Since Hajime still has a remote control mechanism, it should not stay at the devices once the protection completed. It is an interesting future work to turn Hajime into "white worm". In Yamaguchi and Leelaprute (2019), the authors have proposed to extend Hajime to turn it into "white worm" by introducing lifespan to Hajime. In addition, in Yamaguchi (2019), the author has proposed to further extend the time-limited Hajime by introducing the secondary infectivity (the ability to infect a device infected by Mirai). In Molesky, M.J., & Cameron, E.A. (2019), the authors have proposed a perspective of how to utilize white worm technology while overcoming some of its many challenges by balancing individual, business, and government objectives.

Another future work is to develop how to dynamically put Hajime in response to the infection status of Mirai. In Tanaka, Yamaguchi, and Arata (2019), the authors have analyzed the effect of network structure on Mirai's infection. This chapter should become a trigger to interest researchers and engineers in this domain.

REFERENCES

Arzamendi, P., Bing, M., & Soluk, K. (2018). *The ARC of Satori*. Retrieved from https://www.netscout.com/blog/asert/arc-satori

Bertino, E., & Islam, N. (2017). Botnets and Internet of Things Security. *IEEE Computer*, *50*(2), 76–79. doi:10.1109/MC.2017.62

Bonderud, D. (2016). *Leaked Mirai Malware Boosts IoT Insecurity Threat Level*. Retrieved from https://securityintelligence.com/news/leaked-mirai-malware-boosts-iot-insecurity-threat-level/

Devry, J. (2016). Mirai Botnet Infects Devices in 164 Countries. Retrieved from https://www.cybersecurity-insiders.com/mirai-botnet-infects-devices-in-164-countries/

Edwards, S., & Profetis, I. (2016). *Hajime: Analysis of a decentralized internet worm for IoT devices*. Retrieved from https://security.rapiditynetworks.com/publications/2016-10-16/hajime.pdf

Grange, W. (2017). *Hajime battles Mirai for control of the Internet of Things*. Retrieved from https://www.symantec.com/connect/blogs/hajime-worm-battles-mirai-control-internet-things

Grange, W. (2017). *Hajime battles Mirai for control of the Internet of Things*. Retrieved from https://www.symantec.com/connect/blogs/hajime-worm-battles-mirai-control-internet-things

Hiraishi, K. (2001). A Petri-net-based model for the mathematical analysis of multi-agent systems. *IEICE Trans. on Fundamentals, E84-A*(11), 2829–2837.

Kolias, C., Kambourakis, G., Stavrou, A., & Voas, J. (2017). DDoS in the IoT: Mirai and other botnets. *IEEE Computer, 50*(7), 80–84. doi:10.1109/MC.2017.201

Krebs, B. (2016). *KrebsOnSecurity Hit With Record DDoS*. Retrieved from https://krebsonsecurity.com/2016/09/krebsonsecurity-hit-with-record-ddos/

MalwareMustDie. (2016). *MMD-0056-2016 - Linux/Mirai, how an old ELF malcode is recycled*. Retrieved from http://blog.malwaremustdie.org/2016/08/mmd-0056-2016-linuxmirai-just.html

Molesky, M. J., & Cameron, E. A. (2019). Internet of Things: An Analysis and Proposal of White Worm Technology. *Proc. of IEEE ICCE 2019*, 4. 10.1109/ICCE.2019.8662111

Nakahori, K., & Yamaguchi, S. (2017). A support tool to design IoT services with NuSMV. *Proc. of IEEE ICCE 2017*, 84–87. 10.1109/ICCE.2017.7889238

Nakao, K. (2018). Proactive cyber security response by utilizing passive monitoring technologies. *Proc. of IEEE ICCE 2018*. 10.1109/ICCE.2018.8326061

360. netlab. (2017). *Warning: Satori, a Mirai Branch Is Spreading in Worm Style on Port 37215 and 52869*. Retrieved from https://blog.netlab.360.com/warning-satori-a-new-mirai-variant-is-spreading-in-worm-style-on-port-37215-and-52869-en/

Sinaović, H., & Mrdovic, S. (2017), Analysis of Mirai malicious software. Prof. of SoftCOM 2017, 1-5.

Statt, N. (2016). *How an army of vulnerable gadgets took down the web today*. Retrieved from https://www.theverge.com/2016/10/21/13362354/dyn-dns-ddos-attack-cause-outage-status-explained

Tanaka, H., & Yamaguchi, S. (2017). On modeling and simulation of the behavior of IoT devices malwares Mirai and Hajime. *Proc. of IEEE ISCE 2017*, 56–60.

Tanaka, H., Yamaguchi, S., & Arata, T. (2019). Consideration of IoT structure in mitigation against Mirai malware. *Proc. of IEEE ICCE-Berlin 2018*.

US-CERT. (2016). *Heightened DDoS threat posed by Mirai and other botnets*. Retrieved from https://www.us-cert.gov/ncas/alerts/TA16-288A

Yamaguchi, S., Bin Ahmadon, M. A., & Ge, Q. W. (2016). Introduction of Petri Nets: Its Applications and Security Challenges. In B. Gupta, D. P. Agrawal, & S. Yamaguchi (Eds.), *Handbook of Research on Modern Cryptographic Solutions for Computer and Cyber Security* (pp. 145–179). Hershey, PA: IGI Publishing. doi:10.4018/978-1-5225-0105-3.ch007

Yamaguchi, S., & Leelaprute, P. (2019). Hajime worm with lifespan and its mitigation evaluation against Mirai malware based on agent-oriented Petri net PN2. *Proc. of IEEE ICCE 2019*, 4. 10.1109/ICCE.2019.8662079

Yamaguchi, S., & Tanaka, H. (2018), Modeling of infection phenomenon and evaluation of mitigation methods for IoT malware Mirai by agent-oriented Petri net PN2. *Proc. of IEEE ICCE-TW 2018*, 271-272.

Yamaguchi, S., Tanaka, H., & Bin Ahmadon, M. A. (in press). Modeling and Evaluation of Mitigation Methods against IoT Malware Mirai with Agent-Oriented Petri Net PN^2. *International Journal of Internet of Things and Cyber-Assurance*. doi: 10.1504/IJITCA.2019.10021463

York, K. (2016). *Read Dyn's Statement on the 10/21/2016 DNS DDoS Attack*. Retrieved from https://dyn.com/blog/dyn-statement-on-10212016-ddos-attack/

Chapter 17

Leveraging Fog Computing and Deep Learning for Building a Secure Individual Health– Based Decision Support System to Evade Air Pollution

Chitra P.
Thiagarajar College of Engineering, India

Abirami S.
Thiagarajar College of Engineering, India

ABSTRACT

Globalization has led to critical influence of air pollution on individual health status. Insights to the menace of air pollution on individual's health can be achieved through a decision support system, built based on air pollution status and individual's health status. The wearable internet of things (wIoT) devices along with the air pollution monitoring sensors can gather a wide range of data to understand the effect of air pollution on individual's health. The high-level feature extraction capability of deep learning can extract productive patterns from these data to predict the future air quality index (AQI) values along with their amount of risks in every individual. The chapter aims to develop a secure decision support system that analyzes the events adversity by calculating the temporal health index (THI) of the individual and the effective air quality index (AQI) of the location. The proposed architecture utilizes fog paradigm to offload security functions by adopting deep learning algorithms to detect the malicious network traffic patterns from the benign ones.

DOI: 10.4018/978-1-5225-9742-1.ch017

INTRODUCTION

According to 2016 edition of World health statistics, air pollution is considered to be the world's largest single environmental health risk as it is considered to have caused nearly 7 million deaths in the year 2012 globally and around 1.5 million deaths in India. Also, according to WHO's global urban air quality database about 98% of cities in the underdeveloped and developing countries do not meet norms set out in the World Health Organization's (WHO) air quality guidelines. Harmful pollutants from vehicles, industrial exhaust, indoor cook stoves, harmful gases and smokes released during catastrophes such as volcanic eruptions, forest fires etc, are some of the common sources of air pollution. Increased exposure to air pollution causes increased risk of an individual to threats such as heart diseases, stroke, chronic obstructive pulmonary disease, lung cancer, and acute respiratory infections and asthma. Some common harmful health impacts of air pollution on human beings are discussed in Fotopoulou et al. (2016), Khreis, de Hoogh & Nieuwenhuijsen (2018), and Chen et al. (2018). The exploration of the relation between harmful health impacts and exposure of human beings to air pollution can be beneficial only when its assessments are made available to the common people through a decision support system (DSS). This heath impacts assessment through air quality evaluation can bring significant impact on the health status of the enormous urban residents. There are many researches done related to building such a DSS (Kang et al., 2018; Chen et al., 2017; Chen et al., 2018). But, most of them produce only produce general health advisories upon the predicted future values. In this, we propose a DSS which produces individual specific advisories upon the predicted future values and also produce the crucial instantaneous alerts based on the relation evaluated using individual health status and air quality status.

Air quality index (AQI) is an internationally used numerical value used to evaluate the level of air pollution. High AQI values indicate poor air quality and hence adverse health effects. Each country has its own air quality index, corresponding to the national air quality standards. At present, AQI computation are usually done with air pollutant concentration values measured over a specified averaging period by the air quality monitoring sites. Due to the high construction cost these monitoring stations are sparsely placed and hence could give only a limited coverage over the vast urban area. Therefore, the air quality data collected by these monitoring stations is not self-sufficient to portray the real severity of air pollution.

Internet of Things (IoT) is the inter-networking of a collection of physical devices such as sensors and other electronics with software and network connectivity. With recent technology advances in IoT, smart buildings can be equipped with gas sensors to monitor and evaluate the air pollution wrapped with them. The research works has addressed such designs regarding the evaluation of a metropolitan air pollution sensing system (Zheng et al., 2016; Penza et al., 2017; Hu et al., 2016). The AQI values estimated through the analytics of integrating the values obtained from monitoring stations and IoT devices can give clear insights to the air quality of any location than the one obtained from monitoring stations. Min Chen et. al (2018) in his proposed work has utilized this, to predict air quality, through the computation of the multidimensional air quality indicator (M-AQI) based on the air quality values collected through meteorological sites, mobile crowd sourcing and IoT sensing devices. In this proposed work, the same analytics is deployed with additional parameters to calculate a location's effective AQI, using the data from the monitoring stations, IoT devices, meteorological sites and the location's points of interests (POI). A location's effective AQI gives a more precise exploration of air quality in that location than the monitoring stations. The meteorological data imparts the knowledge of the climatic conditions of the location through the parameters like the wind speed, temperature, humidity of the location while the points of interests (POI) data of the location includes data such as the distance of that location from a highly traffic road, the number of peaks at that location, the amount of greeneries at that location etc.

Evolution of IoT has brought wide range of technologies advancement in the field of healthcare. By incorporating new devices and computing technologies IoT serves towards the betterment of human lives by providing latest healthcare facilities from anywhere at any time. These healthcare network and computing infrastructure has rapidly changed the healthcare from closed environments to open environments. Some of the IoT based healthcare works that measure and monitor patients for wide range of diseases are as discussed in Li et al. (2017), Chen et al. (2017), and Hossain and Muhammad (2018). Wearable Internet of Things (wIoT) is an advancement of IoT that includes wearable sensors, internet-connected gateways and has cloud and big data support. Individual health status can be observed through wearable IoT devices that measures individual's health-based data like ECG, respiratory rate and stores them in the cloud. In this proposal, IoT based architectures are incorporated to monitor both the location-based air quality status and individual's health status.

The enormous data collected from monitoring stations, meteorological stations, gas sensors and wIOT continuously flood the cloud data centers. Deployment of an edge infrastructure close to the users for computing, intelligence, and storage can achieve minimum latency and efficient network bandwidth utilization. Fog computing the emerging paradigm in today's network makes this feasible. Fog computing is also known as the cloud on the ground. The basic model of fog computing is as shown in Figure. 1. Smart fog gateways can be employed for devising the process of data collection, data conditioning, intelligent filtering, smart analytics, and selective transfer to the cloud for long-term storage (Constant et al., 2017; Gia et al., 2019; Verma & Sood, 2018). In the proposed work, the entire urban area selected for DSS can be divided into sub-urban areas with every area having a smart fog gateway to perform the data collection and computations.

Figure 1. Basic model of fog computing

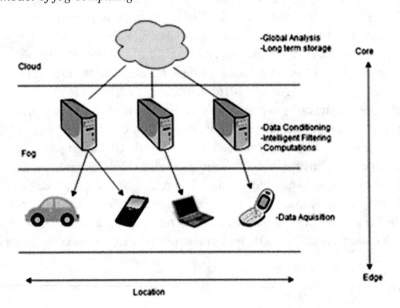

The automatic data collection and the lack of verification are two of IoT's ubiquitous and pervasive nature that makes security breaches and privacy violations more likely in IoT security (Gupta, 2018). Also, the enormous multimedia big data in mobile and cloud computing has created various security and privacy challenges associated to it (Gupta, Yamaguchi & Agrawal, 2018). Individual's health data are sensitive information whose data transfer over public networks would inevitably provoke alteration or unauthorized access by hackers or intruders and therefore necessitates adequate security and privacy solutions (Li et al., 2017; Constant et al., 2017). IoT require a novel shallow and distributed attack detection mechanism due to their architecture and resource constraints so that, the transmission ensures compliance with Health Insurance Portability and Accountability Act (HIPAA). This makes security a priority, rather than an afterthought. Therefore, the healthcare sector can procure the benefits of the IoT, while still ensuring patient safety. The fog nodes set at the edge cloud can be leveraged to offload security functions to handle the expected security issues in IoT thus providing IoT an exclusive opportunity to deploy distributed and collaborative security mechanisms. Among the security mechanism, attack detections can be either signature based or anomaly-based schemes where classical machine learning has been used extensively (Chandola, Banerjee & Kumar, 2009). Fog computing that provides service environment and cloud computing capabilities at the edge of the mobile network can also introduce new modules and functionality in order to provide solutions to analyze network flows and detect network anomalies in real-time applications (Maimó et al., 2018).

Deep learning (DL) is a potential approach used extensively in many applications such as image classification, object recognition, and natural language processing. The self-taught capability of deep learning helps to study the features from the input data hierarchically to illuminate any hidden and unusual patterns from them. This has made deep learning models to be an efficient solution to the most of the IoT security challenges (Maimó et al., 2018; Diro & Chilamkurti, 2018a, 2018b). Also, the supremacy of deep learning algorithms in terms of accuracy when trained with huge amount of data makes it render good performance in air quality predictions (Li et al., 2017; Qi et al., 2018). In this we propose an architecture that integrates an air quality prediction model and a network security model both built using deep learning algorithms.

The objectives of the proposed work are i) Monitoring individuals using wIoT devices. ii) Air quality status and individual's heath status-based event classification for provoking real-time alerts and real-time responses in a secure fog assisted architecture. iii) Build an individual health based DSS through spatial temporal data mining of the predicted air quality values corresponding to individual's health status in the Cloud layer. iv) Exhibit the predicted air quality values on web-based applications and provide health guidance to the individuals.

FOG COMPUTING: PRINCIPLES AND ARCHITECTURE

Fog computing, also known as fog networking or fogging, is an extension of cloud computing. It refers to a decentralized computing structure, where the data and applications resources are placed in logical locations between the data source and the cloud. Such architecture brings the basic analytic services to the network edge, thereby improving the overall network efficiency and performance. Also, fog computing achieves to create a network with lower latency with its capability to process data closer to where it is created. This in turn lessens the amount of bandwidth required compared to that needed for processing in the cloud. Hence, fog computing is a latency-aware computing platform that imperatively supports time-critical applications.

Limitations of the Cloud for IoT Applications

Though the cloud technology allows developers to leverage potential tools to create and deliver IoT applications and services, it also has various limitations, in the implementation of IoT applications. Some of them are

- **High Latency:** The cloud technology cannot guarantee very low latency, the most imperative need of IoT applications due to the long distance between client devices and data processing centers.
- **Inefficient Use of Network Bandwidth:** The vast amount of storage and computing facilities available with the cloud technology makes it more sufficient for processing high volumes of data, but the difficulty is that it cannot provide unlimited bandwidth.
- **Downtime:** The cloud technology in an Internet-based system and is therefore susceptible to technical issues and interruptions in networks. This might raise situations where the customers have to suffer from an outage.
- **Security and Privacy:** In cloud technology, private data in any IoT application has to be globally transferred through interconnected channels alongside with other users' information. This makes the system vulnerable to various cyber-attacks or data loss and hence makes it unsuitable for IoT applications.

Advantages of Fog Computing for IoT Applications

Fog computing, that has decentralized cloud architecture enables data management close to the level where data is generated and most often used. This helps it to meet its three major goals as follows

- It amplifies the efficiency by reducing the amount of data that requires to be transmitted to the cloud for processing and analysis.
- The fog layer being geographically closer to users is highly capable of providing instant responses with reduced latency and reduced bandwidth issues.
- It also provides security and compliance to the data transmission over cloud.

Achievement of the above-mentioned goals makes the fogging approach highly beneficial for the IoT, big data and real-time analytics.

Applications of Fog Computing

The limitations in cloud computing makes it not viable for many IoT applications, and hence fog computing is often used. Its distributed approach addresses the needs of IoT by eliminating the problems such as delay, traffic, processing speed, bandwidth, delivery time, response time, storage data transportation and data processing. Hence, fog computing is ideally suited for all IoT applications. Some of the applications are

- **Connected Cars:** These are semi-autonomous and self-driving cars that operate independently. They demand potential to locally analyze data such as surroundings, driving conditions and directions. Also, they require potential to communicate with the manufacturer to help the progress of vehicle maintenance or track vehicle handling. The fog computing paradigm would enable communications for all of these data sources both at the edge that is the car, and to its end point that is its manufacturer.

- **Health Care:** The fog paradigm can be deployed in many healthcare applications to monitor and serve the patients for a wide range of diseases. In such applications the data transfer requires high security and data integrity. Fog establishes it though its proficient architecture.

- **Smart Cities and Smart Grids:** In applications like smart cities and smart grids, enormous data has to be aggregated from a large number of sensors for processing in order to manage the resources efficiently. Fog computing architectures could be devised to solve this proficiently.

- **Visual Security:** Security and surveillance solutions include everything from the simplest home monitoring systems and burglar alarms, to high-definition, motion-detecting cameras and retina scanning security solutions. The fog computing can be organized for these security and surveillance solutions so as to predict and quickly notify monitoring facilities of any possible security breaches.

- **Real-Time Analytics:** Fog computing deployments can help to facilitate the transfer of data in a wide range of real time application like manufacturing systems that has to instantaneously react to the events as they happen, the financial institutions that use real-time data to inform trading decisions, the detective agencies that monitor for fraud and the organizations that monitor weather and pollution.

Three-Tier Architecture of Fog Computing

The three-tier architecture of fog computing, as shown in Figure 2, is one of the commonly used architectures of fog computing. The components of this architecture are as follows:

- **Tier 1–End Devices:** This layer is occupied by the end devices or the terminal nodes such as IoT enabled sensor nodes and smart hand-held devices such as smart phones, tablets, and smart watches. These end devices are set with global positioning system.

- **Tier 2–Fog Devices:** This layer is the actual fog computing layer that is comprised of fog devices such as router, gateway, switch, and access points that can collaboratively share the available storage and computing facilities.

- **Tier 3–Cloud:** This layer refers to the cloud servers and data centers that have ample amount storage and computing resources.

The three-tier architecture of fog has three interfaces.

1. **The Fog-Cloud Interface:** This interface establishes all services that are distributed from the cloud to the fog devices. It also establishes the links for the fog nodes to pool resources from the cloud.
2. **The Fog-Fog Interface:** This interface associates all fog nodes together so that they can collaborate with each other to share data storage and computing tasks.

Figure 2. Three-tier architecture of fog computing

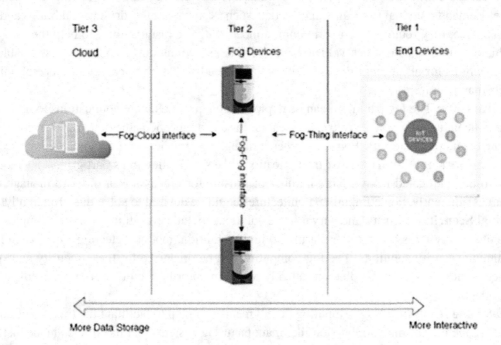

3. **The Fog-Thing Interface:** This interface helps to securely gather data from the IoT devices to the fog nodes for further computations on them.

DEEP LEARNING

A deep structured learning, or more commonly called deep learning is an emerging sub-field of machine learning techniques that utilizes many layers of non-linear information processing for supervised or unsupervised feature extraction, pattern analysis, classification and prediction. It is all about learning multiple levels of prudent and constructive representation and abstraction from data such as images, sound, text and numeric. The most distinctive attribute of deep learning is its efficiency to provide the state-of-the-art accuracy in many tasks, from pattern detection to speech recognition. The reason for it is that, more complex features and input-output relationships are effortlessly learnable through deep learning algorithms. Unlike machine learning algorithms, they can learn automatically, without any manual feature engineering that has to be explicitly coded by the programmers. The massive generation of data- big data that are available for training and the current development in hardware resources such as GPU has an incredible contribution in the success of deep learning over classical machine learning. As an example, Figure 3 shows the procedures involved for utilizing deep learning in AQI forecasting and monitoring.

Some of the popular models within deep learning are as follows:

Figure 3. Procedures involved in AQI monitoring

Multi-Layer Perceptron

Multi-Layer Perceptron (MLP) is a feed forward neural network with three types of layers- the input layer, output layer and hidden layer, as shown in Figure 4. The input layer receives the input signal that has to be processed. The output layer makes decision or prediction on the received input. An arbitrary number of hidden layers that are placed in between the input and output layer are the true computational engine of the MLP. In a MLP the data flows in the forward direction from input to output layer and the neurons in the MLP are trained with the back propagation learning algorithm. MLPs can approximate any continuous function and can solve problems which are not linearly separable. MLPs are widely used for pattern classification, recognition, prediction and approximation.

The computations taking place at every neuron in the output and hidden layer are as follows,

$$o(x) = G(b(2) + W(2)h(x)) \tag{1}$$

Figure 4. Schematic representation of an MLP with single hidden layer

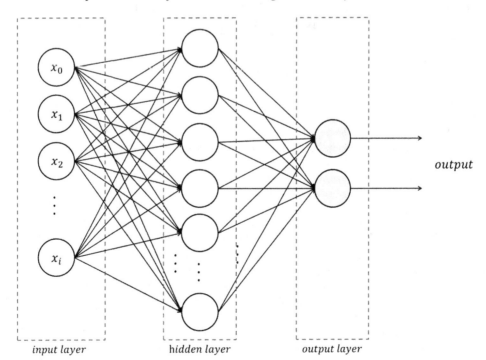

$$h(x) = \mid (x) = s(b(1) + W(1)x) \tag{2}$$

with bias vectors b(1), b(2); weight matrices W(1), W(2)and activation functions G and s. The set of parameters to learn is the set θ= {W(1), b(1), W(2), b(2)}. Typical choices for s include tanh function with tanh(a)=(e^a-e^{-a})/(e^a+e^{-a}) or the logistic sigmoid function, with sigmoid(a)=1/(1+e^{-a}).

Convolutional Neural Networks

Convolutional Neural Networks (CNN) are biologically inspired variants of MLPs that are used for image classification, image clustering and object detection in images. They are also utilized in optical character recognition and natural-language processing. When represented visually as a spectrogram, CNNs can also be applied to sound. In recent times, CNNs have been applied directly to text analytics as well as graph data with graph convolutional networks. This efficacy of CNNs is one of the core reasons for the success of deep learning in many fields.

As, shown in Figure 5, CNN's detect features through the use of filters which are also known as kernels. A filter is just a matrix of values, called weights that are trained to detect specific features. The filter carries out the convolution operation, which is an element-wise product and sum between two matrices. The amount of redundancy present in the input feature is reduced in order to speed up the training process and reduce the amount of memory consumed by the network. This is achieved through many ways and the most common one is max pooling. In max pooling, a window passes over input data and the maximum value within the window is pooled into an output matrix. There are multiple convolutional layers and max pooling operations through which the data is processed to produce the feature maps and is finally converted into a feature vector that is passed into a MLP. This is referred to as a Fully-Connected Layer that performs high-level reasoning in the model.

If the k-th feature map at a given layer is represented as h^k, whose filters are determined by the weights W^k and bias b^k, then the feature map h^k is obtained as follows for tanh activation function

$$h_{ij}^k = \tanh((W^k * x)_{ij} + b^k) \tag{3}$$

The output of the Fully-Connected Layer gives the prediction of the output probabilities of each class. The above described network comprising the convolutional layers, max pooling layers and the fully- connected layer updates its weights and optimize its objective by back propagating the gradients through the same layers.

Figure 5. Schematic representation of convolutional neural networks

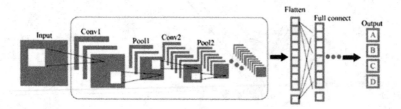

Recurrent Neural Networks

Recurrent Neural Networks (RNN) are powerful set of deep learning algorithms that are good for modeling sequence data such as sound, time series sensor data or written natural language. RNN includes a feedback loop through which the output from step n-1 is fed back to the network and influences the outcome of step n. By this way the RNN differ from feed forward networks. The process of carrying memory forward is mathematically represented as

$$h_t = \Phi(Wx_t + Uh_{t-1})$$
(4)

where h_t is the hidden state at time step t, x_t is the input at the same time step. This is modified by a weight matrix W added to the hidden state of the previous time step h_{t-1} multiplied by its own hidden-state-to-hidden-state matrix U, otherwise known as a transition matrix. The extent of importance to accord for both the present input and the past hidden state is determined by the weight matrices. Through the extension of backpropagation called backpropagation through time, the weights are adjusted in order to minimize the error function. The sum of the weight input and hidden state is squashed by the activation function Φ. Figure 6 shows the complete sequence of a RNN unfolded into a full network.

In traditional RNN during the gradient back-propagation phase, the weights in the transition matrix have a strong impact on the learning process. Small weights in this matrix can lead to a situation where the gradient signal gets too small making the learning process very slow or even stop altogether. This is referred to as vanishing gradients problem. This makes the task of learning long-term dependencies tedious. On the contrary, if the weights are large then it can lead to large gradient signal causing the learning to diverge. This is known as exploding gradients problem. Introduction of the memory cell in the LSTM model, that is composed of four main elements: an input gate, a neuron with a self-recurrent connection, a forget gate and an output gate can handle these issues in RNN as shown in Figure 7.

Updation of memory cells at every time step t is described by the equations below.

$$i_t = \sigma(W_i x_t + U_i h_{t-1} + b_i)$$
(5)

$$\tilde{C}_t = \tanh(W_c x_t + U_c h_{t-1} + b_c)$$
(6)

Figure 6. Schematic representation of recurrent neural networks

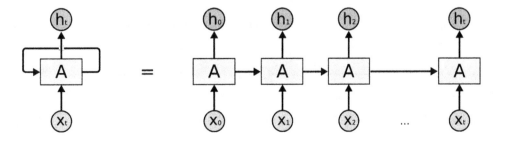

$$f_t = \sigma(W_f x_t + U_f h_{t-1} + b_f) \tag{7}$$

$$C_t = i_t * \tilde{C}_t + f_t * C_{t-1} \tag{8}$$

$$o_t = \sigma(W_0 x_t + U_0 h_{t-1} + b_0) \tag{9}$$

$$h_t = o_t * \tanh(C_t) \tag{10}$$

where x_t is the input to the memory cell layer at time t, W_i, W_f, W_c, W_o, U_i, U_f, U_c, and U_o are weight matrices, b_i, b_f, b_c and b_o are bias vectors.

Restricted Boltzmann Machines

Restricted Boltzmann Machine (RBM) is an undirected graphical model that plays an important role in dimensionality reduction, classification and regression. RBM constitute the building blocks of Deep-Belief Networks. RBM are shallow, two-layer neural networks. The first layer of the RBM is called the

Figure 7. Structure of a memory cell

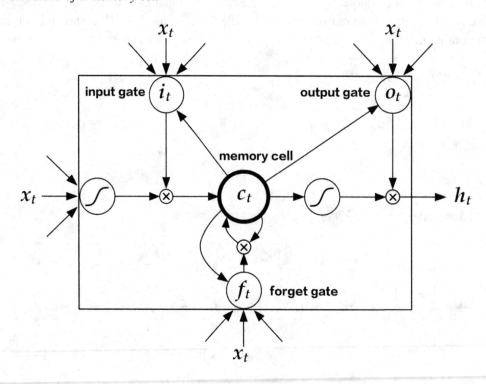

visible or input layer, and the second is the hidden layer. The following Figure 8 shows the graphical model of the RBM where the interconnections between visible units and hidden units are established using symmetric weights.

Each circle represents a node that is connected to each other across layers, but no two nodes of the same layer are linked. Each node is a place of computation that processes input and makes stochastic decisions about whether to transmit it or not. RBM learn to reconstruct data by themselves in an unsupervised fashion, making several forward and backward passes between the visible layer and hidden layer.

Deep Belief Networks

A deep-belief network (DBN) refers to a stack of RBM layers, in which each RBM layer communicates with both the previous and subsequent layers. It is a network assembled out of many single-layer networks. Except the first and final layers each layer in a DBN has a dual role. It serves as the hidden layer to the nodes that come before it and as the input layer to the nodes that come after. Deep-belief networks are used to recognize, cluster and generate images, video sequences and motion-capture data. They model the joint distribution between observed vector x and the l hidden layers h^k is as follows:

$$P(x, h^1, ..., h^l) = (\prod_{k=0}^{l-2} P(h^k \mid h^{k+1})) P(h^{l-1}, h^l) \tag{11}$$

where x=h°, $P(h^k \mid h^{k+1})$ is a conditional distribution for the visible units conditioned on the hidden units of the RBM at level k, and $P(h^{l-1}, h^l)$ is the visible-hidden joint distribution in the top-level RBM. The architecture of a Deep Belief Network with two RBMs is as shown in Figure 9.

Figure 8. Graphical model of the restricted Boltzmann machines

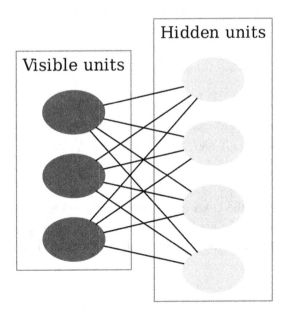

Figure 9. Architecture of a deep belief network with two RBMs

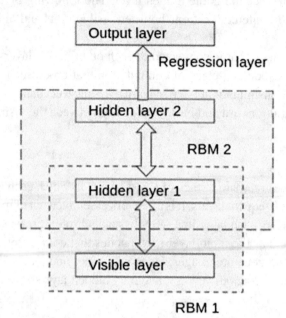

Generative Adversarial Networks

Generative Adversarial Networks (GAN) has huge potential to mimic any distribution of data. They are deep neural network architectures comprising two networks put in opposition against one another. One neural network, called the Generator, generates new data instances, while the other, called the Discriminator, evaluates them for authenticity. Generally, the GANs take a long time to train. When the discriminator is being trained the generator, values are held constant and similarly when the generator is trained the discriminator values are held constant. Both the generator and discriminator train against a static adversary. The training of GAN is done as a fight between generator and discriminator. This can be represented mathematically as,

$$\min_{G} \max_{D} V(G, D) \tag{12}$$

$$V(D,G) = E_{x \sim p_{data}(x)} [\log D(x)] + E_{z \sim p_z(z)} [\log(1 - D(G(z)))] \tag{13}$$

During training, each side of the GAN can overpower the other. If the discriminator is too good, the generator will struggle to read the gradient. If the generator is too good, it will persistently exploit weaknesses in the discriminator that lead to false negatives. Optimal choice of respective learning rates can help to mitigated this.

Deep Autoencoders

A deep autoencoder consists of two symmetrical deep-belief networks with four or five shallow layers, as shown in Figure 10. Among them half of the network represents encoding while the later half represents decoding. Though autoencoders belong to the neural network family, they are closely related to Principal Components Analysis (PCA). But still they are much more flexible than PCA. Autoencoders can represent both linear and non-linear transformation in encoding but PCA can only perform linear transformation. The imperative objective of autoencoder is to minimize reconstruction error between the input and output. Through this, the autoencoders learns significant features present in the data. The number of neurons in the output layer is exactly the same as the number of neurons in the input layer. The different types of Autoencoders are

- Under complete Autoencoders
- Sparse Autoencoders
- Denoising Autoencoders (DAE)
- Contractive Autoencoders (CAE)

Deep Learning for Air Quality Forecasting

City services and monitoring of cities are made more responsive, interactive and efficient in Smart Cities. The people and stakeholders do better interaction in order to benefit in improvising quality of urban services and city life. The air pollution problem is one of the serious issues being faced by the people due to environmental and climate changes induced by them. Air pollution causes various impacts on human health, including respiratory problems, heart and lung diseases, and premature death. Air Quality Index (AQI) is an important parameter that helps in understanding how clean or unhealthy the air is (U.S.E.P.

Figure 10. Deep autoencoders

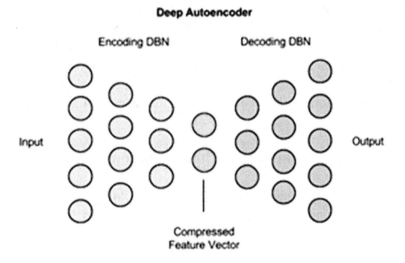

Agency, 2014). Therefore, forecasting AQI parameters could be an important to precautionary measures that could enhance the lifestyle of the common people.

Analysis of environmental time series data implies that they are highly complex, chaotic, high dimensional and noisy in nature. The traditional shallow machine learning models do not have the capacity for modeling them with high accuracy. Deep learning that is often associated with complex real-world data can achieve good accuracy in the problem of time series prediction (Coelho et al., 2017). Due to the efficacy of deep learning several DNN architectures are presented and published for predicting AQI values and also the air pollutants concentration. For instance, in Kim et al. (2009) and Ong, Sugiura, and Zettsu (2016) the authors propose a method using RNN, a family of neural networks for processing sequential data, to predict air quality by using the past information database of several pollutants concentrations. The predicted result of RNN model discussed in the above works gives better modeling performance and higher interpretability than the other data-driven prediction modeling methods. LSTM, a special kind of RNN is also utilized to give efficient results in air quality predictions (Reddy et al., 2018).

A new deep learning-based ozone level prediction model is proposed in Ghoneim and Manjunatha (2017), that considers the pollution and weather correlations integrally. The improved accuracy of deep learning algorithms has attracted researchers to perform time series analysis, interpolation, prediction, and feature analysis of fine-grained air quality using deep learning (Qi et al., 2018). Many machine learning approaches such as Artificial Neural Networks cannot handle non-linear temporal dependency and spatial relationships between multiple spatial time series data. But this is efficiently tackled by the geo-context based diffusion convolutional recurrent neural network proposed in (Lin et al., 2018).

Most advanced deep learning algorithms like the deep auto encoders and deep belief networks are also utilized for air quality prediction as discussed in Eravci and Ferhatosmanoglu (2018) and Lu et al. (2018). Unlike any other baseline approaches the proposed prediction models using deep auto encoders and deep belief networks show enhanced base representations and hence increased prediction accuracy. In Yi et al. (2018), a deep neural network based approach that consists of a spatial transformation component and a deep distributed fusion network is proposed to predict the air quality of next 48 hours for each monitoring station is proposed and compared to be efficient with many state-of-art algorithms.

Apart from the time series prediction, the useful information gathered through these predictions is made available to the local people either through a web service or some decision-based support system. This can be achieved through various big-data and machine learning based techniques as discussed in Kang et al. (2018). A personalized health advisory model based on individual characteristics and exposure information is designed by estimating the high-resolution concentrations of air pollution with big data analytics in Chen et al. (2017). Similarly, in Chen et al. (2018) a big data testbed is set up for the deployment of air quality-aware healthcare applications. While the above approaches aim in building an accuracy efficient model the author in Asgari, Farnaghi, and Ghaemi (2017) discuss a framework utilizing Apache Hadoop to form a cluster of processing machines in order to improve the processing speed of the model.

Deep Learning for Security in Fog-to-Things Communications

The advancements in cloud computing has lead to the emerging IoT applications in various fields that play a crucial role in improving life quality along with various security breaches in the cloud (Negi, Mishra & Gupta, 2013). On the other hand, IoT deployment involves linking traditionally separate multidisciplinary components. This nature of IoT has introduced new security challenges (Stergiou et al, 2018). Various IoT applications require novel cyber security models and decisions distributed at the edge of the network. Success of deep learning in many big data areas indicates that deep learning-based security in fog-to things computing can be a beneficiary approach for attack detection. The massive amount of data produced by IoT devices enable deep models to learn better than shallow algorithms. Because of its high-level feature extraction capability, the use of deep learning for attack detection in the cyberspace could be a tough mechanism to any novel attacks.

Deep learning methods transform the security of IoT systems from secure communication between devices to security-based intelligence systems. Deep learning algorithms are highly capable of data exploration to distinguish between the normal and abnormal behaviour of the traffic patterns within the IoT components and the cloud. The traffic pattern in each part of the IoT system can be scrutinized to identify any malicious behaviour at early stages. Moreover, with their intelligence to predict future, deep learning algorithms can also predict new attacks, which are generally the mutations of previous attacks. The security method, for an IoT application that incorporates healthcare must consider and balance between security and flexible access during emergency situations and hence remains a critical issue (Zhang & Zhang, 2011).

Like any other services, that have fog nodes as a proxy, to offload expensive storage and computations from IoT devices, security procedures in IoT also could be deployed at fog layer. Thus, fog nodes provide a unique opportunity for IoT in setting distributed and shared security mechanisms. Many works related to implementing security handling mechanisms at the fog nodes have been researched and realized (Roman, Lopez & Mambo, 2018).

Leveraging deep learning algorithms that are flexible against morphing attacks with high detection accuracy, for handling security issues at the fog nodes can improvise the IoT systems in many perspectives as discussed in Maimó et al. (2018), Diro and Chilamkurti (2018a, 2018b), and Abeshu and Chilamkurti (2018). In Maimó et al. (2018), the author performs Anomaly Symptom Detection (ASD) model evaluation throughput and anomaly detection performance where deep learning techniques are used to analyze network flows and to detect network anomalies. Deep learning algorithms create high level invariant representations on the training data. This indicates the efficacy of deep learning in security to learn the true face of cyber data on even small variations or changes. The performance comparison of the deep model against traditional machine learning approaches and the distributed attack detection against the centralized detection system are evaluated in Diro and Chilamkurti (2018a).

Some of the limitations of classical machine learning in attack detection that has hindered their penetration into the security market are its low accuracy, lack of automatic feature engineering, reduced scalability, low detection rate, incapability of detecting small mutants of existing attacks and zero-day attacks. In Diro and Chilamkurti (2018b), the author proposes a LSTM based network for distributed cyber-attack detection in fog-to-things communication. This approach mitigates the shortcomings of the classical machine learning algorithms. The distributed deep learning scheme of cyber-attack detection in fog-to-things computing is of ultimate beneficiary than shallow algorithms. A novel distributed cyber-attack detection in fog-to-things computing based on stacked autoencoders shows superior results than shallow models in terms of detection accuracy, false alarm rate, and scalability (Abeshu & Chilamkurti, 2018). In Ieracitano et al. (2018), the authors propose an intrusion detection system (IDS) that leverages the complementary strengths of both automated feature engineering provided by deep learning and manual statistical driven optimized feature engineering based on human-in-the-loop and big data visualization that helps the learning model to better correlate the input-output relationship. In this IDS, the most correlated features were extracted using statistical methods and were fetched as input to a deep autoencoder classifier followed by a shallow MLP classifier for potential threat detection.

PROPOSED SYSTEM

The adverse effects of air pollution due to accelerated growth of globalization are the major concerns that have to be mitigated in order to obtain a better lifestyle among the urban residents. The proposed system aims to build a decision support system based on the location's effective AQI values and the individual's health status in order to enhance the standard of living of the urbanites. Air Quality Index (AQI) is a globally used parameter that denotes the quality of the air stating how good it is to the human beings. Many monitoring stations are been built around cities in order to monitor the air quality of the cities. These values are in turn utilized to govern air quality policies and remedies to overcome the undesirable effects of air pollution. Due to the large amount of cost that has to be invested in the construction of a monitoring station, every city has only a sparse number of monitoring stations. Due to this limitation location based AQI values are not available throughout the cities. In this proposed system, apart from the AQI values obtained from the monitoring stations we also utilize the pollutant concentration values obtained from the IoT sensors along with the meteorological data and location-based Points of Interest (POI) in order to calculate the location based AQI values. The meteorological conditions such a wind, humidity, temperature, precipitation at a particular spatial also influence the AQI values of that location. Also, the POI of the location such as its elevation, its proximity to a road with high traffic, amount of greeneries around the location persuades the value of AQI of the location. Hence, the calculation of the effective AQI of the location using pollutant concentration values obtained from the IoT sensors, meteorological data and POI data along with the one obtained from the monitoring stations would provide a more prominent location based AQI value.

Calculating location based AQI alone could not provide any beneficiaries to the common people unless they are utilized in the right manner for the individual to evade from the hazardous effects of air pollution. In order to achieve this objective, in the proposed system the effect of location based effective AQI value over individual's health is analyzed and the also future effects are predicted. The results of these analyses and prediction are made available to the individual through a decision support system that provides health-based advisories to the individuals. The advisories would include suggestions for sleep, food and amount of risk involved for an individual in the exposure to the air pollution of a particular location. Also, the predicted location based effective AQI values are made available through web-based services for the wellbeing of common people. These objectives of our proposed system are beneficial to the common in two means. One is they help to improvise the health status of the individual by providing health-based advisories to evade from air pollution and the other is they forecast the serious effects every individual undergoes due to air pollution which portrays the impiety of air pollution.

Individual's health data like ECG, respiratory rate are collected from wearable IOT (wIOT) devices and individual's temporal health index (THI) is calculated. The effect of air pollution on individual's health is analyzed by investigating the location based effective AQI value with the THI of the individual. The output of the analysis of THI with respect to the location based effective AQI gives the risk ratio of the individual to that particular AQI. Based on these investigations future effects are also predicted for supporting the individuals through decision support system. The architecture of the proposed system for a single zone is as shown in Figure 11.

The fog paradigm is utilized for full filling the objectives of the proposed system. The entire urban area is divided into different zones or sub-urban areas as shown in Figure 12. The values of location based effective AQI value and the THI of the individuals on every zone is calculated on the edge cloud in order to allow faster analytics and reduce network pressure. After the calculation of these values the risk ratio of every individual to their location based AQI value is also estimated in the edge cloud. Spatio-Temporal mining concept is used to analyze the events adversity at every time instant and timely alerts are generated when an individual's health status to a particular AQI is critical. These alerts can help the individual's to rescue themselves from the adversity of air pollution on that location at that instant of time.

After processing in the edge cloud the values such as location based effective AQI, individual's THI and the risk ratio of the individual are all transferred to the cloud where a prediction model predicts the possible future events and location based AQI to support the decision support system that provides health based advisories to the individual through mobile-client service. Also the forecasted AQI values are made available on web based services in order invoke awareness about the air pollution among the common people.

The transfer of individual's health data from the wIoT to the edge cloud for processing has to take place in a secured manner as the personal data of the individuals are highly confidential. This motivates the idea of implementing the distributed security mechanisms on the fog nodes. By doing so the all types of security malwares can be detected and avoided efficiently without much latency. The proposed system aims to incorporate a distributed deep learning-based security mechanism in the fog nodes in order to analyze the network flows and detect any network anomalies. The implementation of all parameter computations and security mechanism in the fog nodes enhances the utility of the proposed system.

DATABASE REQUIRED FOR THE DECISION SUPPORT SYSTEM

Monitoring Station Data

Based on the observed pollutant concentration values, every monitoring station calculates the AQI value on hour basis. Due to the high cost of construction only limited number of monitoring stations is available along the urban region considered for the proposed architecture.

Meteorology Data

This data includes location-based values of wind speed, temperature, precipitation and humidity on hourly basis. Location based meteorology data is collected from the government's meteorology centre. Researches had proved that the amount of a pollutant concentration and hence the AQI value greatly varies with these meteorology parameters.

Points of Interests (POIs) Data

Location based POIs includes the topography features of that location such as its elevation, distance from the available peaks nearby, distance from the nearby roads with huge traffic flow rate, amount of

Figure 11. Architecture of the proposed system on a sub-urban area

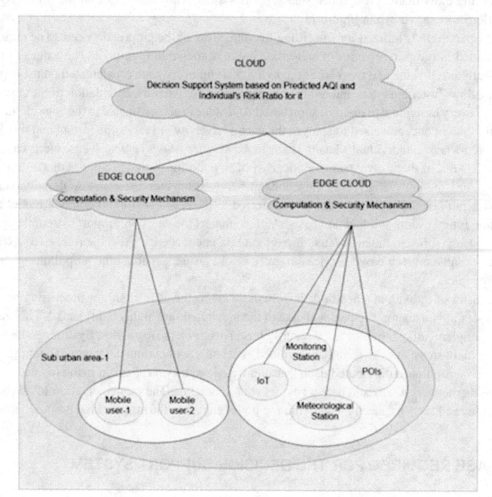

Figure 12. Division of the urban area

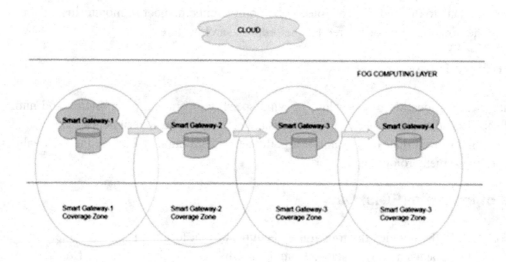

greeneries around it, etc. The POIs in a location greatly manipulate the value of AQI in it. For example, the locations near to traffic roads embrace adverse effects while the locations near to greeneries are less susceptible to the adversity of air pollution.

IoT Gas Sensor Data

The IoT gas sensors such as the Airveda sensor are placed at every location of the urban area to collect the location-based air pollutant concentration values. The AQI value is calculated using the collected pollutant concentration values. This AQI is combined with the AQI values obtained from the monitoring station values in order to calculate the location based effective AQI value.

wIoT Health Sensor Data

Individual's health-based data such as ECG, respiratory rate, body temperature are collected from their wearables (e.g. BodyGuardian Heart remote monitoring system) in order to calculate the individual's temporal health index (THI). This value along with the location based effective AQI value is utilized to analyze the amount of risk ratio an individual carry with respect to a particular location.

Proposed Architecture for Fog Based Decision Support System

The proposed architecture is a four layered architecture as show in Figure 13. The four layers are,

Data Collection Layer

Data Collection Layer performs the task of data retrieval from the monitoring stations, meteorological station and various IoT devices that collect the air pollutant concentration values and individual health status values such as ECG, respiratory rate and body temperature. The POIs of every location is fixed static for every location. The data collected at this layer are heterogeneous in nature and all do not fall on the same time stamp. It is the responsibility of the Fog nodes to synchronize the whole data collected from heterogeneous platforms over a universal time stamp.

Computation and Security Threats Detection Layer

The Computation and Security Threats Detection Layer comprises the fog nodes that perform the actual parameter calculation and monitor the network traffic for security threats. Due to these imparted capabilities the fog nodes acts as smart gateways. The entire urban area is divided into different zones as shown in Figure 12 and each zone has a smart gateway placed exclusively for it. The computations performed in this layer are as follows,

$$
\begin{aligned}
Location\ based\ effective\_AQI =\\
w1.AQI\_MonitoringStation +\\
w2.\ Impact\_MeteorologicaData +\\
w3.AQI\_IoTSensors +\ w4.Impact\_POI
\end{aligned}
\tag{14}
$$

Figure 13. Three-layered fog based architecture of the proposed system

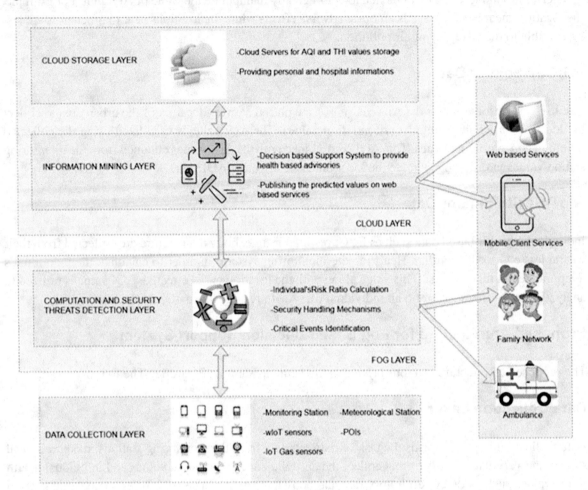

where, AQI _MonitoringStation refers to the AQI value obtained from the monitoring station.
Impact_MeteorologicaData refers to the impact of climate on that location at that instant.
AQI_IoTSensors refers to the AQI value obtained from the IoT Gas sensors.
Impact_POI refers to the impact of POIs in that location.
w1, w2, w3, w4 refers to the weightage given for those corresponding parameters.

$$THI = \; w5.ECG\_value + \; w6.RespiratoryRate\_value + \\ w7.\,BodyTemperature\_value$$

(15)

where, ECG_value refers to the individual's ECG value.
RespiratoryRate_value refers to the individual's Respiratory rate value.
BodyTemperature_value refers to the individual's Body temperature value.
w5, w6, w7 refers to the weightage given for those corresponding parameters.

The THI value corresponds to how sensitive the individual is corresponding to a particular disease the individual is likely to acquire. Hence the values of the weights w5, w6, w7 are determined based on the disease the individual is likely to acquire.

$$Risk\ Ratio = U(\frac{THI}{effective\_AQI}) \tag{16}$$

where, U refers to a weight index that varies with the type of disease the decision support system is supposed to support the individual.

The security mechanisms are imparted through deep learning algorithms distributed at every fog node as shown in Figure 14, in order to detect the malwares from the benign ones. The master security node (fog node) periodically updates the parameters and hence the security model built based on deep learning algorithms in every fog node.

The fog nodes also checks for critical events at every time instant based on the calculated Risk Ratio. During high values the fog nodes are imparted the capability to generate alerts to the individual and their family network and also carry the information to a nearby health center for further necessary actions. The calculated values are further stored in the cloud for building the decision support system.

Information Mining Layer

The information from the fog nodes that are stored in the cloud is processed in this information mining layer for building a well-equipped decision support system. The pattern mining required for forecasting the future AQI values and their impacts on individuals is obtained using online deep learning models that has the capability of updating themselves according to the flow of inputs. Based on the forecasted effects health-based advisories are provided to the individuals that would help them to evade from the adversities of air pollution. This is done via a mobile client service. Also, the predicted AQI values are made available to the public through web services. The advisories from the decision support system are highly beneficial to the vulnerable communities- the individuals suffering from respiratory and heart ail-

Figure 14. Deep learning based distributed attack detection system

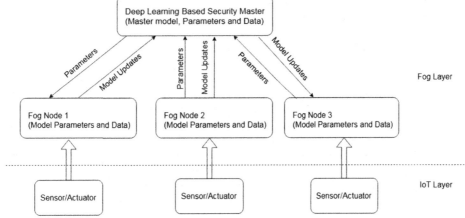

ments- to avoid or reduce their exposure to air pollution on adverse days. Compared to the other decision support systems that are built to support people to avoid air pollution, the architecture of this proposed system is based on fog paradigm and the decision support system is with respect to individual's health status for a particular disease they are likely to acquire. This is the novelty of the proposed system.

Cloud Storage Layer

The cloud storage layer plays receives and aggregates the location based effective AQI and health data summaries from various fog nodes that covers the entire urban area. From the collected data this layer provides information to the information mining layer that has the decision support system. The cloud storage layer also provides the related informations such as individual's family phone numbers, hospital location and other services for handling an emergency situation that might arise in the computation and security threats detection layer. This layer also sends update rules to the fog nodes for handling the proposed applications.

The Development of Fog Based Decision Support System

The flow of data in the proposed architecture is as shown in Figure 15.

Figure 15. Flow chart of the proposed system

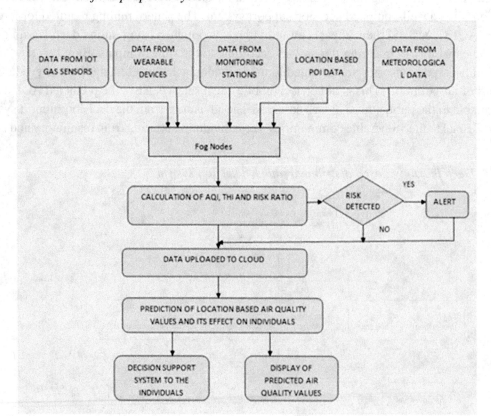

The need for Fog paradigm in the proposed architecture can be fulfilled only when the implemented fog devices are proficient to perform triumphant processing at the very early stage. A wide variety of Fog nodes such as Raspberry Pi or the embedded microprocessor Intel Edison with various hardware and software capabilities can be chosen for the proposed application. The required deep learning security model can be built through any high-level programming languages (e.g. C++, Python, and Java.) using any real time database available for security modeling and are placed on every fog nodes. Similarly the deep learning based prediction model can be developed through any high-level programming languages (e.g. C++, Python, and Java.) in the cloud using the real time database available for air quality modeling. Proper communication link via gateways and are established between the cloud and fog layer. This facilitates the transfer of data that have been aggregated and computed at the fog layer to the cloud and the updates the application rules from the cloud to the fog nodes that are created based on the deeper analytics on the data collected from the fog nodes.

CONCLUSION

The enormous growth of globalization has lead to adverse impacts of air pollution on human health. This has gradually led to the downfall of average life expectancy on earth. Effective measures have to be made without delay in order to improvise the urban lifestyle. The most efficient solution for this would be to create awareness about the menacing effects of air pollution among the common people. The advancement in the computations in today's world has made it possible for proficiently evaluating the effect of air pollution on individual health. The objective of the proposed system is to achieve this through a decision-based support system that incorporates the AQI values and individual health status to particularly support the vulnerable groups suffering from heart and respiratory ailments to evade air pollution.

The proposed system exploits deep learning algorithms for implementing security mechanism and prediction of the effects of air pollution on individual's health. The efficacy of deep learning algorithms makes the proposed system more prudent. The novelty of the proposed system is that the decision support system is built with respect to individual's health status for a particular disease they are likely to acquire by utilizing fog paradigm. The employment of fog nodes for computations and security management creates low-latency network connections which in turn reduces the amount of bandwidth utilized. These benefits of the proposed architecture enhance the utility of the system. In future, more proficient algorithms for prediction of air quality status on individual's health status and security breaches can be developed for improving the accuracy of the proposed application.

REFERENCES

Abeshu, A., & Chilamkurti, N. (2018). Deep learning: The frontier for distributed attack detection in fog-to-things computing. *IEEE Communications Magazine*, *56*(2), 169–175. doi:10.1109/MCOM.2018.1700332

Asgari, M., Farnaghi, M., & Ghaemi, Z. (2017, September). Predictive mapping of urban air pollution using Apache Spark on a Hadoop cluster. In *Proceedings of the 2017 International Conference on Cloud and Big Data Computing* (pp. 89-93). ACM. 10.1145/3141128.3141131

Chandola, V., Banerjee, A., & Kumar, V. (2009). Anomaly detection: A survey. *ACM Computing Surveys*, *41*(3), 15. doi:10.1145/1541880.1541882

Chen, L., Xu, J., Zhang, L., & Xue, Y. (2017, August). Big data analytic based personalized air quality health advisory model. In *2017 13th IEEE Conference on Automation Science and Engineering (CASE)* (pp. 88-93). IEEE. 10.1109/COASE.2017.8256082

Chen, M., Yang, J., Hu, L., Hossain, M. S., & Muhammad, G. (2018). Urban healthcare big data system based on crowdsourced and cloud-based air quality indicators. *IEEE Communications Magazine*, *56*(11), 14–20. doi:10.1109/MCOM.2018.1700571

Chen, M., Yang, J., Zhou, J., Hao, Y., Zhang, J., & Youn, C. H. (2018). 5G-smart diabetes: Toward personalized diabetes diagnosis with healthcare big data clouds. *IEEE Communications Magazine*, *56*(4), 16–23. doi:10.1109/MCOM.2018.1700788

Chen, Y., Shen, H., Smith, K. R., Guan, D., Chen, Y., Shen, G., ... Tao, S. (2018). Estimating household air pollution exposures and health impacts from space heating in rural China. *Environment International*, *119*, 117–124. doi:10.1016/j.envint.2018.04.054 PMID:29957353

Coelho, I. M., Coelho, V. N., Luz, E. J. D. S., Ochi, L. S., Guimarães, F. G., & Rios, E. (2017). A GPU deep learning metaheuristic based model for time series forecasting. *Applied Energy*, *201*, 412–418. doi:10.1016/j.apenergy.2017.01.003

Constant, N., Borthakur, D., Abtahi, M., Dubey, H., & Mankodiya, K. (2017). *Fog-assisted wiot: A smart fog gateway for end-to-end analytics in wearable internet of things*. arXiv preprint arXiv:1701.08680

Diro, A., & Chilamkurti, N. (2018b). Leveraging LSTM networks for attack detection in fog-to-things communications. *IEEE Communications Magazine*, *56*(9), 124–130. doi:10.1109/MCOM.2018.1701270

Diro, A. A., & Chilamkurti, N. (2018a). Distributed attack detection scheme using deep learning approach for Internet of Things. *Future Generation Computer Systems*, *82*, 761–768. doi:10.1016/j.future.2017.08.043

Eravci, B., & Ferhatosmanoglu, H. (2018). Diverse relevance feedback for time series with autoencoder based summarizations. *IEEE Transactions on Knowledge and Data Engineering*, *30*(12), 2298–2311. doi:10.1109/TKDE.2018.2820119

Fotopoulou, E., Zafeiropoulos, A., Papaspyros, D., Hasapis, P., Tsiolis, G., Bouras, T., ... Zanetti, N. (2016). Linked data analytics in interdisciplinary studies: The health impact of air pollution in urban areas. *IEEE Access: Practical Innovations, Open Solutions*, *4*, 149–164. doi:10.1109/ACCESS.2015.2513439

Ghoneim, O. A., & Manjunatha, B. R. (2017, September). Forecasting of ozone concentration in smart city using deep learning. In *2017 International Conference on Advances in Computing, Communications and Informatics (ICACCI)* (pp. 1320-1326). IEEE. 10.1109/ICACCI.2017.8126024

Gia, T. N., Dhaou, I. B., Ali, M., Rahmani, A. M., Westerlund, T., Liljeberg, P., & Tenhunen, H. (2019). Energy efficient fog-assisted IoT system for monitoring diabetic patients with cardiovascular disease. *Future Generation Computer Systems*, *93*, 198–211. doi:10.1016/j.future.2018.10.029

Gupta, B. B. (Ed.). (2018). *Computer and Cyber Security: Principles, Algorithm, Applications, and Perspectives*. CRC Press.

Gupta, B. B., Yamaguchi, S., & Agrawal, D. P. (2018). Advances in security and privacy of multimedia big data in mobile and cloud computing. *Multimedia Tools and Applications*, *77*(7), 9203–9208. doi:10.100711042-017-5301-x

Hossain, M. S., & Muhammad, G. (2018). Emotion-aware connected healthcare big data towards 5G. *IEEE Internet of Things Journal*, *5*(4), 2399–2406. doi:10.1109/JIOT.2017.2772959

Hu, K., Sivaraman, V., Luxan, B. G., & Rahman, A. (2016). Design and evaluation of a metropolitan air pollution sensing system. *IEEE Sensors Journal*, *16*(5), 1448–1459. doi:10.1109/JSEN.2015.2499308

Ieracitano, C., Adeel, A., Gogate, M., Dashtipour, K., Morabito, F. C., Larijani, H., ... Hussain, A. (2018, July). Statistical Analysis Driven Optimized Deep Learning System for Intrusion Detection. In *International Conference on Brain Inspired Cognitive Systems* (pp. 759-769). Springer. 10.1007/978-3-030-00563-4_74

Kang, G. K., Gao, J. Z., Chiao, S., Lu, S., & Xie, G. (2018). Air quality prediction: Big data and machine learning approaches. *International Journal of Environmental Sciences and Development*, *9*(1), 8–16. doi:10.18178/ijesd.2018.9.1.1066

Khreis, H., de Hoogh, K., & Nieuwenhuijsen, M. J. (2018). Full-chain health impact assessment of traffic-related air pollution and childhood asthma. *Environment International*, *114*, 365–375. doi:10.1016/j.envint.2018.03.008 PMID:29602620

Kim, M., Kim, Y., Sung, S., & Yoo, C. (2009, August). Data-driven prediction model of indoor air quality by the preprocessed recurrent neural networks. In 2009 ICCAS-SICE (pp. 1688-1692). IEEE.

Li, P., Xu, C., Luo, Y., Cao, Y., Mathew, J., & Ma, Y. (2017, March). Carenet: Building a secure software-defined infrastructure for home-based healthcare. In *Proceedings of the ACM International Workshop on Security in Software Defined Networks & Network Function Virtualization* (pp. 69-72). ACM. 10.1145/3040992.3041007

Li, X., Peng, L., Yao, X., Cui, S., Hu, Y., You, C., & Chi, T. (2017). Long short-term memory neural network for air pollutant concentration predictions: Method development and evaluation. *Environmental Pollution*, *231*, 997–1004. doi:10.1016/j.envpol.2017.08.114 PMID:28898956

Lin, Y., Mago, N., Gao, Y., Li, Y., Chiang, Y. Y., Shahabi, C., & Ambite, J. L. (2018, November). Exploiting spatiotemporal patterns for accurate air quality forecasting using deep learning. In *Proceedings of the 26th ACM SIGSPATIAL International Conference on Advances in Geographic Information Systems* (pp. 359-368). ACM. 10.1145/3274895.3274907

Lu, H., Song, J., Di, T., Kurdestany, J. M., & Wang, H. (2018). A Deep Belief Network Based Model for Urban Haze Prediction. *Tehnicki Vjesnik (Strojarski Fakultet)*, *25*(2), 519–527.

Maimó, L. F., Celdrán, A. H., Pérez, M. G., Clemente, F. J. G., & Pérez, G. M. (2018). Dynamic management of a deep learning-based anomaly detection system for 5G networks. *Journal of Ambient Intelligence and Humanized Computing*, 1–15.

Negi, P., Mishra, A., & Gupta, B. B. (2013). *Enhanced CBF packet filtering method to detect DDoS attack in cloud computing environment.* arXiv preprint arXiv:1304.7073

Ong, B. T., Sugiura, K., & Zettsu, K. (2016). Dynamically pre-trained deep recurrent neural networks using environmental monitoring data for predicting PM 2.5. *Neural Computing & Applications*, *27*(6), 1553–1566. doi:10.100700521-015-1955-3 PMID:27418719

Penza, M., Suriano, D., Pfister, V., Prato, M., & Cassano, G. (2017, August). Urban Air Quality Monitoring with Networked Low-Cost Sensor-Systems. In Multidisciplinary Digital Publishing Institute Proceedings (Vol. 1, No. 4, p. 573). Academic Press. doi:10.3390/proceedings1040573

Qi, Z., Wang, T., Song, G., Hu, W., Li, X., & Zhang, Z. (2018). Deep air learning: Interpolation, prediction, and feature analysis of fine-grained air quality. *IEEE Transactions on Knowledge and Data Engineering*, *30*(12), 2285–2297. doi:10.1109/TKDE.2018.2823740

Reddy, V., Yedavalli, P., Mohanty, S., & Nakhat, U. (2018). Deep Air: Forecasting Air Pollution in Beijing, China. Academic Press.

Roman, R., Lopez, J., & Mambo, M. (2018). Mobile edge computing, Fog et al.: A survey and analysis of security threats and challenges. *Future Generation Computer Systems*, *78*, 680–698. doi:10.1016/j.future.2016.11.009

Stergiou, C., Psannis, K. E., Kim, B. G., & Gupta, B. (2018). Secure integration of IoT and cloud computing. *Future Generation Computer Systems*, *78*, 964–975. doi:10.1016/j.future.2016.11.031

U. S. E. P. Agency. (2014). *Air Quality Index: A Guide to Air Quality and Your Health.* Author.

Verma, P., & Sood, S. K. (2018). Fog assisted-IoT enabled patient health monitoring in smart homes. *IEEE Internet of Things Journal*, *5*(3), 1789–1796. doi:10.1109/JIOT.2018.2803201

Yi, X., Zhang, J., Wang, Z., Li, T., & Zheng, Y. (2018, July). Deep distributed fusion network for air quality prediction. In *Proceedings of the 24th ACM SIGKDD International Conference on Knowledge Discovery & Data Mining* (pp. 965-973). ACM. 10.1145/3219819.3219822

Zhang, X. M., & Zhang, N. (2011, May). An open, secure and flexible platform based on internet of things and cloud computing for ambient aiding living and telemedicine. In 2011 international conference on computer and management (CAMAN) (pp. 1-4). IEEE. doi:10.1109/CAMAN.2011.5778905

Zheng, K., Zhao, S., Yang, Z., Xiong, X., & Xiang, W. (2016). Design and implementation of LPWA-based air quality monitoring system. *IEEE Access: Practical Innovations, Open Solutions*, *4*, 3238–3245. doi:10.1109/ACCESS.2016.2582153

Compilation of References

360. netlab. (2017). *Warning: Satori, a Mirai Branch Is Spreading in Worm Style on Port 37215 and 52869.* Retrieved from https://blog.netlab.360.com/warning-satori-a-new-mirai-variant-is-spreading-in-worm-style-on-port-37215-and-52869-en/

Abbas, H., Maennel, O., & Assar, S. (2017). Security and privacy issues in cloud computing. *Annales des Télécommunications*, *72*(5-6), 233–235. doi:10.100712243-017-0578-3

Abbosh, O. (2019). *Cybertech Europe.* Retrieved from Accenture: https://www.accenture.com/us-en/event-cybertech-europe-2017?src=SOMS#block-insights-and-innovation

Abbott, R. G., McClain, J., Anderson, B., Nauer, K., Silva, A., & Forsythe, C. (2015). Log analysis of cyber security training exercises. *Procedia Manufacturing*, *3*, 5088–5094. doi:10.1016/j.promfg.2015.07.523

ABC News. (n.d.). *Pat McGrath facebook alleged to have sold information in users' private messages.* Retrieved from http://www.abc.net.au/news/2014-01-03/facebook-sued-for-selling-information-in-users-private-messages/5183904l

Abeshu, A., & Chilamkurti, N. (2018). Deep learning: The frontier for distributed attack detection in fog-to-things computing. *IEEE Communications Magazine*, *56*(2), 169–175. doi:10.1109/MCOM.2018.1700332

Abomhara, M., & Køien, G. M. (2015). Cyber Security and the Internet of Things: Vulnerabilities, Threats, Intruders and Attack. *Journal of Cyber Security*, *4*, 65–88. doi:10.13052/jcsm2245-1439.414

Acar, Y., Stransky, C., Wermke, D., Weir, C., Mazurek, M. L., & Fahl, S. (2017). *Developers Need Support, Too: A Survey of Security Advice for Software Developers. Cybersecurity Development (SecDev)* (pp. 22–26). Cambridge, MA: IEEE.

Adat & Gupta. (2018). Security in Internet of Things: issues, challenges, taxonomy, and architecture. *Telecommunication Systems: Modeling, Analysis, Design and Management, 67*(3-4), 423-441.

Adat, V., & Gupta, B. B. (2018). Security in Internet of Things: Issues, challenges, taxonomy, and architecture. *Telecommunication Systems*, *67*(3), 423–441. doi:10.100711235-017-0345-9

Ahmad, A., Khan, M., Paul, A., Din, S., Rathore, M. M., Jeon, G., & Choi, G. S. (2018). Toward modeling and optimization of features selection in Big Data based social Internet of Things. 2018. *Future Generation Computer Systems*, *82*, 715–726. doi:10.1016/j.future.2017.09.028

Ahmed, M. A. (2015). Novel approach for network traffic pattern analysis using clustering-based collective anomaly detection. *Annals of Data Science*, 111-130.

Aijaz, U. N. (2018). Malware Detection on Server using Distributed Machine Learning. *Perspectives in Communication, Embedded-systems and Signal-processing-PiCES*, 172-175.

Ajzen, I. (1991). The Theory of Planned Behaviour. *Organizational Behavior and Human Decision Processes, 50*(2), 179–211. doi:10.1016/0749-5978(91)90020-T

Akiyama, M., Kawamoto, T., Shimamura, M., Yokoyama, T., Kadobayashi, Y., & Yamaguchi, S. (2007). A proposal of metrics for botnet detection based on its cooperative behaviour. *Applications and the Internet Workshops, 2007. SAINT Workshops in 2007. International Symposium on*, 82–82.

Al Hasib, A. (2009). Threats of online social networks. *International Journal of Computer Science and Network Security*, 88-93.

Albladi, S. M. (2017). *Personality traits and cyber-attack victimisation: Multiple mediation analysis. In Internet of Things Business Models, Users, and Networks*. IEEE.

Albuquerque-Junior, A. E., & Santos, E. M. (2015). Adoption of Information Security Measures in Public Research Institutes. *Journal of Information Systems and Technology Management, 12*(2), 289–316. doi:10.4301/S1807-17752015000200006

Alexopoulos, N., Daubert, J., Mühlhäuser, M., & Habib, S. M. (2017). Beyond the Hype: On Using Blockchains in Trust Management for Authentication. 2017 IEEE Trustcom/BigDataSE/ICESS.

Alge, B. J., Ballinger, G. A., Tangirala, S., & Oakley, J. L. (2006). Information privacy in organizations: Empowering creative and extrarole performance. *The Journal of Applied Psychology, 91*(1), 221–232. doi:10.1037/0021-9010.91.1.221 PMID:16435952

Al-Kahtani, M. S. (2017, February). Security and Privacy in Big data. *International Journal of Computer Engineering and Information Technology, 9*(2), 24–29.

Allen, J., & Howell, K. (n.d.). *Ralph Hood integrating privacy practices into the software development life cycle*. Retrieved from http://resources.sei.cmu.edu/asset_files/Podcast/2009_016_100_47206.pdf

Almomani, A., Gupta, B. B., Atawneh, S., Meulenberg, A., & Almomani, E. (2013a). A Survey of Phishing Email Filtering Techniques. *IEEE Communications Surveys and Tutorials, 15*(4), 2070–2090. doi:10.1109/SURV.2013.030713.00020

Almomani, A., Gupta, B. B., Wan, T., & Altaher, A. (2013b). Phishing Dynamic Evolving Neural Fuzzy Framework for Online Detection Zero-day Phishing Email. *Indian Journal of Science and Technology, 6*(1), 122–126.

Alshboul, A. (2010). Information Systems Security Measures and Countermeasures: Protecting Organisational Assets from Malicious Attacks. Communications of the IBIMA, 9.

Alyasseri, Z. A. A., Khader, A. T., Al-Betar, M. A., & Papa, J. P., & ahmad Alomari, O. (2018, July). EEG-based person authentication using multi-objective flower pollination algorithm. In *2018 IEEE Congress on Evolutionary Computation (CEC)*, (pp. 1-8). IEEE. 10.1109/CEC.2018.8477895

Amazon. (2018). AWS Direct Connect. Retrieved from https://aws.amazon.com/directconnect/

Ambre, A., & Shekokar, N. (2015). Insider threat detection using log analysis and event correlation. *Procedia Computer Science, 45*, 436–445. doi:10.1016/j.procs.2015.03.175

Amellal, H., Meslouhi, A., El Allati, A., & ElHaddadi, A. (2018). Protect the privacy in cloud via data encryption. *The IEEE International Symposium on Advanced Electrical and Communication Technologies*. doi: 10.1109/ISAECT.2018.8618834

Amoroso, E. G. (2013). From the Enterprise Perimeter to a Mobility-Enabled Secure Cloud. *IEEE Security and Privacy, 11*(1), 23–31. doi:10.1109/MSP.2013.8

Anthony, R. (2013). *Detecting security incidents using windows workstation event logs*. SANS Institute, InfoSec Reading Room Paper.

408

Anthonysamy, P., Rashid, A., & Chitchyan, R. (2017). *Privacy requirements: present and future.* Academic Press.

Arachchilage, N. A. G. (2016). *Serious Games for Cyber Security Education.* LAP Lambert Academic Publishing. Retrieved from https://arxiv.org/abs/1610.09511

Arachchilage, N. A. G., Namiluko, C., & Martin, A. (2013). A Taxonomy for Securely Sharing Information among Others in a Trust Domain. In *Internet Technology and Secured Transactions (ICITST). 8th International Conference for 2013.* IEEE.

Arachchilage, N. A. G., & Love, S. (2013). A Game Design Framework for Avoiding Phishing Attack. *Computers in Human Behavior, 29*(3), 706–714. doi:10.1016/j.chb.2012.12.018

Arachchilage, N. A. G., & Love, S. (2014). Security Awareness of Computer Users: A Phishing Threat Avoidance Perspective. *Computers in Human Behavior, 38,* 304–312. doi:10.1016/j.chb.2014.05.046

Arachchilage, N. A. G., Love, S., & Beznosov, K. (2016). Phishing Threat Avoidance Behaviour: An Empirical Investigation. *Computers in Human Behavior, 60,* 185–197. doi:10.1016/j.chb.2016.02.065

Arachchilage, N. A. G., & Martin, A. (2014). *A Trust Domains Taxonomy for Securely Sharing Information: A Preliminary Investigation.* HAISA.

Araiza, A. (2011). Electronic discovery in the cloud. *Duke Law & Technology Review,* 1-19.

Armano, G., & Farmani, M. R. (2016). Multiobjective clustering analysis using particle swarm optimization. *Expert Systems with Applications, 55,* 184–193. doi:10.1016/j.eswa.2016.02.009

Armbrust, M., Fox, A., Griffith, A., Joseph, A., Katz, A., & Konwinski, A. (2009). *Technical Report No. UCB/EECS-2009-28 Above the clouds: a Berkeley view of cloud computing.* University of California at Berkeley.

Armendariz, T. (2018). *Top Malware Threats and How to Protect Yourself.* Retrieved from lifewire: https://www.lifewire.com/top-malware-threats-153641

Armitage, C. J., & Conner, M. (2001). Efficacy of the Theory of Planned Behaviour: A Meta-analysis Review. *British Journal of Social Psychology, 40*(4), 471–499. doi:10.1348/014466601164939 PMID:11795063

Armknecht, F., Boyd, C., Carr, C., Gjosteen, K., Jaschke, A., Reuter, C., & Strand, M. (2015). A Guide to Fully Homomorphic Encryption.

Arzamendi, P., Bing, M., & Soluk, K. (2018). *The ARC of Satori.* Retrieved from https://www.netscout.com/blog/asert/arc-satori

Asgari, M., Farnaghi, M., & Ghaemi, Z. (2017, September). Predictive mapping of urban air pollution using Apache Spark on a Hadoop cluster. In *Proceedings of the 2017 International Conference on Cloud and Big Data Computing* (pp. 89-93). ACM. 10.1145/3141128.3141131

Asghari, H., Guerses, S. F., Mahieu, R., & van Eeten, M. (2016). *Can markets deliver privacy enhanced services on scale?* Academic Press.

Avudaiappan, T., Balasubramanian, R., Pandiyan, S. S., Saravanan, M., Lakshmanaprabu, S. K., & Shankar, K. (2018). Medical image security using dual encryption with oppositional based optimization algorithm. *Journal of Medical Systems, 42*(11), 208. doi:10.100710916-018-1053-z PMID:30244385

Awa, H. O., Ojiabo, O. U., & Emecheta, B. C. (2014). Integrating TAM, TPB and TOE Frameworks and Expanding their Characteristic Constructs for E-commerce Adoption by SMEs. *Journal of Science and Technology Policy Management, 6*(1), 76–94. doi:10.1108/JSTPM-04-2014-0012

Backes, M. A. (2017). walk2friends: Inferring Social Links from Mobility Profiles. In *Proceedings of the 2017 ACM SIGSAC Conference on Computer and Communications Security* (pp. 1943-1957). ACM. 10.1145/3133956.3133972

Bailey, M., Cooke, E., Jahanian, F., Xu, Y., & Karir, M. (2009). *A survey of botnet technology and defenses.* IEEE Cybersecurity Applications & Technology Conf. for Homeland Security. doi:10.1109/CATCH.2009.40

Bakar, A. A., Ismail, R., Ahmad, A. R., & Manan, J. A. (2010). Trust Formation Based on Subjective Logic and PGP Web-of-Trust for Information Sharing in Mobile Ad Hoc Networks. *2010 IEEE Second International Conference on Social Computing.* 10.1109/SocialCom.2010.149

Balystok, E., & Poarch, G. (2014). *Language Experience Changes Language and Cognitive Ability.* Zeitschrift Fur Erziehungswissenschaft; doi:10.100711618-014-0491-8

Banking, T. O., & Sector, F. (2017). *Institute for Development and Research in Banking Technology Applications of Block Chain Technology to Banking and Financial Sector in India.* Retrieved from http://www.idrbt.ac.in/assets/publications/ Best Practices/BCT.pdf

Bansal, A. (2017). *Malicious Web URL Classification using Evolutionary Algorithm.* Academic Press.

Bansal, B., & Sahoo, A. (2015). Full Model Selection Using Bat Algorithm. *Cognitive Computing and Information Processing (CCIP), 2015 International Conference on,* 1-4. 10.1109/CCIP.2015.7100693

Bao, L., Li, Q., Lu, P., Lu, J., Ruan, T., & Zhang, K. (2018). Execution anomaly detection in large-scale systems through console log analysis. *Journal of Systems and Software, 143,* 172–186. doi:10.1016/j.jss.2018.05.016

Barford, P., & Yagneswaran, V. (2006). An Inside Look at Botnets. In *Special Workshop on Malware Detection, Advances in Information Security.* Springer.

Bataev, A. V. (2018). Analysis of the Application of Big Data Technologies in the Financial Sphere. *2018 IEEE International Conference "Quality Management, Transport and Information Security, Information Technologies" (IT&QM&IS),* 568–572. 10.1109/ITMQIS.2018.8525121

Batlin, A., Przewloka, A., & Williams, S. (2016). *Building the trust Engine- How the block chain could transform (and the world) by Hyder Jaffrey Strategic Investment & Fintech Innovation.* UBS Investment Bank Christopher Murphy Global Co-Head of FX, Rates and Credit, UBS Investment Bank-white paper.

Bayramusta, M., & Nasir, V. A. (2016). A fad or future of IT?: A comprehensive literature review on the cloud computing research. *International Journal of Information Management, 36*(4), 635–644. doi:10.1016/j.ijinfomgt.2016.04.006

Beck, R., & Müller-Bloch, C. (2017). Blockchain as Radical Innovation: A Framework for Engaging with Distributed Ledgers as Incumbent Organization. *Proceedings of the 50th Hawaii International Conference on System Sciences,* 5390–5399. 10.24251/HICSS.2017.653

Behl, A. (2011). Emerging security challenges in cloud computing: An insight to cloud security challenges and their mitigation. In *Proceedings of the World Congress on Information and Communication Technologies* (pp. 217–222). Mumbai: Academic Press; . doi:10.1109/WICT.2011.6141247

Ben-Asher, N., & Gonzalez, C. (2015). Effects of cyber security knowledge on attack detection. *Computers in Human Behavior, 48,* 51–61. doi:10.1016/j.chb.2015.01.039

Bensouyad, M., & Saidouni, D. (2015). A discrete flower pollination algorithm for graph coloring problem. *Cybernetics (CYBCONF), 2015 IEEE 2nd International Conference on,* 151-155. 10.1109/CYBConf.2015.7175923

Berlin, K. a. (2015). Malicious behavior detection using windows audit logs. In *Proceedings of the 8th ACM Workshop on Artificial Intelligence and Security* (pp. 35-44). ACM. 10.1145/2808769.2808773

Berman, D. (2018). *The Complete Guide to the ELK Stack*. Retrieved 2 5, 2019, from logz.io: https://logz.io/learn/complete-guide-elk-stack/

Bertino, E., Martino, L. D., Paci, F., & Squicciarini, A. C. (2010). Web services threats, vulnerabilities, and countermeasures. In Security for Web Services and Service-Oriented Architectures. Springer.

Bertino, E., & Islam, N. (2017). Botnets and Internet of Things Security. *IEEE Computer, 50*(2), 76–79. doi:10.1109/MC.2017.62

Bhaladhare, P. R., & Jinwala, D. C. (2014). *A Clustering Approach for the -Diversity Model in Privacy Preserving Data Mining Using Fractional Calculus-Bacterial Foraging Optimization Algorithm*. Advances in Computer Engineering. doi:10.1155/2014/396529

Bhandari, R., Hans, V., & Ahuja, N. J. (2016). Big Data Security – Challenges and Recommendations. *International Journal on Computer Science and Engineering, 4*(1).

Bhushan, K., & Gupta, B. B. (2017). Network flow analysis for detection and mitigation of Fraudulent Resource Consumption (FRC) attacks in multimedia cloud computing. *Multimedia Tools and Applications, 78*(4), 4267–4298. doi:10.100711042-017-5522-z

Biggs, S., & Vidalis, S. (2009). Cloud Computing: The impact on digital forensic investigations. In *Proceedings of the International Conference for Internet Technology and Secured Transactions, (ICITST),* London. doi:10.1109/IC-ITST.2009.5402561

Bilge, L. A. (2017). RiskTeller: Predicting the Risk of Cyber Incidents. In *Proceedings of the 2017 ACM SIGSAC Conference on Computer and Communications Security* (pp. 1299 - 1311). ACM. 10.1145/3133956.3134022

Binkley, J. R., & Singh, S. (2006). An algorithm for anomaly based botnet detection. *Proc. USENIX Steps to Reducing Unwanted Traffic on the Internet Workshop*, 43-48.

Binkley, J., & Singh, S. (2006). An algorithm for anomaly-based botnet detection. *Proceedings of USENIX Steps to Reducing Unwanted Traffic on the Internet Workshop (SRUTI)*, 43–48.

Boes, K., Buhalis, D., & Inversini, A. (2014, December 27). Conceptualising Smart Tourism Destination Dimensions. *Information and Communication Technologies in Tourism,* 391-403.

Bojjagani, S. A. (2016). *Stamba: Security testing for Android mobile banking apps. In Advances in Signal Processing and Intelligent Recognition Systems* (pp. 671–683). Springer.

Bonderud, D. (2016). *Leaked Mirai Malware Boosts IoT Insecurity Threat Level*. Retrieved from https://securityintelligence.com/news/leaked-mirai-malware-boosts-iot-insecurity-threat-level/

Bottou, L. (2014). From Machine Learning to Machine Reasoning. *Machine Learning, 94*(2), 133–149. doi:10.100710994-013-5335-x

Brandis, K., Dzombeta, S., Colomo-Palacios, R., & Stantchev, V. (n.d.). Governance, Risk, and Compliance in Cloud Scenarios. *Applied Sciences, 320*.

Brar, H. S., & Singh, V. P. (2014, September). Fingerprint recognition password scheme using BFO. In *2014 International Conference on Advances in Computing, Communications and Informatics (ICACCI)* (pp. 1942-1946). IEEE. 10.1109/ICACCI.2014.6968600

Brashear, T., Granot, E., Brashear, T. G., & Cesar Motta, P. (2012). A structural guide to in-depth interviewing in business and industrial marketing research. *Journal of Business and Industrial Marketing*, *27*(7), 547–553. doi:10.1108/08858621211257310

Brause, R., Langsdorf, T., & Hepp, M. (1999). *Neural Data Mining for Credit Card Fraud Detection. In Proceedings of the 11th IEEE International Conference on Tools with Artificial Intelligence, ICTAI '99* (p. 103). Washington, DC: IEEE Computer Society. Retrieved from http://dl.acm.org/citation.cfm?id=850950.853684

Brem, A., & Wolfram, P. (2017). Organisation of new product development in asia and europe: Re- sults from western multinationals r&d sites in germany, india, and china. *Review of Managerial Science*, *11*(1), 159–190. doi:10.100711846-015-0183-7

Brin, S., & Page, L. (1998). The Anatomy of a Large-Scale Hypertextual Web Search Engine. *Proceedings of the seventh International Conference on the World Wide Web (WWW1998)*, 107–117. 10.1016/S0169-7552(98)00110-X

Brown, A. J., Glisson, W. B., Andel, T. R., & Choo, K.-K. R. (2018). Cloud forecasting: Legal visibility issues in saturated environments. *Computer Law & Security Review*, *34*(6), 1278–1290. doi:10.1016/j.clsr.2018.05.031

Brown, S. A., & Venkatesh, V. (2005). A Model of Adoption of Technology in the Household: A Baseline Model Test and Extension Incorporating Household Life Cycle. *Management Information Systems Quarterly*, *29*(3), 399–426. doi:10.2307/25148690

Brunton, F., & Nissen, H. (2017, February). Privacy's trust gap: A review. *The Yale Law Journal*, *126*(4), 908–1241.

Bubeck, S., & Eldan, R. (2016). *Multi-scale exploration of convex functions and bandit convex optimization*. Conference On Learning Theory - COLT.

Buyya, R., Yeo, C. S., & Venugopal, S. (2008). Market oriented cloud computing: vision, hype, and reality for delivering IT services as computing utilities. In *Proceedings of the tenth conference on high performance computing and communications (HPCC)*. IEEE Press. 10.1109/HPCC.2008.172

Cabrera, A., Cabrera, E. F., & Barajas, S. (2001). The Key Role of Organizational Culture in a Multi-System View of Technology-Driven Change. *International Journal of Information Management*, *21*(3), 245–261. doi:10.1016/S0268-4012(01)00013-5

Cai, T., & Zou, F. (2012). Detecting HTTP botnet with clustering network traffic. *IEEE 8th Int. Conf. on Wireless Communications, Networking and Mobile Computing*, 1-7. 10.1109/WiCOM.2012.6478491

Calder, A., & Watkins, S. (2008). *IT Governance: A Manager's Guide to Data Security and ISO 27001 / ISO 27002*. Kogan Page Ltd.

CAPGEMINI. (2015). *What You Need to Know About Blockchain and How to Assess the Opportunity Blockchain: A Fundamental Shift for Financial Services Institutions*. Author.

Caputo, D. D., Pfleeger, S. L., Sasse, M. A., Ammann, P., Offutt, J., & Deng, L. (2016). Barriers to usable security? three organizational case studies. *IEEE Security and Privacy*, *14*(5), 22–32. doi:10.1109/MSP.2016.95

Caragliu, A., Bo, D. C., & Nijkamp, P. (2011). Smart Cities in Europe. *Journal of Urban Technology*, *18*(2), 65–82. doi:10.1080/10630732.2011.601117

Carayon, P. K. (2005). Human factors issues in computer and e-business security. In Handbook of integrated risk management for e-business: measuring, modeling and managing risk (pp. 63-85). J. Ross Publishing.

Cárdenas, A. A., Manadhata, K. P., & Rajan, P. S. (2013). Big Data Analytics for Security. *IEEE Security and Privacy*, *11*(6), 74–76. doi:10.1109/MSP.2013.138

Cardullo, P., & Kitchin, R. (2018). Being a 'citizen' in the Smart City: Up and down the scaffold of smart citizen participation in Dublin, Ireland. *GeoJournal*, *84*(1), 1–13. doi:10.100710708-018-9845-8

Carroll, A. B. (1979). A three-dimensional conceptual model of corporate performance. *Academy of Management Review*, *4*(4), 497–505. doi:10.5465/amr.1979.4498296

Cavoukian, A. (2012). Privacy by design. *IEEE Technology and Society Magazine*, *31*(4), 18–19. doi:10.1109/MTS.2012.2225459

Cavoukian, A., Taylor, S., & Abrams, M. E. (2010). Privacy by design: Essential for organizational accountability and strong business practices. *Identity in the Information Society*, *3*(2), 405–413. doi:10.100712394-010-0053-z

Chandola, V., Banerjee, A., & Kumar, V. (2009). Anomaly detection: A survey. *ACM Computing Surveys*, *41*(3), 15. doi:10.1145/1541880.1541882

Chandrakala, D., & Sumathi, S. (2014). Image classification based on color and texture features using frbfn network with artificial bee colony optimization algorithm. *International Journal of Computers and Applications*, *98*(14).

Chang, S., & Daniels, T. E. (2009). P2P botnet detection using behavior clustering & statistical tests. *Proc. 2nd ACM Workshop on Security and Artificial Intelligence*, 23-30. doi:10.1145/1654988.1654996

Chatterjee, Das, Maity, & Sen. (2019). *RF-PUF: Enhancing IoT Security Through Authentication of Wireless Nodes Using In-Situ Machine Learning*. Academic Press.

Chatterjee, S., Sarker, S., & Valacich, J. S. (2015). The Behavioral Roots of Information Systems Security: Exploring Key Factors Related to Unethical IT Use. *Journal of Management Information Systems*, *31*(4), 49–87. doi:10.1080/07421222.2014.1001257

Chaum, D. (1983). *Blind Signatures for Untraceable Payments*. Advances in Cryptology; doi:10.1007/978-1-4757-0602-4_18

Chen, J., Yao, S., Yuan, Q., He, K., Ji, S., & Du, R. (2018). CertChain: Public and Efficient Certificate Audit Based on Blockchain for TLS Connections. *IEEE INFOCOM 2018*.

Chen, L., Xu, J., Zhang, L., & Xue, Y. (2017, August). Big data analytic based personalized air quality health advisory model. In *2017 13th IEEE Conference on Automation Science and Engineering (CASE)* (pp. 88-93). IEEE. 10.1109/COASE.2017.8256082

Chen, Y., & Lin, W. (2009, December). An improved bacterial foraging optimization. In *Robotics and Biomimetics (ROBIO), 2009 IEEE International Conference on* (pp. 2057-2062). IEEE. 10.1109/ROBIO.2009.5420524

Chen, D. A. (2012). Data security and privacy protection issues in cloud computing. In *International Conference on Computer Science and Electronics Engineering* (pp. 647-651). IEEE. 10.1109/ICCSEE.2012.193

Chen, D., Le, J., & Wei, J. (2009). A Peer-to-Peer Access Control Management Based on Web of Trust. *2009 International Conference on Future Computer and Communication*. 10.1109/ICFCC.2009.77

Chen, H., Chiang, R. H., & Storey, V. C. (2012). Business intelligence and analytics: From big data to big impact. *Management Information Systems Quarterly*, *36*(4), 4. doi:10.2307/41703503

Chen, L., & Qi, L. (2011). Social opinion mining for supporting buyer's complex decision making: Exploratory user study and algorithm comparison. *Social Network Analysis and Mining Journal*, *1*(4), 301–320. doi:10.100713278-011-0023-y

Chen, M. A. (2019). A Survey on User Profiling Model for Anomaly Detection in Cyberspace. *Journal of Cyber Security and Mobility, 8*, 75–112.

Chen, M., Hao, Y., Hwang, K., Wang, L., & Wang, L. (2017). Disease Prediction by Machine Learning Over Big Data from Healthcare Communities. *IEEE Access: Practical Innovations, Open Solutions, 5*, 8869–8879. doi:10.1109/AC-CESS.2017.2694446

Chen, M., Mao, S., & Liu, Y. (2014). Big Data: A Survey. *Mobile Networks and Applications, 19*(2), 171–209. doi:10.100711036-013-0489-0

Chen, M., Yang, J., Hu, L., Hossain, M. S., & Muhammad, G. (2018). Urban healthcare big data system based on crowdsourced and cloud-based air quality indicators. *IEEE Communications Magazine, 56*(11), 14–20. doi:10.1109/MCOM.2018.1700571

Chen, M., Yang, J., Zhou, J., Hao, Y., Zhang, J., & Youn, C. H. (2018). 5G-smart diabetes: Toward personalized diabetes diagnosis with healthcare big data clouds. *IEEE Communications Magazine, 56*(4), 16–23. doi:10.1109/MCOM.2018.1700788

Chen, Y., Shen, H., Smith, K. R., Guan, D., Chen, Y., Shen, G., ... Tao, S. (2018). Estimating household air pollution exposures and health impacts from space heating in rural China. *Environment International, 119*, 117–124. doi:10.1016/j.envint.2018.04.054 PMID:29957353

Cheung, A. S. (2014). Location privacy: The challenges of mobile service devices. *Computer Law & Security Review, 30*(1), 41–54. doi:10.1016/j.clsr.2013.11.005

Choo, K.-K. R. (2014). Legal Issues in the Cloud. *IEEE Cloud Computing*, 94-96.

Choo, K. K. R. (2007). *Zombies and Botnets. Trends and issues in crime and criminal justice, no.333*. Canberra: Australian Institute of Criminology.

Chopra, R. (2017). *Cloud Computing: An Introduction*. Mercury Learning and Information.

Chow, C. Y., & Mokbel, M. F. (2009). Privacy in location based services: A system architecture perspective. *SIGSPATIAL Special, 1*(2), 23–27. doi:10.1145/1567253.1567258

Chowdhury, M. A. (2017). *Protecting data from malware threats using machine learning technique*. IEEE. doi:10.1109/ICIEA.2017.8283111

Claar, C. L., & Johnson, J. (2010). Analyzing the Adoption of Computer Security Utilizing the Health Belief Model. *Issues in Information Systems, 11*(1), 286–291.

Claar, C. L., & Johnson, J. (2012). Analyzing Home PC Security Adoption Behaviour. *Journal of Computer Information Systems, 52*(4), 20–29.

Claeys, T., Rousseau, F., & Tourancheau, B. (2017). Securing Complex IoT Platforms with Token Based Access Control and Authenticated Key Establishment. *2017 International Workshop on Secure Internet of Things (SIoT)*. 10.1109/SIoT.2017.00006

Cloud Security Alliance. (2017). *Security Guidance for Critical Areas of Focus in Cloud Computing V4.0*.

Cloud Standards Customer Council. (2015, 4). *Practical Guide to Cloud Service Agreements Version 2.0*. Retrieved from https://www.omg.org/cloud/deliverables/practical-guide-to-cloud-service-agreements.htm

Coelho, I. M., Coelho, V. N., Luz, E. J. D. S., Ochi, L. S., Guimarães, F. G., & Rios, E. (2017). A GPU deep learning metaheuristic based model for time series forecasting. *Applied Energy, 201*, 412–418. doi:10.1016/j.apenergy.2017.01.003

Colombo, P., & Ferrari, E. (2015). Enhancing MongoDB with Purpose-Based Access Control. *IEEE Transactions on Dependable and Secure Computing, 14*(6), 591–604. doi:10.1109/TDSC.2015.2497680

Constant, N., Borthakur, D., Abtahi, M., Dubey, H., & Mankodiya, K. (2017). *Fog-assisted wiot: A smart fog gateway for end-to-end analytics in wearable internet of things.* arXiv preprint arXiv:1701.08680

Corballis, M. (2003). *From mouth to hand: Gesture, speech, and the evolution of right-handedness.* Academic Press. doi:10.1017/S0140525X03000062

Corney, M. A. (2011). Detection of anomalies from user profiles generated from system logs. In *Proceedings of the Ninth Australasian Information Security Conference* (pp. 23--32). Australian Computer Society.

Coskun, B., Dietrich, S., & Memon, N. (2010). Friends of an enemy: identifying local members of peer-to-peer botnets using mutual contacts. *Proc. 26th Annual Computer Security Applications Conf.*, 131-140. 10.1145/1920261.1920283

Costan, V., Lebedev, I., & Devadas, S. (2017). *Secure Processors Part I: Background, Taxonomy for Secure Enclaves and Intel SGX Architecture.* now. Retrieved from https://ieeexplore.ieee.org/xpl/articleDetails.jsp?arnumber=8186867

Council, U. S. N. R. (2005). *Network Science.* Washington, DC: The National Academies Press. doi:10.17226/11516

Crawford, B., Soto, R., Cuesta, R., & Paredes, F. (2014). Application of the artificial bee colony algorithm for solving the set covering problem. *The Scientific World Journal, 2014*, 1–8. doi:10.1155/2014/189164 PMID:24883356

Cremonini, M., & Riccardi, M. (2009). The Dorothy project: an open botnet analysis framework for automatic tracking and activity visualization. *IEEE European Conf. on Computer Network Defense*, 52-54. 10.1109/EC2ND.2009.15

Dagon, D., Gu, G., Lee, C. P., & Lee, W. (2007). A taxonomy of botnet structures. *IEEE 23rd Annual Computer Security Applications Conf.*, 325-339. 10.1109/ACSAC.2007.44

Dagon, D., Gu, G., Lee, C. P., & Lee, W. (2007). A Taxonomy of Botnet Structures. *Proc. 23rd Annual Computer Security Applications Conference (ACSAC 2007)*, 325-339.

Dahbur, K., Mohammad, B., & Tarakji, A. B. (2011). A survey of risks, threats and vulnerabilities in cloud computing. In *Proceedings of International conference on intelligent semantic Web-services and applications.* ACM.

Damanpour, F. (1991). Organisational Innovation: A Meta-analysis of Effects of Determinants and Moderators. *Academy of Management Journal, 34*(3), 555–590.

Damanpour, F., & Wischnevsky, J. D. (2006). Research on Organisational Innovation: Distinguishing Innovation-Generating from Innovation-Adopting Organisations. *Journal of Engineering and Technology Management, 23*(4), 269–291. doi:10.1016/j.jengtecman.2006.08.002

Dantu, R., Kolan, P., & Cangussu, J. (2009). Network risk management using attacker profiling. *Security and Communication Networks, 2*(1), 83–96. doi:10.1002ec.58

Daskal, J. (2018). Microsoft Ireland, the CLOUD Act, and International Lawmaking 2.0. *Stanford Law Review.*

Davies, S. (2010). *Why privacy by design is the next crucial step for privacy protection.* Academic Press.

Davis, F. D. (1989). Perceived Usefulness, Perceived Ease of Use, Acceptance of Information Technology. *Management Information Systems Quarterly, 13*(3), 319–340. doi:10.2307/249008

Davis, F. D., Bagozzi, R. P., & Warshaw, P. R. (1989). User Acceptance of Computer Technology: A Comparison of Two Theoretical Models. *Management Science, 35*(8), 982–1003. doi:10.1287/mnsc.35.8.982

Deci, E. L. (1972). Intrinsic motivation, extrinsic reinforcement, and inequity. *Journal of Personality and Social Psychology*, *22*(1), 113–120. doi:10.1037/h0032355

Delasko, S. A. (2018). Operating Systems of Choice for Professional Hackers. *ICCWS 2018 13th International Conference on Cyber Warfare and Security.*

Delhi, B. C. H. N. (2014). *Bankers ' Clearing House at New Delhi (BCHND) Procedural Guidelines for Cheque Truncation System (CTS).* Author.

Deng, R., Yang, Z., Chow, Y. M., & Chen, J. (2015). A Survey on Demand Response in Smart Grids: Mathematical Models and Approaches. *IEEE Transactions on Industrial Informatics*, *11*(3), 570–582. doi:10.1109/TII.2015.2414719

DeviceHive. (2019). *IoT Privacy and Security Challenges for Smart Home Environments.* Retrieved from hackernoon: https://hackernoon.com/iot-privacy-and-security-challenges-for-smart-home-environments-c91eb581af13

Devry, J. (2016). Mirai Botnet Infects Devices in 164 Countries. Retrieved from https://www.cybersecurity-insiders.com/mirai-botnet-infects-devices-in-164-countries/

Di Giulio, C., Sprabery, R., Kamhoua, C., Kwiat, K., Campbell, R. H., & Bashir, M. N. (2017). Cloud Security Certifications: A Comparison to Improve Cloud Service Provider Security. In *Proceedings of the Second International Conference on Internet of Things, Data and Cloud Computing* (pp. 1–12). Cambridge: ACM; . doi:10.1145/3018896.3025169

Diehl, E. (2016). Law 3: No Security Through Obscurity. In E. Diehl (Ed.), *Ten Laws for Security* (pp. 67–79). Springer.

Diffie, W., & Hellman, M. (1976). New directions in cryptography. *IEEE Transactions on Information Theory*, *22*(6), 644654. doi:10.1109/TIT.1976.1055638

Dimitrakakis, C., & C.A., R. (2012). Bayesian Multitask Inverse Reinforcement Learning. In H. M. Sanner S. (Ed.), *Recent Advances in Reinforcement Learning. EWRL 2011., Lecture Notes in Computer Science* (Vol. 7188). Springer.

Din, S., Paul, A., Hong, H. W., & Seo, H. (2019). Constrained application for mobility management using embedded devices in the Internet of Things based urban planning in Smart Cities. *Sustainable Cities and Society*, *44*, 144–151. doi:10.1016/j.scs.2018.07.017

Dirac, P. A. M. (1947). The Principles of Quantum Mechanics (3rd ed.). Oxford, UK: Clarendon Press.

Diro, A. A., & Chilamkurti, N. (2018a). Distributed attack detection scheme using deep learning approach for Internet of Things. *Future Generation Computer Systems*, *82*, 761–768. doi:10.1016/j.future.2017.08.043

Diro, A., & Chilamkurti, N. (2018b). Leveraging LSTM networks for attack detection in fog-to-things communications. *IEEE Communications Magazine*, *56*(9), 124–130. doi:10.1109/MCOM.2018.1701270

Doku, R., & Rawat, B. D. (2019). Big Data in Cybersecurity for Smart City Applications. *Smart Cities Cybersecurity and Privacy*, 103-112.

Doukas, C., Maglogiannis, I., Koufi, V., Malamateniou, F., & Vassilacopoulos, G. (2012). Enabling data protection through PKI encryption in IoT m-Health devices. *2012 IEEE 12th International Conference on Bioinformatics & Bioengineering (BIBE).*

Dowlin, N., Gilad-Bachrach, R., Laine, K., Lauter, K., Naehrig, M., & Wernsing, J. (2016). *CryptoNets: Applying Neural Networks to Encrypted Data with High Throughput and Accuracy.* Microsoft Research. Retrieved from https://www.microsoft.com/en-us/research/publication/cryptonets-applying-neural-networks-to-encrypted-data-with-high-throughput-and-accuracy/

Du, M., Wang, K., Xia, Z., & Zhang, Y. (2018, April 24). Differential Privacy Preserving of Training Model in Wireless Big Data with Edge Computing. *IEEE Transactions on Big Data.*

Du, M. a. (2017). *Deeplog: Anomaly detection and diagnosis from system logs through deep learning.* ACM. doi:10.1145/3133956.3134015

Du, M., & Li, F. (2018). Spell: Online Streaming Parsing of Large Unstructured System Logs. *IEEE Transactions on Knowledge and Data Engineering*, 1. doi:10.1109/TKDE.2018.2875442

Duncan, B. (2018). *Can EU General Data Protection Regulation Compliance be Achieved When Using Cloud Computing?* Barcelona: Cloud Computing.

Dusuki, A. W., & Yusof, T. F. M. T. M. (2016). The pyramid of corporate social responsibility model: Empirical evidence from Malaysian stakeholder perspective. *Malaysian Accounting Review, 7*(2).

Edla, D. R., Lipare, A., Cheruku, R., & Kuppili, V. (2017). An efficient load balancing of gateways using improved shuffled frog leaping algorithm and novel fitness function for WSNs. *IEEE Sensors Journal, 17*(20), 6724–6733. doi:10.1109/JSEN.2017.2750696

Edwards, S., & Profetis, I. (2016). *Hajime: Analysis of a decentralized internet worm for IoT devices.* Retrieved from https://security.rapiditynetworks.com/publications/2016-10-16/hajime.pdf

Ejaz, W., & Anpalagan, A. (2018, October 13). Dimension Reduction for Big Data Analytics in Internet of Things. *Internet of Things for Smart Cities*, 31-37.

Electronic Privacy Information Center (EPIC). (n.d.). *USA investigations of Google street view.* Retrieved from https://epic.org/privacy/streetview/

Elmrabit, N. H. (2015). Insider threats in information security categories and approaches. In *2015 21st International Conference on Automation and Computing (ICAC)* (pp. 1 - 6). IEEE.

Engrish, K. (2017). *Turning internet of things (not) into the internet of vulnerabilities (Nov): It botnets.* Retrieved from: https://arxiv.org/pdf/1702.03681.pdf

Eravci, B., & Ferhatosmanoglu, H. (2018). Diverse relevance feedback for time series with autoencoder based summarizations. *IEEE Transactions on Knowledge and Data Engineering, 30*(12), 2298–2311. doi:10.1109/TKDE.2018.2820119

Erd, P., & Rényi, A. (1959). On random graphs. *Publicationes Mathematicae, 6*, 290–297.

Eusuff, M. M., & Lansey, K. E. (2003). Optimization of water distribution network design using the shuffled frog leaping algorithm. *Journal of Water Resources Planning and Management, 129*(3), 210–225. doi:10.1061/(ASCE)0733-9496(2003)129:3(210)

Eusuff, M., Lansey, K., & Pasha, F. (2006). Shuffled frog-leaping algorithm: A memetic meta-heuristic for discrete optimization. *Engineering Optimization, 38*(2), 129–154. doi:10.1080/03052150500384759

Evans, M., Maglaras, L. A., He, Y., & Janicke, H. (2016). Human behaviour as an aspect of cybersecurity assurance. *Security and Communication Networks, 9*(17), 4667–4679. doi:10.1002ec.1657

Ezhilarasi, M., & Krishnaveni, V. (2018). *A Survey on Wireless Sensor Network: Energy and Lifetime Perspective* (Vol. 14). Taga Journal of Graphic Technology.

Ezhilarasi, M., & Krishnaveni, V. (2019). An evolutionary multipath energy-efficient routing protocol (EMEER) for network lifetime enhancement in wireless sensor networks. *Soft Computing*, 1–11. doi:10.100700500-019-03928-1

Faerber, F., Dees, J., Weidner, M., Baeuerle, S., & Lehner, W. (2015). Towards a web-scale data management ecosystem demonstrated by SAP HANA. In *2015 IEEE 31st International Conference on Data Engineering* (pp. 1259-1267). Seoul, South Korea: IEEE.

Fahmideh, M., & Beydoun, G. (2019). Big data analytics architecture design—An application in manufacturing systems. *Computers & Industrial Engineering, 128*, 948–963. doi:10.1016/j.cie.2018.08.004

Feily, M., Shahrestani, A., & Ramadass, S. (2009). A survey of the botnet and botnet detection. *3rd Int. Conf. on Emerging Security Information, Systems, and Technologies*, 268-273. 10.1109/SECURWARE.2009.48

Feizollah, A., Anuar, N. B., Salleh, R., & Wahab, A. W. A. (2015). A review on feature selection in mobile malware detection. *Digital Investigation, 13*, 22–37. doi:10.1016/j.diin.2015.02.001

Feng, X., & Zhao, Y.A. (2017). *Digital Forensics Challenges to Big Data in the Cloud.* IoTBDH-2017.

Fernandez, E. B. (2013). Two patterns for cloud computing: Secure virtual machine image repository and cloud policy management point. *Proceedings of the 20th conference on pattern languages of programs*, 15.

Ferraro, P., King, C., & Shorten, R. (2018). Distributed Ledger Technology for Smart Cities, the Sharing Economy, and Social Compliance. *IEEE Access: Practical Innovations, Open Solutions, 6*, 62728–62746. doi:10.1109/ACCESS.2018.2876766

Feruza, Y. S., & Kim, T. (2007). IT Security Review: Privacy, Protection, Access Control, Assurance and System Security. *International Journal of Multimedia and Ubiquitous Engineering, 2*(2), 17–32.

Fichman, R. G., & Kemerer, C. F. (1997). The Assimilation of Software Process Innovations: An Organizational Learning Perspective. *Management Science, 43*(1), 1345–1363. doi:10.1287/mnsc.43.10.1345

Fink, M. (1992). Time reversal of ultrasonic fields. I. Basic principles. *IEEE Transactions on Ultrasonics, Ferroelectrics, and Frequency Control, 39*(5), 555–566. doi:10.1109/58.156174 PMID:18267667

Fishbein, M., & Ajzen, I. (1975). *Belief, Attitude, Intention and Behaviour: An Introduction to Theory and Research.* Addison-Wesley.

Flittner, M., Balaban, S., & Bless, R. (2016). CloudInspector: A Transparency-as-a-Service Solution for Legal Issues in Cloud Computing. In *Proceedings of the IEEE International Conference on Cloud Engineering Workshop (IC2EW)*. Academic Press; . doi:10.1109/IC2EW.2016.36

Flynn, L. A. (2014). *Cloud Service Provider Methods for Managing Insider Threats: Analysis Phase 2, Expanded Analysis and Recommendations.* Carnegie-Mellon Univ.

Forbesthe world's biggest public companies. (n.d.). Retrieved from https://www.forbes.com/global2000/

Fotopoulou, E., Zafeiropoulos, A., Papaspyros, D., Hasapis, P., Tsiolis, G., Bouras, T., ... Zanetti, N. (2016). Linked data analytics in interdisciplinary studies: The health impact of air pollution in urban areas. *IEEE Access: Practical Innovations, Open Solutions, 4*, 149–164. doi:10.1109/ACCESS.2015.2513439

Freed, S. E. (2014). *Examination of personality characteristics among cybersecurity and information technology professionals.* University of Tennessee at Chattanooga.

Freeman, L. C., Bloomberg, W., Koff, S. P., Sunshine, M. H., & Fararo, T. J. (1960). *Local Community Leadership.* Syracuse.

Freeman, L. C., White, D. R., & Romney, A. K. (1989). *Research methods in social network analysis.* George Mason University Press.

Freiling, F., Holz, T., & Wicherski, G. (2005). Botnet Tracking: Exploring a Root-cause Methodology to Prevent Denial of Service Attacks. *Proceedings of 10th European Symposium on Research in Computer Security (ESORICS'05)*. 10.1007/11555827_19

Fromholz, J. M. (2000). The European Union data privacy directive. *Berk. Tech. LJ, 15*, 461.

Froystad, P., & Holm, J. (2015). Blockchain: Powering the Internet of Value. *Whitepaper, 50*. doi:10.3141/2411-03

Fu, Q. G. (2009). Execution anomaly detection in distributed systems through unstructured log analysis. In *Data Mining, 2009. ICDM'09. Ninth IEEE International Conference on* (pp. 149-158). IEEE.

Furnell, S. M., & Thompson, K. L. (2009). From Culture to Disobedience: Recognising the Varying User Acceptance of IT Security. *Computer Fraud & Security, 2009*(2), 5–10. doi:10.1016/S1361-3723(09)70019-3

Galván, A. (2010). Neural plasticity of development and learning. *Human Brain Mapping, 31*(6), 879–890. doi:10.1002/hbm.21029 PMID:20496379

Ganti, R. K., Ye, F., & Lei, H. (2011). Mobile crowdsensing: Current state and future challenges. *IEEE Communications Magazine, 49*(11), 32–39. doi:10.1109/MCOM.2011.6069707

Gartner Research. (2018). Gartner Forecasts Worldwide Public Cloud Revenue to Grow 17.3 Percent in 2019. Stamford.

Gasser, O. A. (2018). In Log We Trust: Revealing Poor Security Practices with Certificate Transparency Logs and Internet Measurements. In *International Conference on Passive and Active Network Measurement* (pp. 173--185). Springer.

Gazalian, P., & Safi, S. M. (2018). Presentation of a method for privacy preserving of people in social networks according to the clustering and sfla. *International Journal of Computer Science and Network Solutions, 6*(1), 1–9.

Ge, L., Liu, H., & Zhang, D. (2012). On effective sampling techniques for host-based Intrusion detection in MANET. *IEEE Military Communications Conf.*, 1-6. 10.1109/MILCOM.2012.6415605

George Jepsen attorney general, state of Connecticut. (n.d.). Retrieved from http://www.ct.gov/ag/cwp/view.asp?Q=520518&A=2341

Gerhardt, E., & Gomes, H. M. (2012). Artificial bee colony (ABC) algorithm for engineering optimization problems. *International Conference on Engineering Optimization*, 1-11.

Ghaffari, F. A. (2016). DroidNMD: Network-based Malware Detection in Android Using an Ensemble of One-Class Classifiers. *The Modares Journal of Electrical Engineering*, 40-47.

Ghahramani, Z. (2015). Probabilistic machine learning and artificial intelligence. *Nature, 521*(7553), 452–459. doi:10.1038/nature14541 PMID:26017444

Ghasemi, C., Yousefi, H., Shin, G. K., & Zhang, B. (2019). On the Granularity of Trie-Based Data Structures for Name Lookups and Updates. *IEEE/ACM Transactions on Networking, 27*(2), 777–789. doi:10.1109/TNET.2019.2901487

Ghoneim, O. A., & Manjunatha, B. R. (2017, September). Forecasting of ozone concentration in smart city using deep learning. In *2017 International Conference on Advances in Computing, Communications and Informatics (ICACCI)* (pp. 1320-1326). IEEE. 10.1109/ICACCI.2017.8126024

Gia, T. N., Dhaou, I. B., Ali, M., Rahmani, A. M., Westerlund, T., Liljeberg, P., & Tenhunen, H. (2019). Energy efficient fog-assisted IoT system for monitoring diabetic patients with cardiovascular disease. *Future Generation Computer Systems, 93*, 198–211. doi:10.1016/j.future.2018.10.029

Ginosar, A., & Ariel, Y. (2017). An analytical framework for online privacy research: What is missing? *Information & Management, 54*(7), 948–957. doi:10.1016/j.im.2017.02.004

Girsang, A. S., Yunanto, A., & Aslamiah, A. H. (2017, August). A hybrid cuckoo search and K-means for clustering problem. In *2017 International Conference on Electrical Engineering and Computer Science (ICECOS)* (pp. 120-124). IEEE. 10.1109/ICECOS.2017.8167117

Giuseppini, G. A. (2005). *Microsoft Log Parser Toolkit: A complete toolkit for Microsoft's undocumented log analysis tool.* Elsevier.

Glaspie, H. W. (2017). *Human Factors in Information Security Culture: A Literature Review.* Springer.

Goebel, J., & Holz, T. (2007). Rishi: identify contaminated bot hosts by IRC nickname evaluation. *Proc. 1st Conf. on 1st Workshop on Hot Topics in Understanding Botnets*, 1-12.

Gong, L., Wang, C., Zhang, C., & Fu, Y. (2019). High-Performance Computing Based Fully Parallel Security-Constrained Unit Commitment with Dispatchable Transmission Network. *IEEE Power & Energy Society, 34*(2), 931–941.

Goodfellow, I., Pouget-Abadie, J., Mirza, M., Xu, B., Warde-Farley, D., Ozair, S., & ... . (2014). Generative Adversarial Nets. In Z. Ghahramani, M. Welling, C. Cortes, N. D. Lawrence, & K. Q. Weinberger (Eds.), Advances in Neural Information Processing Systems (Vol. 27, pp. 2672–2680). Curran Associates, Inc. Retrieved from http://papers.nips.cc/paper/5423-generative-adversarial-nets.pdf

Goodson, S. (2012). *If you're not paying for it, you become the product.* Forbes.com.

Gopalakrishnan, S., & Damanpour, F. (1997). A Review of Innovation Research in Economics, Sociology and Technology Management. *Omega, International Journal of Management Science, 25*(1), 15–28.

Gottling, J. G. (1995). Node and Mesh Analysis by Inspection. *IEEE Transactions on Education, 38*(4), 312–316. doi:10.1109/13.473148

Gou, Z. a. (2017). Analysis of various security issues and challenges in cloud computing environment: a survey. In Identity Theft: Breakthroughs in Research and Practice (pp. 221-247). IGI Global. doi:10.4018/978-1-5225-0808-3.ch011

Gou, Z., Yamaguchi, S., & Gupta, B. B. (2016). Analysis of Various Security Issues and Challenges in Cloud Computing Environment: A Survey. In B. Gupta, D. P. Agrawal, & S. Yamaguchi (Eds.), *Handbook of Research on Modern Cryptographic Solutions for Computer and Cyber Security* (pp. 393–419). Hershey, PA: IGI Global; . doi:10.4018/978-1-5225-0105-3.ch017

Gozman, D., & Willcocks, L. (2019). The emerging Cloud Dilemma: Balancing innovation with cross-border privacy and outsourcing regulations. *Journal of Business Research, 97*, 235–256. doi:10.1016/j.jbusres.2018.06.006

Grange, W. (2017). *Hajime battles Mirai for control of the Internet of Things.* Retrieved from https://www.symantec.com/connect/blogs/hajime-worm-battles-mirai-control-internet-things

Greitzer, F. L. (2010). Combining traditional cyber security audit data with psychosocial data: towards predictive modeling for insider threat mitigation. In *Insider threats in cyber security* (pp. 85–113). Springer. doi:10.1007/978-1-4419-7133-3_5

Grimm, J. (2016). PKI: Crumbling under the pressure. *Network Security, 2016*(5), 5–7. doi:10.1016/S1353-4858(16)30046-0

Grobauer, B., Walloschek, T., & Stocker, E. (2011). Understanding cloud computing vulnerabilities. *IEEE Security and Privacy, 9*(2), 50–57. doi:10.1109/MSP.2010.115

Gross, J. B., & Mary, B. R. (2007). Looking for trouble: understanding end-user security management. In *Proc. The 2007 Symposium on Computer Human interaction For the Management of information Technology*. ACM. 10.1145/1234772.1234786

Gruschka, N. a. (2009). Vulnerable cloud: soap message security validation revisited. In *IEEE International Conference on Web Services* (pp. 625-631). IEEE. 10.1109/ICWS.2009.70

Gu, G., Porras, P., Yegneswaran, V., Fong, M., & Lee, W. (2007). BotHunter: Detecting Malware Infection through ids-driven dialog correlation. *Proceedings of the 16th USENIX Security Symposium (Security'07)*.

Gu, G., Porras, P., Yegneswaran, V., Fong, M., & Lee, W. (2007). BotHunter: Detecting malware infection through ids-driven dialog correlation. *Proceedings of the 16th USENIX Security Symposium*, 167–182.

Gupta, B. B., & Quamara, M. (2018). Multi-layered Cloud and Fog based Secure Integrated Transmission and Storage Framework for IoT based Applications. In *2018 5th International Conference on Signal Processing and Integrated Networks (SPIN)* (pp. 462-467). Noida, India: IEEE.

Gupta, R., & Garg, R. (2015). Mobile Applications Modelling and Security Handling in Cloud-Centric Internet of Things. *2015 Second International Conference on Advances in Computing and Communication Engineering*.

Gupta, B. B. (2018). *Computer and cyber security: Principles, algorithm, applications, and perspectives*. Auerbach Publications.

Gupta, B. B. (2018). *Computer and Cyber Security: Principles, Algorithm, Applications, and Perspectives*. CRC Press.

Gupta, B. B., Arachchilage, N. A. G., & Psannis, K. E. (2018). (2018) Defending against Phishing Attacks: Taxonomy of Methods, Current Issues and Future Directions. *Telecommunication Systems*, 67(2), 247–267. doi:10.100711235-017-0334-z

Gupta, B. B., Yamaguchi, S., & Agrawal, D. P. (2018). Advances in security and privacy of multimedia big data in mobile and cloud computing. *Multimedia Tools and Applications*, 77(7), 9203–9208. doi:10.100711042-017-5301-x

Gupta, B., Agrawal, D. P., & Yamaguchi, S. (2016). *Handbook of Research on Modern Cryptographic Solutions for Computer and Cyber Security*. Hershey, PA: IGI Global; . doi:10.4018/978-1-5225-0105-3

Gürses, S., & del Alamo, J. M. (2016). Privacy engineering: Shaping an emerging field of research and practice. *IEEE Security and Privacy*, 14(2), 40–46. doi:10.1109/MSP.2016.37

Hadar, I., Hasson, T., Ayalon, O., Toch, E., Birnhack, M., Sherman, S., & Balissa, A. (2018). Privacy by designers: Software developers' privacy mindset. *Empirical Software Engineering*, 23(1), 259–289. doi:10.100710664-017-9517-1

Halevi, S., & Shoup, V. (2018). Faster Homomorphic Linear Transformations in HElib.

Hall, M. A. (2009). The WEKA data mining software: an update. *ACM SIGKDD Explorations Newsletter, 11*, 10-18.

Hameed, M. A., & Arachchilage, N. A. G. (2016). A Model for the Adoption Process of Information System Security Innovations in Organisations: A Theoretical Perspective. In *Proc. the 27th Australasian Conference on Information Systems*. ACIS. Retrieved from https://arxiv.org/abs/1609.07911

Hameed, M. A., & Counsell, S. (2012). Assessing the Influence of Environmental and CEO Characteristics for Adoption of Information Technology in Organizations. *Journal of Technology Management & Innovation*, 7(1), 64–84. doi:10.4067/S0718-27242012000100005

Hameed, M. A., & Counsell, S. (2014a). Establishing Relationship between Innovation Characteristics and IT Innovation Adoption in Organisations: A Meta-analysis Approach. *International Journal of Innovation Management*, 18(1), 41. doi:10.1142/S1363919614500078

Hameed, M. A., & Counsell, S. (2014b). User Acceptance Determinants of Information Technology Innovation in Organisations. *International Journal of Innovation and Technology Management, 11*(5), 7. doi:10.1142/S0219877014500333

Hameed, M. A., Counsell, S., & Swift, S. (2012a). A Conceptual Model for the Process of IT Innovation Adoption in Organisations. *Journal of Engineering and Technology Management, 29*(3), 358–390. doi:10.1016/j.jengtecman.2012.03.007

Hameed, M. A., Counsell, S., & Swift, S. (2012b). A Meta-analysis of Relationships between Organisational Characteristics and IT Innovation Adoption in Organisations. *Information & Management, 49*(5), 218–232. doi:10.1016/j.im.2012.05.002

Hanus, B., & Wu, Y. A. (2016). Impact of users' security awareness on desktop security behavior: A protection motivation theory perspective. *Information Systems Management, 13*(1), 2–16. doi:10.1080/10580530.2015.1117842

Hashem, I. A., Yaqoob, I., Anuar, N. B., Mokhtar, S., Gani, A., & Khan, S. U. (2015). The rise of "big data" on cloud computing: Review and open research issues. *Information Systems, 47*, 98–115. doi:10.1016/j.is.2014.07.006

He, P. A. (2018). *A Directed Acyclic Graph Approach to Online Log Parsing.* CoRR, arXiv preprint arXiv:1806.04356

Heartfield, R. A. (2016). *A taxonomy of attacks and a survey of defence mechanisms for semantic social engineering attacks. ACM Computing Surveys.*

He, D., Zeadally, S., Kumar, N., & Lee, H. J. (2016). Anonymous Authentication for Wireless Body Area Networks with Provable Security. *IEEE Systems Journal, 11*(4), 2590–2601. doi:10.1109/JSYST.2016.2544805

Heikkinen, E. (2015). LOGDIG Log File Analyzer for Mining Expected Behavior from Log Files. *14th Symposium on Programming Languages and Software Tools.*

He, P. A. (2016). An evaluation study on log parsing and its use in log mining. In *46th Annual IEEE/IFIP International Conference on Dependable Systems and Networks (DSN)* (pp. 654-661). IEEE. 10.1109/DSN.2016.66

He, P. A. (2017). Drain: An online log parsing approach with fixed depth tree. In *International Conference on Web Services (ICWS)* (pp. 33-40). IEEE. 10.1109/ICWS.2017.13

Hiraishi, K. (2001). A Petri-net-based model for the mathematical analysis of multi-agent systems. *IEICE Trans. on Fundamentals, E84-A*(11), 2829–2837.

Hoboken, J. V., & Rubinstein, I. S. (2014). Privacy and Security in the Cloud: Some Realism About Technical Solutions to Transnational Surveillance in the Post-Snowden Era. *Me. L. Rev., 487.*

Hoehl, M. (2015). Proposal for standard Cloud Computing Security SLAs - Key Metrics for Safeguarding Confidential Data in the Cloud. Retrieved from https://www.sans.org/reading-room/whitepapers/cloud/proposal-standard-cloud-computing-security-slas-key-metrics-safeguarding-confidential-dat-35872

Homoliak, I. A. (2018). *Insight into Insiders: A Survey of Insider Threat Taxonomies, Analysis, Modeling, and Countermeasures.* arXiv preprint arXiv:1805.01612

Horisberger, M. (2013). *Centeractive AG: When SIEM is too much.* Retrieved 10 18, 2018, from Retrospective: https://retrospective.centeractive.com/blog_retrospective_whenSIEM.html

Hossain, M. S., Moniruzzaman, M., Muhammad, G., Ghoneim, A., & Alamri, A. (2016). Big data-driven service composition using parallel clustered particle swarm optimization in mobile environment. *IEEE Transactions on Services Computing, 5*(5), 806–817. doi:10.1109/TSC.2016.2598335

Hossain, M. S., & Muhammad, G. (2018). Emotion-aware connected healthcare big data towards 5G. *IEEE Internet of Things Journal, 5*(4), 2399–2406. doi:10.1109/JIOT.2017.2772959

Hossain, S. M. (2016). Patient State Recognition System for Healthcare Using Speech and Facial Expressions. *Journal of Medical Systems*, *40*(12), 272. doi:10.100710916-016-0627-x PMID:27757715

Hou, S. A. (2017). *Hindroid: An intelligent android malware detection system based on structured heterogeneous information network* ACM. doi:10.1145/3097983.3098026

Hu, B., Dai, Y., Su, Y., Moore, P., Zhang, X., Mao, C., ... Xu, L. (2016). Feature selection for optimized high-dimensional biomedical data using the improved shuffled frog leaping algorithm. *IEEE/ACM Transactions on Computational Biology and Bioinformatics*. PMID:28113635

Hubel, D., & Wiesel, T. (1962). Receptive fields, binocular interaction and functional architecture in the cat's visual cortex. *The Journal of Physiology*, *1*(160), 106–154. doi:10.1113/jphysiol.1962.sp006837 PMID:14449617

Hu, K., Sivaraman, V., Luxan, B. G., & Rahman, A. (2016). Design and evaluation of a metropolitan air pollution sensing system. *IEEE Sensors Journal*, *16*(5), 1448–1459. doi:10.1109/JSEN.2015.2499308

Hu, X. (2015). Adaptive optimization of cloud security resource dispatching SFLA algorithm. *International Journal of Engineering Science*, *4*(3), 39–43.

IBM. (2018). *IBM X-Force Threat Intelligence Index 2018*. IBM.

Ieracitano, C., Adeel, A., Gogate, M., Dashtipour, K., Morabito, F. C., Larijani, H., ... Hussain, A. (2018, July). Statistical Analysis Driven Optimized Deep Learning System for Intrusion Detection. In *International Conference on Brain Inspired Cognitive Systems* (pp. 759-769). Springer. 10.1007/978-3-030-00563-4_74

Indu, I., Anand, P. R., & Bhaskar, V. (2018). Identity and access management in cloud environment: Mechanisms and challenges. *Engineering Science and Technology, an International Journal*, 574-588.

Institute for Development and Research in Banking Technology. (2016). Cyber Security Checklist. Institute for Development and Research in Banking Technology.

Inukollu, V. N., Sailaja, A., & Srinivasa, R. R. (2014). Security issues associated with big data in cloud computing. *International Journal of Network Security & Its Applications, 45.*

IoT: Smart Cities projects share breakdown 2017, by type. (2017). Retrieved February 27, 2019, from The Statistics Portal: https://www.statista.com/statistics/784331/internet-of-things-smart-Cities-projects-by-type/

Jain, A. K., Murty, M. N., & Flynn, P. J. (1999). Data clustering: A review. *ACM Computing Surveys*, *31*(3), 264–323. doi:10.1145/331499.331504

Jansen, W. (2009). Directions in Security Metrics Research. Retrieved from http://csrc.nist.gov/publications/nistir/ir7564/nistir-7564_metrics-research.pdf

Jellinek, R., Zhai, Y., Ristenpart, T., & Swift, M. (2014). A day late and a dollar short: the case for research on cloud billing systems. In *Proceedings of the 6th USENIX conference on Hot Topics in Cloud Computing*, (pp. 21-21). Academic Press.

Jeon, B. N., Han, K. S., & Lee, M. J. (2006). Determining Factors for the Adoption of E-Business: The Case of SMEs in Korea. *Applied Economics*, *38*(16), 1905–1916. doi:10.1080/00036840500427262

Jian, G., Zheng, K., Yang, Y., & Niu, X. (2012). An evaluation model of botnet based on peer to peer. *IEEE 4th Int. Conf. on Computational Intelligence and Communication Networks*, 925-929. 10.1109/CICN.2012.46

Jiang, X. A. (2012). *Dissecting android malware: Characterization and evolution*. IEEE.

Jiang, Y., Perng, C.-s., Li, T., & Chang, R. (2012). Self-Adaptive Cloud Capacity Planning. In *Proceedings of the Ninth International Conference on Services Computing*, Honolulu, HI (pp. 73-80). IEEE.

Jia, T. A. (2017). *LogSeD: Anomaly diagnosis through mining time-weighted control flow graph in logs*. IEEE.

Jindal, Jamar, & Churi. (2018). Future and Challenges Of Internet Of Thing. *International Journal of Computer Science & Information Technology, 10*(2). doi:10.1145/1980822.1980834

Jin, X., Wah, B. W., Cheng, X., & Wanga, Y. (2015). Significance and Challenges of Big Data Research. *Big Data Research, 2*(2), 59–64. doi:10.1016/j.bdr.2015.01.006

Joe, M. M. (2014). A survey of various security issues in online social networks. *International Journal of Computer Networks and Applications*, 11-14.

Jones, C. M., McCarthy, R. V., Halawi, L., & Mujtaba, B. (2010). Utilizing the Technology Acceptance Model to Access the Employee Adoption of Information System Security Measures. *Issues in Information Systems, 11*(1), 9–16.

Jones, G. (2013). Penetrating the cloud. *Network Security*, 5-7. doi:10.1016/S1353-4858(13)70028-X

Kaaniche, N. a. (2014). A secure client side deduplication scheme in cloud storage environments. In *6th International Conference on New Technologies, Mobility and Security (NTMS)* (pp. 1-7). IEEE. 10.1109/NTMS.2014.6814002

Kadir, A. F. (2018). Understanding Android Financial Malware Attacks: Taxonomy, Characterization, and Challenges. *Journal of Cyber Security and Mobility*, 1-52.

Kalaivani, R. (2017). Security Perspectives on Deployment of Big Data using Cloud: A Survey. *International Journal of Advanced Networking & Applications, 8*(5), 5–9.

Kang, G. K., Gao, J. Z., Chiao, S., Lu, S., & Xie, G. (2018). Air quality prediction: Big data and machine learning approaches. *International Journal of Environmental Sciences and Development, 9*(1), 8–16. doi:10.18178/ijesd.2018.9.1.1066

Karaboga, D. (2005). *An idea based on honey bee swarm for numerical optimization* (Vol. 200). Technical report-tr06. Erciyes University, Engineering Faculty, Computer Engineering Department.

Karaboga, D., & Akay, B. (2009). A comparative study of artificial bee colony algorithm. *Applied Mathematics and Computation, 214*(1), 108–132. doi:10.1016/j.amc.2009.03.090

Karim, A., Bin Salleh, R., Shiraz, M., Shah, S. A. A., Awan, I., & Anuar, N. B. (2014). Botnet detection techniques: Review, future trends, and issues. *Journal of Zhejiang University Science C, 15*(11), 943–983. doi:10.1631/jzus.C1300242

Kaspersky lab. (2015). *Damage Control: The Cost of Security Breaches*. Retrieved from https://media.kaspersky.com/pdf/it-risks-survey-report-cost-of-security-breaches.pdf

Kemp, R. (2018). Legal aspects of cloud security. *Computer Law & Security Review, 34*(4), 928–932. doi:10.1016/j.clsr.2018.06.001

Khan, R., Khan, S. U., Zaheer, R., & Khan, S. (2012). Future Internet: The Internet of Things architecture, possible applications and key challenges. *Proc. IEEE 10th Int. Conf. Frontiers of Information Technology*, 257–260.

Khan, M. A. (2016). A survey of security issues for cloud computing. *Journal of Network and Computer Applications, 71*, 11–29. doi:10.1016/j.jnca.2016.05.010

Khosrowshahi, D. (2016). *2016 Data Security Incident*. Retrieved from Uber Newsroom: https://www.uber.com/newsroom/2016-data-incident/

Khreis, H., de Hoogh, K., & Nieuwenhuijsen, M. J. (2018). Full-chain health impact assessment of traffic-related air pollution and childhood asthma. *Environment International, 114*, 365–375. doi:10.1016/j.envint.2018.03.008 PMID:29602620

Kim, M., Kim, Y., Sung, S., & Yoo, C. (2009, August). Data-driven prediction model of indoor air quality by the pre-processed recurrent neural networks. In 2009 ICCAS-SICE (pp. 1688-1692). IEEE.

Kim, D. H. (2018). Attack Detection Application with Attack Tree for Mobile System using Log Analysis. *Mobile Networks and Applications*, 1–9.

Kim, H., Lee, D., & Ham, S. (2013). Impact of Hotel Information Security on System Reliability. *International Journal of Hospitality Management, 35*, 369–379. doi:10.1016/j.ijhm.2012.06.002

Kohler, J., & Specht, T. (2019). Towards a Secure, Distributed, and Reliable Cloud-Based Reference Architecture for Big Data in Smart Cities. *Big Data Analytics for Smart and Connected Cities*, 38-70.

Kolias, C., Kambourakis, G., Stavrou, A., & Voas, J. (2017). DDoS in the IoT: Mirai and other botnets. *IEEE Computer, 50*(7), 80–84. doi:10.1109/MC.2017.201

Kollmitzer, C., & Pivk, M. (2010). *Applied quantum cryptography*. Springer.

Kolosnjaji, B. A. (2016). *Deep learning for classification of malware system call sequences*. Springer. doi:10.1007/978-3-319-50127-7_11

Koppal, A. (2008, April). *The Ising Model and Percolation on Graphs*. Retrieved from http://www1.cs.columbia.edu/coms6998/Notes/lecture22.pdf

Kourai, K. A. (2012). A self-protection mechanism against steppingstone attacks for iaas clouds. In *International Conference on Autonomic Trusted Computing (UIC/ATC)*, (pp. 539–546). IEEE.

Krag, W. B., & Hinson, G. (2016). *Pragmatic security metrics: applying metametrics to information security*. Auerbach Publications.

Kranenburg, R.V. (2008). The Internet of Things: A Critique of Ambient Technology and the All-Seeing Network of RFID, Institute of Network Cultures. ITU work on Internet of things, 2015. *ICTP Workshop*.

Krebs, B. (2016). *KrebsOnSecurity Hit With Record DDoS*. Retrieved from https://krebsonsecurity.com/2016/09/krebsonsecurity-hit-with-record-ddos/

Krizhevsky, A., Sutskever, I., & Hinton, G. E. (2012). ImageNet Classification with Deep Convolutional Neural Networks. In *Advances in Neural Information Processing Systems 25: 26th Annual Conference on Neural Information Processing Systems 2012. Lake Tahoe, Nevada, United States* (pp. 1106–1114). Academic Press.

Krombholz, K. A. (2015). Advanced social engineering attacks. *Journal of Information Security and Applications*, 113-122.

Kugisaki, Y., Kasahara, Y., Hori, Y., & Sarkurai, K. (2007). Bot detection based on traffic analysis. *IEEE Int. Conf. on Intelligent Pervasive Computing*, 303-306.

Kumar, P. (2016). Ranking digital rights: Pushing ict companies to respect users' privacy. In Chi '16 workshop: Bridging the gap between privacy by design and privacy in practice (p. 15). ACM.

Kumar, S. A. (2018). *False information on web and social media: A survey*. arXiv preprint arXiv:1804.08559

Kumaraguru, P. A. (2010). Teaching Johnny not to fall for phish. *ACM Transactions on Internet Technology*, 7.

Kumparak, G. (2019). *Kickstarter hacked, customer addresses and other infor accessed*. Retrieved from Techcrunch: https://techcrunch.com/2014/02/15/kickstarter-hacked-customer-addresses-and-other-info-accessed/

Labrinidis, A., & Jagadish, V. H. (2012). Challenges and opportunities with big data. *Proceedings of the VLDB Endowment International Conference on Very Large Data Bases*, *5*(12), 2032–2033. doi:10.14778/2367502.2367572

Lafuente, G. (2015). The big data security challenge. *Network Security*, *2015*(1), 12–14. doi:10.1016/S1353-4858(15)70009-7

Laha, S. (2015, December). A quantum-inspired cuckoo search algorithm for the travelling salesman problem. In *Computing, Communication and Security (ICCCS), 2015 International Conference on*. IEEE. 10.1109/CCCS.2015.7374201

Lahmer, I., & Zhang, N. (2014). MapReduce: MR model abstraction for future security study. SIN '14 Proceedings of the 7th International Conference on Security of Information and Networks.

Langheinrich, M. (2001). Privacy by design—principles of privacy-aware ubiquitous systems. In *International conference on ubiquitous computing* (pp. 273–291). Academic Press. 10.1007/3-540-45427-6_23

Lazaroiua, C. G., & Rosciab, M. (2012). Definition methodology for the Smart Cities model. *Energy*, *47*(1), 326–332. doi:10.1016/j.energy.2012.09.028

Lecun, Y., Bottou, L., Bengio, Y., & Haffner, P. (1998). Gradient-based learning applied to document recognition. *Proceedings of the IEEE*, 2278–2324.

Lee, C. Y., Kavi, K. M., Paul, R. A., & Gomathisankaran, M. (2015). Ontology of Secure Service Level Agreement. In *Proceedings of the 2015 IEEE 16th International Symposium on High Assurance Systems Engineering*, (pp. 166-172). doi:10.1109/HASE.2015.33

Lee, W. A. (2001). *Information-theoretic measures for anomaly detection*. IEEE.

Lee, Y., & Kozar, K. A. (2005). Investigating Factors Affecting Adoption of Anti-spyware Systems. *Communications of the ACM*, *48*(8), 72–77. doi:10.1145/1076211.1076243

Lee, Y., & Kozar, K. A. (2008). An Empirical Investigation of Anti-spyware Software Adoption: A Multi-theoretical Perspective. *Information & Management*, *45*(2), 109–119. doi:10.1016/j.im.2008.01.002

Legg, P. A., Buckley, O., Goldsmith, M., & Creese, S. (2017). Automated insider threat detection system using user and role-based profile assessment. *IEEE Systems Journal*, *11*(2), 503–512. doi:10.1109/JSYST.2015.2438442

Legris, P., Ingham, J., & Collerette, P. (2003). Why do People Use Information Technology? A Critical Review of the Technology Acceptance Model. *Information & Management*, *40*(3), 191–204. doi:10.1016/S0378-7206(01)00143-4

Leidner, D. E., & Kayworth, T. (2006). Review: A Review of Culture in Information Systems Research: Towards a Theory of Information Technology Culture Conflict. *Management Information Systems Quarterly*, *30*(2), 357–399. doi:10.2307/25148735

Lennvall, Gidlund, & Akerberg. (2017). Challenges when bringing IoT into Industrial Automation. *IEEE Africon Proceedings*.

Lertwongsatien, C., & Wongpinunwatana, N. (2003). E-commerce Adoption in Thailand: An Empirical Study of Small and Medium Enterprises (SMEs). *Journal of Global Information Technology Management*, *6*(3), 67–83. doi:10.1080/1097198X.2003.10856356

Letaifa, B. S. (2015). How to strategize Smart Cities: Revealing the SMART model. *Journal of Business Research*, *68*(7), 1414–1419. doi:10.1016/j.jbusres.2015.01.024

Liang, H., & Xue, Y. (2010). Understanding Security Behaviours in Personal Computer Usage: A Threat Avoidance Perspective. *Journal of the Association for Information Systems*, *11*(7), 394–413. doi:10.17705/1jais.00232

Li, C., Jiang, W., & Zou, X. (2009). Botnet: Survey and case study. *4th International Conference on Innovative Computing, Information and Control*.

Li, D. C. (2015). Online Security Performances and Information Security Disclosures. *Journal of Computer Information Systems*, *55*(2), 20–28. doi:10.1080/08874417.2015.11645753

Li, J. Q., Xie, S. X., Pan, Q. K., & Wang, S. (2011). A hybrid artificial bee colony algorithm for flexible job shop scheduling problems. *International Journal of Computers, Communications & Control*, *6*(2), 286–296. doi:10.15837/ijccc.2011.2.2177

Lin, Y. S., Leu, Y. G., & Lu, W. C. (2012, November). Fuzzy bacterial foraging system and its applications in control of servo motors. In *Fuzzy Theory and it's Applications (iFUZZY), 2012 International Conference on* (pp. 203-207). IEEE. 10.1109/iFUZZY.2012.6409701

Lins, S., Grochol, P., Schneider, S., & Sunyaev, A. (2016). Dynamic Certification of Cloud Services: Trust, but Verify! *IEEE Security and Privacy*, *14*(2), 66–71. doi:10.1109/MSP.2016.26

Lin, W. A. (2012). Traceback Attacks in Cloud--Pebbletrace Botnet. In *32nd International Conference on Distributed Computing Systems Workshops* (pp. 417-426). IEEE.

Lin, Y., Mago, N., Gao, Y., Li, Y., Chiang, Y. Y., Shahabi, C., & Ambite, J. L. (2018, November). Exploiting spatiotemporal patterns for accurate air quality forecasting using deep learning. In *Proceedings of the 26th ACM SIGSPATIAL International Conference on Advances in Geographic Information Systems* (pp. 359-368). ACM. 10.1145/3274895.3274907

Lin, Y., Zhang, X., & Geertman, S. (2015). Toward smart governance and social sustainability for Chinese migrant communities. *Journal of Cleaner Production*, *107*, 389–399. doi:10.1016/j.jclepro.2014.12.074

Li, P., Xu, C., Luo, Y., Cao, Y., Mathew, J., & Ma, Y. (2017, March). Carenet: Building a secure software-defined infrastructure for home-based healthcare. In *Proceedings of the ACM International Workshop on Security in Software Defined Networks & Network Function Virtualization* (pp. 69-72). ACM. 10.1145/3040992.3041007

Li, S., He, H., & Li, J. (2019). Big data driven lithium-ion battery modeling method based on SDAE-ELM algorithm and data pre-processing technology. *Applied Energy*, *242*, 1259–1273. doi:10.1016/j.apenergy.2019.03.154

Liu, J. A. (2018). A survey of mobile crowdsensing techniques: A critical component for the internet of things. *ACM Transactions on Cyber-Physical Systems*, 18 - 43.

Liu, K., & Terzi, E. (2008, June). Towards identity anonymization on graphs. *Proceedings of the 2008 ACM SIGMOD international conference on Management of data*, 93-106. 10.1145/1376616.1376629

Liu, L., Chen, S., Yan, G., & Zhang, Z. (2008) BotTracer: execution based bot-like malware detection. *International Conference on Information Security*, 97-113. 10.1007/978-3-540-85886-7_7

Li, X., Peng, L., Yao, X., Cui, S., Hu, Y., You, C., & Chi, T. (2017). Long short-term memory neural network for air pollutant concentration predictions: Method development and evaluation. *Environmental Pollution*, *231*, 997–1004. doi:10.1016/j.envpol.2017.08.114 PMID:28898956

Lohachab, A., & Karambir. (2019). ECC based inter-device authentication and authorization scheme using MQTT for IoT networks. *Journal of Information Security and Applications, 46*.

Lohachab, A. (2019). A Perspective on Using Blockchain for Ensuring Security in Smart Card Systems. In B. B. Gupta & P. D. Agrawal (Eds.), *Handbook of Research on Cloud Computing and Big Data Applications in IoT* (pp. 418–447). IGI Global. doi:10.4018/978-1-5225-8407-0.ch019

Lohachab, A., & Karambir. (2019). Next Generation Computing: Enabling Multilevel Centralized Access Control using UCON and CapBAC Model for securing IoT Networks. In *2018 International Conference on Communication, Computing and Internet of Things (IC3IoT)* (pp. 159-164). Chennai, India: IEEE.

Lohachab, A., & Bidhan, K. (2018). Critical Analysis of DDoS—An Emerging Security Threat over IoT Networks. *Journal of Communications and Information Networks*, *3*(3), 57–78. doi:10.100741650-018-0022-5

Lonzetta, A. A. (2018). Security Vulnerabilities in Bluetooth Technology as Used in IoT. *Journal of Sensor and Actuator Networks*, 28.

Lopez-Rojas, E. A., Elmir, A., & Axelsson, S. (2016). PaySim: A financial mobile money simulator for fraud detection. *The 28th European Modeling and Simulation Symposium-EMSS, Larnaca, Cyprus*, 174–179. Retrieved from http://www.scopus.com/record/display.url?origin=inward&partnerID=40&eid=2-s2.0-85002406569

Lord, N. (2017). *Insiders vs. outsiders: What's the greater cybersecurity threat?* Retrieved from DATAINSIDER: https://digitalguardian.com/blog/insiders-vs-outsiders-whats-greater-cybersecurity-threat-infographic

Lovas, R., Nagy, E., & Kovács, J. (2018). Cloud agnostic Big Data platform focusing on scalability and cost-efficiency. *Advances in Engineering Software*, *125*, 167–177. doi:10.1016/j.advengsoft.2018.05.002

Lu, H., Song, J., Di, T., Kurdestany, J. M., & Wang, H. (2018). A Deep Belief Network Based Model for Urban Haze Prediction. *Tehnicki Vjesnik (Strojarski Fakultet)*, *25*(2), 519–527.

Luna, J., Taha, A., Trapero, R., & Suri, N. (2015). Quantitative Reasoning About Cloud Security Using Service Level Agreements. *IEEE Transactions on Cloud Computing*, *PP*, 1-1. doi:10.1109/TCC.2015.2469659

Luo, T., Huang, J., Kanhere, S. S., Zhang, J., & Das, K. S. (2019, March 13). Improving IoT Data Quality in Mobile Crowd Sensing: A Cross Validation Approach. *IEEE Internet of Things Journal*.

Luo, L., Guo, D., Ma, B. T., Rottenstreich, O., & Luo, X. (2018, December 24). Optimizing Bloom Filter: Challenges, Solutions, and Comparisons. *IEEE Communications Surveys and Tutorials*.

Lv, Z., Song, H., Val, B. P., Steed, A., & Jo, M. (2017). Next-Generation Big Data Analytics: State of the Art, Challenges, and Future Research Topics. *IEEE Transactions on Industrial Informatics*, *13*(4), 1891–1899. doi:10.1109/TII.2017.2650204

Madini, A., Hussain, R. K., Ghashgari, G., Walters, R. J., & Wills, G. B. (2015). Security in organisations: governance, risks and vulnerabilities in moving to the cloud. *International Workshop on Enterprise Security*, 241-258.

Mahapatra, G., & Banerjee, S. (2015, October). An object-oriented implementation of bacteria foraging system for data clustering application. In *2015 International Conference and Workshop on Computing and Communication (IEMCON)*. IEEE. 10.1109/IEMCON.2015.7344430

Maheswari, K. P., Ramya, P., & Devi, S. M. (2017). *Study and Analyses of Security Levels in Big Data and Cloud Computing*. RTESHM.

Mahmood, T., & Afzal, U. (2013). Security analytics: Big data analytics for cybersecurity: A review of trends, techniques and tools. *2nd National Conference on Information Assurance (NCIA)*, 129–134. 10.1109/NCIA.2013.6725337

Mai, J.-E. (2016). Big data privacy: The datafication of personal information. *The Information Society*, *32*(3), 192–199. doi:10.1080/01972243.2016.1153010

Maimó, L. F., Celdrán, A. H., Pérez, M. G., Clemente, F. J. G., & Pérez, G. M. (2018). Dynamic management of a deep learning-based anomaly detection system for 5G networks. *Journal of Ambient Intelligence and Humanized Computing*, 1–15.

Makanju, A. A.-H. (2009). Clustering event logs using iterative partitioning. In *Proceedings of the 15th ACM SIGKDD international conference on Knowledge discovery and data mining* (pp. 1255-1264). ACM.

MalwareMustDie. (2016). *MMD-0056-2016 - Linux/Mirai, how an old ELF malcode is recycled.* Retrieved from http://blog.malwaremustdie.org/2016/08/mmd-0056-2016-linuxmirai-just.html

Mamaghani, A. S., & Hajizadeh, M. (2014).Software Modularization Using the Modified Firefly Algorithm. *Software Engineering Conference (MySEC), 2014 8th Malaysia*, 321-324. 10.1109/MySec.2014.6986037

Mathew, G. (2012). *Elements of application security in the cloud computing environment. Conference on Open Systems* (pp. 1–6). Kuala Lumpur: IEEE; . doi:10.1109/ICOS.2012.6417637

Mavroeidis, V. A. (2018). Data-Driven Threat Hunting Using Sysmon. *2018 International Conference on Cryptography, Security and Privacy (ICCSP).* 10.1145/3199478.3199490

McMahon, D. (2007). *Quantum computing explained.* Wiley Interscience.

Mell, P., & Grance, T. (2011). *800-145. The NIST Definition of Cloud Computing.* SP: National Institute of Standards & Technology.

Memos, V. A., Psannis, K. E., Ishibashi, Y., Kim, B., & Gupta, B. B. (2017). An Efficient Algorithm for Media-based Surveillance System (EAMSuS) in IoT Smart City Framework. In Future Generation Computer Systems. Elsevier.

Memos, V. A., Psannis, K. E., Ishibashi, Y., Kim, B. G., & Gupta, B. B. (2018). An Efficient Algorithm for Media-based Surveillance System (EAMSuS) in IoT Smart City Framework. *Future Generation Computer Systems, 83*, 619–628. doi:10.1016/j.future.2017.04.039

Mendel, T., & Toch, E. (2017). Susceptibility to social influence of privacy behaviors: Peer versus authoritative sources. In *Proceedings of the 2017 ACM conference on computer supported cooper- ative work and social computing* (pp. 581–593). ACM. 10.1145/2998181.2998323

Menezes, A. J., Van Oorschot, P. C., & Vanstone, S. A. (1996). Handbook of applied cryptography. CRC Press.

Microsoft. (2018). *Five ways blockchain is transforming financial services.* Author.

Mihovska, A., & Sarkar, M. (2017). Smart Connectivity for Internet of Things (IoT) Applications. *New Advances in the Internet of Things, 715*, 105–118.

Mittu, R. A. (2015). Foundations of Autonomy and Its (Cyber) Threats: From Individual to Interdependence. *AAAI Spring Symposium Series.*

Mohammadi, M., & Fuqaha, A. A. (2018). Enabling Cognitive Smart Cities Using Big Data and Machine Learning: Approaches and Challenges. *IEEE Communications Magazine, 56*(2), 94–101. doi:10.1109/MCOM.2018.1700298

Mohammadi, M., Fuqaha, A. A., Sorour, S., & Guizani, M. (2018). Deep Learning for IoT Big Data and Streaming Analytics: A Survey. *IEEE Communications Surveys and Tutorials, 20*(6), 2923–2960. doi:10.1109/COMST.2018.2844341

Mohanty, P. S., Choppali, U., & Kougianos, E. (2016). Everything you wanted to know about Smart Cities: The Internet of things is the backbone. *IEEE Consumer Electronics Magazine, 5*(3), 60–70. doi:10.1109/MCE.2016.2556879

Mohurle, S. A. (2017). A brief study of wannacry threat: Ransomware attack 2017. *International Journal of Advanced Research in Computer Science, 8.*

Molesky, M. J., & Cameron, E. A. (2019). Internet of Things: An Analysis and Proposal of White Worm Technology. *Proc. of IEEE ICCE 2019, 4.* 10.1109/ICCE.2019.8662111

Mongeon, P., & Hus, P. A. (2015). The journal coverage of Web of Science and Scopus: A comparative analysis. *Scientometrics, 106*(1), 213–228. doi:10.100711192-015-1765-5 PMID:25821280

Moore, G. C., & Benbasat, I. (1991). Development of an Instrument to Measure the Perceptions of Adopting an Information Technology Innovation. *Information Systems Research, 2*(3), 173–191. doi:10.1287/isre.2.3.192

Moreno, J. L. (1934). *Who Shall Survive: A New Approach to the Problem of Human Interrelations.* Nervous and Mental Disease Publishing Co. doi:10.1037/10648-000

Moreno, J., Serrano, M. A., & Fernández-Medina, E. (2016). *Main Issues in Big Data Security.* Future Internet; doi:10.3390/fi8030044

Mosegaard, K., & Tarantola, A. (2002). Probabilistic Approach to Inverse Problems. In International Handbook of Earthquake & Engineering Seismology (pp. 237–265). Academic Press.

Moura, J., & Serrão, C. (2016). *Security and Privacy Issues of Big Data.* Retrieved from: https://arxiv.org/abs/1601.06206

Mowbray, M. (2017). *Detecting Security Attacks on the Enterprise Internet of Things: an Overview.* Hewlett Packard Enterprise Development LP.

Muhammad, K., Lloret, J., & Baik, W. S. (2019). Intelligent and Energy-Efficient Data Prioritization in Green Smart Cities: Current Challenges and Future Directions. *IEEE Communications Magazine, 57*(2), 60–65. doi:10.1109/MCOM.2018.1800371

Mukhanov, L. E. (2008). *Using Bayesian Belief Networks for Credit Card Fraud Detection. In Proceedings of the 26th IASTED International Conference on Artificial Intelligence and Applications* (pp. 221–225). Innsbruck, Austria: ACTA Press. Retrieved from http://dl.acm.org/citation.cfm?id=1712759.1712801

Mukkamala, R. R., Vatrapu, R., Ray, P. K., Sengupta, G., & Halder, S. (2018). Converging Blockchain and Social Business for Socio-Economic Development. *2018 IEEE International Conference on Big Data (Big Data)*, 3039–3048. 10.1109/BigData.2018.8622238

Murthy, A. (2014). Moving beyond MapReduce and Batch Processing with Apache Hadoop2. Hortonworks Inc. Arora, M., & Bahuguna, H. (2016). Big Data Security – The Big Challenge. *International Journal of Scientific & Engineering Research, 7*(12).

Nagappan, M. A. (2010). Abstracting log lines to log event types for mining software system logs. In *7th IEEE Working Conference on Mining Software Repositories (MSR)* (pp. 114-117). IEEE. 10.1109/MSR.2010.5463281

Nagarajan, M., & Karthikeyan, S. (2012) *A New Approach to Increase the Life Time and Efficiency of Wireless Sensor Network.* IEEE. doi:10.1109/ICPRIME.2012.6208349

Nakahori, K., & Yamaguchi, S. (2017). A support tool to design IoT services with NuSMV. *Proc. of IEEE ICCE 2017,* 84–87. 10.1109/ICCE.2017.7889238

Nakao, K. (2018). Proactive cyber security response by utilizing passive monitoring technologies. *Proc. of IEEE ICCE 2018.* 10.1109/ICCE.2018.8326061

Narudin, F. A., Feizollah, A., Anuar, N. B., & Gani, A. (2016). Evaluation of machine learning classifiers for mobile malware detection. *Soft Computing*, *20*(1), 343–357. doi:10.100700500-014-1511-6

Negi, P., Mishra, A., & Gupta, B. B. (2013). *Enhanced CBF packet filtering method to detect DDoS attack in cloud computing environment.* arXiv preprint arXiv:1304.7073

Negi, P., Mishra, A., & Gupta, B. B. (2013). Enhanced CBF Packet Filtering Method to Detect DDoS Attack in Cloud Computing Environment. *International Journal of Computer Science Issues*.

Nettitude. (2017). Cloud Penetration Testing. Retrieved from https://www.nettitude.com/uk/cloud-penetration-testing/

Newman, M. E. J. (2004). Detecting community structure in networks. *European Physical Journal. B, Condensed Matter and Complex Systems*, *38*(2), 321–330. doi:10.1140/epjb/e2004-00124-y PMID:15244693

Ng, B. Y., Kankanhalli, A., & Xu, Y. C. (2009). Studying Users' Computer Security Behavior: A Health Belief Perspective. *Decision Support Systems*, *46*(4), 815–825. doi:10.1016/j.dss.2008.11.010

Nia, A. M., & Jha, N. K. (2016). A Comprehensive Study of Security of Internet-of-Things. *IEEE Transactions on Emerging Topics in Computing*.

Ni, J. (2018). *Security and privacy preservation in mobile crowdsensing.* University of Waterloo.

Nokia, N. (2019). *Threat Intelligence Report 2019.* Nokia.

Notario, N., Crespo, A., Martín, Y.-S., Del Alamo, J. M., Le Métayer, D., Antignac, T., . . . Wright, D. (2015). Pripare: Integrating privacy best practices into a privacy engineering methodology. In Security and privacy workshops (SPW), 2015 IEEE (pp. 151–158). IEEE.

Nurse, J. R. (2014). Understanding insider threat: A framework for characterising attacks. *Security and Privacy Workshops (SPW), 2014 IEEE*, 214 - 228.

Oath. (2016). *Yahoo provides notice to additional users affected by previously discussed 2013 data theft.* Retrieved from Oath: https://www.oath.com/press/yahoo-provides-notice-to-additional-users-affected-by-previously/

Oetzel, M. C., & Spiekermann, S. (2014). A systematic methodology for privacy impact assessments: A design science approach. *European Journal of Information Systems*, *23*(2), 126–150. doi:10.1057/ejis.2013.18

Olafsen, A. H., Halvari, H., Forest, J., & Deci, E. L. (2015). Show them the money? the role of pay, managerial need support, and justice in a self-determination theory model of intrinsic work motivation. *Scandinavian Journal of Psychology*, *56*(4), 447–457. doi:10.1111jop.12211 PMID:25810152

Oliner, A., Ganapathi, A., & Xu, W. (2012). Advances and challenges in log analysis. *Communications of the ACM*, *55*(2), 55–61. doi:10.1145/2076450.2076466

Oliveira, R. R., Martins, R. M., & Simao, A. d. (2017). Impact of the Vendor Lock-in Problem on Testing as a Service (TaaS). *International Conference on Cloud Engineering (IC2E).* Vancouver. doi:10.1109/IC2E.2017.30

Ong, B. T., Sugiura, K., & Zettsu, K. (2016). Dynamically pre-trained deep recurrent neural networks using environmental monitoring data for predicting PM 2.5. *Neural Computing & Applications*, *27*(6), 1553–1566. doi:10.100700521-015-1955-3 PMID:27418719

Opara-Martins, J. (2018). Taxonomy of Cloud Lock-in Challenges. In M. Khatib, & N. Salman, *Mobile Computing - Technology and Applications.* IntechOpen. doi:10.5772/intechopen.74459

Oprea, A. F. (2015). Detection of early-stage enterprise infection by mining large-scale log data. In *Dependable Systems and Networks (DSN), 2015 45th Annual IEEE/IFIP International Conference on* (pp. 45-56). IEEE.

Osman, M. (2019). Ecommerce – *Chatbots, Voice, Omni-Channel Marketing*. Retrieved from KINSTA: https://kinsta.com/blog/ecommerce-statistics/

Osman, S. M. (2019). A novel big data analytics framework for Smart Cities. *Future Generation Computer Systems, 91*, 620–633. doi:10.1016/j.future.2018.06.046

Pan, G., Qi, G., Zhang, W., Li, S., Wu, Z., & Yang, T. L. (2013). Trace analysis and mining for Smart Cities: Issues, methods, and applications. *IEEE Communications Magazine, 51*(6), 120–126. doi:10.1109/MCOM.2013.6525604

Pang, Z., Yang, G., Khedri, R., & Zhang, T. Y. (2018). Introduction to the Special Section: Convergence of Automation Technology, Biomedical Engineering, and Health Informatics Toward the Healthcare 4.0. *IEEE Reviews in Biomedical Engineering, 11*, 249–259. doi:10.1109/RBME.2018.2848518

Papazoglou, M. P., & van den Heuvel, W.-J. (2007). Service-Oriented Architecture: Approaches, Technologies, and Research Issues. *Very Large Data Bases, 16*(3), 389–415.

Partners, C. R. (2018). *Insider Threat 2018 Report.*

Passino, K. M. (2002). Biomimicry of bacterial foraging for distributed optimization and control. *IEEE Control Systems, 22*(3), 52-67.

Pavlyukevich, I. (2007). Lévy flights, non-local search and simulated annealing. *Journal of Computational Physics, 226*(2), 1830–1844. doi:10.1016/j.jcp.2007.06.008

Peachey, K. (2019). *Banking by mobile app 'to overtake online by 2019'.* Retrieved from BBC: https://www.bbc.com/news/business-44166991

Pearson, M., & West, P. (2003). Drifting smoke rings: social network analysis and Markov processes in a longitudinal study of friendship groups and risk taking. *Connections: bulletin of the International Network for Social Network Analysis, 25*(2), 59–76. Retrieved from http://eprints.gla.ac.uk/2701/

Pearson, S., & Charlesworth, A. (2009). Accountability as a way forward for privacy protection in the cloud. In IEEE international conference on cloud computing (pp. 131–144). IEEE. doi:10.1007/978-3-642-10665-1_12

Pearson, S., & Benameur, A. (2010). *Privacy, security and trust issues arising from cloud computing. Cloud Computing Technology and Science.* Indianapolis, IN: CloudCom.

Peng, S., Wang, G., & Xie, D. (2016). Social Influence Analysis in Social Networking Big Data: Opportunities and Challenges. *IEEE Network, 31*(1), 11–17. doi:10.1109/MNET.2016.1500104NM

Penza, M., Suriano, D., Pfister, V., Prato, M., & Cassano, G. (2017, August). Urban Air Quality Monitoring with Networked Low-Cost Sensor-Systems. In Multidisciplinary Digital Publishing Institute Proceedings (Vol. 1, No. 4, p. 573). Academic Press. doi:10.3390/proceedings1040573

Petrelli, F., Pucci, L., & Bezzi, P. (2016). Astrocytes and Microglia and Their Potential Link with Autism Spectrum Disorders. *Frontiers in Cellular Neuroscience, 10*, 21. doi:10.3389/fncel.2016.00021 PMID:26903806

Phuang, A. (2017). The flower pollination algorithm with disparity count process for scheduling problem. *Information Technology and Electrical Engineering (ICITEE), 2017 9th International Conference on*, 1-5. 10.1109/ICITEED.2017.8250497

Pierce, J. L., & Delbecq, A. L. (1977). Organisation Structure, Individual Attitudes and Innovation. *Academy of Management Review, 2*(1), 27–37. doi:10.5465/amr.1977.4409154

Piro, G., Cianci, I., Grieco, A., Boggia, G., & Camarda, P. (2014). Information centric services in Smart Cities. *Journal of Systems and Software*, *88*, 169–188. doi:10.1016/j.jss.2013.10.029

Pitrat, J. (1990). Métaconnaissance: Futur de l'intelligence artificielle. *Hermes*.

Pitrat, J. (2010). *Artificial Beings: The Conscience of a Conscious Machine*. Wiley.

Plageras, A. A., Psannis, K. E., Stergiou, C., Wang, H., & Gupta, B. B. (2018). Efficient IoT-based sensor BIG Data collection–processing and analysis in smart buildings. *Future Generation Computer Systems*, *82*, 349–357. doi:10.1016/j.future.2017.09.082

Plohmann, D., Gerhard-Padilla, E., & Leder, F. (2011). *Botnets: Detection, Measurement, Disinfection & Defence*. ENISA.

Point, C. (2018). *2018 Security Report: Welcome to the Future of Cyber Security*. Check Point Research.

Porter, N., Garms, J., & Simakov, S. (2018, 5 3). Introducing Asylo: an open-source framework for confidential computing.

Prasanth, T., & Gunasekaran, M. (2019). Effective Big Data Retrieval Using Deep Learning Modified Neural Networks. *Mobile Networks and Applications*, 1–13.

Premkumar, G., & Ramamurthy, K. (1995). The Role of Inter-organizational and Organizational Factors on the Decision Mode for the Adoption of Inter-organizational Systems. *Decision Sciences*, *26*(3), 303–336. doi:10.1111/j.1540-5915.1995.tb01431.x

Premkumar, G., & Roberts, M. (1999). Adoption of New Information Technologies in Rural Small Businesses. *Journal of Management Science*, *27*(4), 467–484.

Proofpoint. (2018). *Quarterly Threat Report*. Proofpoint.com.

Provos, N. (2004). A virtual honeypot framework. *USENIX Security Symp*.

Puangdownreong, D., Hlungnamtip, S., Thammarat, C., & Nawikavatan, A. (2017). Application of flower pollination algorithm to parameter identification of DC motor model. *Electrical Engineering Congress (iEECON), 2017 International*, 1-4. 10.1109/IEECON.2017.8075889

Punitha, A. A. A., & Indumathi, G. (2018). Centralized cloud information accountability with bat key generation algorithm (CCIA-BKGA) framework in cloud computing environment. *Cluster Computing*, 1–12.

Putnam, H. (1975). Mind, Language and Reality. Cambridge University Press. doi:10.1017/CBO9780511625251

Qiu, M. M., Zhou, Y., & Wang, C. (2013, 6). Systematic Analysis of Public Cloud Service Level Agreements and Related Business Values. In *Proceedings of the 2013 IEEE International Conference on Services Computing* (pp. 729-736). Academic Press. doi:10.1109/SCC.2013.24

Qi, Z., Wang, T., Song, G., Hu, W., Li, X., & Zhang, Z. (2018). Deep air learning: Interpolation, prediction, and feature analysis of fine-grained air quality. *IEEE Transactions on Knowledge and Data Engineering*, *30*(12), 2285–2297. doi:10.1109/TKDE.2018.2823740

Quaddus, M., & Hofmeyer, G. (2007). An Investigation into the Factors Influencing the Adoption of B2B Trading Exchanges in Small Businesses. *European Journal of Information Systems*, *16*(3), 202–215. doi:10.1057/palgrave.ejis.3000671

Quinting, A., Lins, S., Szefer, J., & Sunyaev, A. (2017). Advancing the Adoption of a New Generation of Certifications--A Theoretical Model to Explain the Adoption of Continuous Cloud Service Certification by Certification Authorities. In *Proceedings of Wirtschaftsinformatik* (pp. 1–12). WI: Academic Press.

R Cloud Security Alliance Big data Analytics for Security Intelligence. (n.d.). Retrieved from http://cloudsecurityalliance.org/research/bigdata

Raghavan, S., Sarwesh, P., Marimuthu, C., & Chandrasekaran, K. (2015). Bat Algorithm for Scheduling Workflow Applications in Cloud. *Electronic Design, Computer Networks & Automated Verification (EDCAV), 2015 International Conference on*, 139-144. 10.1109/EDCAV.2015.7060555

Rainer, R. K., & Cegielski, C. G. (2010). *Introduction to information systems: Enabling and transforming business.* John Wiley & Sons.

Rajab, M., Zarfoss, J., Monrose, F., & Terzis, A. (2006). *A multifaceted approach to understanding the botnet phenomenon.* Retrieved October 31, 2009, from http://www.imconf.net/imc-2006/papers/p4-rajab.pdf

Rajab, M. A., Zarfoss, J., Monrose, F., & Terzis, A. (2007). My Botnet is Bigger than Yours (Maybe, Better than Yours): why size estimates remain challenging. *First Workshop on Hot Topics in Understanding Botnets (HotBots'07).*

Rajab, M., Zarfoss, J., Monrose, F., & Terzis, A. (2007). My botnet is bigger than yours (maybe, better than yours): Why size estimates remain challenging. *USENIX Workshop on Hot Topics in Understanding Botnet.*

Rajamohana, S. P., Umamaheswari, K., & Abirami, B. (2017). Adaptive binary flower pollination algorithm for feature selection in review spam detection. *Innovations in Green Energy and Healthcare Technologies (IGEHT), 2017 International Conference on*, 1-4. 10.1109/IGEHT.2017.8094094

Raj, E. D., & Babu, L. D. (2015). A firefly swarm approach for establishing new connections in social networks based on big data analytics. *International Journal of Communication Networks and Distributed Systems*, 15(2-3), 130–148. doi:10.1504/IJCNDS.2015.070968

Rajeswaran, D. a. (2018). *Function call graphs versus machine learning for malware detection.* Springer. doi:10.1007/978-3-319-92624-7_11

Ramachandra, G., Iftikhar, M., & Khan, F. A. (2017). A Comprehensive Survey on Security in Cloud Computing. *Procedia Computer Science*, 110, 465–472. doi:10.1016/j.procs.2017.06.124

Ramzan, Z. (2010). Phishing attacks and countermeasures. In *Handbook of information and communication security* (pp. 433–448). Springer. doi:10.1007/978-3-642-04117-4_23

Ranjani, A. C., & Sridhar, D. M. (2017). *A Proportional Study of Issues in Big Data clustering Algorithm with Hybrid Cs / Pso Algorithm. SSRG International Journal of Electronics and Communication Engineering.*

Rao, R. V., & Selvamani, K. (2015). Data security challenges and its solutions in cloud computing. *Procedia Computer Science*, 48, 204–209. doi:10.1016/j.procs.2015.04.171

Raphael, J. (2019). *7 mobile security threats you should take seriously in 2019.* Retrieved from CSO: https://www.csoonline.com/article/3241727/mobile-security/7-mobile-security-threats-you-should-take-seriously-in-2019.html

Ray, P. P. (2018). A survey on the Internet of Things architectures. *Journal of King Saud University-Computer and Information Sciences*, 30(3), 291–319. doi:10.1016/j.jksuci.2016.10.003

Raza, U., Kulkarni, P., & Sooriyabandara, M. (2017). *Low Power Wide Area Networks: An Overview.* Retrieved from https://arxiv.org/pdf/1606.07360.pdf

Raza, S., Wallgren, L., & Voigt, T. (2013). SVELTE: Real-time intrusion detection in the Internet of Things. *Ad Hoc Networks*, 11(8), 2661–2674. doi:10.1016/j.adhoc.2013.04.014

Razzaq, M. A., Qureshi, M. A., Gill, S. H., & Ullah, S. (2017). Security Issues in the Internet of Things (IoT): A Comprehensive Study. *International Journal of Advanced Computer Science and Applications*, *8*(6), 383–388.

RBI. (1998). *Committees on Computerisation.* Retrieved from https://www.rbi.org.in/scripts/PublicationsView.aspx?id=162

RBI. (2018). *Authorisation of New Retail Payment Systems.* Reserve Bank of India Department of Payment and Settlement Systems Central Office, Mumbai.

Reddy, V., Yedavalli, P., Mohanty, S., & Nakhat, U. (2018). Deep Air: Forecasting Air Pollution in Beijing, China. Academic Press.

Reese, G. (2009). *Cloud application architectures: building applications and infrastructure in the cloud.* Sebastopol, CA: OReilly Media Inc.

Report, S. (2019). *Frequency of online news sources reporting fake news U.S. 2018.* Retrieved from Statista: https://www.statista.com/statistics/649234/fake-news-exposure-usa/

Research, C. P. (n.d.). *2019 Security Report: Security the Cloud, Mobile and IoT.* Academic Press.

Reserve Bank of India - History. (2019). Retrieved February 20, 2019, from https://www.rbi.org.in/Scripts/Project1.aspx

Reserve Bank of India. (2017). *Guidelines on Information security, Electronic Banking, Technology risk management and cyber frauds.* Department of Banking Supervision.

Richman, D. (2017). *Amazon Web Services' secret weapon: Its custom-made hardware and network.* Geekwire.

Riedy, J. (2016). Updating PageRank for Streaming Graphs. In *2016 IEEE International Parallel and Distributed Processing Symposium Workshops (IPDPSW)* (pp. 877-884). Chicago, IL: IEEE. 10.1109/IPDPSW.2016.22

Riquet, D. A. (2012). Large-scale coordinated attacks: Impact on the cloud security. In *Sixth International Conference on Innovative Mobile and Internet Services in Ubiquitous Computing* (pp. 558-563). IEEE.

Rivest, R. L., Hamir, A., & Adleman, L. (1978). Method for obtaining digital signatures and public-key cryptosystems. *Communications of the ACM*, *21*(2), 120-126. doi:10.1145/359340.359342

Rodriguez, K. (2018, April 9). *The U.S. CLOUD Act and the EU: A Privacy Protection Race to the Bottom.* Electronic Frontier Foundation: Retrieved from https://www.eff.org/deeplinks/2018/04/us-cloud-act-and-eu-privacy-protection-race-bottom

Roesch, M. (1999). Snort-lightweight intrusion detection for networks. *Proceedings of the 13th USENIX conference on System administration*, 229–238.

Rogers, E. M. (1983). *Diffusion of Innovations* (3rd ed.). New York: The Free Press.

Romanowski, A. (2019). Big Data-Driven Contextual Processing Methods for Electrical Capacitance Tomography. *IEEE Transactions on Industrial Informatics*, *15*(3), 1609–1618. doi:10.1109/TII.2018.2855200

Roman, R., Lopez, J., & Mambo, M. (2018). Mobile edge computing, Fog et al.: A survey and analysis of security threats and challenges. *Future Generation Computer Systems*, *78*, 680–698. doi:10.1016/j.future.2016.11.009

Rosenschein, J. S., & Pack Kaelbling, L. (1986). The Synthesis of Digital Machines with Provable Epistemic Properties. In J. Halpern (Ed.), *Proceedings of the Conference on Theoretical Aspects of Reasoning About Knowledge* (pp. 83–98). Morgan Kaufmann. 10.1016/B978-0-934613-04-0.50009-0

Rturk, E. (2012). A case study in open source software security and privacy: Android adware. In *World Congress on Internet Security (WorldCIS)*. IEEE; doi:10.1109/IMIS.2012.76.

Ruan, K., Carthy, J., Kechadi, T., & Crosbie, M. (2011). Cloud forensics: An overview. In *Proceedings of the 7th IFIP International Conference on Digital Forensics*, 16-25.

Rubinstein, I., & Good, N. (2012). *Privacy by design: A counterfactual analysis of Google and Facebook privacy incidents*. Academic Press.

Russinovich, M. (2017). How to Go from Responding to Hunting with Sysinternals Sysmon. *RSA Conference*.

Ryan, R. M., & Deci, E. L. (2000). Intrinsic and extrinsic motivations: Classic definitions and new directions. *Contemporary Educational Psychology*, 25(1), 54–67. doi:10.1006/ceps.1999.1020 PMID:10620381

Sable, N. A., & Datar, D. S. (2013). A review-botnet detection and suppression in clouds. *Journal of Information Engineering and Applications*, 3(12), 1–7.

Safa, N. S., Sookhak, M., Solms, R. V., Furnell, S., Abdul-Ghani, N., & Herawam, T. (2015). Information Security Conscious Care Behaviour Formation in Organisations. *Computers & Security*, 53, 65–78. doi:10.1016/j.cose.2015.05.012

Saha, B., & Gairola, A. (2005). *Botnet: An overview*. CERT-In White PaperCIWP-2005-05.

Salleh, K. A., Janczewski, L., & Beltran, F. (2015). SEC-TOE Framework: Exploring Security: Determinants in Big Data Solutions Adoption. *Proc, of the Pacific Asia Conference on Information Systems (PACIS)*, 203.

Sarikaya, R. (2017). The Technology Behind Personal Digital Assistants: An overview of the system architecture and key components. *IEEE Signal Processing Magazine*, 34(1), 67–81. doi:10.1109/MSP.2016.2617341

Sarvas, R., & Frohlich, D. M. (2011). *From snapshots to social media-the changing picture of domestic photography*. Springer Science & Business Media. doi:10.1007/978-0-85729-247-6

Saul, L. K., & Jordan, M. I. (1999). Mixed Memory Markov Models: Decomposing Complex Stochastic Processes as Mixtures of Simpler Ones. *Machine Learning*, 37(1), 75–87. doi:10.1023/A:1007649326333

Saxena, T., & Chourey, V. (2014). A survey paper on cloud security issues and challenges. In *Proceedings of the Conference on IT in Business, Industry and Government (CSIBIG)* (pp. 1–5). Indore: IEEE; . doi:10.1109/CSIBIG.2014.7056957

Schaechter, A. (2002). *Issues in Electronic Banking: An Overview*. International Monetary Fund.

Schaffer, G. (2006). Worms and Viruses and Botnets, Oh My: Rational Responses to Emerging Internet Threats. *IEEE Security and Privacy*, 4(3), 52–58. doi:10.1109/MSP.2006.83

Schwaig, K. S., Kane, G. C., & Storey, V. C. (2006). Compliance to the fair information practices: How are the fortune 500 handling online privacy disclosures? *Information & Management*, 43(7), 805–820. doi:10.1016/j.im.2006.07.003

Schwartz, D., Youngs, N., & Britto, A. (2014). *The Ripple protocol consensus algorithm*. Ripple Labs Inc White Paper. Retrieved from http://www.naation.com/ripple-consensus-whitepaper.pdf

Searchsecurity. (2019). *Access control*. Retrieved from https://searchsecurity.techtarget.com/definition/access-control

Sekhar, Bysani, & Kiranmai. (2018). Security and Privacy Issues in IoT: A Platform for Fog Computing. In *The Rise of Fog Computing in the Digital Era*. IGI Global.

Sekhar, M., Sivagnanam, R., Matt, S. G., Manvi, S. S., & Gopalalyengar, S. K. (2019). Identification of Essential Proteins in Yeast Using Mean Weighted Average and Recursive Feature Elimination. *Recent Patents on Computer Science*, 12(1), 5–10. doi:10.2174/2213275911666180918155521

Sekhar, S. M., & Siddesh, G. M. (2018). *Introduction and Implementation of Machine Learning Algorithms in R*. In *Sentiment Analysis and Knowledge Discovery in Contemporary Business*. IGI Global.

Senarath, A., Arachchilage, N. A., & Slay, J. (2017). Designing Privacy for You: A Practical Approach for User-Centric Privacy. In *International Conference on Human Aspects of Information Security, Privacy, and Trust* (pp. 739-752). Springer. 10.1007/978-3-319-58460-7_50

Sen, J. (2015). *Security and privacy issues in cloud computing.* IGI Global.

Senthilnath, J., Kulkarni, S., Benediktsson, J. A., & Yang, X. S. (2016). A novel approach for multispectral satellite image classification based on the bat algorithm. *IEEE Geoscience and Remote Sensing Letters, 13*(4), 599–603. doi:10.1109/LGRS.2016.2530724

Shahriar, H. A. (2016). Mobile phishing attacks and mitigation techniques. *Journal of Information Security,* 206.

Shanmughapriya, M., Sumathi, G., & Aarthi, K. C. (2018). Bot Net of Things – A Survey. *International Journal of Engineering and Computer Science, 7*(5), 23926–23930.

Shapiro, S. S. (2016). Privacy risk analysis based on system control structures: Adapting system-theoretic process analysis for privacy engineering. In Security and privacy workshops (SPW), 2016 IEEE (pp. 17–24). IEEE.

Sharma, A., & Sehgal, S. (2016). Image Segmentation using Firefly Algorithm. *Information Technology (InCITe)-The Next Generation IT Summit on the Theme-Internet of Things: Connect your Worlds, International Conference on,* 99-102. 10.1109/INCITE.2016.7857598

Sheng, S. A. (2010). Who falls for phish?: a demographic analysis of phishing susceptibility and effectiveness of interventions. In *Proceedings of the SIGCHI Conference on Human Factors in Computing Systems* (pp. 373 - 382). ACM. 10.1145/1753326.1753383

Shridhar, S. V. (2019). The India of Things: Tata Communications' countrywide IoT network aims to improve traffic, manufacturing, and health care. *IEEE Spectrum, 56*(2), 42–47. doi:10.1109/MSPEC.2019.8635816

Shu, K. A. (2017). Fake news detection on social media: A data mining perspective. *ACM SIGKDD Explorations Newsletter,* 22-36.

Silva, A. S.-F. (2016). *ATLANTIC: A framework for anomaly traffic detection, classification, and mitigation in SDN.* IEEE.

Silva, G. C., Rose, L., & Calinescu, R. (2013). *A systematic review of cloud lock-in solutions. Cloud Computing Technology and Science.* Bristol: CloudCom.

Sinaović, H., & Mrdovic, S. (2017), Analysis of Mirai malicious software. Prof. of SoftCOM 2017, 1-5.

Singh, S., Jeong, Y.-S., & Park, J. H. (2016). A survey on cloud computing security: Issues, threats, and solutions. *Journal of Network and Computer Applications, 75,* 200–222. doi:10.1016/j.jnca.2016.09.002

Small, M. L. (2011). How to conduct a mixed methods study: Recent trends in a rapidly growing literature. *Annual Review of Sociology, 37*(1), 57–86. doi:10.1146/annurev.soc.012809.102657

Smart Cities total installed base of connected things 2015-2018. (2018). Retrieved February 25, 2019, from The Statistics Portal: https://www.statista.com/statistics/422886/smart-Cities-connected-things-installed-base/

Snedaker, S., & Rima, C. (2014). *Business Continuity and Disaster Recovery Planning for IT Professionals.* Syngress.

Sobers, R. (2019). 60 Must-Know Cybersecurity. Retrieved from VARONIS: https://www.varonis.com/blog/cybersecurity-statistics/

Solanki, K. V., Makkar, S., Kumar, R., & Chatterjee, M. J. (2018, December 31). Theoretical Analysis of Big Data for Smart Scenarios. *Internet of Things and Big Data Analytics for Smart Generation,* 1-12.

Somani, G., Gaur, M. S., Sanghi, D., Conti, M., & Buyya, R. (2017). DDoS attacks in cloud computing: Issues, taxonomy, and future directions. *Computer Communications, 107*, 30–48. doi:10.1016/j.comcom.2017.03.010

Song, D. X., Wagner, D., & Perrig, A. (2000). Practical techniques for searches on encrypted data. In *Proceeding 2000 IEEE Symposium on Security and Privacy* (pp. 44-55). Academic Press. doi:10.1109/SECPRI.2000.848445

Soomro, Z. A., Shah, M. H., & Ahmed, J. (2016). Information security management needs more holistic approach: A literature review. *International Journal of Information Management, 36*(2), 215–225. doi:10.1016/j.ijinfomgt.2015.11.009

Srivastava, L. (2006). Pervasive, ambient, ubiquitous: the magic of radio. *Proceedings of European Commission Conference From RFID to the Internet of Things.*

Stalmans, E., & Irwin, B. (2011). *A framework for DNS based detection and mitigation of malware infections on a network.* IEEE Information Security South Africa. doi:10.1109/ISSA.2011.6027531

Starck, J.-L., Murtagh F, & J., F. (2015). *Sparse Image and Signal Processing: Wavelets and Related Geometric Multiscale Analysis.* Cambridge University Press.

Statista, R. (2018). *Mobile Internet - Statistics & Facts.* Retrieved 12 30, 2018, from Statista: https://www.statista.com/topics/779/mobile-internet/

Statista, S. (2019). *Share of population using digital banking in the United States from 2018 to 2022.* Retrieved from Statista: https://www.statista.com/statistics/946109/digital-banking-users-usa/

Statista. (2019). *Share of population using digital banking in the United States from 2018 to 2022.* Retrieved from https://www.statista.com/statistics/946109/digital-banking-users-usa/

Statista. (2019, January). *Global market share held by operating systems for desktop PCs, from January 2013 to January 2019.* Retrieved from Statista: https://www.statista.com/statistics/218089/global-market-share-of-windows-7/

Statt, N. (2016). *How an army of vulnerable gadgets took down the web today.* Retrieved from https://www.theverge.com/2016/10/21/13362354/dyn-dns-ddos-attack-cause-outage-status-explained

Stergiou, C., Psannis, K. E., Xifilidis, T., Plageras, A. P., & Gupta, B. B. (2018) Security and privacy of big data for social networking services in cloud. *IEEE INFOCOM 2018.*

Stergioua, C., Psannisa, K. E., & Gupta, B.B. (2016). Secure Integration of IoT and Cloud Computing. In Future Generation Computer Systems. Elsevier.

Stergiou, C. G., Psannis, K. E., Kim, B.-G., & Gupta, B. (2018). Secure integration of IoT and cloud computing. *Future Generation Computer Systems, 78*, 964–975. doi:10.1016/j.future.2016.11.031

Stevanovic, M. A. (2016). On the use of machine learning for identifying botnet network traffic. *Journal of Cyber Security and Mobility*, 11 - 32.

Stevanovic, M., & Pedersen, J. (2014). An efficient flow-based botnet detection using supervised machine learning. *International Conference on Computing, Networking, and Communications (ICNC)*, 797–801. 10.1109/ICCNC.2014.6785439

Stinson, E., & Mitchell, J. C. (2007). Characterizing bots' remote control behaviour. *Proceedings of the 4th GI International Conference on Detection of Intrusions and Malware, and Vulnerability Assessment (DMV A'07).*

Stinson, E., & Mitchell, J. C. (2007). Characterizing bots' remote control behavior. In *Detection of Intrusions and Malware, and Vulnerability Assessment* (pp. 89–108). Springer. doi:10.1007/978-3-540-73614-1_6

Sulaiman, M. H., Mustafa, M. W., Zakaria, Z. N., Aliman, O., & Rahim, S. R. A. (2012). Firefly Algorithm Technique for Solving Economic Dispatch Problem. *Power Engineering and Optimization Conference (PEDCO) Melaka, Malaysia, 2012 IEEE International*, 90-95. 10.1109/PEOCO.2012.6230841

Su, M.-Y. (2011). Using clustering to improve the KNN-based classifiers for online anomaly network traffic identification. *Journal of Network and Computer Applications, 34*(2), 722–730. doi:10.1016/j.jnca.2010.10.009

Sun, Y. A. (2014). Data security and privacy in cloud computing. *International Journal of Distributed Sensor Networks*, 9.

Suo, H. A. (2013). *Security and privacy in mobile cloud computing*. IEEE. doi:10.1109/IWCMC.2013.6583635

Suresh, M. C. V., & Belwin Edward, J. (2017). Optimal Placement Of Distributed Generation In Distribution Systems By Using Shuffled Frog Leaping Algorithm. *Journal of Engineering and Applied Sciences (Asian Research Publishing Network), 12*(3).

Syarif, I. B. (2012). Unsupervised clustering approach for network anomaly detection. In *International Conference on Networked Digital Technologies* (pp. 135-145). Springer. 10.1007/978-3-642-30507-8_13

Symantec, S. C. (2018). *2018 Internet Security Threat Report*. Author.

Symantec. (2016). *Internet Security Threat Report*.

Symantec. (2017). *Internet Security Threat Report*.

Symantec. (2019). *Why hackers love public Wi-Fi*. Retrieved from Norton by Symantec: https://us.norton.com/internet-security-wifi-why-hackers-love-public-wifi.html

Szefer, J. A. (2012). Architectural support for hypervisor-secure virtualization. *ACM SIGARCH Computer Architecture News*, 437-450.

Tabassum, R., & Tyagi, N. (2016). Issues and Approaches for Big Data Security. International Journal of Latest Technology in Engineering, Management & Applied Science, 5(7).

Tan, Z. A. (2014). Enhancing big data security with collaborative intrusion detection. *IEEE Cloud Computing*, 27-33.

Tanaka, H., Yamaguchi, S., & Arata, T. (2019). Consideration of IoT structure in mitigation against Mirai malware. *Proc. of IEEE ICCE-Berlin 2018*.

Tanaka, H., & Yamaguchi, S. (2017). On modeling and simulation of the behavior of IoT devices malwares Mirai and Hajime. *Proc. of IEEE ISCE 2017*, 56–60.

Tarantola, A., & Valette, B. (1982). Generalized nonlinear inverse problems solved using the least squares criterion. *Reviews of Geophysics, 20*(2), 219–232. doi:10.1029/RG020i002p00219

Tarekegn, G. B., & Munaye, Y. Y. (2016, July–August). Big Data: Security Issues, Challenges and Future Scope. *International Journal of Computer Engineering & Technology, 7*(4), 12–24.

Taylor & Francis. (2018). Computer and Cyber Security: Principles, Algorithm, Applications, and Perspectives. CRC Press.

TechTarget. (n.d.). *Chapter 2: Introduction to the Incident Response Process*. Academic Press.

Temizkan, O., Kumar, R. L., Park, S. J., & Subramaniam, C. (2012). Patch release behaviors of software vendors in response to vulnerabilities: An empirical analysis. *Journal of Management Information Systems, 28*(4), 305–338. doi:10.2753/MIS0742-1222280411

Teo, T. S. H., Lin, S., & Lai, K. (2009). Adopters and Non-adopters of E-Procurement in Singapore: An Empirical Study. *Omega. International Journal of Management Sciences, 37*(5), 972–987.

Tep, K. S.-K. (2015). *A taxonomy of cloud attack consequences and mitigation strategies: The Role of Access Control and Privileged Access Management. In Trustcom/BigDataSE/ISPA* (pp. 1073–1080). IEEE.

Tewari, H., Hughes, A., Weber, S., & Barry, T. (2018). A blockchain-based PKI management framework. *NOMS 2018 - 2018 IEEE/IFIP Network Operations and Management Symposium.*

Tewari, A., & Gupta, B. B. (2017). Cryptanalysis of a novel ultra-lightweight mutual authentication protocol for IoT devices using RFID tags. *The Journal of Supercomputing, 73*(3), 1085–1102. doi:10.100711227-016-1849-x

Tewari, A., Jain, A., & Gupta, B. B. (2016). Recent Survey of Various Defense Mechanisms against Phishing Attacks. *Journal of Information Privacy and Security, 12*(1), 3–13. doi:10.1080/15536548.2016.1139423

Thangavel, G., & Adam, T. (2018). Securing Medical Text Data using Cuckoo Search based Advanced Encryption Standard (AES). *IOSR Journal of Computer Engineering,* 35-40.

The Guardian. (n.d.). *Alex Hern uber employees 'spied on ex-partners, politicians and Beyonce.* Retrieved from https://www.theguardian.com/technology/2016/dec/13/uber-employees-spying-ex-partners-politicians-beyonce

The Guardian. (n.d.). *Michael Macegoogle logic: why google does the things it does the way it does.* Retrieved from https://www.theguardian.com/technology/2013/jul/09/google-android-reader-why

The Sydney Morning Herald. (n.d.a). *Adam Turner malware hijacks big four australian banks' apps, steals two-factor SMS codes.* Retrieved from http://www.smh.com.au/technology/consumer-security/malware-hijacks-big-four-australian-banks-apps-steals-twofactor-sms-codes-20160309-gnf528.html

The Sydney Morning Herald. (n.d.b). *Clancy Yeates nab scandal reveals shortcomings with breach re-porting.* Retrieved from http://www.smh.com.au/business/banking-and-finance/nab-scandal-reveals-shortcomings-with-breach-reporting-20150226-13pslp.htmll

Think Tank Ranking Digital Rights. (n.d.). Retrieved from https://rankingdigitalrights.org/ index2015/

Thong, J. Y. L., Yap, C., & Raman, K. S. (1996). Top Management Support, External Expertise and Information Systems Implementation in Small Businesses. *Information Systems Research, 7*(2), 248–267. doi:10.1287/isre.7.2.248

Thovex, C., Le Grand, B., Cervantes, O., Sánchez, A. J., & Trichet, F. (2017). Encyclopedia of Social Network Analysis and Mining. In R. Alhajj & J. Rokne (Eds.), Encyclopedia of Social Network Analysis and Mining (pp. 1–12). New York, NY: Springer. doi:10.1007/978-1-4614-7163-9_381-1

Thovex, C. (2018). Social Network and Surveillance for Society. In T. Özyer, S. Bakshi, & R. Alhajj (Eds.), *Social Network and Surveillance for Society* (pp. 101–113). Springer International Publishing.

Thovex, C., & Trichet, F. (2013). An Epistemic Equivalence for Predictive Social Networks Analysis. *Lecture Notes in Computer Science, 7652,* 201–214. doi:10.1007/978-3-642-38333-5_21

Torkhani, G., Ladgham, A., Sakly, A., & Mansouri, M. N. (2017). A novel optimised face recognition application based on modified shuffled frog leaping algorithm. *International Journal of Applied Pattern Recognition, 4*(1), 27–43. doi:10.1504/IJAPR.2017.082653

Tornatzky, L. G., & Fleischer, M. (1990). The Process of Technological Innovation. Lexington Books.

Tornatzky, L. G., & Klein, K. J. (1982). Innovation Characteristics and Innovation Adoption Implementation: A Meta-analysis of Findings. *IEEE Transactions on Engineering Management, 29*(1), 28–45. doi:10.1109/TEM.1982.6447463

Toshniwal, R., Dastidar, K. G., & Nath, A. (2015). Big Data Security Issues and Challenges. *International Journal of Innovative Research in Advanced Engineering, 2*(2).

Tous, R., Torres, J., & Ayguadé, E. (2015). Multimedia Big Data Computing for In-Depth Event Analysis. In *2015 IEEE International Conference on Multimedia Big Data* (pp. 144-147). Beijing, China: IEEE. 10.1109/BigMM.2015.39

Tracol, X. (2016). "Invalidator" strikes back: The harbour has never been safe. *Computer Law & Security Review, 32*(2), 345–362. doi:10.1016/j.clsr.2016.01.011

Tuncalp, D. (2014). Diffusion and Adoption of Information Security Management Standards across Countries and Industries. *Journal of Global Information Technology Management, 17*(4), 221–227. doi:10.1080/1097198X.2014.982454

Turing, A. M. (1950). Computing Machinery and Intelligence. (O. Academic, Ed.) Mind, 59(236), 433–460. doi:https://doi.org/10.1093/mind/LIX.236.433

Tuttle, H. (2016). Data deluge: what the Panama Papers leak means for business. *Risk Management, 63*(6), 22.

Tyagi, A. K., & Aghila, G. (2011). A wide-scale survey on a botnet. *International Journal of Computers and Applications, 34*(9), 10–23.

U. S. E. P. Agency. (2014). *Air Quality Index: A Guide to Air Quality and Your Health.* Author.

US-CERT. (2016). *Heightened DDoS threat posed by Mirai and other botnets.* Retrieved from https://www.us-cert.gov/ncas/alerts/TA16-288A

USPS. (2019). *Risks and Recommendations for Online Shopping.* Retrieved from CyberSafe at USPS: https://www.uspscybersafe.com/articles/individuals/risks-and-recommendations-for-online-shopping/

Vaarandi, R. (2003). A data clustering algorithm for mining patterns from event logs. In *IP Operations & Management, 2003.(IPOM 2003). 3rd IEEE Workshop on* (pp. 119-126). IEEE.

Vaarandi, R. A. (2014). Using Security Logs for Collecting and Reporting Technical Security Metrics. In *Military Communications Conference (MILCOM)* (pp. 294--299). IEEE. 10.1109/MILCOM.2014.53

Vaarandi, R. A. (2015). LogCluster - A data clustering and pattern mining algorithm for event logs. In *11th International Conference on Network and Service Management (CNSM)* (pp. 1-7). IEEE. 10.1109/CNSM.2015.7367331

Valian, E., Mohanna, S., & Tavakoli, S. (2011). Improved cuckoo search algorithm for global optimization. *International Journal of Communications and Information Technology, 1*(1), 31–44.

Van Blarkom, G., Borking, J., & Olk, J. (2003). *Handbook of privacy and privacy-enhancing technologies. Privacy Incorporated Software Agent (PISA).* The Hague: Consortium.

Varga, P., Plosz, S., Soos, G., & Hegedus, C. (2017). Security Threats and Issues in Automation IoT. *Proc. IEEE 13th International Workshop on Factory Communication Systems (WFCS).* 10.1109/WFCS.2017.7991968

Venkatesh, V., & Bala, H. (2008). Technology Acceptance Model 3 and a Research Agenda on Interventions. *Decision Sciences, 39*(2), 273–315. doi:10.1111/j.1540-5915.2008.00192.x

Venkatesh, V., & Davis, F. D. (2000). A Theoretical Extension of the Technology Acceptance Model: Four Longitudinal Field Studies. *Management Science, 46*(2), 186–204. doi:10.1287/mnsc.46.2.186.11926

Venkatesh, V., Morris, M. G., Davis, G. B., & Davis, F. D. (2003). User Acceptance of Information Technology: Toward a Unified View. *Management Information Systems Quarterly, 27*(3), 425–478. doi:10.2307/30036540

Veracode. (2019). *Data loss prevention guide: learn data loss tips.* Retrieved from https://www.veracode.com/security/guide-data-loss-prevention

Verma, J., Sobhanayak, S., Sharma, S., Turuk, A. K., & Sahoo, B. (2017, May). Bacteria foraging based task scheduling algorithm in cloud computing environment. In *2017 International Conference on Computing, Communication and Automation (ICCCA),* (pp. 777-782). IEEE. 10.1109/CCAA.2017.8229901

Verma, P., & Sood, S. K. (2018). Fog assisted-IoT enabled patient health monitoring in smart homes. *IEEE Internet of Things Journal, 5*(3), 1789–1796. doi:10.1109/JIOT.2018.2803201

Vieane, A., Funke, G., Gutzwiller, R., Mancuso, V., Sawyer, B., & Wickens, C. (2016). Addressing human factors gaps in cyber defense. *Proceedings of the Human Factors and Ergonomics Society Annual Meeting, 60*(1), 770–773. doi:10.1177/1541931213601176

Vijayarani, S., & Sharmila, S. (2016). Research in Big Data – An Overview. *Informatics Engineering, an International Journal, 4*(3).

Villamarin-Salomon, R., & Brustoloni, J. C. (2008). Identifying Botnets Using Anomaly Detection Techniques Applied to DNS Traffic. *Proc. 5th IEEE Consumer Communications and Networking Conference (CCNC2008),* 476-481. 10.1109/ccnc08.2007.112

Visser, W. A. M., & Mcintosh, A. (1998). A short review of the historical critique of usury. *Accounting Business & Financial History, 8*(2), 175–189. doi:10.1080/095852098330503

Vitali, I., Fièvre, S., Telley, L., Oberst, P., Bariselli, S., Frangeul, L., ... Jabaudon, D. (2018). Progenitor Hyperpolarization Regulates the Sequential Generation of Neuronal Subtypes in the Developing Neocortex. *Cell, 174*(5), 1264–1276. doi:10.1016/j.cell.2018.06.036 PMID:30057116

Voelcker, J. (2006). Stalked by satellite - an alarming rise in GPS-enabled harassment. *IEEE Spectrum, 43*(7), 15–16. doi:. doi:10.1109/MSPEC.2006.1652998

Von Neumann, J. (1944). *Theory of Games and Economic Behavior.* Princeton University Press.

Voss, W. G. (2017). European union data privacy law reform: General data protection regulation, privacy shield, and the right to delisting. *Business Lawyer, 72*(1), 221–233.

Wagner, J., & Benecke, A. (2016). National legislation within the framework of the gdpr. *European Data Protection Law Review, 2*(3), 353–361. doi:10.21552/EDPL/2016/3/10

Walravens, N., & Ballon, P. (2013). Platform business models for Smart Cities: From control and value to governance and public value. *IEEE Communications Magazine, 51*(6), 72–79. doi:10.1109/MCOM.2013.6525598

Wang, X., & Zhou, N. (2014).Pattern Search Firefly Algorithm for Solving Systems of Nonlinear Equations. *Computational Intelligence and Design (ISCID), 2014 Seventh International Symposium on,* 228-231. 10.1109/ISCID.2014.222

Wang, H., Wang, W., Cui, L., Sun, H., Zhao, J., Wang, Y., & Xue, Y. (2018). A hybrid multi-objective firefly algorithm for big data optimization. *Applied Soft Computing, 69,* 806–815. doi:10.1016/j.asoc.2017.06.029

Wang, J., Crawl, D., Purawat, S., Nguyen, M., & Altintas, I. (2015). Big data provenance: Challenges, state of the art and opportunities. In *2015 IEEE International Conference on Big Data (Big Data)* (pp. 2509-2516). Santa Clara, CA: IEEE. 10.1109/BigData.2015.7364047

Wang, N., & Mao, B. (2019). The Research on the Problems of Smart Old-Age Care in the Background of Smart City Construction. In *International Conference on Intelligent Transportation, Big Data & Smart City (ICITBS)* (pp. 151-154). Changsha, China: IEEE. 10.1109/ICITBS.2019.00043

Wang, P., Sparks, S., & Zou, C. C. (2010). An advanced hybrid peer-to-peer botnet. *Proc. in Workshop on Hot Topics in Understanding Botnets.*

Wang, Q. (2009). Artificial Neural Network and Hidden Space SVM for Fault Detection in Power System. In *ISNN 2009: Proceedings of the 6th International Symposium on Neural Networks.* Springer Verlag. 10.1007/978-3-642-01510-6_45

Wang, X., Sanders, B. C., & Pan, S. H. (2000). Entangled coherent states for systems with SU (2) and SU (1,1) symmetries. *Journal of Physics. A, Mathematical and General, 33*(41), 7451–7467. doi:10.1088/0305-4470/33/41/312

Wang, Y., Wang, Y., Lin, H., & Tang, T. (2003). Determinants of User Acceptance of Internet Banking: An Empirical Study. *International Journal of Service Industry Management, 14*(5), 501–519. doi:10.1108/09564230310500192

Waters, S., & Ackerman, J. (2011). Exploring privacy management on facebook: Motivations and perceived consequences of voluntary disclosure. *Journal of Computer-Mediated Communication, 17*(1), 101–115. doi:10.1111/j.1083-6101.2011.01559.x

Wee, C. a. (2016). Understanding the Personality Characteristics of Cybersecurity Competition Participants to Improve the Effectiveness of Competitions as Recruitment Tools. In *Advances in Human Factors in Cybersecurity* (pp. 111–121). Springer. doi:10.1007/978-3-319-41932-9_10

What is the purpose of SWIFT India? (2019). Retrieved February 20, 2019, from https://www.swiftindia.org.in/what-purpose-swift-india

Whitmore, A., Agarwal, A., & Xu, L. D. (2015). The Internet of Things—A survey of topics and trends. *Information Systems Frontiers, 17*(2), 261–274. doi:10.100710796-014-9489-2

Wikipedia. (2019). *Investing online.* Retrieved from https://en.wikipedia.org/wiki/Investing_online

Wilinski, P., Solaiman, B., Hillion, A., & Czarnecki, W. (1998). Toward the Border Between Neural and Markovian Paradigms. *IEEE Trans. Systems, Man, and Cybernetics. Part B, 28*(2), 146–159. doi:10.1109/3477.662756

Winters, V. J. (2010). Why are smart cities growing? who moves and who stays. *Journal of Regional Science, 51*(2), 253–270. doi:10.1111/j.1467-9787.2010.00693.x

Wood, D. J., & Logsdon, J. M. (2016). Social issues in management as a distinct field: Corporate social responsibility and performance. *Business & Society.*

Woźniak, M., & Połap, D. (2014, August). Basic concept of cuckoo search algorithm for 2D images processing with some research results: An idea to apply cuckoo search algorithm in 2d images key-points search. In *Signal Processing and Multimedia Applications (SIGMAP), 2014 International Conference on.* IEEE.

Wright, D., & De Hert, P. (2012). Introduction to privacy impact assessment. In *Privacy impact assessment* (pp. 3–32). Springer. doi:10.1007/978-94-007-2543-0_1

Wurm, J. (2014). Security Analysis on Consumer and Industrial IoT Devices. Academic Press.

Wurster, G., & van Oorschot, P. C. (2009). The developer is the enemy. In *Proceedings of the 2008 workshop on new security paradigms* (pp. 89–97). Academic Press.

Wurzinger, P., Bilge, L., Holz, T., Goebel, J., Kruegel, C., & Kirda, E. (2009). *Automatically generating models for botnet detection.* Computer Security ESORICS.

Wynn, D. Jr, Karahanna, E., Williams, C. K., & Madupalli, R. (2012). Preventive Adoption of Information Security Behaviours. *Proc. the 33rd International Conference on Information Systems.*

Xu, H., & Jia, H. (2015). Privacy in a networked world: New challenges and opportunities for privacy research. *Washington Academy of Sciences. Journal of the Washington Academy of Sciences, 101*(3), 73.

Xu, Z. A. (2017). Malware detection using machine learning based analysis of virtual memory access patterns. In *Proceedings of the Conference on Design, Automation and Test in Europe* (pp. 169--174). European Design and Automation Association. 10.23919/DATE.2017.7926977

Xynos, K., Sutherland, I., Read, H., Everitt, E., & Blyth, A. J. (2010). Penetration testing and vulnerability assessments: A professional approach.

Yamaguchi, S., Bin Ahmadon, M. A., & Ge, Q. W. (2016). Introduction of Petri Nets: Its Applications and Security Challenges. In B. Gupta, D. P. Agrawal, & S. Yamaguchi (Eds.), *Handbook of Research on Modern Cryptographic Solutions for Computer and Cyber Security* (pp. 145–179). Hershey, PA: IGI Publishing. doi:10.4018/978-1-5225-0105-3.ch007

Yamaguchi, S., & Leelaprute, P. (2019). Hajime worm with lifespan and its mitigation evaluation against Mirai malware based on agent-oriented Petri net PN2. *Proc. of IEEE ICCE 2019, 4.* 10.1109/ICCE.2019.8662079

Yamaguchi, S., & Tanaka, H. (2018), Modeling of infection phenomenon and evaluation of mitigation methods for IoT malware Mirai by agent-oriented Petri net PN2. *Proc. of IEEE ICCE-TW 2018,* 271-272.

Yamaguchi, S., Tanaka, H., & Bin Ahmadon, M. A. (in press). Modeling and Evaluation of Mitigation Methods against IoT Malware Mirai with Agent-Oriented Petri Net PN^2. *International Journal of Internet of Things and Cyber-Assurance.* doi: 10.1504/IJITCA.2019.10021463

Yang, H. D., & Li, Y. (2014). An Intrusion Detection Method Based on Shuffle Frog Leaping Algorithm. In Advanced Materials Research. Trans Tech Publications. doi:10.4028/www.scientific.net/AMR.1030-1032.1646

Yang, J., Ye, Z., Yan, L., Gu, W., & Wang, R. (2018, September). Modified Naive Bayes Algorithm for Network Intrusion Detection based on Artificial Bee Colony Algorithm. In *2018 IEEE 4th International Symposium on Wireless Systems within the International Conferences on Intelligent Data Acquisition and Advanced Computing Systems (IDAACS-SWS),* (pp. 35-40). IEEE. 10.1109/IDAACS-SWS.2018.8525758

Yang, T. T. (2015). Automated detection and analysis for android ransomware. In *17th IEEE International Conference on High Performance Computing and Communications (HPCC)* (pp. 1338-1343). IEEE.

Yang, X. S. (2010). *Firefly algorithm, stochastic test functions and design optimisation.* arXiv preprint arXiv:1003.1409

Yang, X. S., Karamanoglu, M., & Fong, S. (2012). Bat algorithm for topology optimization in microelectronic applications. *Future Generation Communication Technology (FGCT), 2012 International Conference on,* 150-155. 10.1109/FGCT.2012.6476566

Yang, X. S. (2010). A new metaheuristic bat-inspired algorithm. In *Nature inspired cooperative strategies for optimization (NICSO 2010)* (pp. 65–74). Berlin: Springer. doi:10.1007/978-3-642-12538-6_6

Yang, X. S. (2012, September). Flower pollination algorithm for global optimization. In *International conference on unconventional computing and natural computation* (pp. 240-249). Springer. 10.1007/978-3-642-32894-7_27

Yang, X. S., & Deb, S. (2009, December). Cuckoo search via Lévy flights. *2009 World Congress on Nature & Biologically Inspired Computing (NaBIC),* 210-214. 10.1109/NABIC.2009.5393690

Yang, X., Liu, L., & Zou, R. (2011). A statistical user-behavior trust evaluation algorithm based on cloud model. In *Proceedings of the 2011 6th International Conference on Computer Sciences and Convergence Information Technology (ICCIT)* (pp. 598-603). Academic Press.

Yen, T.-F. A. (2013). *Beehive: Large-scale log analysis for detecting suspicious activity in enterprise networks*. ACM. doi:10.1145/2523649.2523670

Yessad, A., Faron, C., Dieng, R., & Laskri, T. (2008). Ontology-Driven Adaptive Course Generation for Web-based Education. *ED-MEDIA 2008*.

Yimam, D., & Fernandez, E. B. (2016). A survey of compliance issues in cloud computing. *Journal of Internet Services and Applications*, 7(1), 5. doi:10.118613174-016-0046-8

Yin, C., Zhang, S., Xi, J., & Wang, J. (2017). An improved anonymity model for big data security based on clustering algorithm. *Concurrency and Computation*, 29(7), 3902–3904. doi:10.1002/cpe.3902

Yin, R. K. (2013). *Case study research: Design and methods*. Sage Publications.

Yi, X., Zhang, J., Wang, Z., Li, T., & Zheng, Y. (2018, July). Deep distributed fusion network for air quality prediction. In *Proceedings of the 24th ACM SIGKDD International Conference on Knowledge Discovery & Data Mining* (pp. 965-973). ACM. 10.1145/3219819.3219822

Yli-Huumo, J., Ko, D., Choi, S., Park, S., & Smolander, K. (2016). Where Is Current Research on Blockchain Technology?- A Systematic Review. *PLoS One*, 11(10), e0163477. doi:10.1371/journal.pone.0163477 PMID:27695049

York, K. (2016). *Read Dyn's Statement on the 10/21/2016 DNS DDoS Attack*. Retrieved from https://dyn.com/blog/dyn-statement-on-10212016-ddos-attack/

Young, A. L., & Quan-Haase, A. (2009). Information revelation and internet privacy concerns on social network sites: a case study of Facebook. In *Proceedings of the fourth international conference on communities and technologies* (pp. 265–274). Academic Press. 10.1145/1556460.1556499

Yu, H., Yang, Z., & Sinnott, O. R. (2018). Decentralized Big Data Auditing for Smart City Environments Leveraging Blockchain Technology. *IEEE Access: Practical Innovations, Open Solutions*, 7, 6288–6296. doi:10.1109/ACCESS.2018.2888940

Yujuan, Z. A. (2015). Malware detection based on Android permission information. *Jisuanji Yingyong Yanjiu*, 3036–3040.

Yun'an, C. A. (2017). An Andriod Malware Detection Algorithm based on Permissions count. *Computer Applications and Software*, 55.

Yuvaraj, N., & Sabari, A. (2017). Twitter sentiment classification using binary shuffled frog algorithm. *Intelligent Automation & Soft Computing*, 23(2), 373–381. doi:10.1080/10798587.2016.1231479

Zanella, A., Bui, N., Castellani, A., Vangelista, L. Z., & Zorzi, M. (2014). Internet of Things for Smart Cities. *IEEE Internet of Things Journal*, 1(1), 22–32. doi:10.1109/JIOT.2014.2306328

Zang, X., Tangpong, A., Kesidis, G., & Miller, D.J. (2011). *CSE Dept Technical Report on "Botnet Detection through Fine Flow Classification."* Report No. CSE11-001.

Zefan, C., & Xiaodong, Y. (2017, December). Cuckoo search algorithm with deep search. In *2017 3rd IEEE International Conference on Computer and Communications (ICCC)* (pp. 2241-2246). IEEE. 10.1109/CompComm.2017.8322934

Zeidanloo, H. R., & Manaf, A. A. (2010). Botnet Detection by Monitoring Similar Communication Patterns. *International Journal of Computer Science and Information Security, 7*(3).

Zeidanloo, H.R., Manaf, A.B., Vahdani, P., Tabatabaei, F., & Zamani, M. (2010). Botnet Detection Based on Traffic Monitoring. *IEEE Transaction.*

Zeng, E. A. (2017). End user security & privacy concerns with smart homes. *Symposium on Usable Privacy and Security (SOUPS).*

Zeng, G. (2015). Big Data and Information Security. *International Journal of Computational Engineering Research, 5*(6).

Zhang, X. M., & Zhang, N. (2011, May). An open, secure and flexible platform based on internet of things and cloud computing for ambient aiding living and telemedicine. In 2011 international conference on computer and management (CAMAN) (pp. 1-4). IEEE. doi:10.1109/CAMAN.2011.5778905

Zhang, C., Shen, X., Pei, X., & Yao, Y. (2016). Applying big data analytics into network security: Challenges, techniques and outlooks. *IEEE International Conference on Smart Cloud (SmartCloud)*, 325–329. 10.1109/SmartCloud.2016.62

Zhang, C., Sun, J., Zhu, X., & Fang, Y. (2010). Privacy and security for online social networks: Challenges and opportunities. *IEEE Network, 24*(4), 13–18. doi:10.1109/MNET.2010.5510913

Zhang, M., Wang, L., Jajodia, S., Singhal, A., & Albanese, M. (2016). Network diNetwork dversity: A security metric for evaluating the resilience of networks against zero-day attacks. *IEEE Transactions on Information Forensics and Security, 11*(5), 1071–1086. doi:10.1109/TIFS.2016.2516916

Zhang, Y. J. (2014). Cross-tenant side-channel attacks in paas clouds. In *Proceedings of the 2014 ACM SIGSAC Conference on Computer and Communications Security* (pp. 990 - 1003). ACM. 10.1145/2660267.2660356

Zhang, Y. L. (2017). *QoS Prediction in Cloud and Service Computing.* Springer Briefs in Computer Science. doi:10.1007/978-981-10-5278-1

Zhang, Z., Sun, R., & Zhao, C., Wang, J., Chang, C.K., & Gupta, B.B. (2016). CyVOD: A Novel Trinity Multimedia Social Network Scheme. *Multimedia Tools and Applications*, 1–17.

Zheng, K., Zhao, S., Yang, Z., Xiong, X., & Xiang, W. (2016). Design and implementation of LPWA-based air quality monitoring system. *IEEE Access: Practical Innovations, Open Solutions, 4*, 3238–3245. doi:10.1109/ACCESS.2016.2582153

Zhou, J., Cao, Z., Dong, X., & Vasilakos, A. V. (2017, January). Security and Privacy for Cloud-Based IoT:Challenges. *IEEE Communications Magazine, 55*(1), 26–33. doi:10.1109/MCOM.2017.1600363CM

Zhuge, C. A. (2017). Efficient Event Log Mining with LogClusterC. In *Big Data Security on Cloud (BigDataSecurity), IEEE International Conference on High Performance and Smart Computing (HPSC), and IEEE International Conference on Intelligent Data and Security (IDS)* (pp. 261-266). IEEE.

Zhu, W., Cui, P., Wang, Z., & Hua, G. (2015). Multimedia Big Data Computing. *IEEE MultiMedia, 22*(3), 96–c3. doi:10.1109/MMUL.2015.66

Ziegeldorf, J. H., Morchon, O. G., & Wehrle, K. (2014). Privacy in the Internet of Things: Threats and Challenges. *Security and Communication Networks, 7*(12), 2728–2742. doi:10.1002ec.795

Zylva, A. (2016, 3 2). Windows 10 Device Guard and Credential Guard Demystified.

About the Contributors

B. B. Gupta received PhD degree from Indian Institute of Technology Roorkee, India in the area of information security. He has published more than 50 research papers in international journals and conferences of high repute. He has visited several countries to present his research work. His biography has published in the Marquis Who's Who in the World, 2012. At present, he is working as an Assistant Professor in the Department of Computer Engineering, National Institute of Technology Kurukshetra, India. His research interest includes information security, cyber security, cloud computing, web security, intrusion detection, computer networks and phishing.

* * *

Mumtaz Abdul Hameed is currently an Information Technology Consultant and Information Systems Lecturer at the Technovation Consulting and Training Private Limited - Maldives. He received his PhD from Brunel University London - United Kingdom in 2013, after completing his postgraduate studies at the University of Cambridge - United Kingdom. His research interests include: Adoption of IT innovations, Technology acceptance, IS security, Intelligent information processing and IT integration. He has published in Information and Management, Journal of Engineering and Technology Management, among others. Most of his papers were published and presented in the field of innovation adoption in organisations.

Rosni Abdullah is a Professor in Parallel Computing at the School of Computer Sciences, Universiti Sains Malaysia (USM) and is one of the national pioneers in this field. She is the Head of the Parallel and Distributed Processing Research Group at the School since its inception in 1994. Her research areas include Parallel and Distributed Computing, Parallel Numerical Algorithms and Computational Biology. She is currently the Dean of the School of Computer Sciences at USM, as well as the Director of the National Advanced IPv6 Center (Nav6), a center of research excellence in USM that focus on Cybersecurity and Internet of Things (IoT).

G. Aghila received her B.E degree in Computer Science and Engineering from Thiagarajar College of Engineering, India, M.E degree in Computer Science and Engineering from College of Engineering Guindy, India and Ph.D. in knowledge representation and reasoning from College of Engineering Guindy, India. She has 30 years of teaching experience for both U.G and P.G. Her research interests includes Artificial Intelligence, Chem-informatics, Image and Audio Steganography, Big data analytics, Edge computing, Blockchain in banking and Smart & Secure environment.

Mohammed Alauthman received his PhD degree from Northumbria University Newcastle, UK in 2016. He received a B.Sc. degree in Computer Science from Hashemite University, Jordan, in 2002, and received M.Sc. degrees in Computer Science from Amman Arab University, Jordan, in 2004. Currently, he is Assistant Professor and senior lecturer at Department of Computer Science, Zarqa University, Jordan. His main research areas cyber-security, Cyber Forensics, advanced machine learning and data science applications.

Kamal Alieyan received PhD degree from Universiti Sains Malaysia (USM) in 2018. He has published many of research papers in International Journals and Conferences of high repute. Currently he is Postdoctoral Fellow at Dept. of National Advanced IPv6 Centre of Excellence (NAv6) 6th Floor, School of Computer & Mathematical Sciences Building, UNIVERSITI SAINS MALAYSIA, 11800 USM, Penang, Malaysia. His research interest includes network security and network wireless.

Ammar Almomani received PhD degree from Universiti Sains Malaysia (USM) in 2013. He has published many of research papers in International Journals and Conferences of high repute. Currently he is assistant professor and senior lecturer at Dept. of Information Technology, Al-Huson University College, Al-Balqa Applied University, Jordan. His research interest includes advanced Internet security and monitoring.

Badr Almutairi received PhD degree from De Montfort University, UK. Currently he is assistant professor and senior lecturer at Department of Computer Science and Information Technology, Majmaah University, Al Majmaah, KSA.His research interest includes clouds and software Engineering.

Shaswat Anand is a final year student in the Department of Information Science and Engineering at Ramaiah Institute of Technology(MSRIT), Bangalore, India. He has a keen interest in upcoming research areas like Machine Learning, Artificial Intelligence and Blockchain technologies.

Nalin Asanka Gamagedara Arachchilage currently works as a Lecturer in Cyber Security in the Australian Centre for Cyber Security (ACCS) at the University of New South Wales (UNSW Canberra at the Australian Defence Force Academy). He holds a PhD in Usable Security entitled "Security Awareness of Computer Users: A Game Based Learning Approach" from Brunel University London, UK where he developed a game design framework to protect computer users against "phishing attacks". He obtained a BSc (MIS) Hons from University College Dublin, National University of Ireland and has completed a master's degree, MSc in Information Management and Security at the University of Bedfordshire, UK. He is a Sun Certified Java Programmer (SCJP) at Sun Microsystems (now Oracle), USA and professional member of Association for Computing Machinery (ACM).

Vijay Kumar Burugari is working as an Associate Professor in the department of CSE in Malla Reddy Engineering College, Autonomous. His education qualification is B.E CSE from Tirumala Engineering College, M.E CSE from K.S.R. College of Engineering and PhD from Anna University, Chennai. He has 11+ years of experience in teaching and industry. He started his career in Alagappa College of Technology, Chennai and also worked in K.S.Rangasamy College of Engineering, Tiruchengode. He has worked as an Associate Java Consultant and as a Software Engineer Trainee in industry. He is a member of ISTE, CSI, SDIWC, ICSES and IAENG. He has involved in Certification of NBA, NAAC and Autonomous affiliation of the College. He has coordinated project, internship and various departmental activities. His research interests include Computer Networks, Wireless Sensor Networks, IoT, Network Security and Data Mining. He has guided many projects in the diversified fields of information technology where projects are mainly from Wireless Sensor Networks, IoT, Network Security and Data Mining. He worked as a Deputy Placement Officer for KSR college of Engineering. He is a good placement trainer and an Amazon Web Services instructor. He has Organized National/International conference, convener for National/International conference, coordinator of Technical evens and Symposium. He has published 25 papers in various National/International journals and conferences and published a patent titled "Intelligent Shoe for Assisting Blind People". He received "Data Scientist Mastery Award for Educators 2017 V2" from IBM. He was awarded Best Faculty Award from EET CRS Academic Achievement Awards and Best Teacher of the Year (College Level) by International Association of Research and Developed Organization Excellence Awards in 2018 and Young Researcher award 2018 by I2OR.

Sumathi Doraikannan is presently working as a professor, Department of Computer Science and Engineering, at Malla Reddy Engineering College (Autonomous) Hyderabad, Telangana. She received the B.E Computer science and Engineering degree from Bharathiar University in 1994 and M.E Computer Science and Engineering degree from Sathyabama University in 2006, Chennai and completed her doctorate degree in Anna University, Chennai. She has secured 9th rank in the university. She has overall experience of 16 years out of which 6 years in industry, 10 years in teaching field. Her Research interests include Cloud computing, Network Security, Data Mining and Theoretical Foundations of computer science. She has published papers in international journal and conference. She has organized many international conferences and also acted as Technical Chair and tutorial presenter. She is a life member of ISTE. She has published few chapters in books under Wiley and IGI Global publications.

Abderahim El Allati is an Associate Professor, Faculty of Sciences and Techniques Al Hoceima, Abdelmalek Essaadi University, Tétouan Avril, 2014-2018: Assistant Professor, Faculty of Sciences and Techniques Al Hoceima, Mohammed I University, Oujda.

Mohammad Rasool Fatemi is a second-year Master of Computer Science student at University of New Brunswick with an interest in research and development of projects related to machine learning and its applications in cybersecurity. He is Currently a research and development assistant at Canadian Institute for Cybersecurity (CIC).

Siddesh G. M. currently working as Associate professor in Department of Information Science & Engineering, M S Ramaiah Institute of Technology, Bangalore.He is a member of IEEE, ISTE, IETE. He has published good number of research papers in International Conferences and Journals. His research interests are Distributed Computing, Grid/Cloud Computing and IoT.

Nalin Asanka Gamagedara Arachchilage currently works as Lecturer A in the Australian Centre for Cyber Security (ACCS) at the University of New South Wales. Prior to joining as Lecturer, he worked as Research Fellow in Usable Security at the University of British Columbia, Canada. He also worked as Postdoctoral Researcher in Systems Security Engineering at Oxford University. He holds a PhD in Usable Security from Brunel University London, UK. Prior to undertaking his position at Oxford University, Nalin worked on a number of lecturing positions in Computer Science at Brunel University,

University of Bedfordshire, Westminster University and Central Bedfordshire College in the UK. He also worked as Sessional Lecturer in Computer Science at Deakin University, Victoria University and CQUniversity in Australia.

Ali A. Ghorbani has held a variety of positions in academia for the past 35 years and is currently the Canada Research Chair (Tier 1) in Cybersecurity, and the Director of the Canadian Institute for Cybersecurity. He is the co-inventor on 3 awarded patents in the area of Network Security and Web Intelligence and has published over 200 peer-reviewed articles during his career. He has supervised over 160 research associates, postdoctoral fellows, graduate and undergraduate students during his career. His book, Intrusion Detection and Prevention Systems: Concepts and Techniques, was published by Springer in October 2010. In 2007, Dr. Ghorbani received the University of New Brunswick's Research Scholar Award. Since 2010, he has obtained more than $10M to fund 6 large multi-project research initiatives. Dr. Ghorbani has developed a number of technologies that have been adopted by high-tech companies. He co-founded two startups, Sentrant and EyesOver in 2013 and 2015. Dr. Ghorbani is the co-Editor-In-Chief of Computational Intelligence Journal. He was twice one of the three finalists for the Special Recognition Award at the 2013 and 2016 New Brunswick KIRA award for the knowledge industry.

Kevin Jones is Head of Cyber Security Architecture, Innovation and Scouting at Airbus, leading a global network of; teams, projects and collaborations including; research & innovation, state of the art solutions development, and technology scouting for cyber security across; IT, ICS and Product security domains. He holds a BSc in Computer Science and MSc in Distributed Systems Integration from De Montfort University, Leicester where he also obtained his PhD: A Trust Based Approach to Mobile Multi-Agent System Security in 2010. Kevin's specialist areas include; Information Security Management & Risk, Security Auditing, Security Architecture, Cloud Security, Threat & Vulnerability Analysis, and Incident Response and is a recognised expert in SCADA security, and the protection of critical systems. He is active in the cyber security research community, has published numerous papers and holds a number of patents within the domain. Kevin is well known as an innovator, thought leader, and is responsible for multiple cyber security demonstrator platforms and laboratories. He currently acts as an executive consultant to Airbus on matters of cyber security across multiple domains and platforms and works closely with Government agencies on cyber security topics in addition to European programmes and the EU Cyber Security Public Private Partnership. He is a frequent public speaker on cyber security, security innovation, and the protection of critical national infrastructure, in addition to an advisor to numerous cyber security research programmes and events. Kevin is an advocate and champion for cyber security in academia, development of cyber skills and for multi-disciplinary research.

Brian Khieu is a Computer Science master's student at San Jose State University, and he received his bachelor's in Computer Science and Engineering from the University of California Davis. Currently, he is working on his master's thesis which comprises of defending hate speech detection models from common lexical and insertion-based attacks. His research interests are in information flow, inference control, and blockchain applications. He has several years of IT experience providing support and maintenance for a network of health clinics in the Salinas area. In his free time, he enjoys planting trees and tending to his various garden plants.

P. Lalitha Surya Kumari is presently working as Associate Professor in the Department of Computer Science and Engineering, Geethanjali College of Engineering and Technology, Telangana, India. She obtained her Ph. D. in Computer Science and Engineering from Jawaharlal Nehru Technological University, Hyderabad, Telangana, India. Her research area includes Network Security, Information Security and Algorithms.

Ankur Lohachab received his M. Tech degree in Computer Science and Engineering from University Institute of Engineering and Technology, Kurukshetra University, India, in 2018, and B.Tech degree in Computer Science and Engineering from Kurukshetra University, India, in 2015. His research interests include Internet of Things Security, Quantum Computing, Cloud Computing, Blockchain, Data Privacy.

Melody Moh obtained her MS and Ph.D., both in computer science, from Univ. of California - Davis. She joined San Jose State University in 1993 and has been a Professor since Aug 2003. Her research interests include cloud computing, mobile, wireless networking, security/privacy cloud and network systems, and machine learning applications. She has received over 500K dollars of research grants from both NSF and industry, has published over 150 refereed papers in international journals, conferences and as book chapters, and has consulted for various companies.

Kommu Narendra received B.Tech degree in Information Technology from Acharya Nagarjuna University, Guntur, India and M.Tech Degree in Computer Science and Engineering from Jawaharlal Nehru Technological University, Kakinada, India. He is currently working towards the Ph.D. Degree at Department of Computer Science and Engineering, National Institute of Technology Puducherry, India. His current research interests include Blockchain Technology, Big data analytics, and Data mining techniques.

Ira Nath has received her M.Tech degree in Software Engineering from the Maulana Abul Kalam Azad University of Technology, West Bengal, India (MAKAUT) in 2008 formerly West Bengal University of Technology (WBUT), India. She is currently pursuing her Ph.D in Computer Science & Technology at Indian Institute of Engineering Science and Technology (IIEST), Shibpur, India formerly Bengal Engineering and Science University (BESU), Shibpur, India.. She is currently an assistant professor in the department of Computer Science & Engineering, JIS College of Engineering, Kalyani, Nadia. Her research interests include WDM optical Networks, Mobile Adhoc Network and network security, Big data hadoop etc. She is a life time member of CSI.

Chitra P. is an Assistant Professor (Senior Grade) in Department of Computer Science & Engineering, Thiagarajar College of Engineering. She completed her B.E from Madurai Kamaraj University during 1995; subsequently she worked as lecturer and completed her M.E and Ph.D in CSE during 2004 and 2011, respectively. She is a reviewer for many national and international peer reviewed journals and member of technical program committee for many IEEE national and international conferences. She has under her credits many publications in reputed international conferences and journals in the areas of distributed systems, cloud computing, Multicore architectures.

Michael Robinson is a cyber security research engineer at Airbus. As part of the architecture, innovation and scouting team he provides cyber expertise to the business and supports state of the art research into new and novel cyber security solutions. He holds a BSc in Computer Science, an MSc in Computer Security from De Montfort University (UK), and a BA in International Relations from Keele University (UK). He obtained his PhD in cyber security in 2017 from De Montfort University. His research interests include cyber warfare, cyber peacekeeping, cloud security and cyber security risk management.

Abirami S. is a Research Scholar in Department of Computer Science & Engineering, Thiagarajar College of Engineering. She completed her B.E in National Engineering College, Kovilpatti during 2010 and her M.E in Anna University, Coimbatore during 2012.

S. R. Mani Sekhar is currently an Assistant Professor in Department of Information Science & Engineering, Ramaiah Institute of Technology, Bangalore. His research interest includes Data Science, Data Analytics, and Software engineering. He has published a good number of research papers, Book chapter. He is an author of a book titled "Programming with R."

Prabha Selvaraj is working as a Professor in department of CSE in Malla Reddy Institute of Engineering and Technology, Hyderabad. She has completed her B.E CSE in Kongu Engineering College, M.E CSE from College of Engineering, Guindy and PhD from Anna University, Chennai. She has 20+ years of experience in teaching and industry. She started her career in K.S.Rangasamy College of Technology, Tiruchengode and also worked in institution like R.M.K Engineering College, Chennai and Tamilnadu College of Engineering, Coimbatore. She is a member of ISTE, CSI, SDIWC, ICSES and IAENG. She has involved in Certification of NBA, NAAC, Autonomous affiliation, ISO 9001:2001(E) Certification of the institution. She has coordinated project, internship, admission of college and as a BoS coordinator, been a part of the development of curriculum and syllabus of information technology department to improve the quality of education, also worked as a module coordinator to evaluate the standard of syllabus, question paper setting scrutinizing and course outcome analysis. Her research interests include Data Mining, Recommendation System, Query Processing, Security, Web Mining, Information Retrieval System, IoT and Wireless Sensor Networks. She has guided many projects in the diversified fields of information technology where projects are mainly from Information Retrieval, Network, Security, Application Software Development, Product Development, Web Designing, Wireless Sensor Network, IoT and System Software. She has presented guest lecture in different colleges and acted as an external examiner and Question Paper Setter for different autonomous and universities. She has Organized National/International conference, convener for National/International conference, coordinator of Technical evens and Symposium. She has published 25 papers in various National/ International journals and conferences and three book chapters in IGI and Wiley in the area AR, Big data analytics and WBAN. She has published a patent titled "Rear view optimized Safety Helmet". As a student Counselor motivated weak students to improve their studies and coached them in their studies and getting placement. Involved in Green Campus club activities and initiated students to plant trees, blood donation and NSS activities. She is an active member of women empowerment cell. She has received Top 25 Best Faculty Award in CSE from EET CRS, Best Educators Awards by International Association of Research and Developed Organization Excellence Awards in 2018, Outstanding Educator award by I2OR and Distinguished Leader in Engineering Discipline by Higher Education Leadership Awards in 2019.

Awanthika Senarath is a PhD candidate at the Australian Center for Cyber Security, School of Engineering and IT, University of New South Wales – Canberra at the Australian Defence Force Academy, Australia. He Research interests are on usable privacy and developing technological support for organisations and developers to comprehend privacy requirements and concepts.

Dharmpal Singh received his Bachelor of Computer Science and Engineering and Master of Computer Science and Engineering from West Bengal University of Technology. He has about eight years of experience in teaching and research. At present, he is with JIS College of Engineering, Kalyani, and West Bengal, India as an Associate Professor. Currently, he had done his Ph. D from University of Kalyani. He has about 26 publications in national and international journals and conference proceedings. He is also the editorial board members of many reputed/ referred journal.

Pawan Kumar Singh holds M.Tech in Distributed Systems and Mobile Computing, from Jadavpur University, India. He has diverse experience of over a decade working in Mobile applications and Data Analytics. His areas of interest include Mobile application development, Data Security, Identity and Access Management, Multi-Factor Authenticators, FIDO (Fast Identity Online), Machine Learning, Data Analytics, and IOT.

Christophe Thovex is a Senior Researcher, Director of Research and Development at DATA2B - French company specialized in Big Data and Data Science - and a free associated scientist to the International Research Unit LAFMIA (UMI CNRS 3175). He first worked with large production databases for the heavy industry (ALSTOM Marine), before to start his academic research work at the University of Nantes (France). His research domain was first oriented towards social knowledge networks and physics-inspired models, then he generalized that field to Network Science before to start to investigate on bio-inspired models, machine reasoning and meta-computing. He is an editorial member at the Social Networks Analysis and Mining Journal, reviewer for several international conferences and still publishes articles and chapters in international journals and books as a private sector researcher.

Shingo Yamaguchi received B.E., M.E. and D.E. degrees from Yamaguchi University, Japan, in 1992, 1994 and 2002. He was a Visiting Scholar in University of Illinois at Chicago, US, in 2007. He is currently a Professor in Graduate School of Sciences and Technology for Innovation, Yamaguchi University, Japan. His research interest includes service science and cyber security. He is a Board of Governors Member of IEEE Consumer Electronics Society. He is a Senior Member of IEEE and IEICE.

Xichen Zhang is a PhD student at Canadian Institute for Cybersecurity, University of New Brunswick under the supervision of Prof. Ali A. Ghorbani and Prof. Rongxing Lu. He worked as a Research Assistant in Canadian Institute for Cybersecurity from January 2018 to January 2019. He received Master degree of Computer Science from University of New Brunswick in 2018. His research interests include privacy preserving in Mobile Crowdsensing, deep learning, data mining, natural language processing and data visualization. He has involved with many industrial projects, such as malicious advertisement detection, fake news detection, and human-centric solutions for cybersecurity.

Index

A

Access Control 6, 15, 40, 71, 119, 121-122, 151, 157, 211, 282

air pollution 380-381, 393-394, 396-397, 399, 401-403

air quality index 380-381, 393, 396

Artificial Bee Colony 189-191

artificial intelligence 98, 189, 216, 341, 344, 357-358

attacks 8, 25, 35, 39-41, 45, 51-52, 60, 66, 69, 72-76, 78-80, 85, 88, 99, 127, 129, 132-134, 138-139, 141-143, 151-152, 155-165, 168-170, 218, 221, 269, 304, 308, 310, 312, 317, 319, 344-345, 357, 364, 395

attack surface 125, 133, 138

B

bacterial foraging 189-190, 193-194, 196-197

Bat 190, 204-206

big data characteristics 259-260

Bio-Inspired Computing 189-190, 211, 216

blockchain 125-126, 128-139, 249-252, 254, 257-258, 260-261

bootstrap 350-351, 362

bot 307-311, 313, 365-366, 368, 370

C

Certificate authority (CA) 126-127

challenges 1, 3-4, 6, 17, 24, 33-39, 41, 66-67, 69, 78, 84, 86-88, 97, 99, 116, 118-120, 122-123, 126, 141-142, 155, 157, 163, 165, 168-170, 172, 195, 198, 201, 217-219, 224-225, 239, 241, 247, 249, 266, 280, 304, 377, 383, 395

classification 27, 32, 71, 76, 103-105, 109-110, 112, 116, 170, 193, 203, 205, 208, 268, 282, 284, 287, 292, 341, 343, 353, 357, 383, 386-388, 390

cloud computing 2, 11, 14, 41, 64, 78, 84-85, 98-100, 118, 123, 130, 155, 189, 216, 218-219, 264-266, 268, 278, 383-384, 394

Cloud Secure Alliance 24, 41

Cloud Service Agreement 10

clustering 75, 110, 122, 143, 169-171, 184, 196-197, 203, 388

compliance 3, 6, 69, 222, 254, 258, 260, 265, 282-283, 286-287, 289-298, 383

control 1-8, 10, 12-17, 24-25, 34, 40, 46, 52-53, 60, 71, 77, 86, 119, 121-122, 129, 131, 145, 151, 154, 157, 162-163, 173, 211, 219, 248-249, 258, 265, 282, 293, 295-297, 306-307, 310-311, 319, 323-324, 326, 346, 365, 377

convex optimization 357, 362

credit card 48, 51, 55-56, 73, 110-111, 248, 261, 342, 344

cross border transactions 261

cryptography 40, 135, 218, 268

Cuckoo Search 190, 197

customer 1, 3-16, 23, 45, 52, 55, 98, 101, 109, 115, 123, 130, 155, 248-250, 258, 260-261, 269, 283, 291, 294

cyber crime 47, 57

Cyber Forensics 58

cyber security 15-16, 65-67, 88, 99, 144, 344, 367, 395

D

data analysis 36-37, 40, 64, 98, 100-101, 109, 115, 144, 174, 218-222, 224, 229, 232-233, 235-236, 241, 260, 340

data collection 24, 29, 32, 40, 155, 157, 171, 382-383, 399

Data Loss Prevention 23, 71

data mining 27, 29, 40, 68, 70, 75, 84, 86-88, 98, 181, 196, 232, 235, 340, 345, 383

Data Provenance 120-121, 219, 246

Recommended Reference Books

ISBN: 978-1-5225-8876-4
© 2019; 141 pp.
List Price: $135

ISBN: 978-1-5225-8100-0
© 2019; 321 pp.
List Price: $235

ISBN: 978-1-5225-7847-5
© 2019; 306 pp.
List Price: $195

ISBN: 978-1-5225-6313-6
© 2019; 349 pp.
List Price: $215

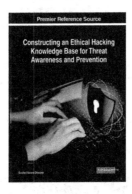

ISBN: 978-1-5225-7628-0
© 2019; 281 pp.
List Price: $220

ISBN: 978-1-5225-5855-2
© 2019; 337 pp.
List Price: $185

Do you want to stay current on the latest research trends, product announcements, news and special offers?
Join IGI Global's mailing list today and start enjoying exclusive perks sent only to IGI Global members.
Add your name to the list at **www.igi-global.com/newsletters.**

Ensure Quality Research is Introduced to the Academic Community

Become an IGI Global Reviewer for Authored Book Projects

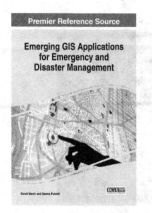

Premier Reference Source

Emerging GIS Applications for Emergency and Disaster Management

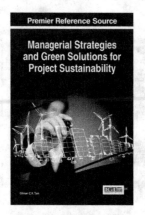

Premier Reference Source

Managerial Strategies and Green Solutions for Project Sustainability

Premier Reference Source

Comparative Approaches to Using R and Python for Statistical Data Analysis

Premier Reference Source

Solutions for High-Touch Communications in a High-Tech World

The overall success of an authored book project is dependent on quality and timely reviews.

In this competitive age of scholarly publishing, constructive and timely feedback significantly expedites the turnaround time of manuscripts from submission to acceptance, allowing the publication and discovery of forward-thinking research at a much more expeditious rate. Several IGI Global authored book projects are currently seeking highly-qualified experts in the field to fill vacancies on their respective editorial review boards:

Applications and Inquiries may be sent to:
development@igi-global.com

Applicants must have a doctorate (or an equivalent degree) as well as publishing and reviewing experience. Reviewers are asked to complete the open-ended evaluation questions with as much detail as possible in a timely, collegial, and constructive manner. All reviewers' tenures run for one-year terms on the editorial review boards and are expected to complete at least three reviews per term. Upon successful completion of this term, reviewers can be considered for an additional term.

If you have a colleague that may be interested in this opportunity,
we encourage you to share this information with them.